Minimal Old Chinese and Later Han Chinese

ABC CHINESE DICTIONARY SERIES

Victor H. Mair, General Editor

The ABC Chinese Dictionary Series aims to provide a complete set of convenient and reliable reference tools for all those who need to deal with Chinese words and characters. A unique feature of the series is the adoption of a strict alphabetical order, the fastest and most user-friendly way to look up words in a Chinese dictionary. Most volumes contain graphically oriented indices to assist in finding characters whose pronunciation is not known. The ABC dictionaries and compilations rely on the best expertise available worldwide and are based on the application of new strategies for the study of Sinitic languages and the Chinese writing system, including the first clear distinction between the etymology of words, on the one hand, and the evolution of shapes, sounds, and meanings of characters, on the other. While aiming for conciseness and accuracy, series volumes also strive to apply the highest standards of lexicography in all respects, including compatibility with computer technology for information processing. Some of the dictionaries in this series are concerned with different varieties of modern Chinese, whereas others present the latest scholarly findings concerning earlier stages of development. All are aimed at facilitating the research and reading of scholars and students alike.

Published Titles in the Series

ABC Chinese-English Dictionary (desk reference and pocket editions)
Edited by John DeFrancis

ABC Dictionary of Chinese Proverbs
Edited by John S. Rohsenow

ABC Chinese-English Comprehensive Dictionary
Edited by John DeFrancis

An Alphabetical Index to the Hanyu Da Cidian
Edited by Victor H. Mair

Handbook of 'Phags-pa Chinese
W. South Coblin

ABC Etymological Dictionary of Old Chinese
Axel Schuessler

Minimal Old Chinese and Later Han Chinese: A Companion to Grammata Serica Recensa
Axel Schuessler

Minimal Old Chinese and Later Han Chinese

A Companion to *Grammata Serica Recensa*

Axel Schuessler

University of Hawai'i Press
Honolulu

Printed in the United States of America
14 13 12 11 10 09 6 5 4 3 2 1

Library of Congress Cataloging-in-Publication Data

Schuessler, Axel.
Minimal old Chinese and later Han Chinese : a companion to Grammata serica recensa / Axel Schuessler.
p. cm. — (ABC Chinese dictionary series)
ISBN 978-0-8248-3264-3 (hardcover : alk. paper)
1. Chinese language—Ancient Chinese, 600–1200—Phonology. I. Karlgren, Bernhard, 1889–1978. Grammata serica recensa. II. Title. III. Title: Companion to Grammata serica recensa.
PL1201.S35 2009
940.54'4910943—dc22

2008061455

University of Hawai'i Press books are printed on acid-free paper and meet the guidelines for permanence and durability of the Council on Library Resources.

Camera-ready copy prepared by the author.

CONTENTS

TABLES

PREFACE

Bernhard Karlgren's Archaic Chinese (= Old Chinese, OC) as presented in his standard work *Grammata Serica Recensa* (*GSR*) of 1957 has long been outdated. This present manual is an attempt to update *GSR* with a relatively simple "Minimal Old Chinese" (OCM, for OC-Minimal) which incorporates those features on which there is broad agreement among investigators today. Though this manual can be thought of as a *Grammata Serica Recensa update*, I will refer to it as *Grammata Serica Companion* (*GSC*) for short.

The perception of the mysterious nature and confusing state of OC has been shaped by several factors. First, *GSR* does not present the data in a transparently organized fashion, so that only patient scrutiny reveals what the OC system is, behind Karlgren's bewildering diacritics and phonetic symbols. The ordinary user has to take Karlgren's, or anyone's, authority at face value. Secondly, the experts' arguments are so specialized and arcane that only the initiated are in a position to follow them. The Introduction to this manual attempts to provide an overview over some of the terms and issues, demystify OC if you will, so that outsiders may have some notion of the data, sources and theories on which expert arguments are based. Thirdly, superficially scholars do not seem to agree on much, because they debate unclear issues and not the many features of OC on which there is a tacit consensus. Furthermore, old settled issues in Middle Chinese (MC) and OC phonology are periodically raised again so that the non-expert must conclude that almost all about OC is still up in the air.

Since the publication of *GSR*, historical linguists have tried to simplify and systematize Karlgren's reconstructions, have suggested emendations or their own OC systems which sometimes look as different from each other as if they were different languages. Compare, for example, (P: = Pulleyblank):

		Karlgren GSR	Baxter 1992	Sagart 1999	Pān 2000	OCM
'today'	今	ki̠əm	k(r)jəm	-ɨm	krŭɯm	kəm
'remember'	念	niəm	nims	[^{a}mə-]^{a}nem-s	mqlɯms	nîms
'offspring'	子	tsi̭əg	tsjəʔ	^{b}tsɨʔ	splŭɯ˙	tsəʔ
'plum'	李	li̭əg	rjəʔ		b-rŭɯ˙	rəʔ
'offense'	罪	dzʻwəd	dzujʔ		sblul˙	dzûiʔ
'think, be'	惟	di̠wər	wjij	^{b}t(ə)-wij		wi
'little bird'	隹	ȶi̠wər		^{b}tu[j]	P: kwjəl	tui

After Karlgren, the field seems to have fallen apart. The occasional user of OC material probably finds it difficult or impossible to tell which OC proposals are just an author's latest theories, ideas and speculations, and what is actually widely accepted.[1] For the purposes of OCM, we will attempt to separate generally agreed OC features from more speculative and probing hypotheses — however valuable and insightful they may be — which are often presented in such definitive language that an unsuspecting reader may think he now has the OC language in front of him to work with.

[1] Witness comments like this by the Indo-Europeanist Douglas Adams: "There are a number of 'competing' systems of [OC] reconstruction (Karlgren, Pulleyblank, Li) whose inherent likelihood and mutual interrelationships can baffle the outsider" (*JIES* 23, 3ε4, 1995: 401).

PREFACE

The Introduction outlines basic issues in OC phonology since *GSR*, and the rationale for OCM, a relatively simple form of OC, a minimum on which most investigators may agree, and which shows that OC is not quite as enigmatic and complex as it often appears. The OCM forms are "minimal" in several respects: they incorporate only the more widely accepted insights into OC gained since *GSR* was published, but leave out more speculative proposals with their often complex OC reconstructions; OCM is based on simple and less complex hypotheses and assumptions than some other proposals (see Intro. sections 6, 8 and 9); OCM is written in a simple form, similar to recordings of modern dialects. Unfortunately, these objectives need to be compromised on occasion because it is necessary to decide a detail on which there is no consensus, in order to be able to put something on paper. But these doubtful cases will be clearly pointed out.

The user will find, it is hoped, a simple, transparent form of OC that may be useful. This is the essence of this endeavor. As pointed out in section 9.2.5 of the Introduction: The user of this manual can add phonemic elements to OCM forms as he may deem appropriate, but it is difficult, even impossible, for an unsuspecting user to visualize an initial cluster presented to him with a questionable or highly hypothetical element deleted or changed; thus a minimalist form *râuk or *tâm is preferable to writing *g-rauk or *qlam.

A manual like the present one is not the place for original contributions to OC; with few exceptions, all proposals and ideas have been offered in the past by others. OCM is to a large extent a mechanical transcription of Karlgren's OC into Baxter's 1992 system with some mostly notational changes. However, the approach to the material on which reconstructions are based is unusual for OC. Often, an investigator asks: could the data possibly support a certain reconstruction? The answer is usually "yes," and then hypotheses are developed and reconstructions built on a possibility — reconstructions that may, or may not, stand the test of time. We will turn the question around and ask: do the data necessarily compel us to postulate a certain (complex) reconstruction for OC? Our answer is usually "no." Therefore typical OC sources of MC forms override irregularities and oddities in the phonetic composition of graphs of the kind that often result in complex OC reconstructions. As a result, OCM is eliminating much that is highly hypothetical in others' (and my former) proposals, is on firmer ground, and appears relatively straightforward.

The user should be aware of some features of *GSC*:

(1) This *GSC* can stand on its own as long as one wishes to look up *pinyin*, MC, LHan and OCM readings of graphs. However, it is really only a companion to *GSR* because it does not repeat other information provided there, such as English glosses, reference to first textual occurrence, and inscriptional forms. In addition to Karlgren's original *GSR*, the following is available:

Pān Wùyún 潘悟雲, translator and editor. 1997. *Hàn wén diǎn* 漢文典. Shanghai.

Pān's is a translation of *GSR*. Its merit is a *pinyin* index of all the graphs in *GSR;* but it refers only to Pān's page, not to the *GSR* series number which is, however, found on that page.[2] Pān also quotes the text passage of a graph's earliest occurrence; and he corrects the occasional error.

[2]*GSR* numbers can also be looked up in Pulleyblank 1991 which, however, does not include graphs which occur only in OC texts; Schuessler *DEZ* (it includes only graphs found in early Zhou texts).

(2) This manual's Introduction provides a broad sketch of major sources and methods for OC for the lay-person (first parts of the Introduction), as well as explanations for what I am doing and why, for the inquisitive reader (later parts). Each can conveniently skip over sections which are irrelevant for his quest. Because of the manual's general survey nature, references to scholars and publications are kept to a minimum. That information, the history of ideas and discoveries with proper credits, as well as more detail and depth, is found in:

Baxter, William. 1992. *A Handbook of Old Chinese Phonology.* Berlin.

(3) For further phonological notes and details on OCM, as well as other information (abbreviations, list of languages, bibliography, complete etymological notes) the reader is referred to:

Schuessler, Axel. 2007. *Etymological Dictionary of Old Chinese* (*EDOC*). Honolulu.

In addition to OCM, *GSC* also provides

• Later Han Chinese (LHan or LH) is the earliest form of Chinese which can be set up without relying heavily on interpretations of phonetic series and morphological speculations. The transcription of LHan forms are much simpler than Karlgren's/Li's traditionally quoted MC in that it avoids most of the diacritical clutter and is written in the way modern Chinese dialects are recorded. It also antedates MC by almost half a millennium. At the very least, LHan can be viewed as MC written in a simple notation and adjusted by evidence from Han data.

Originally I suggested that LHan represents a hypothetical conservative strain of the language of about the 2nd century AD. After completing this manual it occurred to me that a more fitting name for this language should be Mid-Han Chinese (MHan), as that stage still had all those features which survived as archaisms in later dialects, and which have been taken into consideration for the conservative LHan forms for this manual.

• This manual also provides the traditional MC readings of graphs (i.e., Li Fang-kuei's emendations to *GSR's* 'Ancient Chinese') which are often cited for phonological reference. Unlike *GSR*, I will note the *Qieyun* system's so-called *chóngniǔ* doublets and Divisions (see 2.4). The Divisions can be ascertained in:

Shěn Jiānshì 沈兼士. *Guǎngyùn shēngxì* 廣韻聲系. 1977. Taibei.
Liáng Sēngbǎo 梁僧寶. *Sì shēng yùnpǔ* 四聲韻譜. 1967. Taibei.

In addition to these reconstructed stages of pre-modern Chinese, transcriptions in alphabetic scripts, and Chinese transcriptions of foreign names and words have been cited (see Intro. 1.1). For this purpose I have drawn heavily on many relevant publications of W. South Coblin who has analyzed and interpreted transcriptional data from different periods.

Often, I have added in the right margin Baxter's 1992 reconstruction which will show the usual similarity with OCM, but also on occasion differences. Baxter 1992 does not, however, represent its author's current thinking. This will become available in the Baxter-Sagart reconstruction of Old Chinese that provides cutting edge scholarship, with OC forms that may be more complex than OCM and therefore engender discussions for some time before one or other aspect of it (or all) will be widely accepted.

A work like this manual deals with masses of detailed and minute data. *GSR* is nearly error free, Pān Wùyún has caught some of Karlgren's rare oversights; in addition I have still encountered a couple of slips in *GSR* as well as in Pān; these typically involve erroneous tone marks, vowel timbres or diacritics.[3] The compilation of this present *GSC* required manual copying; every effort has been made to prevent new errors from slipping in.

The present work also includes a comprehensive *pinyin* index.

Organization

The original plan was to retain the sequence of *GSR* numbers since this work is meant to be a companion manual. But syllable types that according to our present knowledge should belong together are widely scattered in Karlgren's work — he grouped the phonetic series strictly by syllable finals with his minutely differentiated OC vowel timbres. Thus syllables of the type *KAN are found in *GSR* 139-143, 184-185, 191-192, 196-198, 249, and 1248. For logic and convenience, we list all syllables with similar initial and identical OC rimes together. *GSC* sorts the OC rime categories into sections (1 to 38). Within phonetic series, the graphs are here also rearranged in a way that brings out subgroups with their phonological characteristics.

This being a by-product of the author's *Etymological Dictionary of Old Chinese (EDOC)*, some parts have been taken over from that work, notably Signs and Abbreviations and the References. The *EDOC* ought to be consulted for additional details.

Some OCM and LHan notations differ here occasionally from those in the *EDOC*; they should be considered to supersede the latter.

[3]E.g., *GSR* 1143m cāo 操 should be MC $ts^{h}\hat{a}u^{A}$, not $ts^{h}\hat{a}u^{B}$; *GSR* 866i 醍 'some sort of wine' should be read *tǐ*, not *tí* in Pān's edition. In many instances, dictionaries disagree on Mandarin readings; I usually follow Pān, but in cases of competing pronunciations I often rely on *Gǔdài Hànyǔ cídiǎn*.

ACKNOWLEDGMENTS

This manual is a by-product of the project by A. Schuessler, *Etymological Dictionary of Old Chinese,* Honolulu 2007. Therefore I wish once more to express my gratitude and appreciation to Victor Mair who secured financial support through grants from the Freeman Foundation and other generous sources. Furthermore, this manual has benefitted from helpful suggestions by W. S. Coblin, Victor Mair and especially Ch. Harbsmeier. Of course the mistakes are this author's responsibility.

GSC ENTRIES

>	'developed into, becomes'
<	'derives from an earlier form / from an earlier stage of a language'
->	'loaned to'
<-	'borrowed from'
<>	separates footnote entries
≍	'cognate (to)' or 'allofam' (fellow member in a word family)
§	refer to sections in the introduction to the *EDOC*
~	or, variant

K.	= Karlgren's *GSR* number. Rare graphs which I was unable to find in an available font are referred to by their *GSR* letters
pīnyīn	transcription of Mandarin, followed by the Chinese character(s) *zì* 字. When no character exists (as is often the case with colloquial dialect forms) an empty box □ takes its place.
MC	Middle Chinese or Qièyùn system (QYS), ca. AD 600.
LH	Later Han Chinese (also LHan) of the 1st and 2nd centuries AD. See §12.1.1. In the text, LHan is usually placed in brackets, thus [kɑ] = LHan kɑ unless otherwise identified.
MHan	Middle Han transcriptions of foreign names and words (Pulleyblank 1962; Coblin ms. 1993)
QYS	Qièyùn System = MC
S	alternate Old South form of LHan (from later southern dialects, especially Mǐn)
S.	Siamese (Tai)
OC	Old Chinese
OCB	Baxter's OC (1992)
OCM	Minimal Old Chinese form (starred items)
R.	Rime section (nos. 1 through 38)
R !	the unexpected rime and tone are confirmed by a rhyme in poetry
ac	acute initials (see 1.4)
gr	grave initials (see 1.4)
lab	OC labial[ized] initials (p...m [kw...]); non-lab = non-labial initials
w	OC initial w- (which allows pre-initial velars and s, z)

[D]	Chinese dialect forms; col. = colloquial form (bai 白), lit. = literary or reading form (wén 文). Dialects (actually Sinitic languages) are identified by location. See §12.1.3. Since many of them are not well known, the dialect affiliation is prefixed to the name of the location. These abbreviations are: G = Gàn, K = Kèjiā (Hakka), M = Mǐn, W = Wú, X = Xiāng, Y = Yuè (Cantonese), Mand. = Mandarin, P = Proto-, as in PMin = Proto-Min (also CMin = Common Min). Place names are sometimes shortened: -m = -men, -zh = -zhou, HK = Hongkong.

[E] comments on etymology, especially foreign connections (cognates or loans); details and the key to abbreviations are found in the *EDOC*

[N] introduces further notes or comments

[T] transcriptions of the Chinese word; these are occasionally provided to show a word's later development (see §12.1):
Sin Sukchu or *Sin S.* (EMing = Early Ming period Chinese); SR 'standard reading,' PR 'popular reading,' LR 'left reading'
MGZY = *Měnggǔ zìyùn* ('Phags-pa) of the Yuan (Mongol) period (1270–1308)
ONW(C) = Old Northwest Chinese from about AD 400, as interpreted by Coblin 1994. Occasionally Sui-Tang Chang'an (Coblin's STCA, ca. AD 640) and MTang (Middle Tang, ca. AD 775) forms are also added.
BTD = Buddhist Transcriptional Dialect (later Han period) (Coblin)
MHan = Middle Han (pre-BTD) (Coblin ms. 1993; Pulleyblank 1962); sources are mostly the Hanshu and the Hou-Hanshu (HHanshu)

The OC rime categories are arranged and numbered as follows:

1 a	2 ak	3 aŋ
4 ə	5 ək	6 əŋ
7 e	8 ek	9 eŋ
10 o	11 ok	12 oŋ
13 u	14 uk	15 uŋ
16 au	17 auk	--
--	18 ai	19 oi
20 et, e(t)s	21 at, a(t)s	22 ot, o(t)s
23 en	24 an	25 on
26 i	27 əi	28 ui
29 it, i(t)s	30 ət, ə(t)s	31 ut, u(t)s
32 in	33 ən	34 un
	35 ap, op	36 am, om
	37 əp, ip, up	38 əm, im, um

Within rime categories, the phonetic series are arranged by initial types, usually in the following sequence (OCM initials):

k kw w h(w) ʔ(w) ŋ(w) t l j r n ts s p m

Tables

The entries in the fields consist of MC + LHan + OC *
Horizontal lines = MC (QYS) 'Divisions'
Vertical columns = OC rime categories
Grayed fields show phonologically impossible combinations

R.	= Rime section in *GSC*
ac	acute initials (see 1.4)
gr	grave initials (see 1.4)
lab	OC labial[ized] initials (p...m, kw...);
non-lab	= non-labial[ized] initials
w	OC initial w- (which permits pre-initial velars and s, z)

TRANSCRIPTIONS

Middle Chinese

Karlgren's MC ('Ancient Chinese') of *GSR* with Li Fang-kuei's emendations (Li 1971: 4-7; 1974-1975: 224-227) will be used here with some additional adjustments (see also 2.2).

(1) The tones will be indicated by superscript letters ABCD; see section 2.2.

(2) Glottal stop will be represented by ʔ.

(3) ĕ (ě) will be written e.

(4) ï will be written ɨ.

(5) In Karlgren's/Li's MC, the rounded medial is represented as *-u-* in some syllables (ŋuo, gjuən); as *-w-* in others (mwan, kjwän, kjwei); in some syllable types rather inconsistently: there are both *kjuen* and *kjwen*; *kuât*, but the *qùshēng* counterpart *kwâi*^{C}. To eliminate this confusion, I will write MC *w* for Karlgren's/Li's medial *w* as well as *u*, thus *pwân* (not *puân*), *kjwän*, *kjwən*, etc. Some syllables have a well-established *uo* where I will keep it (kuo, suoŋ). In the Introduction where I specifically cite Karlgren's/Li's MC forms, the *u* may still appear.

After labial initials, the medial *u/w* is redundant — one could write *pân* for *puân*, or *păt* for *pwăt*. The Div. I *u/w* is written systematically and well established; it will be retained here (puân); but the *w* in Div. II is not applied consistently: Li writes pwăi (in analogy to ɣwăi); but phăn in analogy to kăn, and not parallel to kwăn; or pɐk (not pwɐk). Therefore, the *w* will usually be omitted in such Div. II syllables (păt, pɐk), as is done by some writers.

(6) The strong palatal medial in chóngniǔ Div. IV (here '3/4'; see Intro. 2.4) is represented by *ji* in Li's system (e.g., pjiän 4 vs. pjän 3). But in some syllable types, it is written simply as *i* without the *j* which is so characteristic of Div. III, 3/4 syllables: pi 4, si, kwi. In light of MC syllables like kjwie 4 (vs. kjwe), the omission of *j* looks odd, therefore one could write more logically kjiwi instead (parallel to jiwi, and contrasting with Li's kjwi 3). In the *EDOC* I wrote kjiwi, etc., but here I will remain close to Li's system and write kwi 4. The numbers 3 and 4 which are referring to the chóngniǔ division are always added for clarity (pi 4, pji 3).

(7) Like Karlgren, Li omits the medial *j* in syllables with the single vowel *i* (źwi, parallel to kwi 4), but Li inserts a *j* with other finals, e.g., źjwe (Karlgren źwie).

Later Han Chinese

The LHan transcription follows for the most part MC. Note, however, the distinction between *a* and *ɑ;* the latter could also be written *â* if one prefers. See Intro. section 7.

Old Chinese

The Minimal Old Chinese (OCM) phonemes are for the most part Baxter's. The initial consonants are listed in the Introduction 4.6.

Some notational changes to Baxter's system are self-evident, e.g., OCM *kw for Baxter's k^w; since the source of some MC kw- is ambiguous, it could derive from *k^w, *kuV or *kw < k+w. Though aspirated initials p^h k^h t^h ts^h are unit phonemes in LHan and MC, their OC sources are often voiceless sonorants or may be C+h clusters, hence OCM ph, etc.

Voiceless sonorants are marked by an h,but are unit phonemes. See Intro. 5.1.5 for details.

TRANSCRIPTIONS

Some OC pre-initials or prefixes which are weakend or lost by MC are hyphenated to avoid confusion with otherwise identical initial configurations, thus lâm < *g-râm vs. gam < *grâm; or zjwen < s-win vs. sjwen < swin.

Baxter's (and OCM's) six OC vowels are a i u e ə o. The six vowels are written without additional marks in OCM syllables that correspond to MC Div. III (e.g., 張 OCM *taŋ > LHan tśɑŋ, MC tśjaŋ). In MC Div. I/IV and II syllables (no medial j), which seem to have been lax (huǎn 緩) in Later Han Chinese, the OCM vowels are marked with an accent circumflex (as in French *lâche* 'lax') which is here purely symbolic; however:

OC syllable type A (> MC Div. I/IV, II)	â î û ê ə̂ ô
OC syllable type B (> MC Div. III, 3/3, 3/4)	a i u e ə o

E.g., 五 OCM ŋâʔ > LHan ŋɑ^{B}, MC ŋuo^{B}; or 我 OCM *ŋâiʔ > LHan ŋɑi^{B}, MC ŋâ^{B}; note that the MC circumflex *â* represents a darker *a*, as in French *lâche*, and is not (directly) related to the symbolic OCM one.

Elements of diphthongs, including the unstressed ones, are written with vowels (i y u), as in modern dialect transcriptions, instead of semi-vowels (j, w), thus 僚 *riâu, for example.

SYMBOLS AND ABBREVIATIONS

This list is taken from the *EDOC* and may include abbreviations that do not occur in this manual.

□	no Chinese graph exists (for a dialect word)
⋈	cognate, allofam, members of a wf within a language
<>	cognate(s), or loans between languages in either direction; separates forms cited from different language families
=	s. w. as = same word as
~	or, variant
>	develops into
<	derives from
<-	borrowed from
->	loaned into
→	cross-reference
§	section / paragraph of the Introduction to EDOC
a.	and
AA	Austroasiatic (languages)
AAS	Association for Asian Studies
abbr.	abbreviation(s)
ac	acute consonants
acc. to	according to
AM	*Asia Major*
AN	Austronesian (languages)
aux.	auxiliary (e.g., verb)
BEFEO	*Bulletin de l'Ecole Française d'Extrême Orient*
Běidà	Běijīng Dàxué: *Hànyǔ fāngyán cíhuì* 漢語方言詞匯
BI	bronze inscriptions
BIHP	*Bulletin of the Institute of History and Philology* (Academia Sinica, Taiwan) (中央研究院, 歷史語言研究所集刊)
BMFEA	*Bulletin of the Museum of Far Eastern Antiquities*, Stockholm
BSLP	*Bulletin de la société linguistique de Paris*
BSOAS	*Bulletin of the School of Oriental and African Studies*, London
BTD	Han Buddhist Transcriptional Dialect (W. S. Coblin. ms.)
BV	Bahing-Vayu languages (= Kiranti languages; Tibeto-Burman)
[C]	introduces comments on further cognates
CAAAL	*Computational Analysis of Asian and African Languages*
CDC	Common Dialectal Chinese (J. Norman's reconstruction)
CH	Chinese
CLAO	*Cahiers de Linguistique Asie Orientale*
cogn.	cognate
[D]	introduces Chinese dialect forms
DEZ	A. Schuessler, *A Dictionary of Early Zhou Chinese*
ditr.	ditransitive
E	east(ern); early
[E]	introduces etymological comments
EAC	Dobson, *Early Archaic Chinese*
EOC	Early Old Chinese, Shang and early Western Zhou

f. (ff.)	following page(s)
FY	(1) *Fāng yán* 方言 by Yáng Xióng 揚雄; (2) the modern journal *Fāngyán* 方言
G-	Gàn dialects
gr	grave consonants
GSC	*Companion to* Grammata Serica Recensa
GSR	B. Karlgren, *Grammata serica recensa*
GY	Guǎng-yùn 廣韻: Yú Nǎi-yǒng 1974. *Hù zhù jiàozhèng Sòng běn Guǎng-yùn*
GYSX	Shěn Jiānshì 沈兼士. *Guǎngyùn shēngxì*
Hao-ku	Ulrich Unger, *Hao-ku. Sinologische Rundbriefe*
HCT	Li Fangkuei 1977, *A Handbook of Comparative Tai*
HJAS	*Harvard Journal of Asiatic Studies*
HK	Hong Kong
HOCP	William H. Baxter 1992, *Handbook of OC Phonology*
HPTB	Matisoff 2003, *Handbook of Proto-Tibeto-Burman*
HST	W. South Coblin 1986, *A Sinologist's Handlist of Sino-Tibetan Lexical Comparisons*
ICSTLL	International Conference on Sino-Tibetan Languages and Linguistics
id.	idem (the same as above)
IG	indo-germanisch ('Indo-European')
intr.	intransitive
IST	R. Shafer, *Introduction to Sino-Tibetan*
J(.)	Journal
JA	*Journal Asiatique*
JAOS	*Journal of the American Oriental Society*
JAS	*Journal for Asian Studies*
JCL	*Journal of Chinese Linguistics*
JCLTA	*Journal of the Chinese Teachers' Language Association*
JDSW	*Jīngdiǎn shìwén* 經典釋文 by Lù Démíng 陸德明
JGWZ	Lǐ Xiàodìng 李孝定, *Jiǎgǔ wénzì jíshì* 甲骨文字集釋
JIES	*Journal of Indo-European Studies*
JP	Jǐng-pō 景頗 (a Tibeto-Burman language)
JR	rGya-rung = Jia-rong (a Tibeto-Burman language)
JWGL	Zhōu Fǎgō 周法高, *Jīnwén gǔlín (bǔ)* 金文詁林 (補)
K-	Kèjiā (Hakka) dialects
K.	Kachin (a Tibeto-Burman language close to or identical with Jing-po)
Kan.	Kanauri (a Tibeto-Burman language of the Himalayan branch)
KC	Kuki-Chin languages (Tibeto-Burman)
KN	Kuki-Chin-Naga languages (Tibeto-Burman)
KS	Kam-Sui languages
KT	Kam-Tai languages
lab	labial[ized] initial consonants
LAC	Dobson, *Late Archaic Chinese*
LB	Lolo-Burmese languages (a Tibeto-Burman branch)
LB-M	Matisoff's reconstruction of LB
lg. (lgs.)	language(s)
LH, LHan	Later Han Chinese (Eastern Han)
LL	*Language and Linguistics* 語言暨語言學 (Academia Sinica, Taipei)
LOC	Later Old Chinese (Zhànguó)
LTBA	*Linguistics of the Tibeto-Burman Area*
Lush.	Lushai (a Tibeto-Burman language of the Kuki-Naga branch)
M-	Mǐn dialects
M-	Middle (e.g., MM = Middle Mon)
MC	Middle (or ancient) Chinese (ca. AD 600)
MGZY	*Měnggǔ zìyùn*

MK	Mon-Khmer languages
MKS	*Mon-Khmer Studies*
MM, MMon	Middle Mon (an Austroasiatic language)
MS	*Monumenta Serica*
MSOS	*Mitteilungen des Seminars für Orientalische Sprachen*
MY	Miao-Yao (Hmong-Mian) languages
MZYW	*Mínzú yǔwén* 民族語文
[N]	introduces further notes
n.	noun
Oxx	Old xx (e.g., OC = Old Chinese)
OB	Shang dynasty oracle bone inscriptions
OC	Old (or archaic) Chinese
OCB	Old Chinese, Baxter's reconstruction
OCM	Minimal Old Chinese
OE	*Oriens extremus*
OL	*Oceanic Linguistics*
OM	Old Mon (an Austroasiatic language)
ONW(C)	Old Northwest Chinese ca. AD 400 (W. S. Coblin, *Old Northwest Chinese*)
P	Proto
p. c.	personal communication
PCH	Proto-Chinese
perh.	perhaps
PLB	Proto-Lolo-Burmese (= 'Lolo-Burmese,' LB)
PMin	Proto-Min (J. Norman's reconstructions)
poss.	possibly
prob.	probably
PTai	Proto-Tai
PTib.	Proto-Tibetan
PVM	Proto-Viet-Mong languages
PWA	Proto-Western-Austronesian
PWMiao	Proto-Western-Miao
QY	*Qièyùn* 切韻
QY(S)	Qieyun system, i.e., MC (or 'ancient Chinese') reconstructions
R.	Rime section
R!	final confirmed by rime in the *Shijing* or *Chuci*
S.	Siamese
Siam.	Siamese
Skt.	Sanskrit
Sōrui	Shima Kunio 島邦男, *Inkyo bokuji sōrui* 殷墟卜辭綜類
SSYP	*Sì shēng yùnpǔ* 四聲韻普 by Liáng Sēngbǎo
ST	Sino-Tibetan
STC	Paul K. Benedict, *Sino-Tibetan: A Conspectus*
SV	Sino-Vietnamese
sv.	stative verb
SW	Xǔ Shèn 許慎, *Shuōwén jiězì* 說文解字
SWJZGL	Dīng Fúbǎo 丁福保, *Shuōwén jiězì gǔlín* 說文解字詁林
s. w. as	same word as
[T]	introduces transcriptional forms
TB	Tibeto-Burman
TSR	James A. Matisoff, *The Loloish Tonal Split Revisited*
Tib.	Tibetan
tr.	transitive
vb.	verb
Viet.	Vietnamese

W	west(ern)
W-	Wú dialects
w	OC syllables with initial *w-
WB	Written Burmese
wf(s)	word family (families)
W(r)	Written-
WT	Written Tibetan
WTib.	Western Tibetan dialects
X-	Xiāng dialects
XS	xiesheng series (phonetic series)
Y-	Yuè dialects (Cantonese)
YWYJ	*Yǔwén yánjiū* 語文研究
YYWZX	*Yǔyán wénzì xué* 語言文字學
Zang-Mian 1992	Huáng Bùfán 黄布凡 et al., *Zàng-Miǎnyǔ zú yǔyán cíhuì* 藏緬語族語言詞匯
ZGYW	*Zhōngguó yǔwén* 中國語文
ZM92	*Zang-Mian* 1992 (Beijing)
ZWDCD	*Zhōngwén dàcídiǎn* 中文大辭典

INTRODUCTION

1 APPROACHES TO THE HISTORY OF CHINESE

The Chinese language has a long documented history that started with the writing on the Shang Dynasty oracle bones around 1250 BC. The most important pre-modern stages of the language are Old Chinese (ca. 1000 to 200 BC) and Middle Chinese (around AD 600). This 'Companion to *Grammata Serica Recensa*' ('*Grammata Serica* Companion', or *GSC* for short) is concerned with Old Chinese, but cites the conventional Middle Chinese forms, and adds an intermediate layer of Later (Eastern) Han Chinese (ca. 1st cent. AD). Later Han Chinese (LH, LHan) was intended to represent a hypothetical conservative strain of the period; it could, with hindsight, be considered Middle Han Chinese of the first centuries BC and AD.

Records in alphabetic writing provide the best information on the phonology of earlier stages of Chinese; these reach back to the Yuan Dynasty, the late 13th century (see 1.1 below). Beyond that, Chinese transcriptions of foreign words, especially in Buddhist literature, reach back to the Han period (206 BC to AD 220). But these transcriptions tell us only what at the time a Chinese translator found to be the nearest Chinese equivalent to a foreign sound (*bâ-lâ* for Indic *brah-*, for example). The methods of comparative historical phonology offer another approach by comparing modern dialects in order to reconstruct their common ancestor (Common Dialectal Chinese, 1.2), leading us back no farther than the middle of the 1st millennium AD, though. Middle Chinese (MC) is reconstructed with a philological approach, through the rime dictionary *Qièyùn* of AD 601(section 2 below).

Old Chinese (OC) is only indirectly recoverable; its two major foundations are (1) MC, and (2) the writing system and rimes in poetry (3 below) that reveal abstract phonological categories which are filled with MC phonological content. The OC writing system has evolved over a thousand years until it was standardized around 200 BC. Therefore OC is not really 'a language', since the OC reconstructions represent information on the reading of graphs that may come from different centuries and, we must assume, also different dialects. This is the best we can do. When setting up *shéng* 繩 as OC *m-ləŋ 'rope', the *m- disappeared perhaps around 1000 BC, while the *l had lost its lateral feature before 100 BC or so. On the other hand, a simple word like 'five' *ŋa may not have changed much during the first millennium BC. Overall, an OC form gives us a good idea of what a word was, phonemically and historically, during the Zhou period, thus *m-ləŋ is from a historical and linguistic standpoint an early, informative and relevant form — however Confucius might have pronounced it.

1.1 Alphabetic records

The phonologically most accurate recordings of Chinese are in alphabetic scripts. Missionary publications and documents from the 17th century onward have used transcriptions in the Latin alphabet (e.g., Francisco Varo, late 1600; see Coblin 2006). Pre-missionary transcriptions of Chinese in Korean (by Sin Sukchu) and 'Phags-pa alphabets (derived from Tibetan) reach back to the early Ming (14th century) and late Yuan (Mongol) period (13th century AD), Tangut material even to the end of the 12th century (Gong Hwang-cherng 1989). In *GSC*, samples of early transcriptions are provided as an additional 13th-14th century stage of Chinese (after the symbol [T] — these forms kindly provided by W. S. Coblin):

Sin Sukchu or *Sin S.* (EMing = Early Ming period Chinese); *SR* 'standard reading,' i.e., the reading pronunciation; *PR* 'popular reading' is the vernacular; *LR* 'left reading' (by a different recorder).
MGZY = *Měnggǔ zìyùn* 蒙古字韻 ('Phags-pa) of the Yuan (Mongol) period (1270-1308) (Coblin 2007).

Even earlier, Tang period documents found in Dunhuang include Tibetan transcriptions of Chinese words, as do Tibetan inscriptions of AD 822 in Lhasa. However, these transcriptions do not indicate tones, and the material is not as plentiful as the later alphabetic records.

Information on still earlier stages of Chinese is available in the form of transcriptions of foreign words with Chinese graphs, mostly transliterations from Indic (Sanskrit, Prakrit, Gandhari). A corpus of transcriptional forms is the basis of Coblin's

ONW(C) = Old Northwest Chinese of about AD 400 (Coblin 1994).

On a few occasions Sui-Tang Chang'an (Coblin's STCA, ca. AD 640) and MTang (Middle Tang, ca. AD 775) forms are also added. Buddhist transcriptions from the Eastern Han period (2nd cent. AD) have been investigated by Coblin (1982, 1983, 1993); they are utilized here for the reconstitution of Later Han Chinese. Earlier Middle Han (MHan) transcriptions of foreign names and words are quoted from Coblin ms. 1993; his source was primarily Pulleyblank 1962.

1.2 The comparative method and internal reconstruction

The standard approach to historical reconstruction is the comparative method; three or more of today's seven major **'dialects'**, more accurately '**Sinitic languages**', are compared and through 'triangulation' their common proto-forms reconstructed. The Chinese term translated as 'dialect', *fāngyán* 方言, lit. 'regional speech', can refer to any local Chinese language or dialect. The Sinitic languages are: Modern Standard Chinese, conventionally called 'Mandarin' (*guānhuà* 官話, or *pǔtōng-huà* 普通話, *guóyǔ* 國語), Wú 吳 (major cities include Shanghai and Suzhou), Gàn 贛 (Nanchang), Xiāng 湘 (Changsha), Yuè 粵 (= Cantonese), Kèjiā 客家 (= Hakka; a major city is Méixiàn), and Mǐn 閩 dialects (Fuzhou, Xiàmén = Amoy). This list of seven dialects follows a practical convention, yet the lines separating dialect groups can be fuzzy, and other configurations have also been suggested. Except for Mǐn and the oldest colloquial layer in southern dialects (Norman's 'Old South'), the phonological categories of modern dialects correlate with the Middle Chinese (MC) categories of the rime book *Qièyùn* (see 2.1). Since information from modern dialects provides the phonological basis for MC, *GSC* occasionally cites dialect forms for illustration (after the symbol [D]).

J. Norman (2006) has compared modern dialects, excluding Mǐn, and arrived at common forms, Common Dialectal Chinese (CDC). For example, Mandarin mén 門, Shuangfeng *miɛn*, Meixian and Guangzhou *mun* all derive from a CDC *mun²*. With this method one can reach back as far as the Tang period (ca. AD 600-800), perhaps.

Of particular interest for pre-MC are the archaic **Mǐn dialects**, because their phonology and that of Old South cannot always be correlated with the categories of the *Qièyùn*; therefore these dialects must have separated from the rest of Chinese before MC, probably as a consequence of migrations during the Qin-Han dynasties (221 BC-AD 220). (Proto-Mǐn [or 'Common Mǐn'] forms cited here are earlier reconstructions by J. Norman.) For example, the Mǐn and general Old South word for 'I, me' *ŋai^B* (Mand. *wǒ* 我) is not an analogue of MC ŋâ^B; Mandarin *cháng* 長 'long' agrees with MC ḍjaŋ, whereas Mǐn would correspond to a MC dâŋ; *shí* 石 'stone' agrees with MC źjäk, while Mǐn would correlate to a MC (d)źjak; *tiān* 天 'heaven' corresponds to MC tʰien, while Mǐn points to *tʰân; yú* 魚 'fish' corresponds to MC ŋjwo, while some Mǐn forms have initial *h-* instead of *ŋ-*; *liù* 六 'six' has initial *s-* in northern Mǐn dialects. Also the Mǐn vocabulary is more archaic, thus the word for 'dog' is etymologically the *quǎn* 犬 of classical texts, while this has been replaced in other dialects by *gǒu* 狗.

Internal reconstruction is another tool of historical linguistics; it will be successfully applied in section 4.

1.3 The philological approach

The reconstruction of MC and OC are not possible through the above material and methods because of the non-phonetic writing system and the impossibility of triangulation (OC has no known dialects or Sinitic sister languages). The reconstruction of MC is based on rime dictionaries and rime tables; see section 2 below. MC is projected back into OC, i.e., MC forms must by default be assumed to have been the same in OC unless there is OC evidence that requires adjustments. OC evidence is provided by the (fortunately many) graphs which are phonetic compounds with corroborating support from rimes in poetry (section 3), and by phonological distributional patterns (section 4). Sections 5 to 9 of this Introduction are concerned with the philological approach because this is the main path to OC.

This philological procedure for recovering MC and OC is not 'reconstruction' in the usual sense of historical linguistics; it is more like 'interpreting' the Chinese characters (Coblin). But since the term 'reconstruction' is well established, we will continue to use it.

1.4 Segments of a Chinese syllable

Sinitic languages (Chinese dialects) share many areal features with neighbors. With the likely exception of OC, all forms of Chinese, including all modern dialects, are tonal languages. OC and MC were monosyllabic languages (one word = one syllable = one graph), notwithstanding bisyllablic expressives (like Engl. ding-dong) and a few other words, notably names for insects (like Mandarin *húdié* 蝴蝶 'butterfly', *mǎyǐ* 螞蟻 'ant'), which are seized upon by those who want to disprove the 'monosyllabic myth'; technically they may have a point, depending on the definition of a 'monosyllabic language'. It is sometimes hypothesized that OC may also have had 'sesquisyllabic' (Matisoff) or 'iambic' (Sagart) words, i.e., with an unstressed pre-syllable.

What matters for MC and OC phonology is that a Chinese graph writes a **syllable** which linguists analyze as consisting of segmental and supra-segmental phonemes. For example, the MC syllable kjaŋ^B:

k	= initial, initial consonant
jaŋ^B	= final
aŋ	= rime (rhyme), rime category (i.e., the final without medial(s), tone and vowel gradations like ă, ɐ)
j	= medial, medial glide (j, w) or medial vowel (u, i)
a	= vowel
ŋ	= coda, final consonant
B	= tone

Syllables can have an additional medial *u* or *w*, called *hékǒu* 合口 'closed mouth', i.e., 'rounded mouth' (2.4). Thus MC kjaŋ has a *hékǒu* counterpart MC kjwaŋ, or MC kân vs. kwân, etc. A syllable without medial *w/u* (like kjaŋ^B) is called *kāikǒu* 開口 'open mouth'.

Certain initial consonants can occur only before certain categories of finals (see 2.4; 4.1). Occasionally, finals of a rime category differ depending on whether the initial consonant is grave or acute (see more details in 4.6):

> **grave** consonants are all labials (p pʰ b m) and gutturals (velars k kʰ g ŋ, and laryngeals h x ɣ ʔ), i.e., where in articulation the tongue is not involved
> **acute** consonants are all others: dentals (t n s ts etc.), retroflex (tṣ, ṭ ...), palatals (tśj ...), lateral (l), i.e., those where the tongue is involved

After acute initials, the OC final *-un, for example, developed a high glide in front of the dental final (OC *run > LHan luin, MC ljwen), but after grave initials, no glide emerged, or the glide was a less prominent ə (OC *kun > LHan kun > MC kjwən).

1.5 Ancient stages and dialects

Before delving into the matters at hand, it is important to remember that the pre-modern stages of Chinese, which are known only from written records, represent literary standards, koinés, but probably not spoken dialects of specific regions. Yet vernacular variants and dialects must have existed at earlier times, just as today. Literary readings of graphs vs. a vernacular language are attested for the early Ming period (Coblin 1999; 2001). Earlier, the preface to the rime dictionary *Qièyùn* (AD 601), the basis of MC, points out that at that time the reading pronunciations of north and south differed.

Commentators and philologists of the Han period (206 BC-AD 220) were aware of dialectal differences. Yáng Xióng 揚雄 (53 BC-AD 18) has collected dialect words in his *Fāngyán* 方言. Rimes in poetry and sound gloss patterns also allow conclusions about specific regional dialects (Coblin 1983: 20-26). For example, a few features of the Shandong (ancient Qí 齊) dialect are revealed by the commentator Zhèng Xuán 鄭玄 (AD127-200), a native of Shandong who worked in Luòyáng (for a biographical sketch, see Coblin *MS* 34, 1979-1980: 265), as well as by his contemporary and fellow Shandong native Liú Xī 劉熙 (ca. AD 200), author of the *Shìmíng* 釋名 (Bodman 1954; Miller in M. Loewe 1993: 424ff). Their dialect distinguished the OC rimes *-a and *-o, while these have merged in the language of other Han writers and poets. Zhèng's dialect also had lost final *n* in some environments. In Xǔ Shèn's language (d. AD 149), OC *-wa (III) and *-o (III) had merged, as they have in modern dialects. Zhèng Xuán still retained the OC rime *-ai (as do modern Mǐn dialects whose first wave of immigrants came from Shandong during the Qin and Han dynasties). In early Eastern (Late) Han, the dialect of Cháng'ān had a final velar *-ŋ* in fēng 風 'wind', while the Luòyáng dialect in Central China still retained final *-m* (Coblin *AO* 48, 1987: 107).

According to Baxter the OC language of the *Shijing* and the phonetic loans and compounds of graphs had merged the syllable types *mô and *mə̂ (> *mə̂), while there must have been an OC dialect ancestral to MC which distinguished these two (MC 母 məu vs. 每 mwậi).

A historical stage of Chinese is not necessarily a direct descendent from the previous one. For example, what is called 'Mandarin' was until the middle of the 19th century a standard based on the Nanjing dialect, the old capital city of the Ming Dynasty; but after the destruction of Nanjing during the Taiping rebellion in 1864, Mandarin shifted to a standard based on the dialect of Beijing, the capital of the Manchu empire since the 17th century.

2 MIDDLE CHINESE AND THE *QIÈYÙN*

Middle Chinese (MC, Karlgren's 'Ancient Chinese' = Anc. Ch., Zhōnggǔ Hànyǔ 中古漢語) of around AD 600 is the point of departure for investigations of pre-MC stages of the language, because MC is the earliest form of Chinese which is known from a comprehensive rime dictionary and phonological tables. (Chao Yuen Ren started the habit, followed by some authors, of using in Chinese linguistics the English spelling 'rime' for 'rhyme.) The reconstruction of MC is based on the rime dictionary *Qièyùn* and its interpretation through rime tables which have been created centuries later. However, these MC forms include, at least symbolically, all available phonological information for a given syllable and are therefore often cited as points of reference for older stages of Chinese as well as modern dialects.

This present manual on OC is not the place to debate the issues and controversies relating to MC and the *QY*. The following sections summarize only some relevant points about MC.

2.1 The rime dictionary *Qièyùn*

The basis for MC is the rime dictionary ***Qièyùn*** 切韻 (QY) by Lù Fǎ-yán 陸法言 (completed in AD 601). Best known among the later enlarged versions are the ***Guǎngyùn*** 廣韻 (GY; AD 1007-1008) and the ***Jíyùn*** 集韻 (JY; AD 1038-1039). The latter include characters which are rare or not attested in actual texts; some variant readings of graphs may be "informed rationalizing guesses on how a graph ought to be read rather than observations on how they are read, or reports how in earlier sources they were said to be read" (Ch. Harbsmeier, p.c.). Hence one cannot always be sure if one deals with 'real' words or with lexicographic ghosts.

The *QY* lists graphs in homophone groups which are separated by a circle (*niǔ* 紐); these groups are combined into **rime categories**. The sound of a graph or homophone group is suggested by a ***fǎnqiè*** 反切 spelling. This system has been used since the 2nd century AD in commentaries and dictionaries to indicate pronunciation. A word is split into its initial (consonant) and its final (what comes after it; see 1.4 above); each is expressed by a 'speller', the first ('upper') indicates the initial, the second ('lower') the final; for example, *dōng dé hóng fǎn* 東德紅反 means that dōng 東 is spelled dé 德 (t[ək]) + hóng 紅 ([ɣ]uŋ^A) = tuŋ^A (from Baxter 1992: 33).

The *QY* material is organized and interpreted through Sòng Dynasty **rime tables**, the earliest and most important of which is the ***Yùnjìng*** 韻鏡 (prefaces from AD 1161 and 1203). The table format brings out systematic relationships among and within rime categories (or rime groups, *yùnbù* 韻部). Within a rime category, individual finals belong to one of four *děng* 等 'divisions' or 'grades' (see below 2.4).

The often cited rimes of the *QY* as interpreted through the rime tables are summarized in many publications on the subject, for example, in

Baxter 1992: 65-85
Pulleyblank 1962: 72-73; 1984: 238ff.
Lǐ Fāng-kuèi 李方桂 1971. Shànggǔ yīn yánjiù 上古音研究. *Tsing Hua J. of Chinese Studies*, n.s. IX, 1&2: 1-61 (see p. 21f). In English: Gil Mattos, translator, Li Fang-kuei, Studies on Archaic Chinese. *MS* 31 (1974-1975): 219-287 (see p. 226f).
Pān Wùyún 潘悟云 2000. *Hànyǔ lìshǐ yīnyùnxué* 漢語曆史音韻學, p. 83ff.

The *QY* and the rime tables provide only *categories* of initial consonants and of finals. These empty categories need to be filled with phonological content. For this purpose, Karlgren collected the pronunciations of graphs from several modern dialects as well as from Chinese loan readings in Sino-Japanese. Thus he concluded, for example, that the initial consonant of dé 德 was in MC t-, and that the rime must have been MC -ək (cf. Cantonese tɐk[55]).

The nature and linguistic value of the *Qièyùn* and the language it represents has long been a matter of debate which colors one's attitude towards MC as well as OC. Lù Fǎ-yán's preface makes some points clear: the *Qièyùn* was written for those interested in literary pursuits, "for use in writing literature and in vocalizing literary texts" (Coblin, *JCL* 24.1: 95). It incorporated much information from earlier, now lost, dictionaries and commentaries. What prompted the compilation was the realization among Lu and his friends that north and south differed in their pronunciation. Thus the MC of the *QY* does not represent a language that was actually spoken, but reading traditions of the literati (Coblin and Norman *JAOS* 115.4 [1995]: 580).

In light of these and other caveats (see 2.5), Coblin and Norman proposed the term "Qièyùn System" (**QYS**) instead of 'MC' to refer to this somewhat artificial dictionary / rime table construct. 'MC' is a well-established term, but we will occasionally prefer 'QYS', especially when referring to features which are not reflected in an actual language, but only exist in this *QY* system, such as 'categories' and 'Divisions' (see 2.4).

2.2 MC notational systems

Today 'MC' usually means Karlgren's 'Ancient Chinese' as emended by Li Fang-kuei (1971; 1974-1975) who simplified Karlgren's MC by eliminating some non-distinctive diacritics — he replaced Karlgren's *i̯* by *j;* he indicated aspiration by *h* (*phj-* for Karlgren's *p'i̯-*); etc. Those who cite Karlgren/Li have often further eliminated non-contrastive features, such as non-phonemic distinctions between medial *w* and *u* after labials (see the note on Transcriptions in the front matter).

There are alternative proposals for MC, most notably Pulleyblank 1984; 1991. In spite of improvements over Karlgren / Li, Pulleyblank's MC does not have as much practical value because the author introduced his own complex notations (*-ɛjk, -əɛp, puawŋ*, and the like), and because many words which occur only in OC texts are of course not listed in an inventory of MC. Baxter's version of MC (Baxter 1992: 27-85, especially the charts on p. 45 and on pp. 82-85) is a computer-friendly notation without IPA symbols, so that a not immediately transparent phonetic value needed to be assigned to some ordinary English letters. In the end, the Karlgren/Li version appears to be the most often cited.

2.3 Middle Chinese tones

The *QY*'s MC had four tones: A *píngshēng* 平聲 'level' or 'even' tone; B *shǎngshēng* 上聲 'rising' tone; C *qùshēng* 去聲 'departing' or 'falling' tone; D *rùshēng* 入聲 'entering' tone, i.e., a short-stopped syllable ending in *p, t,* or *k.* A 'tone D' syllable can be viewed as toneless so that only three of the traditional four 'tones' remain.

I will use these letters for tone notations as is done in modern dialect studies, and add them as superscript letters to a MC (as well as LHan) syllable: thus MC k^huo^B for Karlgren's *k'uo:*, kuo^C for his *kuo-*. As long as one notes tones B and C, tones A and D can be left unmarked. Occasionally, I may add A for the first MC tone to emphasize that this, and not a potential other one, is intended.

MC still had voiced initial consonants like *gdbz,* but their later devoicing caused a split into so-called *yīn* 陰 (MC ʔjəm^{A1}) tones after voiceless initials (e.g., *ʔ-*), and *yáng* 陽 (MC jiaŋ^{A2}) tones after most voiced initials (e.g., *ji-*), resulting in a post-MC category of four *yīn* series tones A1, B1, C1, D1, and a corresponding *yáng* set A2, B2, C2, D2. As a result, Chinese dialects can have up to eight tones, rare further splits may lead to additional ones. In most dialects, the tones have coalesced again into a smaller number, in Mandarin into four where MC tone A *píngshēng* split into a *yīn píng* (Mand. tone 1) and a *yáng píng* (Mand. tone 2), so that Mand. syllables like *dāng* and *táng* had the same MC tone (tâŋ^A^, dâŋ^A^).

MC	Mand.	MC	Mand.	MC	Mand.
tâŋ^{A} > A1	dāng	dâŋ^{A} > A2	táng	tʰâŋ^{A} > A1	tāng
tâŋ^{B} > B1	dǎng	dâŋ^{B} > B2	dàng	tʰâŋ^{B} > B1	tǎng
tâŋ^{C} > C1	dàng	dâŋ^{C} > C2	dàng	tʰâŋ^{C} > C1	tàng
tâk^{D} > D1	duò	dâk^{D} > D2	duò	tʰâk^{D} > D1	tuò

Also in Mand. and some other dialects, *yángshǎng* 陽上 tone B2 merged with *qùshēng* (tone C) (*shǎng guī qù* 上歸去 "tone B goes to C"). Therefore the four MC tones do not correlate directly with the later four Mandarin tones:

Mand. tone 1	dāng (A1)	tāng (A1)
2	—	táng (A2)
3	dǎng (B1)	tǎng (B1)
4	dàng (B2, C1, C2)	tàng (C1)

This is a simplified summary; some syllable types have their own tonal developments. For instance, after MC nasal initials and l-, the *yángshǎng* tone behaves like a *yīn* tone.

2.4 The QYS (MC) medials and 'Divisions' 等

The rime tables systematize the *QY* material and place the graphs of every rime category into one of four so-called "Grades" or "**Divisions**" ('Div.', děng 等), resulting in up to four different finals within a rime. A *děng* can be envisioned as a row in the rime tables:

- Div. I: Modern words in the first Division have no palatal medial (Mandarin *gai, lang, gong*, etc.), only initial consonants can occur which are non-palatal, not retroflex, not affricated (except ts-...), or not dentilabialized, which leaves MC k-, t-, p-, l-, s-, etc.; see 4.1.
- Div. II: also has no palatal medial, but the MC vowels have a special timbre which caused a rather recent palatalization of velars (家 jiā < ka); MC Div. II vowels in Karlgren's / Li's system are *a, å, ă, ɐ, ɛ*. Only grave (labial and guttural; see 1.4) and retroflex initials (ṭ-, tṣ-, ṣ-) can occur in this Division, but no dentals and palatals.
- Div. III: includes words with a palatal post-initial glide, i.e., Karlgren's MC medial 'yod' *i̯* = Li's *j;* words in this Division have in Mandarin medial *i*, or affricate, sibilant or dentilabial initials, e.g., *liang, jiang, chong, fen*, etc). There are no dental initials (t tʰ d n).
- Div. IV: includes syllables with a prominent medial i after the same initials as in Div. I (Mand. *tiān, diǎo*, etc.). Because of this and because of complementarity (no main vowel *e* in Div. I, only main vowel *e* in Div. IV), Div. IV belongs structurally to Div. I. Therefore one can combine them into 'Div. I/IV'.

A defining feature of a Division is the presence or absence of a medial yod *j* or *i:* there is no medial in Div. I and II, *j* in Div. III, *i* in Div. IV. Div. III *j* mixes freely with Div. I, II and IV syllables in phonetic series (see below) as well as word families (kjän, kân, kăn). The other medial *w* or *u* marks so-called *hékǒu* 合口 'rounded mouth' syllables (MC kjwaŋ, kwân)

(Karlgren/Li write *w* in some syllables, *u* in others); syllables without this bilabial medial are called *kāikǒu* 開口 'open mouth' (MC kjaŋ, kân). The MC *w* is, however, of a completely different nature from medial *j*. The latter is tied to Division III, but the medial bilabial can occur in any Division and freely combine with Div. III *j* (*-jw-*) and Div. IV *i* (*-iwe-*): *kwân, kjwän, kiwen*. The medial *w/u* belongs to a word's root, hence *hékǒu* words do not mix with *kāikǒu* words in phonetic series (see below) and word families. Similarly, Div. IV *i* also belongs to a word's root. For the description of syllable structure *kāikǒu* examples suffice, because the *hékǒu* counterparts are predictable.

Karlgren reconstructed MC finals belonging to the four divisions of rime category *-an*, for instance, as follows:

Div.		Mand.	MC *kāikǒu*		Mand.	MC *hékǒu*
I	寒	hán	ɣân	官	guān	kwân
II	顏	yán	ngan	關	guān	kwan
III	健	jiàn	kjɐn^{C}	綣	quǎn	k^{h}jwɐn^{B}
IV	見	jiàn	kien^{C}	犬	quǎn	k^{h}iwen^{B}

Some rimes, such as *-an*, have an additional set of finals with medial *j*, the so-called **chóngniǔ** doublets. As we have seen, a circle called *niǔ* 紐 'knot, button', marks the start of a set of homophones. In some rimes a set is followed by a superficially identical one (looking like a 'doublet') which is introduced with a 'second button' (*chóngniǔ* 重紐). But one set is placed in Div. III, one in Div. IV. We will write a 3 or 4 after a *chóngniǔ* syllable, and refer to the subdivisions as 3/3 (chóngniǔ Div. III) and 3/4 (chóngniǔ Div. IV) respectively:

Div.		Mand.	MC	*chóngniǔ* doublets	
I	O 寒	hán	ɣân		
II	O 顏	yán	ŋan		
III	O 健	jiàn	kjɐn	3/3	O 蹇 jiǎn, MC kjän^{B} 3
IV	O 見	jiàn	kien	3/4	O 遣 qiǎn, MC k^{h}jiän^{B} 4

These doublets occur only in certain rimes after grave initials (see 1.4 above). Grave initials tend to have more finals (e.g., MC kjɐn, kjän, kjiän) than acute initials (only *tśjän*).

Karlgren considered the finals of 蹇 ki̯än and 遣 k'i̯än (in his MC notation) the same — considered them 'doublets', and the *chóngniǔ* distinctions spurious. Li took note of the *chóngniǔ* doublets in his emendations to Karlgren's MC, thus his *kjän* for Div. 3/3, a stronger medial *kjiän* in Div. 3/4. Traces of this *chóngniǔ* 3 vs. 4 distinction have been uncovered in Chinese dialects, medieval transcriptions, and Chinese loans in Vietnamese and Korean. There is a trace even in Mandarin: jì 悸 (GSR 538e), Karlgren's Anc. Ch. g'i̯wi-, is actually in *chóngniǔ* Div. 4 (Karlgren says that *jì* for the expected *guì* is 'irregular'), vs. kuì 匱 (GSR 540g) Anc. Ch. g'i̯wi- in *chóngniǔ* Div. 3.

With these *chóngniǔ* subdivisions, the QYS has up to six finals within a rime category, actually seven when considering two vowel timbres in Div. II:

Div. I	no MC medial yod	— 寒 hán, MC ɣân, OCM *gân
Div. II	from OC medial *r	— 顏 yán, MC ŋan, *ŋrân
	from OC medial *r	— 間 jiān, MC kǎn, *krên
Div. III	MC medial yod	— 健 jiàn, MC kjɐn^{C}, *kans

Div. 3/3	*chóngniǔ* Div. III after grave initials — 蹇 jiǎn, MC kjän^B 3, *kranʔ
Div. 3/4	*chóngniǔ* Div. IV after grave initials, only in combination with OC front vowels — 遣 qiǎn, MC kʰjiän^B 4, *khenʔ
Div. IV	MC 'pure' Div. IV — 見 jiàn, MC kien^C, *kêns

All these Divisions have, of course, *hékǒu* counterparts: MC ɣwân, ŋwan, kjwɐn... kiwen.

2.5 Problems with the *Qièyùn* and Middle Chinese

The value and reliability of the *Qièyùn*, and with it of MC, has been much debated, among other reasons because of its admittedly and obvious heterogeneous composition as well as its interpretation through much later rime tables.

Some MC features did not exist in AD 600 but have been projected back from the rime tables of later centuries. When these tables were compiled, the main vowel *e* (as opposed to *je*) always combined with a preceding *i*, there was only *ie* as in tiān 天 tʰien. The rime tables placed these syllables into a fourth row, Division IV, which according to Karlgren was characterized by this strong vocalic medial *i*. However, earlier during the Tang period and before, the final was simply *-en*, as transcriptions of foreign words indicate and the syllable structure of MC would require. Thus 天 was really MC tʰen; the vowel *e* warped into *ie* only later (on warping, see 7.6 below). Thus the MC Div. IV syllables are really of the Div. I type, and can be combined into Div. I/IV, as was already noted.

Another rime table feature, which Karlgren and his successors have perhaps misinterpreted and projected back into MC, concerns Div. III syllables with later dentilabial initials (*f, w*). In the tables, Mand. *fan* (Div. III) relates to *ban* (Div. I), as *zhan* (Div. III) does to *dan* (Div. I). It was assumed that a Div. was marked by a single feature, which for Div. III was believed to be the palatal medial *j*. Since *zhan* could derive from MC tśjän, it was then assumed that *fan* must derive from something like *pjwɐn*. However, all dialectal and transcriptional evidence points to a bilabial glide *w*, without a palatal; also phonetically, a medial *w* (or main vowel *u*), not *j*, would explain dentilabialization (*pw- > f; mw- > w-, mut > wut*) (Coblin 1991b). Hence there was no medial *j* in any of these labial-initial syllables; the rime tables may have placed them in Div. III because of the parallelism and complementary distribution with medial *j* syllables after non-labial initials. While Karlgren / Li write, therefore, wù 物 'thing' as MC mjwət, Pulleyblank (Early MC) and Norman (CDC) are certainly correct in postulating EMC and CDC *mut*; the word was the same in LHan. However, QYS forms are customarily quoted for reference, because they contain all the linguistic information of the Chinese philological tradition. Thus *mjwət* tells the reader that historically (i.e., in MC) the initial of wù 物 is *m-*, the rime category is *-ət*, the syllable belongs to Div. III (*-j-*), and it is a *hékǒu* syllable *(-u-)*. A frontish vocalic glide has developed between the vowel *u* and the following dental, thus phonemic *mut* was probably phonetically realized as [muət] so that *-ət* was felt to be the rime. Such off-glides are still clearly heard in Mandarin in careful enunciation so that lún 論 sounds like *luən* or *luin*.

The heterogeneous nature of the *QY* corpus is not only mentioned in its preface, but is also revealed by several syllables which do not fit the system. Thus *dì* 地 (MC di^C) 'earth' and *lěng* 冷 (MC lɐŋ^B) 'cold' are non-canonical syllables, because *d-* cannot occur in combination with final *-i*, and *l-* and Div. II *-ɐ-* are mutually exclusive. Less conspicuous is a word like *jǐn* 緊 MC kjien^B, whose *k-* in front of the Div. 3/4 medial *-ji-* should have palatalized. Its failure to do so betrayes *jǐn* as a Southern intrusion. The *QY* is not in error because the Mandarin pronunciations of these three words are regular analogues to MC. On the one hand, this raises the question: which features of the *QY* reflect regional doublets that should not be projected back into OC? And given this uncertainty, should one dare reconstruct OC at all? And the *QY* has a suspiciously large inventory of phonemes. Some scholars have suspected, for example, that MC *źj-* and *dźj-* reflect dialectal variants. On the other hand, virtually every *QY* distinction has been confirmed by some dialect somewhere. Then again: reconstruction of CDC results in a simple phonological system so that CDC looks like a 'real' language, and the *QY* surreal. On the other hand, CDC is painted with a very broad brush; inclusion of more dialects would probably alter the picture and bring it closer to the *QY*.

Whatever the *QY* may be, it is not fiction; it has preserved pre-*QY* features, as is confirmed by the OC phonetic series. Furthermore the *QY* is all we have to work with when probing into pre-*QY* stages of the languages. We have no choice but to base reconstructions of earlier stages like OC on the QYS reconstructions. Even considering that incongruous readings have slipped in, the bulk of the *QY* material is probably reliable, as long as one restricts oneself to words that are still in use today, or words that occur in actual texts.

3 OLD CHINESE: PHONETIC SERIES

Any reconstruction of Old Chinese (OC = Karlgren's Archaic Chinese = Arch. Ch. *shànggǔ Hànyǔ* 上古漢語), including, of course, Baxter's (OCB = Old Chinese - Baxter) and Minimal Old Chinese (OCM) is based, first, on Middle Chinese which was discussed in the previous section 2; and secondly, on the composite graphs as grouped into phonetic series which are the subject of the present section. Phonetic series are analyzed together with rimes in early texts, especially the **Shījīng** 詩經, a collection of about 300 early and mid Zhou-period songs, but unfortunately redacted during the Han period.

3.1 Composite graphs

Graphs ('characters') are key to OC. They fall into several types (for more details, see, for example, Norman 1988: 65ff; Boltz 1994; Qiu Xigui 2000). The main division is between *wén* 文 'simple non-composite graphs', and *zì* 字 'composite graphs'. *Wén* are semantographs; they indicate the meaning but contain no phonetic information. These include pictograms: *rì* 日 'sun', *mù* 木 'tree'; symbolic graphs: *shàng* 上 'above', *yī* 一 'one'; deictic graphs: *běn* 本 'root' where a stroke at the lower part of *mù* 木 'tree' indicates that the root is meant.

The vast majority of graphs are composites or compounds. They are of two kinds: (1) semantic composites (*huìyì* 會意 'joined meanings'), like *hào* 好 'woman' + 'child' = 'love'. (2) Crucial for the reconstruction of OC are the much more numerous phonetic composites or 'phonograms' (*xiéshēng* 諧聲 or *xíngshēng* 形聲) that consist of a **phonetic** element, which roughly indicates the sound, and of one of 214 **classifiers** or ('**radicals**', 'significs'), which broadly suggests the semantic category. Phonetic compound graphs emerged in order to disambiguate multiple readings and their words. Thus 自 originally wrote both *zì* 'self' and *bí* 'nose', then *bì* 畀 'give' was added to 'nose' as the phonetic element, hence 鼻 'nose', but now *zì* 自 'self' only. Much more common was the inverse process in which a classifier was added to a graph that was borrowed for its sound, as *yán* 言 MC ŋjɐn 'speech' was added as classifier to *wú* 吾 MC ŋuo 'I' serving now as phonetic to write the word *yǔ* 語 MC ŋjwo^{B}.

Graphs with the same phonetic element form a **phonetic series**, or **xiéshēng series** (**XS** series). The implication is that members of a phonetic series sounded similar in OC at the time of their creation, as their MC forms already suggest, e.g., 亶 tân^B, 鱣 tjän, 饘 tśjän, 擅 źjän^C.

The Han period dictionary ***Shuōwén jiězì*** 說文解字 (*SW*) by Xǔ Shèn 許慎 (d. 149 BC) explains the role of a particular element in a graph, whether Xǔ takes it to be phonetic or semantic. The *SW* may therefore furnish information for ambiguous graphs, or confirm what modern scholars already suspect. But the *SW* is to be taken with a grain of salt; see the discussion in 8.1. Many graphs write different words with their distinct readings as, for instance, 長 *cháng* 'long', *zhǎng* 'grow'; or *qū* 區 'conceal' can be borrowed for *gōu* 'crooked'. Commenting on classical texts, the ***Jīngdiǎn shìwén*** 經典釋文 (*JD*) by Lù Dé-míng 陸德明 (556-627) identifies the correct word behind a graph with multiple readings and provides the appropriate *fanqie* spelling.

3.2 The Xiesheng principle

A graph by itself, like 亶, tells us nothing about its OC pronunciation. All we can do is fill in the blanks with MC readings. Thus the graph can only be interpreted through its reconstructed MC reading *tân*. OC is basically MC; we must assume MC phonological values for OC unless there is evidence from OC phonological categories and phonological distributional patterns, and perhaps also other evidence, that the MC forms need adjustment to fit OC categories.

The first step in the reconstruction of OC is to identify the categories of initials through phonetic series, and of rimes through phonetic series and rimes in poetry. As in MC, these are abstract categories with no phonological content. The challenge is to distribute the rather unsymmetrical, reconstructed MC phonological categories over the OC ones (tables at the head of many *GSC* Rime sections illustrate this). The list of the generally accepted OC categories is presented below (5.4) with OCM (basically Baxter's) phonological values. Many dictionaries are organized by rime categories, including Karlgren's *GSR*. Unfortunately, *GSR* numbers the phonetic series without break from 1 through 1260, without making the rime categories explicit. (In this *GSC*, the rime categories are numbered from 1 through 38.)

There was apparently a system behind the creation of OC phonetic compounds, the '*xie-sheng* principle' (XS principle), according to which members of a phonetic series share the same OC rime and the same or similar set of initial consonants. This principle led Karlgren to a number of conclusions about OC, including:

- One set of words in MC -jɐŋ (e.g., 京 kjɐŋ) occurs in XS series consistently with words in OC *-aŋ, another set (e.g., 驚 kjɐŋ) in OC *-eŋ series, hence two distinct OC rimes must have merged in MC (see Table 2-1 under Rime 2).
- The MC final *-jän* must have been *an*-like in OC: note 亶 tân^B, 鱣 tjän, 饘 tśjän, 擅 źjän^C. These words all had the same OC rime, because in phonetic series MC -jän mixes with MC -ân, but not with MC -ien.
- MC -åŋ has systematic XS contacts with MC -uŋ, -jwoŋ; according to the XS principle, *jiāng* 江 must have had the same OC rime as the other graphs in the series; note *gōng* 工 (MC kung), *hóng* 紅 (ɣung), *qióng* 邛 (gjwong). Consequently the OC words were, in OCM notation, kôŋ, gôŋ, goŋ, krôŋ.

Li's XS principle was formulated in simple terms: (1) every OC rime category had one vowel (and not variants correlating to QYS Divisions, such as å, a, â, ɐ). (2) In a XS series only initials from a single manner series (set of homorganic consonants) can occur. This formula advanced our understanding of OC phonology in significant ways.

3.3 Incongruous series

Naturally, a XS concept is apt to have fuzzy edges. The developers of the OC script have occasionally stretched the principle by allowing XS contacts between homorganic final consonants (-k ~ -ŋ ~ open vowel; -t ~ -n; -p ~ -m), and final -i and -n are occasionally written with the same phonetic. Velar initials can also co-occur with laryngeals h- and ʔ-, or even nasal ŋ-.

Many phonetic series are difficult or impossible to reconcile with a XS principle. These are of two kinds: (1) **Systematic** incongruous series in which the initials belong to completely different places of articulation, like MC l co-occurring with k, p, or s. This kind of mix in phonetic series is encountered so often that some principle was followed in their creation. (2) Occasionally phonetic series include initials of different manner series and/or different vowels/final consonants alternating in a rare, even unique and therefore **unsystematic** way; note, for example, 'bird' *zhuī* 隹 which was borrowed for the word *wéi* 'to be' (9.2.6). These cases leave much room for interpretation and speculation, and generate, of course, the most hypotheses and disagreements — and since specialists debate mostly these, they project the skewed impression that virtually *all* about OC is still not settled. I believe that some of these unsystematic series and graphs share only the rime, or initial, or no common phonetic denominator at all so that, I submit, the XS principle does not apply; see 9.2.1.

4 OLD CHINESE THROUGH INTERNAL RECONSTRUCTION

The Preface (p. x) has already defined "Minimal Old Chinese" (OCM). In this section and in section 5 of this Introduction, generally accepted post-Karlgrenian improvements and proposals, which are also incorporated in Baxter's OCB and hence OCM, will be summarized. 'OC' and 'OCM' are for the most part (nearly) identical. Sections 4 and 5 present the rationales for reconstructions in broad outline; for details and proper intellectual credits, consult Baxter 1992. Throughout, particulars of OCM will be pointed out; section 6 summarizes some principles and criteria for OCM; for a fuller account of my rationales for certain OCM details, see the Introduction to *EDOC*. Assumptions, premises, interpretations and sources will be considered in sections 8 and 9.

Karlgren's objective was to reconstruct the *sounds* of OC, not its phonemes. He represented his sounds and their subtle gradations with diacritics and special letters that alone create for the occasional user a formidable barrier for detecting a system. Therefore scholars after Karlgren soon tried to simplify and systematize his Arch. Chin., now called OC.

Some phonemic features of OC can be reconstructed with the methods of internal reconstruction, without reference to graphs, XS principles, and interpretation of phonetic series. Therefore the conclusions generally tend to be well founded.

4.1 The distribution of QY initials

Studying MC in alphabetic transcription, without reference to graphs, already reveals several features of pre-MC, i.e., OC. The MC initial consonants are distributed over the *QY* Divisions (2.4) unevenly, resulting in an unbalanced phonological system. The tabulation on the next page shows:

With Div. I/IV finals can occur all initials except *g*, palatals, and retroflex ones.

With Div. II finals can only occur grave initials (except *g*) and retroflex initials.

All initials can combine with Div. III finals, except *ɣ* and the dentals *t tʰ d n*.

Div.	I/IV -ân/-ien	II -an	III -jän, -jɐn
grave	k kʰ - ŋ ʔ x	k kʰ - ŋ ʔ x	kj kʰj gj ŋj ʔj xj
	ɣ	ɣ	—
	p pʰ b m	p pʰ b m	pj pʰj bj mj
acute	ts tsʰ dz s l	—	tsj tsʰj dzj sj zj lj
	t tʰ d n	—	—
	—	—	tśj tśʰj źj dźj śj ńźj j
	—	ṭ ṭʰ ḍ ṇ	ṭj ṭʰj ḍj ṇj
	—	tṣ tṣʰ dẓ ṣ	tṣj tṣʰj dẓj ṣj

(MC finals of the *-an* rime category are added to the Div. for illustration.) Thus *ɣân, gjän, lân* and *tân* are permissible MC syllables; *ṭân, ṣân, san, lan* or *tjân* are not, but *ṭan, ṭjän* and *ṣan* again are.

4.2 MC initial ɣ-

The tabulation in 4.1 shows that the MC initial *ɣ*- (only in Div. I/IV, II) is in complementary distribution with MC *gj*- (only in Div.III). The earlier, i.e., OC source of *ɣ*- was *g-:

		Mand.	MC	OCM		Mand.	MC	OCM
k-	干	gān	kân	kân	建	jiàn	kjɐnC	kans
kʰ-	看	kàn	kʰânC	khâns	褰	qiān	kʰjän 3	khan
g	—		—	—	乾	qián	gjän 3	gan
ɣ	寒	hán	ɣân	gân	—		—	—

The phonetic series confirm this because *ɣ*- mixes freely with velars. The phoneme *ɣ*- can thus be eliminated from OC, and the system of initials is thereby simplified and regularized.

4.3 MC palatal initials

The tabulation in 4.1 shows that the palatals and dentals are in complementary distribution; palatals are the Div. III counterparts to the Div. I dentals: tśj- relates to t-, as kj- does to k-. Palatals must have resulted from OC dentals + j (tj-), or rather from OC dentals plus the feature which resulted in the QYS Div. III finals with medial *j* (4.6). XS series confirm the affinity of palatals to dentals, as in *GSR* 148, for example: 亶 tânB < OCM *tânʔ, 饘 tśjän < *tan, 擅 źjänC < *dans. Thus the set of palatal consonants is removed from the OC inventory, and phonetic series in question conform now to Li's XS principle. This is confirmed by the near absence of palatals from foreign transcriptions in the Middle Han period and earlier (Coblin ms. 1993:15); for foreign palatals Chinese dental affricates are used (LH 龜茲 *khu-dziə = Kuca [Hanshu]; LH 且末 tsʰiaB-mɑt = Calmadana; LH 丘就 kʰu-dziu = Kujula).

4.4 MC medial w and u

One striking imbalance in the distribution of MC rimes is the association of medial *w* or *u* (*hékǒu* 合口 'rounded mouth') with dental final consonants (-n, -t, Karlgren *-r = OCM *-i) after *all* initials, even after acute ones (短 twân), whereas this medial occurs in velar and most open rimes only after guttural initials in MC; there are no OC *tuang and *tuəŋ, nor *ton and *tun in Karlgren's system:

	MC	OC		MC	OC
干	kân	*kan	剛	kâŋ	*kaŋ
官	kwân (1)	*kwan	光	kwâŋ	*kwaŋ
貫	kwân (2)	*kon	公	kuŋ	*koŋ
短	twân	*ton	東	tuŋ	*toŋ
根	kən	*kən	亙	kəŋ	*kəŋ
壼	kwən (1)	*kwən	肱	kwəŋ	*kwəŋ
睏	kwən (2)	*kun	宮	kjuŋ	*kuŋ
敦	twən	*tun	冬	tuoŋ	*tuŋ

The dental *hékǒu* rimes are parallel to the finals *-oŋ and *-uŋ; therefore, MC twan derives from *ton, twən from *tun. For velar rimes, one assumes labialized unit phonemes such as OCB *k^w-, *$ʔ^w$-, *h^w- (in OCM simply *kw-, *ʔw-, *hw-). Baxter has tried to show that rimes such as *-un, *-on, *-en (rather than *-uən, *-uan, *-ian) formed distinct categories in the XS series and *Shijing* poetry and hence in OC. By and large, the rimes appear to support such narrower categories and simple vowels for OC. At any rate, this phonemic analysis presents a balanced picture, whatever the actual pronunciation might have been around 600 BC.

Neither internal reconstruction nor the XS principle can determine which MC kwân and which MC kwən had an OC labiovelar initial (kwan, kwən), and which a rounded vowel (kon, kun). One must rely on the interpretation of rimes in literature, which are, however, lacking for the majority of words in question.

4.5 OC consonant clusters and *r

MC *l*-, retroflex initials, and Div. II are traced back to an OC *r by using the XS principle together with the method of internal reconstruction.

4.5.1 In not a few phonetic series MC *l*- interchanges with velar, labial, or retroflex initials. Following Karlgren (1933: 57f; 1954) and Li (1971), all investigators assume OC consonant **clusters** in such series. Consider series 36-5/609 which includes *jiàn* 監 'look at' and *lán* 藍 'indigo'. How to apply the XS principle (Karlgren's OC forms):

(a) jiàn 監 (kam) < *klam ~ lán 藍 (lâm) < *lâm
(b) jiàn 監 (kam) < *kam ~ lán 藍 (lâm) < *glâm
(c) jiàn 監 (kam) < *klam ~ lán 藍 (lâm) < *glâm

Karlgren (who used *GSR* 766 各 for illustration) opted for the consonant cluster (c) because this best complied with his principle in making the OC forms most similar, and because of support from Tai where 藍 'indigo' has initial *gr-. He needed two initial OC *g-, though, in order to account for minimal pairs in which one aspirated consonant survived in MC, one unaspirated disappeared:

lán 藍 MC lâm (Div. I) < *glâm vs. xiàn 檻 MC ɣam^B (Div. II) < *g'lam

Bodman, followed by OCB and OCM, symbolized the distinction by hyphenating the suspected pre-initial that was lost in MC: lán < OCM *g-râm vs. xiàn < *grâm. Karlgren cautioned that his choice (c) is not necessarily appropriate in all XS. In some of his series MC l- derives from Arch. Ch. *l-, in others from *gl- or *bl-.

4.5.2 Li's XS principle does not permit initials from more than one manner series to mingle in a XS series (hence MC tśj < OC *tj); when MC *l-* is part of the mix, one assumes clusters, as in *jiàn* 監 above. MC s, ts... and **retroflex** ṣ, tṣ... do mix, though:

24-45/193	shān 山	MC ṣan, ṣǎn
	xiān 仙	MC sjän

Li's XS principle requires clusters here. That the retroflex initial derives from an earlier combination MC s- + r (Li's OC *l) is suggested by XS contacts like this:

4-52/975	shǐ 史	MC ṣɨ^{B} Div. III	< OCM *srəʔ
	lì 吏	MC ljɨ^{C} Div. III	< OCM *rəh

Retroflection develops under the influence of an adjacent retroflex sound; an earlier OC *r is about the only candidate for triggering retroflection. An *r* is in the world's languages, including many cognate Tibeto-Burman ones and other languages in the geographic neighborhood, typically a retroflex flap or trill of some sort. Note, for example, Skt. *varṇa* (not *varna*) 'color', *vṛṣa* 'bull'; Skt. *śiras* nom. 'head', *śirṣṇas* gen. 'of the head'; Written Tibetan (WT) *drag* > modern Tibetan ṭha̱à, WT *bkra* > modern Tib. ṭā; while Vietnamese *traŋ* for MC tjaŋ is most instructive. According to the rule of economy, a single OC phoneme *r accounts for both MC *l* and retroflection, therefore the reconstruction of the OCM forms above.

4.5.3 MC **Div. II** goes back to the same feature as retroflex initials; it must also have been triggered by the loss of an OC medial *r, because

if	彡 shān	MC ṣam	Div. II	< OCM *srâm,
then	監 jiàn	MC kam	Div. II	< OCM *krâm.

(Note that in OCM the circumflex as in *â* does not indicate a special timbre, but is a neutral symbol for the unknown source of later Div. I/IV and II.) Karlgren already reconstructed a medial *l (= OCM *r) in *GSR* 609 (*klam), but he did so because of the XS principle, which can, however, be subject to interpretation (note how he pondered the cluster choices). Now the Div. II medial *r is proven on phonological grounds independent of the XS environment.

The tabulation in 4.1 above shows, furthermore, that MC initial l- in Div. I/IV is in complementary distribution with retroflection and Div. II (the only exception is 冷 MC lɐŋ^{B} [Div. II] > lěng 'cold'), so that l- in MC Div. I/IV and Div. II syllables had the same OC final:

lán	藍	MC lâm	Div. I	< OCM *râm
jiàn	監	MC kam	Div. II	< OCM *krâm
shān	彡	MC ṣam	Div. II	< OCM *srâm

OC medial *r can also occur in MC Div. III syllables:

shǐ	史	MC ṣɨ^{B}	Div. III	< OCM *srəʔ
lì	吏	MC ljɨ^{C}	Div. III	< OCM *rəh

4.5.4 As to the **phoneme sequence**, whether the *r and sonorants followed the main consonant (*kram, *srəʔ) or preceded it (OC *rkam, *rsəʔ), or followed the vowel as Pullayblank has suggested (*karn), a maxim of linguistics holds that not all possible combinations have equal weight. In languages throughout the world the sequence C+r is typical, it is 'unmarked', normal and natural, while the switch of the two would be highly marked, unusual, and requires special pleading. An exceptional (!) language is Written Tibetan (WT) with words like *rta* 'horse'. But even in Tibetan it is the post-initial *r* that triggers retroflection (WT *drag* > ṭha̱à), while pre-initial *r* does not (WT *rta* > tā).

4.6 OC syllable types A and B: QYS Div. III and medial yod

Since MC Div. I/IV and II share the same OC final (4.5.3), only two syllable types remain in OC (Li's Div. III *j* is written in for clarity, though recent OC proposals have eliminated it):

	(A) Div. I/IV/II -ân	(B) Div. III -jan
grave	k k^h g ŋ ʔ h	kj k^hj gj ŋj ʔj hj
	kr k^hr gr ŋr ʔr hr	krj-... inferred from XS series
	p p^h b m	pj p^hj bj mj
	pr p^hr br mr	prj-... inferred from XS series
acute	t t^h d n	tj t^hj dj nj l j
	tr t^hr dr nr	trj t^hrj drj nrj
	ts ts^h dz s r	tsj ts^hj dzj sj zj rj
	tsr ts^hr dzr sr	tsrj ts^hrj dzrj srj

Now the parallelism and balance are perfect; the two OC syllable types are:

type A corresponds to QYS Div. I/IV and II,
type B corresponds to QYS Div. III (including 3/3 and 3/4 with *j*).

In Karlgren's / Li's MC, all Div. III syllables are characterized by a medial *j* which in the past has been projected back into OC. A medial *j* in an OC reconstruction like *ṭjan or *tjan nicely explains both the palatalization as well as the vowel fronting in the MC equivalent *tśjän*.

However, a little more than half of all MC words have this yod; an actual Han period text has 3/4 of all words with MC medial *j*, only 1/4 without (Jakob Dempsey, p.c.). This proportion is very unusual for a language. Pulleyblank has long argued that these yods did not exist in OC, and this is widely believed today. Many Div. III syllables had no *j*, even in MC, according to Pulleyblank (see 2.5), nor in LHan (see below); dentilabialized syllables never had a palatal glide (2.5). The absence of *j* is suggested by the rule of economy and by the transcription of foreign syllables without medial yod, which are rendered by Div. III syllables (Pulleyblank 1994: 73f); and the closely related TB language group, which does not have this phenomenon of a prolific medial palatal, supports the assumption that such medial *j* are typologically unlikely for ST; they seem to be a Chinese innovation.

Two Han period commentators have described the pronunciation of Div. I vs. Div. III syllables, but their phrasing leaves some room for interpretation:

(1) Pān Wùyún (2000: 148-149) quotes and discusses the remarks by Gāo Yòu 高誘 (fl. AD 196-219), the commentator of the texts *Huainanzi* and *Lüshi chunqiu* (all statements cited in Coblin 1983: 228-233). According to Gāo, the Div. III words are pronounced *jí qì* 急氣, the Div. I/IV/II words *huǎn qì* 緩氣. Zhengzhang Shangfang understands these terms to mean 'fast' (*jí* basically means 'urgent') and 'slow' (*huǎn* basically means 'slack') articulation, which he takes to mean 'short' and 'long'. However, the terms could just as well be translated

'tense' and 'lax' pronunciation (Pān and Zhengzhang reject this because they believe that more TB languages make length distinctions than tense/lax distinctions).

(2) Hé Xiū 何休 (AD 129-182), quoted by Bodman (1980: 162), describes the distinction: 言乃 (nậi^B) 者內而深，言而 (ńźjɨ) 者外而淺 "nậi^B (Div. I) is pronounced inside and deep, and ńźjɨ (Div. III) is pronounced outside and shallow" (QYS readings).

Whatever this means, the Han commentator did not describe long vs. short. He might possibly have tried to describe lax (內而深 = 緩氣?) and tense (外而淺 = 急氣?), or pharyngeal vs. plain.

So far the OC origin of the QYS Div. III is a matter of hypotheses and speculation. Pulleyblank considers the distinction prosodic (*JCL* 22.1, 1994: 95). Norman leaves type B syllables unmarked and considers Type A (Div. I/IV) syllables pharyngealized. Zhengzhang Shangfang and Pān Wùyún explain the distinction as differences in length. Most promising is the idea that at some point in OC the difference has been between tense and lax syllables as in Austroasiatic (AA) register languages (Ferlus); in fact, Pulleyblank (1994: 93) has already pointed to parallelism with Khmer registers, after having drawn heavily on the AA languages Vietnamese and Muong in his arguments.

Proposals for OC usually indicate the syllable types with phonologically neutral symbols. For OCM we mark type A syllables (Div. I/IV and II) with a symbolic circumflex accent (as in French *lâche* 'lax') and leave type B syllables unmarked; but the notation of the features is immaterial (*OC > MC):

Syllable	Type A	Type B
OCM > MC	*tân > tân	*tan > tśjän
Norman	*'tan > tân	*tan > tśjän
Recent trend	*ttan > tân	*tan > tśjän
Pulleyblank	*tán > tân	*tàn > tśjän
Sagart 1999	*ᵃtan > tân	*ᵇtan > tśjän
Pān Wùyún	*tan > tân	*tăn > tśjän
Karlgren, Li	*tân > tân	*tjan > tśjän
Baxter 1992	*tɑn > tɑn	*tjɑn > tsyen

5 OLD CHINESE THROUGH THE XIESHENG SYSTEM

The methods of historical linguistics discussed so far (above) have provided fairly reliable reconstructions of some features of OC. However, other aspects of OC are only recoverable through the analysis of the graphs and the phonetic series with the XS principle. For example, if it were not for phonetic series, the connection between MC initial *x-* and nasals could never be known (5.1.5). Unfortunately, the phonetic series do not reveal other OC features as transparently as in the case of MC x-, so that one needs to rely on interpretations based on assumptions and theories (see section 9).

5.1 Initial consonants

5.1.1 The QYS has two **MC initial yod** (*j-*, in Chinese yù 喻), one placed in Div. III (*yù sān* 喻三), one in Div. IV (*yù sì* 喻四):

yù sān = MC jw- Div. III, as in *yuè* 越 MC jwɐt, Karlgren *gi̯wat (OCM *wat)
yù sì = MC ji- Div. IV, as in *yuè* 悅 MC jiwät, Karlgren *di̯wat (OCM *lot)

Since MC *jw-* has XS contacts with gutturals, Karlgren set up Arch. Ch. *gi̯wat 越 with *g-;* for MC *ji-* he variously postulated initial *gi̯-, *bi̯-, *zi̯-, but mostly *di̯- depending on the XS environment, hence 悅 is *di̯wat in his Arch. Ch. To distinguish the voiced stops, which disappear by MC, from ones that survive, he set up the more endurable type as aspirated: *g'i̯-, *b'i̯-, and *d'i̯- (see 4.5.1).

MC *jw-* occurs always with the medial glide *w* (exceptions are the two grammatical words *yān* 焉 and *yǐ* 矣 with plausible sandhi explanations). This initial is now generally written as OC *w-, as required by the rule of economy, and confirmed by Buddhist transcriptions of Indic words in Han-period transliterations where this initial consistently represents Indic *v*, e.g., yuè 越 jwɐt 3 < *wat for Indic *vat*.

The process of elimination and historical phonology both lead to the conclusion that the major source of the **MC *ji-*** was OC *l. MC *ji-* mixes in phonetic series with *d* and t^h, among others; they must all be variants of a distinct OC consonant. The source of MC *ji-* cannot have been a dental stop or *r (they are already identified in OC), nor a palatal (it would not mix with dentals). It cannot have been OC *j-, because too many unusual phonological steps would be required to explain a connection with *d-. This leaves OC *l-: phonetically it is only one step from *l* to *d* (*l* is simply *d* with the air escaping laterally), as illustrated in Línchuān *ti* (< *di*) for Mand. *li* 里. Then, initial *l-* being replaced by *j-* has parallels, e.g., Burmese (*r*, *l* > *j*, note Yangon 'Rangoon'), and Spanish. By the Middle Han period a high medial glide (i or j) had emerged in later Div. III syllables as a result of vowel warping (see 7.6). This medial became the new initial *j-* because the old *l- had to give way to a new *l-* (> MC *l-*) from OC *r-:

because 亮 OC *raŋ > riaŋ > LH liɑŋ
therefore 陽 OC *laŋ > liaŋ > LH Øiɑŋ = jɑŋ
perhaps also 莠 OC *wuʔ (?) > wɨuʔ (?) > LH Øiu^B = ju^B (MC jiəu^B); see below.

Foreign loans and cognates confirm the OC *l (e.g., yè 葉 MC jiäp < *lap 'leaf' ≭ TB *lap 'id.'). Karlgren's Archaic Chinese set of voiced stops is thus replaced by a single phoneme *l-:

Arch. Ch. *gi̯-, *di̯-, *bi̯- = OC *l- (Li OC *r-) = MC ji-
Arch. Ch. *g'i̯-, *d'i̯-, *b'i̯- = OC *g-, *d-, *b- = MC g-/ ɣ-, d-, b-

Thus phonetic series with dental initials fall into two sets, one with OC initial dental stops ('T series'), one with OC *l- ('L series'). They can be distinguished with these diagnostic MC initials (see also tables in *EDOC* §8; §12.1.2):

(1) T series only MC t, ṭ (*tr-), tśj (*t-), źj (*d-)
(2) T and L series MC t^h (*thˆ- / *lhˆ-), d (*dˆ- / *lˆ-), ḍ (*dr- / *r-l-?),
ṭ^h (*thr-, *rh- / *r-lh- ?? — rare), tś^{h}j (*th- / *k-lh- — rare)
(3) L series only MC ji (*l-), śj (*lh-), dźj (*m-l-), zj (*s-l-)

In an OC T series, only initials from sets 1 and 2 can occur; in an L series only, sets 2 and 3. This distinction accords with Li's XS principle. For an example, compare *GSC* 9-11 with 9-17; both are particularly large XS where the absence of any irregular initials cannot be chance. Co-occurrence of MC *ji-* and *t-* is exceptional. Some XS are ambiguous (e.g., only *d-),* some include exceptional graphs, but the distinction is a strongly marked tendency.

Yù sì followed by MC w (jiw-) derives from OC *lu. Thus it would seem that the pre-classical copula *wéi* 惟維 (*GSR* 575; Karlgren *di̯wər) should be something like *lui. Li reconstructed it *rəd, Tibeto-Burmanists took it as something like *wəi. An emerging consensus (Baxter, Sagart, this writer, and others) interprets this syllable type as OC *wi (Baxter *wjij). The high vowel *i* caused the syllable to move into the *yù sì* (Div. IV) category in spite of the initial OC *w-. The OC and Han period form *wi is confirmed by its use for Indic *vi* in Han Buddhist transcriptions, just as *yuè* 越 jwɐt 3 < *wat is used for Indic *vat.*

OCM only: In some XS, MC ji- may derive from OCM *j-, not *l- (see *EDOC* §9, and Table in §12.1.2), but this is difficult to sort out. OCM assumes *j- where the phonetic series includes initial *ts-, as in *yǔn* 允 and *yǒu* 酉; the phonological reasons for these XS contacts are not clear. Also some other phonetic series probably had *j- rather than *l-, such as *yáng* 羊 *jaŋ, as opposed to *yáng* 昜 *laŋ; *yì* 亦 *jak and all its members; *yán* 鹽 *jam < *r-jam 'salt'.

OCM only: I suspect that MC ji- can also reflect earlier (PCH, OC?) *w- which was lost through labial dissimilation when followed by a back vowel; e.g., 莠 yǒu; see previous page.

5.1.2 Karlgren's MC has two voiced palatals, **źj-** and **dźj-**. This QYS distinction has often been thought artificial, but it is confirmed by the *fǎnqiè* of Yán Shīgǔ 顏師古 (581-645) (Coblin 1991: 20f), and in the Chinese of the Miao people of Jīnshuǐxiàng in Húnán who distinguish *shén* 神 (dźj-) ɕiŋ^{A2} from *shí* 石 (źj-) dʑia^{C2} (Pān 2000: 49).

Initial *dźj-* is rare, but *źj-* is as common as *tśj-*, *tś^{h}j-*. This shows that it is *źj-*, not *dźj-*, that derives from an earlier ordinary dental stop *d-, just as MC tśj- derived from *t-, hence 饘 tśjän < *tan, and 擅 źjän^{C} < *dans.

The rare initial MC dźj- (LH ź-) seems to derive from OCM *m-l(i)- (see *EDOC:* 89f.). The OC *m-l cluster is suggested, among others, by the phonetic series 6-24; almost all foreign cognates of syllables with QYS dź- have initial *m-l-, which confirms the OC form.

5.1.3 **MC zj-** can derive from OCM *s-l-, *s-w-, *s-j-, perhaps even *zj- (in non-ST loan words, as probably in *xiàng* 象), because this initial only occurs in XS with OC *l- (see 5.1.1) or with *s-. OCB writes *zl-, but since hyphenation is already introduced (4.5.1), the OCM consonantal inventory can be simplified by replacing *z* with *s- as in *s-l-, etc.

5.1.4 In OCM only: In a few word families and phonetic series **MC dẓ-** alternates with MC l- or ṣ- only. OC *dz- is not a derivational morpheme; therefore OCM *s-r (MC dẓ-) is assumed in such words, which is parallel to *s-l (MC zj-); 4-32/967 is a suggestive XS.

5.1.5 **OC voiceless sonorants** (i.e., nasals, *r, l, j, w*) are clearly revealed by phonetic series. MC initials *t^{h}-*, *śj-* co-occur in XS with *n-* and *ji-*, *t^{h}-* also with *l-;* MC *x-* (*χ-*) co-occurs with *m-* and *ŋ-*, rarely also with other sonorants. Karlgren set up OC clusters like *t'n-, śń-, χŋ-, χm-*. These can be simplified by postulating voiceless sonorants so that the single feature voicelessness explains them all. Since voicelessness is often accompanied by aspiration (as in 'Lhasa'), it is customary to write these initials with an *h:* OCM *nh, *rh, *lh-, *hm-, and *hŋ- — note that these are unit phonemes. In OCM, the *h* is written after the sonorant when the MC outcome is an acute initial, but before it when the MC trace is *x-*, in order to distinguish an OC cluster as in *hrâk > MC xɐk (Div. II) from a voiceless *r as in *rhâk > MC t^{h}âk (Div. I).

A few illustrations: hǎi 海 MC xậi^{B} < *hmə̂ʔ (phonetic is měi 每 *mə̂ʔ), tǐ 體 MC t^{h}iei^{B} < *rhîʔ (phonetic is lǐ 豊 MC liei^{B} < *rîʔ), shì 世 MC śjäi^{C} < *lhats writes yì 勩 MCjiäi^{C} < *lats, xiǎng 饟 MC śjaŋ$^{A/B/C}$ < *nhaŋʔ/h shares the phonetic with ràng 讓 MC ńźjaŋ^{C} < *naŋh.

A summary of OC sonorant initials and their MC reflexes (^ = syllable type A):

Div. I/IV		Div. II instead of I/IV		Div. III	
MC	< OCM	MC	< OCM	MC	< OCM
ŋ x	< *ŋ^ *hŋ^			ŋj xj	< *ŋ *hŋ
m x	< *m^ *hm^			mj xj	< *m *hm
n t^h	< *n^ *nh^			ńźj śj	< *n *nh
d t^h	< *l^ *lh^			ji śj	< *l *lh
(also	< *d^ *th^)			(also	< *j, *hj)
l t^h	< *r^ *rh^			lj ṭ^{h}j	< *r *rh (also < *thr)
		ɣw xw	< *w^ *hw^	jw xjw	< *w *hw
			(also < *gr^, *hr^)		

5.1.6 Not widely acknowledged: **MC tśʰj-** in XS, which include both initial *K- and *l-, derives from *k-hl- (出 k-hlut). **MC ṭʰ-** may perhaps on rare occasions represent a parallel configuration *k-hr- (黜 k-hrut).

5.2 *Chóngniǔ* doublets

The distinction between so-called *chóngniǔ* Div. III and IV doublets has been introduced in 2.4 above.

5.2.1 Chóngniǔ 3/4 syllables mingle in phonetic series and rimes with 'pure' Div. IV syllables (Karlgren's MC -iei, -ien, etc.); they represent the equivalent of Div. III (yod) syllables in association with the high front vowels *i and *e. Above (2.4) we have provided an illustration for the *chóngniǔ* arrangement in the rime tables:

Div.		Mand.	MC	*chóngniǔ* doublets		
I	O 寒	hán	ɣân			
II	O 顏	yán	ŋan	(also O 揀 jiǎn	Anc. Ch. kăn:	MC kɛn^B)
III	O 建	jiàn	kjɐn^C	O 蹇 jiǎn	Anc. Ch. ki̯ɑ̆n:	MC kjän^B 3
IV	O 見	jián	kien	O 遣 qiǎn	Anc. Ch. k'i̯ɑ̆n:	MC k^{h}jiän^B 4

According to Baxter, these fall now into the following OCM rime patterns with the two main vowels *a and *e:

I	寒	ɣân < *gân	IV	見	kien^C < *kêns
II	顏	ŋan < *ŋrân	II	揀	kăn^B < *krênʔ
III	健	kjɐn^C < *kans	3/4	遣	k^{h}jiän^B 4 <*khenʔ
3/3	蹇	kjän^B 3 < *kranʔ (or *kanʔ ?)			

5.2.2 In certain rimes **Div. 3/3** reflects an OC non-front vowel (without *r), thus MC -jau 3 < *-au (苗) vs. -jiau 4 < *-iau (眇); and MC -je 3 < *-ai (皮) vs. -jie 4 < *-e (卑). Baxter accounts for the many other instances of Div. 3/3 by postulating an OC medial *r (hence 蹇 *kranʔ). Such grave initial syllables would then be parallel to retroflex initial syllables in Div. III as *zhāng* 張 *traŋ. He cites examples where TB cognates to such syllables have indeed a medial *r (*jǐ* 几 MC ki^B < OC *kriʔ ⋈ WT k^{h}ri 'seat').

Baxter's medial *r in Div. 3/3 is different from the Div. II medial *r. The latter alternates in XS with other initials, e.g., MC l- < *r- interchanges with Div. II k-, ṣ-, and others (*r- ~ *kr- ~

*sr-...); the consonants seem to be 'movable'. The *chóngniǔ* 3/3 medial *r, as well as the *r in MC retroflex Div. III syllables like *zhāng* 張 *traŋ, have hardly any XS contact with MC l-, they seem to be a firm part of the initial. Gong Hwang-cherng has suggested writing OC *r as a pre-initial in these retroflex syllables; he may write *r-taŋ instead of *traŋ.

Rimes without a QYS Div. 3/3 category are ambiguous as to OC medial *r; Baxter wrote *k(r)jɨ, *k(r)jo, etc. OCM writes *kə, *ko, etc. by default and inserts an *r only when supported by evidence.

5.2.3 The many syllables of *chóngniǔ* Div. 3/3, with Baxter's OC medial *r, result in a suspiciously large number of OC words with *r. For example, according to *SSYP* (p. 336) there are in MC

15 syllables of the type MC	mjwəi III	< OCB *mjəj, OCM *məi
27 syllables of the type MC	mjɨ 3/3	< OCB *mrəj, *mri = OCM *mri ?
0 syllables of the type MC	mi 3/4	— (would be OCB *mjij, OCM *mi)

By comparison we find with OC rime *e, *-ai (*SSYP*, p. 318)

16 syllables of the type MC	mje III	< OCB *mjaj, OCM *mai
3 syllables of the type MC	mje 3/3	< OCB *mrjej, OCM *mre
27 syllables of the type MC	mjie 3/4	< OCB *mje[j], OCM *me

Something is out of balance with these types of syllables. For the sake of simplicity, OCM will try remove *r in some Div. 3/3 finals. Table I-1 provides a synopsis.

Table I-1: MC Div. 3/3 without OCB medial *r (R. = Rime no.)

	Div. III < OCM *-wə-, *-wa-				**Div. 3/3** < OCM *-u-, *-o-			
R.	MC	LHan	**OCM**	OCB	MC	LHan	**OCM**	OCB
34	雲 jwən 君 kjwən	wun kun	*wən *kwən	wjən kjun	允 jiwen^{B} 菌 gjwen^{B}3 愍 mjen^{B} 3 春 tśʰjwen	juin^{B} guɨn^{B} mɨn^{B} tśʰuin	*junʔ *gunʔ *munʔ *thun	 *grjunʔ *mrjən *thjun
31	謂 jwei^{C} 貴 kjwei^{C}	wus kus	*wəs *kwəs	wjəts	位 jwi^{C} 3 匱 gjwi^{C}3	wɨs guɨs	*wus *gus	*(w)rjəps *grjuts
28	圍 jwei 歸 kjwei	wui kui	*wəi *kwəi	 kwjəj	帷 jwi 3 夔 gjwi3 誰 źwi	wɨ guɨ dźui	*wui *gui *dui	
	尾 mjwei^{B}	mui^{B}	*məiʔ	*mjəjʔ	美 mji^{B}3	mɨ^{B}	*muiʔ	*mrjəjʔ
25	遠 jwɐn^{B} 勸 kʰjwɐn^{C}	wɑn^{B} kʰyɑn^{C}	*wanʔ *khwans	*wjanʔ	沿 jiwän4 卷 kjwän^{B}3	juan kyan^{B}	*lon *konʔ	 *krjonʔ
22	越 jwɐt	wɑt	*wat	*wjat	撅 kjwäi^{C}3 稅 śjuäi^{C}	kyɑs śuas	*kots *lhots	 *hljots
21					傑 gjät3 揭 kʰjäi^{C}3	gɨat kʰɨas	*gat *khats	*grjat *khrjats

In some rimes, the proportion of OCB medial-r-syllables to ones without the medial is implausibly high; in some finals there are only syllables with *-r-, as seen above. I suggest that in many rimes in *n, t* and *Vi*, the Div. 3/3 finals had the OCM plain vowel *o* or *u*, while the regular Div. III finals had a *w followed by *a or *ə. Most syllables with OC initial *w- occur in Div. III, while Div. 3/3 is rare with this initial. If MC gjwi^C 3 < OCM *gus, then it follows that the rare 位 jwi^C 3 < OCM *wus, and 美 mji^B3 < OCM *muiʔ (< **miʔ ?). In this proposal, the MC finals after gutturals are the same as after acute initials. See further detailed explanations in Rime 28.

This proposal agrees with the XS series and simplifies OCM, because a medial *r is removed from many syllables, and reconstructions are less complex. In *GSC*, OCB is cited where available so that the reader can adjust OC to Baxter's if the reader wishes (reinserting medial r in most 3/3); the MC readings would provide the necessary information — they are, after all, supplied for such a purpose.

Further elimination of OC *-r-: In the OC rimes *-en (R. 23) and *-e(t)s (R. 20), MC hékǒu Div. II ɣwan (normally < *[g]wrân) and ɣwai^C (normally < *[g]wrats) are very common, I take these to derive from OC *wên and *wê(t)s, also after aspirated *kh-. The rarer MC ɣiwen and ɣiwei^C derive, I assume as a working hypothesis, from OC *gwên and *gwê(t)s; similarly Div. II ɣwăn derives from the expected OC *gwrên.

5.3 OC sources of MC tones

MC tonal categories (see 2.3) agree with corresponding OC ones. That the OC sources of MC tones B (*shǎngshēng*) and C (*qùshēng*) were segmental phonemes *-ʔ and *-s is now widely accepted. Tones A (*píngshēng*) and D (*rùshēng*) had no additional feature, were unmarked. Haudricourt proposed this tonogenesis because of Chinese parallelism with Vietnamese (where *-s became a tone via *-h). Evidence from dialects and transcriptions of foreign words support the reconstructions. Some Chinese dialects have preserved a glottal stop in the *shǎng shēng*; also the creaky phonation of Mand. tone 3 (< *shǎngshēng*) is a typical trace of glottalization. For the sake of simplicity and clarity, I will use the term 'tone' for the categories in spite of earlier OC segmental features.

5.3.1 Comparing the transcriptions of foreign words of the Middle Han period with those of the Later Han period reveals interesting **tonal developments**.

It is striking that in the Middle Han period only tone A and D syllables are normally used in transcriptions while tones B and C do not occur (except in special positions). This implies that the latter were not suitable because of the presence of some additional, interfering segmental feature. The exceptions occur with **tone C syllables** from earlier dental series, which consistently render foreign final *-s* or sibilants (LHan forms after the graphs):

對馬	tuəs-maʔ	Tsushima
柰	nɑs	Japanese (kara)nashi; also in Skt. [Vārā]ṇasī
都賴	tɑ-lɑs	Talas
罽賓	kɨas-pin	Kashmir
貴	kuɨs	Kušan
劫貝	kɨap-pɑs	kārpāsa 'cotton' (an Austroasiatic loan)
央匱	ʔɨaŋ-guɨs	Tocharian B ankwaṣ 'asafoetida'
蒲類	bɑ-luis (*bâ-rus)	Bars (*barus) (Altaic 'tiger', Mongolian *bars*)
謂	wus	Skt. puṣa
貳	nis	Indic niṣ- (Coblin 1982: 132; 1983: 87)
會	ɣuɑs, 衛 was	Skt. vāsa

昧　məs　Skt. (sa-)mādhi (Pulleyblank 1983:100: Skt. dh > Prakrit z)

The last four Indic items are from the later LHan where this final *-s* still survived, but rendered occasionally dentals in general. These transcriptions (and additional ones in BTD material) confirm a Han period and OC final *-s* in the relevant OC rime categories.

Never does tone C from non-dental finals suggest an *s*. Instead, the rare transcriptions suggest an *-h* or *-χ* in such finals:

護澡　ɣuɑh-tsɑuʔ　waxšab
大宛　dɑh-ʔyɑn　? *Taχwār, Tóχαροι (Tocharians) (assuming *dah* rather than *das*)
謝　zah　? šāhi 'Shah'
徑路　keŋh-lɑh (< *-râkh) qiŋiraq 'Hunnish sword'

Otherwise, tone C syllables (from non-dental finals) occur, rarely, in the last syllable of a foreign word when additional sounds are omitted, as if final *-h* reflects some trailing off:

丘就　kʰu-dziuh　Kujula
高附　kɑu-buoh　Κάβουρα (Kabul)

Tone B syllables are rare; they typically occur at the end of a foreign word where they represent a final stop consonant; this seems to confirm the final *-ʔ:*

昆子　kuən-tsiəʔ (*kûn-tsəʔ) *qïrsaq　'arctic fox'
獅子　ṣi-tsiəʔ　Tocharian A śiśäk, B ṣecake 'lion'
史　ṣəʔ (or srəʔ ?)　S(u)liɣ 'Sogdian'
撲挑　pʰok-deuʔ/-theu　Puśkalāvati, Πευκελαῶτις (ambiguous)
護澡　ɣuɑh-tsɑuʔ　waxšab
對馬　tuəs-maʔ　Tsushima (tone B not clear — short syllable?)
奄蔡　ʔɨamʔ-sɑs　Abzoae, Ἀόρσιοι
且末　tsʰiaʔ-mɑt　Calmadana

The last two items with tone B in the middle of the word seem exceptional. In the last name, LHan tsʰia^B was perhaps to be read LHan tsiɑ.

In the BTD of LHan the final *-s* from OC dental final categories was still reserved for Indic syllables ending in *s, ṣ, ś,* but occasionally also for dental stops. But the other tones were now disregarded in transcriptions, except that LHan syllables in tone B tend to avoid Indic long vowels, their brevity is probably a trace of the final glottal stop (e.g., 首陀衛 śu^B-dɑ-was Skt. *śuddhavāsa*). Non-dental *qùshēng* (*-h) has a slight tendency to represent Indic long vowels (e.g., 墮舍利 hyɑi-śah-lih Skt. Vaiśālī). All this suggests that the OC and MHan segmental features were strong and prominent *-ʔ* and *-χ;* but they were giving way to phonemic tones in LHan (BTD).

OCM only, concerning tone C (*qùshēng*). Considering that the Han period *-s* from dental finals is in complementary distribution with the *-h* from non-dental finals, one should reconstruct a single OC phoneme *-s. This is generally done. On the other hand, the *s* / *h* distinction must be maintained for OC as well. OC *qùshēng* words with open syllables (+ s) like OCB *kəs have occasional rime contact with ones in *-k like *kəks; these converged eventually. But if the feature here actually was *-s, one should expect rime contact with *-ts as well. But this is not the case; in OC rimes the two are strictly kept apart, which suggests two distinct phonemes, although at one point in the past their common source was probably an *-s. Furthermore, I suspect that some phonetic series with (almost) exclusively *qùshēng* words (OCB *-ts) actually ended in a simple *-s (see *EDOC* §3.4). Therefore *-s cannot be used for tone C with open syllables, as both MC kuo^{C} and MC kâi^{C} would then derive from OC *kas. Therefore I suggest *-h after open vowels and velar finals, and *-s after dental finals or when by itself:

Table I-2: OCM final *-s

	MC	OCB	OCM
害	ɣâi^{C}	gats	gâts
大	dâi^{C}	lats	dâs
故	kuo^{C}	kas	kâh
路	luo^{C}	raks	râkh

二 OCB *njits, here OCM *nis; 賴 OCB *rats, here OCM *râts; 故 OCB *kas, here OCM *kâh; 織 OCB *tjəks, here OCM *təkh. However, the reader can mechanically rewrite all OCM *-s to *-ts, and all OCM *-h to *-s, if preferred.

5.3.2 MC tones and Karlgren's OC voiced final consonants. One puzzling feature of traditional OC rime categories is the presence of MC open and closed syllables in the same phonetic series, as, for instance, in 5-13/920 (vs. 4-27/962), and also inter-riming in literature. Thus, using OC *-ək and *-ə as an illustration, the MC reflexes seem to form a single rime category:

Table I-3: Karlgren's voiced final *-g

GSR phonetic series	MC	Karlgr. OC	Li OC	OCB '92	OCM
920 職 zhí duty	tśjək	ȶi̯ək	tjək	tjək	tək
織 zhī to weave	tśjək	ȶi̯ək	tjək	tjək	tək
織 zhì cloth	tśɨ^{C}	ȶi̯əg	tjəgh	tjəks	təkh
識 zhì remember	tśɨ^{C}	ȶi̯əg	tjəgh	tjəks	təkh
962 之 zhī walk	tśɨ	ȶi̯əg	tjəg	tjə	tə
志 zhì aim	tśɨ^{C}	ȶi̯əg	tjəgh	tjəs	təh

(A reminder: Baxter 1992 actually wrote ɨ for ə, and he has since eliminated the OC medial *j*.) If 織識 MC tśɨ^{C} were compatible with MC tśək in OC, they must have had a final consonant as well, according to Karlgren: GSR *ȶi̯əg. Then it follows that 志 MC tśɨ^{C} must also derive from *ȶi̯əg, and 之 MC tśɨ as well: *ȶi̯əg. Through this sort of chain-reasoning, the majority of words in MC open syllables ended with a final consonant *-g, *-d, *-b, or *-r in Karlgren's / Li's OC.

Karlgren's successors have projected MC tone categories back into OC where rimes and XS confirm their existence. This revealed that final consonant contacts occur only with a limited number of MC open syllables, all with MC *qùshēng* (tone C), and in XS which include final *-k or *-t. Contacts between final stop consonants and open syllables with tones A (level) and B (rising) stand out as exceptions. For example, the MC final ɨ^{C} resulted apparently from a merger of the two OC finals *-əkh (or OCB *-əks 織識) and *-əh (or OCB *-əs 志). Thus, the OC categories needed to be cut differently from Karlgren, as in the OCB and OCM columns in Table I-3. Consequently, OC final voiced stop consonants *-g, *-d, *-b and *-r are not warranted; this simplified inventory of final consonants brings OC, now with a majority of open syllables, typologically in line with MC, modern dialects and cognate TB languages.

The *Shijing* and other Zhou period poetry occasionally include exceptions where the rimes do not agree in tone, or especially where a short-stopped syllable (-k, -t, -p) rimes with an open one. Some of the incongruous rimes are so consistent that one can assume an OC final which would agree with the OC rime (Mattos) rather than with a MC backward projection; for example, lái 來 OCM *rə ended in the oldest parts of the *Shijing* in a stop consonant, either -k or -ʔ. Occasionally in the *Shijing*, and more frequently later in Han poetry, the last line of a rhymed stanza ends in a short stopped syllable (ending in -k, -t or -p) (see examples in Coblin *JCL* 11.2 [1984]: 6-7 and in Luo and Zhou 1958). In the *Shijing* it can be the second-to-last line. Therefore, some of these exceptional rime contacts reflect poetic prosody.

5.3.3 The inclusion of tones and **elimination of voiced final consonants** had the following consequences for OC:

(a) Karlgren's *-g are eliminated; instead of *-ag, *-əg, *-eg, *-ôg, *-og, *-ug we have now OC *-a, *-ə, *-e, *-u, *-au, *-o. Those with rime and XS contact with *-k are set up by most investigators as OC *-ks, here OCM *-kh. An additional consequence is the combination of GSR *-å, *-o (nos. 32-107) with some *-ag (nos. 801-807 and elsewhere) into the now generally accepted OC rime *-a; and Arch. *-u and *-ug form a single rime OC *-o.

(b) Final *-d with tone C is now *-ts (and also OCM *-s). Words in Arch. Ch. *-d with MC tones other than C derived from *-i (Karlgren's *-r).

(c) Final *-b is eliminated; it either was also OC *-ts; or it was not warranted due to misinterpretation of the phonetic elements, as in *GSR* 642.

(d) Final *-r is replaced by OCM *-i (OCB *-j). Thus *kai (or *kaj) for Karlgren's *kar. Karlgren reconstructed final *-r in order to explain occasional rime / XS contact with *-n. But archaic southern dialects show *-ai, etc. in these finals which would explain the occasional interchange with *-n just as well. Now Arch. Ch. *-â and *-âr actually form one rime group, OCM *-ai (OCB *-aj).

The absence of voiced final stops and the presence of segmental phonemes for later tones are now widely accepted. The only influential authority to retaine the voiced finals was Li Fang-kuei. This was perhaps prompted by his, and a general Chinese, skepticism toward the idea that the MC tones could derive from a toneless form of Chinese. However, Li left the question open, retained the voiced finals, and added the symbols -x and -h to his syllables to indicate sources of later tones B and C.

5.4 Summary of OC rimes

Bodman had proposed and Baxter has worked out a six-vowel system for OC: a, ə (Baxter 1992 ɨ), e, i, o, u; diphthongs OCB aj, əj, uj, aw, jaw, iw, also ej (OCM ai, əi, ui, au, iau, iu; OCB ej = OCM e). As a result, Baxter's system of OC rime categories overlaps exactly with the traditional ones which had been identified by Chinese scholars and adopted by Karlgren. The system is furthermore confirmed by TB cognates (see *EDOC*). All that is necessary to update *GSR* rimes and vowels is simply to substitute mechanically Baxter's 1992 values for Karlgren's: *-u for *-ôg, *-ai for *-â.... OCM is Baxter's system except where indicated:

GSR *-o, *-ag	= OCM *-a; except some *GSR* *-ag in MC tone C
	= OCM *-akh (OCB *-aks), i.e., MC tone C
GSR *-âk, *-âŋ	= OCM *-ak, *-aŋ

GSR *-u, *-ug = OCM *-o, except some *GSR* *-u(g) with MC tone C
= OCM *-okh (OCB *-oks), i.e., MC tone C
GSR *-uk, *-uŋ = OCM *-ok, *-oŋ
GSR *-ôg = OCM *-u, except some *GSR* *ôg with MC tone C
= OCM *-ukh (OCB *-uks), i.e., MC tone C
GSR *-ôk, -ôŋ = OCM *-uk, *-uŋ
GSR *-og = OCM *-au (OCB *-aw); except some *GSR* *-og with MC tone C
= OCM *-aukh (OCB *-awks), i.e., MC tone C
GSR *-ok = OCM *-auk (OCB *-awk)
GSR *-əg = OCM *-ə (OCB 1992 *-ɨ)
= OCM *-əkh (OCB 1992 *-ɨks), i.e., MC tone C
GSR *-ək, *-əŋ = OCM *-ək,*-əŋ
GSR *-eg = OCM *-e; except some *GSR* *-eg with MC tone C
= OCM *-ekh (OCB *-eks), i.e., MC tone C
GSR *-ek, *eŋ = OCM *-ek, *-eŋ

GSR *-â, *-âr = OCM *-ai
GSR *-uâ, *-uâr = OCM *-oi, except after gutturals also *Kwai; not after labials
GSR *-ər = OCM *-əi or *-i
GSR *-uər = OCM *-ui; rarely after gutturals also *Kwi; not after labials
GSR *-ât, *-âd, -ân = OCM *-at, *-a(t)s (OCB *-ats, and similarly passim), *-an
GSR *-uât, *-uâd, *-uân = OCM *-ot, *-o(t)s, *-on, except after gutturals also *Kwat, etc.; not after labials
GSR *iat, *-ian = OCM *-et, *-en
GSR *-ət, *-əd, *-ən = OCM *-ət, *-ə(t)s, *-ən, also after gutturals *Kwət, etc.
GSR *-uət, *-uəd, *-uən = OCM *-ut, *-u(t)s, *-un, after gutturals also *Kwət, etc.; not after labials
GSR *-et, *-en = OCM *-it, *-in
GSR *-âp, *-âm = OCM *-ap, *-am
GSR *-iap,*-iam = OCM *-ep, *-em
GSR *-əp, *-əm = OCM *-əp or *-əm
GSR *-iəp, *-iəm = OCM *-ip, *-im

5.5 Summary of OC initials

This is a list of MC initials and their OC sources which are for the most part Baxter's (1992):

k, k^h, g, ŋ, ʔ < OC k, kh, g, ŋ, ʔ
gjw < OC w
ɣ / ɣw < OC g, rarely perhaps ɦ / gw or w
x < OC hm, hŋ, h, h(w), rarely hl, hn
t, n, l < OC t, n, r
t^h < OC th, nh, lh, rh
d < OC d, l
ṭ, ṇ < OC tr, nr
ṭ^h < OC thr, rh, rarely perhaps t-hl
ḍ < OC dr, dr < rl ?

tś, ź (LH dź), ńź	< OC t, d, n
tś^{h}	< OC th, rarely k-hl-
dź (LH ź)	< OC m-l (also m-d?)
ś	< OC lh, nh, hj
ji	< OC l, j, rarely w
ts, ts^{h}, dz, s	< OC ts, tsh, dz, s (some tsh- perhaps from earlier ks-)
zj / zjw	< OC s-l, s-j / z-w
tṣ, tṣ^{h}, dẓ, ṣ	< OC tsr, tshr, dzr, sr
p, p^{h}, b, m	< OC p, ph, b, m

6 MINIMAL OLD CHINESE: PRINCIPLES AND CRITERIA

As pointed out earlier, OCM simply has selected and adopted more or less commonly accepted proposals for OC and does not claim credit for the OC forms (except for rare suggestions). Two points need to be stressed: First, OCM does not necessarily preclude the validity of other OC reconstructions. Thus *lè* 樂 is OCM *râuk, but it could well have been *g-rauk, or something else. Second, etymological relationships often remain unaffected by the MC system or most OC reconstructions; 五 'five' is cognate to TB *b/l-ŋa whether we read it MC ŋuo^{B}, or Arch. Ch. (Karlgren) *ŋo, or OCB *ŋaʔ.

OCM retains the widely recognized overall categories of *GSR*, while incorporating post-Karlgrenian proposals which have been summarized above. Thus OCM is broadly based on, and agrees *mutatis mutandis* with, Baxter 1992 (OCB) and others' reconstructions, but it errs on the side of simplicity. OCM avoids some finer, debatable distinctions of others' systems. For details of the OCM notations, see under Transcriptions, pp. xix-xx; for Baxter's 1992 *ɨ OCB write *ə, as he does in his later work.

Occasionally, OCM needs to settle on a default form, especially in cases of ambiguous and controversial evidence. The following general principles and criteria serve here as a guide for evaluating proposals and ideas for the purposes of OCM; most have been tacitly assumed by others.

All reconstructions of, and proposals for, OC are based on implicit or explicit premises, assumptions, biases and interpretations. Some will be discussed in more detail in the Introduction sections 8 and 9.

(1) Investigators often approach OC phonology and the interpretation of graphic elements with this question: Is there possibly a phonological connection between two or more elements under consideration? (E.g., *jīn* 今 phonetic in *tān* 貪?) The answer is mostly yes, and then OC forms are reconstructed (rightly or not) on a possibility. For OCM, we ask: are the indications, is the evidence, compelling for postulating a phonological link? The answer is often no, resulting in simpler, more conservative forms for OCM.

(2) I am suspicious of chain reasoning, especially chains that include links which are suppositions and conjectures. This kind of procedure has led to Karlgren's voiced final consonants, for example, or to complex initial clusters.

(3) Following the rule of economy, OCM prefers the smallest number of steps to arrive at a reconstruction — simple hypotheses or OC forms are preferred to complex ones (Occam's razor).

(4) Simplicity. E.g., OCM retains final *-an where Baxter and Starostin suggest *-ar (though they may be right). Or OCM *lè* 樂 is OCM *râuk, but it could well have been *g-râuk.

(5) Because the comparative method of historical reconstruction cannot be applied, we are left with projecting the QYS (MC) back into OC. The QYS values are assumed to reach back unchanged unless evidence (rime, phonetic series, patterns for internal reconstruction) requires adjustments.

(6) Priority of MC. When in doubt, the *typical OC sources of MC forms* will override oddities in phonetic series, because phonological evolution is expected to be regular, whereas the selection of one graphic element over another can be at the whim of a writer (Qiú Xīguī 2000: 269, referring to Zhèng Xuán 鄭玄 [AD 127-200] to that effect).

When there is no scholarly agreement on the same data, the issue is apparently beyond rational explanation, no matter how erudite the argumentation. When a proposal for a reconstruction cannot be proven or disproved, OCM is content with backward projected MC values by default.

(7) In light of most of the above criteria, OCM refrains from sweeping addition of phonemes. Occasionally, pre-initial elements or medial laterals seem to be motivated by the assumption that all members in a phonetic series were more similar in OC than is really required by the overall syllable structure of Sinitic languages and ST. To anticipate what is said in 7.2.1 below: The user of this manual can add phonemic elements to OCM as he deems necessary, but it is very difficult for an unsuspecting user to visualize an initial cluster with an element deleted.

(8) A phonological reconstruction of OC, such as OCM, should be kept separate from an etymological reconstruction. OCM restricts itself to those features which are knowable from within Chinese, as far as possible, without recourse to extensive etymologization. For example, *nèi* 內 MC nuậi^C 'inside' is written with the phonetic element *rù* 入 MC ńźjəp, OCM *nəp 'enter'. There is no rime that would suggest an OC labial final for *nèi* (*nups) or any other word which etymologically might have ended in *-ps. The 'phonetic' element *rù* for *nèi* is explained by the transparent etymological relationship beside some similarity in sound. An etymologizing reconstruction of OC would set up *nûps and *nup respectively; but all that can be safely assumed is OCM *nûts and *nəp.

(9) Foreign cognates or loans are only taken into consideration in cases where they could clarify which of a number of choices within OC would be the likely one, e.g., initial *hm- in *huǒ* 火 'fire' and *huǐ* 虫 'snake', thus ruling out the theoretical alternative *hŋ-. However, TB morphemes and phonemes are not projected into OCM. Thus *huǒ* 火 OCM *hmə̂iʔ 'fire' was not OC *sməiʔ, as TB *sme or *smai may suggest, since there is within Chinese no evidence for an *s- in this word, only for a voiceless nasal. Or: It is suggested that in some words morphological voicing of an initial consonant was due to an earlier nasal prefix, thus *jiàn* 見 OCM *kêns 'to see' > *xiàn* 現 OCM *gêns 'to appear' which could have been at some early period *Nkens. TB parallels as well as MY loans with nasalized initials seem to confirm this (Baxter 1992 writes *ɦ-; L. Sagart 2003 writes *N-; Schuessler 1987 had *m- in some words, now only in *m-l-). But for the sake of not complicating matters, OCM retains the simple voiced initials; there seems to be no compelling evidence within OC for a distinction between ordinary voiced and pre-nasalized initials; furthermore, it would be difficult to sort out which OC initial would be which kind — after all, one of the intended purposes of OCM is its practicality.

7 LATER HAN CHINESE

Later Han Chinese (LHan, LH) represents an older strain of the language of the Eastern Han period from perhaps the 1st century AD. It includes features of Middle Han Chinese (MHan), which must have been present in some LHan speech because they survive in the modern Mǐn dialects as well as in the language of Later Han period writers from Shandong. Thus Mǐn dialects still have traces of the OC / MHan diphthong -ɑi (in rimes as in 歌寄), and of unpalatalized velars as in 支. LHan is based on modern dialect evidence (especially Mǐn), Old Northwest Chinese (ONW, ONWC; Coblin 1991a; 1994b), Han period rimes in poetry (Luó Chángpéi and Zhōu Zǔmó 1958), Wei-Jin rimes (Ting 1975), and Buddhist transcriptions (Coblin 1982; 1993). LHan is discussed in detail in Schuessler 2006. It retains most of the *QY* categories, but is about 500 years older and simpler than MC. The conservative strain of LHan, which is provided in this manual, could perhaps also be called Mid-Han; it can be converted to that of Eastern Han mainstream literature using the following paradigms:

LHan older (MHan)		LHan mainstream literature	
古	kɑ^B	kɔ^B	ɑ > ɔ in open syllables
居	kɨɑ	kɨɔ	ɑ > ɔ in open syllables
無	muɑ	muɔ	ɑ > ɔ in open syllables
寄	kɨɑi	kɨe	merger with the reflex of OC gre, MC gjiɛ 3 技
歌	kɑi	kɑ	ɑi > ɑ in open syllables
支	kie	tśe	palatalization of velars (see 7.3)

7.1 Phonemes

See the note on Transcription in the front matter. The consonants and almost all vowels are the same as in MC, but high medial glides, which are Han period innovations, are written as vowels *i, ɨ, y, u* (in later QYS Div. III), not *j, ji* and *w* (see 7.6). The vowels *ɑ* (could also be written *â*) and *a* are not to be confused.

LHan's notation is phonemic, has shed some of the complexities of MC and follows the transcriptional conventions used for CH dialects (e.g., *-au, -ai, -iau; -yaŋ* for MC *-jwaŋ*).

7.2 No consonant clusters

Like MC and CH dialects, Mid-Han and LHan had no consonant clusters, as transcriptions show: *shī-lì* 師利 LH ṣi-li^C = Skt. śrī; *pó-luó-mén* 婆羅門 LH bâ-lâ-mən 'brahmana' (*fàn* 梵 'brahman' is an earlier transcription, or one that simply ignores some element in a cluster).

7.3 Palatalization of certain velar consonants

This occurred under the influence of the immediately following high vowel *i*, even a secondary one, thus OCM *ke > LH kie > tśe > MC tśje 支. For reasons that are not yet clear, this palatalization of velars did not occur in all rimes (e.g., jí 吉 MC kjet < OCM *kit), nor with aspirated *k^h-*, nor with voiced *g-* in tone A (Schuessler 1996).

7.4 Tones and vowel length

Tones are marked with letters (B, C) as in MC (see 2.3); for the tonal development in MHan and LHan, see 5.3.1. LHan may have preserved earlier segmental features in weakened form, thus one could write LHan *kaa, kaʔ, kah;* however, for the sake of consistency we use the tone letters instead, hence LHan *ka, ka^B, ka^C*. **Vocalic length** distinctions did not exist in LHan syllables. The transcription of Indic syllables with their strict length distinctions reveal no correlation with the later QYS divisions. Only open syllables in tone B tend to be avoided in transcribing Indic long vowels.

7.5 LHan Final -s

As transcriptions show, final *-s survived from OC finals *-(t)s (Karlgren's OC *-d, Baxter's *-ts); see 5.3.1.

7.6 Vowel bending or warping

Vowel bending (or warping) resulted from the distinction between high vocalic onset syllables (HS = Pulleyblank's OC type B syllables) vs. low vocalic onset syllables (LS = OC type A syllables), as explained in Schuessler 2006 (see also 4.6). In HS the onset of a vowel is bent up to the high vowel above it which becomes a medial (*i ɨ y u*); in low onset syllables the vowel is bent down. In Table I-4 the unbent vowels are in the marked boxes; these are *i* and *u* which cannot bend any higher, and *ɑ* cannot bend any lower; the eventual change from *ɑ* 古 kɑ^{B} to *o* 古 ko^{B} is due to a different type of phonological change where the original *ɑ* was pushed into the slot of earlier *o* which had warped to *əu* (狗 kəu^{B}).

Table I-4: LHan vowel bending

HS	脂 (*ki >) tśi 比 pi^{B} 死 si^{B}	支 kie > tśe 卑 pie 知 ṭie	居 kɨɑ 無 muɑ 胥 siɑ	基 kɨə 謀 muə > mu 子 tsiə^{B}	具 kɨo (or kuo) 務 muo 取 tsʰio^{B}	九 ku 浮 bu 秋 tsʰ(i)u
OC	i	e	a	ə	o	u
LS MHan	稽 kei 米 mei^{B} 體 tʰei^{B}	雞 ke 椑 be 啼 de	古 kɑ^{B} 布 pɑ^{C} 土 tɑ^{B}	該 kə 每 mə 才 dzə	狗 ko^{B} 母 mo^{B} 頭 do	告 kou 寶 pou 道 dou^{B}
LHan later stage	稽 kei 米 mei^{B} 體 tʰei^{B}	雞 kei 椑 bei 啼 dei	古 ko^{B} 布 po^{C} 土 to^{B}	該 kɑə > kậi 每 mɑə > mậi^{B} 才 dzɑə > dzậi	狗 kəo > kəu^{B} 母 məo > məu^{B} 頭 dəo > dəu	告 kâu 寶 pâu 道 dâu^{B}

The basic pattern of up-bending is represented in the first row of the table (with initial *k*). Deviations and further changes are the result of other phonological mechanisms. Thus the high glide was assimilated to *u* after labial initials (無 HS [mɨɑ >] muɑ), but was assimilated to *i* after acute initials (子 HS [tsɨə^{B} >] tsiə^{B}). Uncertainties remain, e.g. 秋 qiū < MC tsʰjəu could have been MHan tsʰu (the high vowel *u* does not bend), or it could have been MHan tsʰiu (after acute initials the glide is *i*). The two stages in LS are suggested by transcriptions and rime patterns.

Syllables with diphthongs or final consonants are subject to the same vowel bending, e.g.

	Mand. <	MC <	LHan <	OC	
冬	dōng	tuoŋ	touŋ	tûŋ	NWC (ca. AD 400) tɑuŋ; cf. 告寶 in Table 1-4
表	biǎo	pjäu^{B} 3	pɨɑu^{B}	pauʔ	
標	biāo	pjiäu 4	piau	piau	i in iau cannot bend higher
小	xiǎo	sjäu^{B}	siɑu^{B}	s(i)auʔ	
幾	jǐ	kjei^{B}	kɨi^{B} < kɨəi^{B}	kəiʔ	leveling might have occurred

佛 fó	bjwət	but	—	
吉 jí	kjiet 4	kit	kit	
寮 liáo	lieu	leu < leiɑu	riâu	leveling might have occurred

8 HAN PERIOD SOURCES ON PHONOLOGY

The dictionary *Shuōwén jiězì* and phonological information from Han period sound glosses are considered important sources for the reconstruction of OC. These frequently mentioned materials will be briefly introduced and their utility for OC phonology discussed.

8.1 The *Shuōwén jiězì*

The oldest comprehensive dictionary of graphs, the *Shuōwén jiězì* 說文解字 (*Shuowen* for short [*SW*]) seems to provide answers for puzzling phonetic composites. Its author Xǔ Shèn 許慎 (d. AD 149) was removed from the OC period by only a few centuries. Among others, the eminent philologist Duàn Yùcái 段玉裁 (1735-1815) has made emendations to the transmitted text that had been tampered with over the centuries, and has added comments which are widely taken as authoritative interpretations. The *SW* arranges the Han period corpus of graphs (with a few omissions) under 540 'classifiers' or 'radicals', and identifies the other graphic element, if there is one, as either phonetic or semantic. The *SW* thus provides early information on phonetic series and indirectly on OC phonology. A frequent formula is *cóng A, B shēng* "A is the classifier, B is phonetic"; for example, 語从言吾聲 *yǔ, cóng yán, wú shēng* [*SW* 961] "'to tell': *yán* 'word' is the classifier, *wú* 'I' is phonetic." Occasionally, a graph may serve as an 'abbreviated' phonetic, as in *SW* 2532 梳从木疏省聲 *shū cóng mù shū shěng shēng* "*shū* 'comb': 'wood' is the classifier, *shū* is the abbreviated phonetic"; only the right element of *shū* 疏 is used as phonetic, while the actual phonetic to the left is left out. Occasionally the *SW* uses the formula *cóng A, cóng B, B yì shēng* "A and B are classifiers, B is also phonetic," because no clear line can be drawn between the phonetic and semantic role of a graphic element; for example, *SW* 989: 詔 ... 从言从召召亦聲 *zhào ... cóng yán cóng zhào, zhào yì shēng* "*zhào* 'to tell'... has the classifiers *yán* 'word' and *zhào* 'to call', *zhào* is also phonetic." The phonetic role may be less obvious, or wrongly assumed, in a graph like *guān* 冠 'cap' (*SW* 3357) where Xǔ Shèn states that *yuán* 元 'head' is "also phonetic."

Typically the *SW*'s identification of a graphic element as semantic or phonetic agrees with the obvious structure of the graph and its membership in an OC phonetic series according to the XS principle. However, by "phonetic" Xǔ Shèn may occasionally have meant as little as the rime, the final consonant, the initial consonantal category, or nothing phonetic at all, as in this case:

SW 518 states that in *mǒu* 牡 *mûʔ 'male' (of larger quadrupeds), *tǔ* 土 *thâʔ 'earth' is "phonetic." However, in the OB the element 土 was actually *shì* 士 'male' (Li Xiaoding 1.159), neither *tǔ* nor *shì* can have been phonetic, *mǒu* was originally a semantic compound.

In a few instances, Xǔ Shèn says that a graphic element is semantic (cóng 从) when it must also have been at least partially phonetic. Thus *SW* 1283 analyzes the graph *jiān* 堅 *kîn 'hard' as consisting of the semantic elements *qìn* 臤 *khins 'solid' and *tǔ* 土 *thâʔ 'earth', where *qìn* is clearly (also) phonetic.

Thus Xǔ's explanations for irregular compounds need to be treated with caution. His loose XS "system" was apparently also that of the earlier creators of graphs.

Several additional limitations of the *SW* and its author must be kept in mind.

First, Xǔ and his contemporaries were not aware of the OB and BI and therefore of the paleographic history of graphs. Often Xǔ simply describes the graph he sees without explaining it. Thus the left element in the graph for *shè* 射 'to shoot' he described as *shēn* 身 'body', whereas we know from OB that what appears like *shēn* is the corrupted form of a bow with arrow. See Qiu X. 2000, especially ch. 8 for cases where Xǔ Shèn has misanalyzed graphs.

Secondly, this was not a dictionary of words and their phonology, but only of graphs and graphic relationships – phonetic (phonetic elements / loans) or otherwise (see 8.2.1).

Third, Xǔ Shèn's Later Han Chinese language had simplified and eliminated initial consonant clusters and voiceless sonorants. Evidence for LHan simplification include, for example, writing *chǐ* 耻 LHan ṭʰə^{B} > ṭʰɨ^{B} (the phonetic is *təʔ > LHan tśə^{B}) for the graph *chǐ* 恥 *nhrəʔ > LHan ṭʰə^{B} 'shame' (Qiu 2000: 20). Buddhist transcriptions of Indic words show that LHan had no initial clusters; an Indic cluster with post-consonantal *r* is split into two syllables, see 7.2; conversely, a Div. II syllable like jiā 迦 MC ka (would be OC *krâ) transcribes Indic *ka*. When foreign clusters in Han period loans agree with OC clusters, the loans must go back to Early Han or earlier. In Xǔ's language, the initial consonants of *jiàn* 監 LH kam^{C} and *lán* 藍 LH lɑm were phonetically as irreconcilable as today. When he states that the former is "phonetic" in the latter, he cannot have included the initials if he based this comment on his own language; he can only have meant either the rimes, or he made a guess based on philological traditions and the many parallel k ~ l interchanges in phonetic series.

These instances already show that the *SW*'s notion of "phonetic" is looser than the modern definition of the XS principle, and that we are dealing in the *SW* at least partially with Han period Chinese, not OC. The subsequent discussions will demonstrate that, whatever Xǔ Shèn's insightful pointers, we cannot build an OC reconstruction of a specific word on his statements alone.

8.2 Sound glosses

Late Zhou and especially Han period literature contains sound glosses where one graph is suggesting, or is thought to suggest, the sound of another. The interpretation of such glosses is somewhat uncertain and has been much discussed (see a summary in Coblin 1983: 10-13). Sound glosses fall into different types; most common are loan graph glosses (graph X is to be read as Y, is a loan for Y), so-called *dúruò* glosses (8.2.1), and paronomastic glosses (8.2.2). The phonological parameters for these glosses,which actually are puns, are uncertain. At best, broad tendencies may reveal features of the language or dialect of a writer. But they cannot always be relied upon for the reconstruction of a specific OC word.

8.2.1 *Dúruò* glosses. Occasionally the *SW* and commentators remark that graph X "is read like" graph Y (X dú ruò 讀若 Y, hence the name) (for an introduction to these, see, for example, Coblin 1983: 12f; *JCL* 6.1, 1978: 27-33). Clear are the cases where a *dúruò* gloss tells us which of two or more readings of a graph is at issue. Often a gloss seems to refer only to part of a word's sound, similar to English, "'either' is pronounced like 'eat' and not like 'eye'". For example, *SW* 1440 states, *jué* ⿰目窅, MC ʔiwet, LHan ʔuet, *ʔwît (13-17) is "read like .... 卹", *xù*, MC sjuet, LHan suit, *swit (that is, in the sense of 'care about' as in *wù xù* 勿卹 'don't care', and not like *xù* 卹, MC swət, LHan suət, *sût 'to rub'), i.e., with final *-it, and not like its phonetic *yǎo* 窅, MC ʔieu^{B}, LH ʔeu^{B}, *ʔiûʔ with the vowel *-u.

An example for a misunderstood *dúruò* gloss is the following case, where the *SW* is sometimes thought to confirm that *zì* 自 'self' was phonetically similar to *bí* 鼻 'nose' in OC, hence one encounters OC reconstructions like *zbid.

> *SW* 1472: 自鼻也象鼻形 *zì bí yě, xiàng bí xíng...* "zì 'self' is bí 'nose', the pictograph has the shape of *bí* 'nose'..."

Xǔ Shèn was compiling a dictionary of *wén* 文 'simple graphs' and *zì* 字 'compound characters', not words, sounds, and etymologies. Given his objective, he can only have meant that originally the *graphs* for 'self' and 'nose' were the same (which is indeed true), nothing more. Therefore this statement does not prove complex initials. But elsewhere he has the gloss 自讀若鼻 *zì dú ruò bí* "self is read like nose," which has been discussed in sinological literature. But turning to the complete *SW* passage one discovers that the phrase has been taken out of context and completely misinterpreted:

> *SW* 109 (under *huáng* 皇): ... 自始也 ... 自讀若鼻。今俗以始生子為鼻子 ... *zì shǐ yě... zì dú ruò bí. jīn sú yǐ shǐ shēng zǐ wéi bí zǐ.*

In the seal script, the upper element in *huáng* 皇 was not *bái* 白, but looked like *zì* 自 (its OB source was yet something else). Xǔ explains: "... 自 means 'first'... 自 is read like *bí* 'nose'. Nowadays one customarily considers the first-born offspring *bí zǐ*." Taken out of context, he seems to say that 'self' is to be read like 'nose'. But he suggests nothing of the sort. First, he is referring only to the graph 自, not the word *zì* 'self' or any other behind it. Since the graph originally wrote both *zì* 'self' and *bí* 'nose', Xǔ points out that the graph in question is to be read like *bí* (and not like *zì*) since it stands for a homophone 'first(-born)' (also written 鼻). In sum, a phonetic similarity of the two words 'self' and 'nose' is certainly not suggested by Xǔ Shèn. As to 3000 years ago, there could have been, as today, a mental association of the two because one customarily points to one's nose when pointing to oneself.

8.2.2 Paronomastic glosses. Some late Zhou and Han period texts make use of so-called paronomastic glosses which may indicate a word's sound. The *Shìmíng* 釋名 (written ca. AD 200) is a collection of such glosses by Liú Xī 劉熙 (Bodman 1954). Some glosses, like *Shìmíng* 7.24 provide interesting information on pronunciation:

> 車古者曰車。聲如居，言行所以居人也. *chē gǔzhě yuē jū* (LH kɨɑ). *shēng rú jū* (LH kɨɑ), *yán xíng suǒyǐ jū rén yě.* "'Carriage', the ancients called it *kɨɑ*. It sounds like 'dwell' *kɨɑ*, because one says that when travelling it is that whereby one causes a person to 'dwell' [in it]."
> 今日車聲近舍也。*jīn rì chē shēng jìn shě yě...* "Nowadays, 'carriage' (LH tśʰa) sounds close to 'stay in a place' (LH śa^{B}). ..."

The author's point is that the graph for 'carriage' has two pronunciations, an older one (LH kɨɑ) and a current one (LH tśʰa). These are obviously puns with a phonetic as well as a semantic ingredient.

Apart from clarifications of this kind and general trends which may reveal something about an authors dialect, the utility of paronomastic glosses for the reconstruction of individual OC words is doubtful. A pun does not prove much about an individual graph, especially since the material in the *Shìmíng* does not reveal identifiable phonological patterns (glance through Bodman 1954). The basis of some glosses seems to be even purely graphic rather than phonological, as *fù* 付 in *rǒng* 軵 (Coblin 1978: 50, 51; Bodman 1954: 128-129, notes 274,

347). Furthermore the historical stage and dialect of the punning language are uncertain. Once formulated, a paronomastic gloss "became a philosophical verity.... For example, the gloss 兌, 說也 *duì yuè yě* "The hexagram *dui* means 'pleasure'," occurs in the *Yìjīng*, *Shuowen* and the *Shìmíng*" (Coblin 1983: 15). At least some glosses are phonologically close in LHan, but were quite distinct in OC for which they are thought to be revealing, note 視 shì, LH dźi^B glossed as 是 shì, LH dźe^B — but these are OCM *giʔ vs. *deʔ.

Considering all these caveats, a pun like *sāng wáng yě* 喪亡也 "'Burial' means to 'disappear'", for instance, does by itself not necessarily prove an OC *sm cluster in *sāng;* nor does *shè* 舍 LH śa^C as a gloss for *kù* 庫 LH kʰɑ^C prove a velar in *shè*.

9 INTERPRETATIONS OF IRREGULAR PHONETIC COMPOUNDS

The XS principle is only meaningful when applied to regular and systematic phonetic series (3.2). It has limited, or no, applicability for unsystematic series and irregular graphs. Pushing the XS principle beyond a certain limit into this area can lead to over-interpretation — something that most investigators have understood (Karlgren, Li, Baxter).

9.1 Premises

One's approach to the interpretation of phonetic series, graphs and data is guided by many conscious and unconscious premises and assumptions which can lead to spectacularly different OC forms. There are two premises with which one can approach irregular phonetic compounds: (a) the strictly phonetic premise; and (b) a premise that allows for broader mental or cultural associations and inferences in the choice of graphic elements. In this section 9, some difficult-to-analyze graphs are discussed as examples for the different results of these premises, and for the preference of the 'associative' path. (More practical guidelines have been mentioned in section 6 above.)

9.1.1 The 'phonetic' premise, as it could be called for lack of a better term, approaches XS primarily through deduction. A hypothesis like the XS principle is formulated and with strict logic applied to all phonetic series whose members are assumed to have been as similar as possible. If one postulates *glâm for MC lâm, then one could deduce that *rén* 人 (OCM *nin) was OC *znin because the graph is phonetic in *qiān* 千 (OCM *snhîn) 'thousand'. The hypothetical OC *znin is based purely on this exclusively phonological way of interpreting the XS principle in *all* phonetic series and irregular graphs, yet outside the frame of the phonetic premise there is no evidence for the phoneme *z-, for a XS contact with *snhin itself is not evidence, it merely suggests one of several possible *interpretations.* Evidence would be only MC forms, for example.

9.1.2 The 'associative' premise relies on what we actually know about the language (MC, categories, transcriptions, typology), and approaches irregular phonetic series and graphs with the realization that not only phonological, but *also mental or cultural associations* can have prompted the choice of a graphic element, so that the strict phonological similarity, which strict logic would require, cannot be assumed in irregular cases.

9.2 Illustrations for premises and assumptions

9.2.1 lǐ 李 (4-37/980)

In *SW* 2376 Xǔ Shèn defines *lǐ* 李 'plum' as a 'fruit' (*guǒ* 果), and the graph as consisting of the classifier *mù* 木 'tree' and the "phonetic" *zǐ* 子 'offspring' (子聲).

The phonetic premise: Pān (2000: 307) sets up *lǐ* as OC *b-rŭɯ˙ (the rationale for his *b* is immaterial here); since *zǐ* 子 is 'phonetic', he reconstructs it as *splŭɯ˙ in order to create a phonological link. This exemplifies the strict phonetic premise as well as the rigid application of the deductive mode of reasoning. The reconstructions may be right, but for by now familiar reasons and for the sake of simplicity, we prefer the other method.

The associative premise: First, we have seen that Xǔ Shèn's notion of 'phonetic' was not identical with that of modern investigators; he could mean as little as the rime, or nothing at all. Second, Xǔ Shèn explicitly had *lǐ* the *fruit* on his mind, not the tree. Traditionally, plums are a symbol for prolific offspring (*zǐ* 子). That this symbolism does not derive from the graph, but that the graph probably reflects a folk tradition is suggested by *méi* 梅 'a kind of plum' (without the element *zǐ* 子) which carries the same symbolism. Thus cultural associations have played a role in the choice of the element *zǐ* 子 so that there is no compelling reason to bring the initials together phonetically. Finally, *zǐ* cannot be separated from the prolific TB root *tsa. Consequently, 李 was OCM *rəʔ, and 子 was *tsəʔ.

This example demonstrates several OCM premises and assumptions:

(1) Usually one has reconstructed the OC language by applying the classical XS principle to the writing system. In light of our knowledge of OC (based on MC, etc.), *I now stand the XS principle on its head when considering irregular graphs. The question is: why was the word written in this way — not: what was the puzzling OC word behind the odd graph?* Not: what was the presumably complex word for 'plum' and 'offspring'? But: why was plum (which for all we know was OCM *rəʔ < MC lji^{B}) written in this particular way?

(2) Rather than proposing complex word forms, in odd 'phonetic' compounds the typical OC source of a MC form overrides writing conventions (phonetic series).

(3) Not too much weight should be given to Xǔ Shèn's identification of a "phonetic" when he is proven to be wrong on other occasions, as in *mǒu*, 8.1 above.

(4) This example demonstrates the associative premise: not only phonology entered into the choice of a graphic element, but also cultural and other mental associations. The selection of elements in a composite graph can be on a sliding scale, from purely phonetic (as in *jū* 居 *ka 'dwell', phonetic *gǔ* 古 *kâʔ 'antiquity'), to purely semantic (e.g., *jiān* 尖 'pointed': graph for 'small' on top of 'big'). Many graphic choices fall between these ends, like *lǐ* which still shares the rime with *zǐ*. *The greater the semantic or mental overlap of a graphic element with the word it writes, the greater the chance that phonological similarity has been compromised.* A strict XS principle works only when the compound is strictly phonetic; when other mental associations could have interfered with the selection of a graphic element, a phonology-based XS principle may lead to phonological connections where probably none existed.

9.2.2 xī 犀 (26-33/596)

There are other irregular graphs which share only the rime, if that. Xǔ can only have meant the rime at best when he states (*SW* 540) that in the graph for *xī* 犀 *sâi 'rhinoceros', the element *wěi* 尾 *məiʔ 'tail' was "phonetic." The initials were irreconcilable in Xu's Han period language as well as throughout the preceding archaic stages of Chinese because the words derive from ST *səj 'rhino' and *mrəj or *rməj 'tail' respectively (assuming something like OC *msəj — cf. WT *bse* — drifts into the realm of speculation). When investigating phonetic series, we encounter more examples of just rimes being sufficient as a common denominator (see 8.1). Therefore, we cannot assume that in such instances the initial consonants need to be reconciled for OC.

9.2.3 zuì 罪 (28-20/513)

The graph *zuì* 罪 (dzwậi^B) *dzûiʔ 'crime, offense' was originally written 辠, but for taboo reasons was replaced during the reign of Qin Shi Huangdi by 罪 which originally wrote a word for 'fish trap' (*SW* 3381). *Fēi* 非 looks like a possible phonetic, but initial consonant clusters of the type *sb- did not exist during the Qin dynasty, if they ever existed in OC. Hence the choice of the element *fēi* 非 'is not' could not have been phonetic; it was probably chosen for its mental association with the notion 'wrong, offense'. Because of the possibility of semantic interference I doubt that an OC reconstruction with an initial *sb-* cluster (or the like) is justified. All we can say is that the OC form was something like *dzûiʔ. If the *SW* intended to say that *fēi* was phonetic, it would have referred only to the rime -(u)i.

9.2.4 wèi 位 (31-7/539)

Morphological patterns can be of help in establishing an OC form (see 9.2.9). The problem is that morphology is often a judgement question.

In the OB and BI, the graph 立 stood for both *wèi* 位 MC jwei^C 'position, seat', as well as for *lì* 立 MC ljəp 'to stand'. *Lì* 立 is often believed to be phonetic in *wèi* 位 and thus phonologically very close and perhaps even etymologically related. Thus the two words look similar in some scholars' OC reconstructions. OCM tries to stay on the side of mundane straightforwardness. *Lì* 'stand' would be a prime candidate for a semantic element in a graph for 'position', which weakens the case for phonological similarity (9.2.1 [4]). The final *-ps in *wèi* is based on the possible cognation with lì, and initial *w- is otherwise not known to alternate in word families with initial *r- except in PCH *r-w- configurations which cannot be the case here, in light of the TB cognate *k-rap for *lì* (*EDOC* §10). Hence OCM *wrə(t)s (or even *wus — see 5.2.3) vs. *rəp.

9.2.5 yuè and lè 樂 (17-8/1125)

Many phonetic series include MC features which leave us in a gray area where the application of the XS principle and its premises are debatable. Karlgren and Li applied it in some cases more comprehensively than is proposed here for OCM. For example:

Co-occurrence of MC ŋ- and l- in a series is rare, as in the much-discussed 樂 which writes (a) *lè* 'joy' (MC lâk) OCM *râuk, and (b) *yuè* (MC ŋåk) *ŋrâuk 'music'; the graph was originally invented for (c) *lì* 櫟 (MC liek) *riâuk 'oak' and then borrowed for the other words (樂 is the drawing of an oak tree; U. Unger *Hao-ku* 29, 1984). Because the same graph writes two words with rather different MC initials, Karlgren thought that strict logic requires that *lè* must have had some velar initial in OC as well, in order to make it more similar to *yuè*, thus Karlgren's *ŋlŏk vs. *glåk. Accordingly, he reconstructed almost all graphs in the series with initial *g-, even though not a single one shows a trace of it in MC.

OCM *avoids sweeping creation of OC phonemes* which are based not on tangible evidence (MC or otherwise), and assumes the simplest forms, hence *ŋrâuk vs. *râuk. As already pointed out, the user of this manual can add phonemic elements to OCM as he may deem appropriate, but it is very difficult for an unsuspecting user to visualize an initial cluster, which has been presented to him, with an element deleted; thus *râuk may be less misleading than writing "*g-râuk" — even though, we may speculate (!), this may have been the OC form after all.

9.2.6 wéi 隹惟維 (28-11/575)

Strict phonetic application of the XS principle led to Karlgren's conclusion that *wéi* 隹惟維 'to be' must have been Arch. Ch. *di̯wər (OCM *wi) with an initial dental stop consonant, since the graph was originally invented for zhuī 隹 *ṭi̯wər (OCM *tui) 'little bird' (so *SW* 4685; GSR 575; OB). Sagart follows Karlgren, although he recognizes, like Baxter (as well as OCM), that at least the root of 'to be' was *wi (or *wij, *wjij). He explains the puzzling choice of a word beginning with *t- for phonetic in 'to be' with no dental initial in MC by hypothesizing that the copula must have had an iambic prefix *tə- (*tə-wij) that was regularly lost by MC (Sagart 1999: 91). Thus the iambic prefixes seem to correspond to some extent to Bodman's (and OCM's) hyphenated in OCM.

However, we prefer a simpler solution through the associative premise. All that is *knowable* with some degree of reliability is that, based on MC, 'bird' was *tui and 'to be' was *wi. When in doubt, OCM assumes these MC-based OC forms regardless of phonetic environment in XS. What is *not knowable is the mental association* by which a writer 3200 years ago selected *tui 'bird' to write the grammatical word 'to be' so that a contemporaneous reader could retrieve the intended word.

Just for the sake of argument, an alternative hypothesis for the irregular XS series could run like this: the word 隹 OCM *tui 'little bird' is likely an onomatopoetic imitation of a bird's chirping; the same phonetic writes another imitation of a bird's call, that of a 'female pheasant': *wěi* (yǎo) 鷕 OCM *wiʔ. Classifiers like *kǒu* 口 'mouth' and *niǎo* 鳥 'bird' are later additions to disambiguate graphs, hence 隹 could have originally written both *tui and *wiʔ. From *tui derive some graphs in the phonetic series, from the *wiʔ others like *wéi* 隹 *wi 'to be'. This hypothesis requires fewer assumptions and steps, and is hardly more speculative than alternatives.

The preceding considerations may leave the impression that the OC word 'to be' was the issue, when in fact they were only about the *t-, not the widely agreed-on base *wi. Thus even this t-prefix hypothesis does not invalidate an OCM *wi (and vice versa) which is taken as the minimal foundation on which further hypotheses can be built. This discussion illustrates furthermore how easy it is to become distracted by marginal hypotheses about such things as prefixes, to the point of obfuscating fundamental consensus on OC issues.

A final consideration: **Availability.** The degree of adherence to a phonology-based XS principle seems to depend partly on the number of words in a rime category and, in correlation with this number, *the availability of graphic elements for writing a word.* A rime category with a large corpus of words naturally has a sufficient supply of graphic elements to allow a fairly narrow phonological parameter of a phonetic series. Thus in the common OC rime *-a, words of the type KA and KRA each tend to have their own phonetic (古家假). Rimes which are comprised of relatively few words, such as *-əp, *-en, and *-ui, have a more limited supply of graphic elements, therefore phonetic similarity may occasionally be reduced to the rime or even the final consonant. This could possibly have something to do with irregular graphs and series.

9.2.7 jīn 今, tān 貪, niàn 念 (38-3/651, 652)

The graphs *tān* 貪 MC tʰậm (OCM *rhə̂m) 'to covet' and *niàn* 念 MC niem^C (OCM *nîms) 'think of' share the element *jīn* 今 MC kjəm (OCM *kəm) 'today' which *SW* states is phonetic in the other two. This implies that all three words must have sounded similar in OC; according to strict logic, they should have had some complex initial clusters in OC (see p. ix).

Let us step back for a moment. We know as facts the MC forms tʰậm and niem^C; we know that *tān* would *normally* derive from OC *thəm, *lhəm, *nhəm, or *rhəm in a regular fashion, there is little argument about that; transparent cognates make OC *rhəm a virtual certainty. MC niem^C normally is expected to go back to something like OC *nems, *niams or *nims, depending on one's OC system. It is known that *tān* (*rhə̂m) is related to TB *C-rum and that Chinese regularly unrounds vowels before final labial consonants (ST *-um > OC, MC -əm); and that *niàn* (*nîms) is related to WT *snyam-pa*. On the basis of MC alone, common ST forms like *C-rum (ST *-um > OC *-əm > MC -ậm) and *nim (?) ~ *njam can be postulated. Any OC reconstruction which is significantly out of line with these givens must be suspect, no matter what the XS principle can be construed to imply. The claim of an OC medial *r in *jīn* is probably based on *tān*. An m-prefix for *niàn* is suggested by a meaningless preceding wú 無 *ma in one *Shijing* line. The OC form may well have been *mnîms, but for the sake of simplicity and to avoid arguments about elusive prefixes, we will be content with the minimal form OCM *nîms. When Xǔ Shèn looked at these graphs and stated that 今 was "phonetic," he may have had just the rimes in mind, or he may have presumed that there ought to have been some earlier phonological connection, just as in the case of 監 LHan kam ~ 藍 LHan lâm of his language.

Since we have touched on speculation, let me add my own in order to show that there can be alternative interpretations. It seems that the graph 今 was invented for the word *hàn* 頷 *gə̂m? 'jaw', it shows the downward-turned open mouth (cf. *mìng* 命 'to order', *yuè* 龠 'pan pipe', *líng* 令 'order', *qiān* 僉 'glib-tongued', *hé* 合 'fit' = downward-turned open mouth covering the opening of a vessel like a lid; *shí* 食 'to eat' = open mouth hovering over a full bowl); a stroke points to one side, i.e., the jaw, just as *běn* 本 'root' is *mù* 木 'tree' with a stroke pointing to its lower end. (In 'jaw', the elongated stroke may suggest the tongue, perhaps.) 'Jaw', like 'mouth', is associated with words meaning 'hold in the mouth, hold back, resent'. 'Hold/keep in the mouth' is a widely encountered metaphor for internal psychological processes. Therefore, 今 is at least partially semantic in 貪 'to covet' and *niàn* 念 'to think of', which diminishes the likelihood of a purely phonetic role of 今.

Ruminations as in the preceding paragraph illustrate the above claim (see 9.2.1) that in unsystematic XS the principle is stood on its head. Here, these speculations have no bearing on the OCM forms, because the question we tried to address was: why did they write these OC words with this graphic element? This is the opposite of asking how similar the words that share this graphic element must have sounded. In contemplating the phonological rules and steps required for connecting Pān's forms with MC, OCM seems less complex and hence preferable.

9.2.8 jiàng 匠 (3-52/729)

SW 5729 states that in *jiàng* 匠 'do carpentry work, carpenter' both *jīn* 斤 'axe' and *fāng* 匚 匸 'box' are semantic. In spite of this, it has sometimes been proposed that *fāng* was phonetic after all, and the word should hence be reconstructed OC *zbjaŋ or the like and related to WT *byaŋ-pa* 'skilled, experienced'. However, a phonetic role of *fāng* is not compelling in light of the semantic overlap of graph and word, hence OCM *dzaŋh. This is apparently confirmed by foreign connections: *jiàng* is indirectly connected with Khmer *cāṃṅa* /caŋ/ 'to dress (wood, stone), rough out, trim...' (i.e., do carpentry work), while the WT word is probably cognate to *fāng* 方 'method' ≍ *fàng* 'imitate, conform'.

9.2.9 jì 計 (26-3/1241a)

The word *jì* 計 MC kiei^C 'calculation, accounting' is often reconstructed with an OC final labial, i.e., *-ps, because *shí* 十 *gip 'ten' is suspected to be phonetic. Karlgren refrained from proposing an OC form because he graph for *jì* is not a rime word in poetry, the *SW* (1002) is silent on the question if 十 is phonetic. Because *shí* 'ten' can in a word for 'calculate' play a semantic role, the requirement for close phonological agreement according to the XS principle is weakened (see 9.2.1). A semantic role of 'ten' is, in fact, confirmed by an early variant of the graph written with *qiān* 千 'thousand' instead, so at least these writers made no phonological connection with 十 *gip. Because a phonetic role of 'ten' *gip is not compelling, let us reconsider what the simplest solution could be. MC kiei^C can theoretically derive from many different OC syllables: from OCM *kê(k)h, *kîh, *kê(t)s (< *kê[t]s or *kêps), or from *kî(t)s (< *kî[t]s or *kîps) — these would be in Baxter's system *ke(k)s, *ki(k)s, *kets (< *kets or *keps), or *kits (< *kits or *kips). Since open syllables are more common than closed ones, and final labials are particularly rare, the OC default form should be suspected to be either OCM *kêh or *kîh. Now we should look for possible cognates for confirmation among words with an open syllable. Indeed, it turns out that *jì* is simply an ordinary tone C derivation from *jī* 稽 MC kiei, *kî 'to calculate', hence *jì* was OCM *kîh. If *shí* *gip played a phonetic role, it was only its initial and vowel.

10 CONCLUSION

It was my intention that with this Introduction's summaries and considerations of data, sources, premises and assumptions, the reader may perhaps follow arguments about OC in broad outline. I hope it may help the non-specialist evaluate OC reconstructions by distinguishing (relatively) widely accepted proposals from more probing hypotheses.

REFERENCES

This list of References is taken from the *EDOC;* it may include works that are not mentioned in *GSC*; however, additional works that have been cited are included. For a full bibliography on works on Old Chinese, see Baxter 1992.

Baxter, William H. 1977. *Old Chinese Origins of the Middle Chinese chóngniǔ Doublets: A Study Using Multiple Character Readings.* PhD Diss. Cornell University.

———. 1992. *A Handbook of Old Chinese Phonology.* Berlin, New York.

Baxter, William H., and Laurent Sagart. 1998. "Word formation in Old Chinese." In Packard 1998, 35–76.

Benedict, Paul K. 1972. *Sino-Tibetan. A Conspectus.* London.

Beyer, Stephan V. 1992. *The classical Tibetan language.* Albany, New York.

Bodman, Nicholas C. 1954. *A Linguistic Study of the Shih Ming.* Cambridge, Mass.: Harvard-Yenching Inst. Studies XI.

Bodman, Nicholas C. 1980. Chinese and Sino-Tibetan; evidence towards establishing the nature of their relationship. In Frans van Coetsem and Linda R. Waugh, eds., *Contributions to historical linguistics*, 34–199. Leiden.

Boltz, William G. 1994. *The origin and early development of the Chinese writing system.* New Haven, Conn.

Boodberg, Peter A. 1937. "Some proleptical remarks on the evolution of archaic Chinese." *HJAS* 2: 329–372.

Branner, David Prager. 1995; 2000. *Problems in Comparative Chinese Dialectology. The Classification of Miin and Hakka.* Berlin, NewYork.

Branner, David Prager, ed. 2006. *The Chinese Rime Tables.* Amsterdam.

Chao Yuen Ren. 1941. Distinctions within Ancient Chinese. *HJAS* 5: 203-233.

———. 1968. *A Grammar of Spoken Chinese.* Berkeley, Cal.

Chén Fùhuá 陳复華, ed. 1999. *Gǔdài Hànyǔ cídiǎn* 古代漢語詞典. Beijing.

Chén Zhāngtài 陳章太 and Lǐ Rúlóng 李如龍. 1991. *Mǐnyǔ yánjiù* 閩語研究. Beijing.

Coblin, W. South. 1978. "The initials of Xu Shen's language as reflected in the Shuowen *duruo* glosses." *JCL* 6.1: 27-75.

———. 1979-1980. "The finals of Cheng Hsüan's language as reflected in phonological glosses." *MS* 34: 263-317.

———. 1982. "Notes on the dialect of the Han Buddhist transcriptions". In *Proceedings of the International Conference on Sinology.* Taipei.

———. 1983. *A Handbook of Eastern Han Sound Glosses.* Hong Kong.

———. 1984. "The finals of Yang Xiong's language." *JCL* 11.2: 1-52.

———. 1987. "The rimes of Chang-an in middle Han times. Part II: The early Eastern Han period." *AO* 48: 89-110.

———. 1991a. *Studies in Old Northwest Chinese.* JCL Monograph 4.

———. 1991b. "Thoughts on dentilabialization in the Tang-time dialect of Shazhou." *TP* 77: 88–107.

———. 1993a. "BTD revisited: a reconsideration of the Han Buddhist Transcriptional Dialect." *BIHP* 63.4: 867–943.

———. 1993b. *Beyond BTD: An excursion in Han phonology.* Ms.

———. 1994a. "Remarks on some early Buddhist transcriptional data from Northwest China." *MS* 42: 151–169.
———. 1994b. *A compendium of phonetics in Northwest Chinese*. JCL Monograph 7.
———. 1996. "Marginalia on two translations of the *Qieyun* preface." *JCL* 24.1: 85-97.
———. 1999. "Thoughts on the identity of the Chinese 'Phags-pa dialect." In Simmons, ed. *Issues in Chinese dialect description and classification.*
———. 2006. *Francisco Varo's Glossary of the Mandarin Language.* 2 vols. MS Monograph Series 53/1+2. St. Augustin, Germany.
———. 2007. *A Handbook of 'Phags-pa Chinese.* Honolulu.
Coblin, W. South, and Joseph A. Levi. 2000. *Francisco Varo's Grammar of the Mandarin languages (1703).* Amsterdam/Philadelphia.
Demiéville, Paul. 1950. "Archaïsmes de prononciation en chinois vulgaire." *TP* 40: 1–59.
Dīng Fúbǎo 丁福保. n. d. *Shuōwén jiězì gǔlín* 說文解字詁林. Taipei.
Dobson, W.A.C.H. 1959. *Late Archaic Chinese.* Toronto.
———. 1962. *Early Archaic Chinese.* Toronto.
Downer, G. B. 1959. "Derivation by tone-change in classical Chinese." *BSOAS* 22: 258–290.
Edmondson, Jerold A., and David B. Solnit. 1988. *Comparative Kadai: Linguistic studies beyond Tai.* Summer Inst. of Ling., U. of Texas at Arlington.
Edmondson, Jerold A., and Yang Quan. 1988. "Word-initial preconsonants and the history of Kam-Sui resonant initials and tones." In Edmondson and Solnit 1988: 143-166.
Emmerich, Reinhard, and Hans Stumpfeldt, eds. 2002. *Und folge nun dem, was mein Herz begehrt. Festschrift für Ulrich Unger zum 70. Geburtstag.* Hamburger Sinologische Schriften 8. Hamburg.
Erkes, Eduard. 1956. *Chinesische Grammatik. Nachtrag zur Chinesischen Grammatik von G. v. d. Gabelentz.* Berlin.
Ferlus, Michel. 1998. "Du chinois archaïque au chinois ancien: monosyllabisation et formation des syllables *tendu/lâche.*" ICSTLL (Lund).
———. 1999. "Phonétique historique et écriture du chinois: réflexions à propos de la série phonologique GSR 94." *LTBA* 22.2: 1-20.
Forrest, R. A. D. 1948. *The Chinese Language.* Third ed. 1973. London.
Gabelentz, Georg von der. 1881. *Chinesische Grammatik.* Leipzig.
Gong, Hwang-cherng. 1989. (Articles on Chinese-Tangut/Tangut-Chinese transcriptions, in 2002)
———. 1999. Cóng Hàn-Zàng yǔ de bǐjiào kàn shànggǔ Hànyǔ de cítóu wèntí 從漢藏語的比校看上古漢語的辭頭問題. In Gong 2002, vol. 2: 125–160.
———. 2002. *Hàn-Zàngyǔ yánjiū lùn wénjí* 漢藏語研究論文集. Academia Sinica, Language and Linguistics Monograph III, vol. 2. Taipei.
Graham, A. C. 1973. "The Terminations of the Archaic Chinese Pronouns." *BSOAS* 36:2: 293–298.
Gregerson, Kenneth J. 1976. "Vietnamese hoi and ngã tones and Mon-Khmer -h finals." *Mon-Khmer Studies* 5: 76–83.
Hashimoto, Mantaro. 1976a. The agrarian and the pastoral diffusion of languages. In Hashimoto, ed., *Genetic Relationships, Diffusion, and Typological Similarities of East and SE Asian Languages.* Papers for the 1st Japan-US Joint Seminar on East and SE Asian Linguistics, 1–14. Tokyo.
———. 1976b. "Origin of the East Asian linguistic structure—Latitudinal transitions and longitudinal development." *CAAAL* 22: 35–41.
Haudricourt, André G. 1954a. "Comment reconstruire le chinois archaïque." *Word* 10: 351-364.

———. 1954b. "De l'origine des tons en viêtnamien." *JA* 242: 68-82.

Ho Dah-an (Hé Dà-ān) 何大安. 1993. "Linguistic layers of the Wu dialect during the Six Dynasties." *BIHP* 64:4: 867–875.

Hock, Hans Heinrich. 1988. *Principles of Historical Linguistics.* Berlin, New York, Amsterdam.

Huáng Bùfán 黃布凡, ed. 1992. *Zàng-Miǎnyǔ zú yǔyán cíhuì* 藏緬語族語言詞匯 (A Tibeto-Burman Lexicon). Beijing.

Jenner, Philip N., and Saveros Pou. 1980–1981. A Lexicon of Khmer morphology. *Mon-Khmer Studies* 9-10.

Karlgren, Bernhard. 1923. *Analytical dictionary of Chinese and Sino-Japanese.* Paris.

———. 1924. *Études sur la phonologie chinoise*, fasc. IV. Dictionary of Chinese dialects. Stockholm.

———. 1933. "Word families in Chinese." *BMFEA* 5: 9–120.

———. 1949. *The Chinese language.* New York.

———. 1954. "Compendium of phonetics in Ancient and Archaic Chinese." *BMFEA* 22: 211-367.

———. 1956. "Cognate words in the Chinese phonetic series." *BMFEA* 28: 1–18.

———. 1957. *Grammata serica recensa.* Stockholm.

Keightley, David N., ed. 1983. *The Origins of Chinese Civilization.* Berkeley, L.A.

LaPolla, Randy J. 1994. "Variable finals in Proto-Sino-Tibetan." *BIHP* 65:1: 131–173.

Lehmann, Winfred P. 1993. *Theoretical Bases of Indo-European Linguistics.* London, New York.

Li Fang Kuei (Lǐ Fāng-guì) 李方桂. 1971. "Shànggǔ yīn yánjiù 上古音研究 (Studies on Archaic Chinese phonology)." *Tsing Hua Journal of Chinese Studies* n.s. 9: 1–61.

———. 1974-75. *Fang-kuei Li: Studies on Archaic Chinese.* Translated by Gilbert Mattos. *MS* 31: 219-287.

Lǐ Xiào-dìng 李孝定. 1965. *Jiǎgǔwén zì jíshì* 甲骨文字 集釋. Taipei.

Liáng Sēngbǎo 梁僧寶. 1925. *Sì shēng yùnpǔ* 四聲韻譜. Taipei [reprint].

Loewe, Michael, ed. 1993. *Early Chinese Texts. A Bibliographical Guide.* Berkeley, Cal.

Lù Démíng 陸德明 (556–627). *Jīngdiǎn shìwén* 經典釋文.

Luó Chángpéi 羅常培, and Zhōu Zǔmó 周祖謨. 1958. *Hàn Wèi Jìn nán běi cháo yùnbù yǎnbiàn yánjiù* 漢魏晉南北朝韻部演變研究. Beijing.

Mallory, J. P., and Victor H. Mair. 2000. *The Tarim Mummies.* London, New York.

Maspero, Henri. 1912. "Études sur la phonétique historique de la langue annamite." *BEFEO* 12: 1-126.

Matisoff, James A.1992. "Following the marrow: two parallel Sino-Tibetan etymologies." *LTBA* 15:1: 199–177.

———. 1997a. *Sino-Tibetan numeral systems: prefixes, protoforms and problems.* Pacific Linguistics. Canberra.

———. 2000. "An extrusional approach to *p-/w- variation in Sino-Tibetan." *Language and Linguistics* 1:2: 135–186.

———. 2003. *Handbook of Proto-Tibeto-Burman: a system and philosophy of Sino-Tibetan reconstruction.* Berkeley, Los Angeles.

Matisoff, James A., general editor. 1995. *Languages and dialects of Tibeto-Burman.* STEDT Monograph Series no. 2. Sino-Tibetan Etymological Dictionary and Thesaurus Project. Berkeley.

Mattos, Gilbert L. 1971. "Tonal 'anomalies' in the Kuo Feng odes." *Tsing Hua Journal of Chinese Studies*, n.s IX, nos. 1 and 2: 306–324.

McCoy, John, and Timothy Light, eds. 1986. *Contributions to Sino-Tibetan Studies.* Nicholas Bodman Festschrift. Leiden.

Méi, Tsŭ-lín 梅祖麟. 1970. "Tones and prosody in Middle Chinese and the origin of the rising tone." HJAS 30: 86-110.
———. 1985. Some examples of prenasals and *s-nasals in Sino-Tibetan. In Thurgood et al., eds.
———. 1988. Three examples of internal reconstruction in Chinese. ZGYW 1988.3: 169-181.
Mei, Tsu-Lin, and J. Norman. 1971. "Cl- > s- in some Northern Min dialects." *Tsing Hua Journal of Chinese Studies* 9: 96–105.
Norman, Jerry. 1979. "Chronological strata in the Min dialects." *FY* 4: 268–274.
———. 1983. "Some ancient Chinese dialect words in Min dialects." *FY* 3: 202–211.
———. 1986. The origin of the Proto-Min softened stops. In McCoy and Light, eds., 375–384.
———. 1988. *Chinese*. Cambridge, UK.
———. 1994. "Pharyngealization in early Chinese." *JAOS* 114: 397–408.
———. 2006. Common Dialectal Chinese. In Branner, ed.
Norman, Jerry, and W. South Coblin. 1995. "A new approach to Chinese historical linguistics." *JAOS* 115: 576–84.
Packard, Jerome L. , ed.1998. *New approaches to Chinese word formation*. Berlin, NewYork.
Pān Wù-yún 潘悟云. 1987. "Yuènányŭ zhōng de shànggŭ Hànyŭ jiècí céng 越南語中的上古漢語借辭層 (A layer of OC loan words in Vietnamese)." *YYWZX* 3: 38–47.
———. 2000. *Hànyŭ lìshĭ yīnyùnxué* 漢語曆史音韻學. Shanghai.
Pān Wù-yún et al., transl. 1997. *Hànwén diǎn* 漢文典. (Translation and improvement of Karlgren, *GSR*, with *pinyin* and stroke index.) Shanghai.
Pulleyblank, E. G. 1962. "The consonantal system of Old Chinese." *AM* 9: 58–144, 206–265.
———. 1963. "An interpretation of the vowel systems of Old Chinese and Written Burmese." *AM* 10: 200–221.
———. 1973. "Some new hypotheses concerning word families in Chinese." *JCL* 1:1: 111–125.
———. 1983a. "The Chinese and their neighbors in prehistoric and early historic times." In Keightley, ed., 411–466.
———. 1983b. "Stages in the transcription of Indian words in Chinese from Han to Tang". In Röhrborn, Klaus und Wolfgang Veenker, Hrsg. 1983. *Sprachen des Buddhismus in Zentralasien. Veröffentlichungen der Societas Uralo-altaica,* Bd. 16. Wiesbaden.: 73-102.
———. 1984. *Middle Chinese. A Study in Historical Phonology*. Vancouver, BC.
———. 1991. *Lexicon of reconstructed pronunciation in Early Middle Chinese, Late MC, and Early Mandarin*. Vancouver, BC.
———. 1994. "The Old Chinese Origin of Type A and B Syllables." *JCL* 22.1: 73-99.
———. 1995a. "The historical and prehistorical relationships of Chinese." In W. Wang, *Ancestry*, 145–194.
———. 1995b. *Outline of Classical Chinese Grammar*. Vancouver, BC.
———. 1998. "Qieyun and Yunjing: The essential foundation for Chinese historical linguistics." *JAOS* 118.2: 200–216.
Qiú Xīguī 裘錫圭. 2000. *Chinese writing*. Berkeley, Cal. [*Wénzìxué gàiyào* 文字學概要, Beijing 1988; rev. Taibei 1994.] Translated by G. Mattos and J. Norman.
Revel, Nicole. 1988. *Le riz en Asie du sud-est. Atlas du vocabulaire de la plante*. Paris.
Rosemont, Henry. 1991. *Chinese texts and philosophical contexts: essays dedicated to A. C. Graham*. La Salle, Ill.
Sagart, Laurent. 1999. *The roots of Old Chinese*. Amsterdam and Philadelphia.
———. 2003. "Sources of Middle Chinese Manner Types: Old Chinese Prenasalized Initials in Hmong-Mien and Sino-Tibetan Perspective." *Language and Linguistics* 4.4, 2003: 757-768.
Schuessler, Axel. 1974. "R and l in Archaic Chinese." *JCL* 2.2.
———. 1987. *A dictionary of Early Zhou Chinese*. Honolulu.

———. 1996. Palatalization of Old Chinese velars. *JCL* 24.2: 197-211.

———. 2006. The Qièyùn System 'Divisions' as a Result of Vowel Warping. In Branner, ed., 83–96.

———. 2007. *ABC Etymological Dictionary of Old Chinese*. Honolulu.

Shěn Jiān-shì 沈兼士. 1944. *Guǎngyùn shēngxì* 廣韻聲系. Taipei.

Shima Kunio 島邦男. 1971. *Inkyo bokuji sōrui* 殷墟卜辭綜類. Tokyo.

Simmons, Richard vanNess, ed. 1999. *Issues in Chinese Dialect Description and Classification*. Journal of Chinese Linguistics monograph series no. 15. Berkeley, Cal.

Ting Pang-hsin. 1975. *Chinese Phonology of the Wei-Chin Period: Reconstruction of the Finals as Reflected in Poetry*. Taipei.

Thurgood, Graham, and Randy LaPolla, eds. 2003. *The Sino-Tibetan Languages*. London and New York.

Thurgood, Graham, James A. Matisoff, David Bradley, eds. 1985. *Linguistics of the Sino-Tibetan area: the state of the art*. Paul Benedict Festschrift. Canberra.

Unger, Ulrich. 1982-1995. *Hao-ku. Sinologische Rundbriefe*. Nos. 1–51. Münster.

Wáng Lì 王力. 1958. *Hànyǔ shǐgǎo* 漢語史搞. Beijing.

———. 1982. *Tóngyuán zìdiǎn* 同源字典. Beijing.

Wang, William S-Y., ed. 1995. *The Ancestry of Chinese*. JCL Monograph 8.

Wang, William S-Y. 1995. *The Ancestry of Chinese: Retrospect and Prospect*. In W. Wang, ed., I–XI.

Xǔ Shèn 許慎. ca. 149. *Shuōwén jiězì* 說文解字 (SW); see Dīng Fúbǎo.

Yáng Xióng 揚雄 (Han period). *Fāng yán* 方言. Cited edition: Fāngyán jiàojiān fù tóngjiǎn 方言校箋附通檢 Index du Fang yen, text établi par [Zhou Zumo], Centre franco-chinois d'études sinologiques. Taipei, 1968.

Yú Nǎi-yǒng 余迺永. 1974. *Hù zhù jiàozhèng Sòng běn Guǎng-yùn* 互註校正宋本廣韻. Taipei.

Zhengzhang Shangfang 鄭張尚芳. 1987. Shanggu yunmu xitong he si deng, jieyin, shengdiao de fayuan wenti (The Old Chinese system of initials and the question of the origin of the 4 divisions, the medials, and the tones). *Wenzhou Shifan xueyuan xuebao* 1987.4: 67-90.

Zhōngwén dàcídiǎn 中文大辭典 (*Encyclopedic dictionary of the Chinese language*). 1973. Taipei.

Zhōu Fǎgāo 周法高. 1972. "Shànggǔ Hànyǔ hé Hàn-Zàngyǔ 上古漢語和漢藏語." *Journal of the Institute of Chinese Studies of the Chinese Univ. of Hong Kong* 5: 159–244.

———. n.d. *Jīnwén gǔlín* 金文詁林. Taipei.

1 OCM rime *-a Yú bù 魚部

GSR 32 - 106

Baxter 1992: 478 ff. (§10.2.4)

The OC / Han period value *-a is confirmed by sporadic archaisms in dialects, and MHan transcriptions where the vowel represented foreign a (see examples under the entries).

The OCM final *-wâ has eventually merged everywhere with *-â into MC div. I -uo.

MC div. III -jwo 魚 and -ju 虞 have merged in the North, but in the South (as seen in PMin and some Wu and Gan dialects) QYS -jwo is unrounded -jɤ, while MC -ju is rounded (Mei Tzu-lin *CAAAL* 9, 1978: 44ff; Sagart 1993: 191). The ONWC and BTD also maintain the distinction. Initials *w, *kw- probably developed into LH wuaŋ, kwuɑ etc. in QYS div. III; but we write LH wɑŋ, kyɑ, etc. Sporadic MC -ja III after acute initials has developed in analogy to the regular forms in OCM *-akh > MC ja^{C}, as in 借 MC tsja^{C}, LH tsia^{C} < OCM *tsakh.

Table 1-1: OCM rimes *-aŋ, *-ak, *-a in QYS categories

Div.	*-aŋ R.3	*-ak R.2	*-akh R.2	*-a R.1
I	鋼 kâŋ kɑŋ *kâŋ 光 kwâŋ kuɑŋ *kwâŋ 當 tâŋ tɑŋ *tâŋ	各 kâk kɑk *kâk 郭 kwâk kuɑk *kwâk 落 lâk lɑk *râk 莫 mâk mɑk *mâk	路 luo^{C} lɑ^{C} *râkh	古 kuo^{B} kɑ^{B} *kâʔ 土 t^{h}uo^{B} t^{h}ɑ^{B} *thâʔ 步 buo^{C} bɑ^{C} *bâh
III lab				懼 gju^{C} gyɑ^{C} *gwah 于 ju wɑ *wa 無 mju muɑ *ma
III gr	疆 kjaŋ kɨɑŋ *kaŋ 王 jwaŋ wɑŋ *waŋ 亡 mjwaŋ muɑŋ *maŋ	卻 k^{h}jak k^{h}ɨɑk *khak 攫 kjwak kyɑk *kwak (縛 bjwak buɑk *bak)[1]		居 kjwo kɨɑ *kaʔ
III ac	章 tśjaŋ tśɑŋ *taŋ 陽 jiaŋ jɑŋ *laŋ 相 sjaŋ siɑŋ *saŋ 霜 ṣjaŋ ṣɑŋ *sraŋ	著 ḍjak ḍiɑk *drak (rare)	庶 śjwo^{C} śɑ^{C} *lha(k)h (rare)	書 śjwo śɑ *lha 余 jiwo jɑ *la 所 ṣjwo^{B} ṣɑ^{B} *sraʔ
III ac		石 źjäk dźak *dak 亦 jiäk jak *jak 射 dźjäk źak *m-lak 夕 zjäk ziak *s-jak	柘 tśja^{C} tśa^{C} *takh 射 dźja^{C} źa^{C} *m-lakh	社 źja^{B} dźa^{B} *daʔ 野 jia^{B} ja^{B} *laʔ
3/3 gr	京 kjɐŋ kɨaŋ *kraŋ 兄 xjwɐŋ hyaŋ *hwraŋ 永 jwɐŋ^{B} waŋ^{B} *wraŋʔ 明 mjɐŋ mɨaŋ *mraŋ	戟 kjɐk kɨak *krak 碧 pjɐk pɨak *prak[1]		
II	更 kɐŋ kaŋ *krâŋ 觵 kwɐŋ kuaŋ *kwrâŋ 烹 p^{h}ɐŋ p^{h}aŋ *phrâŋ	客 k^{h}ɐk k^{h}ak *khrâk 宅 ḍɐk ḍak *drâk 百 pɐk pak *prâk 獲 ɣwɛk ɣuak *wrâk		家 ka ka *krâ 寡 kwa^{B} kua^{B} *kwrâʔ 巴 pa pa *prâ

Notes on the Table: In the boxes are provided: 字 / QYS / LHan / *OCM. Abbreviations: gr = grave initials, ac = acute initials, lab = labial(ized) initials. R. in the top row refers to the Rime and section in GSU. Occasionally heavier framed boxes include MC homophonous finals.

[1] The only syllable of this type, MC bjwak and pjɐk (or pjäk 3) are unique.

1 OCM *-a 魚部 (GSR 32-106)

1-1	**= K. 49, 1258a**	**Mand.**	**MC**	**LHan**	**OCM**	
a	古	gǔ	kuo^B	kɔ^B < kɑ^B	kâʔ	
	[T] Sin Sukchu SR ku (上); MGZY gu (上) [ku]; ONW ko <> [E] WT rga-ba 'old'; JP ləga					
m	罟	gǔ	kuo^B	kɑ^B	kâʔ	OCB *kaʔ
q	盬	gǔ	kuo^B	kɑ^B	kâʔ	PTai *klɨo^{A1} 'salt'
r	𥂢	gǔ	kuo^B	kɑ^B	kâʔ	
-	牯 male	gǔ	kuo^B	kɑ^B	-	
	[T] ONW ko <> [D] PMin *k̭o^B					
go	姑蛄	gū	kuo	kɑ	kâ	姑 [D] PMin *ko
k	沽 a river, buy	gū	kuo	kɑ	kâ	
	careless	gǔ	kuo^B	kɑ^B	kâʔ	
p	辜	gū	kuo	kɑ	kâ	
g'	橭	gū, kū	k(ʰ)uo	k(ʰ)ɑ	kâ, khâ	
i	故	gù	kuo^C	kɑ^C	kâh	OCB *kaʔ(s)
	[T] Sin Sukchu SR ku (去); MGZY gu (去) [ku]					
u	苦 bitter	kǔ	kʰuo^B	kʰɑ^B	khâʔ	TB *kha 'bitter'
	[T] Sin Sukchu SR k'u (上); MGZY khu (上) [k'u]; ONW kʰo <> [D] PMin *kho^B					
	苦 bad	gǔ	kuo^B	kɑ^B	kâʔ	
h'	楛 a tree	hù	ɣuo^B	gɑ^B	gâʔ	
	bad	gǔ	kuo^B	kɑ^B	kâʔ	
t	枯	kū	kʰuo	kʰɑ	khâ	Khmer /khah/ 'dry up, wither'
vxy	岵怙祜	hù	ɣuo^B	gɑ^B	gâʔ	
b'	酤	hù	ɣuo^B	gɑ^B	gâʔ	
		gū	kuo(^{C})	kɑ(^{C})	kâ, kâh	
f	固	gù	kuo^C	kɑ^C	kâ(k)h	
	[T] Sin Sukchu SR ku (去); MGZY gu (去) [ku]; ONW ko					
e'	錮	gù	kuo^C	kɑ^C	kâ(k)h	
1258a	涸	hé	ɣâk	gɑk	gâk	
f'	箇個	gè	kâ^C	kɑ^C< kɑi^C	kâih	
	[T] Sin Sukchu SR kɔ (去), LR kɔ; MGZY go (去) [kɔ]; ONW kɑ					
	[D] Y-Taishan kuɔi^{C1}, Kaiping kuai^{C1}; K-Meix ^{55}kɛ^C; PMin *kɑi^C 'bamboo stalk' > 'piece, item' <> [E] PTai *kai^{B1}, Saek kʰal^4 (< gal^A) > kʰan^4 classifier					
a'-	胡 > 鬍	hú	ɣuo	gɔ < gɑ	gâ	'dewlap' > 'beard'
	胡 what	hú	ɣuo	gɑ	gâ	TB *ga 'what'
	胡蝴 butterfly	hú	ɣuo	gɑ	gâ	
i'k'	瑚葫	hú	ɣuo	gɑ	gâ	瑚 see 24-44A; 葫 see 19-19
j'	湖	hú	ɣuo	gɑ	gâ	[D] PMin *ɦo
l'm'	餬鶘	hú	ɣuo	gɑ	gâ	
c'	居 dwell	jū	kjwo	kɨɔ < kɨɑ	kaʔ, kah	⋇ 1-18/85a chǔ 處 'dwell'
	[T] Sin S. SR ky (平); MGZY gy̆u (平) [ky]; MTang ky < kø, ONW kø < kio (?)					
	[D] Y-Guangzh ^{55}kœy^{A1}, Taishan kui^{33}, M-Amoy ^{44}ku^{A1}					
	居 final particle	jū	kjwo, kjɨ	kɨɑ	ka	
o'p'q'	据琚裾	jū	kjwo	kɨɑ	ka	据 ⋇ 1-9/803f
n'r's'	倨踞鋸	jù	kjwo^C	kɨɑ^C	kah	OCB *k(r)jas <> [D] PMin *ky^C
t'	椐	jū	kjwo(^{C}), kʰjwo	kɨɑ(^{C}), kʰɨɑ	ka, kah, kha	
u'	腒	jū, qú	kjwo, gjwo	kɨɑ, gɨɑ	ka, ga	

1 OCM *-a 魚部 (GSR 32-106)

1-2	**= K. 50**	**Mand.**	**MC**	**LHan**	**OCM**	
ag	鼓瞽	gǔ	kuo^B	kɑ^B	kâʔ	

[E] PWa *kloʔ 'bronze-drum', PTai *klɔŋ^{A1} 'drum', Saek tlɔɔŋ^{A1} <> [D] PMin *ko^B

1-3	**= K. 51**	**Mand.**	**MC**	**LHan**	**OCM**	
a	股	gǔ	kuo^B	kɑ^B	kâʔ	
	[E] KS *kwa^1. S. k^{h}aa^{A1} < *k^h- 'leg, thigh'					
b	羖	gǔ	kuo^B	kɑ^B	kâʔ	Kan. k^{h}as 'sheep'

1-4	**= K. 52**	**Mand.**	**MC**	**LHan**	**OCM**
a	蠱	gǔ	kuo^B	kɑ^B	kâʔ

1-5	**= K. 56**	**Mand.**	**MC**	**LHan**	**OCM**	
a	壺	hú	ɣuo	gɑ	gâ	S. kaa^1 'kettle, teapot'

1-6	**= K. 53, 91**	**Mand.**	**MC**	**LHan**	**OCM**	
a	戶	hù	ɣuo^B	gɑ^B	gâʔ	
	[T] Sin Sukchu SR ɣu (上); MGZY Xu (上) [ɣu]; ONW ɣo					
	[E] TB *(C-)ga 'door'; LB *ʔga^1 'door' ⋈ ga^3 'open', NNaga *ga^A 'door', WT sgo 'door'					
c	扈	hù	ɣuo^B	gɑ^B	gâʔ	WB ka^B 'stretched, widen'
-	滬	hù	ɣuo^B	gɑ^B	gâʔ	TB-Lu. k^{h}aar^R < k^{h}aarʔ 'a weir'
de	雇鳸	hù	ɣuo^B	gɑ^B	gâʔ	WB ə-k^{h}a^C 'wages'
g	顧	gù	kuo^C	kɑ^C	kâh	
	[T] Sin Sukchu SR ku (去); MGZY gu (去) [ku]					
91a	所 'whack!'	hǔ	xuo^B	hɑ^B	hâʔ	= 1-30/60i; see also 1-63/91a.

1-7	**= K. 54**	**Mand.**	**MC**	**LHan**	**OCM**
abc	互枑沍	hù	ɣuo^C	gɑ^C	gâh

1-8 **= K. 642a-g** For 盍 and the graphs GSR 642g-x, see 35-1. The phonetic 去 (GSR 642a) resulted from a merger of two different OB graphs that look superficially similar: one of the phonological type KAP showing 'a lid', one of the phonological type KAʔ showing a standing person with an opening indicated between the spread legs (note WT 'excrement').

		Mand.	**MC**	**LHan**	**OCM**	
a	去 put away	qù	k^{h}jwo^B	k^{h}ɨɑ^B	khaʔ	'get rid of'
	go away		k^{h}jwo^C	k^{h}ɨɑ^C	khah	OCB *kh(r)jas
	[T] Sin Sukchu SR k'y (去); MGZY khÿu (去) [k'y]; ONW k^{h}ø < k^{h}io (?)					
	[E] WT skyag-pa, bskyags 'to spend, lay out, expend' ⋈ skyag ~ rkyag 'dirt, excrement'; WB kya^C 'fall, become low, expand' ⋈ k^{h}ya^C 'throw down, put down'					
c	呿	qū	k^{h}jwo(^{C})	k^{h}ɨɑ(^{C})	kha, khah	
de	祛袪	qū	k^{h}jwo	k^{h}ɨɑ	kha	
g	胠 enclose	qū	k^{h}jwo	k^{h}ɨɑ	kha	
f	麮	qù	k^{h}jwo$^{B/C}$	k^{h}ɨɑ$^{B/C}$	khaʔ, khah	

1-9	**= K. 803**	**Mand.**	**MC**	**LHan**	**OCM**
a	豦	qú	gjwo(^{C})	gɨɑ(^{C})	ga, gah
c	遽	jù	gjwo^C	gɨɑ^C	gah

j	籧 mat	qú	gjwo	gɨɑ	ga	
	basket	jǔ	kjwo^{B}	kɨɑ^{B}	kaʔ	籧 = 筥 1-54/76j
k	蘧	qú	gjwo	gɨɑ	ga	
fg	據鐻	jù	kjwo^{C}	kɨɑ^{C}	kah	⋇ jū 据 1-1/49o'
	[T] Sin Sukchu SR ky (去); MGZY gȳu (去) [ky]; MTang ky < kø, ONW kø < kio (?)					
e	醵	jù	gjwo(^{C}),	gɨɑ(^{C}),	ga, gah	
			gjak	gɨɑk	gak	
h	臄	jué	gjak	gɨɑk	gak	
i	劇	jù	gjɐk	gɨak	grak	

1-10	**= K. 74**	**Mand.**	**MC**	**LHan**	**OCM**	
a	車	chē,	tś^{h}ja,	tś^{h}a,	k-lha,	[E] Cf. Toch. B kokale
		jū	kjwo	kɨɑ	ka	OCB *k(r)ja
	[T] Sin Sukchu SR tʂ'je (平); MGZY chȳa (平) [tʂ'jɛ]; ONW tś^{h}a					
e	庫	kù	k^{h}uo^{C}	k^{h}ɑ^{C}	khâh	
-	褲 pants	kù	k^{h}uo^{C}	—	—	= 1-23/43h

1-11	**= K. 32**	**Mand.**	**MC**	**LHan**	**OCM**	
a	家	jiā	ka	ka	krâ	OCB *kra
	[T] Sin Sukchu SR kja (平);MGZY gya (平) [kja]; ONW kä <> [E] WT mk^{h}ar 'house'					
e	嫁	jià	ka^{C}	ka^{C}	krâh	[D] PMin *ka^{C} 'marry'
f	稼	jià	ka^{C}	ka^{C}	krâh	
	[T] ONW kä <> [E] KT: PTai *kla^{C1}, Saek tlaa^{3} > traa^{3} 'rice seedlings', KS *kla^{3} id.					

1-12	**= K. 33**	**Mand.**	**MC**	**LHan**	**OCM**	
acd	叚假椵	jiǎ	ka^{B}	ka^{B}	krâʔ	
	[T] 假 Sin Sukchu SR kja (上); MGZY gya (上) [kja]; ONW kä <> [E] WT kar-skyin 'a loan'					
ef	葭豭	jiā	ka	ka	krâ	
i	蝦	xiā	ɣa	ga	grâ	[D] PMin *ɦa 'shrimp'
hjkl-	瑕遐霞騢椵	xiá	ɣa	ga	grâ	
g	暇	xià	ɣa^{C}	ga^{C}	grâh	

1-13	**= K. 34**	**Mand.**	**MC**	**LHan**	**OCM**
a	斝	jiǎ	ka^{B}	ka^{B}	krâʔ

1-14	**= K. 35**	**Mand.**	**MC**	**LHan**	**OCM**	
a	下 down	xià	ɣa^{B}	ga^{B}	grâʔ	[D] PMin *a^{B}
	descend	xià	ɣa^{C}	ga^{C}	grâh	
	[T] Sin Sukchu SR ɣja (上去); MGZY (Hȳa >) Hya (上去) [ɣja]; ONW ɣä^{B} [D] PMin *ɦa^{C}					
d	苄 rush	xià	ɣa^{C}	ga^{C}	grâh	
	Rehmannia	hù	ɣuo^{B}	gɑ^{B}	gâʔ	

1-15	**= K. 36**	**Mand.**	**MC**	**LHan**	**OCM**	
a	夏 great	xià	ɣa^{B}	ga^{B}	grâʔ (or ɦâʔ ?)	
	summer	xià	ɣa^{C}	ga^{C}	grâh	[D] PMin *ɦa^{C}
cd	廈	xià, shà	ɣa^{B}	ga^{B}	grâʔ	
1236c	嗄	shà	ṣa^{C}, ʔăi^{C}	ṣa^{C}, ʔas ?	srâh, ʔâs ?	'breaking voice'

1-16	= K. 38	Mand.	MC	LHan	OCM	
a	襾	xiǎ	xa^B	ha^B	—	
b	賈 merchant	gǔ	kuo^B	kɑ^B	kâʔ	
	[T] 賈價 Sin Sukchu SR kja (去); MGZY gya (去) [kja]. <> [E] WB ə-kya^C 'price'. <> Tai: Saek khaa^5 < gaa^B 'value, price' ⋈ khaa^6 < k^{h}aa^B 'engage in trade' -> P-Miao *ɴqa^C					
	賈 price	jià	ka^C	ka^C	krâh	[D] PMin *ka^C
c	價 price	jià	ka^C	ka^C	krâh	[E] WB ə-kya^C 'price'
d	檟	jiǎ	ka^B	ka^B	krâʔ	

1-17	= K. 55	Mand.	MC	LHan	OCM	
ae	乎虖	hū	ɣuo	ɦɑ	ɦâ	
	[T] Sin Sukchu SR ɣu (平); MGZY Xu (平) [ɣu]; ONW ɣo					
h	呼	hū	xuo(^{C})	hɑ(^{C})	hâ,hâh	
i	嘑	hū	xuo	hɑ	hâ	

1-18	= K. 57, 78, 85	Mand.	MC	LHan	OCM	
57bf	虎琥	hǔ	xuo^B	hɑ^B	hlâʔ	OCB (post 1992) *hlāʔ
	[T] MHan 虎魄 ἅρπαξ (harpax) <> [D] PMin *kho^B <> [E] AA *kalaʔ 'tiger' > MK *klaʔ > OKhm *klaa					
85a	處 dwell	chǔ	tśʰjwo^B	tśʰɑ^B	k-hlaʔ	⋈ 1-1/49c'
	place	chù	tśʰjwo^C	tśʰɑ^C	k-hlah	
	[T] chù Sin Sukchu SR tʂ'y (去); MGZY chÿu (去) [tʂ'y]; ONW tśʰø < tśʰo					
	[E] WT gda'-ba 'to be there', Mikir kedō 'to dwell'; TGTM *glaː$^{A/B}$ 'place'					
78a	虛 mound	qū	kʰjwo	kʰɨɑ	kha	
	empty	xū	xjwo	hɨɑ	ha	
	虛 [T] Sin Sukchu SR xy (平); MGZY hÿu (平) [xy]; MTang hy, ONW hø < hio ?					
78b	墟 ruins	qū	kʰjwo	kʰɨɑ	kha	
	market	xū	xjwo	hɨɑ		
	墟 [D] Y-Guangzh ^{55}hœy^{A1}, Taish ^{21}hui 'seasonal market'					
78c	歔	xū	xjwo	hɨɑ	ha	
78d	嘘	xū	xjwo(^{C})	hɨɑ(^{C})	ha, hah	
78eg	虡g	jù	gjwo^B	gɨɑ^B	gaʔ	

1-19	= K. 95	Mand.	MC	LHan	OCM	
ace	巨^1 >矩榘	jǔ	kju^B	kyɑ^B	kwaʔ	'carpenter's square'
	矩 jǔ [T] Sin Sukchu SR ky (上); MGZY gÿu (上) [ky]; MTang ky < kuo, ONW kuo					
f	柜	jǔ	kju^B	kyɑ^B	kwaʔ	
i	拒 oppose	jù	gjwo^B	gɨɑ^B	gaʔ	
	拒 troops in sq.	jǔ	kju^B	kyɑ^B	kwaʔ	
a	巨^2 great	jù	gjwo^B	gɨɑ^B	gaʔ	
	[E] ST *wa 'large, wide, distant'; TB-Lushai vak^H 'with force, very hard / much, (open mouth) wide'					
jkno	秬 k 粔秬	jù	gjwo^B	gɨɑ^B	gaʔ	
pqr	詎距鉅	jù	gjwo^B	gɨɑ^B	gaʔ	p 詎 also tone C
gh-	渠蚷佢	qú	gjwo	gɨɑ	ga	

1-20	= K. 96	Mand.	MC	LHan	OCM	
96cdeg	瞿^{2}衢躣鸜	qú	gju	gyɑ	gwa	See 2-7.

1-21	**= K. 41**	**Mand.**	**MC**	**LHan**	**OCM**	
a	瓜	guā	kwa	kua	kwrâ	OCB *kʷra

[T] Sin Sukchu SR kwa (平); MGZY gwa (平) [kwa]; ONW kuä <> [D] PMin *kua

bcd	呱孤罛	gū	kuo	kuɑ	kwâ

罛 [E] WB k^{h}wa^{C} 'kind of net' ⋈ TB *kwan ~ *gwan 'casting net', WT rkon 'net'

孤 [E] Tai: Wuming kla^{C2} < *gl- 'orphan'

efg	苽觚軱	gū	kuo	kuɑ	kwâ	
hi	弧狐	hú	ɣuo	ɣuɑ	gwâ	OCB *gʷa

狐 hú [E] OTib ɦo, Tib. dial. *gwa, WT wa, Bunan goa-nu ~ gwa-nu

1-22	**= K. 42**	**Mand.**	**MC**	**LHan**	**OCM**
a	寡	guǎ	kwa^{B}	kua^{B}	kwrâʔ

1-23	**= K. 97, 43**	**Mand.**	**MC**	**LHan**	**OCM**
97a	于	yú	ju	wɑ	wa

[T] Sin Sukchu SR y (平); MTang y < uo; ONW uo; Han BTD Skt. va. MHan 于闐 wɑ-den Hvatäna (Khotan) <> [E] TB *wa, *s-wa: Newari wa 'to come', JP wa^{31} 'to go back'; Chepang wah-ʔo 'moving', wah-sa 'walk'; WB swa 'to go'; Magari, Chepang hwa 'to walk'

qijkn	雩杅玗盂竽	yú	ju	wɑ	wa
h	宇	yǔ	ju^{B}	wɑ^{B}	waʔ
o	芋	yù	ju^{C}	wɑ^{C}	wah

[D] PMin *uo^{C} <> [E] Area word: MY *vəu^{B2} <> WB wa^{C} 'kind of potato'

p	迂	yú,	ju,	wɑ,	wa,	
		yū	ʔju	ʔyɑ	ʔwa	
y-	紆扜[1]	yū	ʔju	ʔyɑ	ʔwa	
za'	圬杇	wū	ʔuo	ʔuɑ	ʔwâ	
tuv-	吁盱訏扜[2]	xū	xju	hyɑ	hwa	
d'	昬	xǔ	xju^{B}	hyɑ^{B}	hwaʔ	
97b'c'	汙污 /43k 洿	wū	ʔuo	ʔuɑ	ʔwâ	'impure'

[T] Sin Sukchu SR ʔu (平); MGZY 'u (平) [ʔu]; ONW ʔo

	impure, dig	wā	ʔwa	ʔua	ʔwrâ	
43abc	夸誇姱	kuā	k^{h}wa	k^{h}ua	khwrâ	WB krwa^{B} 'be vain, boastful'
d	跨 step over	kuà	k^{h}wa^{C}	k^{h}ua^{C}	khwrâh	
	squat over	kuà !	k^{h}uo^{C}	k^{h}uɑ^{C}	khwâh	
e	荂	kuā,	k^{h}wa,	k^{h}ua,	khwrâ,	
		xū	xjwo	hɨɑ	ha	
fg	刳挎	kū	k^{h}uo^{A} !	k^{h}uɑ	khwâ	
hi	袴絝	kù	k^{h}uo^{C}	k^{h}uɑ^{C}	khwâh	= 1-10/74
j	瓠	hú	ɣuo(^{C})	ɣuɑ(^{C})	gwâ, gwâh	
lm	槬摦	huà	ɣwa^{C}	ɣua^{C}	gwrâh or wâh	

1-24	**= K. 98**	**Mand.**	**MC**	**LHan**	**OCM**
a	羽	yǔ	ju^{B}	wɑ^{B}	waʔ

[T] Sin Sukchu SR y (上); MGZY xÿu (上) [ɦy]

cd	栩詡	xǔ	xju^{B}	hyɑ^{B}	hwaʔ

1-25	**= K. 99**	**Mand.**	**MC**	**LHan**	**OCM**	
ad	禹偊	yǔ	ju^B	wɑ^B	waʔ	
	[T] MTang y < uo, ONW uo					
efg	楀萬踽	jǔ	kju^B	kyɑ^B	kwaʔ	

1-26	**= K. 100**	**Mand.**	**MC**	**LHan**	**OCM**	
a	雨 rain n.	yǔ	ju^B	wɑ^B	waʔ	OCB *w(r)jaʔ [D] PMin *ɦuo^B
	[T] Sin Sukchu SR y (上); MGZY xy̆u (上) [ɦy]; MTang y < uo, ONW uo <> [E] TB *r-waʔ					
	雨 to rain	yù	ju^C	wɑ^C	wah	

1-27	**= K. 44**	**Mand.**	**MC**	**LHan**	**OCM**	

There are no OC syllables with initial w- in Div. I in this rime, only in Div. II; I suspect that they represent OC simple *wâ rather than the more complex *wrâ. This shift into Div. II after OC initial *w- seems to have occurred in other rimes as well. 1-23/97 yú is perhaps phonetic.

a	華[1] flower	huá	ɣwa	ɣua	wrâ or wâ	
	[T] ONW ɣuä <> [D] PMin *hua^{A1}					
c	驊	huá	ɣwa	ɣua	wrâ or wâ	
a-	華[2] a mt., 樺	huà	ɣwa^C	ɣua^C	wrâh or wâh	a mountain
	樺	huà	ɣwa^C	ɣua^C	wrâh or wâh	
	樺 [E] WT gro-ga 'bark of birch'					
d	譁	huá !	xwa	hua	hwrâ or hwâ	

1-28	**= K. 61**	**Mand.**	**MC**	**LHan**	**OCM**	
ad	烏嗚	wū	ʔuo	ʔɑ	ʔâ	
	[T] Sin Sukchu SR ʔu (平); MGZY 'i (平) [ʔu]; ONW ʔo; BTD Skt. o; MHan 烏弋山離 ʔɑ-jɨk-ṣan-liɑi Alexandria; 烏桓 ʔɑ-ɣuɑn *Awar					
e	於 oh	wū	ʔuo	ʔɑ	ʔâ	
	於 be in; honor.	yú	ʔjwo	ʔɨɑ	ʔa	[E] TB *ʔa- honorific prefix
	[T] Sin Sukchu SR ʔy (平);MGZY 'y̆u (平) [ʔy]; MTang ʔy < ʔø, ONW ʔio (?) > ʔø					
	於 satiate	yù	ʔjwo^C	ʔɨɑ^C	ʔah	= 16-10/1242a 飫
g	棜	yù	ʔjwo^C	ʔɨɑ^C	ʔah	
h	瘀	yū !	ʔjwo^C	ʔɨɑ^C	ʔah	
i	菸	yū	ʔjwo	ʔɨɑ	ʔa	
270a	閼	è	ʔât	ʔɑt	ʔât	= 21-1/3131 遏

1-29	**= K. 58**	**Mand.**	**MC**	**LHan**	**OCM**	
ae	五伍	wǔ	ŋuo^B	ŋɑ^B	ŋâʔ	OCB *ŋaʔ
	[T] Sin Sukchu SR ŋu (上); MGZY u (上) [u]; ONW ŋo <> [D] PMin *ŋho^{B2}					
	[E] TB *l-ŋa, *b-ŋa > WT lŋa, WB ŋa^B, PL *ŋa^2, Lushai pa^L-ŋa^H < ŋaa					
f	吾 I, my	wú	ŋuo	ŋɑ	ŋâ	
	[T] Sin Sukchu SR ŋu (平); MGZY u (平) [u]; ONW ŋo					
	[E] TB *ŋa > WT ŋa; WB ŋa 'I' ⋈ ŋa^C, PL *C-ŋa					
	吾 reserved	yú	ŋjwo	ŋɨɑ	ŋa	
m	梧	wú	ŋuo	ŋɑ	ŋâ	
jklno	悟捂晤寤牾	wù	ŋuo^C	ŋɑ^C	ŋâh	晤捂牾 = 1-30/60gh 忤迕
s	衙 to go	yú	ŋjwo	ŋɨɑ	ŋa	
	a place	yá	ŋa	ŋa	ŋrâ	
pq	圄敔	yǔ	ŋjwo^B	ŋɨɑ^B	ŋaʔ	

		Mand.	MC	LHan	OCM	
t	語 to speak	yǔ	ŋjwo^{B}	ŋɨɑ^{B}	ŋaʔ	
	語 [T] Sin Sukchu SR ŋy (上); MGZY xy̆u (上) [ɦy]; MTang ŋy < ŋø < ONW ŋio (?)					
	[E] WT ŋag, dŋags 'speech, talk, word' ⋈ sŋa					
	語 to tell	yù	ŋjwo^{C}	ŋɨɑ^{C}	ŋah	
v-	鋙齬	yǔ	ŋjwo(^{B})	ŋɨɑ(^{B})	ŋa, ŋaʔ	

1-30	= K. 60	Mand.	MC	LHan	OCM	
a	午	wǔ	ŋuo^{B}	ŋɑ^{B}	ŋâʔ	
f	仵	wǔ	ŋuo$^{B/C}$	ŋɑ$^{B/C}$	ŋâʔ, ŋâh	
gh	忤迕	wǔ!	ŋuo^{C}	ŋɑ^{C}	ŋâh	= 1-29/50kl 捂晤
i	許 approve	xǔ	xjwo^{B}	hɨɑ^{B}	hŋaʔ	
	許 whack	hǔ	xuo^{B}	hɑ^{B}	hâʔ	= 1-6/91a 所
k	滸	hǔ	xuo^{B}	hɑ^{B}	hŋâʔ	
	[E] WT dŋo 'shore, bank'					
l	御 drive	yù	ŋjwo^{C}	ŋɨɑ^{C}	ŋah	
	御 meet	yà	ŋa^{C}	ŋa^{C}	ŋrâh	⋈ 2-1/766u' 輅, 1-34/37fe 迓訝
	[E] WB ŋra^{B} 'meet'					
p	禦	yù	ŋjwo^{B}	ŋɨɑ^{B}	ŋaʔ	[E] WT mŋa' 'might'

1-31	= K. 79, 67	Mand.	MC	LHan	OCM	
79agdm	魚漁䰻䱷	yú	ŋjwo	ŋɨɑ	ŋa	
	[T] Sin Sukchu SR ŋy (平); MGZY xy̆u (平) [ɦy]; ONW ŋio (?) > ŋø <> [D] PMin *ŋy					
	[E] TB *ŋya: WT ña; Lushai ŋha^{F}, Tiddim ŋaa^{R} < *ŋaaʔ, Chepang ŋaʔ 'fish'					
67a	穌	sū	suo	sɑ	sŋâ	
67c	蘇	sū	suo	sɑ	sŋâ	OCB *sŋa
	[T] MHan 蘇蓮 sɑ-gɛh soɣd or soɣðak					

1-32	= K. 81	Mand.	MC	LHan	OCM	
a	圉	yǔ	ŋjwo^{B}	ŋɨɑ^{B}	ŋaʔ	= 1-29/58p 圄

1-33	= K. 80	Mand.	MC	LHan	OCM
a	馭	yù	ŋjwo^{C}	ŋɨɑ^{C}	ŋah

1-34	= K. 37	Mand.	MC	LHan	OCM
ad	牙芽	yá	ŋa	ŋa	ŋrâ
	[T] Sin Sukchu SR ŋja (平), PR, LR ja; ONW ŋä <> [D] M-Xiam b. ge^{A2}, giɑ^{A2}, w. ga^{A2}				
	[E] MK: Viet ngà, Bahnar ŋəla 'tusk, ivory'. PTai *ŋa^{A2}; PWMiao *ŋha^{A} <> TB: Lushai ŋho^{L} 'tusk'				
gc	雅庌	yǎ	ŋa^{B}	ŋa^{B}	ŋrâʔ
fe	迓訝	yà	ŋa^{C}	ŋa^{C}	ŋrâh
	⋈ 1-30/60 l <> [E] WB ŋra^{B} 'meet'				
h	鴉	yā	ʔa	ʔa	ʔrâ or ʔa

1-35	= K. 59	Mand.	MC	LHan	OCM
a	吳	wú	ŋuo	ŋuɑ	ŋwâ
de	誤悞	wù	ŋuo^{C}	ŋuɑ^{C}	ŋwâh
fjk	俁虞k	yǔ	ŋju^{B}	ŋyɑ^{B}	ŋwaʔ
gh	娛虞	yú	ŋju	ŋyɑ	ŋwa

1 OCM *-a 魚部 (GSR 32-106)

1-36	**= K. 62**	**Mand.**	**MC**	**LHan**	**OCM**	
a	土 earth	tǔ	tʰuo^B	tʰɑ^B	thâʔ	
	roots	dù	duo^B	dɑ^B	dâʔ	
d	吐	tǔ	tʰuo$^{B/C}$	tʰɑ$^{B/C}$	thâʔ, thâh	[E] TB *(m-/s-)twa 'spit'
g-	杜肚	dù	duo^B	dɑ^B	dâʔ	
e	徒	tú	duo	dɑ	dâ	[E] Tai: S. taa^4 'only, sole'
j	社	shè	źja^B	dźɑ^B	daʔ	

1-37	**= K. 64**	**Mand.**	**MC**	**LHan**	**OCM**	
a	圖	tú	duo	dɑ	dâ	⋈ 2-16/801a
	[T] MHan 浮圖 bu-dɑ Buddha					

1-38	**= K. 45**	**Mand.**	**MC**	**LHan**	**OCM**	
ad	者赭	zhě	tśja^B	tśɑ^B	taʔ	[E] TB *t(y)a: WB tya 'very red'
p	諸	zhū	tśjwo	tśɑ	ta	[T] MTang tśy, ONW tśø < tśo
l'	儲	chǔ !	ḍjwo	ḍiɑ	dra	
klmnq	渚 1 煮鬻陼	zhǔ	tśjwo^B	tśɑ^B	taʔ	
	煮 [T] Sin Sukchu SR tʂy (上); MGZY jȳu (上) [tʂy] <> [D] PMin *tšy^B					
o	翥	zhù	tśjwo^C	tśɑ^C	tah	
r	署	shǔ !	źjwo^C	dźɑ^C	da(k)h	
m'	曙	shǔ, shù	źjwo^C	dźɑ^C	dah or djah ?	
	[E] WT ⋈ ya 'above, up' ⋈ yar 'up, upward' > 'čʰar-ba, šar < *s-yar 'ro rise' (of sun, moon)					
h	豬	zhū	tjwo	ṭiɑ	tra	
	[T] Sin Sukchu SR tʂy (平); MGZY jȳu (平) [tʂy] <> [D] W-Kaihua tɑ^{A1} (Chén Zhōng-mǐn ms.1); W-Wenzhou tsei^{A1} (< tsi), G-Linchuan te^{A1}, M-Xiamen ti^{A1}.					
k'	瀦	zhū	tjwo	ṭiɑ	tra	
i	楮	chǔ	tʰjwo^B,	ṭʰiɑ^B,	thraʔ,	
			tuo^B	tɑ^B	tâʔ	
g	褚	zhǔ	tjwo^B	ṭiɑ^B	traʔ	= 1-39/84g 貯
j	箸	zhù	ḍjwo^C	ḍiɑ^C	drah	[D] PMin *dy^C
n'	著 place n.	zhù	tjwo^C	ṭiɑ^C	trakh	
	[E] WT sta-gon 'preparation' ⋈ stad-pa 'to put on, lay on', Tsangla tʰa 'to put, place', Kanauri ta 'place, set, appoint', Kachin da 'put, place', LB *ta^2, WB tha^B < ʔta^2 'put, place', Lushai daʔ^L 'to put, place, set, put aside'					
	著 to place	zhuó	tjak	ṭiɑk	trak	[T] ONW tak
	著 attach	zhuó	ḍjak	ḍiɑk	drak	[T] MTang ḍak, ONW dak
	著 particle	zhe	tjak, ḍjak	—	—	
	[T] Sin Sukchu SR tʂjaw, dʐjaw (入), LR tʂjawʔ; MGZY jew, cew (入) [tʂɛw ~ dʐɛw]. A Mand. progressive suffix					
o'	躇 advance...	chú	ḍjwo	ḍiɑ	dra	
	jump over	chuò	tʰjak	ṭʰiɑk	tʰrak	= 2-21/1258b
p'	斮	zhuó	tjak	ṭiɑk	trak	
e'	都	dū	tuo	tɑ	tâ	
	[T] MHan 都賴 tɑ-lɑs Talas; 都密 tɑ-mɨt (*tâ-mrit) Tarmita, Termes					
h'	闍	dū	tuo,	tɑ,	tâ,	
			dźja	źɑ	—	
	[T] BTD 術闍 źuit-źɑ Skt. vidhya, Pali vijja					
yb'	堵帾	dǔ	tuo^B	tɑ^B	tâʔ	

c'd'	睹覩	dǔ	tuo^{B}	tɑ^{B}	tâʔ	[T] ONW to [E] TB *ta 'to see'
-	賭	dǔ	tuo^{B}	tɑ^{B}		[E] S. tʰaa^{C2} < *d- 'challenge'
i'j'	屠瘏	tú	duo	dɑ	dâ	
	[T] MHan 浮屠 bu-dɑ Buddha					
s	緒	xù	zjwo^{B}	ziɑ^{B}	s-laʔ	= 1-43/83h 序; 1-42/82o 敍
t	書	shū	śjwo	śɑ	lha	
	[T] Sin Sukchu SR ʂy (平); MGZY shȳu (平) [ʂy] <> [D] PMin *tšy ~ šy					
x	暑	shǔ	śjwo^{B}	śɑ^{B}	lhaʔ	
e	奢	shē	śja	śa	lha	

1-39	**= K. 84**	**Mand.**	**MC**	**LHan**	**OCM**	
a	宁	zhù, chú	ḍjwo(^{B})	ḍiɑ(^{B})	dra, draʔ	
cdf	佇竚羜	zhù	ḍjwo^{B}	ḍiɑ^{B}	draʔ	
-e	苧紵	zhù	ḍjwo^{B}	ḍiɑ^{B}	draʔ	
	紵 [D] PMin *dø^{B} 'flax' <> [E] WT ras 'cotton'					
g	貯	zhù !	ṭjwo^{B}	ṭiɑ^{B}	traʔ	= 1-38/45g 褚

1-40	**= K. 1242b**	**Mand.**	**MC**	**LHan**	**OCM**
b	樗	chū	ṭʰjwo	ṭʰiɑ	thra or rha ?

1-41	**= K. 86**	**Mand.**	**MC**	**LHan**	**OCM**	
a	杵	chǔ	tśʰjwo^{B}	tśʰɑ^{B}	thaʔ	午 1-30/60a is not phonetic

1-42	**= K. 82**	**Mand.**	**MC**	**LHan**	**OCM**	
a	余	yú	jiwo	jɑ	la	
li	餘艅	yú	jiwo	jɑ	la	
	餘 [T] MTang iy < iø < ONW io. <> [E] Tai: S. lia^{A1} < *hl- 'left over'					
f	畬 field	yú	jiwo	jɑ	la	PEMiao *la^{6} 'field'
	畬	shē	śja	śa	hja ?	LB *hja^{1} 'swidden', WB ya
g	悆	yù	jiwo^{C}	jɑ^{C}	lah	= 譽 1-45/89i, 豫 1-43/83e
m	除 eliminate	chú	ḍjwo	ḍiɑ	dra < r-la	
	[T] Sin S. SR dʐy (平); MGZY cȳu (平) [dʐy]; MTang ḍy; ONW dø < dio (?) [D] M-Xiam lit. du^{A2}					
	除 pass away	zhù	ḍjwo^{C}	ḍiɑ^{C}	drah < r-lah	
c'	篨	chú	ḍjwo	ḍiɑ	dra < r-la	
x	茶 tea	chá	ḍa	ḍa	dra < r-lâ	
	[T] Sin Sukchu SR dʐa (平); ONW dä. BTD Skt. ḍa, jhā <> [D] PMin *da^{A} [E] Loloish (TB) *la 'leaf, tea'					
	荼 a bitter plant	tú	duo	dɑ	lâ	
	荼 slowly	shū	śjwo	śɑ	lha	
	荼 a plant EY	shé	dźja	źa	m-la	also 'to scoop, ladle'
	[T] Han BTD Pkt. jha (Coblin 1993: 882)					
uvd'y-	涂途塗梌駼	tú	duo	dɑ	lâ	
	[T] ONW do <> [D] PMin *dho 'soil, earth'. <> [E] S. tʰaa^{A2} < *d- 'smear, paint'					
st	s 賒	shē	śja	śa	lha	ONW śa
-	斜	xié	ja	ja		
pq	徐郐	xú	zjwo	ziɑ	s-la	
o	敍	xù	zjwo^{B}	ziɑ^{B}	s-laʔ	= 序 1-43/83h, 緒 1-38/45s

a’	⿰王余	tú !	t^{h}uo	t^{h}ɑ	lhâ	
b’	稌	tú !,	t^{h}uo(^{B}),	t^{h}ɑ(^{B}),	lhâ, lhâʔ,	
		dù	duo^{B}	dɑ^{B}	lâʔ	

1-43	**= K. 83**	**Mand.**	**MC**	**LHan**	**OCM**	
a	予 ‘I’	yú	jiwo	jɑ^{B}	laʔ !	
	予 give	yǔ	jiwo^{B}	jɑ^{B}	laʔ	
	[T] MTang iy < iø, ONW io					
c	⿺辶予	?				
e	豫 slow, joy	yù	jiwo^{C}	jɑ^{C}	lah	= 悆 1-42/82g, 譽 1-45/89i
	[N] Does not mean ‘elephant’, the right element has a different graphic origin					
f	杼 shuttle	zhù	ḍjwo^{B}	ḍiɑ^{B}	draʔ < r-laʔ	
	oak	shù	dźjwo^{B}	źɑ^{B}	m-laʔ	
	trough	shù	dźjwo^{C}	źɑ^{C}	m-lah	
g	抒	shū !	dźjwo^{B},	źɑ^{B}	m-laʔ	WT ’dag-pa ‘remove’
k	舒	shū	śjwo	śɑ	lha	WT sla-ba ‘easy’
j	紓	shū,	śjwo,	śɑ,	lha,	
		shù	dźjwo	źɑ	mla	
h	序	xù	zjwo^{B}	ziɑ^{B}	s-laʔ	= 敘 1-42/82o, 緒 1-38/45s
i	芧	xù	zjwo^{B}	ziɑ^{B}	s-laʔ	
lm	野墅 country	yě	jia^{B}	jɑ^{B}	laʔ	ONW ia = 埜 1-44/83n
	field hut, villa	shù	źjwo^{B}	dźɑ^{B}	daʔ	

1-44	**= K. 83n**	**Mand.**	**MC**	**LHan**	**OCM**	
n	埜	yě	jia^{B}	jɑ^{B}	laʔ	= 野 1-43/83 l

1-45	**= K. 89, 75**	**Mand.**	**MC**	**LHan**	**OCM**	
a	舁	yú	jiwo^{A} !	jɑ	la	tone A acc. to GY
b	與 give	yǔ	jiwo^{B}	jɑ^{B}	laʔ	= 予 1-43/83a
	[T] Sin Sukchu SR y (上); MGZY yӯu (上) [jy]; MTang iy < iø, ONW io					
	與 participate	yù	jiwo^{C}	jɑ^{C}	lah (or *jah ?)	
	與 a particle	yú	jiwo	jɑ	la	= e 歟
e	歟 a particle	yú	jiwo	jɑ	la	OCB (post-1992) *lǎ
fl	璵旟	yú	jiwo	jɑ	la	
i	譽 praise	yú	jiwo	jɑ	la	WT bla ~ rla ‘above, upper’
	譽 joy	yù	jiwo^{C}	jɑ^{C}	lah	= 悆 1-42/82g, 豫 1-43/83e
j	輿	yú	jiwo	jɑ	la	Tai: S. lɔɔ^{B} ‘car, carriage’
g	⿰月與	yǔ	jiwo^{B}	jɑ^{B}	laʔ	
k	鸒	yù	jiwo^{C}	jɑ^{C}	lah	
n	藇	xù	zjwo^{B},	ziɑ^{B},	s-laʔ,	
		yǔ	jiwo^{B}	jɑ^{B}	laʔ	
o	鱮	xù	zjwo^{B}	ziɑ^{B}	s-laʔ	
75a	舉	jǔ	kjwo^{B}	kɨɑ^{B}	klaʔ	[T] MTang ky < ONW kø < kio (?)

1-45A		**Mand.**	**MC**	**LHan**	**OCM**	
-	与	yǔ	jiwo^{B}	jɑ^{B}	laʔ	

1-46	**= K. 63**	**Mand.**	**MC**	**LHan**	**OCM**	
a	兔	tù	tʰuo^{C}	tʰɑ^{C}	lhâh	Jiarong kɑ-lɑ 'rabbit'
-	䖘 tiger	tù	tʰuo^{C}	tʰɑ^{C}	lhâh	MK *klaʔ 'tiger'
c	菟	tú	duo	dɑ	lâ	

1-47	**= K. 47**	**Mand.**	**MC**	**LHan**	**OCM**
ab	邪耶 a place	yé	jia	ja	la or ja ?
	[T] ONW ia. MHan 莫邪 mɑh-ja Skt māyā				
	slow	xú	zjwo	ziɑ	s-la
abc	邪耶衺 obliq.	xié	zja	zia	s-la or s-ja ? 'oblique'

1-48	**= K. 48**	**Mand.**	**MC**	**LHan**	**OCM**
a	舍 give	shě	śja^{B}	śa^{B}	lhaʔ
	[T] Sin S. SR ʂje (上); MGZY shya̅ (上) [ʂjɛ]; ONW śa <> [E] MMon salah 'to give away, disburse'				
	舍 stop	shè	śja^{C}	śa^{C}	lhah
	[T] BTD 墮舍利 hyɑi-śah-lih Skt. Vaiśālī <> [E] KN-Lushai thlaʔ^{L} (< *slas) 'to let go'				
c	捨	shě	śja^{B}	śa^{B}	lhaʔ

1-49	**= K. 92**	**Mand.**	**MC**	**LHan**	**OCM**	
a	鼠	shǔ	śjwo^{B}	śɑ^{B}~ tśʰɑ^{B}	nhaʔ ?	OCB *hjaʔ (?)
	[T] Sin Sukchu SR ʂy (上); MGZY shy̅u (上) [ʂy]; ONW śo > śø					
	[D] Southern and NW dialects: PMin *tšhy^{B}: Xiam tsʰu^{B}, Fuzh tsʰy^{B}; Ke *tšʰu^{B1}: Meix tsʰu^{B}; Wu Wenzh tɕʰi^{45} (Běidà tsʰei^{B}). NW-Xining tʂʰy^{53}, Dunhuang -tʂʰu^{42}, Lanzh pfʰu^{33}					
b	癙	shǔ	śjwo^{B}	śɑ^{B}	nhaʔ ?	[E] TB *na > WT na-ba 'ill, ache'

1-50	**= K. 93**	**Mand.**	**MC**	**LHan**	**OCM**	
a	黍	shǔ	śjwo^{B}	śɑ^{B}	nhaʔ ?	OCB *hjaʔ [T] ONW śo > śø

1-51	**= K. 69**	**Mand.**	**MC**	**LHan**	**OCM**	
ad	⿸虍田盧	lú	luo	lɑ	râ	
	[T] BTD 比盧持 pi^{C}-lɑ-ḍiə Skt. vairaṭi-					
jkl	壚櫨爐	lú	luo	lɑ	râ	
mno	鑪籚纑	lú	luo	lɑ	râ	
p	顱	lú	luo	lɑ	râ	S. pʰaak < *pʰr/l- 'forehead'
-	艫 'boat'	lú	luo	lɑ	—	TB-WB hlo- 'boat'; KS *lwa^{A}
e	虜	lǔ	luo^{B}	lɑ^{B}	râʔ	
qr	廬臚	lú !	ljwo	liɑ	ra	WT gra-ma 'the awn, bristles'
-	驢	lǘ	ljwo	liɑ	ra	WB la^{B} 'mule'
	驢 [T] Sin Sukchu SR ly (平); MGZY ly̅u (平) [ly], ONW lio					
u	蘆	lǘ	ljwo	liɑ	ra	[D] PMin *lho^{C}
f	慮	lǜ	ljwo^{C}	liɑ^{C}	rah	
	[T] Sin Sukchu SR ly (去); MGZY ly̅u (去) [ly]; ONW lio; BTD Skt. lo					
	[E] ST *rwa- ?: WT bgro-, bgros 'to consider', Lushai ruat^{F} 'to think, believe, consider'					
vy	鑢⿰金膚	lǜ	ljwo^{C}	liɑ^{C}	rah	
-	勴濾	lǜ	ljwo^{C}	liɑ^{C}	rah	
t	儢	lǚ	ljwo^{B}	liɑ^{B}	raʔ	
x	攎	chū	ṭʰjwo	ṭʰiɑ	rha	

g 膚 fū pju puɑ pra OCB *prja
[E] Cf. TB *s-pak > WT -lpags 'skin'.<> Tai-S. plɨak^{D1L} < *pl- 'husk, bark'

1-52	= K. 70	Mand.	MC	LHan	OCM	
ae	魯櫓	lǔ	luo^B	lɑ^B	râʔ	OCB *C-rjaʔ

1-53	= K. 71	Mand.	MC	LHan	OCM	
a	鹵	lǔ	luo^B	lɑ^B	râʔ	TB *s-la 'salt'

1-54	= K. 76	Mand.	MC	LHan	OCM	
ade	呂侶梠	lǚ	ljwo^B	liɑ^B	raʔ	= 旅 1-55/77a
	[T] Sin Sukchu SR ly (上); MGZY lÿu (上) [ly]; ONW lio					
-	鋁	lǚ	ljwo^B	liɑ^B ?	raʔ (?)	WT ra-gan 'brass' < rag
g	閭	lǘ	ljwo	liɑ	ra	
h	郘	lǚ	ljwo^B	liɑ^B ?	raʔ	
j l	筥莒	jǔ	kjwo^B	kɨɑ^B	kaʔ = 籧 1-9/803j [E] LB *kak 'large basket'	

1-55	= K. 77	Mand.	MC	LHan	OCM	
ae	旅膂	lǚ	ljwo^B	liɑ^B	raʔ	= 呂 1-54/76a
f	旅	lú	luo	lɑ	râ	= 盧壚 1-51/69dj OCB *g-rjaʔ

1-56	= K. 94	Mand.	MC	LHan	OCM	
a	女 woman	nǚ	ṇjwo^B	ṇiɑ^B	nraʔ	OCB *nrjaʔ
	[T] Sin Sukchu SR ny (上); MGZY ñÿu (上) [ṇy]; ONW nø < nio <> [D] PMin *ny^B					
	[E] WT mna'(-ma) 'd.-in-law'; West Tib. ñag(-mo) 'woman'; JP na̱^{33} 'older sister, sister-i.l.'					
	女 give a wom.	nǜ	ṇjwo^C	ṇiɑ^C	nrah	
f	籹	nǚ	ṇjwo^B	ṇiɑ^B	nraʔ	WT mna' 'cake'
j	汝	rǔ	ńźjwo^B	ńɑ^B	naʔ	
	[D] PMin *ny^B, Amoy li^{B1} <> [E] TB: *na ~ *naŋ 'you'					
g	如	rú	ńźjwo,	ńɑ,	na,	Mru na 'be so'
			ńźjwo^C	ńɑ^C	nah	see 21-27/318
	[T] Sin Sukchu SR ry (平); MGZY Zhÿu (平) [ry]; ONW ńo > ńø					
r	茹 madder	rú	ńźjwo	ńɑ	na	
	茹 interlaced	rú	ńźjwo(^{C})	ńɑ(^{C})	na, nah	
	茹 rotten	rǔ	ńźjwo^B	ńɑ^B	naʔ	
	茹 to swallow	rú !	ńźjwo$^{B/C}$	ńɑ$^{B/C}$	naʔ, nah	MY: *naʔ^7 'to swallow'
	Also: PVM *s-ɲaːʔ 'to chew, masticate'; Kharia ɲoʔ 'to eat'					
	茹 deliberate	rù	ńźjwo^C	ńɑ^C	nah	WT mno-ba 'to think'
q	洳	rù	ńźjwo(^{C})	ńɑ(^{C})	na, nah	WT na 'meadow'
s	駑	rú	ńźjwo	ńɑ	na	
o	帤	nú, rú	ṇjwo	ṇiɑ	nra	
p	袽	rú !	ṇjwo	ṇiɑ	nra	
t	恕	shù	śjwo^C	śɑ^C	nhah	
u	絮 silk	xù	sjwo^C	siɑ^C	snah	
	to season	chù	ṭʰjwo^C	ṭʰiɑ^C	nhrah ?	
l	奴	nú	nuo	nɑ	nâ	
	[T] Sin S. SR nu (平); MGZY nu (平) [nu]; ONW no. 匈奴 LH huoŋ-nɑ Xiōng-nú, Huns					
vy	拏砮	nú	nuo	nɑ	nâ	

b'c'	拏 c'	ná	ṇa	ṇa	nrâ	[T] BTD Skt. ṇā
d'	砮	nú, nǔ	nuo(^{B})	nɑ(^{B})	nâ, nâʔ	
e'	笯	nú,	nuo(^{C}),	nɑ(^{C}),	nâ, nâh	
		ná	ṇa	ṇa	nrâ	
f'	駑	nú	nuo	nɑ	nâ	
-	努	nǔ	nuo^{B}	nɑ^{B}	nâʔ	
a'	怒	nù	nuo$^{B/C}$	nɑ$^{B/C}$	nâʔ, nâh	
	[E] ST *nwar: Lushai nɔr^{F} < nɔɔrʔ 'press, push' ⋇ Lushai nuar^{H} / nɔrʔ^{L} < nuar < nɔrʔ/h 'be displeased, disgruntled', Khami *nuar 'get angry'					
z	弩	nǔ	nuo^{B}	nɑ^{B}	nâʔ	
	[T] Sin Sukchu SR nu (上); MGZY nu (上) [nu]; ONW no					
	[E] PTai *hnaa^{C}, PVM *s-naːʔ; Khmer snaa, PSBahn. *sənaː 'crossbow'					
-	瘏	nà	ṇa^{C} !, i.e., prob. na^{C} [JY]			TB *na 'ill'

1-57	**= K. 46**	**Mand.**	**MC**	**LHan**	**OCM**	
ab'	且[1] > 祖 ancest	zǔ	tsuo^{B}	tsɑ^{B}	tsâʔ	ONW tso 'ancestor'
h'	粗	cū,	tsʰuo,	tsʰɑ,	tshâ,	[D] PMin *tsho
		zù	dzuo^{B}	dzɑ^{B}	dzâʔ	
i'j'	徂殂	cú	dzuo	dzɑ	dzâ	
m'	駔	zù,	dzuo^{B},	dzɑ^{B},	dzâʔ,	
		zǎng	tsâŋ^{B}	tsɑŋ^{B}	tsâŋʔ	
d'	租	zū	tsuo	tsɑ	tsâ	
q'	蒩	zū,	tsuo,	tsɑ,	tsâ,	
		qū, jū	ts(ʰ)jwo	ts(ʰ)iɑ	tsa, tsha	
e'	組	zǔ	tsuo^{B}	tsɑ^{B}	tsâʔ	
k'	虘	cuó	dzuo	dzɑ	dzâ	
v's'u'	叡樝楂	zhā	tṣa	tṣa	tsrâ	
r'	齟	chǔ	tṣʰjwo^{B}	tṣʰɑ^{B}	tshraʔ	
i	柤	zhā	tṣa	tṣa	tsrâ	
j	担	zhā, jiě,	tṣa, tsja^{B}	tṣa, tsia^{B},	tsrâ, tsaʔ,	
		jiè	dzja^{B}	dzia^{B}	dzaʔ	
46a	且[2] moreover	qiě	tsʰja^{B}	tsʰia^{B}	tshaʔ	
	[T] Sin S. SR ts'je (上); MGZY tshȳa (上) [ts'jɛ]; ONW tsʰia. MHan 且末-mɑt = Calmadana					
	且 obstruct	qū	tsʰjwo	tsʰiɑ	tsha	
	且 many	jū	tsjwo	tsiɑ	tsa	
h	罝	jiē	tsja	tsia	tsa	
k	沮 leak	jù	dzjwo^{B}	dziɑ^{B}	dzaʔ	WT 'dzag-pa 'to drop, drip'
	沮 marshy	jù	tsjwo^{C}	tsiɑ^{C}	tsah	
n'	菹	jū !	tṣjwo	tṣɑ	tsra	
u	咀	jǔ !	dzjwo^{B}	dziɑ^{B}	dzaʔ	TB *dzaʔ 'eat'
m	蛆	jū	tsjwo	tsiɑ	tsa	
opqrs	狙疽砠雎鴡	jū !	tsʰjwo	tsʰiɑ	tsha	
t	苴 hemp, straw	jū !	tsʰjwo	tsʰiɑ	tsha	
	straw shoe	qū, jū	ts(ʰ)jwo	ts(ʰ)iɑ	tsa,tsha	
	dung straw	zhǎ	tṣa^{B}	tṣa^{B}	tṣâʔ	
n	岨	jū !	tsʰjwo	tsʰiɑ	tsha	

vy	組阻	zǔ	tsjwo^{B}	tṣɑ^{B}	tsraʔ	
x	詛	zǔ !	tsjwo^{C}	tṣɑ^{C}	tsrah	
a'	鉏	jǔ !	dzjwo^{B}	dẓɑ^{B}	dzraʔ	
z	助	zhù	dzjwo^{C}	dẓɑ^{C}	dzrah	

[T] Sin Sukchu SR dẓu (上); MGZY cu (上) [dẓu]

o'	耡	zhù, chú	dzjwo(^{C})	dẓɑ(^{C})	dzra, dzrah	
p'	鋤	chú	dzjwo	dẓɑ	dzra	

[D] W-Kaihua zɑ^{A2}; PMin *dhy, dy, ḏy <> [E] OKhmer /crās/ 'to scrape', OKhmer ⋙ OKhmer caṃrās 'to rake, hoe' ⋙ Khmer rā'sa /roəh/ 'to scrape, rake, hoe, harrow'

1-58	**= K. 65**	**Mand.**	**MC**	**LHan**	**OCM**	
a	麤	cū	tsʰuo	tsʰɑ	tshâ	

1-59	**= K. 66**	**Mand.**	**MC**	**LHan**	**OCM**	
a	鱻	cū	tsʰuo	tsʰɑ	tshâ	

1-60	**= K. 87**	**Mand.**	**MC**	**LHan**	**OCM**	
a	初	chū	tṣʰjwo	tṣʰɑ	tshra	

[T] Sin Sukchu SR tṣ'u (平); MGZY chu (平) [tṣ'u]; MTang tṣʰy, ONW tṣʰø < tṣʰo

[D] PMin *tšhø, Xiamen lit. tsʰɔ^{A1}, col. tsʰue^{A1}

1-61	**= K. 68**	**Mand.**	**MC**	**LHan**	**OCM**	
a	素	sù	suo^{C}	sɑ^{C}	sâh	Khmer /saa/ 'white, colorless'

1-62	**= K. 90, 88**	**Mand.**	**MC**	**LHan**	**OCM**	
90a	疋	shū	ṣjwo	ṣɑ	sra	
bd	疏蔬	shū	ṣjwo	ṣɑ	sra	

[T] MHan 疏問 ṣɑ-mun^{C} (*sra-məns) Skt. śramaṇa <> [D] PMin *šø

-	梳	shū	ṣjwo	ṣɑ		[D] PMin *šø

[E] ST *Crja(t): TB *hryat 'to comb': KN-Lai hriat / hriaʔ, WT(g)šad-pa < *(g-)rhjat

88a	楚	chǔ	tṣhjwo^{B}	tṣʰɑ^{B}	tshraʔ	

[T] Sin Sukchu SR tṣ'u (上); MGZY chu (上) [tṣ'u]; ONW tṣʰo > tṣʰø.

[E] Khmu /cərlaʔ/ 'thorn'

90e	胥	xū	sjwo	siɑ	sa	
f	湑	xǔ	sjwo^{B}	sɑ^{B}	sraʔ	

[N] Probably with OCM *r because *shū* 釃 ṣjwo^{A} 7-21/878h) is the same word

[E] Khmer /srak/ 'to drop, drip'

g-	稰諝	xǔ	sjwo^{B}	siɑ^{B}	saʔ	
h	糈	xǔ	sjwo^{B},	siɑ^{B},	saʔ,	
		shǔ	ṣjwo^{B}	ṣɑ^{B}	sraʔ	
i-	壻婿	xù	(—)	siɑ^{C}	sah	son-in-law
			~ siei^{C}	se(i)^{C}		

[T] Coll. Shazhou siei (si?) <> [D] PSMin *sai^{C}: Xiam col. sai^{C}, lit. se^{C}, Chaozh sai^{C}, Fuzhou sa^{C}; W-Wenzh sei^{C}, K-Meix sɛ^{C}, Guangzh ʃai^{C2}

1-63	**= K. 91**	**Mand.**	**MC**	**LHan**	**OCM**	
a	所 'place'	suǒ	ṣjwo^{B}	ṣɑ^{B}	sraʔ	OCB *s(k)rjaʔ

[T] Sin Sukchu SR ṣu (上), LR ṣwɔ; MGZY (zhu >) shu (上) [ṣu]; ONW ṣø < ṣo

[E] TB *sra 'place': JP ʃă^{31}-ra^{31} 'place', WB ra 'place, situation, thing, subject'.

[N] It seems that the graph for 'whack' 1-6 所 may have been borrowed for an obsolete **ga 'place', cf. JP *ga*^{55} 'earth, place', and then used for the synonym suǒ. This **ga is perhaps represented by hù 戶 1-6a 'to stop', and perh. also by the meaning 'household' (i.e., 'dwelling'?) which folk etymology may have associated with the homophonous 'door' as a *pars pro toto* (words for 'stop, dwell, place' tend to be related).

-	齭	chǔ	tṣʰjwo^{B}	tṣʰɑ^{B}	—	SW

1-64	**= K. 72**	**Mand.**	**MC**	**LHan**	**OCM**	
a	普	pǔ	pʰuo^{B}	pʰɑ^{B}	phâʔ	

1-65	**= K. 73**	**Mand.**	**MC**	**LHan**	**OCM**	
a	步	bù	buo^{C}	bɑ^{C}	bâh	

[T] Sin Sukchu SR bu (去); MGZY pu (去) [bu]; MTang bu < bo, ONW bo
[D] PMin *b̯-: Jiànyáng vo^{6}; Yao bia^{6} (< *nb-) <> [E] TB-Mru pak 'go, walk

1-66	**= K. 101**	**Mand.**	**MC**	**LHan**	**OCM**	
a	夫 man	fū	pju	puɑ	pa	TB *pa > JP wa^{33} 'man'
	夫 that	fú	bju	buɑ	ba	PL *m-ba^{1}, WT pʰa 'there'

[T] Sin Sukchu SR fu (平); MGZY Hwu (平) [fu]; MTang pfu < pfuo, ONW puo

f	扶 assist	fú	bju	buɑ	ba	also a pre-syllable [D] PMin *bhuo
	扶 a measure	fú	pju	puɑ	pa	

[T] MTang bvu < bvuo, ONW buo <> [D] PMin *bhio <> [E] TB *pa 'palm of hand'

	扶 crawl	fú, pū	bju, pʰuo	buɑ, pʰɑ	ba, phâ	
e	鈇	fū	pju	puɑ	pa	~ 1-67/102h
gh	枎芙	fú	bju	buɑ	ba	

1-67	**= K. 102, 771**	**Mand.**	**MC**	**LHan**	**OCM**	
102ah	父 > 斧 axe	fǔ	pju^{B}	puɑ^{B}	paʔ	OCB *p(r)jaʔ

[T] Sin Sukchu SR fu (上); MGZY Hwu (上) [fu]; MTang pfu < pfuo, ONW puo
[D] PMin *puo^{B} <> [E] TB *r-pa 'axe'

a	父 father	fù	bju^{B}	buɑ^{B}	baʔ	TB *pa, Lu. pa^{F} < *paaʔ

[T] Sin Sukchu SR fu (上); MGZY hwu (上) [vu]; MTang bvu < bvuo, ONW buo

	父 honorific	fǔ	pju^{B}	puɑ^{B}	paʔ	
f	釜	fǔ	bju^{B}	buɑ^{B}	baʔ	
n	甫 honorific	fǔ	pju^{B}	puɑ^{B}	paʔ	WT -pa masculine suffix
rst	脯莆黼	fǔ	pju^{B}	puɑ^{B}	paʔ	
u	簠	fǔ	pju(^{B}/^{C})	puɑ(^{B}/^{C})	pa, paʔ, pah	
v	輔	fǔ	bju^{B}	buɑ^{B}	baʔ	[E] OKhmer /βnak/ 'support'
y	y	fǔ	bju^{B}	buɑ^{B}	baʔ	
i'j'	哺捕	bǔ !	buo^{C}	bɑ^{C}	bâh	

哺 [D] PMin *bo^{C}, but Jian'ou piɔ^{44} (prob. from *bo^{C} via bɔo^{C})

z	圃	pǔ !	puo$^{B/C}$	pɑ$^{B/C}$	pâʔ, pâh	OCB *pas
e'	餔	bù	puo(^{C})	pɑ(^{C})	pâ, pâh	TB *wa (or *pa) 'bite, chew'
c'	補	bǔ	puo^{B}	pɑ^{B}	pâʔ	

[T] MTang pu < po, ONW po <> Also WB pʰa 'mend, patch' <> [D] PMin *puo^{B}
[E] MK: PVM *k-paːʔ 'to repair, sew', Khmer /pah/ (i.e., prob. = paʔ) 'to patch'

f'	浦	pǔ	pʰuo^{B}	pʰɑ^{B}	phâʔ	Viet phá < pʰaʔ 'inlet, cove'
n'o'	蒲蒱	pú	buo	bɑ	bâ	

[T] 蒲類 bɑ-lus Bars (*barus) 'tiger' [Hanshu]

d' 逋 bū puo pɑ pâ

[E] TB: WT sbas 'hide, conceal', 'ba-bo 'hole, cave, cavern', Kitanti bha 'anus', Mikir iŋbò < *m-ba^{A} 'lose, get lost'

k' 酺 drinking pú buo bɑ bâ

deity bù buo^{C} bɑ^{C} bâh

g'h' 痡鋪 pū, fū p^{h}uo, p^{h}ju p^{h}ɑ, p^{h}uɑ phâ, pha

l' 匍匐 pú-fú buo, bju bɑ, buɑ bâ, ba

[D] Mand. col. pá 爬 'to climb'

\- 葡萄 pú-táo buo-dâu bɑ-dɑu 'grape'

<- Iranian *budāwa or *bādāwa

j 布 bù puo^{C} pɑ^{C} pâh

[T] Sin Sukchu SR pu (去); MGZY bu (去) [pu]; ONW po <> [D] Min *pio^{C}. W-Qingtian paʔ (Pān 1991:238) <> [E] Lushai p^{h}aʔ^{L} (< *phah) 'to spread' (as cloth)

m 怖 pù p^{h}uo^{C} p^{h}ɑ^{C} phâh

[T] ONW p^{h}o^{C} <> [D] Mand. col. pà 怕 'to fear' <> [E] TB-Lushai p^{h}ɔɔk^{F} 'be afraid'

p'q't' 尃 q' 敷 fū p^{h}ju p^{h}uɑ pha [T] ONW p^{h}uo

u' 傅 assist fù pju^{C} puɑ^{C} pah

attach bju^{C} buɑ^{C} bah

v' 榑 fú bju buɑ ba

x' 賻 fù bju^{C} buɑ^{C} bah

y' y' pū p^{h}uo p^{h}ɑ phâ

771a 博 bó pâk pɑk pâk [T] ONW pɑk

d 搏 beat, seize bó pâk pɑk pâk

drum bó, fù pâk, pju^{C} pɑk, puɑ^{C} pâk, pakh

n 簙 bó pâk pɑk pâk

gj 鎛 j bó pâk pɑk pâk

\- 膊髆 bó pâk pɑk pâk [E] PMon *pnah 'shoulder'

l 膊 pò p^{h}âk p^{h}ɑk phâk

Also TB-LB *pak ~ *ʔpak > Lahu phâʔ 'unfasten, dismantle' ⋇ pâʔ 'collapse, come undone'; Akha pa^{HS} 'break, split.

f 溥 a river bó pâk pɑk pâk

great pǔ p^{h}uo^{B} p^{h}ɑ^{B} phâʔ

o 簿 bó buo^{B} bɑ^{B} bâʔ

p 薄 trellis, thin bó bâk bɑk bâk [E] TB *ba 'thin'

[T] Sin Sukchu SR baw (入), LR bawʔ; MGZY paw (入) [baw]; ONW bɑk <> [D] PMin *ḅok

薄 a sound pò p^{h}âk p^{h}ɑk phâk

qr 礴鑮 bó bâk bɑk bâk

鑮 Also PMonic *c(l)-m-ɔk 'a hoe, spade', in Yue dial. like Taishan pɔŋ$^{35/A1}$

m 縛 fù bjwak buɑk bak

[T] MTang bvuak, ONW buak < bak <> [D] PMin *buk > Amoy bak^{D2}, Fuzh puoʔ^{D2}, Jiany po^{D2} 'to tie'. <> [E] MK-Khmer p̈ā'ka /pak/ 'to enlace, embroider' ⋇ /bamnak/ 'to be enlacing, stitching together'; Mon /pa̤k/, Semai /bək/, Temiar /bəg/ 'to bind'

1-68 = K. 39 Mand. MC LHan OCM

a 巴 bā pa pa prâ

[T] Sin Sukchu SR pa (平); MGZY: suppl. ba (平) [pa]); ONW pä

\- 笆 bamboo bā ba^{B}, pa ba^{B}, pa — WT spa ~ sba 'cane'

笆 fence bā pa — — TB: *rpa 'fence'

\- 疤 bā pa pa — WT ’bar ‘uneven, rough’

c 芭 bā pa pa prâ

d 豝 bā pa pa prâ MK-Wa-L.-B. *bras ‘wild boar’

b 把 bǎ pa^B pa^B prâʔ

[T] Sin S. SR pa (上); MGZY: suppl. ba (上) [pa]) <> [E] WT spar-ba ‘the grasping hand’

\- 葩 pā p^{h}a p^{h}a —

[E] WT ’bar-ba ‘to blossom’; Lepcha bor ‘to bloom’ a-bor ‘blossom’; Lushai paar^H ‘flower, blossom’ ⋟ parʔ^L ‘to open’ (as flower) ⋟ p^{h}arʔ^L ‘to open’ (as hand, flower), KN-Khami par ‘flower’; WB pan^B ‘flower’; JP ^{1}nam-^{2}pan

-e 耙杷 pá, bà ba(^{C}) ba(^{C}) brâ(h) [T] ONW bä

[E] ? JP braʔ^{56} ‘forked’ (road); Kanauri pra ‘spread, stretch’, WB pra^B ‘divided into several parts’, JP braʔ^{55} < brak^{55} ‘be forked’

1-69 = K. 103 Mand. MC LHan OCM

agh 無 > 舞h wǔ mju^B muɑ^B maʔ ‘dance’ OCB *m(r)jaʔ

無 not have wú mju muɑ ma [E] ST *ma: TB *ma ‘not’

[T] Sin Sukchu SR, LR vu (平); MGZY wu (平) [vu]; MTang mvu < muo, ONW muo

i 廡 wǔ mju^B muɑ^B maʔ

[E] S maa^{C1} (WrSiam hmaa) ‘beautiful’

j 憮 stupefied wǔ mju^B, huo muɑ^B, hɑ maʔ, hmâ

憮 love wǔ mju^B muɑ^B maʔ ⋟ 2-40/802h 慕

[T] ONW muo^B <> [E] WB maŋ^A ‘to like, love’; KS *maŋ^4 ‘to like’

k 甒 wǔ mju^B muɑ^B maʔ

[E] S. mɔɔ^{C1} < *hm- ‘cooking pot’

lm 蕪譕 wú mju muɑ ma

n 幠 hū xuo hɑ hmâ

o 膴 hū, xǔ xuo, xju^B, mju hɑ, hɨɑ^B, muɑ hmâ, hmaʔ, ‘big slice of dried meat’

膴 big wǔ mju^B muɑ^B maʔ

q 鄦 a state xǔ xjwo^B hɨɑ^B hmaʔ ~ 許 *hŋaʔ 1-30/60i

p 撫 fǔ p^{h}ju^B p^{h}uɑ^B phaʔ

1-70 = K. 106 Mand. MC LHan OCM

a 无 wú mju muɑ ma = 無 1-70/103a

1-71 = K. 104 Mand. MC LHan OCM

a 武 wǔ mju^B muɑ^B maʔ OCB *Np(r)jaʔ

[T] MTang mvu < muo, ONW muo. <> [E] WT dmag ‘army’

f 鵡 wǔ mju^B muɑ^B maʔ

g 賦 fù pju^C puɑ^C pah WT dpya ‘tax, duty, tribute’

The ‘phonetic’ wǔ may have been chosen because tax collection was until not too long ago enforced with the help of the military

1-72 = K. 105 Mand. MC LHan OCM

a 巫覡 wū mju muɑ ma

[N] The original graph shows two hands holding up some object. <> [E] WT ’ba-po < *ɴba ‘shaman(ess), sorcerer’

b 誣 wū mju muɑ ma [E] Chepang maʔ- ‘to lie, deceive’

1 OCM *-a 魚部 (GSR 32-106)

1-73	**= K. 40**	**Mand.**	**MC**	**LHan**	**OCM**	
a	馬	mǎ	ma^B	ma^B	mrâʔ	OCB *mraʔ
	[T] Sin Sukchu SR ma (上); ONW $mä^B$ <> [D] PMin $*ma^B$ <> [E] TB *mraŋ					
f	禡	mà	ma^C	ma^C	mrâh	
h	罵	mà	$ma^{B/C}$	$ma^{B/C}$	mâʔ, mâh	

2 OCM rime *-ak Duó bù 鐸部

GSR 766 - 807

Baxter 1992: 484 ff. (§10.2.5)

See Table 1-1 for OCM rimes *-aŋ, *-ak, *-a in QYS categories.

Table 2-1: Comparison of OCM rimes *-aŋ,*-ak with *-eŋ, *-ek

Div.	*-aŋ R.3	*-ak R.2	*-ek R.	*-eŋ R.9
I	鋼 kâŋ kɑŋ *kâŋ 光 kwâŋ kuɑŋ *kwâŋ 當 tâŋ tɑŋ *tâŋ	各 kâk kɑk *kâk 郭 kwâk kuɑk *kwâk 落 lâk lɑk *râk 莫 mâk mɑk *mâk		
IV			擊 kiek kek *kêk 鶪 kiwek kuek *kwêk 厤 liek lek *rêk 覓 miek mek *mêk	經 kieŋ keŋ *kêŋ 扃 kiweŋ kueŋ *kwêŋ 定 dieŋ[C] deŋ[C] *dêŋh
III	疆 kjaŋ kiɑŋ *kaŋ 王 jwaŋ wɑŋ *waŋ 亡 mjwaŋ muɑŋ *maŋ 章 tśjaŋ tśɑŋ *taŋ	卻 kʰjak kʰiɑk *khak 攫 kjwak kyɑk *kwak (縛 bjwak buɑk *bak) 著 ḍjak ḍiɑk *drak		
III ac		石 źjäk dźak *dak 亦 jiäk jak *jak 射 dźjäk źak *m-lak 夕 zjäk ziak *s-jak	刺 tsʰjäk tsʰiek *tshek 易 jiäk jek *lek 役 jiwäk wek *wek	正 tśjäŋ tśeŋ *teŋ 盈 jiäŋ jeŋ *leŋ 營 jiwäŋ4 weŋ *weŋ
3/4 gr			益 ʔjiäk4 ʔiek *ʔek 辟 pjiäk4 piek *pek	勁 kjiäŋ[C]4 kieŋ[C] *keŋh 頃 kʰjiwäŋ4 kʰyeŋ *khweŋ 名 mjiäŋ4 mieŋ *meŋ
III gr	京 kjɐŋ kɨaŋ *kraŋ 兄 xjwɐŋ hyaŋ *hwraŋ 永 jwɐŋ[B] waŋ[B]*wraŋʔ 明 mjɐŋ mɨaŋ *mraŋ	戟 kjɐk kɨak *krak 碧 pjɐk pɨak *prak		驚 kjɐŋ kɨɛŋ *kreŋ 榮 jwɐŋ wɛŋ *wreŋ 鳴 mjɐŋ mɨɛŋ *mreŋ
II	更 kɐŋ kaŋ *krâŋ 觥 kwɐŋ kuaŋ *kwrâŋ 烹 pʰɐŋ pʰaŋ *phrâŋ	客 kʰɐk kʰak *khrâk 宅 ḍɐk ḍak *drâk 百 pɐk pak *prâk		生 ṣɐŋ ṣɛŋ *srêŋ (irreg.)
II		獲 ɣwɛk ɣuak *wrâk (irreg.)	搹 kɛk kɛk *krêk 畫 ɣwɛk ɣuɛk *wrêk 脈 mɛk mɛk *mrêk 責 tṣɛk tṣɛk *tsrêk	耕 kɛŋ kɛŋ *krêŋ 爭 tṣɛŋ tṣɛŋ *tsrêŋ

2 OCM *-ak 鐸部 (GSR 766-807)

See Table 17-1 for comparison of OCM rimes *-ek, *-ak, *-auk, *-uk that shows the shift from OC *-auk to MC -jak, and *-ak to MC -jäk after acute initials in div. III where the latter final merged with the reflexes of OCM *-ek in standard Chinese (Table 2-1), but has the expected QYS analogue -jɑk in Min dialects. In the OC rimes *-ak,*-ek, *-ok and *-auk, syllables with MC retroflex initials, especially of the expected type ḍjak, djäk, ḍjwok, tend to be rare in Div. III and seem to have shifted into Div. II ḍɐk, ḍåk, ḍɛk, ḍɔk.

MC xâk (LH hɑk) is rare, if not unique, while MC xɐk II, LH hak occurs more often. Perhaps MC xɐk is the regular reflex of OCM *hâk (not *hrâk), while MC xâk may derive from OCM *hŋâk or *hmâk.

2-1	**= K. 766**	**Mand.**	**MC**	**LHan**	**OCM**	
axz	各 > 佫 格[1]	gé	kɐk	kak	krâk	'go to, arrive'
	[T] Sin Sukchu SR kaw (入); MGZY gyay (入) [kjaj] ⋇ jiǎ 假 *krâʔ 1-12/33c					
	各 each	gè	kâk	kɑk	kâk	
	[T] Sin Sukchu SR kaw (入), LR kawʔ, kɔʔ; MGZY gaw (入) [kaw]; ONW kɑk 'each'					
de	胳[1] 袼 armpit	gē	kâk	kɑk	kâk < *klak	
	[E] PMon *knlak 'armpit'; TB *g-lak > WB lak-kali^B 'armpit'					
f	閣	gè	kâk	kɑk	kâk	
gp'	恪 p'	kè	k^{h}âk	k^{h}ɑk	khâk	
hj	貉[1] j animal	hé	ɣâk	gɑk	gâk	
h	貉[2] a tribe	mò	mɐk	mak	mrâk	= 貊
	a sacrifice	mà	ma^C	ma^C	mrâkh	
c'	骼	gé	k(^{h})ɐk	k(^{h})ak	k(h)râk,	
			kâk	kɑk	kâk < klak	[E] KS *k-la:k^D, *tla:k^{D1}
d	胳[2] haunch	gé, gè	kɐk	kak	krâk	
b'	觡	gé	kɐk	kak	krâk	
g'	垎	hè	ɣɐk	gak	grâk	[E] LB *ʔkrak 'dry'
z	格[2] obstruct	hè	ɣɐk	gak	grâk	
	branch	gè	kâk	kɑk	kâk	[E] TB *ka:k 'branch'
d'	客	kè	k^{h}ɐk	k^{h}ak	khrâk	
	[T] Sin Sukchu SR k'əj (入), LR k'əjʔ; MGZY khyay (入) [k'jaj]					
o'	喀	kè	k^{h}ɐk	k^{h}ak	khrâk	[E] PMV *krha:k 'to spit'
-	咯	kǎ				'cough up phlegm'
	[D] Min: Xiàmén k^{h}ak^{D2} and keʔ^{D1}					
	咯	luò	lâk	lɑk	râk	Tai: S. raak^{D2} 'to vomit'
j'	額	é	ŋɐk	ŋak	ŋrâk	
	[D] PMin *ŋhiak: Xiam giɑʔ^{D2}, hiɑʔ^{D2}, lit. gik^{D2}					
h'	詻	é	ŋɐk	ŋak	ŋrâk	
	[T] Sin Sukchu SR əj (入), PR ŋəjʔ; MGZY yay (入) [jaj]					
k	洛	luò	lâk	lɑk	râk	OCB *g-rak
	[T] Sin Sukchu SR law (入), LR lawʔ; MGZY law (入) [law]; ONW lɑk					
q'	落	luò	lâk	lɑk	râk	OCB *g-rak
	[D] PMin *lhək 'to fall'					
n	烙	luò	lâk	lɑk	râk	S. k^{h}lɔɔk^{D2L} < *gl- 'burn'

o	絡	luò	lâk	lɑk	râk	
	[E] LB *ʔkrak 'rope', WT 'grags-pa 'bind'					
p	酪 yoghurt	lào	lâk	lɑk	râk < *g-rak	
	[T] Cf. Mongol *aɣiraɣ (Pulleyblank 1962: 253)					
qrst	雒輅駱駱	luò	lâk	lɑk	râk	q OCB *C-rak
u	珞	luò,	lâk,	lɑk,	—	
		lì	liek	leuk	riâuk	= 17-8/1125j 礫
v	略	lüè	ljak	liɑk	rak	
	[T] Sin Sukchu SR ljaw (入); MGZY lew (入) [lɛw]; ONW l(i)ak					
k'	賂	lù	luo^C	lɑ^C	râkh	OCB *g-raks
n'	輅 chariot	lù	luo^C	lɑ^C	râkh	
	crosspiece	hè	ɣɐk	gak	grâk	
	to meet	yà	ŋa^C	ŋa^C	ŋrâh	
	= 御 1-30/60l; 迓訝 1-34/37fe <> [E] WB ŋra^B 'meet'					
x'	簬	lù	luo^C	lɑ^C	râkh	
l'	路	lù	luo^C	lɑ^C	râkh	OCB *g-raks
	[T] Sin S. SR lu (去), PR, LR lu; MGZY lu (去) [lu]; ONW lo. MHan 徑路 keŋ^C-lɑ^C qiŋiraq (Hunnish sword) <> [D] W-Wenzh løy^{21}; PMin *d̬uo^C: Yǒng'ān tiɯ^{C1}, Jiàny tiɔ^{C2}, Fuzh tuo^{C2}					
s'	簵	lù	luo^C	lɑ^C	râkh < *g-rakh	
	[E] Tai: S. kʰlaa^{C2} (WrSiam glaa) 'bamboo'					
t'u'	露 u'	lù	luo^C	lɑ^C	râkh	OCB *g-raks
	[T] ONW lo. Transcribes a pre-Han TB word for 'black' (cf. WT rog, rag-po); Unger *Hao-ku* 50, 1995 <> [D] PMin *lho^C > Jiàn'ou su^{44} -/- 'appear' <> Middle Viet tlô' 'to show'					
v'	鷺	lù	luo^C	lɑ^C	râkh	
r'	璐	lù	luo^C	lɑ^C	râkh	

2-2	**= K. 776**	**Mand.**	**MC**	**LHan**	**OCM**	
a	谷	jué	gjak	gɨɑk	gak	
bc	卻却	què	kʰjak	kʰɨɑk	khak	
def	綌郤郄	xì	kʰjɐk	kʰɨak	khak	
g	腳脚	jiǎo	kjak	kɨɑk	kak	[T] MTang kiak, ONW kak

2-3	**= K. 785**	**Mand.**	**MC**	**LHan**	**OCM**
ab	a 戟	jǐ	kjɐk	kɨak	krak

2-4	**= K. 786**	**Mand.**	**MC**	**LHan**	**OCM**
a	丮	jí	kjɐk	kɨak	krak

2-5	**= K. 787**	**Mand.**	**MC**	**LHan**	**OCM**	
ab	㡿	qì	kʰjɐk	kʰɨak	khrak	
c	隙	xì	kʰjɐk	kʰɨak	khrak	
d	虩	xì	xjɐk	hɨak	hrak	= 2-11/789a 覤

2-6	**= K. 774**	**Mand.**	**MC**	**LHan**	**OCM**	
a	郭	guō	kwâk	kuɑk	kwâk	[T] ONW kuɑk
ef	椁槨	guǒ	kwâk	kuɑk	kwâk	
ghi	廓鞟鞹	kuò	kʰwâk	kʰuɑk	khwâk	[E] TB *(r-)kwâk 'skin'

2-7	**= K. 96, 778**	**Mand.**	**MC**	**LHan**	**OCM**	
96a	䀠	jù	kju^{C}	kyɑ^{C}	kwakh	
96c	瞿[1] anxious	jù,	kju^{C}	kyɑ^{C}	kwakh	OCB *gʷ(r)jas
96i	懼	jù	gju^{C}	gyɑ^{C}	gwakh	
	[T] Sin Sukchu SR gy (去); MGZY kȳu (去) [gy]; MTang gy < guo, ONW guo					
778a	矍	jué,	kjwak,	kyɑk,	kwak,	
		xuè	xiwak	hyɑk	hwak	
778b	攫	jué	kjwak	kyɑk	kwak	
	[E] WT 'gog-pa, bkog 'snatch, seize, take away'					
778c	玃	jué	kjwak	kyɑk	kwak	
778d	躩	què, jué	k(^{h})jwak	k(^{h})yɑk	kwak, khwak	
778e	戄	xuè, jué	xjwak	hyɑk	hwak	
96c	瞿[2] lance	qú	gju	gyɑ	gwa	
96deg	衢躣鸜	qú	gju	gyɑ	gwa	
96h	臞	qú	gju(^{C})	gyɑ(^{C})	gwa, gwah	
	[E] WB kʰwak 'concave' (as a cup), 'sunken' (face)					

2-7A	**= K. 783**	**Mand.**	**MC**	**LHan**	**OCM**
a	虢	guó	kwɐk	kuak	kwrâk

2-8 **= K. 784** The proportion of syllables with initial or medial *w- in MC Div. II is suspiciously high; I suspect that such syllables represent OC simple *wâk > ɣwɛ/ak, rather than a complex *(g)wrâk.

		Mand.	**MC**	**LHan**	**OCM**	
ad	蒦獲	huò	ɣwɛk	ɣuak	gwrâk or wâk	[T] ONW ɣuëk
e	韄	huò,	ɣwɛk,	ɣuak,	gwrâk or wâk,	[E] WT 'grogs-pa 'to bind'
		wò	ʔwɐk	ʔuak	ʔwrâk or ʔwâk	
hi	穫鑊	huò	ɣwâk	ɣuɑk	gwâk	
l	擭	huò	ɣwa^{C},	ɣua^{C},	gwrâkh or wâkh,	
			ʔwɐk	ʔuak	ʔwrâk or ʔwâk	
k	護	hù	ɣuo^{C}	ɣuɑ^{C}	gwâkh	
	[T] MHan 護澡 ɣuɑ^{C}-tsɑuʔ = waxšab <> [E] WT 'gogs-pa 'to prevent'					
fg	彠 矱	huò,	ɣwɛk,	ɣuak,	gwrâk or wâk,	
		yuē	ʔjwak	ʔyɑk	ʔwak	
j	濩 boil	huò	ɣwâk	ɣuɑk	gwâk	
	濩 a dance	hù	ɣuo^{C}	ɣuɑ^{C}	gwâkh	
m	臒	wò	ʔwâk	ʔuɑk	ʔwâk	
n	蠖	huò !	ʔwâk	ʔuɑk	ʔwâk	

2-9	**= K. 767**	**Mand.**	**MC**	**LHan**	**OCM**
a	壑	hè	xâk	hɑk	hâk

2-10	**= K. 779**	**Mand.**	**MC**	**LHan**	**OCM**	
a	赫	hè	xɐk	hak	hrâk	OCB *xrak
	[E] TB *s-ryak 'ashamed, shy'					
b	嚇	xià,	xa^{C},	ha^{C},	hrâkh	
		hè	xɐk	hak	hrâk	

2-10A = K. 1259a		**Mand.**	**MC**	**LHan**	**OCM**	
a	謋	huò !	xɐk	hak	hrâk	

2-11	**= K. 789**	**Mand.**	**MC**	**LHan**	**OCM**	
a	覤	xì	xjɐk	hɨak	hrak	= 2-5 虩

2-12	**= K. 775**	**Mand.**	**MC**	**LHan**	**OCM**	
ae	霍藿	huò	xwâk	huɑk	hwâk	
f	臛	huò	xuok	houk	hûk	

2-13	**= K. 805**	**Mand.**	**MC**	**LHan**	**OCM**	
a	亞	yà	ʔa^{C}	ʔa^{C}	ʔrâkh	

Div II (< *-r-) occurs suspiciously often sound symbolic words so that one may doubt of a medial *r in some OC syllables.

e	弫	yā	ʔa	ʔa	ʔ(r)â
f	啞 laugh	è	ʔak	ʔak	ʔ(r)âk
	mute	yǎ	ʔa^{B}	ʔa^{B}	ʔ(r)âʔ

(ʔa^{B}) [D] M-Xiam b. e^{B1}, w. a^{B1} <> [E] TB *(m-)a 'mute' > PL *ʔa$^{2/3}$, WB a^{C} 'mute'

g	堊	è	ʔâk	ʔɑk	ʔâk
h	惡 bad	è	ʔâk	ʔɑk	ʔâk

[T] Sin Sukchu SR ʔaw (入), LR ʔawʔ; MGZY 'aw (入) [ʔaw]; ONW ʔɑk,

	惡 hate	wù	ʔuo^{C}	ʔɑ^{C}	ʔâkh

[T] Sin Sukchu SR ʔu (去); MGZY 'u (去) [ʔu] <> [E] WT ʔag-po 'bad'

	惡 how	wū	ʔuo	ʔɑ	ʔâ

2-14	**= K. 788**	**Mand.**	**MC**	**LHan**	**OCM**	This series prob. belongs to 2-34.
ac	a 逆	nì	ŋjɐk	ŋɨak	ŋrak	OCB *ŋrjak

[T] Sin Sukchu SR i (入), PR ŋi; MGZY ngi (入) [ŋi]; ONW ŋek

fg	f 咢	è	ŋâk	ŋɑk	ŋâk	[E] WT rŋa 'drum'
-	顎	è	ŋâk	ŋɑk	ŋâk	[E] PTai *ŋɨak, WB ŋak 'gills'
hli	愕鄂遻	è	ŋâk	ŋɑk	ŋâk	= 噩

[D] Xiamen giɑʔ^{D2}, lit. gok^{D2}

kmn	諤鍔鶚	è	ŋâk	ŋɑk	ŋâk	
j	遻	wù	ŋuo^{C}	ŋɑ^{C}	ŋâkh	
792 hij	溯泝訴	sù	suo^{C}	sɑ^{C}	sŋâkh	= 愬 2-34/769b

2-15	**= K. 768**	**Mand.**	**MC**	**LHan**	**OCM**	
a	噩	è	ŋâk	ŋɑk	ŋâk	= 2-14/788hli 愕鄂遻
-	鱷	è	ŋâk	ŋɑk	ŋâk	
d	蘁	wù	ŋâk, ŋuo^{C}	ŋɑk, ŋɑ^{C}	ŋâk(h)	

2-16	**= K. 801**	**Mand.**	**MC**	**LHan**	**OCM**	
a	度 to measure	duó	dâk	dɑk	dâk	[E] WB t^{h}wa 'a measure'

[T] Sin Sukchu SR daw (入); MGZY taw (入) [daw]

	度 a measure	dù	duo^{C}	dɑ^{C}	dâkh	[T] ONW do
b	渡	dù	duo^{C}	dɑ^{C}	dâkh	[E] WT 'da-ba, das 'pass over'
c	剫	duó	dâk	dɑk	dâk	

2 OCM *-ak 鐸部 (GSR 766-807)

2-17	**= K. 795**	**Mand.**	**MC**	**LHan**	**OCM**	
ahd	石鼫祏	shí	źjäk	dźak	dak	
	Xiam. tsioʔ^{D2}			dźɑk	dak	[D] PMin *džiɔk
	[T] Sin Sukchu SR ẓi (入); MGZY zhi (入) [ẓi]; MTang źek < dźek, ONW dźek					
e	碩	shuò !	źjäk	dźak	dak	
i	跖	zhí	tśjäk	tśak	tak	
j	磔	zhé	ṭɐk	ṭak	trâk	
no	妬妒	dù	tuo^C	tɑ^C	tâkh	
l	柘	zhè	tśja^C	tśa^C	takh	[T] ONW tśa
k	斫	zhuó	tśjak	tśɑk	tak or tauk ?	
	[T] ONW tśak. <> [E] TB *tuk > LB *ɴtök ~ *ʔtök 'to cut by a blow, hack away at', WB tok 'cut by a single light blow', JP tok^{55} 'cut into pieces'					
m	拓	tuò	tʰâk	tʰɑk	thâk	
pq	橐 q	tuó	tʰâk	tʰɑk	thâk	q = 2-23/792e
r	蠹	dù	tuo^C	tɑ^C	tâkh	

2-18	**= K. 804**	**Mand.**	**MC**	**LHan**	**OCM**
a	庶 all	shù	śjwo^C	śɑ^C	lha(k)h < *tlha(k)h ?
	庶 a title	zhù	tśjwo^C	tśɑ^C	ta(k)h
d	遮	zhē	tśja	tśa	ta
ef	摭蹠	zhí	tśjäk	tśak	tak

2-19	**= K. 791**	**Mand.**	**MC**	**LHan**	**OCM**
a	炙	zhì	tśjäk	tśak	tak = *tjak?
	[E] LB *kyik, WB kʰyac 'burnt'				
	炙	zhè	tśja^C	tśa^C	takh = *tjakh?

2-20	**= K. 794**	**Mand.**	**MC**	**LHan**	**OCM**
a	尺	chǐ	tśʰjäk	tśʰak	thak ?

2-21	**= K. 1258b**	**Mand.**	**MC**	**LHan**	**OCM**	
b	辵	chuò	ṭʰjak	ṭʰiɑk	tʰrak	= 1-38/45o' 踖

2-22	**= K. 780**	**Mand.**	**MC**	**LHan**	**OCM**
a	乇	zé	ṭɐk	ṭak	trâk
b	宅	zhái	ḍɐk	ḍak	drâk
	[T] Sin Sukchu SR dẓəj (入), LR dẓəjʔ; MGZY cay (入) [dẓaj]; MTang ḍĕk, ONW dĕk				
hi	詫侘	chà	ṭʰa^C	ṭʰa^C	thrâkh
g	吒	zhà	ṭa^C	ṭa^C	trâkh
	[T] BTD Skt ṭa, ṭha, e.g. 阿迦貳吒 ʔɑ-ka-ńis-ṭa^C Skt. akaniṣṭa				
f	秅	chá,	ḍa,	ḍa,	drâ,
		dù	tuo^C	tɑ^C	tâ(k)h
j	詫	dù	tuo^C	tɑ^C	tâkh
e	託	tuō	tʰâk	tʰɑk	thâk
	[T] Sin Sukchu SR t'aw (入); MGZY thaw (入) [t'aw]				

2-23 **= K. 792** The central element in 㡿 writes words with the meaning 'oppose, disobedient'. Therefore this graph and its derivative 斥 plays partially a semantic role here in 2-23, and also in 2-14; 2-34.

		Mand.	MC	LHan	OCM	
abc	㡿斥厈 rebuff	chì	tśʰjäk	tśʰak	k-lhak	
	spy	chì	tśʰjäk	tśʰak	k-lhak	⋈ 2-25/790a 睪 *lak 'spy'
	spread	chì	tśʰjäk	tśʰak	k-lhak	⋈ 18-8/3t *k-hlai?
d	坼	chè	ṭʰɐk	ṭʰak	thrâk	
	⋈ 2-17/795j 磔 *trâk; ⋈ 18-8/3j 拸 *thrai?					
ef	㯩柝 a rattle	tuò	tʰâk	tʰɑk	thâk	= 2-17/795q

2-24	**= K. 793**	**Mand.**	**MC**	**LHan**	**OCM**	
a	赤 red	chì	tśʰjäk	tśʰak	k-lhak	OCB *KHjAk [T] ONW tśʰek
	expel	cì	tsʰjäk	tsʰiak	s-lhak ?	
d	赦	shè	śja^{C}	śa^{C}	lhakh	
e	螫	shì	śjäk	śak	lhak	
-	郝	hè	xâk	hɑk	hâk	

2-25	**= K. 790**	**Mand.**	**MC**	**LHan**	**OCM**	
abce	睪圛懌繹	yì	jiäk	jak ~ jɑk	lak	懌 'pleased' ⋈ 1-42/82g *lah
fghi-	譯醳驛睪曎	yì	jiäk	jak ~ jɑk	lak	
	繹 [T] Sin Sukchu SR iʔ (入); MGZY yi (入) [ji]					
d	斁[1] fed up	yì, dù	jiäk, duo^{C}	jak, dɑ^{C}	lak, lâkh	= 2-26/807a
dq	斁[2] 殬 destroy	dù	tuo^{C}	tɑ^{C}	tâkh < tlâkh ?	
k	𥼶	shì	śjäk	śak	lhak	
l	釋	shì	śjäk	śak	lhak	
	Xiam.	tsʰioʔ^{A1}		tśʰɑk		
	[T] Sin Sukchu SR ṣi (入); MGZY shi (入) [ṣi]; ONW śek; BTD 釋迦文 śak-k(j)a-mun Skt. śākyamuni <> [E] KS *s-lak or ʔlak[7] 'to wash clothes'; <> ? PTai *zək 'wash clothes'					
o	澤 marsh	zé	ḍɐk	ḍak	drak < r-lak	
	[T] MHan 澤散 ḍak-sɑn^{C} Alexandria					
	lay open	shì	śjäk	śak	lhak	
	wine	yì	jiäk	jak ~ jɑk	lak	
n	擇	zé	ḍɐk	ḍak	drak < r-lak	
	[T] Sin Sukchu SR dẓəj (入); MGZY cay (入) [dẓaj]; MTang ḍĕk, ONW dĕk					
	[E] KT: KS *la:i[6] 'to pick, select', Tai: S. lɨak^{D2} 'to choose'					
	[N] The expected MC div. III ḍjak has shifted to div. II ḍɐk in this rime					
r	蘀	tuò	tʰâk	tʰɑk	lhâk	
m	檡	zé,	ḍɐk,	ḍak,	drak < r-lak,	
		shì	śjäk	śak	lhak	
p -	鐸澤	duó	dâk	dɑk	lâk	

2-26	**= K. 807**	**Mand.**	**MC**	**LHan**	**OCM**	
a	射 hit w. bow	shí	dźjäk	źak,	m-lak	
	Fuzh. sioʔ^{D2}			źɑk		[D] PMin *žiɔk ~ *žiak,
	射 shoot	shè	dźja^{C}	źa^{C}	m-lakh	[T] ONW ia [D] PMin *žia^{C}
	射 fed up	yì	jiäk	jak ~ jɑk	lak	= 2-25/790d

-	麝	shè	dźja^{C}	źa^{C}	m-lah	[E] WT gla-ba 'musk deer'
eg	榭謝	xiè	zja^{C}	za^{C}	s-lakh	[T] MHan šāhi

2-27	**= K. 800**	**Mand.**	**MC**	**LHan**	**OCM**	
aml	亦[1] > 腋	yè	jiäk	jak	jak	armpit

腋 [E] TB-Mru yak, Lushai zak^{L} (< *jak) 'armpit', Newari jaːk-wa 'armpit'

a	亦[2] also	yì	jiäk	jak	jak	

[T] ONW iek <> [E] Lushai ve^{L} < veʔ/h 'also' ⪥ vek^{R} < vek 'again, over again'

def	奕帟弈	yì	jiäk	jak	jak	
n	液	yè !	jiäk	jak	jak	[E] TB *ryak 'grease'
j	夜	yè	jia^{C}	ja^{C}	jah > jakh	OCB *(l)jAks

[T] Sin Sukchu SR je (去); ONW ia < ja <> [E] TB *yaʔ 'night'

l	掖	yè	jiäk	jak	jak	
gh	跡迹	jī, jì	tsjäk	tsiak	tsjak	

[T] ONW tsiek <> [E] Limbu yok[2] 'trace, track', Lushai hniak^{H} 'footprint, hoofprint'

2-28	**= K. 796**	**Mand.**	**MC**	**LHan**	**OCM**	
a	夕	xī, xì	zjäk	ziak	s-jak	

[T] ONW ziek <> [E] TB *s-ryak '24 hr day'

-	汐	xī, xì	zjäk	ziak	s-jak	'evening tide'
e	穸	xī, xì	zjäk	ziak	s-jak	

2-29	**= K. 797**	**Mand.**	**MC**	**LHan**	**OCM**	
a	席	xí	zjäk	ziak,	s-lak	[T] ONW ziek
	Xiam.	tsʰioʔ^{D2}		ziɑk		[D] PMin *dzhiɔk
b	蓆	xí	zjäk	ziak	s-lak	

2-30	**= K. 777**	**Mand.**	**MC**	**LHan**	**OCM**	
a	若	ruò	ńźjak,	ńɑk	nak	

[T] Sin S. SR rjaw (入), LR rjawʔ; MGZY Zhew (入) [rɛw]; ONW ńak
ńźja^{B} GY ONW ńa

g	箬	ruò	ńźjak	ńɑk	nak	[E] Lushai hnaʔ^{L} 'leaf'
i	鄀	ruò	ńźjak	ńɑk	nak	
f	諾	nuò	nâk	nɑk	nâk	[T] ONW nɑk
k	婼	chuò	ṭʰjak	ṭʰiɑk	nhrak ?	
	婼羌	ruò-qiāng	ńźjak-	ńɑk-kʰiɑŋ		name of a TB people

[T] 婼 may transcribe TB *nak (WT nag) 'black' (cf. Pulleyblank 1983: 417); or the ethnonym WT mi-ñag for the later Mi-niaɯ (Tangut, Xixia) people; GY reads MC ńźie in this sense.

l	匿	nì	ṇjək	ṇɨk	nrək < *r-nək ?	
n	暱	nì	ṇjək	ṇɨk	nrək	[E] KN-Lai neek 'familiar'
o	慝	tè	tʰək	tʰək	nhək	[E] WT nag 'black'

[T] Sin Sukchu SR t'əj (入), LR t'əjʔ; MGZY (cʰiy > thʰiy) (入) [t'əj]

2-31	**= K. 806**	**Mand.**	**MC**	**LHan**	**OCM**	
af	乍咋	zhà	dẓa^{C}	dẓa^{C}	dzrâkh	
g	詐	zhà	tṣa^{C}	tṣa^{C}	tsrâkh	
k	笮	zé	tṣɐk	tṣak	tsrâk	[E] Khmer /craɑk/ 'insert'

p	柞 oak	zuò,	tsâk,	tsɑk,	tsâk,	
		zuó	dzâk	dzɑk	dzâk	
	柞 clear away	zé	tṣɐk	tṣak	tsrâk	
l	作	zuò	tsâk	tsɑk	tsâk	

[T] Sin SR tsaw (入), tsɔ (去), tsu, PR tsɔ, LR tsawʔ; MGZY dzaw (入)[tsaw], dzu (去) [tsu]

m	迮	zuò	tsâk	tsɑk	tsâk	
rv	怍 v	zuò	dzâk	dzɑk	dzâk	
s	昨	zuó	dzâk	dzɑk	dzâk	

[T] Sin Sukchu SR dzaw (入), LR dzawʔ; MGZY tsaw (入) [dzaw]

t	酢	zuò	dzâk	dzɑk	dzâk	= 2-32/798t 醋
-	飵 eat	zuò	dzâk	dzɑk	dzâk	[E] ST *dza
hij	祚胙阼	zuò	dzuo^{C}	dzɑ^{C}	dzâkh	

2-32	**= K. 798**	**Mand.**	**MC**	**LHan**	**OCM**	
a	昔	xī	sjäk	siak	sak or sjak ?	

昔 [T] Sin Sukchu SR si (入); MGZY si (入) [si]. — The OB graph shows a sun under water, i.e., the notion of 'yesterday' (Pankenier *EC* 7, 1981-82: 19)

fg	惜腊	xī	sjäk	siak	sak or sjak ?	
u	借	jiè	tsjäk,	tsiak,		[T] ONW tsiek
	Xiam.	tsioʔ^{D1}		tsiɑk,	tsak,	[D] PMin *tsiɔk
	借	jiè	tsja^{C}	tsia^{C}	tsakh	
v	唶	jiè	tsja^{C}	tsia^{C}	tsakh	
k	踖 walk rev.	jí	tsjäk	tsiak	tsak or tsjak ?	
	踖 trample	jí	dzjäk	dziak	dzak or dzjak ?	
	踖 reverent	qì, què	ts^{h}jäk,ts^{h}jak	ts^{h}iak	ts^{h}ak	
ln	趞鵲	què	ts^{h}jak	ts^{h}iɑk	ts^{h}ak	
y	蜡 maggot	qù	ts^{h}jwo^{C}	ts^{h}iɑ^{C}	tshakh	
	sacrifice	zhà	dẓa^{C}	dẓa^{C}	dzrâkh	
ia'	耤籍	jí	dzjäk	dziak	dzak or dzjak ?	
b'	藉 a field	jí	dzjäk	dziak	dzak	
	a mat	jiè	dzja^{C}	dzia^{C}	dzakh	
pq	厝逪	cuò	ts^{h}âk	ts^{h}ɑk	tshâk	[T] ONW ts^{h}ɑk
s	錯 mistake	cuò	ts^{h}âk	ts^{h}ɑk	—	

[T] Sin Sukchu SR ts'aw (入), LR ts'awʔ; MGZY tshaw (入) [ts'aw]; ONW ts^{h}ɑk

t	醋	zuò	dzâk	dzɑk	dzâk	= 2-31/806t 酢
o	斮	zhuó	tṣjak	tṣɑk	tsrak	
z	矠	zé	dẓɛk	dẓɛk	dzrêk	
x	措	cuò	ts^{h}uo^{C}	ts^{h}ɑh	tshâkh	
c'	簎	cè	tṣ^{h}ɐk	tṣ^{h}ak	tshrâk	

2-33	**= K. 770**	**Mand.**	**MC**	**LHan**	**OCM**	
a	索 twist rope	suǒ	sâk	sɑk	sâk	

[T] Sin Sukchu SR saw (入), PR, LR sawʔ; MGZY saw (入) [saw]; ONW sɑk

[E] MK-PVM *ɟaːk 'rope' PMonic *ɟook 'creeper, vine, rope' <> Tai: S. čʰïak^{D2L} < PTai ǰ- 'rope', Saek saak^{D2} < z- 'vines, rope'

	索 fear	suǒ	sâk	sɑk	sŋâk	WT sŋaŋ-ba 'be afraid'

		Mand.	MC	LHan	OCM	
	索 select	sè	ṣɐk	ṣak	srâk	

2-34	= K. 769	Mand.	MC	LHan	OCM	
a	朔	shuò	ṣåk	ṣak ?, ṣɔk ?	sŋrak ?, srok ?	
	The left element 'go against' is partly semantic. This series prob. belongs to 2-14.					
	[T] Sin Sukchu SR ṣaw (入), PR ṣwawʔ; MGZY shwaw (入) [ṣwaw]					
b	愬	sù	suo^C	sɑ^C	sŋâkh	
c	謝	sù	suo^C	sɑ^C	sŋâkh	= 2-14/792h 泝訴
d	遡	sù	suo^C	sɑ^C	sŋâkh	

2-35	= K. 799	Mand.	MC	LHan	OCM	
ae	舄潟	xì	sjäk	siak	sak	
f	寫	xiě	sja^B	sia^B	saʔ	[T] ONW sia
h	瀉	xiè !	sja^B	sia^B	saʔ	

2-36	= K. 773	Mand.	MC	LHan	OCM
a	亳	bó	bâk	bɑk	bâk

2-37	= K. 781	Mand.	MC	LHan	OCM	
a	百	bǎi	pɐk	pak	prâk	[E] ST *(p)ria: TB *r-ya
	[T] Sin Sukchu SR pəj (入), LR pəjʔ; MGZY bay (入) [paj]; ONW pëk					
fg	貊陌	mò	mɐk	mak	mrâk	= 2-1h

2-38	= K. 782	Mand.	MC	LHan	OCM	
a	白	bái	bɐk	bak	brâk	
	[T] Sin Sukchu SR bəj (入); LR bəjʔ; MGZY pay (入) [baj]; ONW bëk					
f	帛	bó	bɐk	bak	brâk	
i	伯	bó	pɐk	pak	prâk	
	[E] TB-Kukish prak 'eldest br.'					
j	柏	bǎi, bó	pɐk	pak	prâk	
k	迫	pò	pɐk	pak	prâk	
m	拍 beat	pāi !	p^{h}ɐk	p^{h}ak	phrâk	
	shoulder	bó	pâk	pɑk	pâk	
	[E] TB *p(r)ak, *r-pak 'shoulder'					
o	魄	pò	p^{h}ɐk	p^{h}ak	phrâk	= 2-39/772b 霸
	[T] MHan 虎魄 ἅρπαξ (harpax)					
l	怕 quiet	pò	p^{h}ɐk	p^{h}ak	phrâk	
	fear	pà	p^{h}a^C	—		
	[T] Sin Sukchu SR p'a (去); MGZY pha (去) [p'a]; Sui-Tang pä^C					
pq	粕胉	pò	p^{h}âk	p^{h}ɑk	phâk	
r	泊	bó	bâk	bɑk	bâk	
s	碧	bì	pjɐk	pɨak	prak	(not MC pjäk: Baxter 1977:192)

2-39	= K. 772	Mand.	MC	LHan	OCM	
a	霏	pò	p^{h}âk	p^{h}ɑk	phâk	'hide soaked in rain'
b	霸 hegemon	pò	p^{h}ɐk	p^{h}ak	phrâk	
	lead	bà	pa^C	pa^C	prâkh	

2-40 = K. 802 The phonetic is perhaps 3-64/709

		Mand.	MC	LHan	OCM	
ad	莫[1] > 暮	mù	muo^C	mɑ^C	mâkh	evening
	[T] MHan 莫邪 mɑh-ja Skt māyā					
	莫[2] nobody	mò	mâk	mɑk	mâk	
	[T] Sin Sukchu SR maw (入), LR mawʔ; MGZY maw (入) [maw]; ONW mɑk					
ar	莫[3]嗼 silent	mò	mɐk	mak	mrâk	
npq	寞漠瘼	mò	mâk	mɑk	mâk	
o	幕	mù	mâk	mɑk	mâk	
-	暯	mò	mâk	mɑk	mâk	
k	膜 membrane	mó	mâk	mɑk	mâk	
	kneel	mó	muo	mɑ	mâ	
e	募	mù	muo^C	mɑ^C	mâkh	
f	墓	mù	muo^C	mɑ^C	mâkh	
	[T] Sin Sukchu SR mu (去); MGZY mu (去) [mu]; ONW mo <> [D] PMin *mhuo^C					
h	慕	mù	muo^C	mɑ^C	mâh !	≍ 4-65 慔
gj	嫫模	mó	muo	mɑ	mâ	
l	謨	mó	muo	mɑ	mâʔ !	[T] ONW mo
m	(蝦) 蟆	xiā-má	ɣa-ma	ga-ma	grâ-mrâ or ga-ma?	
s	冪	mì	miek	mek	mêk	

3 **OCM rime *-aŋ** Yáng bù 陽部

GSR 697 - 765

Baxter 1992: 489 ff. (§10.2.6)

See Table 1-1 for OCM rimes *-aŋ, *-ak, *-a in QYS categories. Some OC finals in *-aŋ have converged with ones in *-eŋ (Rime 9) in QYS Div. III -jɐŋ, see Table 2-1. For the QYS syllables with this final, which pattern like *chóngniǔ* Div. 3/3 syllables, Baxter reconstructs an OC medial *r.

3-1	**= K. 698**	**Mand.**	**MC**	**LHan**	**OCM**	
a	亢^{1}	gāng	kâŋ	kɑŋ	kâŋ < klaŋ ?	
	[E] MY *klaːŋ^{A} 'neck'					
abc	亢^{2} 抗伉	kàng	k^{h}âŋ^{C}	k^{h}ɑŋ^{C}	khâŋh	'to oppose'
-	囥 to store	kàng	k^{h}âŋ^{C}	k^{h}ɑŋ^{C}		
	[E] Tai: S. k^{h}aŋ^{A1} < *k^{h}l- 'to hold water, confine'					
d	忼	kāng	k^{h}âŋ$^{B/C}$	k^{h}ɑŋ$^{B/C}$	khâŋʔ/h	≭ 3-12/746m 慷
hi	坑阬	kēng	k^{h}ɐŋ	k^{h}aŋ	khrâŋ	
eg-	杭頏航	háng	ɣâŋ	gɑŋ	gâŋ	[T] ONW ɣɑŋ
f	沆	hàng	ɣâŋ^{B}	gɑŋ^{B}	gâŋʔ	

3-2	**= K. 697**	**Mand.**	**MC**	**LHan**	**OCM**	
a	岡	gāng	kâŋ	kɑŋ	kâŋ	TB *kaŋ 'mountain, spur'
be	剛綱	gāng	kâŋ	kɑŋ	kâŋ	
f	犅	gāng	kâŋ	kɑŋ	kâŋ < klaŋ	
	[T] Sin Sukchu SR kaŋ (平); MGZY gang (平) [kaŋ] <> [E] TB: WT glaŋ 'ox'					
h	鋼	gāng	kâŋ(^{C})	kɑŋ(^{C})	kâŋ(h)	[E] Lushai k^{h}aŋ^{F} 'solidified'

3-3	**= K. 710**	**Mand.**	**MC**	**LHan**	**OCM**	
ab	畺壃	jiāng	kjaŋ	kɨɑŋ	kaŋ	
h	疆 boundary	jiāng	kjaŋ	kɨɑŋ	kaŋ	
	[D] Min Xiamen col. kiũ^{A2}, lit. kioŋ^{A2}					
	疆 hard	jiàng	gjaŋ^{B}	gɨɑŋ^{B}	gaŋʔ	
c	僵	jiāng,	kjaŋ,	kɨɑŋ,	kaŋ,	
		qiáng	gjaŋ	gɨɑŋ	gaŋ	
e	彊 fierce	jiāng	kjaŋ	kɨɑŋ	kaŋ	
	彊 strong	qiáng	gjaŋ	gɨɑŋ	gaŋ	= 3-4/713a 強
	彊 effort	qiǎng !	gjaŋ^{B}	gɨɑŋ^{B}	gaŋʔ	
d	薑	jiāng	kjaŋ	kɨɑŋ	kaŋ or kjaŋ ?	
	[D] PMin *kiɔŋ <> [E] TB- SChin-Areng kachiŋ; WB k^{h}yaŋ^{B} 'ginger'. AA: PVM *s-gəːŋ 'ginger'; PTai *xiŋ^{A1}: S. k^{h}iŋ^{2}, KS siŋ 'ginger'					

3-4	= K. 713	Mand.	MC	LHan	OCM	
a	強 strong	qiáng	gjaŋ	gɨɑŋ	gaŋ	= 3-3/710e 彊

[T] Sin Sukchu SR gjaŋ (平); MGZY (kÿang >) kyang (平) [gjaŋ]; MTang giaŋ < gaŋ, ONW gaŋ; BTD Skt. kaṅ[giya] <> [D] Min Xiam col. kiũ^{A2}, lit. kioŋ^{A2}

	強 effort	qiǎng !	gjaŋ^{B}	gɨɑŋ^{B}	gaŋʔ
cd	繈襁	qiǎng !	kjaŋ^{B}	kɨɑŋ^{B}	kaŋʔ

3-5	= K. 711	Mand.	MC	LHan	OCM
a	姜	jiāng	kjaŋ	kɨɑŋ	kaŋ or kjaŋ ?

[T] MTang kiaŋ < kaŋ, ONW kaŋ. — 姜羌 the element 羊 *jaŋ 'sheep' in the graphs may be phonetic, but could also be semantic (names referring to nomads).

3-6	= K. 712	Mand.	MC	LHan	OCM
ae	羌蜣	qiāng	k^{h}jaŋ	k^{h}ɨɑŋ	khaŋ or khjaŋ ?

3-7	= K. 752	Mand.	MC	LHan	OCM	
a	竟 boundary	jìng	kjɐŋ^{B}	kɨaŋ^{B}	kraŋʔ	
	end	jìng	kjɐŋ^{C}	kɨaŋ^{C}	kraŋh	[T] ONW keŋ
b	境	jìng	kjɐŋ^{B}	kɨaŋ^{B}	kraŋʔ	
c	鏡	jìng	kjɐŋ^{C}	kɨaŋ^{C}	kraŋh	

[T] Sin S. SR kiŋ (去); MGZY ging (去) [kiŋ]; ONW keŋ
[D] PMin *kiaŋ^{C} > Amoy kiã^{C1}, Fuzh kiaŋ^{C1}

d	滰	jiǎng	gjaŋ^{B}	gɨɑŋ^{B}	gaŋʔ

3-8	= K. 753	Mand.	MC	LHan	OCM
a	慶	qìng	k^{h}jɐŋ^{C}	k^{h}ɨaŋ^{C}	khraŋ(h)

[E] ? WT g-yaŋ 'blessing'

3-9	= K. 754	Mand.	MC	LHan	OCM
a	競	jìng	gjɐŋ^{C}	gɨaŋ^{C}	graŋh

3-10	= K. 755	Mand.	MC	LHan	OCM
a	京	jīng	kjɐŋ	kɨaŋ	kraŋ

[T] ONW keŋ <> [E] Khmer /kraŋ/ 'steep knoll, bluff or crag overlooking a plain'

d	景	jǐng	kjɐŋ^{B}	kɨaŋ^{B}	kraŋʔ	[T] ONW keŋ
h	憬	jiǒng	kjwɐŋ^{B}	kyaŋ^{B}	kwraŋʔ ?	
eg	勍黥	qíng	gjɐŋ	gɨaŋ	graŋ	
f	鯨	jīng	gjɐŋ	gɨaŋ	graŋ	
l	涼	liáng	ljaŋ	liɑŋ	raŋ	[E] WT graŋ-ba 'be cold'
ijm	倞亮諒	liàng	ljaŋ^{C}	liɑŋ^{C}	raŋh	OCB *C-rjaŋs
k	掠	lüè,	ljak,	liɑk,	rak,	
		liàng	ljaŋ^{C}	liɑŋ^{C}	raŋh	

[D] Min: Amoy lŋ^{C} 'to beat' <> [E] Lushai rɔk^{L} 'to plunder'

3-11	= K. 745	Mand.	MC	LHan	OCM
a	更 change	gēng	kɐŋ	kaŋ	krâŋ

[T] Sin S. SR kəjŋ (平), PR kəŋ ~ kiŋ, LR kiŋ; MGZY gÿing (平) [kjiŋ]; ONW këŋ

	更 still more	gèng	kɐŋ^{C}	kaŋ^{C}	krâŋh

cd	哽鯁	gěng	kɐŋ^B	kaŋ^B	krâŋʔ	
e	梗	gěng	kɐŋ^B	kaŋ^B	krâŋʔ	

[E] Lepcha kraŋ 'be strong on legs', Lushai ṭaŋ^H / ṭan^L < ṭanh (< traŋs) 'put forth all one's strength'.

f	綆	gěng	kɐŋ^B	kaŋ^B	krâŋʔ	'well rope'

See also 23-25/221.

-	硬	yìng	ŋɛŋ^C			

[T] Sin Sukchu SR ŋiŋ (去); MGZY ying (去) [jiŋ]

3-12	**= K. 746, 700**		**MC**	**LHan**	**OCM**	
746a	庚	gēng	kɐŋ	kaŋ	krâŋ	
g	賡	gēng	kɐŋ(C)	kaŋ(C)	krâŋ, krâŋh	
h	康	kāng	kʰâŋ	kʰɑŋ	khâŋ = khlaŋ	

[E] Lushai tlaŋ^R / tlan^L adv. 'peaceably, quietly, calmly', vb. 'be good, kindly, peaceably'

k	康 empty	kāng	kʰâŋ	kʰɑŋ	khâŋ	
no	穅糠	kāng	kʰâŋ	kʰɑŋ	khâŋ = khlaŋ	

[E] WT: lgaŋ 'shell, husk'

m	慷	kāng !	kʰâŋ^B	kʰɑŋ^B	khâŋʔ	× 3-1/698d
700a	唐	táng	dâŋ	dɑŋ	g-laŋ	

[T] Sin S. SR daŋ (平); MGZY tang (平) [daŋ]; ONW dɑŋ

cde	塘糖螗	táng	dâŋ	dɑŋ	lâŋ = g-laŋ	

塘 [E] PYao *glaaŋ^2 'pond'

3-13	**= K. 747**	**Mand.**	**MC**	**LHan**	**OCM**
a	羹	gēng	kɐŋ	kaŋ	krâŋ

3-14	**= K. 748**	**Mand.**	**MC**	**LHan**	**OCM**	
a	行 road	xíng	ɣɐŋ	gaŋ	grâŋ	

[T] Sin Sukchu SR ɣiŋ (平); MGZY Hÿing (平) [ɣjiŋ]; ONW ɣëŋ <> [D] M-Xiam kiã^{A2}
[E] Khmer /rɔɔŋ/ 'way, line, row or bed, gutter'

	行 go round	xìng	ɣɐŋ^C	gaŋ^C	grâŋh	
	行 a row	háng	ɣâŋ	gɑŋ	gâŋ	
	行 strong	háng	ɣâŋ(C)	gɑŋ(C)	gâŋ, gâŋh	
e	荇	xìng	ɣɐŋ^B	gaŋ^B	grâŋʔ	
f	桁 lid	héng	ɣɐŋ	gaŋ	grâŋ	
	fetters	háng	ɣâŋ	gɑŋ	gâŋ	
g	珩	héng	ɣɐŋ	gaŋ	grâŋ	
h	衡 crosswise	hóng	ɣwɐŋ	ɣuaŋ	gwrâŋ	= 3-23/707l 橫
	crosspiece	héng	ɣɐŋ	gaŋ	grâŋ	

[T] Sin Sukchu SR ɣiŋ (平), SR ɣujŋ (平), PR ɣuŋ; MGZY Hÿing (平) [ɣjiŋ]; ONW ɣuëŋ.

j	蘅	héng	ɣɐŋ	gaŋ	grâŋ

3-15	**= K. 749**	**Mand.**	**MC**	**LHan**	**OCM**
a	杏	xìng	ɣɐŋ^B	gaŋ^B	grâŋʔ

3-16	**= K. 714**	**Mand.**	**MC**	**LHan**	**OCM**
a	皀	xiāng	xjaŋ	hɨɑŋ	haŋ
lm	膷薌	xiāng	xjaŋ	hɨɑŋ	haŋ

		Mand.	MC	LHan	OCM	
c	鄉 village	xiāng	xjaŋ	hɨɑŋ	haŋ	
	towards	xiàng	xjaŋ^{C}	hɨɑŋ^{C}	haŋh < hnaŋh?	
	to feast	xiǎng	xjaŋ^{B}	hɨɑŋ^{B}	haŋʔ	= j
i	嚮	xiàng	xjaŋ^{C}	hɨɑŋ^{C}	haŋh < hnaŋh?	= 3-18/715a 向
n	響	xiǎng	xjaŋ^{B}	hɨɑŋ^{B}	haŋ^{A} !	
j	饗	xiǎng	xjaŋ^{B}	hɨɑŋ^{B}	haŋ^{A} !	= 3-17/716a 享

[T] Sin Sukchu SR xjaŋ (去); MGZY (hȳang >) hyang (去) [xjaŋ]; MTang hiaŋ < ONW haŋ

k	曏	xiàng,	xjaŋ$^{B/C}$,	hɨɑŋ$^{B/C}$,	haŋʔ/h,
		shǎng	śjaŋ$^{B/C}$	śɑŋ$^{B/C}$	hjaŋʔ/h
o	卿	qīng	kʰjɐŋ	kʰɨaŋ	khraŋ

3-17	**= K. 716**	**Mand.**	**MC**	**LHan**	**OCM**	
ab	享亨 feast	xiǎng	xjaŋ^{B}	hɨɑŋ^{B}	haŋ^{A} !	= 3-16/714cj 鄉饗
	penetrate	hēng	xɐŋ	haŋ	hraŋ	

The word 'to feast, meal' MC xjaŋ(^{B}) ~ śjaŋ(^{B}) is written with additional graphs: 3-16/714cj 鄉饗, 3-18/715e 餉, 3-42/730 饟.

3-18	**= K. 715**	**Mand.**	**MC**	**LHan**	**OCM**	
a	向	xiàng	xjaŋ^{C}	hɨɑŋ^{C}	haŋh	= 3-16/714ic 嚮鄉

[T]Sin Sukchu SR xjaŋ (去); MGZY (hȳang >) hyang (去) [xjaŋ]; MTang hiaŋ < ONW haŋ
[D] Min: Xiam col. hiɑ̃^{C1}, ŋ^{C1}.

e	餉	xiǎng	śjaŋ$^{A/B/C}$	śɑŋ$^{B/C}$	hjaŋʔ, hjaŋh

~ 3-42/730c 饟 [T] ONW śaŋ

3-19	**= K. 717**	**Mand.**	**MC**	**LHan**	**OCM**
a	香	xiāng	xjaŋ	hɨɑŋ	haŋ

3-20	**= K. 718**	**Mand.**	**MC**	**LHan**	**OCM**
a	央 center	yāng	ʔjaŋ	ʔɨɑŋ	ʔaŋ

[T] Sin Sukchu SR ʔjaʔ (平); MGZY ('ȳang >) 'yang (平) [ʔjaŋ]; BTD Skt. aṅ. MHan 央匱 ʔɨɑŋ-guis Tocharian B ankwaṣ 'asafoetida'

	央 brilliant	yīng	ʔjɐŋ	ʔɨaŋ	ʔraŋ	
e	殃	yāng	ʔjaŋ	ʔɨɑŋ	ʔaŋ	
-	秧	yāng	ʔjaŋ	ʔɨɑŋ	ʔaŋ	

[D] PMin *ɔŋ^{A1} <> [E] MY *ʔzon^{A} 'young rice plant'

g	泱	yāng	ʔjaŋ	ʔɨɑŋ	ʔaŋ	
h	鴦	yāng,	ʔjaŋ,	ʔɨɑŋ,	ʔaŋ,	
		āng	ʔâŋ	ʔɑŋ	ʔâŋ	
c	佒	yǎng,	ʔjaŋ^{B},	ʔɨɑŋ^{B},	ʔaŋʔ,	
		āng	ʔâŋ	ʔɑŋ	ʔâŋ	
f	鞅	yǎng	ʔjaŋ^{B}	ʔɨɑŋ^{B}	ʔaŋʔ	
d	怏	yàng	ʔjaŋ$^{B/C}$	ʔɨɑŋ$^{B/C}$	ʔaŋʔ/h	
k	英	yīng	ʔjɐŋ	ʔɨaŋ	ʔraŋ	OCB *ʔrjaŋ

[T] Sin Sukchu SR ʔiŋ (平); MGZY 'ing (平) [ʔiŋ]; ONW ʔeŋ (ʔæŋ?)

ij	盎 j	àng	ʔâŋ^{C}	ʔɑŋ^{C}	ʔâŋh	[E] Khmer /ʔaaŋ/ 'jar'

3-21	**= K. 756**	**Mand.**	**MC**	**LHan**	**OCM**	
a	影	yǐng	ʔjɐŋ^B	ʔɨaŋ^B	ʔraŋʔ	

[D] Coastal Min *ʔɔŋ^B > Fuzhou ouŋ^{B1}, Amoy ŋ^{B1}; Jiàn'ou, Jiànyang ioŋ^{B1} (< *ʔioŋ^B)

3-22	**= K. 706**	**Mand.**	**MC**	**LHan**	**OCM**	
a	光	guāng	kwâŋ	kuɑŋ	kwâŋ	

[T] Sin Sukchu SR kwaŋ (平); MGZY gwang (平) [kwaŋ]; ONW kuɑŋ

f	洸	guāng	kwâŋ	kuɑŋ	kwâŋ	
g	絖	kuàng	k^{h}wâŋ^C	k^{h}uɑŋ^C	khwâŋh	
h	侊	guāng,	kwâŋ,	kuɑŋ,	kwâŋ,	
		gōng	kwɐŋ	kuaŋ	kwrâŋ	
i	觥	guāng	kwɐŋ	kuaŋ	kwrâŋ	= 3-23/707l 觵

[T] ONW kuëŋ <> [E] MY *krɔŋ^A 'horn'. MY <- TB (*kruŋ^A ~) *k-rwaŋ^A

j	恍	huǎng	xwâŋ^B	huɑŋ^B	hwâŋʔ	

3-23	**= K. 707**	**Mand.**	**MC**	**LHan**	**OCM**	
a	黃	huáng	ɣwâŋ	ɣuɑŋ	gwâŋ	

[T] Sin Sukchu SR ɣwaŋ (平); MGZY Xong (平) [ɣɔŋ]; ONW ɣuɑŋ
[E] WB waŋ^B 'brightly yellow'

ceg	璜潢簧	huáng	ɣwâŋ	ɣuɑŋ	gwâŋ	
-	蟥	huáng	ɣwâŋ	ɣuɑŋ	gwâŋ	
m	橫 crossw.	hóng, héng	ɣwɐŋ	ɣuaŋ	gwrâŋ	

= 3-14748h 衡 [T] ONW ɣuëŋ

	fully	guàng	kwâŋ^C	kuɑŋ^C	kwâŋh	
l	觵	guāng	kwɐŋ	kuaŋ	kwrâŋ	= 3-22/706i 觥
h	廣 wide	guǎng	kwâŋ^B	kuɑŋ^B	kwâŋʔ	

[T] Sin Sukchu SR kwaŋ (上); MGZY gwang (上) [kwaŋ]; ONW kuɑŋ

	廣 cohort	guàng	kwâŋ^C	kuɑŋ^C	kwâŋh	
s	獷	guǎng	kwɐŋ^B	kuaŋ^B	kwrâŋʔ	
nop	壙曠纊	kuàng	k^{h}wâŋ^C	k^{h}uɑŋ^C	khwâŋh	
r -	應懭	kuàng	k^{h}wâŋ$^{B/C}$,	k^{h}uɑŋ$^{B/C}$,	khwâŋʔ/h,	
			k^{h}âŋ^B	k^{h}ɑŋ^B	khâŋʔ	
t	擴	kuò	k^{h}wâk	k^{h}uɑk	khwâk	

3-24 **= K. 708** Wáng 王 3-26/739 may be phonetic, see Introd.

		Mand.	**MC**	**LHan**	**OCM**
ag	皇煌	huáng	ɣwâŋ	ɣuɑŋ	wâŋ

煌 [T] ONW ɣuɑŋ. MHan 敦煌 tuən-ɣuɑŋ Sogd. *ðruwan, Θρόανα (Dunhuang)

defh	徨偟湟篁	huáng	ɣwâŋ	ɣuɑŋ	wâŋ
ijkl	遑隍餭凰	huáng	ɣwâŋ	ɣuɑŋ	wâŋ
[o]	艎	huáng	ɣwâŋ	ɣuɑŋ	wâŋ
m	蝗	huáng,	ɣwâŋ,	ɣuɑŋ,	wâŋ
		hóng	ɣwɐŋ	ɣuaŋ	

[N] MC Div. II vocalism because the syllable is onomatopoetic, cf. EDOC §7.2.2.

n	喤	huáng,	ɣwɐŋ,	ɣuaŋ,	wâŋ,
		hōng	xwɐŋ	huaŋ	hwâŋ

[N] MC Div. II vocalism because the syllable is onomatopoetic, cf. EDOC §7.2.2.

3-25	**= K. 763**	**Mand.**	**MC**	**LHan**	**OCM**	
a	冏	jiǒng	kjwɐŋ^B	kyaŋ^B	kwraŋʔ	

3-26	**= K. 739**	**Mand.**	**MC**	**LHan**	**OCM**
a	王 king	wáng	jwaŋ	waŋ	waŋ
	[T] Sin Sukchu SR waŋ (平); MGZY xwang (平) [ɦwaŋ]; ONW uaŋ				
	王 govern	wàng	jwaŋ^C	waŋ^C	waŋh
ki	往 i	wǎng	jwaŋ^B	waŋ^B	waŋʔ
	[T] Sin S. SR waŋ (上); MGZY xwang (上) [ɦwaŋ]; ONW uaŋ <> [E] TB *waŋ 'to come'				
-	旺暀	wàng	jwaŋ^C	waŋ^C	waŋh
l	迋 to go	wàng	jwaŋ^C	waŋ^C	waŋh
	frighten	wǎng	jwaŋ^B	waŋ^B	waŋʔ
	迋 deceive	guǎng, kuàng	kjwaŋ^B, gjwaŋ^B	kyaŋ^B, gyaŋ^B	kwaŋʔ, gwaŋʔ
m	匡	kuāng	k^{h}jwaŋ	k^{h}yaŋ	khwaŋ
	[E] WB kwaŋ^B 'bend, curved'				
v-	筐恇	kuāng	k^{h}jwaŋ	k^{h}yaŋ	khwaŋ
u-	眶框	kuàng !	k^{h}jwaŋ	k^{h}yaŋ	khwaŋ
o	狂	kuáng	gjwaŋ	gyaŋ	gwaŋ
x	誑	kuáng !	kjwaŋ^C	kyaŋ^C	kwaŋh
y	俇	guàng	gjwaŋ^B	gyaŋ^B	gwaŋʔ
q	枉	wǎng	ʔjwaŋ^B	ʔyaŋ^B	ʔwaŋʔ
rt	汪尪	wāng	ʔwâŋ	ʔuaŋ	ʔwâŋ

3-27	**= K. 764**	**Mand.**	**MC**	**LHan**	**OCM**	
a	永	yǒng	jwɐŋ^B	waŋ^B	wraŋʔ	OCB *wrjaŋʔ
	[T] Sin Sukchu SR jujŋ (上), PR, LR juŋ; MGZY xÿung (上) [ɦjuŋ]; ONW ueŋ					
gi	咏詠	yǒng	jwɐŋ^C	waŋ^C	wraŋh	
j	泳	yǒng	jwɐŋ^C	waŋ^C	wraŋh	

3-28	**= K. 765**	**Mand.**	**MC**	**LHan**	**OCM**
a	兄	xiōng	xjwɐŋ	hyaŋ	hwraŋ
	[T] Sin Sukchu SR xjujŋ, xjuŋ (平), LR xjuŋ; MGZY (Hÿing >) hÿing (平) [xjiŋ]				
f	怳	huǎng	xjwaŋ^B	hyaŋ^B	hwaŋʔ
	'confused', also xwâŋ^B/hwaŋ^B				
g	況	kuàng !	xjwaŋ^C	hyaŋ^C	hwaŋh
	[T] Sin Sukchu SR xwaŋ (去), PR xyaŋ; MGZY (Hwyang >) hwyang (去) [xyaŋ]				
h	貺	kuàng !	xjwaŋ^C	hyaŋ^C	hwaŋh
i	軦	huàng	xjwaŋ^C	hyaŋ^C	hwaŋh

3-29	**= K. 699**	**Mand.**	**MC**	**LHan**	**OCM**
a	卬 high	áng	ŋâŋ	ŋaŋ	ŋâŋ
	look up	yǎng	ŋjaŋ^B	ŋɨaŋ^B	ŋaŋʔ
b	昂	áng	ŋâŋ	ŋaŋ	ŋâŋ
c	仰 look up	yǎng	ŋjaŋ^B	ŋɨaŋ^B	ŋaŋʔ
	[T] Sin S. SR ŋaŋ (上), PR jaŋ, ŋjaŋ, LR jaŋ; MGZY (ngÿang >) ngyang (上) [ŋjaŋ]; ONW ŋaŋ <> [D] PMin *ɔŋ^C > Amoy ŋ^{C1}, Fuzh auŋ^{C1}; G-Ruijin ȵiaŋ^C ȵiu^{A2} 仰牛 'to tend livestock'				

d	迎 meet	yíng	ŋjɐŋ	ŋɨaŋ	ŋraŋ

[T] ONW ŋeŋ <> [D] PMin *ŋiaŋ > Jiany ŋiaŋ^{A1}; Xiam col. ŋiã^{A2} / giã, lit. geŋ^{A2} / giŋ 'to receive ceremoniously' <> [E] ST *ŋraŋ: TB *ŋraŋ > WB ŋraŋ^{B} 'contradict, deny'

	迎 receive	yìng	ŋjɐŋ^{C}	ŋɨaŋ^{C}	ŋraŋh

3-30	**= K. 701**	**Mand.**	**MC**	**LHan**	**OCM**
a	宕	dàng	dâŋ^{C}	dɑŋ^{C}	dâŋh

3-31	**= K. 723**	**Mand.**	**MC**	**LHan**	**OCM**
aef	章彰樟	zhāng	tśjaŋ	tśɑŋ	taŋ
hj	璋鄣	zhāng	tśjaŋ	tśɑŋ	taŋ
k	障	zhàng	tśjaŋ(^{C})	tśɑŋ(^{C})	taŋ, taŋh
g	獐	zhāng,	tśjaŋ	tśɑŋ,	taŋ or
	Xiam.	kiũ^{A1}		kiɑŋ	kjaŋ ?

3-32 **= K. 725** Since TB cognates to words in this series have root initial *j-, some OC forms may also have had a *j in the initial.

		Mand.	**MC**	**LHan**	**OCM**	
a	尚	shàng	źjaŋ^{C}	dźɑŋ^{C}	daŋh, probably = djaŋh	

[T] Sin Sukchu SR zjaŋ (去); MGZY zhang (去) [zaŋ]; MTang źaŋ, ONW dźaŋ.
[E] ST *jaŋ: WT yaŋ 'again, still, once more'

d	裳	cháng	źjaŋ	dźɑŋ	daŋ = djaŋ	

[D] PMin dźiɔŋ <> [E] WT g-yaŋ 'animal skin clothing'

e	常	cháng	źjaŋ	dźɑŋ	daŋ = djaŋ	
fi	嘗 i	cháng	źjaŋ	dźɑŋ	daŋ = djaŋ	

[T] Sin Sukchu SR dzjaŋ (平); MGZY zhang (平) [zaŋ]; MTang źaŋ
[D] PMin *d̥źiɔŋ points to earlier *m-d(j)aŋ
[E] TB *m-yaŋ 'taste', Chepang yaŋ-sā 'to taste', WT myoŋ-ba, myaŋs / myoŋ 'to taste'

v	鱨	cháng	źjaŋ	dźɑŋ	daŋ = djaŋ	
n	賞	shǎng	śjaŋ^{B}	śaŋ^{B}	hjaŋʔ	[T] ONW śaŋ
y	償	cháng, shàng	źjaŋ(^{C})	dźɑŋ(^{C})	daŋ(h)	'indemnify, pay back'
j	掌	zhǎng	tśjaŋ^{B}	tśɑŋ^{B}	taŋʔ	'palm of hand'
l	惝	chǎng	tśʰjaŋ^{B}	tśʰɑŋ^{B}	thaŋʔ	
mx-	敞𢢍憋	chǎng	tśʰjaŋ^{B}	tśʰɑŋ^{B}	thaŋʔ	
k	倘	chǎng,	tśʰjaŋ^{B},	tśʰɑŋ^{B},	thaŋʔ,	'stop suddenly'
		tǎng	tʰâŋ(^{B})	tʰɑŋ(^{B})	thâŋ(ʔ)	
q	當 match	dāng	tâŋ	tɑŋ	tâŋ	

[T] Sin Sukchu SR taŋ (平); MGZY dang (平) [taŋ]; ONW tɑŋ

	當 ought	dàng	tâŋ^{C}	tɑŋ^{C}	tâŋh	
r	黨	dǎng	tâŋ^{B}	tɑŋ^{B}	tâŋʔ	
za'b'c'	儻擋曭矘	tǎng	tʰâŋ^{B}	tʰɑŋ^{B}	thâŋʔ	
std'	堂棠螳	táng	dâŋ	dɑŋ	dâŋ	
e'	鏜	tāng	tʰâŋ	tʰɑŋ	thâŋ	
f'	瞠	chēng	ṭʰɐŋ	ṭʰaŋ	thrâŋ	⋈ 4-30/976a'

'Look straight at' [Zhuang].

u	定	chéng	ḍɐŋ	ḍaŋ	drâŋ	= 3-35/721n
-	撐	chéng	ḍɐŋ	ḍaŋ	[T] 撐犁 ḍaŋ-li Xiongnu tengri 'sky'	

3-33	**= K. 726**	**Mand.**	**MC**	**LHan**	**OCM**	
a	上 rise	shàng	źjaŋ^{B}	dźɑŋ^{B}	daŋʔ, probably = djaŋʔ	
	[T] Sin S. SR ʐjaŋ (上去); MGZY zhang (上去) [ʐaŋ]; MTang źaŋ, ONW dźaŋ					
	[D] PMin *d̥žioŋ^{B} < PCH *m-daŋʔ or rather *m-jaŋʔ?					
	[E] WT yaŋ as in yaŋ-rtse 'highest point, summit' ≭ ya 'above, up'					
	上 up	shàng	źjaŋ^{C}	dźɑŋ^{C}	daŋh = djaŋh	[D] PMin *dziɔŋ^{C}

3-34	**= K. 724**	**Mand.**	**MC**	**LHan**	**OCM**	
aefg	昌猖菖閶	chāng	tśʰjaŋ	tśʰɑŋ	k-hlaŋ or thaŋ ?	[T] ONW tśʰaŋ
cd	倡唱	chàng	tśʰjaŋ^{C}	tśʰɑŋ^{C}	k-hlaŋh	
	[D] PMin *tšhiɔŋ <> [E] WB ə-kʰraŋ^{B} 'a song'					

3-35	**= K. 721**	**Mand.**	**MC**	**LHan**	**OCM**	
a	長 grow	zhǎng	ṭjaŋ^{B}	ṭiɑŋ^{B}	traŋʔ	OCB *trjaŋʔ
	[T] Sin Sukchu SR tʂjaŋ (上); MGZY jang (上) [tʂaŋ]					
	長 long	cháng	ḍjaŋ	ḍiɑŋ	draŋ	OCB *ɦtrjaŋ
	[T] MTang ḍaŋ, ONW daŋ, BTD Skt. -ḍiyānika					
	長 length	zhàng	ḍjaŋ^{C}	ḍiɑŋ^{C}	draŋh	
h	張 stretch	zhāng	ṭjaŋ	ṭiɑŋ	traŋ	
	[E] WT draŋ(s) 'draw, drag, pull, draw tight' (a rope), LB *raŋ 'draw, pull, drag'					
	張 swell	zhàng	ṭjaŋ^{C}	ṭiɑŋ^{C}	traŋh	
g	帳	zhàng	ṭjaŋ^{C}	ṭiɑŋ^{C}	traŋh	
ij	粻餦	zhāng	ṭjaŋ	ṭiɑŋ	traŋ	
lm	悵韔	chàng	ṭʰjaŋ^{C}	ṭʰiɑŋ^{C}	thraŋh	
f	萇	cháng	ḍjaŋ	ḍiɑŋ	draŋ	
k	倀	chāng,	ṭʰjaŋ,	ṭʰiɑŋ,	thraŋ,	
		chèng	ṭʰɐŋ^{C}	ṭʰaŋ^{C}	thrâŋh	
n	棖	chéng	ḍɐŋ	ḍaŋ	drâŋ	= 3-32/725n
	[E] Tai: S. soŋ^{A2} [WrSiam drŋ]; or TB-Lepcha tă-raŋ 'upright beam in house'					

3-36	**= K. 722**	**Mand.**	**MC**	**LHan**	**OCM**
a	丈	zhàng	ḍjaŋ^{B}	ḍiɑŋ^{B}	draŋʔ
	[T] Sin Sukchu SR dʐjaŋ (上); MGZY cang (上) [dʐaŋ]; MTang ḍaŋ, ONW daŋ				
b	杖 stick	zhàng	ḍjaŋ^{B}	ḍiɑŋ^{B}	draŋʔ
	lean on	zhàng	ḍjaŋ^{C}	ḍiɑŋ^{C}	draŋh

3-37	**= K. 719**	**Mand.**	**MC**	**LHan**	**OCM**
a	鬯	chàng	ṭʰjaŋ^{C}	ṭʰiɑŋ^{C}	thraŋh
	[E] WT čʰaŋ 'fermented liquor'				

3-38 **= K. 720** This phonetic 昜 originally wrote OC l-initial words, the series 羊 3-39/732 wrote OC j-initial words; but after the initials had merged, one finds crossovers.

		Mand.	**MC**	**LHan**	**OCM**	
aeh	昜陽暘	yáng	jiaŋ	jɑŋ	laŋ	[E] WB laŋ^{B} 'be bright'
jp	揚颺	yáng	jiaŋ	jɑŋ	laŋ	[E] WT laŋ-ba 'to rise, arise'
q	楊	yáng	jiaŋ	jɑŋ	laŋ	[E] WT lčaŋ < *lhjaŋ 'willow'
st	瘍鍚	yáng	jiaŋ	jɑŋ	laŋ	

i	煬 melt	yáng	jiaŋ	jɑŋ	laŋ	'melt metal'
	roast	yàng	jiaŋ^{C}	jɑŋ^{C}	laŋh	
z	湯 flowing	shāng	śjaŋ	śɑŋ	lhaŋ	
	湯 hot liq.	tāng	tʰâŋ	tʰɑŋ	lhâŋ	
j'	傷	shāng	śjaŋ	śɑŋ	lhaŋ	[E] Tai: S. laaŋ^{A2} 'destroy'
k'l'	殤觴	shāng	śjaŋ	śɑŋ	lhaŋ	
h'g'	禓裼	shāng	śjaŋ	śɑŋ	lhaŋ	
i'	⿰矢昜	shāng,	śjaŋ,	śɑŋ,	lhaŋ,	
		qiāng	tsʰjaŋ	tsʰiɑŋ	s-lhaŋ	

[E] Tai: S. sa-lɛɛŋ 'harmful'

x	場	cháng	ḍjaŋ	ḍiɑŋ	draŋ < r-laŋ
y	腸	cháng	ḍjaŋ	ḍiɑŋ	draŋ < r-laŋ

[D] PMin *tɔŋ^{A2}. <> [E] WT loŋ-ka 'intestines, entrails, guts', Chepang yoŋ-kliʔ ~ lyoŋ-ki. <> MY: *gl-: PY klaaŋ^{2} 'intestines' MTang ḍaŋ, ONW daŋ

uv	畼暢	chàng	ṭʰjaŋ^{C}	ṭʰiɑŋ^{C}	thraŋh (or t-lhaŋh, k-hraŋh ?)
c'	餳	táng	dâŋ	dɑŋ	—
n'	盪 eliminate	dàng	dâŋ^{B}	dɑŋ^{B}	lâŋʔ
	push	tàng	tʰâŋ^{C}	tʰɑŋ^{C}	lhâŋh
m'o'	璗簜	dàng	dâŋ^{B}	dɑŋ^{B}	lâŋʔ
p'	蕩 immense	dàng	dâŋ^{B}	dɑŋ^{B}	lâŋʔ
	purify	dàng	dâŋ^{C}	dɑŋ^{C}	lâŋh
e'	愓 carefree	dàng	dâŋ^{B}	dɑŋ^{B}	lâŋʔ
	directly	shāng	śjaŋ	śɑŋ	lhaŋ
f'	碭	dàng	dâŋ^{C}	dɑŋ^{C}	lâŋh
-	逿	dàng	dâŋ^{C}	dɑŋ^{C}	—

3-39 = K. 732 This phonetic 羊 originally wrote OC j-initial words, the series 昜 3-38/720 wrote OC l-initial words; but after the initials had merged, one finds crossovers.

		Mand.	MC	LHan	OCM	
a	羊 goat	yáng	jiaŋ	jɑŋ	jaŋ	

[T] Sin Sukchu SR jaŋ (平); MGZY yang (平) [jaŋ]; ONW iaŋ <> [E] Lushai -jaaʔ 'a wild goat', JP ja^{55} 'blue sheep' <> ? PTai *l-: S. liaŋ^{A2} -pʰaa^{A1} 'goat, antelope'.

	羊 a fly	yáng	jiaŋ	jɑŋ	jaŋ	

[D] PMin *ziɔŋ^{A2} <> [E] TB *yaŋ^{A} 'a fly'

ef	佯徉	yáng	jiaŋ	jɑŋ	jaŋ	
h	洋	yáng	jiaŋ	jɑŋ	jaŋ	[E] WT yaŋs- 'wide, broad'
i	痒 disease	yáng,	jiaŋ,	jɑŋ,	jaŋ,	
		xiáng	zjaŋ	ziɑŋ	s-jaŋ	
	ulcer	yǎng	jiaŋ^{B}	jiɑŋ^{B}	- (Zhouli)	~ 3-38/720s 瘍 (Zuo)
g	恙	yàng	jiaŋ^{C}	jɑŋ^{C}	jaŋh	
j	養 nourish	yǎng	jiaŋ^{B}	jɑŋ^{B}	jaŋʔ	? S. liaŋ^{C2} 'feed, nourish'
	養 support	yàng	jiaŋ^{C}	jɑŋ^{C}	jaŋh	
r	癢 itch	yǎng	jiaŋ^{B}	jɑŋ^{B}	jaŋʔ	

[D] PMin *dzioŋ^{B} < *N- <> [E] WT g-ya-ba 'to itch'

ks-	羕漾	yàng	jiaŋ^{C}	jɑŋ^{C}	jaŋh
-	樣	yàng	jiaŋ^{C}	jɑŋ^{C}	jaŋh

[T] Sin Sukchu SR jaŋ (去); MGZY yang (去) [jaŋ]; ONW iaŋ

mnp	庠祥翔	xiáng	zjaŋ	ziɑŋ	s-jaŋ	
q	詳	xiáng	zjaŋ	ziɑŋ	s-jaŋ	

[T] LMing c'iâm [ts'iaŋ]; Sin SR zjaŋ (平), LR zjaŋ; MGZY (zȳang >) zyang (平) [zjaŋ]

3-40	**= K. 734**	**Mand.**	**MC**	**LHan**	**OCM**
af	商賓	shāng	śjaŋ	śɑŋ	lhaŋ

The graph is used to write the name of a place; it is therefore the drawing of some building.

3-41	**= K. 728**	**Mand.**	**MC**	**LHan**	**OCM**	
a	象	xiàng	zjaŋ^B	ziɑŋ^B	s-jaŋʔ	OCB *zaŋʔ

[T] Sin Sukchu SR zjaŋ (上); MGZY (zȳang >) zyang (上) [zjaŋ]; MTang ziaŋ < ONW zaŋ.
[D] M-Xiamen col. tsʰiũ^{C2}, lit. sioŋ^{C2} <> [E] PTai *ǰaŋ^C, Saek saaŋ^{C2} < z- 'elephant'; MK-PMonic *ciiŋ <> TB-LB *tsaŋ 'elephant' > WB chaŋ^A

ef	像橡	xiàng	zjaŋ^B	ziɑŋ^B	s-jaŋʔ

3-42	**= K. 730**	**Mand.**	**MC**	**LHan**	**OCM**	
a	襄	xiāng	sjaŋ	siɑŋ	snaŋ	
b	纕	xiāng	sjaŋ	siɑŋ	snaŋ	
fg	瀼穰	ráng	ńźjaŋ	ńɑŋ	naŋ	瀼 [E] WB hnaŋ^B 'dew, fog'
h	穰	ráng	ńźjaŋ(^{B})	ńɑŋ(^{B})	naŋ, naŋʔ	
e	攘 steal	ráng	ńźjaŋ	ńɑŋ	naŋ	
	oppose	rǎng	ńźjaŋ^B	ńɑŋ^B	naŋʔ	
d	壤	rǎng	ńźjaŋ^B	ńɑŋ^B	naŋʔ	

[E] S. daaŋ^{B1} < *ʔd- (< *ʔn- ?) 'potash, lye', Li Ngam ʔnăŋ^{B1}

i	讓	ràng	ńźjaŋ^C	ńɑŋ^C	naŋh	[E] WT gnaŋ 'to concede'
j	釀	ràng	ńźjaŋ^C	ńɑŋ^C	naŋh	
c	饟	xiǎng	śjaŋ$^{A/B/C}$	śɑŋ$^{B/C}$	nhaŋʔ, nhaŋh	~ 3-18/715e

A late graph? See also 3-17/716. [T] ONW śaŋ

-	孃	niáng	ṇjaŋ	—	—	= 娘

[T] Sin S. SR njaŋ (平); MGZY ñang (平) [ṇaŋ]; ONW naŋ <> [E] Tai: S. naaŋ^{A2} < *n- 'lady'

l	囊	náng	nâŋ	nɑŋ	nâŋ	ONW nɑŋ
k	曩	nǎng	nâŋ^B	nɑŋ^B	nâŋʔ	[E] WT gna' 'ancient'

3-43	**= K. 735**	**Mand.**	**MC**	**LHan**	**OCM**	
a	良 good	liáng	ljaŋ	liɑŋ	raŋ	cf. 9-19/823a
e	粮	liáng	ljaŋ	liɑŋ	raŋ	= 3-45/737d
f	俍	liáng,	ljaŋ,	liɑŋ,	raŋ,	
		làng	lâŋ^C	lɑŋ^C	râŋh	
il	桹狼	láng	lâŋ	lɑŋ	râŋ	
k	浪 river	láng	lâŋ	lɑŋ	râŋ	
	浪 reckless	làng	lâŋ^C	lɑŋ^C	râŋh	
n	琅 tinkle	láng	lâŋ	lɑŋ	râŋ	
	licentious	làng	lâŋ^C	lɑŋ^C	râŋh	
oqt	稂蜋廊	láng	lâŋ	lɑŋ	râŋ	
p	筤	láng	lâŋ	lɑŋ	râŋ	

[E] Tai: Po'ai laaŋ^{A2} < *nl/raŋ 'bamboo shoot'

r	郎	láng	lâŋ	lɑŋ	râŋ

[T] Sin Sukchu SR laŋ (平); MGZY lang (平) [laŋ]; ONW lɑŋ

s	閬	láng, làng	lâŋ$^{(C)}$	lɑŋ$^{(C)}$	râŋ, râŋh	
g	埌	làng	lâŋ^{C}	lɑŋ^{C}	râŋh	
h	朗	lǎng	lâŋ^{B}	lɑŋ^{B}	râŋʔ	

3-44	**= K. 736**	**Mand.**	**MC**	**LHan**	**OCM**
a	兩 two	liǎng	ljaŋ^{B}	liɑŋ^{B}	raŋʔ

[T] Sin Sukchu SR ljaŋ (上); MGZY (lÿang >) lyang (上) [ljaŋ]; MTang liaŋ < laŋ, ONW laŋ

[D] PMin *l̥ɔŋ$^{B/C}$ 'two', liɔŋ^{B} 'a tael' > NMin Jiànyáng sɔŋ^{C1} 'two', liɔŋ^{B1} 'tael'

	兩 arrange	liǎng	ljaŋ$^{B/C}$	liɑŋ$^{B/C}$	raŋʔ/h
	兩 chariot	liàng	ljaŋ^{C}	liɑŋ^{C}	raŋh
c	輛	liàng	ljaŋ^{C}	liɑŋ^{C}	raŋh
d-	蜽魎	liǎng	ljaŋ^{B}	liɑŋ^{B}	raŋʔ

3-45	**= K. 737**	**Mand.**	**MC**	**LHan**	**OCM**	
a	量 to meas.	liáng	ljaŋ	liɑŋ	raŋ	

[D] PMin *liɔŋ 'measure' > Fuzh lioŋ^{A2} <> [E] WT 'graŋ-ba 'to count'

	量 a measure	liàng	ljaŋ^{C}	liɑŋ^{C}	raŋh	[E] WT graŋs 'number'
d	糧	liáng	ljaŋ	liɑŋ	raŋ	= 3-43/735e

3-46	**= K. 738**	**Mand.**	**MC**	**LHan**	**OCM**
a	梁	liáng	ljaŋ	liɑŋ	raŋ

[D] PMin *liɔŋ 'beam' > Amoy niũ^{A2}, Fuzh lioŋ^{A2}

b	粱	liáng	ljaŋ	liɑŋ	raŋ

3-47	**= K. 702**	**Mand.**	**MC**	**LHan**	**OCM**	
a	葬	zàng	tsâŋ^{C}	tsɑŋ^{C}	tsâŋh	ONW tsɑŋ

3-48	**= K. 703**	**Mand.**	**MC**	**LHan**	**OCM**	
a	倉	cāng	ts^{h}âŋ	ts^{h}ɑŋ	tshâŋ < k-sâŋ	OCB *tshaŋ

[T] Sin Sukchu SR ts'aŋ (平); MGZY tshang (平) [ts'aŋ]. <> [E] WT gsaŋ-ba 'conceal'

d	滄	cāng	ts^{h}âŋ	ts^{h}ɑŋ	tshâŋ
e	蒼	cāng	ts^{h}âŋ	ts^{h}ɑŋ	tshâŋ < k-sâŋ

[E] ? ST *saŋ 'live, green': TB-Garo t^{h}aŋ < *saŋ 'live' ⋡ gat^{h}aŋ *k-saŋ 'green'

f	鶬 crane	cāng	ts^{h}âŋ	ts^{h}ɑŋ	tshâŋ
	tinkle	qiāng	ts^{h}jaŋ	ts^{h}iɑŋ	tshaŋ
hijk	瑲槍蹌牄	qiāng	ts^{h}jaŋ	ts^{h}iɑŋ	tshaŋ
g	搶 to rush	qiǎng	ts^{h}jaŋ$^{(B)}$	ts^{h}iɑŋ$^{(B)}$	tshaŋ, tshaŋʔ
	beat	chuǎng	tṣ^{h}jaŋ^{B}	tṣ^{h}ɑŋ^{B}	tshraŋʔ
l	創 wound	chuāng	tṣ^{h}jaŋ	tṣ^{h}ɑŋ	tshraŋ
	begin	chuàng	tṣ^{h}jaŋ^{C}	tṣ^{h}ɑŋ^{C}	tshraŋh
m	愴	chuàng	tṣ^{h}jaŋ^{C}	tṣ^{h}ɑŋ^{C}	tshraŋh
n	瘡	chuāng	tṣ^{h}jaŋ	tṣ^{h}ɑŋ	tshraŋ
c	滄	chuàng,	tṣ^{h}jaŋ^{C},	tṣ^{h}ɑŋ^{C},	tshraŋh,
		cāng	ts^{h}âŋ	ts^{h}ɑŋ	tshâŋ

3-49	**= K. 727**	**Mand.**	**MC**	**LHan**	**OCM**	
ad	爿斨	qiāng	tsʰjaŋ	tsʰiɑŋ	tshaŋ	
f	將 bring	jiāng	tsjaŋ	tsiɑŋ	tsaŋ	
	[E] WT 'čʰaŋ-ba 'to hold, keep'					
	將 intend	jiāng	tsjaŋ	tsiɑŋ	tsaŋ	
	[T] Sin Sukchu SR tsjaŋ (平); MGZY (dzÿang >) dzyang (平) [tsjaŋ]; MTang tsiaŋ < tsaŋ, ONW tsaŋ <> [E] AA: OKhmer caṅ /cɔŋ/, Khmer ca'ṅa /cɑŋ/ 'to want, desire, hope for, be willing to, about to, on the point of'					
	將 to lead	jiàng	tsjaŋ^{C}	tsiɑŋ^{C}	tsaŋh	
	將 beg	qiāng	tsʰjaŋ	tsʰiɑŋ	tshaŋ	
z	鏘	qiāng	tsʰjaŋ	tsʰiɑŋ	tshaŋ	
v	漿	jiāng	tsjaŋ	tsiɑŋ	tsaŋ	
x	蔣 a plant	jiǎng !	tsjaŋ	tsiɑŋ	tsaŋ	
	a state	jiǎng	tsjaŋ^{B}	tsiɑŋ^{B}	tsaŋʔ	name of a state
u	獎	jiǎng	tsjaŋ^{B}	tsiɑŋ^{B}	tsaŋʔ	
y	醬	jiàng	tsjaŋ^{C}	tsiɑŋ^{C}	tsaŋh	
a'	鬺	shāng	śjaŋ	śɑŋ	lhaŋ ? or hjaŋ ?	
g	戕	qiāng !	dzjaŋ	dziɑŋ	dzaŋ	
jlmj'	牆墻廧嬙	qiáng	dzjaŋ	dziɑŋ	dzaŋ	
--	檣薔	qiáng	dzjaŋ	dziɑŋ	dzaŋ	
oq	妝莊	zhuāng	tsjaŋ	tṣɑŋ	tsraŋ	
n	壯	zhuàng	tsjaŋ^{C}	tṣɑŋ^{C}	tsraŋh	
i'	裝	zhuāng	tsjaŋ(^{C})	tṣɑŋ(^{C})	tsraŋ, tsraŋh	
r	牀床 bed	chuáng	dẓjaŋ	dẓɑŋ	dzraŋ	
	[T] ONW dẓaŋ (?) <> [D] PMin *dzhɔŋ					
s	狀	zhuàng	dẓjaŋ^{C}	dẓɑŋ^{C}	dzraŋh	
	[T] Sin Sukchu SR dẓaŋ (去), PR dẓwaŋ; MGZY cʰang (去) [dẓAŋ]; ONW dẓaŋ (?)					
	[E] Tai: S. raaŋ^{B2} 'form, shape' ← Khmer rāṅa /rííəŋ/ 'body build, form, figure, shape'					
t	牂[牜羊]	zāng	tsâŋ	tsɑŋ	tsâŋ	
f'	臧	zāng	tsâŋ	tsɑŋ	tsâŋ	[E] WT bzaŋ-po 'good'
g'	藏 to store	cáng	dzâŋ	dzɑŋ	dzâŋ	OCB *fitsʰaŋ
	[T] Sin Sukchu S dzaŋ (平); MGZY tsang (平) [dzaŋ]; ONW dzɑŋ					
	藏 a store	zàng	dzâŋ^{C}	dzɑŋ^{C}	dzâŋh	
h'	贓	zāng	tsâŋ	tsɑŋ	tsâŋ	

3-50	**= K. 727mj'**	**Mand.**	**MC**	**LHan**	**OCM**
mj...	廧嬙檣薔	qiáng	dzjaŋ	dziɑŋ	dzaŋ
	= 727j... w/o phonet. 爿 3-49, q.v.				

3-51		**Mand.**	**MC**	**LHan**	**OCM**	
-	床 bed	chuáng	dẓjaŋ	dẓɑŋ	dzraŋ	= 3-49/727r 牀

3-52	**= K. 729**	**Mand.**	**MC**	**LHan**	**OCM**
a	匠	jiàng	dzjaŋ^{C}	dziɑŋ^{C}	dzaŋh
	See Intro. 9.2.8. [T] Sin Sukchu SR dzjaŋ (去); MGZY (tsÿang >) tsyang (去) [dzjaŋ] [E] Khmer /caŋ/ 'to dress (wood, stone), rough out, trim...'				

3-53	= K. 704	Mand.	MC	LHan	OCM	
a	桑	sāng	sâŋ	sɑŋ	sâŋ	
	[T] ONW sɑŋ. MHan 桑門 sɑŋ-mən śramaṇa					
b	顙	sǎng	sâŋ^{B}	sɑŋ^{B}	sâŋʔ	

3-54	= K. 705	Mand.	MC	LHan	OCM	
a	喪 burial	sāng	sâŋ	sɑŋ	sâŋ	⅏ 3-47/702 葬
	[T] Sin Sukchu SR saŋ (平); MGZY sang (平) [saŋ] <> [E] WB saŋ- 'grave'					
	喪 destroy	sàng	sâŋ^{C}	sɑŋ^{C}	sâŋh = smâŋh	OCB *smaŋs
	⅏ ? 3-65/742 亡. Some graphic forms incorporate the element wáng 亡 *maŋ 'lose, ruin', but its role may be semantic and only apply to the meaning 'destroy'.					

3-55	= K. 731	Mand.	MC	LHan	OCM
a	相 look at	xiàng	sjaŋ^{C}	siɑŋ^{C}	saŋh
	相 appear	xiàng	sjaŋ(^{C})	siɑŋ(^{C})	saŋ, saŋh
	相 mutually	xiāng	sjaŋ	siɑŋ	saŋ
	[T]Sin Sukchu SR sjaŋ (平); MGZY (sȳang >) syang (平) [sjaŋ]; MTang siaŋ < saŋ, ONW saŋ				
d	想	xiǎng	sjaŋ^{B}	siɑŋ^{B}	saŋʔ
ef	湘箱	xiāng	sjaŋ	siɑŋ	saŋ
	霜	shuāng	ṣjaŋ	ṣɑŋ	sraŋ
	[T] ONW ṣaŋ; MHan 貴霜 Kuṣāṇa <> [D] W-Wenzh ɕyɔ$^{44/32}$-peŋ$^{44/33}$ 'ice', PMin *šɔŋ: Xiamen sŋ^{55}, Chaozhou sɯŋ^{33}				
h	孀	shuāng	ṣjaŋ	ṣɑŋ	sraŋ

3-56	= K. 733	Mand.	MC	LHan	OCM
a	爽 go astray	shuǎng	ṣjaŋ^{B}	ṣɑŋ^{B}	sraŋʔ
	爽 bright	shuǎng	ṣjaŋ^{B}	ṣɑŋ^{B}	sraŋʔ

3-57	= K. 740	Mand.	MC	LHan	OCM	
a	方 square	fāng	pjwaŋ	puɑŋ	paŋ	
	[T] Sin Sukchu SR faŋ (平); MGZY Hwang (平) [faŋ]; MTang pfuaŋ, ONW puaŋ < paŋ					
	方 begin	fāng	pjwaŋ	puɑŋ	paŋ	[E] NNaga *praŋ 'begin'
	方 method	fāng	pjwaŋ	puɑŋ	paŋ	
	[E] WT byaŋ- 'skill, practice'					
	方 tossed	páng	bwâŋ	bɑŋ	bâŋ	
l	牥	fāng	pjwaŋ	puɑŋ	paŋ	
o	邡	fāng	pjwaŋ	puɑŋ	paŋ	
k	枋 a tree	fāng	pjwaŋ	puɑŋ	paŋ	
	a handle	bìng	pjɐŋ^{C}	piaŋ^{C}	praŋh	= 3-61 柄
g	舫	fǎng	pjwaŋ^{C}, pwâŋ^{C}	puɑŋ^{C}, pɑŋ^{C}	paŋh	
i	放 let go	fàng	pjwaŋ^{C}	puɑŋ^{C}	paŋh	
	[T] Sin Sukchu SR faŋ (去); MGZY Hwang (去) [faŋ]; MTang pfhuaŋ (?), ONW pʰuaŋ < pʰaŋ					
	[E] WT 'pʰaŋs 'to fling, throw'					
	放 imitate	fǎng	pjwaŋ^{B}	puɑŋ^{B}	paŋʔ	
j	昉	fǎng	pjwaŋ^{B}	puɑŋ^{B}	paŋʔ	
mn	瓬旊	fǎng	pjwaŋ^{B}	puɑŋ^{B}	paŋʔ	
q	妨	fáng	pʰjwaŋ	pʰuɑŋ	phaŋ	

s	芳	fāng	p^hjwaŋ	p^huɑŋ	phaŋ	
uv	髣仿	fǎng	p^hjwaŋ^B	p^huɑŋ^B	phaŋʔ	
r	紡	fǎng	p^hjwaŋ^B	p^huɑŋ^B	phaŋʔ	
	[T] MTang pfhuaŋ (?), ONW p^huaŋ < p^haŋ <> [E] WT p^haŋ 'spindle'					
t	訪	fǎng	p^hjwaŋ^C	p^huɑŋ^C	phaŋh	⋈ 9-27/817a pìn 聘
xza'	坊防 a'	fáng	bjwaŋ	buɑŋ	baŋ	
y	房	fáng	bjwaŋ	buɑŋ	baŋ	
	[T] Sin Sukchu SR vaŋ (平); MGZY h(w)ang (平) [vaŋ]; ONW buaŋ < baŋ					
	[E] WT baŋ-ba 'storeroom'					
b'	魴	fáng	bjwaŋ	buɑŋ	baŋ	
e'	彷	páng	bwâŋ	bɑŋ	bâŋ	
j'	祊	bēng	pɐŋ	paŋ	prâŋ	= 3-58/750e
f'	旁 side	páng	bwâŋ	bɑŋ	bâŋ	
	[E] Lushai paŋ^L 'side of body'					
	bang!	bēng	pɐŋ	paŋ	pâŋ !	
n'	騯 bang!	páng,	bwâŋ,	bɑŋ,	bâŋ	
		péng	bɐŋ	baŋ		
m'	傍	páng	bwâŋ(C)	bɑŋ(C)	bâŋ, bâŋh	
o'	徬	bàng	bwâŋ^C	bɑŋ^C	bâŋh	
-	艕	bàng	pwâŋ^C	pɑŋ^C	pâŋh	
	[E] AN *qaBaŋ 'two boats lashed together'					
k'	謗	bàng	pwâŋ^C	pɑŋ^C	pâŋh	
l'd'c'	滂汸雱	páng !	p^hwâŋ	p^hɑŋ	phâŋ	
p'	榜	bàng !	pɐŋ^C	paŋ^C	prâŋh	[E] WT spaŋ 'board, plank'
r'	蒡	bēng,	pɐŋ,	paŋ,	prâŋ,	
		páng	bwâŋ	bɑŋ	bâŋ	

3-58	**= K. 741**	**Mand.**	**MC**	**LHan**	**OCM**	
a	匚匚	fāng	pjwaŋ	puɑŋ	paŋ	

3-59	**= K. 750**	**Mand.**	**MC**	**LHan**	**OCM**	
a	彭 Pl.N.	péng	bɐŋ	baŋ	brâŋ	
	forceful	páng	bwâŋ	bɑŋ	bâŋ	
	bang!	pāng	pwâŋ	pɑŋ	pâŋ	
e	髣	bēng	pɐŋ	paŋ	prâŋ	= 3-57/740j'

3-60	**= K. 751**	**Mand.**	**MC**	**LHan**	**OCM**
a	亨	pēng	p^hɐŋ	p^haŋ	phrâŋ

3-61	**= K. 757**	**Mand.**	**MC**	**LHan**	**OCM**	
a	丙	bǐng	pjɐŋ^B	pɨaŋ^B	praŋʔ	
g	怲	bǐng	pjɐŋ$^{B/C}$	pɨaŋ$^{B/C}$	praŋʔ/h	OCB *prjaŋs
h	柄	bìng	pjɐŋ^C	pɨaŋ^C	praŋh	[D] PMin *paŋ^C
i-j	炳昺邴	bǐng	pjɐŋ^B	pɨaŋ^B	praŋʔ	
k	病	bìng	bjɐŋ^C	bɨaŋ^C	braŋh	
	[T] ONW beŋ <> [D] PMin *baŋ^C > Fuzh paŋ^{C2}, Amoy pĩ^{C2}					

3-62	**= K. 758**	**Mand.**	**MC**	**LHan**	**OCM**	
a	秉	bǐng	pjɐŋ^{B}	pɨaŋ^{B}	praŋʔ	[T] ONW peŋ
d	棅	bìng	pjɐŋ^{C}	pɨaŋ^{C}	praŋh	

3-63	**= K. 759**	**Mand.**	**MC**	**LHan**	**OCM**
a	兵	bīng	pjɐŋ	pɨaŋ	praŋ
	[T] Sin Sukchu SR piŋ (平); MGZY bing (平) [piŋ]; ONW peŋ				

3-64	**= K. 709**	**Mand.**	**MC**	**LHan**	**OCM**
-a	茻莽[1]	mǎng	mwâŋ^{B}	maŋ^{B}	mâŋʔ
	SW 483. [E] TB-Chep. maŋʔ 'grass'				
	莽[2]	mò	muo^{B}	mɑ^{B}	mâʔ < mlaʔ ?
	[E] TB *m-lyak 'grass'				
-	蟒	mǎng	mwâŋ^{B}	mɑŋ^{B}	mâŋʔ

3-65	**= K. 742**	**Mand.**	**MC**	**LHan**	**OCM**	
a	亡	wáng	mjwaŋ	muɑŋ	maŋ	
	[T] Sin S. SR, LR vaŋ (平); MGZY wang (平) [vaŋ] <> [E] Lushai maŋ^{F} 'to die, die out'					
i	忘	wàng	mjwaŋ$^{(C)}$	muɑŋ$^{(C)}$	maŋ (!)	
	[T] MTang mvuaŋ, ONW muaŋ					
la'	罔[1]網 net	wǎng	mjwaŋ^{B}	muɑŋ^{B}	maŋʔ	[E] PTai *mɯaŋ^{A2} 'fishnet'
	罔[2] dejected	wǎng	mjwaŋ^{B}	muɑŋ^{B}	maŋʔ	
	[E] S. pʰraaŋ^{A2} < *br- 'deceive'					
b'	惘	wǎng	mjwaŋ^{B}	muɑŋ^{B}	maŋʔ	
k	芒 sharp	máng	mwâŋ, mjwaŋ	mɑŋ, muɑŋ	mâŋ, maŋ	
	芒 great	máng	mwâŋ,	mɑŋ,	mâŋ	
	芒 confused	máng	mwâŋ, xwâŋ$^{(B)}$	mɑŋ, huɑŋ$^{(B)}$	mâŋ, hmâŋ, hmâŋʔ	
c'	鋩	máng !	mjwaŋ	muɑŋ	maŋ	
d'	茫	máng	mwâŋ	mɑŋ	mâŋ	
g	妄	wàng	mjwaŋ^{C}	muɑŋ^{C}	maŋh	
m	望	wàng	mjwaŋ$^{A/C}$	muɑŋ$^{A/C}$	maŋ^{A}	= 3-66/743
	[T] Sin Sukchu SR, LR vaŋ (去); MGZY wang (去) [vaŋ]; MTang mvuaŋ , ONW muaŋ < maŋ					
	[E] TB *mraŋ 'to see'					
op	忙汒	máng	mwâŋ	mɑŋ	mâŋ	
q	盲	máng	mɐŋ	maŋ	mrâŋ	[T] ONW mëŋ
-st	虻蝱蝱	méng	mɐŋ	maŋ	mrâŋ	
	[E] WT sbraŋ 'a fly'					
ur	氓甿	méng	mɛŋ	mɛŋ	mrə̂ŋ or mrâŋ	
	[E] WT dmaŋs 'people'					
y	肓	huāng	xwâŋ	huɑŋ	hmâŋ	
z	衁	huāng	xwâŋ	huɑŋ	hmâŋ	
	[E] MK: PMnong *mham 'blood'					
v	巟	huāng	xwâŋ	huɑŋ	hmâŋ	
e'	荒	huāng	xwâŋ	huɑŋ	hmâŋ	
	[T] Sin Sukchu SR xwaŋ (平); MGZY hwang (平) [xwaŋ]					
f'	謊	huǎng	xwâŋ$^{(B)}$	huɑŋ$^{(B)}$	hwâŋ(ʔ)	

g'	慌	huǎng	xwâŋ^{B}	huɑŋ^{B}	hwâŋʔ	
h'i'	幒幌	máng	mwâŋ	mɑŋ	mâŋ	

3-66	**= K. 743**	**Mand.**	**MC**	**LHan**	**OCM**	
adg	朢望謹	wàng	mjwaŋ^{C}	muɑŋ^{C}	maŋh	望 = 3-65/742m

3-67	**= K. 744**	**Mand.**	**MC**	**LHan**	**OCM**	
ac-	网蝄魍	wǎng	mjwaŋ^{B}	muɑŋ^{B}	maŋʔ	网 = 3-65/742a' 網

3-68	**= K. 760**	**Mand.**	**MC**	**LHan**	**OCM**	
a	明	míng	mjɐŋ	mɨaŋ	mraŋ	OCB *mrjaŋ
	[T] Sin S. SR miŋ (平); MGZY ming (平) [miŋ]; ONW meŋ <> [D] PMin *maŋ 'next' (year)					
e	盟	méng	mjɐŋ	mɨaŋ	mraŋ	
g	萌	méng	mɛŋ	mɛŋ	mrâŋ or mrêŋ ?	
	[E] Viet. mãm 'sprout, shoot'; TB-Lepcha mlam 'shoots from stump of tree'					

3-69	**= K. 761**	**Mand.**	**MC**	**LHan**	**OCM**	
a	皿	mǐn	mjɐŋ^{B}	mɨaŋ^{B}	mraŋʔ	
	[E] Viet. mâm 'food tray'					
e	孟	mèng	mɐŋ^{C}	maŋ^{C}	mrâŋh	[T] ONW mëŋ
g	猛	měng	mɐŋ^{B}	maŋ^{B}	mrâŋʔ	

4 OCM rime *-ə Zhī bù 之部

GSR 936 - 1001

Baxter 1992: 464 ff. (§10.2.1)

Table 4-1: OCM rimes *-əŋ, *-ək, *-ə in QYS categories

Div.	*-əŋ R.6	*-ək R.5	*-əkh R.5	*-ə R.4
I	恆 kəŋ^{C} kəŋ^{C} *kə̂ŋh 肱 kwəŋ kuəŋ *kwə̂ŋ 登 təŋ təŋ *tə̂ŋ 崩 pəŋ pəŋ *pə̂ŋ	克 kʰək kʰək *khə̂k 或 ɣwək ɣuək *wə̂k 得 tək tək *tə̂k 北 pək pək *pə̂k	塞 sậi^{C} sə^{C} *sə̂kh 背 pwậi^{C} pə^{C} *pə̂kh	改 kậi^{B} kə^{B} *kə̂ʔ 恢 kʰwậi kʰuə *khwə̂ 每 mwậi^{B} mə^{B} *mə̂ʔ 在 dzậi^{B} dzə^{B} *dzə̂ʔ
III lab	弓 kjuŋ kuŋ *kwəŋ 雄 juŋ3 wuŋ *wəŋ 夢 mjuŋ^{C} muŋ *məŋ	福 pjuk puk *pək 牧 mjuk muk *mək	富 pjəu^{C} pu^{C} *pəkh	丘 kʰjəu kʰu < kʰwuə *khwə 有 jəu^{B} wu^{B}< wuə^{B} *wəʔ 婦 bjəu^{B} bu^{B} < buə^{B} *bəʔ
3/3 lab	冰 pjəŋ pɨŋ *prəŋ	逼 pjək pɨk *prək	備 bji^{C}3 bɨ^{C} < bɨə^{C} *brəkh	龜 kjwi3 kuɨ<kwɨə *kwrə 鄙 pji^{B}3 pɨ^{B} < pɨə^{B} *prəʔ
III non -lab	兢 kjəŋ kɨŋ *kəŋ 承 źjəŋ dźɨŋ *dəŋ 孕 jiəŋ^{C} jɨŋ^{C} *ləŋh	亟 kjək kɨk *kək 洫 xjwək huɨk *hwək 域 jwək wɨk *wək 織 tśjək tśɨk *tək 弋 jiək jɨk *lək 色 ṣjək ṣɨk *srək	亟 kʰjɨ^{C} kʰɨə^{C} *khəkh 織 tśɨ^{C} tśə^{C} *təkh 異 jiɨ^{C} jə^{C} *ləkh	其 gjɨ gɨ < gɨə *gə 以 jiɨ^{B} jɨ < jə^{B} *ləʔ 子 tsɨ^{B} tsɨ^{B}< tsiə^{B} *tsəʔ 史 ṣɨ^{B} ṣɨ^{B} < ṣiə^{B} *srəʔ
II	黽 mɛŋ^{B} mɛŋ^{B} *mrə̂ŋʔ	革 kɛk kɛk *krə̂k 麥 mɛk mɛk *mrə̂k	憊 bǎi^{C} bɛ^{C} *brə̂kh	戒 kǎi^{C} kɛ^{C} *krə̂h 怪 kwǎi^{C} kuɛ^{C} *kwrə̂h

In this section are also found phonetic series in OCM *-u (section 13) that are suspected of including words in OCM *wə. In late Western Han poetry, these words tend to rime with ones in OC *-ə (Coblin 1986: 103f). By LHan these words seem to have ended in -u. The multitude of MC rimes with medial u/w in this OC category and their multiple OC sources are interpreted as follows:

	Mand.	MC	LHan	< earlier	OCM
九	jiǔ	kjəu^{B}	ku^{B}		kuʔ
丘	qiū	kʰjəu	kʰu	< kʰwuə	khwə
有	yǒu	jəu^{B}	wu^{B}	< wuə^{B}	wəʔ
負	fù	bjəu^{B}	bu^{B}	< buə^{B}	bəʔ
龜	guī	kjwi 3	kuɨ	< kwiə	kwrə
丕	pī	pʰji 3	pʰɨ	< pʰiə	phrə
恢	huī	kʰwậi	kʰwə		khwə̂
灰	huī	xwậi	hwə		hwə̂
誨	huì	xwậi^{C}	hwə^{C}		hmə̂h

MC and modern dialects distinguish between OC syllable types *Po,*Mo and *Pə, *Mə; but these have merged in the language of the *Shijing* and phonetic series (Baxter 1992); this has led to some confusion of these finals.

See Table 26-1 for OC rimes *-i, *-əi, *-ui and *-ə in QYS categories.

4 OCM *-ə 之部 (GSR 936-1001)

4-1	**= K. 936**	**Mand.**	**MC**	**LHan**	**OCM**	
	改	gǎi	kậi^{B}	kə^{B}	kə̂ʔ < kləʔ	

[T] Sin Sukchu SR kaj (上); MGZY gay (上) [kaj]; ONW kɑi
[E] PTai *klai^{A1} 'to pass by, change into'

4-2	**= K. 937**	**Mand.**	**MC**	**LHan**	**OCM**	
a	亥	hài	ɣậi^{B}	gə^{B}	gə̂ʔ	
h	孩	hái	ɣậi	gə	gə̂	
g	咳 smile	hái	ɣậi	gə	gə̂	
	咳 cough	ké !	k^{h}ậi^{C}	k^{h}ə^{C}	khə̂kh	
s	欬 cough	ké	k^{h}ậi^{C}	k^{h}ə^{C}	khə̂kh	
			k^{h}ək	k^{h}ək	khə̂k	

[D] Min: Amoy lit. k^{h}ek^{D1} 'sound of coughing' <> [E] TB *ka:k: Lushai k^{h}aak^{H} 'eject forcibly from the throat' ≭ k^{h}aak^{R} 'phlegm', WT k^{h}ogs 'cough', WB hak 'to hawk, raise phlegm'; <> Tai: S. k^{h}aak^{D1} 'to spit out', Saek k^{h}aak^{6} 'cough up phlegm', PVM *k-ha:k / krha:k 'to spit'

i	恢	hài	ɣậi^{C}	gə^{C}	gə̂h	
j	侅 N.Pr.	gāi	kậi	kə	kə̂	
	swallow	ài	ŋậi^{C}	ŋə^{C}	ŋə̂h	
klm	垓姟晐	gāi	kậi	kə	kə̂	
opq	胲該賅	gāi	kậi	kə	kə̂	
r	陔	gāi	kậi	kə	kə̂	

[E] WB hle-ka^{B} 'stairs, ladder' (hle 'ladder'), JP lǎ^{33}-ka^{33} 'steps', ? WT skras, skas-ka, skad 'ladder'

n	絯	gāi, xié	kậi, ɣai	kə, gɛ	kə̂, grə̂	
y	駭	hài	ɣăi^{B}	gɛ^{B}	grə̂ʔ	
z	骸	hái	ɣăi	gɛ	grə̂	
a'	核	hé	ɣɛk	gɛk	grə̂k	= 5-3/1260a 覈

[E] TB: WT rag 'fruit stone, bead', Mikir rak 'fruit stone'

tu	硋閡	ài	ŋậi^{C}	ŋə^{C}	ŋə̂kh	= 4-23/956g 礙
v	刻	kè	k^{h}ək	k^{h}ək	khə̂k	
x	劾	hé, hài	ɣək, ɣậi^{C}	gək, gə^{C}	gə̂k(h)	

4-3	**= K. 990**	**Mand.**	**MC**	**LHan**	**OCM**
ac	戒誡	jiè	kăi^{C}	kɛ^{C}	krə̂h

[T] Sin Sukchu SR kjaj (去), PR kjej; MGZY gyay (上) [kjaj]; ONW këi

d	械	xiè	ɣăi^{C}	gɛ^{C}	grə̂h
e	駴	xiè	ɣăi^{B}	gɛ^{B}	grə̂ʔ
f	祴	gāi	kậi	kə	kə̂

4-4	**= K. 952**	**Mand.**	**MC**	**LHan**	**OCM**	
af	其^{1} > 箕	jī	kjɨ	kɨ < kɨə	kə	'basket', OCB *k(r)jə
a	其^{2} this	qí	gjɨ	gɨə	gə	

[T] Sin Sukchu SR gi (平); MGZY ki (平) [gi]; ONW giə

	其^{3} probably	jì	kjɨ^{C}	kɨə^{C}	kəh	
g	基	jī	kjɨ	kɨə	kə	OCB *k(r)jə

[T] Sin Sukchu SR kjej (平), PR, LR ki; MGZY gi (平) [ki]; BTD 基耶今波羅 kɨə-ja-kɨm-pɑ-lɑ Skt. keśakambala

e'	琪	qí	gjɨ	gɨə	gə

jl	朞稘	jī	kjɨ	kɨə	kə	[T] ONW kiə
k	期 time	qí	gjɨ	gɨə	gə	
	year	jī	kjɨ	kɨə	kə	[T] ONW kiə
m	萁 stalks	qí	gjɨ	gɨə	gə	
	a vegetab.	jī	kjɨ	kɨə	kə	
n	諆 plan	jī	kjɨ	kɨə	kə	
	deceive	qī	k^hjɨ	k^hɨə	khə	
	[T] Sin Sukchu SR k'jej (平), PR k'i; MGZY khi (平) [k'i]; MTang k^hi, ONW k^hiə,					
pqf'	倛欺僛	qī	k^hjɨ	k^hɨə	khə	
-	魌	qī	k^hjɨ	k^hɨə	khə	
rtuv	綦基棋旗	qí	gjɨ	gɨə	gə	
xya'b'	琪祺騏麒	qí	gjɨ	gɨə	gə	
z	綦 grey	qí	gjɨ	gɨə	gə	
	cord	qí, jì	gjɨ(C)	gɨə(C)	gə(h)	
c'	惎	jì	gjɨ^C	gɨə^C	gəh	OCB *g(r)jəʔ(s)
	= 4-5/953su 忌諅					
d'	諅	jì	gjɨ^C	gɨə^C	gəh	

4-4A		Mand.	MC	LHan	OCM	
-	丌	jī	kjɨ	kɨ < kɨə		SW 2003
-	迈	jì	kjɨ^C	kɨə^C		SW 2004

4-5	= K. 953	Mand.	MC	LHan	OCM	
a	己	jǐ	kjɨ^B	kɨ^B < kɨə^B	kəʔ	
	[T] Sin Sukchu SR kjej (上), PR, LR ki; MGZY gi (上) [ki]					
f	改	jǐ	kjɨ^B	kɨə^B	kəʔ	
i	紀	jì	kjɨ^B	kɨə^B	kəʔ	OCB *k(r)jəʔ
j	記	jì	kjɨ^C	kɨə^C	kəh	[T] ONW kiə
s	忌 dread	jì	gjɨ^C	gɨə^C	gəh	OCB *g(r)jəʔ(s)
	= 4-4/952c' 惎					
	忌 a particle	jì	kjɨ^C	kɨə^C	kəh	
u	諅	jì	gjɨ^C	gɨə^C	gəh	
xy	跽 y	jì	gjɨ^B	gɨə^B	gəʔ	
k	屺	qǐ	k^hjɨ^B	k^hɨə^B	khəʔ	
l	杞	qǐ	k^hjɨ^B	k^hɨə^B	khəʔ	
	[E] ? TB: WT k^hri-šiŋ 'a creeper'					
q	芑	qǐ	k^hjɨ^B	k^hɨə^B	khəʔ	[E] ? TB: WT k^hre 'millet'
r	起	qǐ	k^hjɨ^B	k^hɨə^B	khəʔ	
	[T] Sin Sukchu SR k'jej (上), PR k'i; MGZY khi (上) [k'i]; ONW k^hiə					

4-6	= K. 985	Mand.	MC	LHan	OCM	
a	龜	guī	kjwi 3	kuɨ < kwɨə ~ ku	kwrə R!	OCB *kwrjə
	[T] 龜茲 *ku-dzə = Kuca [Hanshu] <> [D] PMin *kui ~ *ku. In Han and Wei-Jin poetry the word rimes with both *-ə and *-u.					

4-7	= K. 986	Mand.	MC	LHan	OCM	
a	簋	guǐ	kjwɨ^B 3	kuɨ^B < kwɨə^B	kruʔ R!	OCB *k^wrjuʔ
	= 4-8/987 ⋇ 31-2/540a,g-j guì 匱櫃					

4-8	**= K. 987**	**Mand.**	**MC**	**LHan**	**OCM**	
a	毁	guǐ	kjwɨ^{B} 3	kuɨ^{B} < kwɨə^{B}	kruʔ R!	OCB *kʷrjuʔ
	= 4-7/986					
eg	匓廏	jiù	kjəu^{C}	ku^{C}	kuh	

4-9	**= K. 988**	**Mand.**	**MC**	**LHan**	**OCM**	
a	頯 face	kuí	gjwɨ 3	guɨ < gwɨə	gru	OCB *gʷrju
	= 4-12/992e 頄					
	mien	kuǐ	kʰjwɨ^{B} 3	kʰuɨ^{B} < kʰwɨə^{B}	khruʔ	
	[T] ONW gui <> [E] Lepcha tă-gryu 'cheek'					
b	頮	huì	huậi^{C}	huə^{C}	hwə̂h	
	= 31-2/540f 靧 *hwə̂s 'wash the face'					

4-10	**= K. 989**	**Mand.**	**MC**	**LHan**	**OCM**	
a	逵	kuí	gjwɨ 3	guɨ < gwɨə	gru R!	OCB *gʷrju
	= 4-12/992m 馗					

4-11	**= K. 991**	**Mand.**	**MC**	**LHan**	**OCM**	
a	怪	guài	kwăi^{C}	kuɛ^{C} < kwɛ^{C}	kwrə̂h ?	[T] ONW kuëi
	The phonetic could be yòu 又 . Seems to be cognate to 傀 28-1/569d guī (kwậi) *kûi.					

4-12	**= K. 992**	**Mand.**	**MC**	**LHan**	**OCM**	
a	九	jiǔ	kjəu^{B}	ku^{B} R!	kuʔ / kwəʔ ?	OCB *kʷjuʔ
	[N]The graph was perh. invented for a word 'to bend, elbow' → jú 鞠鞫.					
	[T] Sin Sukchu SR kiw (上); MGZY giw (上) [kiw]; MTang keu < kiu, ONW ku					
	[D] PEMin *kəu^{B1}: M-Xiamen, Fuzhou kau^{B}; PWMin *kiu^{B1}.					
	[E] ST *kwəʔ: TB *d-kuw, Lushai kua^{R} < *kuaʔ (< *ʔ, not *-h < *-s)(kɔ^{11})					
e	頄	kuí, qiú	gjwɨ 3,gjəu	guɨ < gwɨə,gu	gru, gu	OCB *gʷrju
	= 4-9/988a 頯 [T] ONW gui					
m	馗	kuí	gjwɨ 3	guɨ < gwɨə	gru	OCB *gʷrju
	= 4-10/989a 逵					
n	鳩	jiū	kjəu	ku	ku	
	[T] MTang keu < kiu, ONW ku. <> [D] Y-Guǎngzhōu, Hongkong kɐu^{A1} ~ kʰɐu^{A1}, Foshan, Nanhai et al., have kʰ-; M-Xiàmén kiu^{A1} ~ kʰiu^{A1} <> [E] TB *kuw 'dove'					
fgj	宄 㝅 氿	guǐ	kjwɨ^{B} 3	kuɨ^{B} < kwɨə^{B}	kwrəʔ	
	宄: Wei-Jin rime -wə (Ting: 53)					
k	軌	guǐ	kjwɨ^{B} 3	kuɨ^{B} < kwɨə^{B} R! kruʔ		OCB *kʷrjuʔ
l	匭	guǐ	kjwɨ^{B} 3	kuɨ^{B} < kwɨə^{B}	kruʔ	= 4-7/986 簋
o	究	jiū !	kjəu^{C}	ku^{C}	kuh	OCB *k(r)jus
				< kwuə^{C} R!	~ kwəh	ж 4-15/1066a 求
	[T] MTang keu < kiu, ONW ku. In Han poetry jiù rimes sometimes with *-u, sometimes with *-ə (Luo / Zhou p. 132).					
p	仇	qiú	gjəu	gu < gwuə R! <	*gwə, gu R!	= 4-15/1066 逑
qrst	厹叴艽䡅	qiú	gjəu	gu	gwə or gu	
u	尻	kāo	kʰâu	kʰou	khû	
v	虓	xiāo	xau	hɔu	hû	
	An onomatopoetic word, hence no *r in spite of QYS Div. II.					
x	旭	xù	xjwok	huok	hok	

4-13	**= K. 993**	**Mand.**	**MC**	**LHan**	**OCM**	
ac	久玖	jiǔ	kjəu^B	ku^B < kwuə^B R!	kwəʔ R!	OCB *kʷjəʔ
	[T] Sin Sukchu SR kiw (上); MGZY giw (上) [kiw] <> [D] PMin *kiu^B: Xiamen ku^B					
b	灸	jiǔ	kjəu$^{B/C}$	ku$^{B/C}$	kwəʔ/h	
de	疚宊	jiù	kjəu^C	ku^C < kwuə^C R!	kwəh R!	
g	柩	jiù	gjəu^C	gu^C	gwəh	
f	羑	yǒu	jəu^B	wu^B < wuə^B	wəʔ	

4-14	**= K. 994**	**Mand.**	**MC**	**LHan**	**OCM**	
a	丘	qiū	kʰjəu	kʰu < kʰwuə R!	khwə R!	OCB *kʷhjə
	In Han poetry, qiū rimes with both *-ə and *-u. <> [T] MTang kʰeu < kʰiu, ONW kʰu; BTD Prakr. khu, Skt kṣu. MHan 丘就 kʰu-dziu^C = Kujula <> [E] ST *kwə: TB-Phön kəwa, Lushai kʰua^H 'village', Lai kʰua 'cosmos, village'.					
d	蚯	qiū	kʰjəu	kʰu	khwə	

4-15	**= K. 1066**	**Mand.**	**MC**	**LHan**	**OCM**	
ae	求¹ > 裘	qiú	gjəu	gu < gwuə R!	gwə R!	OCB *gʷjə 'fur'
a	求² seek	qiú	gjəu	gu	gu R!	OCB *g(r)ju
	⋈ 4-12/992o 究 <> [T] Sin S. SR giw (平); MGZY kiw (平) [giw]; MTang geu < giu, ONW gu					
f	球	qiú	gjəu	gu	gu R!	
	[D] PMin *ǧiu <> PTai *gwa^{C2} 'to search' <> [E] Tai: Wu-ming klau^{A2} 'ball'					
g	捄 curved	qiú	gjəu	gu	gu	
	collect	jiū	kjəu	ku	ku	
k	逑	qiú	gjəu	gu	gu R!	OCB *g(r)ju
	= 4-12/992p 仇					
lh	銶絿	qiú	gjəu	gu	gu R!	
n	俅	qiú	gjəu	gu	gwə R!	
m	救	jiù	kjəu^C	ku^C	kuh R!	OCB *k(r)jus
j	賕	qiú	gjəu	gu	gu	
i	觩	qiú,	gjeu,	giu,	giu,	
		jiū	kjeu	kiu	kiu	= 13-8/1064ef 虯觓

4-16	**= K. 1067**	**Mand.**	**MC**	**LHan**	**OCM**	
a	臼	jiù	gjəu^B	gu^B R!	guʔ	
	[D] PMin *ghiu^B: Xiam kʰu^{C2}, Fuzh kʰou^{C2} <> [E] PVM *t-koːlʔ 'rice mortar'					
b	舅	jiù	gjəu^B	gu^B	guʔ R!	OCB *g(r)juʔ
	[D] PMin *giu^B > Xiam ku^{C2}, Fu'an kou^{C2} <> [E] TB *kuw 'uncle'					
c	舊	jiù	gjəu^C	gu^C	gwəʔ/h R!	OCB *gʷjəʔ(s)
	[T] MTang geu < giu, ONW gu <> [D] PMin *giu^C					
f	匶	jiù	gjəu^C	gu^C	guh or gwəh	

4-17	**= K. 995**	**Mand.**	**MC**	**LHan**	**OCM**	
a	又	yòu	jəu^C	wu^C < wuə^C	wəh	OCB *wjə(k)s
	Original graph for 右 <> [T] Sin Sukchu SR iw (去); MGZY ngiw (去) [ŋiw]					
e	友	yǒu	jəu^B	wu^B < wuə^B	wəʔ	[T] ONW u
i	右	yòu	jəu^B, jəu^C	wu$^{B/C}$ < wuə$^{B/C}$	wəʔ, wəh	OCB *wjəʔ(s)
	[T] Sin S. SR iw (去); MGZY ngiw (去) [ŋiw]; MTang eu < u, ONW u					
kl	佑祐	yòu	jəu^C	wu^C < wuə^C	wəh	

m	䀁	yòu	jəu$^{B/C}$	wu$^{B/C}$ < wuə$^{B/C}$	wəʔ/h	
n	醢	hǎi	xậi^{B}	hə^{B}	hwə̂ʔ ?	
o	有	yǒu	jəu^{B}	wu^{B} < wuə^{B}	wəʔ	OCB *wjəʔ

[T] Sin Sukchu SR iw (上); MGZY ngiw (上) [ŋiw]; MTang eu < u, ONW u; Han BTD *wu
[D] PMin *u^{B} ~ iu^{B}: Xiamen u^{C2}, Fuzhou ou^{C2}

qr	侑宥	yòu	jəu^{C}	wu^{C} < wuə^{C}	wəh	
u	囿	yòu	jəu^{C},	wu^{C} < wuə^{C},	wəkh,	OCB *wjə(k)s
			juk	wuk < wuək	wək	
xy	痏鮪	wěi	jwi^{B}	wi^{B} < wiə^{B}	wrəʔ	
z	賄	huì	xwậi^{B}	hwə^{B}	hmə̂ʔ ! (Baxter 1992: 352)	
a'	郁	yù	ʔjuk	ʔuk < ʔwək	ʔwək	

4-18	**= K. 996**	**Mand.**	**MC**	**LHan**	**OCM**
adef	尤訧疣肬	yóu	jəu	wu < wuə	wə

[T] ONW iu <> [E] WT yus 'blame'

4-19	**= K. 997**	**Mand.**	**MC**	**LHan**	**OCM**
a	郵	yóu	jəu	wu < wuə	wə

4-19A		**Mand.**	**MC**	**LHan**	**OCM**	
-	詯	huì	ɣwậi^{C}	ɣuə^{C}	wə̂h	SW 1042

自 'nose' is semantic, not phonetic

4-20	**= K. 950**	**Mand.**	**MC**	**LHan**	**OCM**	
a	灰	huī	xwậi	huə	hwə̂	

[T] Sin Sukchu SR xuj (平); MGZY hue (平) [xuɛ]. The phonetic could be yòu 又, hence OCM *hwə̂; also the graphic derivatives *huī, kuī* point to OCM *hw- rather than *hm-.

b	恢	huī !	kʰwậi	kʰuə	khwə̂	
-	盔	kuī	kʰwậi	—	—	'helmet; basin'
c	脄	méi	mwậi(^{C})	mə(^{C})	mə̂(h)	= 4-64/947m 脢

This graph occurs late (first in Liji) as a loan graph for 脢 when *hm- and *hw- had already merged. Note 4-17/995z 賄 for a similar graphic confusion of *m- vs. *w-.

4-21	**= K. 955**	**Mand.**	**MC**	**LHan**	**OCM**	
ad	喜憘	xǐ	xji^{B}	hiə^{B} > hi^{B}	həʔ	

[T] Sin Sukchu SR xi (上); MGZY hi (上) [xi]; MTang hi, ONW hiə

efg	嘻譆嬉	xī	xji	hiə	hə	
ijk	暿熺熹	xī	xji	hiə	hə	
lm	糦饎	chì	tśʰi^{C}	tśʰə^{C}	k-hjəʔ	OCB *KHjəʔ(s)

= 4-34/960k [食+巸]

4-22	**= K. 958**	**Mand.**	**MC**	**LHan**	**OCM**
a	醫	yī	ʔi	ʔiə > ʔi	ʔə

[E] KT: PHlai ja[1] 'medicine', KS *gja[2] 'medicine, to cure', PTai *ʔia^{A1} 'medicine'

4-22A	毐	ǎi	ʔậi(^{B})	ʔə(^{B})		SW 5653

4-23	**= K. 956**	**Mand.**	**MC**	**LHan**	**OCM**	
a	疑 doubt	yí	ŋjɨ	ŋɨə > ŋɨ	ŋə	

[T] MTang ŋi [ŋgi], ONW ŋiə

	疑 stop	yì	ŋjək	ŋɨk	ŋək	
b	儗	nǐ	ŋjɨ^{B}	ŋɨə^{B}	ŋəʔ	[T] BTD Skt. jña
c	嶷 a mount.	yí	ŋjɨ	ŋɨə	ŋə	
	firmly	yì	ŋjək	ŋɨk	ŋək	
d	擬	nǐ	ŋjɨ^{B}	ŋɨə^{B}	ŋəʔ	
e	薿	yǐ, nǐ	ŋjɨ^{B}, ŋjək	ŋɨə^{B}, ŋɨk	ŋəʔ, ŋək	
f	⿱羽疑	yí, ní	ŋjɨ, ŋjək	ŋɨə, ŋɨk	ŋə, ŋək	
g	礙	ài	ŋâi^{C}	ŋə^{C}	ŋə̂kh	= 4-2/937t 硋

[T] Sin Sukchu SR ŋaj (去); MGZY ngay (去) [ŋaj]; ONW ŋɑi^{C}
[E] ? TB: WT 'geg(s)-pa, bkag, dgag 'to hinder, prohibit, shut'

h	凝	níng	ŋjəŋ	ŋɨŋ	ŋəŋ	

4-24	**= K. 998**	**Mand.**	**MC**	**LHan**	**OCM**	
a	牛	niú	ŋjəu	ŋu < ŋwuə R!	ŋwə	OCB *ŋ^{w}jə

[T] Sin S. SR ŋiw, iw (平); PR, LR niw; MGZY ngiw (平) [ŋiw]; ONW ŋu <> [D] PMin *ŋiu: Xiamen gu^{A2}, Fuzhou ŋu^{A2} <> [E] Tai: S. ŋua^{A2} < *ŋwue ? 'ox', TB *ŋwa 'bovine'

4-25	**= K. 939**	**Mand.**	**MC**	**LHan**	**OCM**
a	臺	tái	dậi	də	də̂
-	嬯	tái	dậi	də	də̂

[E] AA: Khmer tai /ɗəj/ 'female human, female slave'

4-26	**= K. 961**	**Mand.**	**MC**	**LHan**	**OCM**	
ag	止趾	zhǐ	tśɨ^{B}	tśə^{B} > tśɨ^{B}	təʔ	
hj	沚芷	zhǐ	tśɨ^{B}	tśə^{B}	təʔ	
k	祉	zhǐ !	ṭ^{h}ɨ^{B}	ṭ^{h}iə^{B}	thrəʔ	
l	齒 see 4-29					
m	寺	sì	zɨ^{C}	ziə^{C}	s-ləh ?	OCB *sdjəs ?
d'	詩	shī	śɨ	śə	lhə ?	OCB *stjə

[E] ? TB: Lushai hlaa^{R} 'song, poem, poetry'

e'	邿	shī	śɨ	śə	lhə ?	
z	時^{1} this	shí	źɨ	dźə	də	OCB *djə(ʔ)

[E] WT da 'there'

zb'	時^{2}旹 time	shí	źɨ	dźə	dəʔ (tone!)	

[T] Sin Sukchu SR ʐi (平), PR, LR ʐʅ; MGZY zhi (平) [ʐi]; MTang źi < dźi, ONW dźə

j'	塒	shí	źɨ	dźə	də	OCB *djə
y	恃	shì	źɨ^{B}	dźə^{B}	dəʔ	OCB *djəʔ
x	侍	shì	źɨ^{C}	dźə^{C}	dəh	

[T] MTang źi < dźi, ONW dźə

v	洔	zhǐ	tśɨ^{B}	tśə^{B}	təʔ
p	持	chí	ḍjɨ	ḍiə	drə

[T] BTD 比盧持 pi^{C}-lɑ-ḍiə Skt. vairaṭi-

qrst	峙畤庤痔	zhì	ḍjɨ^{B}	ḍiə^{B}	drəʔ
u	跱	zhì	ḍjɨ^{B}	ḍiə^{B}	drəʔ

g' 待 dài dậi^{B} də^{B} dəʔ
[T] BTD nán-dài 難待 Skt. nanda
k' 偫 zhì ḍjɨ^{B} ḍiə^{B} drəʔ
h' 特 single tè ! dək dək dək = 5-12/919f 犆
[T] Sin Sukchu SR dəj (入), LR dəjʔ; MGZY t^{h}iy (入) [dəj]; ONW dək.
[E] ? ST: tak 'one' in Western Himalayan languages, e.g., Darmiya taku 'one'
特 male tè dək dək dək OCB *dək
[E] Tai: S. t^{h}ɨk^{D1}S < *th- (in northern dial. *d-) 'young male animal' <> NNaga *te:k 'buffalo'
i' 等 děng təŋ^{B} təŋ^{B} təŋʔ

4-27 = K. 962 Mand. MC LHan OCM
ac 之芝 zhī tśɨ tśɨ < tśə tə
[T] Sin Sukchu SR tʂi (平), PR, LR tʂɿ; MGZY ji (平) [tʂi]; ONW tśə
[E] WT čʰa-ba 'to go, become, be going to'; WB ca^{C} 'begin, at first' ≭ ə-ca^{C} 'beginning'
ef 志誌 zhì tśɨ^{C} tśə^{C} təh
\- 痣 zhì tśɨ^{C} tśə^{C}, kiə^{C} ? [D] PMin *ki^{C}
d 蚩 chī tś^{h}ɨ tś^{h}ə thə

4-28 = K. 963 Mand. MC LHan OCM
a 市 shì źɨ^{B} dźɨ^{B} < dźə^{B} dəʔ [D] PMin *džhi
[T] MTang źi < dźi, ONW dźə <> [E] ? PTai *ǰɨ^{C2} 'to buy', Ahom 'come to terms, consent'
\- 柿 shì dẓɨ^{B} dẓiə^{B} -əʔ [D] PMin *ghi^{B}

4-29 = K. 961-l Mand. MC LHan OCM
l 齒 chǐ tś^{h}ɨ^{B} tś^{h}ɨ^{B} < tś^{h}ə^{B} k-hjəʔ
[T] Sin Sukchu SR tʂ'i (上); PR, LR tʂ'ɿ; MGZY chi (上) [tʂ'i]; MTang tś^{h}i, ONW tś^{h}ə
[D] PMin *khi^{B1} ~ tʃhɨ^{B1} <> [N] The phonetic 止 was added later.

4-30 = K. 976 Mand. MC LHan OCM
ab 目以 yǐ jiɨ^{B} jɨ^{B} < jə^{B} ləʔ OCB *ljəʔ
[T] Sin Sukchu SR i (上); MGZY yi (上) [ji]; MTang i, ONW iə. <> [E] ? ST *lə: Lushai la^{L} < laah / laak 'to take, get', Tiddim laa^{R} / laak^{R} < laaʔ / laak 'to take', Newari laa-
fg 苢苡 yǐ jiɨ^{B} jə^{B} ləʔ
h 似 sì zɨ^{B} ziə^{B} s-ləʔ
[T] Sin Sukchu SR zɿ (上); MGZY z^{h}i (上) [zɿ]
ik 姒耜 sì zɨ^{B} ziə^{B} s-ləʔ
p 台[1] my yí jiɨ jə lə
u 怡 yí jiɨ jə lə
v 詒 give yí jiɨ jə lə
deceive dài dậi^{B} də^{B} ləʔ
xy 貽飴 yí jiɨ jə lə [T] ONW iə
d' 枲 xǐ ! sɨ^{B} siə^{B} səʔ
p' 冶 yě jia^{B} ja^{B} laʔ [T] ONW ia
e' 始 shǐ śɨ^{B} śə^{B} lhəʔ
z 治[1] regulate zhì ḍɨ(C) ḍiə(C) drə, drəh < r-lə, r-ləh
[T] Sin Sukchu SR dʐi (去); MGZY ci (去) [dʐi]; MTang ḍi, ONW diə; OCB *lrjə
p 台[2] rounded tāi t^{h}ậi t^{h}ə lhə

-	苔 moss	tái	dâi	də	lə̂	

[D] PMin *dhəi, *dhi <> [E] PTai *glai^{A2} 'moss'

z	治^2 kill	tái	dâi	(dəi)		

[D] 'To kill' in Min: PMin *dhai^{A2}, dhi <> [E] Area word: Tai: S. taai^{A1}, Zhuang t^{h}ai$^{A1/2}$ 'to die' (< PTai *trai, *prai), MY *təjH 'to kill' ⵅ *dəjH 'to die' from a hypothetical **pə-təjH and **mətəjH respectively (M. Ratliff, p.c.)

n'o'	迨 o'	dài	dâi^B	də^B	lə̂ʔ	

[E] TB *la: LB *la, WB la 'come, reach in degree'

q'	箈	dài	dâi^B	də^B	lə̂ʔ	
h'	胎	tāi	t^{h}âi	t^{h}ə	lhə̂	
t	佁	yǐ, chì	jiɨ^B, ṭ^{h}ɨ^C	jə^B, ṭ^{h}iə^C	ləʔ, rhəh < r-lhəh ?	
a'	眙	chì,	ṭ^{h}ɨ^C,	ṭ^{h}iə^C,	rhəh	ⵅ 3-32/725f'
		zhèng	ḍjəŋ^C	ḍɨŋ^C	drəŋh	
b'	笞	chī	ṭ^{h}ɨ	ṭ^{h}iə	rhə < r-lhə ?	
1240a	咍 laugh	hāi	xâi	hə	hə̂	
976c'	鈶	sì	zɨ^B	ziə^B	s-ləʔ	
i'	炱	tái	dâi	də	lə̂	
j'	駘 ugly	tái	dâi	də	lə̂	
	slack	dài	dâi^B	də^B	lə̂ʔ	
k'l'm'	怠殆紿	dài	dâi^B	də^B	lə̂ʔ	
l	矣	yǐ	jɨ^B 3!	jə^B	ləʔ	final enclitic particle
mno	俟竢涘	sì	dẓɨ^B	dẓiə^B	s-rəʔ	
938ab	唉埃	āi	ʔâi	ʔə	ʔə̂	
c	挨	ǎi, āi	ʔâi, ʔǎiʔ	ʔə, ʔɛʔ	ʔə̂, ʔ(r)ə̂ʔ	
d	欸	āi	ʔǎi	ʔɛ	ʔə̂	onomatopoetic, no *r
ef	娭誒	xī	xjɨ	hɨə	hə	

4-31	**= K. 977**	**Mand.**	**MC**	**LHan**	**OCM**	
a	已	yǐ	jiɨ^B	jɨ^B < jə^B	ləʔ	OCB *ljəʔ

[T] Sin Sukchu SR i (上); MGZY yi (上) [ji]; MTang i, ONW iə

b	异	yì	jiɨ^C	jə^C	ləkh	= 5-17/954a 異

4-32	**= K. 967**	**Mand.**	**MC**	**LHan**	**OCM**	
adi	巳祀汜	sì	zɨ^B	zɨ < ziə^B	s-ləʔ	
k	戺	shì	dẓɨ^B	dẓiə^B	dzrəʔ < s-rəʔ	

4-33	**= K. 968**	**Mand.**	**MC**	**LHan**	**OCM**	
a	辭	cí	zɨ	zɨ < ziə	s-lə	= 4-53/972j 詞

[T] Sin Sukchu SR zɿ (平), LR zɿ; MGZY z^{h}i (平) [zɿ]

4-34	**= K. 960**	**Mand.**	**MC**	**LHan**	**OCM**	
acd	臣頤 d	yí	jiɨ	jɨ < jə	jə	
k	饎	chì	tś^{h}ɨ^C	tś^{h}ə^C	k-hjəʔ !	OCB *KHjəʔ(s); = 4-21 饎
i	茝	chǐ,	tś^{h}ɨ^B,	tś^{h}ə^B,	k-hjəʔ,	
		zhǐ	tśɨ^B	tśə^B	k-jəʔ ?	
j	熙	xī	xjɨ	hɨə	hə (*hjəʔ)	
f	姬	jī	kjɨ	kɨə	kə (*kjəʔ)	

[N] The phonetic suggests hjə (j) and kjə, but such words should have become palatalized.

4-35	**= K. 978**	**Mand.**	**MC**	**LHan**	**OCM**	
a	里	lǐ	ljɨ^{B}	lɨ^{B} < liə^{B}	rəʔ	OCB *C-rjəʔ
	[T] ONW liə <> [E] ST *rwə: TB *rwa > WB rwa 'town, village'					
d	理	lǐ	ljɨ^{B}	liə^{B}	rəʔ	OCB *C-rjəʔ
	[T] ONW liə <> [E] TB *riy 'draw, paint, write, delimit'					
e-	裹裡	lǐ	ljɨ^{B}	liə^{B}	rəʔ	
j	鯉	lǐ	ljɨ^{B}	liə^{B}	rəʔ	OCB *C-rjəʔ
c	梩	lí	ljɨ	liə	rə	
hi	貍狸	lí	ljɨ	liə	rə or C-rə (because of Min)	
	OCB *C-rjə (*pʰrə ~ *pʰə-rə >) *rə ? <> [T] ONW liə <> [D] Min: Jiànōu sɛ^{A2}					
mn	薶霾	mái	mǎi	mɛ	mrə̂	
l	埋	mái	mǎi	mɛ	mrə̂	
-	堇	chì, lí	ṭʰjək, xjuk, ṭʰjuk	ṭʰiək	—	SW 272

4-36	**= K. 979**	**Mand.**	**MC**	**LHan**	**OCM**
a	孷	lí	ljɨ	lɨ < liə	rə
		xī	xjɨ	hɨə	hə
c	嫠	lí	ljɨ	liə	rə
fglk	嫠犛氂 k	lí	ljɨ	liə	rə
ijk	氂犛	lí	ljɨ	liə	rə
	[E] TB: WT 'bri-mo 'domesticated female yak'				
1237q	漦	chí	dẓɨ, ljɨ	dẓiə	s-rə

4-37	**= K. 980**	**Mand.**	**MC**	**LHan**	**OCM**
a	李	lǐ	ljɨ^{B}	lɨ^{B} < liə^{B}	rəʔ or C-rəʔ (because of Min)
	See Intro. 9.2.1. OCB *C-rjəʔ <> [T] ONW liə <> [D] Min: Jiànyōu sɛ^{C2}				

4-38	**= K. 945**	**Mand.**	**MC**	**LHan**	**OCM**	
a	乃	nǎi	nậi^{B}	nə^{B}	nə̂ʔ	
	[T] Sin Sukchu SR naj (上); MGZY nay (上) [naj]; ONW nɑi^{B}; BTD Skt. 不乃 pūrṇa					
-	奶	nǎi	nậi^{B}	—	—	
	(an OC form might have been *nə̂ʔ or, unlikely, *nə̂iʔ) <> [D] Min: Xiam lit. lãi^{B}, col. lẽ^{B}					
d	鼐	nài	nậi$^{B/C}$	nə$^{B/C}$	nə̂ʔ/h	
e	仍	réng	ńźjəŋ	ńɨŋ	nəŋ	[E] TB *(s-)naŋ 'follow'
fgh	扔艿礽	réng	ńźjəŋ	ńɨŋ	nəŋ	
j	孕 See 6-14/945l.					

4-39	**= K. 946**	**Mand.**	**MC**	**LHan**	**OCM**
a	迺	nǎi	nậi^{B}	nə^{B}	nə̂ʔ
	[N] xī 西 26-32/594 'west, nest' is sometimes thought to be phonetic				

4-40	**= K. 981, 959**		**MC**	**LHan**	**OCM**
a	耳	ěr	ńźɨ^{B}	ńɨ^{B} < ńə^{B}	nəʔ
	[T] Sin Sukchu SR ri (上), PR, LR ɻ; MGZY Zhi (上) [ri]; ONW ńə^{B} [E] TB *r-na 'ear / hear' > WT rna-ba 'ear'				
de	珥衈	ěr, èr	ńźɨ^{C}	ńə^{C}	nəh
cf	刵佴	èr	ńźɨ^{C}	ńə^{C}	nəh

g	咡	èr	ńźɨ(^{B})	ńə(^{B})	nə(ʔ)	
h	餌	ěr	ńźɨ^{C}	ńə^{C}	nəh	[T] ONW ńə

[E] PTai: *hň-: S. jɨa^{B1} 'bait' // ST *njə: WT: ña 'tendon, sinew'

i	眲	èr, nè	ńźɨ^{C}, ṇɛk	ńə^{C}, ṇɛk	nəh, nrə̂k	
959a	恥	chǐ	ṭʰɨ^{B}	ṭʰiə^{B}	rhəʔ or nhrəʔ ?	OCB *hnrjəʔ

4-41	**= K. 982**	**Mand.**	**MC**	**LHan**	**OCM**	
a	而	ér	ńźɨ	ńə > ńɨ	nə	

[T] Sin Sukchu SR ri (平), PR, LR ɽɿ; MGZY Zhi (平) [ri]; ONW ńə

cdef	栭耏胹鴯	ér	ńźɨ	ńə	nə	
g	鮞	ér	ńźɨ, ńźjuk	ńə, ńuk	nə, nuk	
h	耐	nài	nậi^{C}	nə^{C}	nə̂h	
ij	隭陾	réng,	ńźjəŋ,	ńɨŋ,	nəŋ,	= 4-38/945e 仍
		nú	nəu^{B}	no^{B}	nôʔ	

4-42	**= K. 940**	**Mand.**	**MC**	**LHan**	**OCM**	
ad	災灾	zāi	tsậi	tsə	tsə̂	= 4-45/943z 烖

[E] ? ST *tsə > TB: JP tsa^{31} 'be damaged' ⋈ ʃă^{31}-tsa^{31} 'to destroy'

[N] This may be phonetic in 4-50/969.

4-43	**= K. 941**	**Mand.**	**MC**	**LHan**	**OCM**
a	再	zài	tsậi^{C}	tsə^{C}	tsə̂h

[T] Sin Sukchu SR tsaj (去); MGZY dzay (去) [tsaj]; ONW tsɑi^{C}

4-44	**= K. 942**	**Mand.**	**MC**	**LHan**	**OCM**
ad	采^{1}採 gath.	cǎi	tsʰậi^{B}	tsʰə^{B}	tshə̂ʔ
	采^{2} color	cǎi	tsʰậi^{B}	tsʰə^{B}	tshə̂ʔ

[E] ? WT tsʰos 'paint, dye, to color'

	采^{3} appana.	cài	tsʰậi^{C}	tsʰə^{C}	tsʰə̂h
e	菜	cài	tsʰậi^{C}	tsʰə^{C}	tsʰə̂h

[T] Sin Sukchu SR ts'aj (去); MGZY tshay (去) [ts'aj]; ONW tsʰɑi

[E] ST *tsə: LB*tsyak^{H} 'to pluck'

4-45	**= K. 943**	**Mand.**	**MC**	**LHan**	**OCM**	
agh	才材財	cái	dzậi	dzə	dzə̂	

[T] Sin Sukchu SR dzaj (平); MGZY tsay (平) [dzaj]; ONW dzɑi (dzɛi ?)

i	在	zài	dzậi^{B}	dzə^{B}	dzə̂ʔ	
lo	𢦏𢦔	zāi	tsậi	tsə	tsə̂	
p	䣢	zài	tsậi^{C}	tsə^{C}	tsə̂h	
z	烖	zāi	tsậi	tsə	tsə̂	= 4-42/940a 災
v	哉	zāi	tsậi	tsə	tsə̂	
y	栽 plant	zāi	tsậi	tsə	tsə̂	
	erect	zài	dzậi^{C}	dzə^{C}	dzə̂h	
a'	載 carry	zài	tsậi^{C}	tsə^{C}	tsə̂h	

[T] Sin Sukchu SR tsaj (去); MGZY dzay (去) [tsaj]; LTang tsɑi^{C} or tsɛi^{C}, ONW tsɑi^{C}

	載 load	zài	dzậi^{C}	dzə^{C}	dzə̂h
	載 year	zǎi	tsậi$^{B/C}$	tsə$^{B/C}$	tsə̂ʔ/h

[T] Sin Sukchu SR tsaj (上); MGZY dzay (上) [tsaj]; ONW tsɑi^{B}

c'	裁	zài, cái	dzậi$^{(C)}$	dzə$^{(C)}$	dzə̂(h)	
r	鼒	zī	tsɨ	tsiə	tsə	
s	紂 black	zī	tṣɨ	tṣiə	tsrə	= 4-50/969e, ~ 4-49/966a
d'	胾	zì	tṣɨ^{C}	tṣiə^{C}	tsrəh	
t	豺	chái	dẓăi	dẓɛ	dzrə̂	
e'	戴	dài	tậi^{C}	tə^{C}	tə̂h	

4-45A = K. 1240b		**Mand.**	**MC**	**LHan**	**OCM**
b	猜	cāi	tsʰậi	tsʰə	tshə̂

[N] MC tsʰậi can derive from OCM *tshə̂; OCM tshə̂i would be MC tsʰiei. See EDOC 8.2.5.

4-46		**Mand.**	**MC**	**LHan**	**OCM**	
-	纔	cái	dzậi	dzə	dzə̂	[T] ONW dzɑi (dzɛi ?)

The 'phonetic' looks like 36-23/612.

4-47	**= K. 964**	**Mand.**	**MC**	**LHan**	**OCM**	
a	子	zǐ	tsɨ^{B}	tsɨ^{B} < tsiə^{B}	tsəʔ	

See Intro. 9.2.1. [T] Sin Sukchu SR tsɿ (上); MGZY dzʰi (上) [tsɿ]; ONW tsiə; MHan 昆子 *kûn-tsəʔ = Kïrsaq; 獅子 ṣi-tsiəʔ Tocharian A śiśäk, B ṣecake 'lion' <> [E] TB *tsa or *za > WT tsʰa-bo 'grandchild', Atsi tso, Maru tsō, PBurm. *tsa^{B}; Lushai faF 'child, son, daughter'

	子	zì	tsɨ^{C}	tsiə^{C}	tsəh	
m	耔	zǐ	tsɨ^{B}	tsiə^{B}	tsəʔ	

[E] ? WT tsʰi-ba 'furrow' (in a ploughed field)

k	仔	zī, zǐ	tsɨ$^{(B)}$	tsiə$^{(B)}$	tsə(ʔ)	
l	孜	zī	tsɨ	tsiə	tsə	
n	字	zì	dzɨ^{C}	dziə^{C}	dzəh	= 4-49/966k 孳

[T] Sin Sukchu SR dzɿ (去); MGZY tsʰi (去) [dzɿ]; ONW dziə

4-48	**= K. 965**	**Mand.**	**MC**	**LHan**	**OCM**
a	梓	zǐ	tsɨ^{B}	tsɨ^{B} < tsiə^{B}	tsəʔ
b	宰	zǎi	tsậi^{B}	tsə^{B}	tsə̂ʔ

4-49	**= K. 966**	**Mand.**	**MC**	**LHan**	**OCM**	
a	兹 black	zī	tsɨ	tsɨ < tsiə	tsə	~ 4-45/943s, 4-50/969e
b	茲 mat; this	zī	tsɨ	tsiə	tsə	

[T] ONW tsiə; MHan 龜茲 *ku-tsə = Kuca

ghi	嗞滋鎡	zī	tsɨ	tsiə	tsə	
j	慈	cí	dzɨ	dziə	dzə	

[E] TB: WT *mdza'-ba 'to love', WB ca 'to feel for'

k	孳 multiply	zī	tsɨ	tsɨə	tsə	
	孳 copulate	zì	dzɨ^{C}	dziə^{C}	dzə^{C}	= 4-47/964n 字

[T] Sin Sukchu SR dzɿ (去); MGZY tsʰi (去) [dzɿ]; ONW dziə

[N] The two readings are not distinguished consistently.

4-50 **= K. 969** K. 940 災 may be phonetic.

		Mand.	**MC**	**LHan**	**OCM**	
ab	甾	zī	tṣɨ	tṣiə	tsrə	[T] BTD Skt. ci
cd	菑 a field	zī	tṣɨ	tṣiə	tsrə	

		Mand.	MC	LHan	OCM	
	菑 stump	zī, zì	tṣɨ(^{C})	tṣiə(^{C})	tsrə(h)	
ef	緇 black	zī	tṣɨ	tṣiə	tsrə	= 4-45/943s, ~ 4-49/966a
ghij	輜錙	zī	tṣɨ	tṣiə	tsrə	[T] 輜 BTD Skt. ji
-	椔	zī	tṣɨ	tṣiə	tsrə	

4-51	**= K. 970**	**Mand.**	**MC**	**LHan**	**OCM**
ad	士仕	shì	dẓɨ^{B}	dẓiə^{B} < ẓə	s-rəʔ

[T] Sin Sukchu SR ẓi (上去), PR ẓʅ; MGZY c^{h}i (上) [dẓʅ]; MTang dẓi (?), ONW dẓə (?)

4-52	**= K. 975, 971**	**Mand.**	**MC**	**LHan**	**OCM**	
975a	史	shǐ	ṣɨ^{B}	ṣiə^{B}	srəʔ	

[T] Sin Sukchu SR ṣi (上), PR, LR ṣʅ; MGZY sh^{h}i (上) [ṣʅ]; MTang ṣi, ONW ṣə; MHan ṣəʔ (or srəʔ ?) S(u)liɣ 'Sogdian' <> [D] PMin *šai^{B} 'to use'

-	駛	shǐ	ṣɨ$^{B/C}$	ṣiə$^{B/C}$	—	[T] BTD Skt. ṣya
n	使 command	shǐ	ṣɨ^{B}	ṣiə^{B}	srəʔ	
	envoy	shì	ṣɨ^{C}	ṣiə^{C}	srəh	
k	k	shì	ṣɨ^{C}	ṣiə^{C}	srəh	
g	吏	lì	ljɨ^{C}	liə^{C}	rəh	[T] MTang li, ONW liə
971a	事	shì	dẓɨ^{C}	dẓiə^{C}	s-rəʔ R!	

[T] Sin Sukchu SR ẓi (去), PR, LR ẓʅ; MGZY c^{h}i (去) [dẓʅ]; MTang dẓi (?), ONW dẓə (?)
[D] PMin *dɨ^{C} ~ šai^{C} 'matter'

d	剚	zì	tṣɨ^{C}	tṣiə^{C}	tsrəh

4-53	**= K. 972**	**Mand.**	**MC**	**LHan**	**OCM**	
a	司	sī	sɨ	sɨ < siə	sə	[T] ONW siə

[E] ST *zə: WT mdzad-pa, mdzod (< m-za-t) 'to do, act' ※ bzo 'work, labor', Kuhish ca, Mru caŋ 'to do, make'

f	伺	sī, sì	sɨ(^{C})	siə(^{C})	sə(h)	
g	笥	sì	sɨ^{C}	siə^{C}	səh	
h	祠	cí	zɨ	ziə	s-lə	
j	詞	cí	zɨ	ziə	s-lə	= 4-33/968 辭

[T] Sin S. SR zɿ (平), LR zɿ; MGZY z^{h}i (平) [zɿ] <> [E] ST *s-lə: WT zla-ba, zlas 'to say, tell'

k	嗣	sì	zɨ^{C}	ziə^{C}	s-ləh	
-	飼	sì	zɨ^{C}	ziə^{C}	s-ləkh	= 5-19/921ae

4-54 **= K. 973** Contrary to SW 4643, 囟 *sins or *səns 'head' (32-34/1241l) is not phonetic, but probably semantic.

		Mand.	**MC**	**LHan**	**OCM**	
a	思 think	sī	sɨ, sɨ^{C}	sɨ < siə	sə	OCB *sjə

[T] Sin Sukchu SR sɿ (平); MGZY s^{h}i (平) [sɿ]; ONW siə

	思 brood	sì	sɨ^{C}	siə^{C}	səh	OCB *sjəs
	思 bearded	sāi	sɨ, sậi	s(i)ə	sə, sə̂	
b	緦	sī	sɨ	siə	sə	
cd	葸諰	xǐ !	sɨ^{B}	siə^{B}	səʔ	
e	颸	sī, chī	tṣ^{h}ɨ	tṣ^{h}iə	tshrə < k-srə	
f	偲 forceful	cāi	ts^{h}ậi	ts^{h}ə	tshə̂ < k-sə̂	
	偲 forcible	sī	sɨ	siə	sə	

-	腮 jaw	sāi				

4-55	**= K. 974**	**Mand.**	**MC**	**LHan**	**OCM**	
a	絲	sī	sɨ	sɨ < siə	sə	

4-56	**= K. 951**	**Mand.**	**MC**	**LHan**	**OCM**	
ac	佩珮	pèi	bwậi^{C}	bə^{C} R!	bêh	

4-57	**= K. 983**	**Mand.**	**MC**	**LHan**	**OCM**	
a	a	bǐ	pjɨ^{B} 3	pɨ^{B} < pɨə^{B}	prəʔ	
e	鄙	bǐ	pjɨ^{B} 3	pɨə^{B}	prəʔ	

4-58	**= K. 1237a'**	**Mand.**	**MC**	**LHan**	**OCM**	
a'	圮	pǐ	bjɨ^{B} 3	bɨ^{B} < bɨə^{B}	brəʔ	

4-59	**= K. 1237r**	**Mand.**	**MC**	**LHan**	**OCM**	
r	奰	bì	bjɨ^{C} 3	bɨ^{C} < bɨə^{C}	brə(k)h	⋈ 4-61/999k 丕

4-60	**= K. 1237y**	**Mand.**	**MC**	**LHan**	**OCM**	
y	轡	pèi	pjɨ^{C} 3	pɨ^{C} < pɨə^{C}	prəh	? ⋈ 紱韍 *brəh (5-36/935)

4-61	**= K. 999**	**Mand.**	**MC**	**LHan**	**OCM**	
a	不 soar	fǒu	pjəu^{B}	pu^{B} < puə^{B}	pəʔ	
	[T] BTD Skt. 不乃 pūrṇa <> [E] Cf. WT 'p^{h}ag-pa 'to rise, raise, soar up'.					
	不 not	bù	pjəu($^{B/C}$)	pu < puə R!	pə	[T] ONW pu
e	否[1] = 不 not	fǒu	pjəu^{B}	pu^{B} < puə^{B}	pəʔ R!	OCB *pjəʔ
	[T] Sin Sukchu SR fəw (上); MGZY Hwuw (上) [fuw]					
g	紑	fóu	p^{h}jəu(^{B})	p^{h}u(^{B}) < p^{h}uə(^{B})	phə	OCB *phjə
h	罘	fú	bjəu	bu < buə R!	bu R!	
	loan for = 罦 *bu (13-73/1233j)					
i	芣	fú	bjəu	bu < buə	bə	
q	阫	pēi, péi	p^{h}wậi	p^{h}ə	phə̂	
s	坏	péi	bwậi	bə	bə̂	
j	抔	póu	bəu	bo	bô	
e	否[2] bad	pǐ	pjɨ^{B} 3	pɨ^{B} < pɨə^{B}	prəʔ	
	否[3] obstruct	bèi	bjɨ^{B} 3	bɨə^{B}	brəʔ	
-	邳	pí	bjɨ 3	bɨə	brə	
-	豾	pī	p^{h}ji 3	p^{h}ɨə	phrə?	
klm	丕伾駓	pī	p^{h}ji 3	p^{h}ɨə	phrə R!	
n	秠	pī	p^{h}ji 3,	p^{h}ɨə^{B} < p^{h}ɨə,	phrə,	
			p^{h}jəu	p^{h}u < p^{h}uə	p^{h}ə R!	
-	胚	pēi	p^{h}wậi	p^{h}ə	phə̂	
tu	杏音 spit	pòu	p^{h}əu^{C}	p^{h}o^{C}	phôh	
	[N] The initial t^{h}- may be an error (Karlgren) or due to paronomastic attraction, see 34-12/459 涒.					
v	剖	pōu !	p^{h}əu^{B}	p^{h}o^{B}	phôʔ	
z	部	pǒu, bù	bəu^{B}	bo^{B} R!	bôʔ	
	[E] Tai: PTai *bu̯o^{A2}, Po'ai poo^{A1} < *p- 'mountain' <> WT 'bog 'small hillock'					

g'	菩	bù, pǒu	bəu^{B}, p^{h}əu^{B}	bo^{B}, p^{h}o^{B}	bôʔ, phôʔ	
a'	培 mound	pǒu	bəu^{B}	bo^{B} R!	bôʔ	
	earth up	péi	bwậi	bə	bə̂	
-	菩	pú	bəu	bo		[T] BTD Skt. bo(dhi)
x	棓	pǒu, póu	p^{h}əu^{B}, bəu	p^{h}o^{B}, bo	phôʔ, bô	
y	瓿	bù	bəu^{B}	bo^{B}	bôʔ	
d'	掊	bǒu, pǒu	p(^{h})əu^{B}	p(^{h})o^{B}	p(h)ôʔ	
po	桮杯	bēi	pwậi	pə	pə̂	
	[T] ONW pɑi <> [E] TB: WT p^{h}or-pa 'bowl, cup'					
b'	陪	péi	bwậi	bə	bə̂	
	[T] Sin Sukchu SR buj (平); PR bəj; MGZY pue (平) [buɛ]; ONW bɑi					
c'	倍 double	bèi	bwậi^{B}	bə^{B}	bə̂ʔ	
	[T] ONW bɑi. <> [E] WT 'p^{h}ar-ma 'double, manifold'					
	倍 turn back	bèi	bwậi^{C}	bə^{C}	bə̂kh	= 5-32/909e 背
	[T] ONW bɑi; BTD -pa(ka)					
e'	踣	bó, pòu	bək, p^{h}əu^{C}	bək, p^{h}o^{C}	bə̂k, phə̂kh	
f'	韸	běng	puŋ^{B}	poŋ^{B}	pôŋʔ	

4-62	**= K. 1000**	**Mand.**	**MC**	**LHan**	**OCM**	
a	負	fù	bjəu^{B}	bu^{B} < buə^{B}	bəʔ R!	OCB *ɦpjə(k)?
	[T] MTang bvu, ONW bu <> [E] ? TB *buw 'carry on back or shoulder'. Or ST *bə: WT 'ba-ba 'to bring, carry'					
bc	偩萯	fù	bjəu^{B}	bu^{B} < buə^{B}	bəʔ	

4-63	**= K. 1001**	**Mand.**	**MC**	**LHan**	**OCM**	
a	婦	fù	bjəu^{B}	bu^{B} < buə^{B} R!	bəʔ R!	OCB *bjəʔ
	[T] Sin S. SR vu (去), vŵ (上), LR vu (去); MGZY Hwow (上) [vɔw]; MTang bvu, ONW bu					
	[D] PMin *bu^{C}: Xiamen pu^{C2} <> [E] Tai *baa^{A} 'wife'					

4-64	**= K. 947**	**Mand.**	**MC**	**LHan**	**OCM**	
a	母 mother	mǔ	məu^{B}		< *môʔ	
				mə^{B} R!	< məʔ R!	
	[T] Sin Sukchu SR mu, məw (上), LR mu; MGZY muw (上) [muw]; ONW mou^{B}					
	[N] OC and Han poetry, mǔ rimes consistently with *-ə (Luo / Zhou p. 266).					
	[E] TB *mow 'woman, bride' > WT -mo 'female suffix', Chepang mo 'wife'					
107a	毋 don't	wú	mju	muɑ //	mə	OCB *m(r)jo
	毋 a cap	móu	mjəu	mu < muə	mə	
947f	姆	mǔ	məu^{B}	mo^{B}	môʔ	
g	拇	mǔ	məu^{B}	mo^{B}	môʔ	[E] TB: PL: *C-ma^{3} 'thumb'
-	莓	mù	məu^{C}	mo^{C}	—	
h	坶	mù	mjuk	mok	mok	
i	每 flourish	mèi	mwậi(^{C})	mə(^{C})	mə̂(h)	
	每 each	měi	mwậi^{B}	mə^{B}	mə̂ʔ	
	[T] Sin Sukchu SR muj (上), PR, LR məj; MGZY mue (上) [muɛ]; ONW mɑi					
1251q	敏	mǐn	mj(w)en^{B}	mɨən^{B} R! //	mə̂ʔ R!	
947 l	梅	méi	mwậi	mə	mə̂ and mə̂ʔ	
	[E] ? Old Japanese ume^{2} 'plum'					
m	脢	méi	mwậi(^{C})	mə(^{C})	mə̂(h)	= 4-20/950c 脉

n	鋂	méi	mwậi	mə	mə̂	
o	晦	mǔ, mǒu	məu^B	mo^B	mə̂ʔ	= 4-66/949a
t	晦	huì	xwậi^C	huə^C	hmə̂ʔ R!	OCB *hmə(k)ʔ(s)
u	誨	huì	xwậi^C	huə^C	hmə̂h	

[T] Sin Sukchu SR xuj (去); MGZY hue (去) [xuɛ] <> [E] PL *s-ma^2 'to teach'

q	痗	mèi, huì	mwậi^C, xwậi^C	mə^C, huə^C	(h)mə̂h	

[E] WT rma 'wound, JP məmà 'wound, scar'

r	𩰣	huì	xwậi^C	huə^C	hmə̂h	
st	悔晦	huǐ !	xwậi^C	huə^C	hmə̂h	
x	海	hǎi	xậi^B	hə^B	hmə̂ʔ R!	

MC is irregular. <> [T] Sin Sukchu SR xaj (上); MGZY hay (上) [xaj]; ONW hɑi

138a	侮	wǔ	mju^B	muo^B	moʔ R!	

4-65	**= K. 948**	**Mand.**	**MC**	**LHan**	**OCM**	
a	某 > 梅	méi	mwậi	mə	mə̂(ʔ)	'plum tree'
	某 a certain	mǒu	məu^B	mo^B	mə̂ʔ	

[T] Sin Sukchu SR məw, mu (上), LR mu; MGZY muw (上) [muw]; ONW mou

f	謀	móu	mjəu	mu < muə R!	mə R!	

[T] Sin Sukchu SR məw (平); MGZY (khuw >) wuw (平) [vuw]

ce-	媒禖腜	méi	mwậi	mə	mə̂	'go-between'
d	煤	méi	mwậi	mə	mə̂	

[E] TB-Lushai maŋ^R / man^L < maŋʔ / maŋs 'be sooty, grimy'

-	㷵	mǔ	muo^B [GY], mju(^{B})	mɑ^B, muɑ^B	—	⋈ 2-40/802h 慕

[N] GY muo^B writes a Han period dialect variant of wǔ *maʔ 憮 1-69/103j 'love'

4-66	**= K. 949**	**Mand.**	**MC**	**LHan**	**OCM**	
a	畝	mǔ	məu^B <		*moʔ	= 4-64/947o
				mə^B R!	mə̂ʔ R!	OCB *mo/əʔ

[T] Sin Sukchu SR mu, məw (上); MGZY muw (上) [muw] <> [D] W-Suzhou col. m^{C2}, Wenzh mɛ^{B2}; X-Changsha mɤu^B; G-Nanchang mɛu^B; Y-Guangzhou mau^{B2}; M-Xiamen bɔ^B
[E] WT rmo-ba 'to plow', Mikir -mò classifier for strips of fields

5 OCM rime *-ək Zhí bù 職部

GSR 903 - 935

Baxter 1992: 472 ff. (§10.2.2)

See Table 4-1 for OCM rimes *-əŋ, *-ək, *-ə in QYS categories. See also Rime 14 *-uk for mergers after labial initials. Instead of LHan kɨk one could also write kɨək, instead of jək one could write jɨk, etc.

5-1	**= K. 903**	**Mand.**	**MC**	**LHan**	**OCM**	
afg	克尅剋	kè	kʰək	kʰək	khə̂k	

5-2	**= K. 931**	**Mand.**	**MC**	**LHan**	**OCM**	
a	革 skin	gé	kɛk	kɛk	krə̂k	
	extreme	jí	kjək	kɨək	kək	= 5-4d
c	愅 change	gé	kɛk	kɛk	krə̂k	
d	翮	hé	ɣɛk	gɛk	grə̂k	~ 8-2/855g 翮

5-3	**= K. 1260a**	**Mand.**	**MC**	**LHan**	**OCM**	
a	覈	hé	ɣɛk	gɛk	grə̂k	= 4-2/937a' 核

5-4	**= K. 910**	**Mand.**	**MC**	**LHan**	**OCM**	
a	亟 urgently	jí	kjək	kɨk	kək	
	often	qì	kʰjɨᶜ	kʰɨəᶜ	khəkh	
cd	悈殛 urgent	jí	kjək	kɨk	kək	= 5-2a
e	極	jí	gjək	gɨk	gək	

[T] Sin Sukchu SR gi (入); MGZY ki (入) [gi]; ONW gik

[E] LB *kak 'expensive, intense, at its peak'

5-5	**= K. 911**	**Mand.**	**MC**	**LHan**	**OCM**	
a	棘	jí	kjək	kɨk	kək	OCB *krjək
c	襋	jí	kjək	kɨk	kək	

5-6 **= K. 929** There are hardly any MC jwuk < *wək, hence no OC medial *r here. One could also write LHan wək instead of LHan wɨk.

		Mand.	**MC**	**LHan**	**OCM**	
ae	或[1] > 域	yù	jwək	wɨk	wək	OCB *wrək
gj	棫罭	yù	jwək	wɨk	wək	
kn	閾緎	yù,	jwək,	wɨk,	wək,	
		xù	xjwək	huɨk	hwək	
l	淢	xù	xjwək	huɨk	hwək	= 5-7/930a 洫 ¤ 域
m	窢	xù	xjwək	huɨk	hwək	

aq	或² 惑	huò	ɣwək	ɣuək	wə̂k	
	[T] Sin Sukchu SR ɣuj (入), LR xujʔ; MGZY Xue (入) [ɣuɛ]; ONW ɣuək					
r	蜮	huò,	ɣwək,	ɣuək,	wə̂k,	
		yù	jwək	wɨk	wək	
suv	膕馘聝	guó	kwɛk	kuɛk	kwrə̂k	
t	蟈	guō	kwɛk	kuɛk	kwrə̂k	
o	國	guó	kwək	kuək	kwə̂k	OCB *k-wək
	[T] Sin Sukchu SR kuj (入), PR, LR kujʔ; MGZY gue (入) [kuɛ]; ONW kuək					
y	彧	yù	ʔjuk	ʔuk	ʔuk	

5-7	= K. 930	Mand.	MC	LHan	OCM	
a	洫	xù	xjwək	huɨk //	hwit	
	= 淢 5-6L 'moat' < 'boundary', 'threshold'. See also 29-7/410d; GSR 410 'moat'					
b	侐	xù,	xjwək,	huɨk,	hwək,	
		huì	hjwɨ^C	huɨ^C	hwəkh	
c	殈	xù	xiwek,	huek,	hwêk,	= 8-7/1260f 砉
			xjwäk	hyek	hwek	

5-8	= K. 914	Mand.	MC	LHan	OCM
a	赫	xì	xjək	hɨk	hək

5-9	= K. 915	Mand.	MC	LHan	OCM
a	抑	yì	ʔjək	ʔɨk	ʔək

5-10	= K. 957	Mand.	MC	LHan	OCM	
a	意	yì	ʔɨ^C	ʔɨə^C	ʔəkh	OCB *ʔ(r)jəks
	[T] Sin Sukchu SR ʔi (去); MGZY 'i (去) [ʔi]; MTang ʔi, ONW ʔiə					
c	鷾	yì	ʔɨ^C	ʔɨə^C	ʔəkh	
d	醷 a drink	yì	ʔjək,	ʔɨk,	ʔək,	
			ʔɨ^B	ʔɨə^B	ʔəʔ	
	醷 a breath	ài	ʔăi^C	ʔɛ^C	ʔə̂h ! an onomatopoetic syllable	
efghi	億憶檍繶臆	yì	ʔjək	ʔɨk	ʔək	OCB *ʔ(r)jək
	[T] ONW ʔik.					
b	噫 oh!	yì	ʔɨ	ʔɨə	ʔə	
	to belch	ài	ʔăi	ʔɛ	ʔə̂ ! an onomatopoetic syllable	

5-11	= K. 905	Mand.	MC	LHan	OCM
ad	㝵得	dé	tək	tək	tə̂k
	[T] Sin Sukchu SR təj (入), LR təjʔ; MGZY dʰiy (入) [təj]; ONW tək				

5-12	= K. 919	Mand.	MC	LHan	OCM	
a	直 straight	zhí	ḍjək	ḍɨk	drək	
	[T] Sin Sukchu SR dẓi (入); MGZY ci (入) [dẓi]; ONW dik.					
	[E] LB *N-d(y)ak^L 'truly, very', WB tyak-tyak 'very'; Lushai tak^L 'real, true, genuine, very'					
	直 take place	zhì	ḍɨ^C	ḍiə^C	drəkh	
b	稙	zhí	tjək	ṭɨk	trək	ONW tik
g	置	zhì	ṭɨ^C	ṭiə^C	trəkh	
	[T] MTang ṭi, ONW tiə <> [E] TB: WT 'ǰog-pa, bžag 'to put, place, arrange'					

		Mand.	MC	LHan	OCM	
h	值	zhí	ḍɨ^C	ḍiə^C	drəkh	
	[T] MTang ḍi, ONW diə					
cd	埴殖	zhí	źjək	dźɨk	dək	
e	植	zhí, zhì	źjək, ḍɨ^C	dźɨk, ḍiə^C	dək, drəkh	[T] ONW dźik
ki	德悳	dé	tək	tək	tə̂k	
	[T] ONW tək. MHan 粟德 siok-tək Soɣd or soɣðik					
f	犆 single	tè	dək	dək	də̂k	= 4-26/961h' 特
	[E] ? ST: tak 'one' in Western Himalayan languages, e.g., Darmiya taku 'one'					
	犆 hem	zhí	ḍjək	ḍɨk	drək	

5-13 **= K. 920** There is no paleographic connection with 5-10/957 (Unger, Hao-ku 78, 2003: 84)

		Mand.	MC	LHan	OCM	
a	戠	zhī, shì	tśjək	tśɨk	tək	
gi	職膱	zhí	tśjək	tśɨk	tək	
f	織 to weave	zhī	tśjək	tśɨk	tək	[T] ONW tśik
	[E] TB *tak > WT 't^{h}ag-pa 'to weave' ⋈ t^{h}ags 'texture, web'; LB *tak/*dak 'weave, spin'					
	織 material	zhì	tśɨ^C	tśə^C	təkh	[T] ONW tśə^C
	[E] WT btags 't^{h}ag- 'woven' ⋈ t^{h}ags 'texture, web', JP daʔ[31] < dak[31] 'woven material'					
e	樴	zhí, dé	tśjək, dək	tśɨk, dək	tək, də̂k	
k	識 remember	zhì	tśɨ^C	tśə^C	təkh	
	識 know	shì	śjək	śɨk	lhək	
	[T] Sin Sukchu SR ʂi (入); MGZY shi (入) [ʂi]; ONW śik					
j	幟	shì,	śjək, śjɨ^C,	śɨk, śɨ^C,	lhək(h),	
		zhì	tś^{h}ɨ^C	tś^{h}ə	thəkh	
l	熾	chì	tś^{h}ɨ^C	tś^{h}ə	thəkh	

5-14	= K. 916	Mand.	MC	LHan	OCM	
a	陟	zhì	ṭjək	ṭɨk	trək	[T] ONW tik
	[E] LB *ɴtak 'ascend' > WB tak 'go up, ascend, advance, increase', WB ə-t^{h}ak 'upper part, prior time', WT ltag-pa 'the upper part / place'					
1257d	騭	zhì	ṭjək (tśjet)	ṭɨk	trək	Coblin 1983: 222

5-15	= K. 917	Mand.	MC	LHan	OCM
a	敕	chì	ṭ^{h}jək	ṭ^{h}ɨk	rhək

5-16	= K. 918	Mand.	MC	LHan	OCM	
ace	弋妋杙	yì	jiək	jɨk	lək	
	[T] MHan 烏弋山離 ʔɑ-jik [lɨk?]-ṣan-liɑi Alexandria; 粟弋 siok-jik Soɣd or Soɣðik					
g	忒	tè	t^{h}ək	t^{h}ək	lhə̂k	
h	貣	tè	t^{h}ək, dək	t^{h}ək	lhə̂k	
i	代	dài	dậi^C	də^C	lə̂kh	
	[T] Sin Sukchu SR daj (去); MGZY tay (去) [daj]; ONW dɑi; BTD 秫代 Skt. śuddha					
qr	岱黛	dài	dậi^C	də^C	lə̂kh	
p	貸	dài, tè	t^{h}ậi^C	t^{h}ə^C	lhə̂kh	
s	蟘	tè !	dək	dək	lə̂k	
fkl	式拭軾	shì	śjək	śɨk	lhək	[T] ONW śik
no	試栻	shì	śɨ^C	śə^C	lhəkh	[T] MTang śi, ONW śə
m	侙	chì	ṭ^{h}jək	ṭɨk	rhək	

5-17	**= K. 954**	**Mand.**	**MC**	**LHan**	**OCM**	
a	異	yì	jiɨ^{C}	jə^{C}	ləkh	OCB *ljəks
	= 4-31/977b 异					
di	翼瀷	yì	jiək	jɨk	lək or jək	OCB *ljək
	= 5-18/912 翼 [T] ONW ik					
e	廙	yì	jiək, jiɨ^{C}	jɨk, jə^{C}	lək(h)	
g	趩	chì	ṭ^{h}jək	ṭ^{h}ɨk	rhək	
-	禩	zì	zjɨ^{B}	ziə^{B}	—	

5-18 **= K. 912** The rimes are very irregular, the phonetic role of lì 立 is not clear; perhaps these do not form a single phonetic group.

		Mand.	**MC**	**LHan**	**OCM**	
ab	翊 翌	yì	jək	jək	lək or jək	= 5-17/954d
-	昱 bright	yù	jiuk	juk	luk or juk	
	SW 2928: lì 立 *rəp is phonetic, hence Baxter 1992: 556 *(w)rjɨ/up					
-	煜 bright	yù, yì	jiuk, jiəp	juk, jəp	luk/juk or ləp/jəp	

5-19	**= K. 921**	**Mand.**	**MC**	**LHan**	**OCM**	
ad	食[1]蝕	shí	dźjək	źɨk	m-lək	
	[T] Sin Sukchu SR zị (入); MGZY ci (入) [dzị]; ONW źik. <> [E] TB *m-lyak 'lick'					
	[N] Any or all words in this XS may have had an OC medial *j					
ae	食[2]飤	sì	zɨ^{C}	ziə^{C}	s-ləkh	
	= 4-53/972[m] <> [T] ONW ziə^{C} <> [D] PMin *džhi^{C} 'raise livestock'					
	[E] TB *s-lyak > LB *ʔljak 'to feed an animal'; Garo srak 'lick'					
h	飾	shì	śjək	śɨk	lhək	
g	飭	chì	ṭ^{h}jək	ṭɨk	rhək	⋊ 5-21/928 力

5-20	**= K. 913**	**Mand.**	**MC**	**LHan**	**OCM**	
a	奭	shì	śjäk,	śak,	hjak,	[D] Am ts^{h}io$ʔ^{A1}$
			xjək	hɨk	hək	
b	襫	shì	śjäk	śak	hjak ?	

5-20A	**= K. 1260b**	**Mand.**	**MC**	**LHan**	**OCM**
	疒	nè	ṇɛk	ṇɛk	nrə̂k or nrêk

5-21	**= K. 928**	**Mand.**	**MC**	**LHan**	**OCM**	
a	力	lì	ljək	lɨk	rək	OCB *C-rək
	⋊ 飭 5-19/921g <> [T] Sin Sukchu SR li (入); MGZY li (入) [li]; ONW lik					
	[E] ST *rə > LB *(k-)ra² 'strength, power' > PL *ra² 'strength', WB a^{B} <> Viet sủ'c 'force'					
c	仂	lè, lì	lək, ljək	lək, lɨk	rə̂k, rək	
deh	扐阞泐	lè	lək	lək	rə̂k	[T] ONW lək
f	勒	lè	lək	lək	rə̂k	
	Middle Viet mlạc > nhạc (only in certain expressions)					
-	朸	lì	ljək	lɨk	rək	OCB *C-rjək

5-22	**= K. 944, 932**	**Mand.**	**MC**	**LHan**	**OCM**	
944a	來 > 麥 wheat	mài	mɛk	mɛk	mrə̂k	OCB *mrək
	[E] ? TB: LB *g-ra² 'buckwheat', WT bra-bo 'buckwheat'					

932a	麥 > 來 come	lái	lậi	lə	rə̂ < rə̂k R!	OCB *C-rə(k)

[T] Sin Sukchu SR laj (平), LR laj; MGZY lay (平) [laj]; ONW lɑi) <> [E] ST *rə > TB *ra

944j	萊	lái	lậi(^{C})	lə(^{C})	rə̂(h)	
m	騋	lái	lậi	lə	rə̂	
- -	鯠郲	lái	lậi	lə	—	
fg	倈逨	lái	lậi	lə	rə̂	
ki	賚勑	lài	lậi^C	lə^C	rə̂kh	
-	睞	lài	lậi^C	lə^C	—	SW 1042

5-23	**= K. 907**	**Mand.**	**MC**	**LHan**	**OCM**
a	賊	zéi	dzək	dzək	dzə̂k

[T] ONW dzək <> [E] ? TB: WT ǰag < 'robbery'

5-24	**= K. 906**	**Mand.**	**MC**	**LHan**	**OCM**	
a	則	zé	tsək	tsək	tsə̂k	

[T] Sin Sukchu SR tsəj (入), LR tsəjʔ; MGZY dzʰiy (入) [tsəj]; ONW tsək

c	側	cè	tṣjək	tṣɨk	tsrək	= 5-27/924 仄昃
ef	惻測	cè	tṣʰjək	tṣʰɨk	tshrək	= 5-25/922a 畟

[T] Sin Sukchu SR tṣ'əj (入); MGZY chʰiy (入) [tṣ'əj]; ONW tṣhik

g	廁	cè	tṣʰɨ^C	tṣʰiə^C	tshrəkh

[T] Sin Sukchu SR tṣ'ʅ (去); LR tṣ'ʅ; MGZY chʰi (去) [tṣ'ʅ]

[E] TB *ts(y)i 'urinate' > WT gči(d)-pa 'to urinate'; WB tsʰi^B 'urine', NN *C-chi

5-25	**= K. 922**	**Mand.**	**MC**	**LHan**	**OCM**	
a	畟	chì,	tṣʰjək,	tṣʰɨk,	tshrək,	= 5-24/906ef 測惻

[T] Sin Sukchu SR tṣ'əj (入); MGZY chʰiy (入) [tṣ'əj]; ONW tṣhik

	畟	jì	tsjək	tsɨk	tsək
b	稷	jì	tsjək	tsɨk	tsək
c	謖	sù	ṣjuk	ṣuk	ṣuk ?

5-26 **= K. 923** 即 also serves as phonetic for MC tsjet, see 29-30/399

		Mand.	**MC**	**LHan**	**OCM**
ab	即 蝍	jí	tsjək	tsɨk	tsək
d	鵖	jí	tsjək, tsjäk	tsɨk, tsiak	tsək, tsek

5-27	**= K. 924**	**Mand.**	**MC**	**LHan**	**OCM**	
adefc	夨仄昊昃 c	zè	tṣjək	tṣɨk	tsrek	= 5-24/906c 側

5-28	**= K. 908**	**Mand.**	**MC**	**LHan**	**OCM**
a	塞 to block	sài, sāi, sè	sək, sậi^C	sək, sə^C	sə̂k(h)

[T] ONW sək, sɑi. MHan sək Saka <> [E] ? AA-Khmer suka /sok/ 'to stop up, block, cram...'

	塞 frontier	sài	sậi^C	sə^C	sə̂kh
b	寋	sè	sək	sək	sə̂k

5-29	**= K. 925**	**Mand.**	**MC**	**LHan**	**OCM**
a	息	xī	sjək	sɨk	sək

[T] Sin Sukchu SR si (入); MGZY si (入) [si]; ONW sik. MHan 安息 Arśak

[E] TB *sak: LB *C-sak 'breath, air, breath of life': WB ə-sak 'breath, life'; Mru chak 'heart, life'; JP saʔ^{31} 'to breathe' ≭ n^{31}-saʔ^{31} 'breath, force'

b	熄	xī	sjək	sɨk	sək	

5-30	= K. 926	Mand.	MC	LHan	OCM	
ae	嗇穡	sè	ṣjək	ṣɨk, S ṣək	srək	OCB *srjək

[T] ONW ṣik <> [E] ? TB: LB *C-šak 'pluck, pick'

5-31	= K. 927	Mand.	MC	LHan	OCM	
a	色	sè	ṣjək	ṣɨk, S ṣək	srək	OCB *srjək

[T] Sin Sukchu SR ʂəj (入), LR ʂəjʔ; MGZY sh^{h}iy (入) [ʂəj]; ONW ṣik

[E] TB-Lushai saar^{H} < saar 'prismatic colors' ⋇ saar^{R} / sarh^{R} 'healthy looking, rosy, ruddy'

5-32	= K. 909	Mand.	MC	LHan	OCM	
a	北	běi	pək	pək	pə̂k	

[T] Sin Sukchu SR pəj (入), LR pəʔ; MGZY bue (入) [puɛ]; ONW pək

e	背[1] the back	bèi	pwậi^{C}	pə^{C}	pə̂kh	'the back'

[T] Sin Sukchu SR puj (去); PR pəj; LR pəj; MGZY bue (去) [puɛ]

ef	背[2]偝 turn b.	bèi	bwậi^{C}	bə^{C}	bə̂kh	= 4-61/999c' 倍

[N] 'turn the back' <> [T] ONW bɑi

[E] TB: Lepcha buk 'back, wrong side' -/- 'carry on back'; ST *bək: TB *bak > JP baʔ^{31} (< *bak) 'carry' (child on back), Lushai pua^{L} / puak^{F} 'carrying on the back as a child'

-	邶	bèi	bwậi^{C}	bə^{C}	bə̂kh	

5-32A		Mand.	MC	LHan	OCM	
-	僰 name	bó	pək	pək	pə̂k	'name of a people'

5-33	= K. 933	Mand.	MC	LHan	OCM	
a	畐	fú	bjuk	buk < buək	bək	
-	愊	fú	bjuk	buk		
m	匐	fú, bó	bjuk, bək	buk, bək	bək, bə̂k	
dij	福葍輻	fú	pjuk	puk	pək	

福 [T] Sin Sukchu SR fu (入), PR, LR fu; MGZY Hwu (入) [fu]; MTang pfuk, ONW puk

k	幅 width	fú	pjuk	puk	pək	
	幅 strap	fú, bī	pjuk, pjək	puk, pɨk	pək, prək	
l	楅	fú, bī	pjuk, pjək	puk, pɨk	pək, prək	
-	蝙蝠 a bat	biān-fú	pien-pjuk	pen-puk	—	

[E] TB *ba:k > Lushai baak^{R}, Garo do-bak (do 'bird') 'bat', Mikir plàk-wúk ~ -plàk-bat

r	富	fù	pjəu^{C}	pu^{C}	pəkh	

[T] MTang pfu, ONW pu; BTD Skt. pu. <> [E] WT: p^{h}yug-pa 'rich' ⋇ p^{h}yugs 'cattle'

o	湢	bì	pjək	pɨk	prək	
p	逼	bī	pjək	pɨk	prək	
n	偪 crowd	bī	pjək	pɨk	prək	OCB *prjək

[T] ONW pik < ? TB-Lushai pik^{L} 'be thick, dense, impenetrable, overcrowded, overgrown'

	偪 Pl.N.	fú	pjuk	puk	pək	
s	副 cleave	pì	p(h)jək	p(h)ɨk	p(h)rək	OCB *p(h)rək ?
	副 aid	fù	p^{h}jəu^{C}	p^{h}u^{C}, p^{h}uə^{B} R!	phəkh	
q	疈	pì, bò	p^{h}jək, pɛk	p^{h}ɨk, pɛk	phrək, prə̂k	

? Tai: S. pliik^{4} 'divide into small pieces, evade'

5-34	**= K. 984**	**Mand.**	**MC**	**LHan**	**OCM**	
a	葡^1 > 箙	fú	bjuk	buk < buək	bək	'a qiver'
ad	葡^2 備 prepar	bèi	bjɨ^C 3	bɨ^C < bɨə^C	brəkh	OCB *brjəks

[T] Sin Sukchu SR bi (去), LR bi; MGZY pue (去) [buɛ] 'prepare'
[E] Cf. WT 'byor-ba ~ 'byar-ba 'be prepared' <> Tai: S. p^{h}rak ^{D2} < *b- 'prepare'

fg	精犕	bèi	bjɨ^C 3	bɨ^C < bɨə^C	brəkh	
h	僃	bèi	bǎi^C	bɛ^C	brə̂kh	

5-35	**= K. 934**	**Mand.**	**MC**	**LHan**	**OCM**	
a	𠬝	fú	bjuk	buk	bək	
d	服 submit	fú	bjuk	buk	bək	= 5-36/935a 伏

[T] Sin Sukchu SR vu (入); MGZY hwu (入) [vu]; MTang bvuk, ONW buk; OCB *bjək

	服 box	fù	bjəu^B	bu^B	bəʔ	'carriage box'
g	箙	fú	bjuk	buk	bək	

5-36	**= K. 935**	**Mand.**	**MC**	**LHan**	**OCM**	
a	伏 lie down	fú	bjuk	buk	bək	OCB *bjək

[E] TB-Lushai bɔk^L / bɔʔ^L 'to lie down'

	伏 to hatch	fù	bjəu^C	bu^C	bəkh	

'To hatch' [Li] <> [D] PMin bu^C: Fúzh pou^{C2}, Xiàmén pu^{C2}
[E] TB: Chepang bhyuk-sa 'to hatch' <> Tai: S. vak^{D2} 'to hatch'

-	坿	fù	bju^C	buo^C	boh	= 10-39/136k 附
- -	絥鞴	bì	bjɨ^C 3	bɨə^C	brə(k)h	

[N] 'harness a horse' [SW]. ? ⋈ 轡 'reins' 4-60/1237y

5-37	**= K. 1062**	**Mand.**	**MC**	**LHan**	**OCM**
a	冒 covetous	mò	mək	mək	mə̂k

For additional items of GSR 1062, see 13-74.

5-38	**= K. 904**	**Mand.**	**MC**	**LHan**	**OCM**
a	黑	hēi	xək	hək	hmə̂k

[T] Sin Sukchu SR xəj (入), LR xəjʔ; MGZY hiy (入) [xij]
[E] WT smag 'dark, darkness', mog-pa 'dark-colored'; Limbu mak 'black, dark' (of color) ⋈ makt- 'to become night', JP maʔ^{31} < mak^{31} 'black'

c	墨	mò	mək	mək	mə̂k

[T] Sin Sukchu SR məj (入), LR məjʔ; MGZY mue (入) [muɛ]

f	纆	mò	mək	mək	mə̂k
de	默嘿	mò	mək	mək	mə̂k

5-39	**= K. 1037**	**Mand.**	**MC**	**LHan**	**OCM**	
a	牧	mù	mjuk	muk	mək	OCB *mjək

[T] Sin Sukchu SR mu (入); MGZY wu (入) [vu]; ONW muk
[E] ST *m/brək ?: WT 'brog-pa < *ɴbrak 'summer pasture, solitude, wilderness, nomad'

6 OCM rime *-əŋ Zhēng bù 蒸部

GSR 881 - 902

Baxter 1992: 476 ff. (§10.2.3)

See Table 4-1 for OCM rimes *-əŋ, *-ək, *-ə in QYS categories.
Note: the OC final *əŋ is rare with MC tone B; words with this tone (OC *-ʔ) have either lost the nasal, or changed the nasal to a different place of articulation (-n, -m), or have doublets. OC *-uŋ (Rime 15) has no tone B words at all.

6-1	**= K. 881**	**Mand.**	**MC**	**LHan**	**OCM**	
a	亙	gèng, gèn	kəŋ^C	kəŋ^C	kə̂ŋh	
d	恆 constant	héng	ɣəŋ	gəŋ	gə̂ŋ	
	[T] Sin Sukchu SR ɣiŋ (平), PR ɣəŋ (平); MGZY Xing (平) [ɣiŋ]; ONW ɣəŋ; BTD Skt. gaṅga					
	恆 moon	gèng	kəŋ^C	kəŋ^C	kə̂ŋh	'increasing moon'
	[T] Sin Sukchu SR kəjŋ (去), PR kiŋ (去)					
fg	f 縆	gēng	kəŋ	kəŋ	kə̂ŋ	
h	堩	gèng	kəŋ^C	kəŋ^C	kə̂ŋh	

6-2	**= K. 882**	**Mand.**	**MC**	**LHan**	**OCM**	
ba	肯¹肎 meat	kěn,	k^{h}əŋ^B,	k^{h}əŋ^B,	khə̂ŋʔ,	'meat on bones'
		kǎi	k^{h}ậi^B	k^{h}ə^B	khə̂ʔ < khə̂ŋʔ	
	[T] Sin Sukchu SR k'əjŋ (上), PR, LR k'ən; MGZY kh^{h}ing (上) [k'əŋ]					
	[D] PMin *kheŋ^B, which is the analog to MC k^{h}əŋ^B and k^{h}ieŋ^B					
b	肯² willing	kěn	k^{h}əŋ^B	k^{h}əŋ^B	khə̂ŋʔ	

6-3	**= K. 888**	**Mand.**	**MC**	**LHan**	**OCM**
a	兢 fear	jīng	kjəŋ	kɨŋ	kəŋ
	兢 strong	jīng	gjəŋ	gɨŋ	gəŋ

6-4	**= K. 901**	**Mand.**	**MC**	**LHan**	**OCM**
a	弓	gōng	kjuŋ	kuŋ	kwəŋ
	[T] ONW kuŋ <> [D] K-Meix ^{44}t^{h}iɛn-^{44}kiuŋ^{A1} 天弓 'rainbow'; PMin *kyŋ				
	[E] TB *ku:ŋ$^{A/B}$ > WB ə-k^{h}uiŋ^B 'large branch, bough of tree', kuiŋ^A 'hang over in a curve' <> Tai: S. koŋ^4 'to arch, bend (bow)'				
e	穹	qióng !	k^{h}juŋ	k^{h}uŋ	khwəŋ

6-5	**= K. 887**	**Mand.**	**MC**	**LHan**	**OCM**
abf	厶厷肱	gōng	kwəŋ	kuəŋ	kwə̂ŋ
g	弘	hóng	ɣwəŋ	ɣuəŋ	gwə̂ŋ
hijk	宏竑紘閎	hóng	ɣwɛŋ	ɣuɛŋ	gwrə̂ŋ
m	鞃	gōng,	kwəŋ,	kuəŋ,	kwə̂ŋ,
		kōng	k^{h}wəŋ	k^{h}uəŋ	khwə̂ŋ

6 OCM *-əŋ 蒸部 (GSR 881-902)

1	雄	xióng	juŋ 3	wuŋ	wəŋ	OCB *wjəŋ
	[N] rimes with *-əŋ in Shijing, also in Zuozhuan (Shaughnessy EC 20: 231)					

6-6	**= K. 889**	**Mand.**	**MC**	**LHan**	**OCM**	
a	興 raise	xīng	xjəŋ	hɨŋ	həŋ	ONW hiŋ
	elated	xìng	xjəŋ^C	hɨŋ^C	həŋh	

6-7		**Mand.**	**MC**	**LHan**	**OCM**
-	擤	xǐng	xjəŋ^C	hɨŋ^C	həŋh

6-8	**= K. 890**	**Mand.**	**MC**	**LHan**	**OCM**	
ac	雁鷹	yīng	ʔjəŋ	ʔɨŋ	ʔəŋ	ONW ʔiŋ
e	膺	yīng	ʔjəŋ	ʔɨŋ	ʔəŋ	? Lushai eŋ^H 'the breast'
d	應 ought	yīng	ʔjəŋ	ʔɨŋ	ʔəŋ	
	應 answer	yìng	ʔjəŋ^C	ʔɨŋ^C	ʔəŋh	ONW ʔiŋ

6-9	**= K. 883**	**Mand.**	**MC**	**LHan**	**OCM**
aeij	a 登鐙燈	dēng	təŋ	təŋ	tə̂ŋ
	[T] Sin Sukchu SR təjŋ (平), PR, LR təŋ; MGZY d^{h}ing (平) [təŋ]; ONW təŋ				
k	隥	dèng	təŋ^C	təŋ^C	tə̂ŋh
l	鄧	dèng	dəŋ^C	dəŋ^C	də̂ŋh
m	澄	chéng	ḍjəŋ, ḍɐŋ	ḍɨŋ, ḍaŋ	drəŋ
	[E] Tai: S. rɨaŋ^{A2} 'limpid, clear'				
n	證	zhèng	tśjəŋ^C	tśɨŋ^C	təŋh
	[T] Sin Sukchu SR tʂiŋ (去); MGZY jing (去) [tʂiŋ]; ONW tśiŋ				

6-10	**= K. 896**	**Mand.**	**MC**	**LHan**	**OCM**
a	丞	chéng	źjəŋ	dźɨŋ	dəŋ
c	承	chéng	źjəŋ	dźɨŋ	dəŋ
	[T] Sin Sukchu SR dʐiŋ (平); MGZY zhing (平) [ʐiŋ]; ONW dźiŋ				
d	丞	chéng	źjəŋ	dźɨŋ	dəŋ
g	丞	chéng	źjəŋ	dźɨŋ	dəŋ
h	烝	zhēng	tśjəŋ	tśɨŋ	təŋ
k	蒸	zhēng	tśjəŋ	tśɨŋ	təŋ
	[T] ONW tśiŋ <> [E] TB *taŋ: WT t^{h}aŋ 'pine, fir, evergreen tree', WB t^{h}aŋ^B 'firewood'				
j	脀	zhēng	tśjəŋ	tśɨŋ	təŋ
i	拯	zhěng	tśjəŋ^B	tśɨŋ^B	təŋʔ

6-11	**= K. 891**	**Mand.**	**MC**	**LHan**	**OCM**	
a	徵 examine	zhēng	ṭjəŋ	ṭɨŋ	trəŋ	[T] MTang ṭiŋ, ONW tiŋ
	徵 suppress	chéng	ḍjəŋ	ḍɨŋ	drəŋ	
	徵 a note	zhǐ	ṭjɨ^B	ṭiə^B	trəʔ < trəŋʔ ?	
b	懲	chéng	ḍjəŋ	ḍɨŋ	drəŋ	

6-12	**= K. 894**	**Mand.**	**MC**	**LHan**	**OCM**
ad	爯偁	chēng	tś^{h}jəŋ	tś^{h}ɨŋ	k-hləŋ (or thəŋ?)
g	稱 weigh	chēng	tś^{h}jəŋ	tś^{h}ɨŋ	k-hləŋ (or thəŋ?, but note Khmer)
	[T] ONW tś^{h}iŋ <> [E] ? MK: Khmer thlɤŋ 'to weigh'				

	稱 equal to	chèng	tś^{h}jəŋ^{C}	tś^{h}ɨŋ^{C}	k-hləŋh (or thəŋh?)	

6-13	**= K. 893**	**Mand.**	**MC**	**LHan**	**OCM**	
ac	灷[illegible]	yìng	jiəŋ^{C}	jɨŋ^{C}	ləŋh	
kl	媵賸	yìng	jiəŋ^{C}	jɨŋ^{C}	ləŋh	
f	朕 I, my	zhèn	ḍjəm^{B}	ḍɨm^{B}	drəŋʔ < r-ləŋʔ	
	a seam	zhèn	ḍjen^{B}	ḍɨn^{B}	drənʔ < r-lənʔ or r-ləŋʔ	
j	栚	zhèn	ḍjəm^{B}	ḍɨm^{B}	drəŋʔ < r-ləŋʔ	
p	勝 equal to	shēng	śjəŋ	śɨŋ	lhəŋ	
	勝 vanquish	shèng	śjəŋ^{C}	śɨŋ^{C}	lhəŋh	ONW śiŋ
qrtv	滕 r 縢騰	téng	dəŋ	dəŋ	lə̂ŋ	ONW dəŋ
u	螣 a snake	téng	dəŋ	dəŋ	lə̂ŋ	
	an insect	tè	dək	dək	lə̂k	
n	塍	chéng	dźjəŋ	źɨŋ	m-ləŋ	

6-14	**= K. 945j**	**Mand.**	**MC**	**LHan**	**OCM**	
j	孕	yùn	jiəŋ^{C}	jɨŋ^{C}	ləŋh	= 6-24/892c [illegible]
	[T] ONW iŋ					
-	[illegible]	yùn [JY] = 鱦				
	The element 乃 'contain' (4-38/945a) is semantic; it also occurs in yíng 盈 'full'					

6-15	**= K. 895**	**Mand.**	**MC**	**LHan**	**OCM**
a	乘 to mount	chéng	dźjəŋ	źɨŋ	m-ləŋ
	乘 chariot	shèng	dźjəŋ^{C}	źɨŋ^{C}	m-ləŋh

6-16	**= K. 897**	**Mand.**	**MC**	**LHan**	**OCM**
acd	升昇陞	shēng	śjəŋ	śɨŋ	lhəŋ
	[T] Sin Sukchu SR ṣiŋ (平); MGZY shing (平) [ṣiŋ]; ONW śiŋ				
e	抍	shēng,	śjəŋ,	śɨŋ,	lhəŋ,
		zhěng	tśjəŋ	tśɨŋ	təŋ
	OC *təŋ is the reading of a synonym like 6-10/896hj				

6-17	**= K. 898**	**Mand.**	**MC**	**LHan**	**OCM**	
ac	夌陵	líng	ljəŋ	lɨŋ	rəŋ	陵 [T] BTD Skt. lavim[k]
f	凌 ice	líng	ljəŋ	lɨŋ	rəŋ	OCB *b-rjəŋ
	~ 9-19/823h 冷 <> [T] ONW liŋ					
	凌 repress	líng	ljəŋ	lɨŋ	rəŋ	OCB *b-rjəŋ
eghi	淩菱鯪蔆	líng	ljəŋ	lɨŋ	rəŋ	
-	㥄	líng	ljəŋ	lɨŋ	—	
	A Han period dialect variant of 怜 [FY 1.6]					

6-18	**= K. 885**	**Mand.**	**MC**	**LHan**	**OCM**	
a	能 bear n.	néng	nəŋ	nə(ŋ)	nə̂ !	[T] ONW nəŋ
	[E] AA: Kharia bɔnɔi 'bear', Santali bana 'Indian black bear' → TB-Lepcha să-na 'bear'					
	能 able	néng	nəŋ	nəŋ	nə̂ŋ, nə̂ʔ	
	[T] Sin Sukchu SR nəjŋ (平), PR, LR nəŋ; MGZY n^{h}ing (平) [nəŋ]; ONW nəŋ					
f	態	tài	t^{h}ậi^{C}	t^{h}ə^{C}	nhə̂h	

6-19	**= K. 884**	**Mand.**	**MC**	**LHan**	**OCM**
a	曾 to add	zēng	tsəŋ	tsəŋ	tsə̂ŋ

[T] Sin Sukchu SR tsəjŋ (平), PR tsəŋ; MGZY dz^{h}ing (平) [tsəŋ]; ONW tsəŋ

	曾 pf. tense	céng	dzəŋ	dzəŋ	dzə̂ŋ
cde	增憎橧	zēng	tsəŋ	tsəŋ	tsə̂ŋ
fg	罾矰	zēng	tsəŋ	tsəŋ	tsə̂ŋ
h	繒	zēng,	tsəŋ,	tsəŋ,	tsə̂ŋ,
		qíng	dzjəŋ	dziɨŋ	dzəŋ
i	層	céng	dzəŋ, tsəŋ	dzəŋ, tsəŋ	dzə̂ŋ, tsə̂ŋ

[T] Sin Sukchu SR dzəjŋ (平), PR, LR dzəŋ; MGZY ts^{h}ing (平) [dzəŋ]

j	贈	zèng	dzəŋ^{C}	dzəŋ^{C}	dzə̂ŋh
k	甑	jìng, zèng	tsjəŋ	tsɨŋ	tsəŋ
-	僧	sēŋ	səŋ	səŋ	—

[T] BTD 僧伽 səŋ-ga Skt. saṃgha

6-20	**= K. 886**	**Mand.**	**MC**	**LHan**	**OCM**
afgj	朋倗傰鵬	péng	bəŋ	bəŋ	bə̂ŋ

[T] Pre-ONW bəŋ

m	崩	bēng	pəŋ	pəŋ	pə̂ŋ

[T] ONW pəŋ <> [D] PMin *p̆-: Jiànyáng vaiŋ[9]; Yao baaŋ[1] (< *nb-) 'collapse, fall over'

[E] ? TB-Chepang bəŋh- 'to slip, slide' (earth, rock) ⋈ bəŋh- 'landslide'

kl	k 堋	bèng	pəŋ^{C}	pəŋ^{C}	pə̂ŋh

[E] TB: WT 'bum 'tomb, sepulcher', Lushai p^{h}uum^{H} 'to bury, inter'

o	繃	bēng	pɛŋ	pɛŋ	prə̂ŋ

[E] ? TB: WT (')p^{h}reŋ 'string on which things are filed' ⋈ 'p^{h}reŋ-ba 'string of beads, rosary' ⋈ 'breŋ-ba 'strap, rope', 'p^{h}reŋ 'to love'

n	掤	bīng	pjəŋ	piɨŋ	prəŋ

6-21	**= K. 899**	**Mand.**	**MC**	**LHan**	**OCM**	
ab	冫冰	bīng	pjəŋ	piɨŋ	prəŋ	OCB *prjəŋ

[T] ONW piŋ

[E] ? TB *pam > Tangkhul Naga p^{h}am, Kanauri pom 'snow', Jiarong ta-rpam 'ice'

de	馮憑	píng	bjəŋ	biɨŋ	brəŋ

[T] Sin Sukchu SR biŋ (平); MGZY ping (平) [biŋ]

6-22	**= K. 900**	**Mand.**	**MC**	**LHan**	**OCM**
a	凭	píng	bjəŋ(^{C})	biɨŋ(^{C})	brəŋ(h)

6-23	**= K. 902**	**Mand.**	**MC**	**LHan**	**OCM**
a	夢[1]c dream	mèng	mjuŋ^{C}	muŋ(^{C})	məŋ (tone A!)

[T] Sin Sukchu SR muŋ (去); MGZY wung (去) [vuŋ]; MTang moŋ, ONW muŋ

[E] ST *məŋ: WT rmaŋ-lam 'dream'

	夢[2] blind	méng	muŋ	moŋ	môŋ < mloŋ ?	= 12-27/1181 ca 矇蒙
d	瞢	méng	mjuŋ	muŋ	məŋ	
			mwəŋ	məŋ	mə̂ŋ	
g	薨	hōng	xwəŋ	huəŋ	hmə̂ŋ	
e	甍	méng	mɛŋ	mɛŋ	mrə̂ŋ	
f	甍	máng	mwâŋ	maŋ	mâŋ	

6-24	**= K. 892, 1252d**		**MC**	**LHan**	**OCM**	
1252d 黽	frog	mǐn	meŋ^B	meŋ^B	mrə̂ŋʔ	
黽	Pl.N.	méng	meŋ	meŋ	mrə̂ŋ	
黽池	Pl.N.	miǎn-	mjiän^B 4, mjien^B 4	mian^B, min^B	menʔ, minʔ	
黽勉		mǐn-miǎn	mjen^B 3 ! -mjän^B 3	mɨn^B -mɨan^B	mrənʔ-mranʔ	= 33-36/475m 忞
892a 蠅		yíng	jiəŋ	jɨŋ	ləŋ	

[E] Old Sino-Viet. lAŋ 'a fly'

b 繩	rope	shéng	dźjəŋ	źɨŋ	m-ləŋ	

[T] Sin Sukchu SR ʐiŋ (平); MGZY cing (平) [dʐiŋ]

[E] ? ST *mləŋ: WB ə-hmyaŋ^B 'string, thread, fiber, nerve' ~ mín 緡

繩	full	yìng	jiəŋ^C	jɨŋ^C	ləŋ^C	

= yùn 孕 *ləŋh (6-14/945j) 'pregnant'

- 䑈	pregnant	shèng	dźjəŋ^C	źɨŋ^C	m-ləŋh	

⋙ yùn 孕 *ləŋh (6-14/945j) 'pregnant'

- 鱦		shéng, shèng,	dźjəŋ$^{A/C}$,	źɨŋ(^{C}),	—	'spawn' n. (of fish) [EY]
鱦		yùn	jiəŋ^C	jɨŋ^C		

Same word as = 鱊 and = yùn 孕 *ləŋh (6-14/945l) 'pregnant'

鱦		mǐn	meŋ^B	meŋ^B	mrə̂ŋʔ	

GY: 'a kind of frog'; Pl.N.; *JY:* 'a kind of fish'. Prob. s. w. as 黽.

7 OCM rime *-e Zhī bù 支部

GSR 861 - 880

Baxter 1992: 491 ff. (§10.2.7)

See Table 8-1 for OCM rimes *-eŋ, *-ek, *-e in QYS categories.

Table 7-1: Comparison of OC *-i, *-e and *-ai in QYS Divisions

Div,	*-i R.26	*-e R.7	*-ai R.18
I			何 ɣâ gɑi *gâi 跛 puâ pɑi^{B} *pâiʔ 多 tâ tɑi *tâi
IV	啟 kʰiei^{B} kʰei^{B} *khîʔ 米 miei^{B} mei^{B} *mîʔ 睽 kʰiwei kʰuei *khwî 氐 tiei^{B} tei^{B} *tîʔ	雞 kiei ke *kê 圭 kiwei kue *kwê 啼 diei de *dê	
3/3 gr	耆 gji3 gɨ *gri 戣 gjwi3 gwɨ *gwri	技 gje^{B}3 gɨe^{B} *greʔ	騎 gje3 gɨɑi *gai 皮 bje3 bɨɑi *bai
3/4 gr	伊 ʔi4 ʔi *ʔi 癸 kwi^{B}4 kwi^{B} *kwiʔ 比 pi^{B}4 pi^{B} *piʔ	歧 gjie4 gie *ge 規 kjwie4 kye *kwe 卑 pjie4 pie *pe	
III ac	死 si^{B} si^{B} *siʔ 維 jiwi4 wi *wi	支 tśje tśe < kie *ke 知 tje ṭie *tre	離 lje liɑi *rai
III ac			蛇 dźja źai *m-lai
II	階 kăi kɛi *krî	解 kaɨ^{B} kɛ^{B} *krêʔ 卦 kwaɨ^{C} kuɛ^{C} *kwrêh 買 maɨ^{B} mɛ^{B} *mrêʔ	加 ka kai *krâi 麻 ma mai *mrâi 沙 ṣa ṣai *srâi

The table shows how most OC finals of rime *-e have merged in MC with reflexes of other rimes.

While there are virtually no syllables of the type *Tai (Rime 18), here type *Te abounds; conversely, syllables of the type *(C)le are rare while *(C)lai is rather common. See the introductory comments to Rime no. 18 *-ai. For the palatalization of velars with *chóngniǔ* div. 4/4 vocalism (as in series 7-3 to 7-6), see Schuessler, *JCL* 24.2, 1996: 197-211.

7 OCM *-e 支部 (GSR 861-880)

7-1	**= K. 876**	**Mand.**	**MC**	**LHan**	**OCM**	
a	系	xì	ɣiei^{C}	ge^{C}	gêh	OCB *N-keks

= 8.1 繫 <> [T] ONW ɣėi

c	係	xì	kiei^{C}	ke^{C}	kêh	OCB *keks = 8.1 繫; 7-2 繼
dgkl	奚㜎豀蹊	xī	ɣiei	ge	gê	
m-	鼷騱	xī	ɣiei	ge	gê	
i	徯	xī	ɣiei, ɣiei^{B}	ge, ge^{B}	gê, gêʔ	
j	謑 disgrace	xǐ	ɣiei^{B}	ge^{B}	gêʔ	
	perverse	xǐ	ɣiei, ɣiei^{B}	ge, ge^{B}	gê, gêʔ	
np	雞鷄	jī	kiei	ke	kê	

[T] Sin Sukchu SR kjej (平), PR, LR ki; MGZY gÿi (平) [kji]; ONW kėi <> [D] PMin *kei, Ke: Meix kai^{A1} <> [E] KT, MY: PTai kəi^{B1} < *k- 'chicken', KS *kaːi^{5}, MY *kai

q	谿	xī, qī	k^{h}iei	k^{h}e	khê < khle	
-	溪	xī	k^{h}iei	k^{h}e	khê < khle	

[E] ? PWMiao *kle^{A1} 'water, river'

7-2	**= K. 1241b**	**Mand.**	**MC**	**LHan**	**OCM**	
b	繼	jì	kiei^{C}	ke^{C}	kêh	OCB *keks

= 7-1/876c 係, 8-1/854a 繫 <> [T] ONW kėi

7-3	**= K. 864**	**Mand.**	**MC**	**LHan**	**OCM**	
abc	支枝肢	zhī	tśje	tśe < kie	ke	'branch > limb'

[T] ONW tśe (kie?); BTD Skt. ke, tye, Pkt. ce. MHan 一支 ʔit-kie Iki, 條支 deu-kie Taokē
[D] PMin *ki <> [E] TB: Chepang gweʔ 'finger', Tani *ke(ŋ) 'finger'; WT bkye 'to divide'

e	翅 wing	chì	śje^{C} //	kie	ke	

[N] 'Wing' *ke is the same etymon as 'branch, limb' above. The reading *chì* has been transferred from the synonym shì 翨 *lheh ? 'wing'.
[T] Sin SR tʂ'ʅ, ʂi (去), PR ʂʅ, LR tʂ'ʅ; MGZY shi (去) [ʂi]; MTang śi, kie (?), Sui-Tang kɨ, ONW kie (?); see Coblin 1994, Compendium of Phonetics in Northwest Chinese: 209f.

	翅 only	chì	śje^{C}	śe^{C}	lhekh	= 7-12/877k 啻

[N] The graph 翅 was borrowed for 'only' because of its reading for 'wing'

d	忮	zhì	tśje^{C}	tśe^{C} < kie^{C}	keh	

[E] Tai: S. keek^{D1} 'wicked, perverted'

ih-	歧岐蚑	qí	gjie 4	gie	ge	[T] ONW gie
g	跂 tiptoe	qǐ, qì	k^{h}jie$^{B/C}$ 4	k^{h}ie$^{B/C}$	kheʔ, kheh	= 7-4/862a 企

[T] Sin Sukchu SR k'jej (上), PR k'i; MGZY khÿi (上去) [k'ji]; Sui-Tang k^{h}ɨ, ONW k^{h}ie

	跂 6 toes	qí	gjie 4	gie	ge	
f	[illegible]	qì	k^{h}jie^{C} 4	k^{h}ie^{C}	kheh	

[E] TB: JP k^{h}yè, n^{31}-k^{h}yeŋ^{31} 'oblique, slanting'

m	頍	kuǐ	k^{h}jwie^{B} 4	k^{h}uie^{B}	khweʔ	
j	伎 talented	jì	gje^{B} 3	gɨe^{B}	greʔ	
	run	qí	gje 3	gɨe	gre	
k	技	jì	gje^{B} 3	gɨe^{B}	greʔ	
l	芰	jì	gje^{C} 3	gɨe^{C}	greh	
-	妓	jī, jì	kje 3, gje^{B} 3	gɨe^{B}	—	

[T] Wei-Jin kɨe, gɨe^{B} 'prostitute' <> [E] MK: PVM *keːʔ 'woman' > Viet. cái / gái 'feminine', PWa *krih 'girl'; Bahnar North kadri, PNBahn. *kadrì 'female'

-	鬾	jì	gje(^{C}) 3			

-	庋	jǐ	kje^B 3			
1259b	屐	jī	gjɐk	gɨak	grak	OCB 1977: 193 *grjek

7-4	= K. 862	Mand.	MC	LHan	OCM	
a	企	qǐ	k^{h}jie$^{B/C}$ 4	k^{h}ie$^{B/C}$	kheʔ/h	= 7-3/864g 跂

[T] Sin Sukchu SR k'jej (上), PR k'i; MGZY khÿi (上去) [k'ji]; Sui-Tang k^{h}ɨ, ONW k^{h}ie

7-5	= K. 865	Mand.	MC	LHan	OCM	
a	只 a particle	zhǐ	tśje^B	tśe^B < kie^B	keʔ	
	只 only	zhǐ	tśje^B	tśe^B	—	~ 7-6/867i 祇

[T] ONW kie ~ tśe ?

cd	軹咫	zhǐ	tśje^B	kie^B	keʔ	
e	枳 (枳椇)	zhǐ	kjie^B 4 !	kie^B	keʔ	'Hovenia dulcis'

[T] ONW kie, Mid-Tang kɨ

	枳 a citrus	zhǐ	tśje^B	kie^B	keʔ	'Poncirus trifoliata' (citr.)
b	胑	zhī	tśje	kie	ke	= 7-3/864c 肢
-	伿	xì	ɣiei^B	ge^B	—	SW
-	迟	—	k^{h}jiäk	k^{h}iek	—	SW

7-6 **= K. 867** There is some confusion with 26-14/GSR 59.

		Mand.	MC	LHan	OCM	
a	氏 clan	shì	źje^B	dźe^B < gie^B	geʔ	
	月氏 Yuè-zhī		-tśje	-tśe < -kie	-ke	

[N] Yue-zhī does not mean 'Moon *clan*'

de	坻抵	zhǐ	tśje^B	kie^B	keʔ	
g	疧 illness	qí	gjie 4	gie	ge	

For the synonym 867h, see 26-14/590

j -	軝蚔	qí	gjie 4	gie	ge	
i	祇 spirit	qí	gjie 4	gie	ge	
	祇 only	zhī	tśje	tśe < kie	ke	~ 7-5/865a 只

[T] BTD Skt. je(tavana), -khye-, khya ~ khyeya

f	舐	shì	dźje^B	źe^B	(m-leʔ)	OCB *m-lajʔ

Said to be the vulgar form of 8-12/850 弛; = 7-18/1238e 咶 etc. <> [T] ONW źe^B <> [D] Yue-Guangzh lai^{31} <> [E] Kam-Tai: S. lia^{A2} < *dl- 'to lick', KS *lja^2 ? <> [N] [Zhuang]. The phonetic element has been added after palatalization.

-	紙 paper	zhǐ	tśje^B	tśɑi^B < kiɑi^B ?		

[T] ONW tśe <> [D] PMin *tšiɑi^B <> [E] Viet. giấy, PVM *k-cajʔ

[N] LHan kiɑi^B, not kɨɑi^B, would account for palatalization

7-7	= K. 861	Mand.	MC	LHan	OCM	
a	解 unloose	jiě	kaɨ^B	kɛ^B	krêʔ	

[T] Sin Sukchu SR kjaj (上); PR, LR kjej; MGZY gyay (上) [kjaj]; ONW këi

[E] ? Area *C-re: TB: Chepang greh- 'to sever, chop off, cut cleanly'

	解 residence	jiě !	kaɨ^C	kɛ^C	krêh	
	解 underst.	xiè	ɣaɨ^B	gɛ^B	grêʔ	

[D] Min: Jiànyáng hai^C, Fuzhou a^{C2}, Xiàm ue^{C2}

	解 careless	jiè, xiè	kaɨ^C, ɣaɨ^B	kɛ^C, gɛ^B	krêh, grêʔ	[T] ONW ɣëi
bc	懈繲	xiè, jiè	kaɨ^C	kɛ^C	krêh	

d	蟹	xiè	ɣaɨ^{B}	gɛ^{B}	grêʔ ?

[D] PMin *he^{B} <> [E] TB *d-ka:y / *d-gra:y > NNaga *gra:n, JP tʃă^{55}-k^{h}an^{51}, Mikir čehē 'crab', Lushai cha^{L}-kai^{L} < -kaih 'crab', Tangkhul khai 'fish'; Adi take

e	邂逅	xiè-hòu	ɣaɨ^{C}-ɣəu^{C}	gɛ^{C}-go^{C}	grêh-grôh

7-7A	= K. 1240fg	Mand.	MC	LHan	OCM
fg	瀣薤	xiè	ɣaɨ^{C}	gɛ^{C}	grê(k)h or grə̂(k)h ?

[T] 蘇薤 sɑ-gɛh soɣd or soɣðak

7-8	= K. 879	Mand.	MC	LHan	OCM
abc	圭珪	guī	kiwei	kue	kwê
d	桂	guì	kiwei^{C}	kue^{C}	kwêh
e	閨	guī	kiwei	kue	kwê
g	鮭 porpoise	guī	kiwei	kue	
	a demon	huá, xié	ɣwa, ɣaɨ	ɣuai, gɛ	gwrâi, gwrê
j	畦	qí !	ɣiwei	ɣue	gwê
h	刲	kuī	k^{h}iwei	k^{h}ue	khwê

[D] ua^{A1} in Jiang-Huai Mand. 'stab something with a knife, slaughter'

i	奎	kuí	k^{h}iwei	k^{h}ue	khwê

[E] TB: WB kwai^{B} 'be divided, split, parted' ⋈ k^{h}wai^{B} 'divide, split', JP gai^{31}-gai^{31} 'walk with legs spread wide'

l	跬	kuǐ	k^{h}jwie^{B} 4	k^{h}ye^{B}	khweʔ
stu	卦挂掛	guà	kwaɨ^{C}	kuɛ^{C}	kwrêh
v	絓	huà,	ɣwaɨ^{C},	ɣuɛ^{C},	gwrêh,
		guà	kwaɨ^{C}	kuɛ^{C}	kwrêh
x	哇	wā	ɣwaɨ(^{C})	ɣuɛ(^{C})	gwrê, gwrêh
n	佳	jiā	kaɨ	kɛ	krê
o	街	jiē	kaɨ	kɛ	krê
pqr	厓崖涯	yá, ái	ŋaɨ	ŋɛ	ŋrê
a'	睚	yá, ái	ŋaɨ^{C}	ŋɛ^{C}	ŋrêh

[T] Sin Sukchu SR ŋja, jaj (平), PR, LR ja; MGZY yay (平) [jaj]

y	鼃 frog	wā	ʔwa, ʔwaɨ	ʔuai, ʔuɛ	ʔwrâi, ʔwrê
		huá	ɣwa, ɣwaɨ	ɣuai, ɣuɛ	wrâi, wrê
z	蛙 frog	wā	ʔwaɨ	ʔuɛ	ʔwrê

[E] PT *kw-: Boai kwɛɛ^{C1}, Wuming klwe 'small green frog'; KS *k-wai^{C} 'small frog'

f	窐	wā,	ʔwa,	ʔuai,	ʔwrâi,
		guī	kiwei	kue	kwê

Guī may just be the reading of the phonetic.

b'	窪	wā	ʔwa	ʔuai	ʔwrâi
k	洼	wā	ʔiwei	ʔue	ʔwê
m	恚	huì	ʔjwie^{C} 4	ʔye^{C}	ʔweh

7-9	= K. 880	Mand.	MC	LHan	OCM
ab	巂懏	xí, xī	ɣiwei	ɣue	wê
c	攜	xié	ɣiwei	ɣue	wê
d	蠵	xì, xī	ɣiwei	ɣue	wê
ef	觿鑴	xī, huī	ɣiwei, xjwie	ɣue, hye	wê, hwe

7-10	**= K. 875**	**Mand.**	**MC**	**LHan**	**OCM**	
a	規	guī	kjwie 4	kye	kwe	

[T] Sin Sukchu SR kuj (平); MGZY gÿue (平) [kyɛ] <> [E] TB: Chepang *gweʔ 'circular in shape' ¤ kweʔ 'hook, fishhook'; TB *koy 'bend round, be curved, coil et al.'

b	䂓	guī	kjwie 4	kye	kwe	
cd	窺闚	kuī	k^{h}jwie 4	k^{h}ye	khwe	

7-11	**= K. 873**	**Mand.**	**MC**	**LHan**	**OCM**	
a	兒	ér	ńźje	ńe	ŋe	OCB *ŋje

[T]- Sin Sukchu SR ri (平), PR, LR rɿ; MGZY Zhi (平) [ri]; ONW ńe. MHan 臨兒 lim-ńe Skt. Lumbini <> [D] Xiang: ŋa <> [E] Area word: TB: JP ŋa̱i^{33} (< ŋ̇ai ?), tʃă^{33}-ŋ̇ai^{33} 'baby', Mru ŋia 'child'. AA: PSBahn. *ŋe 'baby'

e	唲	ér	ńźje	ńe	ne	[T] ONW ńe

[E] TB *m-nwi(y) 'to laugh', KN *m-nui > Lushai nui^{H} / nuiʔ^{L}, Bodo, Dimasa mini, JP mă^{31}-ni^{33} 'to laugh'

f	倪	ní	ŋiei	ŋe	ŋê	[T] ONW ŋėi

[E] WB ŋai 'small, little, inferior'

ijl	輗郳鯢	ní	ŋiei	ŋe	ŋê	
o	麑	ní	ŋiei,	ŋe,	ŋê	
			miei, mjie	me, mie	mê, me	

This is the reading of the syn. 麛 7-31/360e

mn	霓蜺	ní, yè	ŋiei, ŋiet	ŋe, ŋet	ŋê, ŋêt	
g	掜	nǐ	$ŋiei^{B/C}$	$ŋe^{B/C}$	ŋêʔ/h	
h	睨	nì	$ŋiei^{B/C}$	$ŋe^{B/C}$	ŋêʔ/h	
p	鶂	yì	ŋiek	ŋek	ŋêk	= 8-5/849f
q	鬩	xì	xiek	xek	hŋêk	

7-12	**= K. 877**	**Mand.**	**MC**	**LHan**	**OCM**	
a	帝	dì	$tiei^{C}$	te^{C}	têh	

[T] Sin Sukchu SR ti (去), PR, LR ti; MGZY di (去) [ti]; ONW tėi. OCB *teks; but the *Shijing* rimes do not compel the assumption of OCM *têkh.

[E] WT t^{h}e 'celestial gods', JP mă^{31}-tai^{33} 'sky god'

e	揥	dì, tì,	$t(^{h})iei^{C}$,	$t(^{h})e^{C}$,	têh, thêh,	
		chì	$ṭ^{h}jäi^{C}$	$ṭ^{h}ies$	thres	
f	諦	dì	$tiei^{C}$	te^{C}	têh	
gh	啼蹄	tí	diei	de	dê	
j	締	dì, tí	$diei(^{C})$	$de(^{C})$	dê(h)	
i	禘	dì	$diei^{C}$	de^{C}	dêh	
k	啻 only	chì	$śje^{C}$	$śe^{C}$	lhekh	= 7-3/864e
s	適 go to etc.	shì	śjäk	śek	lhek	[T] ONW śek. OCB *stjek
	go to	zhī	tśjäk	tśek	tek	only 'go to'
t	擿	zhì	ḍjäk	ḍiek	drek	
mn	嫡鏑	dí	tiek	tek	têk	
o	蹢 hoof	dí	tiek	tek	têk	
	to stop	zhí	ḍjäk	ḍiek	drek	
-	滴	dī	tiek	tek	têk	

[E] WT: gtig(s)-pa ~ 't^{h}ig-pa, t^{h}igs 'to drop, drip' ¤ 't^{h}ig-pa, btigs 'cause to fall in drops' ¤ t^{h}igs-pa 'a drop', JP theʔ^{31} < t^{h}ek^{31} 'dropping, dripping'

		Mand.	MC	LHan	OCM	
q	敵	dí	diek	dek	dêk	

[E] TB *m-ta:y (or rather *taiʔ): JP tai^{31} 'avenge, retaliate', mətài 'vengeance', Lushai tai^{R} < taiʔ 'be at enmity with one another, have a grudge against'

p	摘	tì,	t^{h}iek,	t^{h}ek,	thêk,	
		zhāi	ṭɛk	ṭɛk	trêk	
r	謫 blame	zhé	ṭɛk, ḍɛk	ṭɛk, ḍɛk	trêk, drêk	OCB *trek
	sun ch.	zhé	ḍɛk	ḍɛk	drêk	'change in the sun'
u	讁 blame	zhé	ṭɛk, ḍɛk	ṭɛk, ḍɛk	trêk, drêk	

7-13	**= K. 863**	**Mand.**	**MC**	**LHan**	**OCM**	
a	知	zhī	tje	ṭie	tre	

[T] Sin Sukchu SR tʂi (平); MGZY ji (平) [tʂi]; ONW te

[E] Lushai hria^{R} / hre^{H} / hriat^{F} 'to know', JP tʃe^{33} < rje^{33} 'to know'

b	智	zhì	tje^{C}	ṭie^{C}	treh	

[T] Sin Sukchu SR tʂi (去); MGZY ji (去) [tʂi]; ONW te

d	蜘蛛	zhī-zhū	tje-tju	ṭie-ṭio	tre-tro	'spider'
e	踟躕	chí -chú	ḍje-ḍju	ḍie-ḍio	dre-dro	

[E] Tai: S. rii^{A2}-rɔɔ^{A2} 'walk hesitatingly, undecided'

7-14	**= K. 866**	**Mand.**	**MC**	**LHan**	**OCM**	
a	是	shì	źje^{B}	dźe^{B}	deʔ	

[T] Sin Sukchu SR ʐi (上), PR ʐɿ; MGZY zhi (上) [ʐi]; ONW dźe.

[E] TB *day: WT de 'that'; JP n^{55}-deʔ^{55} 'this, there', n^{55}-de^{51} 'so (many...), thus'

d	諟	shì	źje^{B}	dźe^{B}	deʔ	
g	隄	dī	tiei	te	tê	
h	鞮	dī, tí	tiei, diei	te, de	tê, dê	
i	醍 wine	tǐ	t^{h}iei^{B}	t^{h}e^{B}	thêʔ	
j	緹	tí, tǐ	diei, t^{h}iei^{B}	de, t^{h}e^{B}	dê, thêʔ	
k	堤	dī !	diei	de	dê	
lm	媞偍	tí	diei	de	dê	
o	蝭	tí	diei	de	dê	
-	騠	tí	diei	de	—	'A type of horse'
n	提 lift	tí	diei	de	dê	

[T] Sin Sukchu SR djej (平), PR, LR di; MGZY ti (平) [di]; ONW dėi; BTD Skt. de[va]

	提 cut off	dǐ	tiei^{B}	te^{B}	têʔ	
	提 flock	chí	źje	dźe	de	
p	題 forehead	tí	diei	de	dê	
	look at	dì	diei^{C}	de^{C}	dêh	
r	鯷	dì, tí,	diei^{C}, diei	de^{C}, de	dêh, dê	
		shì	źje^{B}	dźe^{B}	deʔ	
q	踶 kick	dì	diei^{C}	de^{C}	dêh	

[E] WT rdeg, LB *tek^{H} 'kick', Garo ga-tek, Tangkhul Naga kəkət^{h}ək

	踶 effort	zhì	ḍje^{B}	ḍie^{B}	dreʔ	
e	禔	zhī, shí, tí	tśje,źje,diei	tśe, dźe, de	te, de, dê	[E] WT bde-ba 'happy'
f	翨 wing	shì	śje^{C}	śe^{C}	lheh	

[N] The alternate reading jì, MC kjie^{C} 4 probably has been transferred from the old reading of the synonym 7-3/864e 翅 *ke (tone C here is probably borrowed from the reading MC śje^{C}). In turn, the regular reading of 翨 has later been applied to the synonym chì 翅.

s 寔 shí źjək dźɨk dək ~ 29-18/398a 實

[E] TB: LB *dyak 'truly, very, intensive', WB tyak-tyak 'very', Lushai tak^L 'real, true'

[N] This word *dək is probably written with 是 *deʔ 'this, be right' because the semantics outweighed the less than perfect phonetic fit.

t 湜 shí źjək dźɨk dək

7-15 = K. 1238d Mand. MC LHan OCM

d 卮 zhī tśje tśe te or ke or tai

7-16 = K. 1238b Mand. MC LHan OCM

b 豸 zhì ḍje^B ḍie^B dreʔ ~ zhì , zhài 7-17 廌

This graph is perhaps phonetic in 32-21/372 紖 *drinʔ

7-17 Mand. MC LHan OCM

\- 廌 zhì,zhài ḍje^B, ḍaɨ^B ḍie^B, ḍɛ^B dreʔ ~ zhì 7-16 豸

[E] MK *draay > OMon *dray 'hog deer' (→ WB darai 'hog deer'), Biat ɗraai 'swamp deer', PVM *k-ɗe: 'deer'

7-18 = K. 1238e Mand. MC LHan OCM

e 咶 lick shì dźje^B źe^B m-leʔ [Zhuang]

Also written 7-6/867f 舐 [Zhuang], 8-12/850 䑛 [SW], 18-9/4 䑙 [Yupian]

7-19 = K. 1238f Mand. MC LHan OCM

f 豕 shǐ śje^B śe^B lheʔ ?

[E] ? MK: PMonic *cliik, Mon klot, kloik 'pig', PWa *lik 'pig'. Theoretically, the OC rime could also be *-aiʔ.

7-20 = K. 359 Mand. MC LHan OCM OCB *-ej (1992: 419)

a 爾 you, part. ěr ńźje^B ńe^B neʔ

[T] Sin Sukchu SR ri (上), PR ɽ; MGZY Zhi (上) [ri]; ONW ńe. OCB *njajʔ (1992: 453), *njəjʔ <> [E] TB: Chepang ni 'you' ⋈ niŋ 'you' (plural), WB ñañ^B

爾 luxuriant nǐ niei^B ne^B nêʔ

\- 你 you nǐ nɨ^B

[T] Sin Sukchu SR njej (上), PR, LR ni; MGZY ñi (上) [ɲi]; STang nɨ^B > ni^B, ONW nii

c 邇 ěr ńźje^B ńe^B neʔ OCB *njəjʔ (1992: 453)

[T] ONW ńe. <> [E] TB *ney > WT ñe-ba 'near' ⋈ sñen-pa 'come near'; JP ni^{31}, PL *b-ni^{55}, WB ni^B (< ne^B); but Lushai in^L-hnai^R < hnaiʔ 'near, close', LB *nay^2

d 嬭 nǎi ! niei^B ne^B nêʔ

gh 濔禰 nǐ niei^B ne^B nêʔ

i 薾 luxuriant nǐ niei^B ne^B nêʔ

oblivious niè niet net nêt

j 璽 xǐ sje^B sie^B sneʔ

lk 獮𤣽 xiǎn sjän^B sian^B snenʔ

LH actually = sien^B, but for consistency's sake we write rimes in -n as -ian.

m 彌 complete mí mjie 4 mie me = 7-31/360a

[T] MTang mɨ, ONW mie [i.e. QYS div. 3], BTD Skt. mai-, -me, -mi-

彌 finish mǐ mjie^B 4 mie^B meʔ

o 瀰 mǐ, mjie^B 4, mie^B meʔ = 7-31/360a 弭

mí mjie, miei^B = 26-40/598h 敉

7-20A		**Mand.**	**MC**	**LHan**	**OCM**	
	尒	ěr	ńźje^{B}	ńe^{B}	neʔ	SW 492

7-21	**= K. 878**	**Mand.**	**MC**	**LHan**	**OCM**	
acde	麗儷攦欐	lì	liei^{C}	le^{C}	rêh	
f	驪	lí	liei, lje	le, lie	rê, re	
g	纚 rope	lí	lje	lie	re	
	band	shǐ, shǎi	ṣje^{B}, ṣai^{B}	ṣie^{B}, ṣɛ^{B}	sreʔ, srêʔ	= 7-28/871g 屣
h	釃	shī	ṣje	ṣie	sre	

[E] ST *s-lai: Lushai tʰlei^{R} < sleʔ 'to sift' (by side to side motion) <> Viet. rây 'to strain, sift, sieve' <> [N] Also shū, ṣjwo, LHan ṣɑ, OCM *sra, it is the same etymon as 1-62/90f.

i	灑	sǎ, shǐ	ṣaɨ$^{B/C}$, ṣje$^{B/C}$	ṣɛ$^{B/C}$, ṣie$^{B/C}$	srêʔ/h, sreʔ/h	[T] ONW ṣä
-	曬	shài, shì	ṣje^{C}	ṣie^{C}	sreh	
j	躧	xǐ	ṣje^{B}	ṣie^{B}	sreʔ	= 7-28/871g 屣

7-22	**= K. 1241o-q**		**MC**	**LHan**	**OCM**	
-	[illegible]	xié	gaɨ	gɛ	grê	
o	蠡 worm	lǐ	liei^{B}	le^{B}	rêʔ	'wood-worm'
	itch	luǒ	luâ^{B}	loi^{B}	rôiʔ	
pq	劙𧓍欚	lǐ, lí	liei$^{B/C}$, lje	le$^{B/C}$, lie	rêʔ/h, re	

See GYSX p. 292 for more graphs in this XS series.

7-23	**= K. 1241r**	**Mand.**	**MC**	**LHan**	**OCM**
r	荔	lì	liei^{C}, lje^{C}	le^{C}, lie^{C}	rêh, reh

7-24	**= K. 872**	**Mand.**	**MC**	**LHan**	**OCM**
a	詈	lì	lje^{C}	lie^{C}	reh

7-25	**= K. 358**	**Mand.**	**MC**	**LHan**	**OCM**	OCB *-ej (1992: 419)
a	此	cǐ	tsʰje^{B}	tsʰie^{B}	tsheʔ	OCB *tshjejʔ

[T] Sin Sukchu SR ts'ɿ (上); MGZY tshʰi (上) [ts'ɿ]; ONW tsʰe

c	佌	cǐ	tsʰje^{B}	tsʰie^{B}	tsheʔ	
d	庛	cì	tsʰje^{C}	tsʰie^{C}	tsheh	
hi	泚玼	cǐ	tsʰje^{B},tsʰiei^{B}	tsʰie^{B},tsʰe^{B}	tsheʔ, tshêʔ	
fg	雌鴜	cī	tsʰje	tsʰie	tshe	OCB *tshje

[D] Wu-Suzhou ts'ɿ^{44}-ȵiɤ$^{24/21}$ 雌牛 'cow'; opposite xióng 雄 'male'

e	跐	cǐ	tsʰje^{B}	tsʰie^{B}	tsheʔ	
mno	貲髭頿	zī	tsje	tsie	tse	
j	紫	zǐ	tsje^{B}	tsie^{B}	tseʔ	
kl	訾訿 sland.	zǐ	tsje^{B}	tsie^{B}	tseʔ	'slander'
	訾 measure	zī	tsje	tsie	tse	
	訾 fault	sí	zje	zie	s-le or s-je	
p	疵 flaw	cí	dzje	dzie	dze	
q	觜	cī	dzje(^{C})	dzie(^{C})	dze(h)	= 18-13/5 髊 [Lüshi ch.]
r	胔 carcass	zì	dzje^{C}	dzie^{C}	dzeh	OCB *dzjejs
	胔 intestines	zì	dzje, tsʰje	dzie, tsʰie	dze, tshe	'small intestines'

[E] PTai *sai^{C1} 'intestines'

		Mand.	MC	LHan	OCM	
s	眥	zì, jì	dzje^{C},dziei^{C}	dzie^{C}, dze^{C}	dzeh, dzêh	
t	觜 beak	zuǐ , zī	tsjwe^{B}, tsje	tsye^{B}, tsie	tsoiʔ, tse or tsai ?	

[E] ? TB: WT mts^{h}ul-pa 'lower part of face, muzzle, beak'.

-	嘴	zuǐ	tsjwe^{B} ?			
x	柴 wood	chái	dẓaɨ	dẓɛ	dzrê	

[T] Sin Sukchu SR dẓaj (平); MGZY cay (平) [dẓaj]

	柴 heap	zì	dzje^{C}, tsje^{C}	dzie^{C}, tsie^{C}	dzeh, tseh	OCB *dzjejs
uv	茈祡	chái	dẓaɨ	dẓɛ	dzrê	
1236a	些 a particle	suò	sâ^{C}	sɑi^{C} or sɑ^{C}		
	a few	xiē	sja			

7-26	= K. 869	Mand.	MC	LHan	OCM	
a	斯 cleave	sī	sje	sie	se	

[T] MTang si, ONW se <> [E] ST *ser: WT ser-ka 'cleft, split', Chepang ser- 'divide, split cleanly'

	斯 complet.	sì	sje^{C}	sie^{C}	seh	'completely'
cd	凘廝	sī	sje	sie	se	
ef	嘶撕	sī !	siei	se	sê	

7-27	= K. 870	Mand.	MC	LHan	OCM
a	虒	sī	sje	sie	sle
d	嗁	tí	diei	de	lê
e	遞	dì	diei$^{B/C}$	de$^{B/C}$	lêʔ, lə̂h
-	傂	yí	je	je	le
c	篪箎	chí	ḍje	ḍie	dre < r-le ?
b	褫	chǐ,	ṭ^{h}je^{B},	ṭ^{h}ie^{B},	rheʔ
		chí, zhì	ḍje(^{B})	ḍie(^{B})	dre, dreʔ

7-28	= K. 871	Mand.	MC	LHan	OCM	
abf	徙征蓰	xǐ	sje^{B}	sie^{B}	seʔ	

徙 [T] Sui-Tang si, ONW se, LHan

[E] ? TB: WB sai 'carry from one place to another, remove by repeated processes'

gh	屣縰	xǐ	ṣje^{B}	ṣie^{B}	sreʔ	= 7-12/878j 纚

7-29	= K. 874	Mand.	MC	LHan	OCM
a	卑	bēi	pjie 4	pie	pe

[T] ONW pie. LHan 鮮卑 sian-pie *Särbi

d	碑	bēi	pjie 4	pie	pe
e	裨 add	bì	pjie 4	pie	pe
	a robe	bēi, péi	pjie, bjie 4	pie, bie	pe, be
c	俾	bǐ	pjie^{B} 4	pie^{B}	peʔ

[T] Sin Sukchu SR pi (上), PR pəj; 'Phags-pa: MGZY bi (上) [pi]; ONW *pie

x	鞞	bǐ,	pjie^{B} 4,	pie^{B},	peʔ,
		bǐng	pieŋ^{B}	peŋ^{B}	pêŋʔ
gi	綼陴	pí	bjie 4	bie	be
h	脾	pí	bjie 4	bie	be

[T] ONW bie <> [E] TB *r-pay, *pay ~ *play: JP pāi, Mru pai, but Angami Naga ú-prì, Mikir pli-ha < *-i, Garo pilai, Chepang leh

		Mand.	MC	LHan	OCM	
k	埤 accumul.	pí	bjie 4	bie	be	
	low gr.	bì	bjie^{B} 4	bie^{B}	beʔ	'low ground'
lm	婢庳	bì	bjie^{B} 4	bie^{B}	beʔ	
n	頼	pǐ	p^{h}iei^{B}	p^{h}e^{B}	phêʔ	
p	鼙	pí	biei	be	bê	
q	椑 shaft	pí	biei	be	bê	
	coffin	bì	biek, bjäk	bek, biek	bêk, bek	
f	髀	bì	biei^{B}, pjie^{B},pji^{B} 4	be^{B}, pie^{B}	bêʔ, peʔ	

[D] Yue dial 'thigh': Guangzhou tai^{22}-pei^{35} 大髀 'thigh'

[E] TB *pey 'leg', Lushai p^{h}ei^{L} 'foot, leg'; ? WT dpyi 'hip, hipbone'

r	捭 open	bǎi	paɨ^{B}	pɛ^{B}	prêʔ	

[E] ST *prai: WB prai^{B} 'to gape'

	捭 cleave	bò	pɛk	pɛk	prêk	cf. 8-19/853p
st	稗粺	bài	baɨ^{C}	bɛ^{C}	brêh	
u	蜱	pí	baɨ	bɛ	brê	
v	蠯	pái, pí, bèng	baɨ,bjie 4, bɛŋ^{B}	bɛ, bie, bɛŋ^{B}	brê, be, brêŋʔ	
-	箄	pái	baɨ	bɛ	brê ?	

7-30		**Mand.**	**MC**	**LHan**	**OCM**
-	屄	bī	pjie 4		

[D] *pe, *pet <> [E] ST *bet ? : LB *b(y)et^{L} 'vulva', Kanauri p^{h}ɛ:ts

7-31	**= K. 360**	**Mand.**	**MC**	**LHan**	**OCM**	OCB *-ej (1992: 419)
a	弭	mǐ	mjie^{B} 4	mie^{B}	meʔ	= 26-40/598h 敉

[T] MTang mi, ONW me [i.e., QYS div. 3] = 7-20/359m 彌

d	渳	mǐ	mjie^{B} 4	mie^{B}	meʔ	
e	麛	mí	miei	me	mê	syn. 7-11/873o 麑

7-32		**Mand.**	**MC**	**LHan**	**OCM**	
-	芈	mǐ	mjie^{B} 4	mie^{B}	meʔ	'to bleat; bear' n.

[E] KS *mu:i^{1}-fi, PTai *hm-: S. mii^{A1}, Po-ai muui^{A1}; Hlai mui^{4} 'bear' n.

7-33	**= K. 1240c,e**	**Mand.**	**MC**	**LHan**	**OCM**
c	買	mǎi	maɨ^{B}	mɛ^{B}	mrêʔ

[T] Sin Sukchu SR maj (上); MGZY may (上) [maj]; ONW mëi

[E] TB *b/m-rey > WT rje-ba (< *N-rje ?) 'to barter', JP ma^{31}-ri^{33} 'to buy'

e	賣	mài	maɨ^{C}	mɛ^{C}	mrêh	[T] ONW mëi

7-34		**Mand.**	**MC**	**LHan**	**OCM**	
-	乜	miē	mjia^{B} 4		—	'to squint, glance (sideways)'

This is a unique syllable [GY]. <> [D] Canton mêt, Hakka mak, Ningpo mi^{C}

[E] Area etymon *Cmit or *Cmet 'wink / signal with eyes or finger'

8 OCM rime *-ek Xī bù 錫部

GSR 844 - 860

Baxter 1992: 494 ff. (§10.2.8)

In the OC rimes *-ak, *-ek, *-ok and *-auk, syllables with MC retroflex initials, especially of the expected MC type ḍjak, ḍjäk, ḍjwok, tend to be rare in Div. III and seem to have shifted into Div. II ḍɐk, ḍåk, ḍɛk, ḍɔk. See Table 2-1 for a comparison of OCM rimes *-aŋ,*-ak with *-eŋ, *-ek; Table 17-1 for comparison of OCM rimes *-ek, *-ak, *-auk, *-uk.

Table 8-1: OCM rimes *-eŋ, *-ek, *-e in QYS categories

Div.	*-eŋ R.9	*-ek R.8	*-ekh R.8	*-e R.7
IV	經 kieŋ keŋ *kêŋ 扃 kiweŋ kueŋ *kwêŋ 定 dieŋ^C deŋ^C *dêŋh	擊 kiek kek *kêk 鶪 kiwek kuek *kwêk 厤 liek lek *rêk 覓 miek mek *mêk	縊 ʔiei^C ʔe^C *ʔêkh	雞 kiei ke *kê 圭 kiwei kue *kwê 啼 diei de *dê
3/3	驚 kjɐŋ kɨɛŋ *kreŋ			技 gje^{B}3 gɨe^B *greʔ
3/4 gr	勁 kjiäŋ^{C}4 kieŋ^C *keŋh 頃 k^{h}jiwäŋ4 k^{h}yeŋ *khweŋ 名 mjiäŋ4 mieŋ *meŋ	益 ʔjiäk4 ʔiek *ʔek 辟 pjiäk4 piek *pek	臂 pjie^{C}4 pie^C *pekh	歧 gjie4 gie *ge 規 kjwie4 kye *kwe 卑 pjie4 pie *pe
III ac	正 tśjäŋ tśeŋ *teŋ 盈 jiäŋ jeŋ *leŋ 營 jiwäŋ4 weŋ *weŋ	刺 ts^{h}jäk ts^{h}iek *tshek 易 jiäk jek *lek 役 jiwäk wek *wek	刺 ts^{h}je^C ts^{h}ie^C *tshekh 易 jie^C je^C *lekh	支 tśje tśe < kie *ke 知 tje ṭie *tre
II	耕 kɛŋ kɛŋ *krêŋ 爭 tṣɛŋ tṣɛŋ *tsrêŋ 生 ṣɐŋ ṣɛŋ *srêŋ (irreg.)	槅 kɛk kɛk *krêk 畫 ɣwɛk ɣuɛk *wrêk 脈 mɛk mɛk *mrêk 責 tṣɛk tṣɛk *tsrêk	阨 ʔaɨ^C ʔɛ^C *ʔrêkh 畫 ɣwaɨ^C ɣuɛ^C *wrêkh	解 kaɨ^B kɛ^B *krêʔ 卦 kwaɨ^C kuɛ^C *kwrêh 買 maɨ^B mɛ^B *mrêʔ

8-1	**= K. 854**	**Mand.**	**MC**	**LHan**	**OCM**	
a	毄	qī	k^{h}iek	k^{h}ek	khêk	
b	擊	jī	kiek	kek	kêk	
c	[illegible]	jì	kiei^C	ke^C	kêkh	
d	繫 attach	xì	kiei^C,	ke^C,	kêh,	OCB *keks
	[T] ONW kėi. = 7-1/876c 係; 7-2/1241b 繼					
	be attached	xì	ɣiei^C	ge^C	gêh	OCB *N-keks
	[T] ONW ɣėi, = 7-1/876a 系					

8-2	**= K. 855**	**Mand.**	**MC**	**LHan**	**OCM**
a	鬲 a pot	lì	liek	lek	rêk
	鬲 handful	gè	kɛk	kɛk	krêk

d	搹	gè	kɛk	kɛk	krêk	
ef	膈隔	gé	kɛk	kɛk	krêk	[T] ONW këk
-	鬲阝	gé	kɛk	kɛk	krêk	

[T] MHan 鬲阝昆 gé-kūn LH kɛk-kuən < krêk-kûn Qyrqyz < qyrqyŕ (Pulleyblank 1983: 455)

g	翮	hé	ɣɛk	gɛk	grêk	~ 5-2/931d 翯
h	鷊	yì	ŋiek	ŋek	ŋêk	

8-3	= K. 1260d	Mand.	MC	LHan	OCM
d	覡	xí	ɣiek	gek	gêk

Prob. not *giâuk or *giûk, the initial and vowel of 見 may be partially phonetic

8-4 **= K. 844** Words with initial OC *ʔ- and *w- do not occur in MC Div. I, but almost exclusively in Div. II; hence there was probably no OC medial *r in the Div. II items in 8-4, 8-5 and 8-9.

		Mand.	MC	LHan	OCM	
ab	戹厄	è	ʔɛk	ʔɛk	ʔrêk or ʔêk (passim)	= 8-5/849h
def	軶軛扼	è	ʔɛk	ʔɛk	ʔrêk	[T] ONW ʔëk
gh	阸阨	è, ài	ʔaiᶜ	ʔɛᶜ	ʔrêkh	

8-5	= K. 849	Mand.	MC	LHan	OCM	See comment under 8-4.
a	益	yì	ʔjiäk 4	ʔiek	ʔek	
cd	嗌膉	yì	ʔjiäk 4	ʔiek	ʔek	
g	縊	yì	ʔieiᶜ	ʔeᶜ	ʔêkh	

[E] TB *ʔik > Nung i < ik 'strangle'; WB ac 'squeeze, throttle'

e	搤	è	ʔɛk	ʔɛk	ʔrêk or ʔêk (passim)	
h	隘 distress	è	ʔɛk	ʔɛk	ʔrêk	
	narrow	ài	ʔaiᶜ	ʔɛᶜ	ʔrêkh	= 8-4/844ah
f	鷁	yì	ŋiek	ŋek	ŋêk	= 7-11/873p

8-6	= K. 860	Mand.	MC	LHan	OCM
abc	狊鶪鵙	jú	kiwek	kuek	kwêk
d	闃	qù	kʰiwek	kʰuek	khwêk

8-7	= K. 1260f	Mand.	MC	LHan	OCM	
f	砉	xū,	xiwek,	huek	hwêk	= 5-7/930c
		huò	xwɐk			

8-8	= K. 851	Mand.	MC	LHan	OCM
abc	役垼疫	yì	jiwäk	wek	wek

[T] Sin Sukchu SR ŋyj (入); MGZY ywi (入) [yi]

8-9	= K. 847	Mand.	MC	LHan	OCM	See comment under 8-4.
a	畫	huà	ɣwaiᶜ	ɣuɛᶜ	wrêkh or wêk	

[T] MGZY Xway (去) [ɣwaj]; ONW ɣuä

	畫	huò	ɣwɛk	ɣuɛk	wrêk or wêk

[T] Sin Sukchu SR ɣuj (入); MGZY Xway (入) [ɣwaj]

e	繣	huà,	ɣwaiᶜ,	ɣuɛᶜ,	wrêkh or wêkh
		huò	xwɛk	huɛk	hwrêk or hwêk

8 OCM *-ek 錫部 (GSR 844-860)

\- 劃 huà ɣwɛk ɣuɛk wrêk or wêk

8-10 = K. 856 **Mand.** **MC** **LHan** **OCM**

a 狄 dí diek dek lêk

[E] For the initial OC *l-, see Pulleyblank 1983: 448)

狄鞮 dí-dī diek-diei dek-de 'translators, interpreters'

d 荻 dí diek dek lêk

e 惖 tì tʰiek tʰek lhêk

f 逖 tì tʰiek tʰek lhêk

8-11 = K. 1260c **Mand.** **MC** **LHan** **OCM**

c 隻 zhī tśjäk tśek tek

[T] ONW tśek <> [E] TB *tyik ~ tyak > LB *C-tik^{L}, ti^{2} 'one' > WB tac ⋠ LB *ʔdik 'only'; WT gčig 'one'; JR kətiag

8-12 = K. 850 **Mand.** **MC** **LHan** **OCM**

a 易 change yì jiäk jek lek

[E] Tai: S. lɛɛk^{D2L} < *dl- 'to change, exchange'; KS *hlik^{7} 'exchange'

易 easy yì jie^{C} je^{C} lekh

[T] Sin Sukchu SR i (去); MGZY yi (去) [ji]; Sui-Tang i, ONW ie <> [E] TB *lway 'easy': WB lwai 'easy, yielding', JP loi^{31} 'easy'; WT legs 'good, happy, comfortable'

fg 蜴埸 yì jiäk jek lek

p 睗 shì śjäk śek lhek

\- 暘 shì śjäk śek lhek

n 錫 xí siek sek slêk

[T] MTang sɨk, ONW sėk-- [E] MK: Late OMon slāk /slaik/ 'bronze'. Tai: Longzh hik^{D1}S, Po'ai liik < *tʰr- 'tin'; Nung xlek < Chinese

l 緆 cloth xī siek sek slêk

ornament tì tʰiei^{C} tʰe^{C} lhêkh

m 裼 bare xī siek sek slêk

wrapper tì tʰiei^{C} tʰe^{C} lhêkh

t 賜 cì sje^{C} sie^{C} slekh

[T] Sin Sukchu SR sɿ (去); MGZY sʰi (去) [sɿ]

i 惕 tì tʰiek tʰek lhêk

'Be anxious, to respect, to grieve' [Shi, Shu]

hk 剔逷 tì tʰiek tʰek lhêk cf. tì 26-15/591 剃

r 鬄 cut off tī, tʰiek, tʰek, lhêk, cf. tì 26-15/591 剃

tì tʰiei^{C} tʰe^{C} lhêkh = tī 剃 (tʰiei^{C})

[T] ONW tʰėi. <> [D] PMin *thie^{C}

鬄 false hair dì, diei^{C}, de^{C}, lêkh,

xī sjäk siek slek

s 髢 false hair dì diei^{C} de^{C} lêkh

\- 舓 lick shì dźje^{B} źe^{B} m-leʔ [SW] = 7-18/1238e 咶 etc.

8-13 = K. 858 **Mand.** **MC** **LHan** **OCM**

ac 秝厤 lì liek lek rêk

eh	歷曆		lì	liek	lek	rêk	
	[T] Sin Sukchu SR li (入); MGZY li (入) [li]; ONW lėk <> [E] WB re 'to count', Kanauri ri, WT rtsi-ba < *rhji < *rhi 'to count' ⋈ rtsis-pa 'astronomer'						
i	磿		lì	liek	lek	rêk	
-	轣轆		lì-lù	liek-luk	lek-lok	—	'spinning wheel'

8-14	= K. 868		Mand.	MC	LHan	OCM	
a	朿		cì	ts^{h}je^C	ts^{h}ie^C	tshekh	
d	刺	to kill	cì	ts^{h}je^C	ts^{h}ie^C	tshekh	
	[T] Sin Sukchu SR ts'ʅ (去); 'Phags-pa: MGZY tsh^{h}i (去) [ts'ʅ]						
	刺	to stab	cì	ts^{h}jäk	ts^{h}iek	tshek	
	[E] WT ts^{h}er-ma 'thorn, thorn bush' ⋈ gzer-ba 'to bore into' ⋈ gzer 'nail'						
ef	莿誎		cì	ts^{h}je^C	ts^{h}ie^C	tshekh	
j	趚		qì	ts^{h}jäk	ts^{h}iek	tshek	
l	策		cè	tṣ^{h}ɛk	tṣ^{h}ɛk	tshrêk	
m	責	to exact	zé	tṣɛk	tṣɛk	tsrêk	OCB *tsr(j)ek (< *Strek?)
		debt	zhài	tṣaɨ^C	tṣɛ^C	tsrêkh	
-	債		zhài	tṣaɨ^C	tṣɛ^C	tsrêkh	
o	嘖		zé	tṣɛk, dẓɛk	tṣɛk, dẓɛk	tsrêk, dzrêk	
p	幘	kerchief	zé	tṣɛk	tṣɛk	tsrêk	
		reg. teeth	cè	tṣ^{h}ɛk	tṣ^{h}ɛk	tshrêk	
q	簀		zé	tṣɛk	tṣɛk	tsrêk	
r	皟		cè	tṣ^{h}ɛk	tṣ^{h}ɛk	tshrêk	
s	賾		zé	dẓɛk	dẓɛk	dzrêk	
uh	蹟迹		jì	tsjäk	tsiek	tsek	⋈ *tsjak
t	積	collect	jī	tsjäk	tsiek	tsek	[T] ONW tsiek
	積	store	jì	tsje^C	tsie^C	tsekh	
	[E] WT rtseg-pa 'to put on top, pile up, stack'						
x	漬		zì	dzje^C	dzie^C	dzekh	
v	績		jī	tsiek	tsek	tsêk	

8-15	= K. 845	Mand.	MC	LHan	OCM	
a	冊	cè	tṣ^{h}ɛk	tṣ^{h}ɛk	tshrêk	= 8-14/868la 策
	[T] ONW tṣ^{h}ëk					= 8-16/846a 筴
g	柵	cè	tṣ^{h}ɛk, tṣ^{h}ɐk	tṣ^{h}ɛk, tṣak	tshrêk	

8-16	= K. 846	Mand.	MC	LHan	OCM	
a	筴	cè	tṣ^{h}ɛk	tṣ^{h}ɛk	tshrêk	= 8-15/845a 冊
	[T] ONW tṣ^{h}ëk					

8-17	= K. 852		Mand.	MC	LHan	OCM
a	脊	spine	jí	tsjäk	tsiek	tsek
	脊	trample	jí	dzjäk	dziek	dzek
cd	瘠膌		jí	dzjäk	dziek	dzek
b	蹐		jí	tsjäk	tsiek	tsek

8-18	**= K. 857**	**Mand.**	**MC**	**LHan**	**OCM**	
a	析	xī	siek	sek	sêk	
	[E] ST *sek: Mikir iŋsèk < *m-sèk 'to split' (Mikir -ek can derive from both -ik or -ek), JP se$ʔ^{55}$ < sek 'cut'					
cde	晳晢淅	xī	siek	sek	sêk	

8-19	**= K. 853**	**Mand.**	**MC**	**LHan**	**OCM**	
a	辟 ruler	bì	pjiäk 4	piek	pek	[T] ONW piek
	辟 law	bì	bjiäk 4	biek	bek	
	辟 coffin	pì	biek	bek	bêk	
dgh	璧躃躄	bì	pjiäk 4	piek	pek	
	[T] MHan 璧流離 piek-liu-liɑi Skt. vaidurya, Pkt. veluriya					
i	僻	pì	p^hjiäk 4	p^hiek	phek	
k	闢	pì	bjiäk 4	biek	bek	
	[E] ST *pe: WT 'byed-pa, p^hyes, dbye 'to open'; Lushai p^hen^R < p^henʔ 'to open'					
j	擗	bì	bjiäk 4	biek	bek	
s	臂	bì	$pjie^C$ 4	pie^C	pekh	
	[E] TB: Lepcha a-ká pek, Limbu phuk-bek 'forearm'					
t	譬	pì	p^hjie^C 4	p^hie^C	phekh	
	[T] ONW p^hie <> [E] TB: WT dpe 'pattern, model'					
u	避	bì	$bjie^C$ 4	bie^C	bekh	
	[T] Sin Sukchu SR bi (去); MGZY pi (去) [bi] <> [E] Lushai pai^R < paiʔ 'oblique'					
l	壁	bì	piek	pek	pêk	
m	澼	pì	p^hiek	p^hek	phêk	
	[T] Sin Sukchu SR p'i (入); MGZY phi (入) [p'i]					
-	劈	pī	p^hiek	p^hek	phêk	
	[E] ? TB: JP $bjek^{31}$ 'to divide; JP $p^hjaʔ^{55}$ < p^hjak^{55} 'split open'					
n	甓	pì	biek	bek	bêk	
v	嬖	bì	$piei^C$	pe^C	pêkh	
	[T] ONW pėi <> [E] KT: KS *jaak 'woman, girl'; PT *ʔb-: Boai bik^{D1} 'girl'					
x	薜 a plant	bì	$biei^C$	be^C	bêkh	
	crack	bò	pɛk	pɛk	prêk	
p	擘	bò	pɛk	pɛk	prêk	cf. 7-29/874r 捭
	[D] Y-Guangzh $ma:k^7$ 'to break', G-Nanchang $miɛ^3$, Hakka mak^7 'to open, break', note KS *$hma:k^7$ 'to split, chop'. <> [E] TB-Chepang prek- 'cleave, divide down center'. <> KT (OC loan?) KS *$pra:k^7$-ti 'break, tear'; PT *pr-: S $tɛɛk^{D1L}$					
q	繴	bò	bɛk	bɛk	brêk	
o	幦	mì	miek	mek	mêk	= 9-30/841 幂冥 榠

8-20		**Mand.**	**MC**	**LHan**	**OCM**
	覓	mì	miek	mek	mêk
	[T] MTang mɨk, ONW mėk <> [D] Min: Quanzhou $baʔ^{D2}$, Amoy ba^{C2}, bai^{D2}, lit. bek^{D2}				

8-21	**= K. 859**	**Mand.**	**MC**	**LHan**	**OCM**
a	鼏 cover	mì	miek	mek	mêk

8-22	**= K. 1260e**	**Mand.**	**MC**	**LHan**	**OCM**	
e	簚 cover	mì	miek	mek	mêk	= 8-21/859a
	20-18/311 蔑 may be partially phonetic.					

8-23		**Mand.**	**MC**	**LHan**	**OCM**	
-	糸	mì	miek	mek	mêk	SW 5790

8-24	**= K. 848**	**Mand.**	**MC**	**LHan**	**OCM**	
ab	脈	mài	mɛk	mɛk	mrêk	
	[E] TB: Lushai mar^H < *mar 'the pulse'					
c	霢霂	mài-mù	mwɛk-muk	mɛk-mok	mrêk-mrôk	
d	覛	mài, mì	mɛk, miek	mɛk, mek	mrêk	SW 5790

9 OCM rime *-eŋ Gēng bù 耕部

GSR 808 - 843

Baxter 1992: 497 ff. (§10.2.9)

See Table 8-1 for OCM rimes *-eŋ, *-ek, *-e in QYS categories, and Table 2-1 for a comparison of OCM rimes *-aŋ,*-ak with *-eŋ, *-ek.

After grave initials, some OC finals in *-eŋ have converged with ones in *-aŋ in MC Div. III -jɐŋ, see the table under Rime 3. Since these pattern like chóngniǔ Div. 3/3 syllables, Baxter reconstructs an OC medial *r. Syllables that pattern like chóngniǔ Div.3/4 syllables (MC -jiäŋ) had the OC final *-eŋ (Baxter 1992 *-jeŋ).

9-1	**= K. 831**	**Mand.**	**MC**	**LHan**	**OCM**	
a	巠	jīng	kieŋ	keŋ	kêŋ	
c	經 norm	jīng	kieŋ	keŋ	kêŋ	OCB *keŋ
	[T] Sin Sukchu SR kiŋ (平); MGZY gÿing (平) [kjiŋ]; MTang kieŋ < kɨŋ, ONW kėŋ					
	[E] TB: WB ə-k^{h}yaŋ^B 'diameter', WT kyaŋ 'straight, slender'					
	經 warp	jìng	kieŋ^C	keŋ^C	kêŋh	
g	涇	jīng	kieŋ	keŋ	kêŋ	
fi	徑逕	jìng	kieŋ^C	keŋ^C	kêŋh	
	徑 [T] MHan 徑路 keŋ^C-lɑ^C qiŋiraq (Hunnish sword)					
e	剄	jǐng	kieŋ^B	keŋ^B	kêŋʔ	
j	窒	qìng	k^{h}ieŋ^C	k^{h}eŋ^C	khêŋh	
l	陘	xíng	ɣieŋ	geŋ	gêŋ	
k	脛	xìng, jìng	ɣieŋ^C	geŋ^C	gêŋh	[E] TB-Mikir keŋ^L 'foot, leg'
m	勁	jìng	kjiäŋ^C 4	kieŋ^C	keŋh	
n	頸	jǐng,	kjiäŋ^B,	kieŋ^B,	keŋʔ,	OCB *kjeŋʔ, *gjeŋ
		qíng	gjiäŋ 4	gieŋ	geŋ	
o	輕 light	qīng	k^{h}jiäŋ 4	k^{h}ieŋ	kheŋ	
	[T] ONW k^{h}ieŋ <> [E] TB *r-ya:ŋ ~ *gya:ŋ, WT yaŋ 'light'					
	輕 swift	qìng	k^{h}jiäŋ^C 4	k^{h}ieŋ^C	kheŋh	
p	罄	qīng,	k^{h}jiäŋ 4,	k^{h}ieŋ,	kheŋ,	
		qìng	k^{h}ieŋ^C	k^{h}eŋ^C	khêŋh	
s	硜	kēng	k^{h}ɛŋ	k^{h}ɛŋ	khrêŋ	
t	誙	kēng, héng	k^{h}ɛŋ, ɣɛŋ	k^{h}ɛŋ, gɛŋ	khrêŋ, grêŋ	
q	牼	kēng, héng	k^{h}ɛŋ, ɣɛŋ	k^{h}ɛŋ, gɛŋ	khrêŋ, grêŋ	
u	莖	héng, jīng	ɣɛŋ	gɛŋ	grêŋ	
	[E] TB *r-k(l)aŋ > WT rkaŋ 'marrow, leg bones, stalk'; WB k^{h}raŋ-chi < *skraŋ 'marrow' (chi 'oil, lymph')					
v	娙	yíng	ŋɛŋ	ŋɛŋ	ŋrêŋ	
x	桱 red	chēng	ṭ^{h}jäŋ	ṭ^{h}ieŋ	threŋ	
	A late graph [Yili] for = 9-12/834m 赬 [Shijing]					

9 OCM *-eŋ 耕部 (GSR 808-843)

9-2	= K. 832, 822	Mand.	MC	LHan	OCM	
832ac	殸 > 磬	qìng	kʰieŋ^{C}	kʰeŋ^{C}	khêŋh	
d	罄	qìng	kʰieŋ^{C}	kʰeŋ^{C}	khêŋh	
e	謦	qǐng	kʰieŋ^{B}	kʰeŋ^{B}	khêŋʔ	
f	馨	xīng	xieŋ	heŋ	hêŋ	

[E] ST *hiŋ: Lushai hiiŋ^{H} / hiin^{L} 'be sour, nasty smelling, stinking'

822a	聲	shēng	śjäŋ	śeŋ	hjeŋ	OCB *xjeŋ

[T] Sin Sukchu SR ʂiŋ (平); MGZY shing (平) [ʂiŋ]; ONW śeŋ
[D] M-Xiamen siã^{A1}, Fuzhou siaŋ^{A1}; K-Meixian saŋ^{A1}.

9-3	= K. 813	Mand.	MC	LHan	OCM	
a	敬	jìng	kjɐŋ^{C}	kɨɛŋ^{C}	kreŋh	[T] ONW keŋ
g	驚	jīng	kjɐŋ	kɨɛŋ	kreŋ	

[T] Sin Sukchu SR kiŋ (平); MGZY ging (平) [kiŋ]; ONW keŋ

hi	儆憼	jǐng	kjɐŋ^{B}, gjɐŋ^{C}, kjäŋ^{B}	kɨɛŋ^{B}, gɨɛŋ^{C} kɨeŋ^{B}	kreŋʔ, greŋh keŋʔ

[E] ? MK: OKhmer krēṅa /krɛɛŋ/ 'be stiff or rigid with fear, to fear, afraid of' → Tai: S. kreeŋ^{A1} 'to fear'

j	警	jǐng	kjɐŋ^{B}, kjäŋ^{B}	kɨɛŋ^{B}, kɨeŋ^{B}	kreŋʔ, keŋʔ
kl	擎檠	qíng	gjɐŋ	gɨɛŋ	greŋ

9-4	= K. 808	Mand.	MC	LHan	OCM	
a	耕	gēng	kɛŋ	kɛŋ	krêŋ	

[T] Sin Sukchu SR kəjŋ (平), PR kiŋ ~ kəŋ; MGZY gÿing (平) [kjiŋ]

bd	刑形	xíng	ɣieŋ	geŋ	gêŋ	OCB *geŋ

[T] Sin Sukchu SR ɣiŋ (平); MGZY Hÿing (平) [ɣjiŋ]; MTang ɣieŋ < ɣɨŋ, ONW ɣėŋ

efgh	侀硎鉶鈃	xíng	ɣieŋ	geŋ	gêŋ
i	荊	jīng	kjɐŋ	kɨɛŋ	kreŋ

9-5	= K. 810	Mand.	MC	LHan	OCM
ab	幸倖	xìng	ɣɛŋ^{B}	gɛŋ^{B}	grêŋʔ
cd	婞涬	xìng	ɣieŋ^{B}	geŋ^{B}	gêŋʔ

9-6	= K. 809	Mand.	MC	LHan	OCM
a	耿	gěng	kɛŋ^{B}	kɛŋ^{B}	krêŋʔ

[E] TB: WB krañ < kriŋ 'clear, bright'

c	褧	jiǒng	kʰiweŋ^{B}	kʰueŋ^{B}	khwêŋʔ

9-7	= K. 828	Mand.	MC	LHan	OCM	
a	頃 slanting	qīng	kʰjiwäŋ4	kʰyeŋ	khweŋ	
	interval	qǐng	kʰjiwäŋ^{B}4	kʰyeŋ^{B}	khweŋʔ	
b	傾	qīng	kʰjiwäŋ4, kʰjiäŋ 4	kʰyeŋ,	khweŋ	[T] ONW kʰueŋ
c	穎 pointed	yǐng	jiwäŋ^{B}	weŋ^{B}	weŋʔ	
	a cushion	jǐng, jiǒng	kjiäŋ^{B} 4, kiweŋ^{B}	kieŋ^{B}, kueŋ^{B}	kwêŋʔ	

d	熲	jiǒng	kiweŋ^{B}	kueŋ^{B}	kwêŋʔ	
e	顈	jiǒng, qiǒng	k^{h}iweŋ^{B}	k^{h}ueŋ^{B}	khwêŋʔ	

9-8	**= K. 842**	**Mand.**	**MC**	**LHan**	**OCM**	
ac	冋坰	jiōng	kiweŋ	kueŋ	kwêŋ	
e	駉	jiōng	kiweŋ	kueŋ	kwêŋ	
d	扃 bolt	jiōng	kiweŋ	kueŋ	kwêŋ	
	clear-mind	jiǒng	kiweŋ^{B}	kueŋ^{B}	kwêŋʔ	
f	絅	jiǒng	k^{h}iweŋ^{B}	k^{h}ueŋ^{B}	khwêŋʔ	
h -	泂迥	jiǒng	ɣiweŋ^{B}	ɣueŋ^{B}	gwêŋʔ or wêŋʔ	

9-9	**= K. 843**	**Mand.**	**MC**	**LHan**	**OCM**	
a	熒	yíng	ɣiweŋ($^{B/C}$)	ɣueŋ($^{B/C}$)	wêŋ(ʔ/h)	
i	螢	yíng	ɣiweŋ	ɣueŋ	wêŋ	
cfj	塋營謍	yíng	jiwäŋ 4	weŋ	weŋ	OCB *wjeŋ
	營 [T] Sin Sukchu SR jujŋ (平), PR juŋ, iŋ, LR iŋ; MGZY yÿung (平) [juŋ]; ONW iueŋ					
k	瑩	yíng,	jwɐŋ,	wɛŋ,	wreŋ,	OCB *wrjeŋ
		yìng	ʔieŋ^{C}	ʔeŋ^{C}	ʔêŋh	
d	榮	róng	jwɐŋ	wɛŋ	wreŋ	[T] ONW ueŋ
e	禜	róng	jwɐŋ(^{C})	wɛŋ(^{C})	wreŋ(h)	
h	縈	yíng	ʔjiwäŋ 4	ʔyeŋ	ʔweŋ	OCB *ʔ^{w}jeŋ
	[E] TB: Lushai veŋ^{R} / ven^{L} 'to gird / wear round the waist'					
l	鶯	yīng	ʔɛŋ	ʔɛŋ	ʔrêŋ	
m	崢嶸	chéng-róng	dẓɛŋ-jwɐŋ,			
			-ɣwɛŋ	dẓɛŋ-ɣuɛŋ	dzrêŋ-wrêŋ ?	
b	檾	qǐng !	k^{h}iweŋ^{B},	k^{h}ueŋ^{B},	khwêŋʔ,	
			k^{h}jiwäŋ^{B}4	k^{h}yeŋ^{B}	khweŋʔ	
g	煢	qióng	gjiwäŋ 4	gyeŋ	gweŋ	
	= 32-8/830 惸, 23-10/829, 256 嬛					

9-10	**= K. 814**	**Mand.**	**MC**	**LHan**	**OCM**
ace	嬰攖纓	yīng	ʔjiäŋ 4	ʔieŋ	ʔeŋ
d	癭	yǐng	ʔjiäŋ^{B} 4	ʔieŋ^{B}	ʔeŋʔ
fgh	嚶鸚罌	yīng	ʔɛŋ	ʔɛŋ	ʔrêŋ

9-11	**= K. 833**	**Mand.**	**MC**	**LHan**	**OCM**	
a	丁 cyclic.	dīng	tieŋ	teŋ	têŋ	'cyclical character'
	[T] Early Han 丁靈 Dīng-líng LH teŋ-leŋ < *têŋ-rêŋ Turk. Tägräg					
	sound	zhēng	ṭɛŋ	ṭɛŋ	têŋ (!)	'sound of beating'
-	打 hit	dǐng	tieŋ^{B}	teŋ^{B}	—	
		dǎ	ṭɐŋ^{B}	ṭaŋ^{B}		
	[T] Sin Sukchu SR tiŋ (上), LR ta <> [D] Suzhou taŋ^{B}, Xiamen tã^{B}					
	[E] TB: Lushai deŋ^{H} / den 'to throw, strike, hit'					
e	頂	dǐng	tieŋ^{B}	teŋ^{B}	têŋʔ	⋈ 32-16/375mn 顛巔
-	酊	dǐng	tieŋ^{B}	teŋ^{B}		
g	町 banks	dìng	dieŋ^{B}	deŋ^{B}	dêŋʔ	
	trampled	tǐng	t^{h}ieŋ^{B}	t^{h}eŋ^{B}	thêŋʔ	

h 亭 tíng dieŋ deŋ dêŋ

i 停 tíng dieŋ deŋ dêŋ

[T] MTang dieŋ < dɨŋ, ONW dėŋ

[E] TB *diŋ > Lushai diŋ^{H} / din^{L} 'to stand, stop, halt, stand up, go straight up', Lepcha diŋ 'be erect, stand', JP diŋ^{33} 'be perfectly straight', WB tañ 'to place in position, build'

f 汀 tīng tʰieŋ tʰeŋ — 'island' [Chuci]

z 定 settle dìng dieŋ^{C} deŋ^{C} dêŋh = 9-13/363a

[T] Sin Sukchu SR diŋ (去); MGZY ting (去) [diŋ]; ONW dėŋ

[E] ST *diŋ or *deŋ: LB *ʔdiŋ^{1} 'put, place on, set up, establish', WB tañ 'place in position, build', Lepcha diŋ 'be erect, to stand'

定 forehead dìng tieŋ^{C} teŋ^{C} têŋ < tleŋ

\- 顁 forehead dìng tieŋ^{C} teŋ^{C} têŋ < tleŋ

[E] AA: Mon tneŋ 'forehead', PVM *tlañ^{B} 'forehead'; Bahnaric *kliâŋ 'forehead'; Pearic kliŋ^{2}. Wa-Lawa-Bulang *k/sṇtɑŋ 'forehead'.

j 正 first zhēng tśjäŋ tśeŋ teŋ OCB *tjeŋ [T] ONW tśeŋ

正 correct zhèng tśjäŋ^{C} tśeŋ^{C} teŋh

[T] Sin Sukchu SR tʂiŋ (去); MGZY jing (去) [tʂiŋ]; ONW tśeŋ

o 征 zhēng tśjäŋ tśeŋ teŋ

v 鉦 zhēng tśjäŋ tśeŋ teŋ

ru 政証 zhèng tśjäŋ^{C} tśeŋ^{C} teŋh

t 整 zhěng tśjäŋ^{B} tśeŋ^{B} teŋʔ

[T] Sin Sukchu SR tʂiŋ (上); MGZY jing (上) [tʂiŋ] <> [E] TB-Lushai diiŋ^{F} 'to go straight or direct, go straight through without breaking the journey, etc.'; Chepang dʰeŋ- 'be straight'; JP teŋ^{31} 'right, correct', Lepcha atʰáŋ 'right, correct', WB tañ^{C} 'straightforward, direct'

y 竀 look chēng ṭʰɐŋ ṭʰɐŋ — 'look straight at' [SW]

[N] ~ 3-32/725f'. The graph seems to be at least partially semantic. <> [E] Tai: S. tʰlɨŋ (WSiam tʰa-lɨŋ) 'a fierce stare, to stare hard at'

red chēng ṭʰjäŋ ṭʰieŋ threŋ = 9-12/834m

The graph occurs in Zuozhuan for = 9-12/834m 赬 [Shijing]

1248b 綻 zhàn ḍăn^{C} ḍɛn^{C} drîns

9-12	= K. 834	Mand.	MC	LHan	OCM	
a	鼎	dǐng	tieŋ^{B}	teŋ^{B}	têŋʔ	

[T] Sin Sukchu SR tiŋ (上); MGZY ding (上) [tiŋ]; ONW tėŋ

g	貞	zhēn	tjäŋ	ṭieŋ	treŋ	[T] MTang ṭeŋ, ONW teŋ
j	禎	zhēn	tjäŋ	ṭieŋ	treŋ	
k	偵	zhēng,	tjäŋ,	ṭieŋ,	treŋ,	
		zhēn	ṭʰjäŋ(C)	ṭʰieŋ(C)	threŋ(h)	
l	楨	zhēn	tjäŋ	ṭieŋ	treŋ	
m	赬 red [Shi]	chēng	ṭʰjäŋ	ṭʰieŋ	threŋ	= 9-1/831x; 9-11/833y

[E] Tai: S. dɛɛŋ^{A1} < *ʔdl/riɛŋ 'red', Saek riiŋ^{A1} 'red', Be liŋ^{13} 'purple'; PMiao *ʔl_N^{A} 'red'

9-13	= K. 363	Mand.	MC	LHan	OCM	
a	奠 present,	diàn,	dien^{C},	den^{C},	dîns	= 9-11/833z
	settle	dìng	dieŋ^{C}	deŋ^{C}	dêŋh	
	stagnant	tíng	dieŋ	deŋ	dêŋ	
e	鄭	zhèng	ḍjäŋ^{C}	ḍieŋ^{C}	dreŋh	
f	躑	zhí	ḍjäk	ḍiek	drek	

9-14	**= K. 818**	**Mand.**	**MC**	**LHan**	**OCM**	
a	成 complete	chéng	źjäŋ	dźeŋ	deŋ	
	[T] Sin S. SR dẓiŋ (平); MGZY zhing (平) [ẓiŋ]; ONW dźeŋ <> [D] PMin *d̑žiaŋ 成 'percent'					
e	城	chéng	źjäŋ	dźeŋ	deŋ (or geŋ ?)	OCB *djeŋ
	[E] ? TB: WT gyaŋ, gyeŋ 'pisé, stamped earth, wall' ⋈ rgyaŋ 'wall' ⋈ 'geŋs-pa 'to fill'					
h	誠	chéng	źjäŋ	dźeŋ	deŋ	
i	盛 put into	chéng	źjäŋ	dźeŋ	deŋ	
	ample	shèng	źjäŋ^{C}	dźeŋ^{C}	deŋh	
	[T] Sin Sukchu SR ẓiŋ (去); MGZY zhing (去) [ẓiŋ]					

9-15	**= K. 815**	**Mand.**	**MC**	**LHan**	**OCM**	
a	盈	yíng	jiäŋ	jeŋ	leŋ	OCB *(l)jeŋ
	[E] TB *bliŋ, *pliŋ 'fill' > Chepang bliŋh-ʔo 'full' ⋈ leŋʔ- 'be full', PL-B *m-bliŋ^{3} > OBurm plañ, WB prañ^{C} 'full'					
c	楹	yíng	jiäŋ	jeŋ	leŋ	= 9-17/835y

9-16	**= K. 816**	**Mand.**	**MC**	**LHan**	**OCM**	
aef	嬴瀛贏	yíng	jiäŋ	jeŋ	leŋ	f = 9-15/815a OCB *(l)jeŋ

9-17	**= K. 835**	**Mand.**	**MC**	**LHan**	**OCM**	
a	壬	tǐng	tʰieŋ^{B}	tʰeŋ^{B}	lhêŋʔ	
d	廷	tíng, dìng	dieŋ(^{C})	deŋ(^{C})	lêŋ, lêŋh	
h	庭 court	tíng	dieŋ	deŋ	lêŋ	OCB *leŋ
	庭 [T] MTang dieŋ < dɨŋ, ONW dėŋ <> [D] M-Xiam tĩã^{A2}					
	庭 distant	tìng	tʰieŋ^{C}	tʰeŋ^{C}	lhêŋh	
i	挺 pull out	tǐng	dieŋ^{B}	deŋ^{B}	lêŋʔ	
	straight	tǐng	tʰieŋ^{B}	tʰeŋ^{B}	lhêŋʔ	[E] TB: *pleŋ 'straight'
j	梃	tǐng !	dieŋ^{B}	deŋ^{B}	lêŋʔ	
o	鋌 rod	dìng	dieŋ^{B}	deŋ^{B}	lêŋʔ	
	to rush	tǐng	tʰieŋ^{B}	tʰeŋ^{B}	lhêŋʔ	
m	霆	tíng	dieŋ	deŋ	lêŋ	OCB *leŋ
kl	筳莛	tíng	dieŋ	deŋ	lêŋ	
	[E] Perh. ST *C-liŋ: TB *r-kliŋ > Mikir arkleŋ, Lushai tʰliŋ^{R} 'marrow', Mru kliŋ 'id.'; WT gliŋ-bu 'flute', LB *kliŋ > PL *ʔliŋ^{1} ~ *hliŋ^{1} 'flute', WB kyañ 'tube'					
n	蜓	dìng,	dieŋ^{B},	deŋ^{B},	lêŋʔ,	
		diàn	dien^{B}	den^{B}	lînʔ	
pq	珽脡	tǐng	tʰieŋ^{B}	tʰeŋ^{B}	lhêŋʔ	
rt	呈程	chéng	ḍjäŋ	ḍieŋ	dreŋ < r-leŋ (?)	
u	裎	chéng	ḍjäŋ	ḍieŋ	dreŋ	
	裎 [E] TB-Mikir -reŋ^{L} angse^{H} 'naked', WT sgren-mo 'naked', JP krin^{31} 'naked', Lushai ṭeen^{R} 'be bare (as a hill side)' <> [N] In an L-series, the MC initial should derive from OCM *r-l-, but the TB cognate speaks in favor of *dr-					
s	珵 a stone	chéng	ḍjäŋ	ḍieŋ	dreŋ	
	tablet	tīng	tʰieŋ	tʰeŋ	rhêŋ	
v	酲	chéng	ḍjäŋ, ṭʰjäŋ	ḍieŋ, ṭʰieŋ	dreŋ, rheŋ	'dead drunk' OCB *lrjeŋ
x	逞	chěng	ṭʰjäŋ^{B}	ṭʰieŋ^{B}	rheŋʔ	= 9-27/817a 騁
	The OC form could also be *threŋʔ or *r-lheŋʔ					
y	桯	tīng !	jiäŋ	jeŋ	leŋ	= 9-15/815c

z 聖 shèng śjäŋ^{C} śeŋ^{C} lheŋh ⋇ 9-17/835d'
[T] Sin Sukchu SR ʂiŋ (去); MGZY shing (去) [ʂiŋ]; ONW śeŋ
d' 聽 listen tīng t^{h}ieŋ t^{h}eŋ lhêŋ OCB *lheŋ
[T] Sin Sukchu SR t'iŋ (平); MGZY thing (平) [t'iŋ]; MTang t^{h}ieŋ < t^{h}ɨŋ, ONW t^{h}ėŋ
聽 obey tìng t^{h}ieŋ^{C} t^{h}eŋ^{C} lhêŋh
c' 檉 chēng ṭ^{h}jäŋ ṭ^{h}ieŋ rheŋ

9-18 = K. 836 Mand. MC LHan OCM
a 霝 líng lieŋ leŋ rêŋ ~ rîn R! = 9-19/823u 零
[T] MTang lieŋ < lɨŋ, ONW lėŋ. The OB graph shows 'cloud' with raindrops, not mouths
i 靈 líng lieŋ leŋ rêŋ
[T] Sin Sukchu SR liŋ (平); MGZY ling (平) [liŋ]; ONW lėŋ. Early Han 丁靈 LH teŋ-leŋ < *têŋ-rêŋ Dīng-líng = Turk. tägräg
egh 孁蘦蠕 líng lieŋ leŋ rêŋ

9-19 = K. 823 Mand. MC LHan OCM
a 令 command lìng ljäŋ(^{C}) lieŋ(^{C}) reŋ(h) ~ rin(s)
[T] Sin Sukchu SR liŋ (平去); MGZY ling (平去) [liŋ]; ONW lieŋ
good líng ljäŋ lieŋ reŋ cf. 3-43/735a
Pl.N. lián ljän lian ren
f 領 lǐng ljäng^{B} lieŋ^{B} reŋʔ OCB *C-rjeŋʔ
[T] Sin Sukchu SR liŋ (上); MGZY ling (上) [liŋ]; ONW lieŋ
[D] 'Collar' in PMin *liaŋ^{B}: Fuzh liaŋ^{B1}, Xiàm niã^{B1} <> [E] TB: Lushai riŋ^{F} 'neck'
j 泠 líng lieŋ leŋ rêŋ
gikl 伶囹玲苓 líng lieŋ leŋ rêŋ
npq 舲蛉軨 líng lieŋ leŋ rêŋ
rvx 鈴鴒齡 líng lieŋ leŋ rêŋ
ou 苓零 líng lieŋ leŋ rêŋ ~ rîn R!
零 = 9-18/836a 霝 <> [T] MTang lieŋ < lɨŋ, ONW lėŋ
h 冷 lěng lieŋ^{B}, lɐŋ^{B} leŋ^{B} rêŋʔ ~ 6-17/898f 陵凌
[T] Sin Sukchu SR ləjŋ (上), PR, LR ləŋ; MGZY l^{h}ing (上) [ləŋ] <> [D] Yue laŋ^{2} 'cold' < ?
[E] TB: Mikir niŋ-kreŋ 'cold weather, winter' (niŋ 'season')
\- 岭 líng lieŋ
\- 怜 líng lieŋ leŋ ?
~ líng 愣 a Han period dialect variant [FY 1.6]

9-20 = K. 837 Mand. MC LHan OCM
abc 寧寍寧 níng nieŋ neŋ nêŋ
[T] ONW nėŋ <> [E] WB hñaŋ^{B} 'soft, gentle, quiet'
g 濘 nìng nieŋ^{C} neŋ^{C} nêŋh
h 嬣 néng ṇɛŋ ṇɛŋ nrêŋ

9-21 = K. 820 Mand. MC LHan OCM
a 晶 jīng tsjäng tsieŋ tseŋ

9-22 = K. 819 Mand. MC LHan OCM
a 井 jǐng tsjäŋ^{B} tsieŋ^{B} tseŋʔ
[T] Sin Sukchu SR tsiŋ (上); MGZY dzing (上) [tsiŋ]

f 姘 jìng dzjäŋ^B dzieŋ^B dzeŋʔ
hi 穽阱 jǐng dzjäŋ^B dzieŋ^B dzeŋʔ

9-23 = K. 811 **Mand.** **MC** **LHan** **OCM**

a 爭 zhēng tṣɛŋ tṣɛŋ tsrêŋ OCB *tsr(j)eŋ
[T] Sin Sukchu SR tṣəjŋ (平), PR, LR tṣəŋ; MGZY j^{h}ing (平) [tṣəŋ]; ONW tṣëŋ
[E] TB: WT 'dziŋ-ba 'quarrel, contend, fight', WB cac 'war, battle'

d 淨 jìng dzjäŋ^C dzieŋ^C dzeŋh [T] ONW dzieŋ

e 竫 jìng dzjäŋ^B dzieŋ^B dzeŋʔ = 9-25/812m' 靖

c 崢嶸 chéng-róng dẓɐŋ-jwɐŋ,
dẓɛŋ-ɣwɛŋ dẓɛŋ-ɣuɛŋ dzrêŋ-wrêŋ

9-24 = K. 821 Acc. to Karlgren the phonetic is unrelated to 32-33/382a xīn 辛

Mand. **MC** **LHan** **OCM**

ab 觲騂 xīng sjäŋ sieŋ seŋ
c 騂 xīng sjäŋ sieŋ seŋ

9-25 = K. 812 **Mand.** **MC** **LHan** **OCM**

aeh 生牲笙 shēng ṣɐŋ ṣeŋ sreŋ OCB *srjeŋ
生 [T] Sin Sukchu SR ṣəjŋ (平), PR, LR ṣəŋ; MGZY sh^{h}ing (平) [ṣəŋ]; ONW ṣëŋ
[E] TB *s-riŋ (*śriŋ) > Manchati sriŋ 'to live, alive'

g 甥 shēng ṣɐŋ ṣeŋ sreŋ OCB *srjeŋ
[E] WT sriŋ-mo 'sister', Lower Kanauri riŋs

i 眚 shěng sjäŋ^B, ṣjɐŋ^B ṣeŋ^B sreŋʔ

l 省 observe xǐng sjäŋ^B sieŋ^B seŋʔ
reduce shěng sjäŋ^B, ṣjɐŋ^B ṣeŋ^B sreŋʔ

qs 姓性 xìng sjäŋ^C sieŋ^C seŋh
[T] Sin Sukchu SR siŋ (去); MGZY sing (去) [siŋ]; ONW sieŋ

tu 狌鼪 xìng, shēng ! sjäŋ^C sieŋ^C seŋh 'weasel'
[T] WT *sre(ŋ) > sre-moŋ, sre-mo 'weasel', Lepcha să-myóŋ 'marmot', Mikir iŋren < *m-ren 'mongoose', WB hrañ^C 'squirrel'

x 星[1] star xīng sieŋ seŋ, S ts^{h}eŋ sêŋ
[T] MTang sieŋ < sɨŋ, ONW sėŋ <> [D] Y-Guangzh ^{55}sɛŋ^{A1}, Taish ^{33}ɬen^{A1}, Enping ^{35}siaŋ^{A1}; PMin *tshaŋ ~ *seŋ: Xiam col. ts^{h}ĩ^{A1} ~ san^{A1}, lit. siŋ^{A1}

x - 星[2]晴 qíng dzjäŋ dzieŋ dzeŋ 'clearing sky' OCB *ɦtshjeŋ

z 猩 to bark xīng sieŋ seŋ sêŋ
[E] KN-Liangmei t^{h}aŋ, Zemei ^{1}ke-^{5}t^{h}aŋ 'to bark'
猩 monkey shēng ṣɐŋ ṣeŋ sreŋ

a' 腥 xīng sieŋ(^{C}) seŋ(^{C}) sêŋ(h)
[T] MTang sieŋ < sɨŋ, ONW sėŋ <> [E] TB: JP siŋ^{33} 'smell; scent; odor of fresh, raw food', Chepang səyŋ- 'emit smell, odor, be rotten', Lepcha mŭŋ-šiŋ, Rawang pušë:ŋ 'stench'

b' 醒 xǐng sieŋ($^{B/C}$) seŋ($^{B/C}$) sêŋ(ʔ/h)
[T] Sin Sukchu SR siŋ (上), LR siŋ; MGZY sing (上) [siŋ]
[E] ST *seŋ: WT seŋ-po ~ bseŋ-po 'clear, white, airy, pale' ⋇ gseŋ-po 'clear and sharp' (sound), JP seŋ^{33} 'clean'; Lushai t^{h}iaŋ^H / thian^L 'be clear, clean'

v 旌 jīng tsjäŋ tsieŋ tseŋ

c' 青 green qīng ts^{h}ieŋ ts^{h}eŋ tshêŋ < k-sêŋ ? OCB *sreŋ (!)
[E] ST *siŋ: WT gsiŋ-ma < *k-siŋ 'pasture land, meadow', Mikir reŋ-seŋ < *-se/iŋ 'green', Rawang məsëŋ 'green', măšiŋ 'blue'

青 luxuriant jīng tsieŋ tseŋ tsêŋ OCB *tseŋ
i' 清 qīng ts^{h}jäŋ ts^{h}ieŋ tsheŋ < k-seŋ ? OCB *tshjeŋ
[T] Sin Sukchu SR ts'iŋ (平); MGZY tshing (平) [ts'iŋ]; ONW ts^{h}ieŋ
e' 蜻 qīng ts^{h}ieŋ ts^{h}eŋ tshêŋ
g' 精 jīng tsjäŋ tsieŋ tseŋ
f' 菁 jīng tsjäŋ, tsieŋ ts(i)eŋ tseŋ, tsêŋ
k' 請 qǐng ts^{h}jäŋ^B, ts^{h}ieŋ^B, tsheŋʔ,
dzjäŋ dzieŋ dzeŋ
[E] TB-PKiranti *sìŋ 'ask', Garo siŋʔ 'to inquire, question, ask'
h' 凊 qìng ts^{h}jäŋ^C ts^{h}ieŋ^C tsheŋh
l' 情 qíng dzjäŋ dzieŋ dzeŋ [T] ONW dzieŋ
m'n's' 靖靜靚 jìng dzjäŋ^B dzieŋ^B dzeŋʔ 靖 = 9-23/811e 竫
t' 綪 tuck in zhēng tṣɛŋ tṣɛŋ tsrêŋ
dark red qiàn ts^{h}ien^C ts^{h}en^C tshîns
1250cd 倩蒨 red qiàn ts^{h}ien^C ts^{h}en^C tshîns
OCB tshins 'dark red' (Baxter 1992: 433)

9-26 = K. 825 Mand. MC LHan OCM
a - 平坪 píng bjɐŋ bɨɛŋ breŋ OCB *brjeŋ
[T] ONW beŋ <> [D] PCoastal Min *baŋ > Amoy pĩ^{A2} < *baŋ 'even, flat' ⋈ p^{h}ĩ^{A2} < *b^{h}aŋ 'to flatten'; Fuzh paŋ^{A2}; PNMin *piaŋ 'level' 平, 'yard' 坪
[E] TB *pleŋ 'flat surface' > Tamang pleŋ 'big flat stone'; Mikir kapleŋ 'plank'
- 評 píng bjɐŋ bɨɛŋ breŋ
c 苹 Artemisia píng bjɐŋ bɨɛŋ breŋ
duckweed píng bieŋ beŋ bêŋ
- 泙 píng bieŋ beŋ bêŋ
d 萍 rain m. píng bieŋ beŋ bêŋ < bleŋ 'rain master'
[E] AA: Khmer bhlieŋ 'rain', PNB *plíñ 'sky', Pearic phliŋ 'sky'
蓱 duckweed píng bieŋ beŋ bêŋ
e 伻 bēng, pēng p(h)ɛŋ p(h)ɛŋ prêŋ, phrêŋ
[E] ? TB-WT spriŋ-ba, spriŋs 'to send a message'
fg 怦砰 pēng p^{h}ɛŋ p^{h}ɛŋ phrêŋ

9-27 = K. 839, 817 MC LHan OCM
a 甹 pīng p^{h}ieŋ p^{h}eŋ phêŋ
cd 娉聘 pìn p^{h}jiäng^C 4 p^{h}ieŋ^C pheŋh ⋈ 3-57/740t 訪
817a 騁 chěng ṭ^{h}jäng^B ṭ^{h}ieŋ^B rheŋʔ = 9-17/835x 逞 OCB *hlrjeŋ
(a) 'gallop, drive rapidly'; (b) 'develop one's potential'. According to *SW* 4326, 甹 is phonetic that can mean as little as the rime; the element could be semantic ('inquire'). The OC form could also be *threŋʔ or *r-lheŋʔ.

9-28 = K. 840 Mand. MC LHan OCM
ab 竝並 bìng bieŋ^B beŋ^B bêŋʔ
[T] Sin Sukchu SR piŋ (去); MGZY bing (去) [piŋ]; ONW bėŋ
- 碰 pèng bɐŋ^C [Zìhuì],
bâŋ^C [Duan Yucai]

9-29	= K. 824	Mand.	MC	LHan	OCM	
ab	a 并	bìng	pjiäŋ$^{(C)}$ 4	pieŋ$^{(C)}$	peŋ, peŋh	[T] ONW bieŋ
e	瓶	pīng	p^{h}ieŋ$^{(B)}$	p^{h}eŋ$^{(B)}$	phêŋ, phêŋʔ	
f	屏 screen	píng	bieŋ	beŋ	bêŋ	OCB *beŋ
	remove	bìng	pjiäŋ$^{B/C}$ 4	pieŋ$^{B/C}$	peŋʔ/h	OCB *pjeŋʔ
	anxious	bīng	pjäŋ ?	pieŋ	peŋ	
g	偋	bìng	bjiäŋ^{C} 4	bieŋ^{C}	beŋh	
-	軿	píng	bieŋ	beŋ	bêŋ	
d	併	bìng	bieŋ^{B},	beŋ^{B},	bêŋʔ,	
			pjäŋ^{C} ?	pieŋ^{C}	peŋh	
h	洴 beat	píng	bieŋ	beŋ	bêŋ	[T] BTD Skt. bim[bisara]
ij	缾瓶	píng	bieŋ	beŋ	bêŋ	[T] BTD Skt. bim[bisara]

[E] AA: Khmer bīṅa /piiŋ/ 'swollen, pot-bellied, earthen water pot'

k	荓 a plant	píng	bieŋ	beŋ	bêŋ	
	to cause	pēng	p^{h}ɛŋ	p^{h}ɛŋ	phrêŋ	
l	絣	bēng	pɛŋ	pɛŋ	prêŋ	
m	迸	bèng	pɛŋ^{C}	pɛŋ^{C}	prêŋh	
n	駢 horses s.	pián	bien,	ben,	bên or bîn, 'horses side by side'	
			bieŋ	beŋ	bêŋ	

[E] ? TB: Chepang b^{h}iŋ- 'be close together (lay object, friends), double up'

	駢 double	pián	bien	ben	bîn	'side by side'
o	骿 double	pián	bien	ben	bîn	'side by side'
pq	胼跰	pián	bien	ben	bîn	

9-30	= K. 841	Mand.	MC	LHan	OCM	
a	冥 dark	míng	mieŋ$^{(B)}$	meŋ$^{(B)}$	mêŋ(ʔ)	

[T] MTang mieŋ < mɨŋ, ONW mėŋ <> [D] PMin *maŋ^{A2} 'night'
[E] TB *miŋ > WB mañ^{B} ~ mai^{B} 'dark, black' <> MY *mhwaaṆ^{1C} [Purnell] or *m̥weŋ^{C1} [Wang Fushi 20/140] 'evening, night', MK: PNBahn. măŋ 'night'

	冥 cover	mì	miek	mek	mêk	
-	暝	míng	mieŋ$^{(B)}$	meŋ$^{(B)}$	mêŋ, mêŋʔ	
c	溟	míng	mieŋ	meŋ	mêŋ	
b	瞑 sleep	míng,	mieŋ,	meŋ,	mêŋ,	
		mián	mien	men	mîn	= 32-40/457e 眠
	瞑 dizzy	miàn	mien^{C}	men^{C}	mîns	
d	螟蛉	míng-líng	mieŋ-lieŋ	meŋ-leŋ	mêŋ-rêŋ	

[E] Tai: S. ma-lɛɛŋ^{A2} < *ml/r- 'insect'

efg	塓冪幎	mì	miek	mek	mêk	= 8-19/853o 幦

[T] MTang mian < mɨan, ONW mėn

9-31	= K. 826	Mand.	MC	LHan	OCM
a	名	míng	mjiäŋ 4	mieŋ	meŋ R!

[T] Sin Sukchu SR miŋ (平); MGZY ming (平) [miŋ]; MTang mieŋ, ONW mieŋ
[E] TB *r-miŋ > WT miŋ, OTib myiŋ 'name', Jiarong termi, LB *ʔ-miŋ$^{1/3}$, Lushai hmiŋ^{H} 'name' <> [N] In Chuci míng rimes also with *-in.

d	銘	míng	mieŋ	meŋ	mêŋ

[T] MTang mieŋ < mɨŋ, ONW mėŋ

9-32	= K. 762	Mand.	MC	LHan	OCM	
a	命	mìng	mjɐŋ^{C}	miɛŋ^{C}	min R! ~mreŋ R!	OCB *mrjiŋ(s)

[T] Sin Sukchu SR miŋ (去); MGZY ming (去) [miŋ]; ONW meŋ <> [D] PMin *miaŋ^{C} 'life'

9-33	= K. 827	Mand.	MC	LHan	OCM	
a	鳴	míng	mjɐŋ	miɛŋ	mreŋ	OCB *mrjeŋ

[E] TB: WB mrañ 'to sound'; Mikir marèŋ 'make noise, cry', Lushai riŋ^{H} / rin^{F} 'be loud'

10 OCM rime *-o Hóu bù 侯部

GSR 108 - 138; 1229 - 1235

Baxter 1992: 500 ff. (§10.2.10)

Table 10-1: OCM rimes *-oŋ, *-ok, *-o in QYS categories

MC	*-oŋ R.12	*-ok R.11	*-o, *-okh R.10, 11
I	公 kuŋ koŋ *kôŋ 蒙 muŋ moŋ *môŋ 東 tuŋ toŋ *tôŋ	谷 kuk kok *kôk 木 muk mok *môk 獨 duk dok *dôk	口 kʰəu^{B} kʰo^{B} *khôʔ 豆 dəu^{C} do^{C} *dôh 彀 kəu^{C} ko^{C} *kôkh
III	共 gjwoŋ^{C} guoŋ^{C} *goŋh 縫 bjwoŋ buoŋ *boŋ 龍 ljwoŋ lioŋ *roŋ 種 tśjwoŋ^{B} tśoŋ^{B} *toŋʔ 重 ḍjwoŋ^{B} ḍioŋ^{B} *droŋʔ 用 jiwoŋ^{C} joŋ^{C} *loŋh	曲 kʰjwok kʰuok *khok 俗 zjwok ziok *s-lok 蜀 źjwok dźok *dok	拘 kju kuo *ko 付 pju^{C} puo^{C} *poh 朱 tju ṭio *tro 俞 jiu jo *lo 裕 jiu^{C} jo^{C} *lokh
II	江 kåŋ kɔŋ *krôŋ 邦 påŋ pɔŋ *prôŋ 撞 ḍåŋ ḍɔŋ *drôŋ	角 kåk kɔk *krôk 璞 pʰåk pʰɔk *phrôk 濁 ḍåk ḍɔk *drôk	No Div. II

10-1 **= K. 108** Kǒu 口 10-3 may be phonetic.

		Mand.	MC	LHan	OCM	
a-c	句[1]勾鉤	gōu	kəu	ko	kô	'hook'
	[E] WT dgu-ba 'to bend'					
a	句[2] phrase	jù	kju^{C}	kuo^{C}	—	
	[T] 句決 kuo^{C} (or kɨo^{C})-kuet 'a kind of hat', cf. Mongol kökül (Pulleyblank 1983: 453)					
d	狗	gǒu	kəu^{B}	ko^{B}	kôʔ < kloʔ	
	[D] PMin *k̥əu^{B} <> [E] MY *klu^{2}					
efh	笱耇苟	gǒu	kəu^{B}	ko^{B}	kôʔ	
i	雊	gòu	kəu^{C}	ko^{C}	kôh	
qr	痀駒	jū	kju	kuo	ko	OCB *k(r)jo
p	拘 grasp	jū	kju	kuo	ko	
	[T] ONW kuo; BTD Skt. ku; 拘律陀 kuo-luit-da Skt. kolita					
	拘 receive	gōu	kəu	ko	kô	
	拘 tree st.	qú	gju	guo	go	'tree stump'
o	枸 a tree	jǔ	kju^{B}	kuo^{B}	koʔ	
	crooked	gōu	kəu	ko	kô	
tuv	劬絇朐	qú	gju	guo	go	
xy	軥鴝	qú	gju	guo	go	

l	袧	kōu	kʰəu	kʰo	khô	
k	敂	kòu !	kʰəu^{B}	kʰo^{B}	khôʔ	= 10-3/110f 釦
j	怐	kòu	kʰəu^{C}	kʰo^{C}	khôh	
m	詾	hòu	ɣəu^{C},xəu^{C}	ɣo^{C}, ho^{C}	ɦôh, hôh	⋈ 10-5/112f
n	蚼	hǒu	xəu^{B}	ho^{B}	hôʔ	
-	齁	hōu	xəu	ho	—	

[E] WT ŋur-ba 'to grunt' ⋈ sŋur-ba 'to snore'

z	竘	qǔ, kōu !	kʰju^{B}, kʰəu^{B}	kʰ(ɨ)o^{B}	khoʔ, khôʔ	
a'	呴	xū	xju(^{C})	huo(^{C})	ho,hoh	
b'	姁	xǔ	xju^{B}	huo^{B}	hoʔ	
-c'	昫煦 warm	xù	xju^{C}	huo^{C}	hoh	煦 also MC xju^{B}

10-2	**= K. 109**	**Mand.**	**MC**	**LHan**	**OCM**	
a	冓	gòu	kəu^{C}	ko^{C}	kôh	OCB *k(r)os
efgjkl	媾搆構覯購遘	id.				

遘 [E] TB *gow > WB ku^{B} 'cross over, transfer', JP gau^{33} 'pass over'

hi	溝篝	gōu	kəu	ko	kô	
1198a	講	jiǎng	kåŋ^{B}	kɔŋ^{B}	krôŋʔ	

10-3	**= K. 110**	**Mand.**	**MC**	**LHan**	**OCM**	
a	口	kǒu	kʰəu^{B}	kʰo^{B}	khôʔ	OCB *kh(r)oʔ

[T] Sin Sukchu SR k'əw (上); MGZY khʰiw (上) [k'əw]; ONW kʰou

[E] TB: JP kʰu^{33} 'hole, hollow', Lushai kua^{L} (kɔ^{L}) < kuaʔ/h 'a hollow, cavity' ⋈ kua^{L} / kuak^{F} 'to open up (a path)'

de	叩扣	kòu	kʰəu$^{B/C}$	kʰo$^{B/C}$	khôʔ/h	

[E] ? WB kʰok < *kʰuk 'knock, rap'

f	釦	kòu !	kʰəu^{B}	kʰo^{B}	khôʔ	= 10-1/108k 敂

10-4	**= K. 111**	**Mand.**	**MC**	**LHan**	**OCM**
a	寇	kòu	kʰəu^{C}	kʰo^{C}	khôh

[E] TB *r-kuw > Chepang kuʔ 'steal', WT rku-ba 'to steal', JP lǎ^{31}-ku^{55} 'to steal', NNaga *C/V-kə:w, WB kʰui^{B} < *C-kui^{B}, PL *ko^{2} 'to steal' <> [N] Baxter 1992: 238 considers 25-19/257m 完 phonetic, but it could also be semantic, cf. SW 1358.

10-5	**= K. 112**	**Mand.**	**MC**	**LHan**	**OCM**	
a	后	hòu	ɣəu$^{B/C}$	go$^{B/C}$	gôʔ/h	OCB *g(r)oʔ
c	邂逅	hòu	ɣai^{C}-ɣəu^{C}	gɛ^{C}-go^{C}	grêh-grôh	OCB *gres-gros
d	垢	gòu	kəu^{B}	ko^{B}	kôʔ	

[T] MTang kəu, ONW kou <> [E] ? TB: WT bsgo-ba 'to soil, stain, defile, infect'

e	姤	gòu	kəu^{C}	ko^{C}	kôh	
f	詬	hòu,	xəu^{C},	ho^{C},	hôh,	⋈ 10-1/108m
		kòu, gòu	kʰəu^{C}, kəu^{B}	kʰo^{C}, ko^{B}	khôh, kôʔ	

[E] WT 'kʰu-ba 'insult, offend'

g	呴	hòu	xəu$^{B/C}$	ho$^{B/C}$	hôʔ/h

10-6	**= K. 113**	**Mand.**	**MC**	**LHan**	**OCM**	
a	侯 target	hóu	ɣəu	go	gô	OCB *g(r)o

[E] ? AA: Khmer koḥ /kaoh/ 'to raise (crossbow) with a view to aiming' ⋈ kpoḥ 'be raised up, clearly visible'; or goḥ /kóh/ 'to hit (squarely)'

		Mand.	MC	LHan	OCM	
	侯 be, have	hóu	ɣəu	go	gô	
	[E] AA: PVM *kɔːʔ 'to be, have, there is', PMonic *gooʔ 'to get, possess, obtain'					
e	候 watch	hòu	ɣəu^{C}	go^{C}	gôh	
f	喉	hóu	ɣəu	go	gô	
	[E] ? TB: Chepang guk 'throat' <> MK *kɔʔ 'neck'					
g	猴	hóu	ɣəu	go	gô	
	[D] PMin *ğəu < *ɴgo ? < ? TB: PL *ʔ-ko$^{2/1}$					
hj	猴餱	hóu	ɣəu	go	gô	
i-	鍭睺	hóu	ɣəu(C)	go(C)	gô, gôh	

10-7	**= K. 114**	**Mand.**	**MC**	**LHan**	**OCM**	
a	厚 thick	hòu	ɣəu^{B}	go^{B}	gôʔ	OCB *g(r)oʔ
	[T] Sin Sukchu SR ɣəw (上); MGZY Xiw (上) [ɣiw] <> [D] ğəu^{B}					
	厚 thickness	hòu	ɣəu^{C}	go^{C}	gôh	

10-8	**= K. 115**	**Mand.**	**MC**	**LHan**	**OCM**	
a	後 behind	hòu	ɣəu^{B}	ɣo^{B}	ɦôʔ	OCB *ɦ(r)oʔ
	[T] Sin Sukchu SR ɣəw (上); MGZY Xiw (上) [ɣiw]; MTang ɣəu, ONW ɣou <> [D] PMin *ɦəu^{B} <> [E] TB *ok > WT 'og (not ʔog) 'below, afterward, later, after'; LB *ʔok 'lower side, below' > WB ok 'under part, space under'; Limbu yo 'down, below, downhill'					
	後 support	hòu	ɣəu^{C}	ɣo^{C}	ɦôh	

10-9	**= K. 121**	**Mand.**	**MC**	**LHan**	**OCM**
a	具	jù	gju^{C}	guo^{C}	goh
	[T] MTang gy < guo, ONW guo				
d	俱	jū	kju	kuo	ko
	[T] Sin Sukchu SR ky (平); MGZY gȳu (平) [ky]; MTang ky < kuo, ONW kuo				
e	椇	jǔ	kju^{B}	kuo^{B}	koʔ

10-10	**= K. 122**	**Mand.**	**MC**	**LHan**	**OCM**
a	區[1] conceal	ōu	ʔəu	ʔo	ʔô
l	甌	ōu	ʔəu	ʔo	ʔô
	[E] WB ui^{B} 'pot, jar, chatty'				
m-	謳歐	ōu	ʔəu	ʔo	ʔô
	歐 [T] Sin Sukchu 歐 SR ʔəw (平); MGZY 歐 'ʰiw (平) [ʔəw]; ONW ʔou				
j	毆	ǒu !	ʔəu^{B}	ʔo^{B}	ʔôʔ
i	嘔 vomit	oǔ	ʔəu^{B}	ʔo^{B}	ʔôʔ
	babble	ōu	ʔəu	ʔo	ʔô
k	漚 soak	où	ʔəu^{C}	ʔo^{C}	ʔôh
	seagull	ōu	ʔəu	ʔo	ʔô
n	傴	yǔ	ʔju^{B}	ʔuo^{B}	ʔoʔ
o	嫗 warm	yù, yǔ	ʔju^{B}	ʔuo^{B}	ʔoʔ
	[E] ST *ʔo: WB u^{B} (i.e., /ʔu^{B}/) 'lay an egg' ⋇ ə-u^{B} 'egg'				
	嫗 mother	yù	ʔju^{C}	ʔuo^{C}	ʔoh
-	蓲 brood	yòu	ʔjəu^{C}	ʔu^{C}	—
	[D] Min: Jiàn'ōu iu^{C1}, Chóngān ieu^{C1}				
p	饇	yù,	ʔju^{C},	ʔuo^{C},	ʔoh,
		qū	kʰju	kʰuo	kho < kʔo ?

a 區[2] conceal qū k^hju k^huo kho < kʔo ?
crooked gōu kəu ko kô = late graphic loan for 句鉤枸

h 摳 kōu k^həu, k^hju k^ho, k^huo kho
[E] ? TB *ku > WB k^hu^B 'take out or up and put in dish, gather'; Yakha k^hu 'lift up, raise'; Bahing ku-to 'bring up'

g 軀 qū k^hju(C) k^huo(C) kho ! OCB *kh(r)jo
[T] MTang k^hy < k^huo, ONW k^huo <> [E] TB *(s-)kuw > WT sku, WB kui 'body'

cd 驅毆 qū k^hju(C) k^huo(C) kho, khoh
[E] ? WT 'k^hyug-pa 'to run, dart, hasten' ⋇ 'k^hyu-ba, k^hyus 'to run' ⋇ dkyu-ba 'a race' ⋇ 'gyu-ba, 'gyus 'to move quickly'

q 樞 pivot shū tś^{h}ju tś^{h}o k-hlo ? or khjo ?
[D] Yue: HK-NT $^{232}k^hy^{A1}$, Conghua k^hy^{55}, Doumen k^hui^{45}; Hakka: Huizhou ky^{33}, Dongguan k^hi^{33}

樞 an elm shū, ōu ʔəu ʔo ʔô

r 貙 wild cat chū ṭ^{h}ju ṭ^{h}io thro ? or rho ?

10-11 = K. 124 **Mand.** **MC** **LHan** **OCM**

a 禺 monkey yù $ŋju^C$ $ŋuo^C$ ŋoh
[E] TB: Kuki-Naga *ŋa:w 'ape' > Lushai $ŋau^H$ < ŋau 'grey monkey'

禺 a fish yú ŋju ŋuo ŋo

c 寓 yù $ŋju^C$ $ŋuo^C$ ŋoh

fi 嵎隅 yú ŋju ŋuo ŋo

g 愚 yú ŋju ŋuo ŋo
[T] MTang ŋy < ŋuo, ONW ŋuo <> [D] K-Sung Him Tong $ŋɔŋ^C$, Meixian $ŋuŋ^C$ 'stupid'
[E] Tai: PTai *$ʔŋua^{B2/C2}$ 'stupid, idiot, ignorant', S. $ŋoo^{C1}$ 'stupid'

jk 腢髃 yú, ǒu ŋju, $ŋəu^B$ ŋuo, $ŋo^B$ ŋo, ŋôʔ

l 齵 yú, ǒu ŋju, ŋəu ŋuo, ŋo ŋo, ŋô

h 遇 yù $ŋju^C$ $ŋuo^C$ ŋoh
[T] Sin Sukchu SR ŋy (去); MGZY xy̆u (去) [ɦy]

o 耦 a pair ǒu $ŋəu^B$ $ŋo^B$ ŋôʔ

n 偶 a pair ǒu $ŋəu^B$ $ŋo^B$ ŋôʔ
unexpected òu $ŋəu^C$ $ŋo^C$ ŋôh

m 喁 yú, ŋju, $ŋəu^B$, ŋuo, $ŋo^B$, ŋo, ŋôʔ,
yóng ŋjwoŋ ŋuoŋ ŋoŋ

p 顒 yóng ŋjwoŋ ŋuoŋ ŋoŋ

10-12 = K. 117 **Mand.** **MC** **LHan** **OCM**

a 兜 dōu təu to tô
[T] BTD 兜術陀 to-źuit-dɑ Skt. tuṣita

10-13 = K. 116 **Mand.** **MC** **LHan** **OCM**

ab 斗枓 bushel dǒu $təu^B$ to^B tôʔ [D] PMin *$təu^B$
斗枓 ladle zhǔ $tśju^B$ $tśo^B$ toʔ

10-14 = K. 1246a **Mand.** **MC** **LHan** **OCM**

a 豛 dòu $təu^C$ to^C tôh

10-15 = K. 1235		**Mand.**	**MC**	**LHan**	**OCM**	
a	𠁁	dòu	dəu^{B}	do^{B}	dôʔ	
b	斲	zhuó	ṭåk	ṭɔk	trôk	
c	鬭	dòu	dəu^{C}	do^{C}	dôh	= 10-17/1234a 鬥

10-16 = K. 118		**Mand.**	**MC**	**LHan**	**OCM**
a	豆	dòu	dəu^{C}	do^{C}	dôh
	[T] Sin Sukchu SR dəw (去); MGZY tʰiw (去) [dəw] <> [D] PMin *dəu^{C}				
-	荳	dòu	dəu^{C}	do^{C}	—
	[E] TB *tu-ŋ 'bean'				
d	脰	dòu	dəu^{C}	do^{C}	dôh
	[D] PMin *d̯əu^{C}: Fúzhou tau^{C2}-kauk^{D1}, Jiànyáng lo^{C2}				
	[E] TB *tuk ⋈ *du(k) 'neck, head', JP duʔ^{31} 'neck', Garo gitok, Mikir tśethok, Lepcha tŭk-tok 'neck', Abor-Miri a-tuk, Atong dək-əm, Kaike tʰoppā (< *tʰok-pa) 'head'				
-	逗	dòu	dəu^{C}	do^{C}	
e	頭	tóu	dəu	do	dô
	[T] ONW dou; BTD Skt. dhu <> [D] PMin *dhəu^{A2}: Jiànglè tʰəu^{D1}, Fuzh ^{52}tʰau, Xiàmen tʰau^{A2}-kʰak; W-Wenzh ^{21}dɦeu				
fg	裋豎	shù	źju^{B}	dźo^{B}	doʔ
169a	短	duǎn	twân^{B}	tuɑn^{B}, S toiʔ	tônʔ
	[T] Sin Sukchu SR twɔn (平); MGZY don (平) [tɔn]; ONW tuɑn. <> [D] PMin *toi^{B}				

10-17 = K. 1234		**Mand.**	**MC**	**LHan**	**OCM**	
a	鬥	dòu	dəu^{C}	do^{C}	dôh	= 10-15/1235c
	[T] ONW dou <> [E] TB *daw > WB do^{B} 'interfere in a quarrel'; Lushai do^{H} 'be at enmity'					

10-18 = K. 128		**Mand.**	**MC**	**LHan**	**OCM**	
af	朱[1] > 株	zhū	tju	ṭio	tro	'tree trunk'
ar	朱[2]袾[1] red	zhū	tśju	tśo	to	
	[T] ONW tśuo <> [E] MK: PVM *tɔh 'red'					
de	侏珠	zhū	tśju	tśo	to	
gh	蛛鼄	zhū	tju	ṭio	tro	
klm	誅跦邾	zhū	tju	ṭio	tro	
u	咮	dòu, zhòu	təu^{C}, tjəu^{C}	to^{C}, ṭu^{C}	tôkh, trokh	= 11-13/1218b 啄
s	殊	shū	źju	dźo	do	
	[T] Sin Sukchu SR ʐy (平); MGZY zhÿu (平) [ʐy]; BTD Skt. ju					
	[E] ST *do(k): JP doʔ^{31} < tok^{31} 'cut off'					
t	銖	zhū	źju	dźo	do	
pr	姝袾[2]	shū !	tśʰju	tśʰo	tho	'beautiful'

10-19 = K. 129		**Mand.**	**MC**	**LHan**	**OCM**	
a	主	zhǔ	tśju^{B}	tśo^{B}	toʔ	
	[T] Sin Sukchu SR tʂy (上); MGZY jÿu (上) [tʂy]; ONC tśuo^{B} <> [D] PMin *tšo^{B}					
-	麈	zhǔ	tśju^{B}	tśo^{B}	toʔ	'large kind of deer in the mountains'
b-	罜炷	zhù	tśju^{C}	tśo^{C}	toh	
c	注 touch	zhù	tśju^{C}, tju^{C}	tśo^{C}, ṭio^{C}	toh, troh	
	[E] ST *tu: WB tui^{C} 'touch lightly', Lushai tuuk^{F} 'to touch' (as in a game)					
	注 pour	zhù	tśju^{C}, tju^{C}	tśo^{C}, ṭio^{C}	toh, troh	= 13-22/1090a' 鑄

注 flow in   zhù   tśju^{C}, tju^{C} tśo^{C}, ṭio^{C} toh, troh

[E] WT mdo 'confluence, lower part of valley'

d 註   zhù   tśju^{C}, tju^{C} tśo^{C}, ṭio^{C} toh, troh

e 拄   zhǔ   tju^{B} ṭio^{B} troʔ

f 鉒   zhù   tju^{C} ṭio^{C} troh

g 住   zhù   ḍju^{C} ḍio^{C} droh   [D] PMin *diu^{C}

h 柱   zhù   ḍju^{B} ḍio^{B} droʔ

[T] Sin Sukchu SR dzy (上); MGZY cÿu (上) [dzy] <> [D] PMin *dhiu^{B}

[E] TB-WB tuiŋ 'post, column'; SChin Daai ktuŋ 'post', JP toʔ^{31} < tok^{31}

i 黈   tǒu   tʰəu^{B} tʰo^{B} thôʔ

10-20 = K. 1232   Mand.   MC   LHan   OCM

a 㸑   zhù   tśju^{C} tśo^{C} toh

10-21 = K. 130   Mand.   MC   LHan   OCM

a 殳   shū   źju   dźo   do

c 投   tóu   dəu   do   dô

[T] ONW dou <> [E] WT 'dor-ba 'to throw or cast away, throw out, eject, decline, reject' ※ gtor-ba 'to strew, scatter, throw, waste'

323a 祋   dài !   twâi^{C} tuɑs   tôs

10-22 = K. 127   Mand.   MC   LHan   OCM

a 壴   zhù   tju^{C} ṭio^{C} troh

eh 侸尌   shù   źju^{C} dźo^{C} doh

j 樹 to plant   shǔ   źju^{B} dźo^{B} doʔ

樹 [T] Sin Sukchu SR ʐy (上); MGZY zhÿu (上) [ʐy]

[E] ? Area word: TB-Lushai tuʔ^{L} (< *tus) 'to plant (a seed)'

樹 tree   shù   źju^{C} dźo^{C} doh

[T] Sin Sukchu SR ʐy (去); MGZY zhÿu (去) [ʐy]; ONW dźuo <> [D] PMin *džhiu^{C}

m 廚厨   chú   ḍju   ḍio   dro

n 躕 (踟躕)   chú   ḍju   ḍie-ḍio   dre-dro

[E] Tai: S. rii^{A2}-rɔɔ^{A2} 'walk hesitatingly, undecided'

10-23 = K. 125   Mand.   MC   LHan   OCM

a 俞 canoe   yú   jiu   jo   lo   'dug-out, canoe' SW 3803

The original graph consisted of 'boat' and 'knife'. The upper element was either part of the knife, or the downward turned mouth, thus writing *yù* 'instruct'. — 舠舠 look like the original graph for 'canoe', but appear only later (JY) and are read *dāo* 'a small, knife-shaped boat', i.e., the word is taken as a special meaning of 'knife'.

俞 agree   yú   jiu   jo   lo   'say yes'

[E] WB lyo 'suit, agree with, be proper'

fghi 愉榆渝瑜   yú   jiu   jo   lo

愉 [E] WB lyo^{C} 'loose, slack, subside' ※ hlyo^{C} 'loosen, make lax, lessen, diminish'

no 踰逾   yú   jiu   jo   lo

[T] Sin Sukchu SR y (平); MGZY yÿu (平) [jy]

k 揄   yú   jiu   jo   lo

l 覦   yú   jiu(^{C})   jo(^{C})   lo, loh

cm 喻諭   yù   jiu^{C} jo^{C} loh   [E] ? WT blo 'mind, intellect'

q	窬	yú, tóu	jiu, dəu	jo, do	lo, lô	

[E] MK: Old Sino-Viet. lo 'small hole' (Pan Wuyun 1987: 29), Loven luh 'hole', Khmer /tluh/ 'perforate' ⋇ /luh/ 'pass through, pierce, perforate...'

p	揄	yú	jiu, dəu^{B}	jo, doʔ	lo, lôʔ	
r	蝓	yú, chú	jiu, dźju	jo, źo	lo, m-lo	
dj	愈瘉	yù	jiu^{B}	jo^{B}	loʔ	
s	輸	shū	śju	śo	lho	

[T] MTang śu < śuo, ONW śuo <> [D] PMin *šo

uv	偷媮	tōu	t^{h}əu	t^{h}o	lhô	偷 [E] WB lu^{C} 'take by force'
t	歈	tóu	dəu	do	lô	

[E] WT glu 'song', Mru klö 'sound, melody', WB kyu^{B} 'produce melodious sound'

10-24 = K. 126 The OCM initial was either *j- or *l-.

		Mand.	MC	LHan	OCM
a	臾 drag	yú	jiu	jo	jo < r-jo (cf. 10-29/123a)
ef	腴諛	yú	jiu	jo	jo
bcdg-	庾斞楰[illegible][illegible]	yǔ	jiu^{B}	jo^{B}	joʔ

10-25 = K. 1243b	Mand.	MC	LHan	OCM	
b 瓥	yú	jiu^{B}	jo^{B}	loʔ	⋇ 10-23/125f,u

10-26 = K. 1243c	Mand.	MC	LHan	OCM
c 戍	shù	śju^{C}	śo^{C}, tś^{h}o^{C}	hjoh ?

[T] ONW śuo <> [D] PMin *tšhio^{C}; Yue-Guangzh ^{33}ts^{h}y^{CD}, Taish ts^{h}ui^{21} 'house'

10-27 = K. 120	Mand.	MC	LHan	OCM
a 漏	lòu	ləu^{C}	lo^{C}	rôh or rôkh

[T] Sin S. SR ləw (去); MGZY l^{h}iw (去) [ləw]; MTang ləu, ONW lou <> [D] PMin *ləu^{C}
[E] Old Sino-Viet. rɔ <> Tai: S. rua^{B2} < *r- 'to leak'

10-28 = K. 1246b	Mand.	MC	LHan	OCM
b 陋	lòu	ləu^{C}	lo^{C}	rôh

10-29 = K. 123, 1207		MC	LHan	OCM	GYSX 1024
123a 婁 drag	lǘ	lju	lio	ro = rjo (cf. 10-24/126a)	
bind	lǚ	lju^{B}	lio^{B}	roʔ	
empty	lóu	ləu	lo	rô	
mound	lóu	ləu(^{B})	lo(^{B})	rô, rôʔ	
j 塿	lǒu	ləu^{B}	lo^{B}	rôʔ	[T] ONW lou
b 僂	lóu, lǚ	ləu, lju^{B}	lo, lio^{B}	rô, roʔ	
c 膢	lǘ, lóu	lju, ləu	lio, lo	ro, rô	
d 摟	lǘ, lǒu !	lju, ləu	lio, lo	ro, rô	
e 蔞	lǘ, lóu	lju(^{B}), ləu	lio(^{B}), lo	ro, roʔ, rô	
f 屢	lǚ !	lju^{C}	lio^{C}	roh	⋇ 10-29/1207a
g 瘻	lǘ	lju	lio	ro	
h 縷	lǚ	lju^{B}	lio^{B}	roʔ	
i 鞻	lóu, lù,	ləu, lju^{C},	lo, lio^{C},	rô, roh,	
	jù	kju^{C}	kuo^{C}	kroh	

k	樓		lóu	ləu	lo	rô	

[T] BTD Skt. ro[hita]. MHan 樓蘭 Krorayina <> [D] PMin *ləu

l	螻	cricket	lóu	ləu	lo	rô	
		sickness	lòu	ləu^{C}	lo^{C}	rôh	
m	鏤		lòu	ləu^{C}	lo^{C}	rô, rôh	

[E] WT 'bru-ba 'chisel, carve, cut'; Nung ə-ru 'carve, write' <> Tai: S. pɔɔk^{D1} 'to peel', but also PTai *dlɔɔk : S. lɔɔk^{D2} 'to skin, peel' ⋈ plɔɔk^{D1} 'an encasement'

n	髏		lóu	-ləu	[dok-]lo	rô	= a 'empty'
op	窶寠		jù	gju^{B}	guo^{B}	groʔ	
123q	屨		jù	kju^{C}	kuo^{C}	kroh	
123r	數	to count	shǔ	ṣju^{B}	ṣo^{B}	sroʔ	

[T] Sin Sukchu SR ṣu (上); MGZY (zhu >) shu (上) [ṣu]; ONW ṣuo

[E] ? AA: Mon ruih [røh], hypoth. sruih 'to count', lros id.

	數	number	shù	ṣju^{C}	ṣo^{C}	sroh	
1207a	數	frequent	shuò	ṣåk	ṣɔk	srôk	⋈ 10-29/123f
	數	net	cù	ts^{h}jwok	ts^{h}iok	tshok < k-sok	
b	籔	a measure	shǔ	ṣju^{B}	ṣo^{B}	sroʔ	'a measure of capacity' [Yili]
		container	sǒu	səu^{B}	so^{B}	sôʔ	'container for rinsing rice' [SW]
c	藪		sǒu	səu^{B}	so^{B}	sôʔ	= 10-35/131o 棷

[T] ONW sou <> [E] ? OTib. sog 'grassland'

10-30 = K. 133			**Mand.**	**MC**	**LHan**	**OCM**	
ad	須[1]鬚	beard	xū	sju	sio, ts^{h}io	sno	[D] PMin *tshiu ~ siu
	須[2]	wait	xū	sju	sio, ts^{h}io	sno	= 10-31/134a 需 'wait'

[T] Sin Sukchu SR sy (平); MGZY sÿu (平) [sy]; MTang sy, ONW suo; BTD Skt. su

[D] PMin *tshiu^{A1} ~ *siu^{A1}

e	嬃		xū	sju	sio	sno	
f	盨		xǔ	sju^{B}	sio^{B}	snoʔ	

10-31 = K. 134 There is some confusion between this series and 25-35/238 耎 ruǎn

			Mand.	**MC**	**LHan**	**OCM**	
a	需	wait	xū	sju	sio, ts^{h}io	sno	= 10-30/133a 須 'wait'

[T] MTang sy, ONW suo

	需	soft	ruǎn,	ńźjwän^{B},	ńuan^{B},	nonʔ,	
			nuǎn	nuân^{B}	nuɑn^{B}	nônʔ	
b	繻		xū, rú	sju, nźju	sio, ńo	sno, no	
c	儒		rú	ńźju	ńo	no	
-	嚅唲,儒兒		rú-ér	ńźju-ńźie	ńo-ńe	no-ne	

'Forced laugh, strong laughter' [Chuci] is a reduplicated form.

fg	濡	g	rú	ńźju	ńo	no	
h	臑	soft	rú	ńźju	ńo	no	
		shoulder	nào	nâu(C)	nɑu(C)	nâu, nâuh	
					or nou(C)	or nû, nûh	
i	襦		rú	ńźju	ńo	no	
e	懦	weak	rú	ńźju	ńo	no	

[E] TB *now 'tender, soft' > PL *C-nu^{2} , WB nu^{C} < no^{C} 'young, tender' ⋈ nu^{B} 'be made soft' ⋈ hnu^{B} 'make soft, mollify', Lushai no^{R} < nooʔ 'young, tender, soft, young of animals'

			Mand.	MC	LHan	OCM	
	懦	weak	ruǎn,	ńźjwän^{B},	ńuan^{B},	nonʔ,	
			nuǎn,	nuân^{B},	nuɑn^{B},	nônʔ,	
			nuò	nuâ^{C}	nuɑi^{C}	nôih	
j	醹		rú	ńźju(^{B})	ńo(^{B})	no, noʔ	

[E] WT rno-ba, rnon-po 'sharp, acute (of taste, intellect)'

		Mand.	MC	LHan	OCM	
d	穤	rú	ńźju^{C}	ńo^{C}	noh	[T] ONW ńuo
-	糯	nuò	nuâ^{C} [Jiyun]			'glutinous rice'

[E] Tai khâu nua (Savina, khâu 'rice')

10-32 = K. 135		Mand.	MC	LHan	OCM
a	乳	rǔ	ńźju^{B}	ńo^{B}	noʔ

[T] Sin Sukchu SR ry (上); MGZY Zhȳu (上) [ry]; ONW ńuo <> [E] TB *nuw ~ *now > WT nu-ma 'breast' ⋇ nu-ba 'to suck' ⋇ nud-pa 'to suckle', Tsangla nu 'milk'

		Mand.	MC	LHan	OCM
-	穀	nòu, gòu	nəu^{C}	no^{C}	nôh

10-33 = K. 119		Mand.	MC	LHan	OCM
a	走	zǒu	tsəu^{B}	tso^{B}	tsôʔ

[T] Sin Sukchu SR tsəw (上); MGZY dzʰiw (上) [tsəw]; ONW tsou^{B} <> [D] PMin *tsəu^{B}

10-34 = K. 1229		Mand.	MC	LHan	OCM
a	奏	zòu	tsəu^{C}	tso^{C}	tsôh
bc	湊腠	còu	tsʰəu^{C}	tsʰo^{C}	tshôh

10-35 = K. 131, 325			MC	LHan	OCM	
131a	取[1]	qǔ, cǒu	tsʰju^{B},tsʰəu^{B}	tsʰio^{B},tsʰo^{B}	tshoʔ, tshôʔ	

[T] Sin Sukchu SR ts'y (上); MGZY tshȳu (上) [ts'y]; MTang tsʰy < tsʰuo, ONW tsʰuo

			MC	LHan	OCM	
ae	取[2] 娶	qù	tsʰju^{C}	tsʰio^{C}	tshoh	
k	聚	jù	dzju$^{B/C}$	dzio$^{B/C}$	dzoʔ/h	OCB *dzjos

[T] Sin Sukchu SR dzy (上去); MGZY tsȳu (上去) [dzy]; MTang dzy, ONW dzuo

[E] ST *tso: WB cu^{C} 'to collect, gather together', WT 'tsʰogs-pa 'to assemble, gather, meet'

			MC	LHan	OCM	
i	娵	jū	tsju	tsio	tso	
j	諏	zōu !	tsju	tsio	tso	
m	掫	zōu,	tsəu, tṣjəu^{B},	tso, tṣuo^{B},	tsroʔ !,	
		jù	tsju	tsio	tso	
n	緅	zōu,	tsəu, tṣjəu,	tso, tṣuo,	tsro !,	
		jū	tsju^{C}	tsio^{C}	tsoh	
l	陬	zōu	tsəu, tsju	tso, tsio	tsô, tso	

[E] WT zur 'edge, corner, side, aside'; Lepcha sur 'angle, corner'

				MC	LHan	OCM	
g	趣	hasten	qù	tsʰju^{C}	tsʰio^{C}	tshoh < ? C-soh	
	趣	interest	qù	tsʰju^{C}	tsʰio^{C}	—	

[T] Sin Sukchu SR ts'y (去); MGZY tshȳu (去) [ts'y]; MTang tsʰy, ONW tsʰuo

				MC	LHan	OCM	
	趣	groom	cù !	tsʰəu^{B}	tsʰo^{B}	tshôʔ	cf. 11-19/1219d
o	棷		sǒu	səu^{B}	so^{B}	sôʔ	= 10-29/1207c 藪

[T] ONW sou

				MC	LHan	OCM	
q	騶		zhòu !	dẓjəu^{C}	dẓu^{C}	dzroh	OCB *dzrjos

= 10-36/132g 騶

				MC	LHan	OCM	
p	菆	hemp st.	zōu	tṣjəu	tṣuo	tsro	'hemp stalk'
	菆	gather w.	cuán	dzwân	dzuɑn	dzôn	'gather wood'

- 轍 zǎo tzâu^B tsou^B —

325ab a 最 zuì tswâi^C tsuɑs tsôs OCB *tsots

[T] MTang tsuɑi, ONW tsuɑC. Words in final *-t or *-s are occasionally included in an open syllable series, e.g., GSR 61, and 605.

c 蕞 zuì dzwâi^C dzuɑs dzôs

d 嘬 chuài tṣʰwăi^C, tṣʰuɛs,

tṣʰwai^C tṣʰuas tshrôs

e 撮 pinch cuō tsʰwât tsʰuɑt tshôt

[E] TB: LB *tswat ⋇ caus. *ʔtswat 'to pluck' > WB cʰwat

撮 pointed zuì tswât [GY] tsuɑt tsôt or

tswâi^C [JY] tsuɑs tsôts

10-36 = K. 132 MC (t)ṣjəu can derive from both OC (t)sro and (t)sru.

		Mand.	MC	LHan	OCM	
a	芻	chú	tṣʰju	tṣʰo	tshro	

[T] ONW tṣʰuo <> [E] AA: PMon *ksɔɔy 'useless fiber, hay', PWa *sɔh 'cut grass'

c	趨 hasten	qū	tṣʰju	tṣʰo	tshro	

[T] Sin Sukchu SR ts'y (平); MGZY tshȳu (平) [ts'y]

	趨馬 groom	cǒu-mǎ	tsʰəu^B-	tsʰo^B-	tshôʔ	= 10-35/131g
de	雛鶵	chú	dẓju	dẓo	dzro	

[T] Sin Sukchu SR dẓu (平); MGZY cu (平) [dẓu]

-	皺	zhōu	tṣjəu	tṣu		
f	縐	zhòu	tṣjəu^C	tṣu^C	tsruh	[E] ? TBLepcha a-sŭr 'wrinkle'
h	齺	zōu	tṣjəu	tṣu	tsru	
g	騶 groom	zōu	tṣjəu	tṣuo	tsro	[D] Min: Xiam (lit.) tsɔ^{A1}
	騶 run	zòu	dẓjəu^C	dẓuo^C	dzroh	OCB *dzrjos

= 10-35/131q 驟

10-37 = K. 1097

		Mand.	MC	LHan	OCM	
abm	a 叟傻	sǒu	səu^B	so^B	sôʔ	
n	瞍	sǒu	səu^B	so^B	sôʔ	
d	搜 move	sǒu	səu^B	so^A R!	sô	'move'

[E] TB *m-sow 'awake', Tamang ^{2}so 'live'; WT gson-pa 'be alive, to wake, rouse, urge on'

	搜 search	sōu	ṣjəu	ṣu	sru R!	OCB *srju 'search'
e-	廋鄋	sōu	ṣjəu	ṣu R!	sru	
h	獀 hunt	sōu	ṣjəu	ṣuo	sro or sru = 13-62/1098a	
	獀 dog	sōu	ṣjəu	ṣuo	sro	

[N] Leibian səu^B < *sôʔ, SW náo-sōu 獿獀 [nɑu-ṣu])

[E] AA: Palaung-Wa *sɔʔ 'dog', PSBahn. *sɔː, PVM *ʔa-cɔːʔ

fg	溲 soak	sǒu	ṣjəu^B	ṣu^B	sruʔ	

= 13-32/1077r 滫; = 13-60/1112h 糔

	溲 urinate	sōu	ṣjəu	ṣu	sru	
j	醙	sōu !	ṣjəu^B	ṣu^B	sruʔ	
i	瘦	shòu !	ṣjəu^C	ṣu^C	sruh	
k	嫂	sǎo	sâu^B	sou^B	sûʔ	
l	謏	xiǎo	sieu^B	seu^B	siûʔ	

10-38 = K. 1230		**Mand.**	**MC**	**LHan**	**OCM**	
a	裒	póu	bəu	bo	bû R!	

10-39 = K. 136		**Mand.**	**MC**	**LHan**	**OCM**	
a	付	fù	pju^C	puo^C	poh	
	[T] MTang pfu < pfuo, ONW puo					
d	柎 raft	fū	pju	puo	po	
	board	fù, bòu	bju^C, bəu^C	buo^C, bo^C	boh, bôh	
e	趺	fū	pju	puo	po	
cr	府俯	fǔ	pju^B	puo^B	poʔ	
m	符	fú	bju	buo	bo	
n	腐	fǔ	bju^B	buo^B	boʔ	
	[E] ? TB: Lepcha por, pór 'to spoil, smell'					
ij	坿祔	fù	bju^C	buo^C	boh	
k	附	fù	bju^C	buo^C	boh	
	[T] MHan 高附 kau-buo^C Κάβουρα (Kabul)					
	附婁	fù-lóu	bju^C-ləu^B	buo^C-lo^B		
lpq	駙蚹鮒	fù	bju^C	buo^C	boh	
o	胕 intestines	fù	bju^C	buo^C	boh	'belly'
	[E] ST and area word: TB *(s-)pu ⋈ (s-)bu 'belly, stomach'					
	胕 foot	fū	pju	puo	po	
h	泭	fū	p^hju	p^huo	pho	= 13-73/1233k 桴
fg	弣拊	fǔ	p^hju^B	p^huo^B	phoʔ	

10-40 = K. 137		**Mand.**	**MC**	**LHan**	**OCM**
a	鳧	fú	bju	buo	bo

10-41		**Mand.**	**MC**	**LHan**	**OCM**
-	冃	mòu	məu^C	mo^C	môh ?

11 OCM rime *-ok Wū bù 屋部

GSR 1202 - 1228

Baxter 1992: 503 ff. (§10.2.11)

See Table 10-1 for OCM rimes *-oŋ, *-ok, *-o in QYS categories. In the OC rimes *-ak, *-ek, *-ok and *-auk, syllables with MC retroflex initials, especially of the expected QYS type ḍjak, ḍjäk, ḍjwok, tend to be rare in Div. III and seem to have shifted into Div. II ḍɐk, ḍåk, ḍɛk, ḍɔk.

11-1	**= K. 1203**	**Mand.**	**MC**	**LHan**	**OCM**	
a	哭	kū	kʰuk	kʰok	khôk	

[E] TB-Lushai kuuk^{H} 'shriek'

11-2	**= K. 1225**	**Mand.**	**MC**	**LHan**	**OCM**		
a	角	jiǎo, jué	kåk	kɔk	krôk	OCB *krok	[T] ONW käk
d	桷	jué	kåk	kɔk	krôk		
e	确	què	ɣåk	gɔk	grôk		
f	斛	hú	ɣuk	gok	gôk		

11-3	**= K. 1226**	**Mand.**	**MC**	**LHan**	**OCM**	
a	㱿	què	kʰåk	kʰɔk	khrôk	
bc	愨	què	kʰåk	kʰɔk	khrôk	
-	殼	ké	kʰåk	kʰɔk	khrôk	

[D] M-Xiam lit. kʰok^{D1}, col. kʰɑk^{D1}, Y-Guǎngzh ^{33}hɔk^{D}

d	穀	jué	kåk	kɔk	krôk	
h	穀 a tree	gǔ	kuk	kok	kôk	
i	穀 husked	gǔ	kuk	kok	kôk	

[E] AA: PVM *rkoʔ 'husked rice', Khmu /rŋkŏʔ/ <> TB-WB kok 'rice plant'

j	轂	gǔ	kuk	kok	kôk	
k	縠	hú	ɣuk	gok	gôk	
l	斛 a meas.	hú	ɣuk	gok	gôk	
	poor	xué, què	ɣåk, kʰåk	gɔk, kʰɔk	grôk, khrôk	
m	瑴	gòu	kəu^{C}	ko^{C}	kôkh	'to suckle' [GY]
p	彀	gòu	kəu^{C}	ko^{C}	kôkh	
q	鷇	kòu	kʰəu^{C}	kʰo^{C}	khôkh	

[E] JP kroʔ^{55} < krok^{55} 'to hatch'

g	嗀	xuè, hù	xåk, xuk	hɔk, hok	hrôk	

[E] PTai *r̥ak^{D2}, KS *trwak^{7} 'vomit'

11-4	**= K. 1213**	**Mand.**	**MC**	**LHan**	**OCM**	
a	曲	qū	kʰjwok	kʰuok	khok	OCB *kh(r)jok

[T] Sin Sukchu SR k'y (入); MGZY khÿu (入) [k'y]; ONW kʰuok

11-5	**= K. 1214**	**Mand.**	**MC**	**LHan**	**OCM**	
ab	局跼	jú	gjwok	guok	gok	OCB *ɦkh(r)jok
	[T] ONW guok					
cd	挶梮	jú	kjwok	kuok	kok	

11-6	**= K. 1204**	**Mand.**	**MC**	**LHan**	**OCM**
a	屋	wū	ʔuk	ʔok	ʔôk
	[T] Sin Sukchu SR ʔu (入); MGZY 'u (入) [ʔu]; ONW ʔok				
b	剭	wū	ʔuk	ʔok	ʔôk
cdef	偓喔幄握	wò	ʔåk	ʔɔk	ʔrôk
h	腛	wò	ʔåk	ʔɔk	ʔrôk
g	渥 moisten	wò	ʔåk	ʔɔk	ʔrôk
	soak	òu	ʔəu^C	ʔo^C	ʔrôkh

11-7	**= K. 1217**	**Mand.**	**MC**	**LHan**	**OCM**
a	勖	xù	xjwok	huok	hok

11-8	**= K. 1227**	**Mand.**	**MC**	**LHan**	**OCM**	
a	岳	yuè	ŋåk	ŋɔk	ŋrôk	= 11-10/1215c 嶽
	[T] ONW ŋäk					

11-9	**= K. 1216**	**Mand.**	**MC**	**LHan**	**OCM**
a	玉	yù	ŋjwok	ŋuok	ŋok
d	頊	xù	xjwok	huok	hŋok
	[T] ONW huok <> [E] WT sŋog-pa, bsŋogs 'to vex, annoy'				

11-10	**= K. 1215**	**Mand.**	**MC**	**LHan**	**OCM**	
a	獄	yù	ŋjwok	ŋuok	ŋok	OCB *ŋ(r)jok
cd	嶽鸑	yuè	ŋåk	ŋɔk	ŋrôk	c = 11-9/1227a 岳

11-11	**= K. 1205**	**Mand.**	**MC**	**LHan**	**OCM**	
a	禿	tū	t^{h}uk	t^{h}ok	thôk	cf. 28-13/544c

11-12	**= K. 1224**	**Mand.**	**MC**	**LHan**	**OCM**	
a	蜀	shǔ	źjwok	dźok	dok	
d	蠋	zhú	źjwok	dźok	dok	
e	燭	zhú	tśjwok	tśok	tok	
	[T] ONW tśuok <> [E] LB *duk 'burn, be blazing' ⪤ *ʔduk 'kindle, set on fire' > WB tok 'blaze, flame'; WT dugs-pa 'to make warm, to light'; Lushai duk^L 'be glowing with heat'					
f	矚	chù	tś^{h}jwok	tś^{h}ok	thok	
g	觸	chù	tś^{h}jwok	tś^{h}ok	thok	
	[T] ONW tś^{h}uok <> [D] Min: Xiam lit. ts^{h}iok^{D1}, col. ts^{h}ik^{D1} <> [E] ST *tok WT t^{h}ogs-pa 'to strike, stumble, run against', Lushai tɔɔk^H 'to knock (against)', Mikir tòk- 'to strike, beat'					
-	歜	chù	tś^{h}jwok	tś^{h}ok	thok	'angry', N.Pr.
h	躅	zhú	ḍjwok	ḍiok	drok	
j	襡	dú	duk	dok	dôk	

kl 韣韣 dú, shǔ, zhú — duk, źjwok, tśjwok — dok, dźok, tśok — dôk, dok, tok

m 髑 dú duk- dok- dôk

i 獨 dú duk dok dôk

[D] 'To be alone, alone'. Acc. to FY 79/111, this was a Han period 'Southern Chǔ' dialect word for 'one', note also Fuzhou sioʔ[8] (corresponding to QYS źjwok < *dok) 'one' that may be related (Norman FY 1983.3: 208).

n 噣 peck zhuó ṭåk ṭɔk trôk

beak dòu, zhòu $təu^C$, $tjəu^C$ to^C, $ṭio^C$ tôkh, trokh

p 濁 zhuó ḍåk ḍɔk drôk OCB *drok

[N] The GSR reading ṭåk is not supported by the QY (Coblin 1983: 154).

o 斀 zhuó ṭåk ṭɔk trôk

q 鐲 zhuó ḍåk ḍɔk drôk

s 屬 attached zhǔ tśjwok tśok tok

[E] WT gtogs-pa 'to belong to, be part of' ⋊ t^hog-pa 'to gather', rdogs-pa 'to bind, fasten'

屬 attach shǔ źjwok dźok dok [T] ONW dźuok

t 斸 zhǔ tjwok ṭiok trok = 11-12/1224v 钃

u 欘 zhú tjwok ṭiok trok

v 钃 zhuó tjwok ṭiok trok = 11-12/1224t 斸

x 躅 zhú ḍjwok ḍiok drok

[E] WT 'dug-pa 'to sit, dwell, stay, remain', WT rdog-pa 'step, kick, walk'; JP t^hoŋ[31] 'stop'

r 擉 chuō $tṣ^h$åk $tṣ^h$ɔk tshrôk

[E] AA: Khmer cūka /còok/ 'lift with tool...' ⋊ cpūka /cbòok/ 'trident for lifting fish'

11-13 = K. 1218		**Mand.**	**MC**	**LHan**	**OCM**
a	豖	chù	t^hjwok	$ṭ^h$iok	throk
-	豚	zhuó	tjuk	ṭiok	trok

豚 [E] TB: Chepang tuʔ 'female genitals'

cd	椓㧻	zhuó	ṭåk	ṭɔk	trôk

[E] ? TB : WT rdug-pa 'to strike against, to stumble at'
[D] Min: Amoy col. teʔ[D1], lit. tok[D1], Zhangzh tøʔ

f	琢	zhuó	ṭåk, tjuk	ṭɔk, ṭiok	trôk, trok	
eg	涿諑	zhuó	ṭåk	ṭɔk	trôk	
b	啄 peck up	zhuó	ṭåk, tuk	ṭɔk, tok	trôk	⋊ 10-18/128u 咮

[E] LB *tok 'peck, strike with a curved instrument, hook onto', WB tok-hra 'woodpecker'; Lushai tśu[L] / tśuk[L] (Lorr. chu) 'to bite (as snake)', 'peck'

h-	冢塚	zhǒng	$tjwoŋ^B$	$ṭioŋ^B$	troŋʔ

[E] TB: WT rduŋ 'a small mound, hillock', WB toŋ 'hill, mountain' <> MY *tr²ɔŋ¹ 'mountain'

11-14 = K. 1202, 1220			**MC**	**LHan**	**OCM**	
a	谷 valley	gǔ	kuk	kok	klôk = klok	

[E] ? Mikir arlók < *r-lók 'valley'

	谷 good	yù	jiwok	jok	lok	
	title	lù	luk	lok < *lok		part of a Xiongnu title

f	浴	yù	jiwok	jok	lok	

[T] Sin Sukchu SR y (入); MGZY yȳu (入) [jy]
[E] WT ldug(s)-pa, ldugs (< *ɴluk) 'to pour (water into vessel, on hands)' > 'cast, found'

deg	欲慾鵒	yù	jiwok	jok	lok	ONW iuok
h	裕	yù	jiu^C	jo^C	lokh	
1220a	俗	sú	zjwok	ziok	s-lok	

[T] Sin Sukchu SR zy (入); MGZY zȳu (入) [zy]; ONW zuok
[D] M-Xiam lit. siok^D2, col. sioʔ^D2

11-15 = K. 1208, 1228			MC	LHan	OCM	
aef	彔盝琭	lù	luk	lok	rôk	
ghi	睩祿簶	lù	luk	lok	rôk	
klm-	綠菉錄逯	lù	ljwok	liok	rok	
1228a	剝	bō	påk	pɔk	prôk	[D] Guangzh mɐk^7
-	鵦	fù	bjuk	buk	—	SW

11-16 = K. 1209		Mand.	MC	LHan	OCM	
a	鹿	lù	luk	lok	rôk	
e	摝	lù	luk	lok	rôk	

[E] WT dkrug-pa 'stir up' ⋈ 'kʰrug-pa 'be disturbed, quarrel' ⋈ sprug-pa 'to shake, stir up'

h	麓	lù	luk	lok	rôk	

[E] AA: PVM *m-ruːʔ 'forest'

fg	漉麗	lù	luk	lok	rôk	
-	轆 (lì 轣-)	lù	liek-luk	lek-lok	—	'spinning wheel'

[E] Tai rɔɔk^8 'pulley' (?)

11-17 = K. 1223		Mand.	MC	LHan	OCM
a	辱	rǔ, rù	ńźjwok	ńok	nok
bcd	溽縟蓐	rù	ńźjwok	ńok	nok
ef	槈耨	nòu	nuok, nəu^C	nouk, no^C	nûk, nôkh

[T] ONW nouk or nauk ? <> [N] The OB graph shows two hands holding an agricultural implement, a hoe. Hence a 辱 is the original graph for ef.
[E] Lushai hnu^F < hnuʔ (< *-ʔ) 'work finished, weeded or harvested area'

-	嗕		nok	nok	

11-18 = K. 1206		Mand.	MC	LHan	OCM
a	族	zú	dzuk	dzok	dzôk
d	鏃	zú	tsuk	tsok	tsôk
e	瘯	cù	tsʰuk	tsʰok	tshôk
f	蔟 nest	cù	tsʰuk	tsʰok	tshôk
	a pipe	còu	tsʰəu^C	tsʰo^C	tshôkh
g	嗾	sǒu,	səu^B/C,	so^B/C,	sôʔ/h,
		còu	tsʰəu^C	tsʰo^C	tshôh < k-sôh

11-19 = K. 1219		Mand.	MC	LHan	OCM
a	足 foot	zú	tsjwok	tsiok	tsok

[T] Sin Sukchu SR tsy (入), PR, LR tsuʔ; MGZY dzȳu (入) [tsy]; ONW tsuok
[E] WT čʰog-pa 'be sufficient'

	足 add	jù	tsju^{C}	tsio^{C}	tsokh	
c	哫	zú	tsjwok	tsiok	tsok	
d	促	cù	ts^{h}jwok	ts^{h}iok	tshok	= 11-21/1222g

cf. 10-35/131g; 10-36/132c

e	捉	zhuō	tṣåk	tṣɔk	tsrôk	

11-20- = K. 1221		**Mand.**	**MC**	**LHan**	**OCM**	
a	粟	sù	sjwok	siok	sok	OCB *sjok

[T] MHan 粟德 siok-tək Soɣd or soɣðik <> [D] PEMin *tshuok^{D1}, PWMin *ʃuok^{D1} 'unhusked rice'

11-21 = K. 1222 How MC śj- can serve as phonetic in words with MC s- is quite puzzling; perhaps some of the words in Div. I derive from OC *sl-.

		Mand.	**MC**	**LHan**	**OCM**	
a	束	shù	śjwok	śok	lhok	

[E] ? WB hluiŋ^{B} 'bind into a bundle'

i	速	sù	suk	sok	sôk	

[T]Sin S. SR su (入); MGZY su (入) [su]; ONW sok. <> [D] M-Xiam lit. sok^{D1}, col. sɑk^{D1}

k	餗	sù	suk	sok	sôk	
pr	樕遫	sù	suk	sok	sôk	
g	誎	cù	ts^{h}jwok	ts^{h}iok	tshok < k-sok ?	= 11-19/1219d
q	蔌	sù	suk	sok	sôk	

[D] M-Xiam sok^{D1} <> [E] WT 'tsho-ba, sos 'to live, revive, last; feed'

s	嗽	sòu	səu^{C}	so^{C}	sôkh	

[E] TB *su(w) > Magari su, Garo, Dimasa gu-su, WT sud-pa 'cough'

t	漱	sòu	səu^{C}, ṣjəu^{C}	so^{C}, ṣu^{C}	srokh or sroh	⋈ 10-37/1097f etc.
o	欶	shù, shuò	ṣåk	ṣɔk	srôk	

[D] Gan-Changsha so^{33}, Yue-Guangzh ʃɔk^{33}, Min-Xiamen suʔ^{32} (D1)
[E] WB sok 'drink, smoke'

l	驌	sǒng,	sjwoŋ^{B},	sioŋ^{B},	soŋʔ,	
		sǒu	səu^{B}	so^{B}	sôʔ	
mn	悚竦	sǒng	sjwoŋ^{B}	sioŋ^{B},	soŋʔ	

[D] M-Xiam lit. sioŋ^{B1}, su ts^{h}ɑŋ^{C1} = 12-22/1191j 聳

-	踈	shū	ṣjwo	ṣɑ	—	

11-22 = K. 1210		**Mand.**	**MC**	**LHan**	**OCM**
a	卜	bǔ	puk	pok	pôk

[T] ONW pok <> [E] LB *ɴpök^{H} ~ *ʔpök^{H} ~ *ʔbök^{L} 'explode, pop'

e	扑	pū	p^{h}uk	p^{h}ok	phôk
f	朴	pǔ	p^{h}åk	p^{h}ɔk	phrôk
g	仆	fù, pòu	p^{h}ju^{C}, p^{h}əu^{C},	ph(u)o^{C},	phokh,
			p^{h}jəu^{C}, bək	p^{h}u^{C}, bək	phəkh, bək
hi	訃赴	fù	p^{h}ju^{C}	p^{h}uo^{C}	phokh

11-23 = K. 1211		**Mand.**	**MC**	**LHan**	**OCM**	
a	a	bú	buk	bok	bôk	
b	僕 servant	pú	buk, buok	bok	bôk	OCB *bok

[E] WT bu 'son, boy'

	僕 crowd	pú	p^huk	p^hok	phôk	
g	樸 shrubby	bú	puk, buk	pok, bok	pôk, bôk	
	rough	pǔ	p^huk	p^hok	phôk	
	to trim	pò	p^håk	p^hɔk	phrôk	
i-	轐濮	bú	puk	pok	pôk	
j	撲	pū	p^huk	p^hok	phôk	
	[T] MHan 撲挑 p^hok-deuʔ/-t^heu < *phôk-liâuʔ Puśkalāvati, Πευκελαῶτις					
m	墣	pú, pò	p^huk, p^håk	p^hok, p^hɔk	phôk, phrôk	
n	璞	pú	p^håk	p^hɔk	phrôk	

11-24	**= K. 1212**	**Mand.**	**MC**	**LHan**	**OCM**	
ae	木沐	mù	muk	mok	môk	
	木 [T] Sin Sukchu SR mu (入); MGZY mu (入) [mu]; ONW mok					
f	霢霂	(mài-)mù	-muk	-mok	-môk or -mrôk	OCB *-mok

12 OCM rime *-oŋ Dōng bù 東部

GSR 1172 - 1201

Baxter 1992: 505 ff. (§10.2.12)

See Table 10-1 for OCM rimes *-oŋ, *-ok, *-o in QYS categories.

12-1	**= K. 1172**	**Mand.**	**MC**	**LHan**	**OCM**	
ad	工功	gōng	kuŋ	koŋ	kôŋ = kloŋ	
	[T] Sin Sukchu SR kuŋ (平); MGZY gung (平) [kuŋ]; ONW koŋ					
	[E] ? Area word: TB-WB kiuŋ^B 'employ, order, commission' <> AA-OMon kloñ /kloŋ/ 'to work'?, 'work as a cultivator'					
e	攻	gōng	kuŋ, kuoŋ	koŋ, kouŋ	kôŋ, kûŋ	
g	貢	gòng	kuŋ^C	koŋ^C	kôŋh	
lm	鳿瑲	hòng	ɣuŋ	goŋ	gôŋ	
g'	鴻	hóng	ɣuŋ	goŋ	gôŋ = gloŋ ?	
	[N] Transcribes a pre-Han TB word for 'river' (cf. WT kluŋ); Unger *Hao-ku* 50, 1995					
j	虹 rainbow	hóng	ɣuŋ	goŋ	gôŋ = gloŋ ?	
	[D] PMin *ghioŋ^B, but Jiànyáng leŋ^{C1}, Gan-Shànggāo has lɑn^B-luŋ^H					
	[E] PY *kluŋ^A 'rainbow'					
	虹 rainbow	jiàng	kåŋ^C	kɔŋ^C	krôŋh	[D] Gan: Wuning dial. kɔŋ^{C1}
i	紅	hóng	ɣuŋ	goŋ	gôŋ	OCB *goŋ
	[T] Sin Sukchu SR ɣuŋ (平); MGZY Xung (平) [ɣuŋ]					
k	訌	hóng	ɣuŋ	goŋ	gôŋ	
h	空 hollow	kōng	k^{h}uŋ	k^{h}oŋ	khôŋ	
	[T] Sin Sukchu SR k'uŋ (平); MGZY khung (平) [k'uŋ]; ONW k^{h}oŋ					
	[E] WT k^{h}uŋ 'hole, pit, cavity; hollow'; WB k^{h}oŋ^B 'be hollow'					
	空 exhaust	kòng	k^{h}uŋ^C	k^{h}oŋ^C	khôŋh	
	空 hole	kǒng	k^{h}uŋ^B	k^{h}oŋ^B	khôŋʔ	
z	悾	kōng	k^{h}uŋ(^{C}), k^{h}åŋ^C	k^{h}oŋ(^{C}), k^{h}ɔŋ^C	khôŋ, khôŋh, khrôŋh	
a'	控 throw	kòng	k^{h}uŋ^C	k^{h}oŋ^C	khôŋh	
	to beat	qiàng	k^{h}åŋ^C	k^{h}ɔŋ^C	khrôŋh	
b'	椌	qiāng	k^{h}åŋ	k^{h}ɔŋ	khrôŋ	'hollow wooden instrument'
v	江	jiāng	kåŋ	kɔŋ	krôŋ	
	[E] AA: PMonic *krooŋ, Bahnar kroŋ, Katu karuŋ					
u	杠	gāng	kåŋ	kɔŋ	krôŋ	
x	矼	gāng, kòng	kåŋ, k^{h}uŋ^C	kɔŋ, k^{h}oŋ^C	krôŋ, khôŋh	
y	項	xiàng	ɣåŋ^B	gɔŋ^B	grôŋʔ	
	[T] ONW ɣäŋ^B <> [D] Chéngdu ^{53}tɕin-^{13}xaŋ 頸 項, Yángzh ^{42}tɕiŋ-^{55}xɑŋ (col.); Amoy haŋ^{C2}					
	[E] TB Chepang groŋ-ko 'stretch the neck'					
s	邛	qióng	gjwoŋ	guoŋ	goŋ	
	[E] WT gyoŋ 'want, need, indigence'					

pc'	p 鞏	gǒng	kjwoŋ^B	kuoŋ^B	koŋʔ
d'	恐	kǒng	k^{h}jwoŋ^B	k^{h}uoŋ^B	khoŋʔ

[T] Sin Sukchu SR k'juŋ (上), PR, LR k'uŋ; MGZY khÿung (上) [k'juŋ]; ONW k^{h}uoŋ
[E] WT 'goŋ(s)-pa, bkoŋ 'to despond, be in fear'

e'	蛩	qióng	gjwoŋ	guoŋ	goŋ
f'	跫	qióng,	gjwoŋ,	guoŋ,	goŋ,
		qiāng	k^{h}åŋ	k^{h}ɔŋ	khrôŋ

12-2	**= K. 1174**	**Mand.**	**MC**	**LHan**	**OCM**	
a	孔	kǒng	k^{h}uŋ^B	k^{h}oŋ^B	khôŋʔ	[T] ONW k^{h}oŋ

12-3	**= K. 1182**	**Mand.**	**MC**	**LHan**	**OCM**	
a	廾	gǒng	kjwoŋ^B	kuoŋ^B	koŋʔ	
c	共 join hands	gǒng	kjwoŋ^B	kuoŋ^B	koŋʔ	
	共 together	gòng	gjwoŋ^C	guoŋ^C	goŋh	[T] ONW guoŋ
e	拱	gǒng	kjwoŋ^B	kuoŋ^B	koŋʔ	
m	拲	gǒng,	kjwoŋ^B,	kuoŋ^B,	koŋʔ,	
		jú	kjwok	kuok	kok	
f	供	gōng	kjwoŋ(^{C})	kuoŋ(^{C})	koŋ, koŋh	

[T] Sin Sukchu SR kjuŋ (平), PR kuŋ; MGZY gÿung (平) [kjuŋ]

gk	龏龔	gōng	kjwoŋ	kuoŋ	koŋ
l	恭	gōng	kuŋ, kjwoŋ	kuoŋ	kroŋ
n	輁	gǒng,	kjwoŋ^B,	kuoŋ^B,	koŋʔ,
		qióng	gjwoŋ	guoŋ	goŋ
o	洪	hóng	ɣuŋ	goŋ	gôŋ
pq	鬨 q	hòng,	ɣuŋ^C,	goŋ^C,	
		xiàng	ɣåŋ^C	gɔŋ^C	grôŋh
r	烘	hōng	xuŋ	hoŋ	hôŋ
s	巷	xiàng	ɣåŋ^C	gɔŋ^C	grôŋh
-	港	gǎng	kåŋ^B	kɔŋ^B	krôŋʔ

[T] Sin Sukchu SR kjaŋ (上); MGZY gyang (上) [kjaŋ]

t	輂	jú	kjwok	kuok	kok

12-4	**= K. 1184**	**Mand.**	**MC**	**LHan**	**OCM**	
a	邕	yōng	ʔjwoŋ	ʔuoŋ	ʔoŋ	

[E] WB uiŋ 'pond, lake' (~ aŋ^B 'pond, pool'?), Mru öŋ 'id.', JP ʔuŋ^{33} 'fill (as a lake)'

c	雝 harmon.	yōng	ʔjwoŋ	ʔuoŋ	ʔoŋ	'harmonious'
	cover	yōng	ʔjwoŋ($^{B/C}$)	ʔuoŋ($^{B/C}$)	ʔoŋ, ʔoŋʔ, ʔoŋh	
j	廱	yōng	ʔjwoŋ	ʔuoŋ	ʔoŋ	
l	癰	yōng	ʔjwoŋ	ʔuoŋ	ʔoŋ	

[E] WB uiŋ^C 'bulge of anything' ⋈ uiŋ^B 'collection of humors (boil)'

h	雍 harmon.	yōng	ʔjwoŋ	ʔuoŋ	ʔoŋ
	obstruct	yǒng	ʔjwoŋ$^{B/C}$	ʔuoŋ$^{B/C}$	ʔoŋʔ/h
k	擁	yōng !	ʔjwoŋ^B	ʔuoŋ^B	ʔoŋʔ
i	壅 obstruct	yōng, yǒng	ʔjwoŋ$^{A/B/C}$	ʔuoŋ$^{B/C}$	ʔoŋ, ʔoŋʔ, ʔoŋh
m	饔	yōng	ʔjwoŋ	ʔuoŋ	ʔoŋ

op	罋甕	wèng	ʔuŋ^C	ʔoŋ^C	ʔôŋh	= 12-13/1173g 瓮
	[T] ONW ʔoŋ <> [N] 罋 has additional readings MC ʔjwoŋ(^{C})					

12-5	**= K. 1183**	**Mand.**	**MC**	**LHan**	**OCM**	
1183a	凶	xiōng	xjwoŋ	huoŋ	hoŋ	
b	兇 bad	xiōng	xjwoŋ	huoŋ	hoŋ	[T] ONW huoŋ
	兇 fear	xiǒng	xjwoŋ^B	huoŋ^B	hoŋ, hoŋʔ	
c	訩	xiōng	xjwoŋ	huoŋ	hoŋ	
def-	匈胷胸恟	xiōng	xjwoŋ	huoŋ	hoŋ	
	[T]匈奴 LH huoŋ-nɑ Xiōng-nú, Skt. Hūna, Hunns. 匈奴 renders foreign *hona* or *huna*; transcriptions tend to have the last sound of a syllable anticipate the initial of the next one, but in LH there was no syllable *hon*, hence *huoŋ* (note many Chinese cannot pronounce Engl. *town*, they say [tʰɑwŋ] instead).					
g	洶	xiōng	xjwoŋ(^{B})	huoŋ(^{B})	hoŋ, hoŋʔ	
1243a	酗	xù	xju^C	huo^C	hoh	

12-6	**= K. 1175**	**Mand.**	**MC**	**LHan**	**OCM**
a	東	dōng	tuŋ	toŋ	tôŋ
	[T] Sin Sukchu SR tuŋ (平); MGZY dung (平) [tuŋ]; ONW toŋ				
g	涷	dòng	tuŋ$^{A/C}$	toŋ^C	tôŋh
	[E] Yao languages have a back vowel: blŭŋ^6, bjŭŋ^6, bŭŋ^6, biŋ^6				
fe	棟凍	dòng	tuŋ^C	toŋ^C	tôŋh
h	蝃蝀	(dì)-dōng	tiei^C-tuŋ	tes-toŋ	-tôŋ

12-7	**= K. 1189**	**Mand.**	**MC**	**LHan**	**OCM**
a	妐	zhōng	tśjwoŋ	tśoŋ	toŋ
	[N] 公 gōng is semantic and probably not phonetic, hence only the rimes agree.				

12-8	**= K. 1188**	**Mand.**	**MC**	**LHan**	**OCM**
a	重 heavy	zhòng	ḍjwoŋ^B	ḍioŋ^B	droŋʔ
	重 double	chóng	ḍjwoŋ	ḍioŋ	droŋ
	[T] Sin Sukchu SR dʐjuŋ (平), PR dʐuŋ; MGZY cÿung (平) [dʐjuŋ]; ONW duoŋ				
c	湩	zhòng	ṭjwoŋ^C, tuŋ^C	ṭioŋ^C, toŋ^C	troŋh, tôŋh
b	偅	zhòng	tśjwoŋ^C	tśoŋ^C	toŋh
d	種 seed, hair	zhǒng	tśjwoŋ^B	tśoŋ^B	toŋʔ
	[T] ONW tśuoŋ <> [E] TB: Chepang tuŋʔ- 'to plant' ⋈ duŋ 'shoot, sprout', Tangsa (Barish) ¹toŋ(ʔ) <> ? AA-PVM *k-co:ŋʔ 'seed'				
	種 sow	zhòng	tśjwoŋ^C	tśoŋ^C	toŋh
efu	腫踵煄	zhǒng	tśjwoŋ^B	tśoŋ^B	toŋʔ
	[T] Sin Sukchu SR tʂjuŋ (上); MGZY jung (上) [tʂuŋ]				
g	鍾 a vessel	zhōng	tśjwoŋ	tśoŋ	toŋ
kd'	尰瘇	zhòng	źwoŋ^B	dźoŋ^B	doŋʔ
	[E] TB: Limbu thɔŋt- 'to swell'				
j	衝	chōng	tśʰjwoŋ	tśʰoŋ	thoŋ
-	衝	chōng	tśʰjwoŋ	tśʰoŋ	thoŋ
l	董	dǒng	tuŋ^B	toŋ^B	tôŋʔ
m	動	dòng	duŋ^B	doŋ^B	dôŋʔ
	[T] Sin Sukchu SR duŋ (上); MGZY tung (上) [duŋ]; ONW doŋ				

n 慟 tòng ! duŋ^C doŋ^C dôŋh
o 童 boy tóng duŋ doŋ dôŋ
[T] MGZY tung (平) [duŋ] <> [E] TB-KN-Khami doŋ 'boy' <> MY: Mong tuŋ^{55} 'son, male'
童 shaman tóng duŋ doŋ —
[D] PMin *doŋ^A > Amoy col. daŋ^{A2} 'sorcerer, medium' < MK: Viet. døong 'to shamanize', WrMon doŋ 'to dance'
r 僮 tóng duŋ doŋ dôŋ
s 瞳 tóng ! t^{h}uŋ t^{h}oŋ thôŋ = 12-9/1176j 侗
t 穜 chóng, ḍjwoŋ, ḍioŋ, droŋ,
tóng duŋ doŋ dôŋ
x 鐘 bell zhōng tśjwoŋ tśoŋ toŋ
a' 衝 chōng tś^{h}jwoŋ tś^{h}oŋ thoŋ
b' 憧 chōng, tś^{h}jwoŋ, tś^{h}oŋ, thoŋ,
zhuàng ḍåŋ^C ḍɔŋ^C drôŋh
c' 罿 chōng, tś^{h}jwoŋ, tś^{h}oŋ, thoŋ,
tóng duŋ doŋ dôŋ
e' 幢 chuáng ḍåŋ ḍɔŋ drôŋ
f' 撞 chuáng, ḍåŋ, ḍɔŋ, drôŋ,
zhuàng ḍåŋ^C ḍɔŋ^C drôŋh
[T] Sin Sukchu SR tʂaŋ (去), PR, LR tʂwaŋ; MGZY cwang (去) [dʐwaŋ]
[E] WT rduŋ-ba, brduŋs 'to beat, hammer, pound'; WB t^{h}oŋ^B 'pound' (vb?), JP t^{h}oŋ^{31} 'kick'
1248a 畽 tuǎn t^{h}wân^B thuɑn^B thônʔ

12-9 = K. 1176 The phonetic tóng was prob. OCM *dôŋ (not *lôŋ), because most foreign connections have a T-like initial, tóng 'tube' is a late character; 'copper' is perh. a loan.

		Mand.	**MC**	**LHan**	**OCM**	
a	同	tóng	duŋ	doŋ	dôŋ	

[T] Sin Sukchu SR duŋ (平); MGZY tung (平) [duŋ]; ONW do

d	銅	tóng	duŋ	doŋ	lôŋ	

[E] Cf. Tai-Wuming luːŋ², MK-Palaung məlɔŋ 'copper'

ei	桐詷	tóng	duŋ	doŋ	dôŋ	
g	筒	tóng, tǒng	duŋ	doŋ	lôŋ	= 12-10/1185t 筩

Late graph [Lüshi] (*l-> d-) <> [T] Sin Sukchu SR duŋ (平); MGZY tung (平) [duŋ]

h	洞	dòng	duŋ^C	doŋ^C	dôŋh	

[E] TB *dwaːŋ 'pit, hole', Tiddim Chin waːŋ 'hole, make a hole', WT doŋ 'deep hole, pit'

j	侗 stupid	tōng,	t^{h}uŋ(^{C}),	t^{h}oŋ(^{C}),	thôŋ, thôŋh	= 12-8/1188s
		tóng	duŋ	doŋ	dôŋ	
	simple	dòng	duŋ^B	doŋ^B	dôŋʔ	
k	恫	tōng	t^{h}uŋ	t^{h}oŋ	thôŋ	

12-10	**= K. 1185**	**Mand.**	**MC**	**LHan**	**OCM**
a	用	yòng	jiwoŋ^C	joŋ^C	loŋh

[T] Sin Sukchu SR juŋ (去); MGZY yʸung (去) [juŋ]; ONW iuoŋ
[E] WT loŋs 'the use or enjoyment of something' (e.g., wealth)

f	甬	yǒng	jiwoŋ^B	joŋ^B	loŋʔ
xa'	庸鏞	yōng	jiwoŋ	joŋ	loŋ
y	傭 hire	yōng	jiwoŋ	joŋ	loŋ

	傭 fair	chōng	tśʰjwoŋ	tśʰoŋ	k-lhoŋ	
z	墉	yōng	jiwoŋ	joŋ	loŋ	= 12-10A/1186a
h	甬	yǒng	jiwoŋ^{B}	joŋ^{B}	loŋʔ	
jkm	俑勇蛹	yǒng	jiwoŋ^{B}	joŋ^{B}	loŋʔ	
n	踊	yǒng	jiwoŋ^{B}	joŋ^{B}	loŋʔ	
lu	涌湧	yǒng	jiwoŋ^{B}	joŋ^{B}	loŋʔ	

[D] M-Amoy col. yiŋ^{B} 'wave'

r	通	tōng	tʰuŋ	tʰoŋ	lhôŋ	

[T] Sin Sukchu SR t'uŋ (平); MGZY thung (平) [t'uŋ]; ONW tʰoŋ

p	桶	tǒng	tʰuŋ^{B}	tʰoŋ^{B}	thôŋʔ	(late graph [Lüshi])

[E] ? PTai *thuaŋ$^{C1/A1}$ 'bucket' <> ? TB: Chepang dʰuŋ 'container'

q	痛	tòng	tʰuŋ^{C}	tʰoŋ^{C}	lhôŋh	[T] ONW tʰoŋ
t	筩	tóng	duŋ	doŋ	lôŋ	= 12-9/1176g 筒

[T] Sin S. SR duŋ (平); MGZY tung (平) [duŋ] <> [E] Area word: WT doŋ-po ~ ldoŋ-po < *N-loŋ 'tube', Chepang tʰoŋ 'tube'. <> PTai *kl-: S. klɔɔŋ^{C1} 'tube, cylinder'; Li loŋ, IN t'luŋ

o	誦	sòng	zjwoŋ^{C}	zioŋ^{C}	s-loŋh	

[T] Sin Sukchu SR zjuŋ (去), PR suŋ; MGZY zyung (去) [zjuŋ]; ONW zuoŋ

[D] M-Xiam (lit.) sioŋ^{C2} = 訟 <> [E] TB: WT luŋ 'exhortation, admonition, instruction'

12-10A	**= K. 1186**	**Mand.**	**MC**	**LHan**	**OCM**		
a	𩫖	yōng !	jiwoŋ	joŋ	loŋ	SW	= 12-10/1185z

12-11	**= K. 1187**	**Mand.**	**MC**	**LHan**	**OCM**
a	容 contain	róng	jiwoŋ	joŋ	loŋ

'countenance' = 12-13/1190d. The original phonetic was 12-13 公 (Unger, *Hao-ku* 63, 1999). [T] Sin Sukchu SR juŋ (平); MGZY yyung (平) [juŋ]; ONW iuoŋ

[E] TB: WT loŋ 'leisure, free time' <> Tai: S. loŋ^{B2} ~ looŋ^{B2} 'feel at ease'

bc	溶蓉	róng	jiwoŋ	joŋ	loŋ

12-12	**= K. 1192**	**Mand.**	**MC**	**LHan**	**OCM**
ac	舂摏	chōng	śjwoŋ	śoŋ	lhoŋ

[E] KT: S. *klooŋ 'hull rice', Kam-Sui *tyuŋ^{B}

d	惷	chōng	śjwoŋ,	śoŋ,	lhoŋ,
			ṭʰjwoŋ^{C},	ṭʰioŋ^{C},	rhoŋh,
			ṭʰåŋ	ṭʰɔŋ	rhôŋ

12-13 = K. 1173, 1190 The element 公 seems to been the original graph for 瓮 wēng (Unger, *Hao-ku* 63, 1999). A *wèng* was a bellied vessel with a small opening, two handles and outward turned lips. The graph was also used as a phonetic in *wēng* 'old man, uncle', and perhaps than transferred to the similar sounding synonym *gōng* 'uncle'.

		Mand.	**MC**	**LHan**	**OCM**	
1173a	公 prince	gōng	kuŋ	koŋ	klôŋ	

[T] Sin Sukchu SR kuŋ (平); MGZY gung (平) [kuŋ] <> [D] Min-Xiamen kaŋ^{A1} 'grandfather'; 'clan head' <> [E] Tai: S. luŋ^{A2} < *l- 'parent's elder brother, uncle' <> ? MK etymon: Khmer /looŋ/ 'chief' ⋇ /klooŋ/ 'dignitary higher than' /looŋ/

	公 impartial	gōng	kuŋ	koŋ	kôŋ	'impartial, fair, public'

[E] TB: WT (d)guŋ 'middle'

1190a	松	sōng	zjwoŋ	zioŋ	s-loŋ

[T] ONW zuoŋ <> [D] Min: Xiam lit. sioŋ^{A2}, col. tsiŋ^{A2}

b 訟 litigate sòng zjwoŋ(^{C}) zioŋ(^{C}) s-loŋ, s-loŋh

d 頌 eulogy sòng zjwoŋ^{C} zioŋ^{C} s-loŋh

[T] Sin Sukchu SR zjuŋ (去), PR suŋ; MGZY zÿung (去) [zjuŋ]; ONW zuoŋ

[D] M-Xiam (lit.) sioŋ^{C2} = 誦 <> [E] WT luŋ 'exhortation, admonition, instruction'

頌 counten. róng jiwoŋ joŋ loŋ 'countenance' = 12-11/1187a

f 崧 sōng sjuŋ siuŋ suŋ < sluŋ ? = 15-11/1012 嵩

[D] M-Xiam lit. sioŋ^{A1}, col. siŋ^{A1}

[E] MK *sluuŋ > PMonic *slooŋ 'be high up, high, tall', OMon s-lūŋ 'be high'

\- 鬆 sōng suoŋ, tsʰjwoŋ souŋ, tsʰioŋ — [D] M-Xiam lit. soŋ^{A1}, col. saŋ^{A1}

1173g 翁 wèng ʔuŋ^{C} ʔoŋ^{C} ʔôŋh = 12-4/1184op 齆齈

\- 翁 wēng ʔuŋ ʔoŋ ʔôŋ

[T] Sin Sukchu SR ʔuŋ (平); MGZY 'ung (平) [ʔuŋ]; ONW ʔoŋ

[E] TB-Lushai un^{L} 'be old, elderly, venerable, ancient', WB u^{B} 'uncle'

12-14 = K. 1180 Mand. MC LHan OCM

a 弄 lòng luŋ^{C} loŋ^{C} rôŋh

12-15 = K. 1193 Mand. MC LHan OCM

a 龍 dragon lóng ljwoŋ lioŋ roŋ OCB *C-rjoŋ

[E] AA: Viet. rồng 'dragon', Khmer roŋ ~ rôŋ <> KT: Siam. maḥroŋ ~ măroŋ

龍 variegat. máng mång mɔŋ mrôŋ = 12-26/1201 尨駹哤

h 蘢 lóng luŋ, ljwoŋ loŋ, lioŋ rôŋ, roŋ

ik i 礱 lóng luŋ loŋ rôŋ

l 籠 lóng luŋ(^{B}) loŋ(^{B}) rôŋ, rôŋʔ

[T] ONW luoŋ <> [E] Area word: AA: OKhmer /kruŋ/ 'to cover, shelter, protect, to pen (animals)' ⋇ druṅa /truŋ/ 'pen, cage, coop for birds and animals' <> WB khruiŋ^{C} 'cage for birds' <> KT: PTai *kroŋ^{B1} 'cage', AN *kuruŋ 'cage'

m 聾 lóng luŋ loŋ rôŋ [D] Min: Jiànyáng soŋ^{A}

o 蠪 lóng luŋ loŋ rôŋ

fg 壟隴 lǒng ljwoŋ^{B} lioŋ^{B} roŋʔ

p 寵 chǒng ṭʰjwoŋ^{B} ṭʰioŋ^{B} rhoŋʔ

12-16 = K. 1194 Mand. MC LHan OCM

a 茸 róng ńźjwoŋ ńoŋ noŋ ⋇ 氄, 15-10/1013e 莪

12-16A 軵 rǒng ńźjwoŋ^{B} ńoŋ^{B} — 'push a cart' SW 6456

12-17 = K. 1195 Mand. MC LHan OCM

a 氄 rǒng ńźjwoŋ^{B} ńoŋ^{B} noŋʔ ⋇ 茸, 15-10/1013e 莪

12-18 = K. 1196 Mand. MC LHan OCM

a 宂 rǒng ńźjwoŋ^{B} ńoŋ^{B} noŋʔ

12-19 = K. 1199 Most graphs have two forms, one with element a, the other with b.

Mand. MC LHan OCM

ab 囪匆 chuāng tṣʰåŋ tṣʰɔŋ tshrôŋ

-lm 窗窻窓 chuāng tṣʰåŋ tṣʰɔŋ tshrôŋ

cdf 悤怱聰 cōng tsʰuŋ tsʰoŋ tshôŋ

		Mand.	MC	LHan	OCM	
h	葱 onion	cōng	ts^{h}uŋ	ts^{h}oŋ	tshôŋ	
	[E] TB: WT btsoŋ 'onion', Mru choŋ					
g	蔥 onion	cōng	ts^{h}uŋ	ts^{h}oŋ	tshôŋ	
	a wagon	chuāng	tṣ^{h}åŋ	tṣ^{h}ɔŋ	tshrôŋ	
ijk	i 總摠	zǒng	tsuŋ^B	tsoŋ^B	tsôŋʔ	

12-20	**= K. 1177**	**Mand.**	**MC**	**LHan**	**OCM**
a	a	zōng	tsuŋ(^{C})	tsoŋ(^{C})	tsôŋ, tsôŋh
bcef	愡椶稯鬷	zōng	tsuŋ	tsoŋ	tsôŋ

12-21	**= K. 1178**	**Mand.**	**MC**	**LHan**	**OCM**
a	叢	cóng	dzuŋ	dzoŋ	dzôŋ
	Because of semantic overlap, 取 is not necessarily phonetic.				

12-22	**= K. 1191**	**Mand.**	**MC**	**LHan**	**OCM**	
a	从	cóng	dzjwoŋ	dzioŋ	dzoŋ	
d	從 follow	cóng	dzjwoŋ	dzioŋ	dzoŋ	
	[T] Sin Sukchu SR dzjuŋ (平), PR, LR dzuŋ; MGZY tsÿung (平) [dzjuŋ]; ONW dzuoŋ					
	從 follower	zòng	dzjwoŋ^C	dzioŋ^C	dzoŋh	
	從 longitud.	zōng	tsjwoŋ	tsioŋ	tsoŋ	
	從 leisure	cōng	ts^{h}jwoŋ	ts^{h}ioŋ	tshoŋ	
	從 hairdress	zǒng	tsuŋ^B	tsoŋ^B	tsôŋʔ	
h	縱 let off	zòng	tsjwoŋ^C	tsioŋ^C	tsoŋh	
	縱 quickly	zǒng	tsuŋ^B	tsoŋ^B	tsôŋʔ	[E] WB cuiŋ^B 'drive fast'
i	樅	zōng, cōng	ts(^{h})jwoŋ	ts(^{h})ioŋ	tsoŋ, tshoŋ	
k	豵	zōng	tsuŋ	tsoŋ	tsôŋ	
j	聳	sǒng	sjwoŋ^B	sioŋ^B	soŋʔ,	= 11-21/1222mn 竦悚
				ts^h(i)oŋ^C	tshoŋh < k-soŋh	
	[D] M-Xiam lit. sioŋ^{B1}, col. ts^{h}ɑŋ^{C1}					
-	慫	sǒng	sjwoŋ^B	sioŋ^B	soŋʔ	= 11-21/1222m 悚

12-23	**= K. 1179**	**Mand.**	**MC**	**LHan**	**OCM**
a	送	sòng	suŋ^C	soŋ^C	sôŋh
	[T] Sin Sukchu SR suŋ (去); MGZY sung (去) [suŋ]; ONW soŋ				
	[D] M-Xiam lit. soŋ^{C1}, col. sɑŋ^{C1}				

12-24	**= K. 1200**	**Mand.**	**MC**	**LHan**	**OCM**	
a	雙	shuāng	ṣåŋ	ṣɔŋ	srôŋ	OCB *sCr(j)oŋ)
	[T] Sin Sukchu SR ṣaŋ (平), PR ṣwaŋ; MGZY sh^{h}ang (平) [ṣAŋ]					
	[E] TB: WT zuŋ 'a pair, single', Mru choŋ 'pair'					

12-25	**= K. 1197**	**Mand.**	**MC**	**LHan**	**OCM**	
a	丰	fēng	p^{h}jwoŋ	p^{h}uoŋ	phoŋ	
e	邦	bāng	påŋ	pɔŋ	prôŋ	
	[T] Sin Sukchu SR paŋ (平); MGZY bang (平) [paŋ]					
d	蚌	bàng	båŋ^B	bɔŋ^B	brôŋʔ	= g'
m	夆	féng,	bjwoŋ,	buoŋ,	boŋ,	
		fēng	p^{h}jwoŋ	p^{h}uoŋ	phoŋ	

o	逢 meet	féng	bjwoŋ	buoŋ	boŋ	[T] ONW buoŋ
	a sound	péng	buŋ	boŋ	bôŋ	
v	摓	féng	bjwoŋ	buoŋ	boŋ	
x	縫 to sew	féng	bjwoŋ	buoŋ	boŋ	
	[T] Sin Sukchu SR vuŋ (平); MGZY Hwung (平) [vuŋ]; ONW buoŋ <> [D] Min: Xiam lit. hoŋ^{A2}, col. pɑŋ^{A2}					
	縫 a seam	fèng	bjwoŋ^{C}	buoŋ^{C}	boŋh	
	[D] Min: Xiam lit. hoŋ^{C2}, col. p^{h}ɑŋ^{C2}					
r	烽	fēng	p^{h}jwoŋ	p^{h}uoŋ	phoŋ	
st	蜂蠭	fēng	p^{h}jwoŋ	p^{h}uoŋ	phoŋ	
	[T] Sin S. SR fuŋ (平); MGZY hwung (平) [fuŋ] <> [D] Min: Xiam lit. hoŋ^{A1}, col. 蜂 p^{h}ɑŋ^{A1} <> [E] TB: WT buŋ-ba 'bee' (HST: 40)					
u-	鋒峰	fēng	p^{h}jwoŋ	p^{h}uoŋ	phoŋ	
y	蓬	péng	buŋ	boŋ	bôŋ	
-	篷 sail	péng	buŋ	—	—	
	[T] Sin Sukchu SR buŋ (平); MGZY pung (平) [buŋ]) 'sail' <> [D] PMin *b^{h}oŋ					
i	封	fēng	pjwoŋ	puoŋ	poŋ	
	[D] Min: Xiam lit. hoŋ^{A1}, col. pɑŋ^{A1} <> [E] Area etymon: WT p^{h}uŋ-po 'heap'; Lushai puŋ^{H} / puŋ^{L} 'increase, assemble' ⪤ vuuŋ^{R} 'a heap, a mound'					
-	犎	fēng	pjwoŋ	puoŋ	poŋ	
	[N] Hanshu 96A: humped cattle of India, zebu					
k	葑	fēng	p^{h}jwoŋ	p^{h}uoŋ	phoŋ	
l	紺	běng, bǎng	puŋ^{B}, påŋ^{B}	poŋ^{B}, pɔŋ^{B}	pôŋʔ, prôŋʔ	
z	奉	fèng	bjwoŋ^{B}, p^{h}jwoŋ^{B}	buoŋ^{B}, p^{h}uoŋ^{B}	boŋ^{B}, phoŋ^{B}	[D] Min: Xiam (lit.) hoŋ^{C2}
	[T] Sin Sukchu SR fuŋ (上), LR vuŋ; MGZY Hwung (上) [vuŋ]; ONW buoŋ					
b'	捧	pěng !	p^{h}jwoŋ^{B}	p^{h}uoŋ^{B}	phoŋ^{B}	
c'	俸	fèng	bjwoŋ^{C}	buoŋ^{C}	boŋh	
d'	唪	běng, bèng	puŋ^{B}, buŋ^{B}	poŋ^{B}, boŋ^{B}	pôŋʔ, bôŋʔ	
e'	琫	běng	puŋ^{B}	poŋ^{B}	pôŋʔ	
f'	菶	běng	puŋ^{B}, buŋ^{B}	poŋ^{B}, boŋ^{B}	pôŋʔ, bôŋʔ	
-	棒	bàng	båŋ^{B}	bɔŋ^{B}	brôŋʔ	
	[E] Tai: S. p^{h}lɔɔŋ^{A2} < *b- 'club, cudgel'					
g'	蚌	bàng	båŋ^{B}	bɔŋ^{B}	brôŋʔ	= d

12-26	**= K. 1201**	**Mand.**	**MC**	**LHan**	**OCM**	
acde	尨哤駹厖	máng	måŋ	mɔŋ	mrôŋ	a = 12-13/1193a 龍

12-27	**= K. 1181**	**Mand.**	**MC**	**LHan**	**OCM**	
adf	蒙濛饛	méng	muŋ	moŋ	môŋ	
c	矇 blind	méng	muŋ	moŋ	môŋ	= 6-23/902a 夢
	[E] TB *mu:ŋ > WB hmuiŋ 'dull, downcast' ⪤ hmuiŋ^{B} 'very dark'; JP muŋ^{33} 'overcast'					
b	幪 cover	méng	muŋ	moŋ	môŋ	
	dense	měng	muŋ^{B}	moŋ^{B}	môŋʔ	
e	蠓	měng	muŋ(^{B})	moŋ(^{B})	môŋ, môŋʔ	

13 OCM rime *-u Yōu bù 幽部

GSR 1040 - 1116

Baxter 1992: 507 ff. (§10.2.13)

Table 13-1: OCM rimes *-uŋ, *-uk, *-u in QYS categories

Div.	*-uŋ R.15	*-uk R.14	*-u R.13, *-ukh R.14
I	冬 tuoŋ touŋ *tûŋ	告 kuok kouk *kûk 毒 duok douk *dûk	好 xâu^B hou^B *hûʔ 寶 pâu^B pou^B *pûʔ 道 dâu^B dou^B *lûʔ 誥 kâu^C kou^C *kûkh
III	宮 kjuŋ kuŋ *kuŋ 豐 p^{h}juŋ p^{h}uŋ *phuŋ 終 tśjuŋ tśuŋ *tuŋ 中 ţjuŋ ṭuŋ *truŋ 嵩 sjuŋ siuŋ *suŋ	匊 kjuk kuk *kuk 目 mjuk muk *muk 竹 ţjuk ṭuk *truk 六 ljuk liuk *ruk	浮 bjəu bu *bu 覆 p^{h}jəu^C p^{h}u^C *phukh 舟 tśjəu tśu *tu 祝 tśjəu^C tśu^C *tukh 劉 ljəu liu *ru
II	降 kåŋ^C kɔŋ^C *krûŋh 戇 ṭåŋ^C ṭɔŋ^C *trûŋh	學 ɣåk gɔk *grûk	包 pau pɔu *prû 爪 tṣau^B tṣɔu^B *tsrûʔ 窖 kau^C kɔu^C *krûkh
IV		惄 niek neuk *niûk 篴 diek deuk *liûk	梟 kieu keu *kiû 窈 ʔieu^B ʔeu^B *ʔiûʔ 鳥 tieu^B teu^B *tiûʔ 翏 lieu leu *riû
3/4 gr			糾 kjieu^{B}4 kiu^B *kiuʔ 謬 mjieu^{C}4 miu^C *mriuh
III ac			鏐 ljeu liu *riu
II			坳 ʔau ʔɔu *ʔriû

All phonetic series that are suspected to include words with the OCM rime *-wə (Div. III) are found under Rime 4.

No LHan high vocalic onset need to be postulated with the high vowel *u*; however, *i* is inserted after acute initials. LHan -iu after gutturals is a survival of OC *-iu (Baxter *-iw). Table 16-1 for comparison of OCM rimes *-auk, *-uk, *-(i)au, *-(i)u.

13-1	**= K. 1040**	**Mand.**	**MC**	**LHan**	**OCM**	
abc	臯皋槔	gāo	kâu	kou	kû	
d	嘷	háo	ɣâu	gou	gû	
efg	ef 皞	hào	ɣâu^{B}	gou^{B}	gûʔ	
	⋈14-1/1039h 皓; 13-2/1244c 杲					
h	翱	aó	ŋâu	ŋou	ŋû	

13-2	**= K. 1244c**	**Mand.**	**MC**	**LHan**	**OCM**	
c	杲	gǎo	kâu^{B}	kou^{B}	kûʔ	
	= 14-1/1039h 皓; ⋈ 13-1/1040g 皞					

13-3 **= K. 1041** 号 GSR 1041p etc. constitute a separate series, see 16-8.

		Mand.	**MC**	**LHan**	**OCM**	
aj	丂攷	kǎo	k^{h}âu^{B}	k^{h}ou^{B}	khûʔ	
do	考栲	kǎo	k^{h}âu^{B}	k^{h}ou^{B}	khûʔ R!	OCB *khuʔ
l	巧	qiǎo	k^{h}au$^{B/C}$	k^{h}ɔu$^{B/C}$	khrûʔ, khrûh	
	[T] Sin-SR k^{h}jaw^{B}; MGZY k^{h}jaw^{B}; ONW k^{h}äu; BTD k^{h}ɹau; MHan k^{h}ɹu					
mn	朽死	xiǔ	xjəu^{B}	hu^{B}	huʔ	

13-4	**= K. 1042**	**Mand.**	**MC**	**LHan**	**OCM**	
a	昊	hào	ɣâu^{B}	gou^{B}	gûʔ	[T] ONW ɣau

13-5	**= K. 1043**	**Mand.**	**MC**	**LHan**	**OCM**	
a	顥	hào	ɣâu^{B}	gou^{B}	gûʔ	

13-6	**= K. 1065**	**Mand.**	**MC**	**LHan**	**OCM**	
ab	韭韮	jiǔ	kjəu^{B}	ku^{B}	kuʔ	OCB *k(r)juʔ
	[D] PMin *kiu^{B}: Xiamen ku^{B} <> [E] TB: WT sko 'onion'					

13-7	**= K. 1068**	**Mand.**	**MC**	**LHan**	**OCM**	
a	咎 fault	jiù	gjəu^{B}	gu^{B}	guʔ	OCB *g(r)juʔ
	Pl.N.	gāo	kâu	kou	kû	
c	櫜	gāo	kâu(^{B})	kou(^{B})	kû, kûʔ	
ef	鼛櫜	gāo	kâu	kou	kû < klu ?	

13-7A	**= K. 1070mn**	**Mand.**	**MC**	**LHan**	**OCM**	
mn	臭溴	xiāo !	kieu	keu	kiû	
	There is nothing to suggest that 13-11/1070 休 is phonetic.					

13-8	**= K. 1064**	**Mand.**	**MC**	**LHan**	**OCM**	
ab	丩 > 糾[1] twist	jiū !	kjieu^{B} 4	kiu^{B}	kiuʔ	OCB *k(r)jiwʔ
	丩 has tone A.					
ef	虯觓	qiú,	gjieu 4,	giu,	giu,	
		jiū	kjieu 4	kiu	kiu	= 4-15/1066i 觩
ghi	叫訆嘂	jiào	kieu^{C}	keu^{C}	kiûh	
	叫 [T] Sin Sukchu SR kjew (去); PR kjaw; MGZY gÿaw (去) [kjɛw]; ONW kėu; MHan kɨu; BTD kėu					
d	赳 elegant	jiū !	kjieu^{B} 4	kiu^{B}	kiuʔ	a lexicographic ghost?

bc	糾²糺 eleg.	jiào, jiǎo	gjäu^{B} 3, -kjäu^{B} 3	gɨɑu^{B}, -kɨɑu^{B}	gauʔ, kauʔ	
1103a	收	shōu	śjəu	śu	hjuʔ or nhiu ?	OCB *xjiw

[T] Sin Sukchu SR ʂiw (平); MGZY shiw (平) [ʂiw]; ONW śu
[N] SW says that 丩 is phonetic, but it may have been chosen for other unknown reasons.

1139a	荍	qiáo	gjiäu 4	giau	giau

SW says that 收 is phonetic. Although the latter is a phonological oddity in this series, qiáo fits within the range of the phonetic GSR 1064a.

13-9	**= K. 1044**	**Mand.**	**MC**	**LHan**	**OCM**	
a	好 good	hǎo	xâu^{B}	hou^{B}	hûʔ	OCB *xūʔ

[T] Sin Sukchu SR xaw (上); MGZY haw (上) [xaw]; ONW hɑu. See also p. 10.

	好 love, like	hào	xâu^{C}	hou^{C}	hûh

[E] TB *hu 'rear, raise, nourish'

13-10	**= K. 1244d**	**Mand.**	**MC**	**LHan**	**OCM**	
d	薅	hāo	xâu	hou	hû	= 13-11/1070k 茠

[E] TB: Chepang huʔ- 'to weed'

13-11	**= K. 1070**	**Mand.**	**MC**	**LHan**	**OCM**	See also 13-7A.
ag	休咻	xiū	xjəu	hu	hu	
hij	貅鵂髤	xiū	xjəu	hu	hu	
k	茠	hāo	xâu	hou	hû	= 13-10/1244d 薅
l	烋	xiāo	xau	hɔu	hrû or hû	

13-12	**= K. 1088**	**Mand.**	**MC**	**LHan**	**OCM**
a	臭	chòu	tśʰjəu^{C}	tśʰu^{C}	k-hjuh

[D] M-Xiam lit. tsʰiu^{C1}, col. tsʰɑo^{C1}, Fuzh tsʰau^{C}
[T] Sin Sukchu SR tʂ'iw (去); MGZY chiw (去) [tʂ'iw]; MTang tśʰeu < tśʰu, ONW tśʰu

c	嗅	xiù	xjəu^{C}	hu^{C}	huh

[T] MTang hiu > heu, ONW hu <> [D] M-Xiam lit. hiu^{C1} 'bad smelling'

d	糗	qiǔ	kʰjəu^{B}	kʰu^{B}	khuʔ

13-13	**= K. 1089**	**Mand.**	**MC**	**LHan**	**OCM**
a	醜	chǒu	tśʰjəu^{B}	tśʰu^{B}	k-hju

13-14 **= K. 1071** 憂 is probably not phonetic in 16-27/1152 náo.

		Mand.	**MC**	**LHan**	**OCM**	
-	㥑	yōu	ʔjəu	ʔu	ʔu	SW

This may be the original graph for the next item a, hence has nothing to do with 16-27.

a	憂	yōu	ʔjəu	ʔu	ʔu	
d	優	yōu	ʔjəu	ʔu	ʔu	[T] BTD Skt. u[pā...], ut[pa...]
fghi	瀀纋耰櫌	yōu	ʔjəu	ʔu	ʔu	

耰櫌 [E] TB: Lushai *vuur*^{F} 'fill (with earth), cover'

e	懮	yǒu	ʔjəu^{B}	ʔu^{B}	ʔuʔ

13-15	**= K. 1072**	**Mand.**	**MC**	**LHan**	**OCM**
a	麀	yōu	ʔjəu	ʔu	ʔu

13-16	**= K. 1115**	**Mand.**	**MC**	**LHan**	**OCM**	
a	幺	yāo	ʔieu	ʔeu	ʔiû	
b	幽	yōu	ʔjieu 4, ʔjəu	ʔiu	ʔiu	
c	幽	yōu	ʔjieu 4	ʔiu	ʔiu	OCB *ʔ(r)jiw(ʔ)
	[T] ONW ʔiu <> [E] Mru iu (i.e. ʔiu) 'dark'					
f	幼	yòu	ʔjieu^{C} 4	ʔiu^{C}	ʔiuh	
	[T] Sin Sukchu SR ʔiw (去); MGZY Yiw (去) [ʔjiw] <> [E] WT *yu-bo* 'without horns'					
g	呦	yōu	ʔjieu 4	ʔiu	ʔiu	
	[E] Lushai euʔ^{L} (i.e., ʔeuʔ) 'to bark or call (as sambhur deer)'					
h	黝	yǒu	ʔjieu^{B} 4	ʔiu^{B}	ʔiuʔ	
i	窈	yǎo	ʔieu^{B}	ʔeu^{B}	ʔiûʔ	see 16-20/1145q 窕
j	坳	āo, ào	ʔau	ʔɔu	ʔriû	= 13-16A 凹
	> later 凹 'concave'; ⋇ 13-17/1245a 窅 *ʔiûʔ 'eye socket'					

13-16A	凹 concave	āo, ào	ʔau	—		= 13-16/1115j 坳

13-17	**= K. 1245ab**	**Mand.**	**MC**	**LHan**	**OCM**	
ab	窅杳	yǎo	ʔieu^{B}	ʔeu^{B}	ʔiûʔ	⋇ 13-16/1115c 幽
-	䁵	jué !	ʔiwet	ʔuet	ʔuît < ʔiût ?	SW 1440
	For other instances of a *-uiC < *-iuC metathesis, see *EDOC* něi (p. 397).					

13-18	**= K. 1244h**	**Mand.**	**MC**	**LHan**	**OCM**
h	饕餮	tāo-tiè	tʰâu-tʰiet	tʰɑ/ou-tʰet	?
	[N] The 號 16-8 element may be semantic.				

13-19	**= K. 1084, 1085**		MC	LHan	OCM	
afg	舟	zhōu	tśjəu	tśu	tu	
	[E] MK: Khmer du:k 'boat', Bahn. *du:k 'boat', PVM *ɗo:k -> Tai-S. tu:k^{D1} 'boat'					
fg	侜輈	zhōu	tjəu	ṭu	tru	
1085a	受 receive	shòu	źjəu^{B}	dźu^{B}	duʔ	
	[T] Sin Sukchu SR ʐiw (上); MGZY zhiw (上) [ʐiw]; ONW dźu					
d	授 give	shòu	źjəu^{C}	dźu^{C}	duh	ONW dźu
e	綬	shòu	źjəu^{B}	dźu^{B}	duʔ	

13-20	**= K. 1086**	**Mand.**	**MC**	**LHan**	**OCM**	
ad	州洲	zhōu	tśjəu	tśu	tu	
	[T] Sin Sukchu SR tʂiw (平); MGZY jiw (平) [tʂiw]					
e	酬	chóu	źjəu	dźu	du	= 13-22/1090o 醻

13-20A	**= K. 1087**	**Mand.**	**MC**	**LHan**	**OCM**
a	帚箒 broom	zhǒu	tśjəu^{B}	tśu^{B}	tuʔ
	The same graph writes a synonym sǎo, see 13-61.				

13-21	**= K. 1091**	**Mand.**	**MC**	**LHan**	**OCM**	
[a']a	雠讎	chóu	źjəu	dźu	du	
	[T] MTang źeu < dźu, ONW dźu <> [E] Lushai do^{H} 'to counter contributions...'					
e	售	shòu	źjəu^{C}	dźu^{C}	duh	
cd	犨犫	chōu	tśʰjəu	tśʰu	thu	WB huik 'to pant'

13-22	**= K. 1090**	**Mand.**	**MC**	**LHan**	**OCM**	
abl	a𠷎 > 疇[1]	chóu	ḍjəu	ḍu	dru	'ploughed fields'
ldf	疇[2]𠷎𠷎	chóu	ḍjəu	ḍu	dru	'who'
	[T] Sin Sukchu SR dẓiw (平); MGZY ciw (平) [dẓiw] <> [E] Kuki-Chin *tuʔ/h 'who'					
kmn	儔籌躊	chóu	ḍjəu	ḍu	dru	WT do 'two, a pair'
q	譸	zhōu	ṭjəu	ṭu	tru	
op	醻魗	chóu	źjəu	dźu	du	= 13-20/1086e 酬
g	壽	shòu	źjəu^{B}	dźu^{B}	duʔ	
a'	鑄	zhù	tśju^{C}	tśo^{C}	toh	= 10-19/129c 注
r	擣 beat	dǎo	tâu^{B}	tou^{B}	tûʔ	
	[D] Yue-Taishan au^{55}-^{m}bai^{55} 搗米 <> [E] JP t^{h}u^{55}, WB tui^{B} 'push'					
	pain	zhòu	ḍjəu^{C}	ḍu^{C}	druh	
s	禱	dǎo	tâu$^{B/C}$	tou$^{B/C}$	tûʔ, tûh	= 13-26/1083n 裯
t	檮	táo	dâu	dou	dû	
u	幬 to cover	dào	dâu^{C}	dou^{C}	dûh	
	covering	chóu	ḍjəu	ḍu	dru	
xz	燾翿	dào, tāo	dâu(^{C})	dou(^{C})	dû, dûh	

13-23	**= K. 1073**	**Mand.**	**MC**	**LHan**	**OCM**	
ab	肘疛	zhǒu	ṭjəu^{B}	ṭu^{B}	truʔ	WT gru-mo 'elbow'
c	酎	zhòu	ḍjəu^{B}	ḍu^{B}	druʔ	
d	討	tǎo	t^{h}âu^{B}	t^{h}ou^{B}	thûʔ	

13-24	**= K. 1074**	**Mand.**	**MC**	**LHan**	**OCM**
a	盩	zhōu	ṭjəu	ṭu	tru

13-25	**= K. 1116**	**Mand.**	**MC**	**LHan**	**OCM**
a	鳥	niǎo //	tieu^{B}	teu^{B}	tiûʔ
	[T] Sin Sukchu SR njew (上); MGZY dyaw (上) [tjɛw] <> [E] TB: Garo *doʔ, Karen *to 'bird'				
b	蔦	niǎo //	tieu$^{B/C}$	teu$^{B/C}$	tiûʔ, tiûh
c	島	dǎo	tâu^{B}	tou^{B}	tûʔ

13-26	**= K. 1083**	**Mand.**	**MC**	**LHan**	**OCM**
ahi	周	zhōu	tśjəu	tśu	tiu
	[T] ONW tśu <> [E] Tai: S. diw[3] 'strips of rattan or bamboo bent in a circle to which ribs of a cage are fastened'				
fhi	婤賙輖	zhōu, chōu	tśjəu	tśu	tiu
m	綢 wrap	chóu	ḍjəu	ḍu	driu
	In 綢繆 ḍjəu-mjieu, OCB *drjiw-mrjiw 'be tied round' <> [T] MTang ḍeu < ḍu, ONW du				
	綢 envelop	tāo	t^{h}âu	t^{h}ou	lhû
	graph borrowed late [Liji] for 13-27/1078g				
n	裯	chóu	ḍjəu	ḍu	driu
j	啁	zhōu, zhāo	ṭjəu, ṭau	ṭu, ṭɔu	tru, trû
l	稠	chóu	ḍjəu	ḍu	driu
k	惆	chóu !	ṭ^{h}jəu	ṭ^{h}u	thriu
o	凋	diāo	tieu	teu	tiû
	[E] S. tok^{D1} 'to become faded'				

prs	琱彫錭	diāo	tieu	teu	tiû	
tu	雕鵰	diāo	tieu	teu	tiû	
v	蜩	tiáo	dieu	deu	diû	
x	調 tune	tiáo	dieu	deu	diû	OCB *diw
	[T] BTD Skt. deva					
	morning	zhōu !	tjəu^C	ṭu^C	tru(k)h	a loan for 14-9/1075a
y	裯	dǎo	tâu^B	tou^B	tûʔ	
z	倜	tì	t^{h}iek	t^{h}ek < t^{h}euk	thiûk	

13-27	**= K. 1078**	**Mand.**	**MC**	**LHan**	**OCM**	
a	舀	yóu	jiəu,	ju,	lu,	
		~ yǎo	jiäu^B	jau^B	lauʔ	
bcf	慆搯謟	tāo	t^{h}âu	t^{h}ou	lhû	
g	韜	tāo	t^{h}âu	t^{h}ou	lhû	= 13-26/1083m
d	滔 overflow	tāo	t^{h}âu	t^{h}ou	lhû	
	滔 crowd	táo	t^{h}âu, dâu	t^{h}ou, dou	lhû, lû	
h	稻	dào	dâu^B	dou^B	lûʔ < g-luʔ	MY *nblau^A
	[E] Borrowed by Tocharian as klu 'rice' (Mallory a. Mair 2000: 310) <> [D] PMin *tiu^{B2} 粙 (corresponds to QYS ḍjəu^C [JY]) may possibly be a variant (Norman, p.c.)					
l	蹈	dǎo, dào	dâu^C	dou^C	lûh	

13-28	**= K. 1046**	**Mand.**	**MC**	**LHan**	**OCM**
ac	叏弢	tāo	t^{h}âu	t^{h}ou	lhû ?

13-29	**= K. 1047**	**Mand.**	**MC**	**LHan**	**OCM**	
a-e	匋掏綯	táo	dâu	dou	lû R! (綯)	OCB *b-lu
	匋 Sin Sukchu SR daw (平); MGZY taw (平) [daw]; ONW dɑu					
d	陶 kiln	táo	dâu	dou	lû R!	
	gallop	dào	dâu^C	dou^C	lûh	
	pleased	yáo	jiäu	jau	lau	

13-30 **= K. 1079** The initial could be either OCM *li- or *j-; the default initial is here *j- (~ *li-).

		Mand.	**MC**	**LHan**	**OCM**	
a	由	yóu	jiəu	ju	ju	
	[T] Sin Sukchu SR iw (平); MGZY yiw (平) [jiw]; ONW iu					
c	油	yóu	jiəu	ju	ju	= 13-32/1077q 滺
d	鼬	yòu	jiəu^C	ju^C	juh	[E] TB *yuʔ or *b-yəw 'rat'
b	柚 pumelo	yòu	jiəu^C	ju^C	juh	
	cylinder	zhú	ḍjuk	ḍuk	druk < r-liuk	
m	袖 sleeve	xiù	zjəu^C	ziu^C	s-juh	OCB *zjus
n	褏 sleeve	xiù	zjəu^C	ziu^C	s-juh	
	dress	yòu	jiəu^C	ju^C	juh	
	The graphs n 褏 and o 褎 are often substituted for each other, o 褎 being the more common.					
o	褎 big, tall	yoù	jiəu^C	ju^C	juh < wuh ?	
	'big, tall (of grain)' <> [E] Lushai *vu^R* 'be ripe and yellow (as standing rice)', 'show up / be conspicuous (as flowers)'					

e	妯	chōu,	ṭ^{h}jəu,	ṭh^{h}u,	rhiu or t-hliu,	
		zhóu	ḍjəu^C	ḍu^C	driuh < r-liuh	
f	抽	chōu	ṭ^{h}jəu	ṭh^{h}u	rhiu or t-hliu	OCB *hlrju

[T] MTang ṭ^{h}eu < ṭ^{h}u, ONW t^{h}u <> [E] TB: Chepang klu- 'pull out (hair)' ⋊ glu- 'pull out (larger) weeds, cultivate crop' ⋊ blu- 'remove, root out'. <> Tai: S. t^{h}lok^{D1} 'id.'

ghil	宙胄冑軸	zhòu	ḍjəu^C	ḍu^C	driuh < r-liuh	
p	軸	zhóu !	ḍjuk	ḍuk	driuk < r-liuk	
q	迪	dí	diek	dek < deuk	liûk	
-	笛	dí	diek	dek < deuk	liûk	OCB *liwk

= 14-13/1022d 篴 <> [T] Sin Sukchu SR di (入); MGZY ti (入) [di]

13-31	**= K. 1082**	**Mand.**	**MC**	**LHan**	**OCM**	
a	牖	yǒu	jiəu^B	ju^B	luʔ or juʔ	

13-32 **= K. 1077** The phonetic writes words with initials OCM ju ~ liu ~ s(l)iu.

		Mand.	**MC**	**LHan**	**OCM**	
a	攸	yōu !	jiəu	ju	ju	[E] WT yul 'place'
-	滺	yóu	jiəu	ju	ju	
c	悠	yōu !	jiəu	ju	ju	OCB *ljiw
q	滺	yōu !	jiəu	ju	ju	OCB *ljiw

= 13-30/1079c 油 *ju <> [T] Sin Sukchu SR iw (平); MGZY yiw (平) [jiw]

k	莜	diào	dieu^C	deu^C	liûkh	= v
f	條 pull down	tiāo	t^{h}ieu	t^{h}eu	lhiû	
	條 a tree	tiáo	dieu	deu	liû	OCB *liw

[T] MTang diau, ONW dėu

ghjt	鞗鋚鰷鯈	tiáo	dieu	deu	liû	OCB *liw
v	蓧	diào	dieu^C	deu^C	liûkh	= k
	蓧	dí	diek	dek < deuk	liûk	
x	滌	dí	diek	dek < deuk	liûk	OCB *liwk
s	蓨	tiāo	t^{h}iek	t^{h}ek	lhiûk	
e	脩	xiū	sjəu	siu	siu	OCB *sljiw

[E] TB: Lushai t^{h}u^F < suuʔ 'dried (as fish)', 'dried and rotten'

r	滫	xiǔ	sjəu^B	siu^B	siuʔ	

= 13-60/1112h 糔; = = 10-37/1097f 溲 *sruʔ

u	筱	xiǎo	sieu^B	seu^B	siûʔ	
d	修	xiū	sjəu	siu	siu	

[T] ONW su; BTD Skt. śu

l	儵 rapid	xiāo,	sieu,	seu,	siû,	
		shū	śjuk	śuk	hjuk	
mop	倏儵倐	shù	źjuk	dźuk	diuk	

MC ź- can occasionally derive from an OC j-like initial, see EDOC §9.3.

13-33	**= K. 1080**	**Mand.**	**MC**	**LHan**	**OCM**	
afgh	斿游遊蝣	yóu	jiəu	ju	ju	OCB *ju

遊 = 13-34/1081g 逌 <> [T] Sin Sukchu SR iw (平); MGZY yiw (平) [jiw]; ONW iu [D] PMin *ziu <> [E] WT rgyu-ba < *r-ju 'to go, walk, move, wander, range (of men, animals, etc.)', Lepcha yǔ

13-34	**= K. 1081**	**Mand.**	**MC**	**LHan**	**OCM**	
a	卣	yóu	jiəu(^{B})	ju(^{B})	ju, juʔ	
g	逌	yóu	jiəu	ju	ju	= 13-33/1080 游遊
	[T] Sin Sukchu SR iw (平); MGZY yiw (平) [jiw]; ONW iu					

13-35	**= K. 1094**	**Mand.**	**MC**	**LHan**	**OCM**	
a	囚	qiú	zjəu	ziu	s-ju	OCB *zju
c	泅	qiú	zjəu	ziu	s-ju	⋇ 13-33/1080
	[D] M-Xiam, Fuzh siu^{A2} 'to swim'					

13-36	**= K. 1096**	**Mand.**	**MC**	**LHan**	**OCM**	
a	酉	yǒu	jiəu^{B}	ju^{B}	juʔ	
h	庮	yóu, yǒu	jiəu(^{B})	ju(^{B})	ju, juʔ	[E] KN *m-hew 'spoiled'
ij	槱標	yǒu, yòu	jiəu$^{B/C}$	ju$^{B/C}$	juʔ, juh	
r	猶	yóu	jiəu	ju	ju	OCB *ju
	[T] Sin Sukchu SR iw (平); MGZY yiw (平) [jiw]; ONW iu					
a'	蕕	yóu	jiəu	ju	ju	
ty	猷輶	yóu	jiəu	ju	ju	
k	酒	jiǔ	tsjəu^{B}	tsiu^{B}	tsiu, tsiuʔ	
	[T] Sin Sukchu SR tsiw (上); MGZY dziw (上) [tsiw]; MTang tseu < tsiu, ONW tsu					
	[D] PMin *tsiu^{B} > Xiam, Fuzh tsiu^{B} <> [E] PTB *yu(w) 'wine'					
ln	酋蝤	qiú	dzjəu	dziu	dziu	
o	遒	qiú, jiū	dzjəu, tsjəu	dziu, tsiu	dziu, tsiu	
pq	緧鰌	qiū	ts^{h}jəu	ts^{h}iu	tshiu	
z	蹜	zú, cù	ts(^{h})juk	ts(^{h})iuk	tsiuk, tshiuk	

13-37	**= K. 1246c**	**Mand.**	**MC**	**LHan**	**OCM**
c	狖 monkey	yòu	jiəu^{C}	ju^{C}	juh < wuh ? = 28-11/575q

13-38	**= K. 1102, 1048**		MC	LHan	OCM	
1102a	首 head	shǒu	śjəu^{B}	śu^{B}	lhuʔ	
	[T] BTD 首陀衛 śu^{B}-dɑ[i]-was Skt. śuddhavāsa <> [E] TB *lu 'head'					
	首 turn head	shòu	śjəu^{C}	śu^{C}	lhuh	
1048a	道 way	dào	dâu^{B}	dou^{B}	lûʔ	OCB *luʔ
	[T] Sin Sukchu SR daw (上去); MGZY taw (上) [daw]; ONW dɑu <> [E] Yao klău^{B} 'road'					
	道 lead	dào	dâu^{C}	dou^{C}	lûh	
d	導 lead	dào	dâu^{C}	dou^{C}	lûh	

13-39 **= K. 1095** The initial could be OCM *l- or *j- (< **w-?).

		Mand.	**MC**	**LHan**	**OCM**	
a	秀	xiù	sjəu^{C}	siu^{C}	siuh < *swuh ?	OCB *sljus
	[T] Sin Sukchu SR siw (去); MGZY siw (去) [siw]					
	[E] ? TB: Chepang syu- 'to prosper, flourish', Lushai vuul^{H} 'be in full bloom (as flowers)'					
c	琇	xiù, yòu	sjəu^{C}, jiəu^{B}	siu^{C}, ju^{B}	siuh, juʔ	
d	莠	yǒu	jiəu^{B}	ju^{B}	juʔ < *wuʔ ?	OCB *ljuʔ
	[E] WT yur-ma 'weeds' from < *wur					
e	誘	yòu	jiəu^{B}	ju^{B}	luʔ (?)	OCB *ljuʔ
	[E] WT slu 'entice'; also PTai *l-: S. lɔɔ^{B2} 'to lure, deceive'					

13-40 **= K. 1099** The OC initial could have been *nh, *lh, or *hj; *hj is the default initial.

		Mand.	MC	LHan	OCM	
a	守 keep	shǒu	śjəu^B	śu^B	hjuʔ	
	[T] Sin Sukchu SR ṣiw (上); MGZY shiw (上) [ṣiw]; ONW śu					
	守 fief	shòu	śjəu^C	śu^C	hjuh	OCB *stjus
c	狩 hunt	shòu	śjəu^C	śu^C	hjuʔ !	

13-41 **= K. 1100** The initial consonant is unknown, it probably is the same as in the possible cognate 狩 13-40c.

		Mand.	MC	LHan	OCM
a	獸	shòu	śjəu^C	śu^C	hjuh
	[T] Sin Sukchu SR ṣiw (去); MGZY shiw (去) [ṣiw]				

13-42 **= K. 1101** The OC initial consonant is uncertain, the default here is *hj-; the word could possibly be related to foreign ones with initial *n-.

		Mand.	MC	LHan	OCM	
a	手	shǒu	śjəu^B	śu^B, S tśʰu^B	hjuʔ or nhuʔ ?	OCB *hjuʔ ?
	[T] Sin Sukchu SR ṣiw (上); MGZY shiw (上) [ṣiw]; ONW śu					
	[D] PMin *tšhiu^B1 > Xiam tsʰiu^B, PWMin *ʃiu^B1					

13-43	**= K. 1055**	**Mand.**	**MC**	**LHan**	**OCM**	
a	老	lǎo	lâu^B	lou^B	rûʔ	Old Sino-Viet. reu
	[T] ONW lɑu <> [E] TB *raw > WT ro 'corpse'; Lep hryu 'be dry, dead' (of leaf); Lushai ro^H 'be dry, dead'; WB ro (= rau) 'very old' ≭ rwat 'old, tough', NNaga *rəw 'old' (of person)					

13-44	**= K. 1056**	**Mand.**	**MC**	**LHan**	**OCM**	
a	牢	láo	lâu	lou	rû	Viet. rào 'enclosure'
	[T] Sin Sukchu SR law (上); MGZY law (上) [law]					

13-45	**= K. 1069**	**Mand.**	**MC**	**LHan**	**OCM**	
a	翏 fly high	liáu	lieu	leu	riû	SW 1499
	whistling	liù, liào	ljəu^C, ljeu^C, ljäu^C	liu^C	riuh	'whistling of wind'
b	鏐	liú	ljeu, ljəu	liu	riu	
f	飂	liú	ljəu	liu	ru, probably riu (cf. a)	
j	勠	liú, lù	ljəu(^C), ljuk	liu(^C), liuk	riu, riuh, riuk	
k	瘳	chōu, liáo	ṭʰjəu, lieu	ṭʰu, leu	rhiu, riû	
no	寥漻	liáo	lieu	leu	riû	
p	蓼 a plant	liǎo	lieu^B	leu^B	riûʔ	
	a plant	lù	ljuk	liuk	riuk	
g	摎	liú, jiū	ljəu, kjieu 4	liu, kiu	riu, kiu	
i	璆	qiú	gjieu 4	giu	giu	
h	樛	jiū	kjieu 4	kiu	kiu	

		Mand.	MC	LHan	OCM	
l	繆 twist	jiū	kjieu 4	kiu	kiu	OCB *k(r)jiw

[E] PTai *kliəu^{A1} (?): S. kliau^{A1} 'to wind around, twist a string', Saek tlɛɛu^{C1}; note however PTai *kiəu^{C1} : S. kiau^{C1} 'to wind around, twist'

	繆 bind	miù	mjieu^{C} 4	miu^{C}	miuh	
m	謬	miù	mjieu^{C} 4	miu^{C}	miuh	OCB *mrjiws

[T] Sin Sukchu SR miw (去); MGZY miw (去) [miw]

s	膠 unite, glue	jiāo	kau(^{B})	kɔu(^{B})	kriû R!	
	to crow	jiāo	kau	kɔu	kriû R!	OCB *kriw
	frost	jiāo	kau	kɔu or kau ? (krû or krâu ?)		[Chuci]

[E] PWMiao *klau^{7} 'ice, snow'

u	僇	lù	ljuk	liuk	ruk	[E] TB-Mru ruk 'shame'
vx	戮穋	lù	ljuk	liuk	ruk	
r	醪	láo	lâu	lou	rû	

[E] WT ru-ma 'curdled milk', also JP ru^{31}- 'liquor' <> PTai *xl-: S. lau^{C1} 'liquor', KS *khlaau^{3} 'rice wine'

t	嘐	xiāo	xau	hɔu	hrû or h(i)û	
q	熮 sharp taste	liào	ljäu^{C}	liau^{C}	riauh	

13-46	**= K. 1104**	**Mand.**	**MC**	**LHan**	**OCM**
ac	流旒	liú	ljəu	liu	ru or riu

[T] Sin Sukchu SR liw (平); MGZY liw (平) [liw]; MTang leu < liu, ONW lu < lu. MHan 璧流離 piek-liu-liɑi Skt. vaidurya, Pkt. veluriya <> [D] M-Xiam, Fuzh lau^{A2}

13-47	**= K. 1114**	**Mand.**	**MC**	**LHan**	**OCM**	
aa'	丣^{1} > 劉	liú	ljəu	liu	ru	'to butcher'

劉 [T] Sin Sukchu SR liw (平); MGZY liw (平) [liw]; MTang leu < liu, ONW lu < lu [D] Jiànyáng seu^{A2} <> [E] TB-Tiddim gou^{53} / gɔʔ^{11} < rouh / rɔʔ/h 'to kill, slaughter'

b'	懰	liǔ	ljəu^{B}	liu^{B}	ruʔ	
c'	瀏	liú	ljəu(^{B})	liu(^{B})	ru, ruʔ	
pq-	留 q 榴	liú	ljəu	liu	ru	

[T] MTang leu < liu, ONW lu < lu <> [D] M-Xiam, Fuzh lau^{A2}

stz	st 騮	liú	ljəu	liu	ru	
v	溜	liù	ljəu^{C}	liu^{C}	ruh	[E] Tai: S. riau^{B2} 'rapids'
y	霤	liù	ljəu^{C}	liu^{C}	ruh	
lm	柳 m	liǔ	ljəu^{B}	liu^{B}	ruʔ	
x	罶	liǔ	ljəu^{B}	liu^{B}	ruʔ	
-	籀	zhòu	ḍjəu^{C}	ḍu^{C}	druh	
u	聊	liáo	lieu	leu	riû	
a	丣^{2} cyclic. s.	mǎo	mau^{B}	mɔu^{B}	mrûʔ	OCB *mruʔ
g	昴	mǎo	mau^{B}	mɔu^{B}	mrûʔ	
f	茆	mǎo, liǔ	mau^{B}, ljəu^{B}	mɔu^{B}, liu^{B}	mrûʔ, ruʔ	
i	窌	pào,	p^{h}au^{C},	p^{h}ɔu^{C},	phrûh,	
		jiào	kau^{C}	kɔu^{C}	krûh or krûkh	

Jiào is a synonym (14-1/1039o) written with the graph for pào.

j	貿 barter	mào	məu^{C}	mo^{C}	mûh	
	bad eyes	mòu	mjəu^{C}	mu^{C}	muh	※ 13-76/1109q

13-48	**= K. 1105**	**Mand.**	**MC**	**LHan**	**OCM**	
a	柔	róu	ńźjəu	ńu	nu	[E] JP nu^{33} 'relaxed, slack'
b	揉	ròu	ńźjəu(^{C})	ńu^{C}	nuh	[T] ONW ńu
c	暒	róu	ńźjəu	ńu	nu	
e	輮	róu !	ńźjəu$^{B/C}$	ńu$^{B/C}$	nuʔ, nuh	
d	蹂	róu	ńźjəu($^{B/C}$)	ńu($^{B/C}$)	nu, nuʔ, nuh	
	[E] Lushai *hnuʔ 'footprint'					
f	糅	róu, niù	ṇjəu^{C}	ṇu^{C}	nruh	
	[E] WT snor-ba 'mix, disturb'					
g	猱 monkey	náo	nâu	nou	nû	
	~ 16-27/1152b 獿 (*nâu); 13-49 夒					

13-49		**Mand.**	**MC**	**LHan**	**OCM**
-	夒	náo	nâu	nou	nû
	~ 13-48/1105g 猱; 16-27/1152b 獿 (*nâu)				

13-50	**= K. 1076**	**Mand.**	**MC**	**LHan**	**OCM**	
af	丑^{1} > 狃	niǔ	ṇjəu^{B}	ṇu^{B}	nruʔ	'claw'
	狃 'Finger, toe, claws' <> [E] TB-LB *s-nyuw^{1,2} 'digit, finger' > WB lak-hñui^{B} 'forefinger' <> PTai *niu^{C2} 'finger', Shan niw 'finger, toe, fingernail, toenail'					
e	杻	niǔ	ṇjəu^{B}	ṇu^{B}	nruʔ	
g	紐	niǔ	ṇjəu^{B}	ṇu^{B}	nruʔ	OCB *nrjuʔ
	[T] Sin Sukchu SR niw (上); MGZY ñiw (上) [ṇiw]; ONW nu					
k	忸	niǔ	ṇjuk	ṇuk	nruk	
h	羞	xiū	sjəu	siu	snu	
	Qiu X. 2000, p. 224: the element 丑 was originally 又. <> [T] BTD Skt. śu					
a	丑^{2} cycl.s.	chǒu	ṭʰjəu^{B}	ṭʰu^{B}	rhuʔ or nhruʔ	OCB *hnrjuʔ
	[E] PVM *c-luː > kluː / tluː 'buffalo' > Viet. trâu [ṭəw]					

13-51	**= K. 1049**	**Mand.**	**MC**	**LHan**	**OCM**	
a	早	zǎo	tsâu^{B}	tsou^{B}	tsûʔ	
	[T] Sin Sukchu SR tsaw (上); MGZY dzaw (上) [tsaw]; ONW tsɑu					
b	草 grass	cǎo	tsʰâu^{B}	tsʰou^{B}	tshûʔ	= 13-52/1052c 艸
	[T] Sin Sukchu SR ts'aw (上); MGZY tshaw (上) [ts'aw]; ONW tsʰɑu					
	草 anxious	cǎo	tsʰâo^{B}	tsʰou^{B}	tshûʔ < *C-sûʔ ?	= 13-60/1112e 慅

13-52	**= K. 1052**	**Mand.**	**MC**	**LHan**	**OCM**	
ac	a 艸	cǎo	tsʰâu^{B}	tsʰou^{B}	tshûʔ	= 13-51/1049b 草

13-53	**= K. 1050**	**Mand.**	**MC**	**LHan**	**OCM**	
a	棗	zǎo	tsâu^{B}	tsou^{B}	tsûʔ	OCB *tsuʔ

13-54 **= K. 1051** The element gào 告 *kluk 'report' is semantic, not phonetic; the word 造 *tshûh originally meant 'to go and offer (a sacrifice)', 'go and appear in court', which usually would involve some 告 announcement or report. Therefore, this phonetic series did not have an *sk-like initial.

		Mand.	**MC**	**LHan**	**OCM**
a	造 make	zào	dzâu^{B}	dzou^{B}	dzûʔ
	造 to go to	cào	tsʰâu^{C}	tsʰou^{C}	tshûh

d	慥	cào	tsʰâu^C	tsʰou^C	tshûh	
e	簉	chòu	tṣʰjəu^C	tṣʰu^C	tshruh	

13-55	**= K. 1053**	**Mand.**	**MC**	**LHan**	**OCM**	
ad	曹螬	cáo	dzâu	dzou	dzû	

[T] Sin Sukchu SR dzaw (平); MGZY tsaw (平) [dzaw] <> [E] WT 'dzog- 'heap together'

e	漕 transport	zào	dzâu^C	dzou^C	dzûh	
	Pl.N.	cáo	dzâu	dzou	dzû	
fgh	傮糟遭	zāo	tsâu	tsou	tsû	[T] ONW tsau

13-56	**= K. 1054**	**Mand.**	**MC**	**LHan**	**OCM**	
a	皂	zào	dzâu^B	dzou^B	dzûʔ	

13-57	**= K. 1092**	**Mand.**	**MC**	**LHan**	**OCM**	
a	秋	qiū	tsʰjəu	tsʰiu	tshiu	OCB *tshjiw

[D] M-Xiam, Fuzh tsʰiu^{A1} ≭ shōu 收 *nh(i), hence < *C-nh(i)u?

bcd	楸萩鶖	qiū	tsʰjəu	tsʰiu	tshiu	
e	啾	jiū	tsjəu	tsiu	tsiu	
f	湫	qiū,	tsjəu,	tsiu,	tsiu,	
		jiǎo	tsieu^B	tseu^B	tsiûʔ	
g	揫	jiū !	dzjəu	dziu	dziu	
j	愀	qiǎo,	tsʰjäu^B,			
		jiù	dzjəu^B	dziu^B	dziuʔ	
i	愁	chóu	dẓjəu	dẓu	dzru or dzriu	
h	甃	zhòu	tṣjəu^C	tṣu^C	tsruh or tsriuh	

13-58	**= K. 1093**	**Mand.**	**MC**	**LHan**	**OCM**	
a	就	jiù	dzjəu^C	dziu^C	dzuh R !	OCB *dzjus

[T] Sin Sukchu SR dziw (去); MGZY tsiw (去) [dziw]; MTang dzeu < dziu, ONW dzu. MHan 丘就 kʰu-dziu^C = Kujula

bc	蹴 c trample	zú, cù	tsjuk, tsʰjuk	tsiuk, tsʰiuk	tsuk, tshuk	
	anxiously	cù, zú	tsjuk, dzjuk	tsiuk, dziuk	tsuk, dzuk	

13-59	**= K. 1111**	**Mand.**	**MC**	**LHan**	**OCM**	
a	爪	zhǎo	tṣau^B	tṣɔu^B	tsrûʔ	= 13-60/1112a 叉
c	抓	zhuā	tṣau(^{B}/^{C})	tṣɔu(^{B}/^{C})	tsrû, tsrûʔ, tsrûh	

[D] M-Xiam tsua^{A1}

13-60	**= K. 1112**	**Mand.**	**MC**	**LHan**	**OCM**	
a	叉	zhǎo	tṣau^B	tṣɔu^B	tsrûʔ	= 13-59/1111a 爪

[D] M-Xiam b. liāō^{B1} (< ?)

d	蚤	zǎo	tsâu^B	tsou^B	tsûʔ	
e	慅	sāo,	sâu(^{B}),	sou(^{B}),	sû, sûʔ,	
		cǎo	tsʰâo^B	tsʰou^B	tshûʔ < C-sûʔ ?	= 13-51/1049b 草
f	搔	sāo	sâu	sou	sû	TB-Chepang saw- 'itch'
g	騷	sāo	sâu	sou	sû	

[E] MK-OKhmer /sook/ 'sorrow'

h	糔	xiǔ	sjəu	su^B	suʔ	
	= 13-32/1077r 滫; = 10-37/1097f 溲					
i	鼜	qì	tsʰiek	tsʰek < tsʰeuk	tshiûk	

13-61	**= K. 1087**	**Mand.**	**MC**	**LHan**	**OCM**
gf	掃埽	sǎo	sâu$^{B/C}$	sou$^{B/C}$	sûʔ/h

The same graphic element 帚 writes a synonym zhǒu; see 13-20A.

13-62	**= K. 1098**	**Mand.**	**MC**	**LHan**	**OCM**	
a	蒐 a plant	sōu	ṣjəu	ṣu	sru	
	a hunt	sōu	ṣjəu	ṣu	sru or sro	= 10-37/1097h

13-63	(cf. K. 647)	**Mand.**	**MC**	**LHan**	**OCM**	
-	犙	sōu	ṣjəu, ṣjeu	ṣu	sru	'three-year-old calf'

[E] KD: PHlai *sr-: Baoding fu^3, Zhong-shan tshu^3 'three'. <> Cf. 38-29/647

13-64	**= K. 1057**	**Mand.**	**MC**	**LHan**	**OCM**
afg	保葆褓	bǎo	pâu^B	pou^B	pûʔ
h	褒 robe	bāo	pâu	pou	pû
	salute	bào	pâu^C	pou^C	pûh

13-65	**= K. 1058**	**Mand.**	**MC**	**LHan**	**OCM**
a	報	bào	pâu^C	pou^C	pûh

13-66 **= K. 1059** In the BI, 13-69 缶 has been added as phonetic (Qiu 2000: 232).

		Mand.	**MC**	**LHan**	**OCM**
a	寶	bǎo	pâu^B	pou^B	pûʔ

[T] Sin Sukchu SR paw (上); MGZY baw, ba'o (上) [paw]; ONW pɑu <> [E] TB *puw 'value'

13-67	**= K. 1060**	**Mand.**	**MC**	**LHan**	**OCM**
ab	a 鴇	bǎo	pâu^B	pou^B	pûʔ

13-68	**= K. 1061**	**Mand.**	**MC**	**LHan**	**OCM**
a	虣	bào	bâu^C	bou^C	bûh

13-69	**= K. 1107**	**Mand.**	**MC**	**LHan**	**OCM**
a	缶	fǒu	pjəu^B	pu^B	puʔ R!
d	d	piáo	bjiäu 4	biau	biau

13-70	**= K. 1108**	**Mand.**	**MC**	**LHan**	**OCM**	
a	阜	fù	bjəu^B	bu^B	buʔ R!	OCB *b(r)juʔ

[T] MTang bvu, ONW bu

13-71	**= K. 1154, 1106**		**MC**	**LHan**	**OCM**
1154a	髟	biāo	pjieu 4,	piu,	piu,
			pjiäu 4	piau	piau

[N] The graph 髟 also writes a synonym shān *srâm 36-24/1154.
[E] PMiao *preu^{2A}, PYao *pyʲei^1 'hair'

This graph 髟 seems to be the abbreviated phonetic in the following:

1106a	彪	biāo	pjieu 4	piu	piu
b	滮	biāo	bjieu 4, bjəu	biu	biu

13-72	= K. 1113	Mand.	MC	LHan	OCM	
ab	包[1] > 胞	bāo,	pau,	pɔu,	prû,	[E] WT p^{h}ru-ma 'uterus'
		pāo	p^{h}au	p^{h}ɔu	phrû	
a	包[2] wrap	bāo	pau	pɔu	prû	OCB *pru

[T] Sin Sukchu SR paw (平); MGZY baw (平) [paw], MHan pɹu; BTD pɹɑu; ONW päu
[E] WT 'p^{h}ur- 'wrap up'

c	苞 mat	bāo	pau	pɔu	prû	OCB *pru
	reed	biào	bjäu^{B} 3?	bɨɑu^{B}	bauʔ	
eg	庖炮	páo	bau	bɔu	brû	
h	鮑	bào	bau^{B}	bɔu^{B}	brûʔ	
d	飽	bǎo	pau^{B}	pɔu^{B}	prûʔ	

[T] Sin Sukchu SR paw (上); MGZY baw (上) [paw]; ONW päu
[E] TB: Lushai puar^{H} 'full, satiated'

f	匏 gourd	páo	bau	bɔu	brû	[E] Lushai buur^{H} 'gourd'
-	跑 run	pǎo	—			[E] Miao plau^{C1} 'to flee'
i	袍 robe	páo	bâu	bou	bû	
	lapel	bào	bâu^{C}	bou^{C}	bûh	
j	抱	bào	bâu^{B}	bou^{B}	bûʔ	

[T] Sin Sukchu SR baw (上); MGZY paw (上) [baw] <> [D] PMin *bhâu ~ *bâu
[E] WB puik 'hold in arms, hug'

kl	枹⿱罒包	fú	bjəu	bu	bu	
m	鞄	pò,	p^{h}åk,	p^{h}ɔk,	phrûk,	
		páo, bào	bau(^{B}/^{C})	bɔu(^{B}/^{C})	brû, brûʔ, brûh	
n	雹	báo	båk	bɔk	brûk	

13-73	= K. 1233	Mand.	MC	LHan	OCM	
ad	孚 > 俘	fú	p^{h}ju irreg!	p^{h}u	phu R!	OCB *ph(r)ju
f	莩	fú	p^{h}ju	p^{h}u	phu	
g	郛	fú	p^{h}ju	p^{h}u R!	phu	
j	罦	fú	p^{h}ju, bjəu	p^{h}u	phu	OCB *ph(r)ju

= 罘 4-61/999h

l	浮	fú	bjəu	bu	bu R!	OCB *b(r)ju

[T] Sin Sukchu SR vəw (平); MGZY Hwow (平) [vow]; MTang bvu, ONW bu. MHan 浮圖 bu-dɑ Buddha <> [D] PMin *bhu ~ bu: Xiamen, Fuzhou p^{h}u^{A2}. Yao bjou^{2} < *nb-

n	蜉	fú	bjəu	bu	bu	[E] WT sbur 'ant'
h	垺	fú, fōu	p^{h}ju, p^{h}jəu,	p^{h}u(o),	pho, phu,	
		pēi	p^{h}uậi	p^{h}ə	phə̂	

[E] WB p^{h}u^{C} 'to swell' ⋈ pu 'to bulge', WT 'bo-ba, 'bos 'to swell (up), rise'

k	桴 drum stick	fú	bjəu	bu	bu	
	raft	fú !	p^{h}ju	p^{h}uo	pho	= 10-3/136h 泭
i	殍	piǎo,	bjäu^{B} 3?,	bɨɑu^{B},	bauʔ,	
		fū	p^{h}ju	p^{h}u	phu	
o	捊	páu, póu	bau, bəu	bɔu, bou	brû, bû	

13-74	**= K. 1062**	**Mand.**	**MC**	**LHan**	**OCM**	
-ab	冃 > 冒[1]	mào	mâu^{C}	mou^{C}	mûh	OCB *muks
ab	冒[2] to look at	mào	mâu^{C}	mou^{C}	mûh	

[D] Gan-Wuning mɑu^{C1} 'to look at' <> [E] JP mu^{31} 'to see'

ab	冒[3]	mò	mək	mək	—	

Alternate reading for 'covetous' and the name Mào-dùn 冒頓, then read Mò-dú LH mək-tuət

-cd	帽媢瑁	mào	mâu^{C}	mou^{C}	mûh	

For an additional item of GSR 1062, see 5-37.

13-75	**= K. 1063**	**Mand.**	**MC**	**LHan**	**OCM**	
a	牡	mǔ, mǒu	məu^{B}	mu^{B}	muʔ R!	OCB *m(r)juʔ

[E] OKhmer jmol [cmo̤o̤l] 'male of animals'. See *EDOC;* Intro. 8.1.1.

13-76 **= K. 1109** See Baxter 1992: 467 for these rimes.

		Mand.	**MC**	**LHan**	**OCM**	
a	矛	máo	məu < mjəu	mu	mu R!	OCB *m(r)ju
c	茅	máo	mau	mɔu	mrû R!	OCB *mru
d	楙	mào !	mâu	mou	mû	
f	懋	mào	məu^{C}	mou^{C}	mûh	OCB *m(r)jus
h	敄	wù	mju$^{B/C}$	muo$^{B/C}$	moʔ, moh	
kl	婺騖	wù	mju^{C}	muo^{C}	moh	
o	鍪	móu	mjəu	mu	mu	
mnp	蝥蟊髳	máo	mjəu	mu	mu	
q	瞀	mào, mòu	måk, məu^{C}	mɔk, mo^{C}	mrôk(h)	

[E] WT rmogs-pa 'eyes heavy with sleep, inert'

r	楘	mù	muk	mok	môk	
s	鶩	wù	muk	mok	môk	
j	務	wù	mju^{C}	muo^{C} R!	moh	OCB *m(r)jos

[T] MTang mvu < mvuo, ONW muo 'make effort' <> [E] TB *mow > PL *mi(aw)^{2} 'work', WB mu 'do, perform'. <> PTai *hm-: S. mok^{D1} 'apply oneself'

t	霧	wù	mju^{C}	muo^{C}	moh	

[D] Yue-Guangzh mou^{22}, Min-Xiam bu^{33}, bɔ^{24}, Fuzh muɔ^{52} <> [E] TB *mu:k 'fog'

13-77 **= K. 1110** See Baxter 1992: 467 for these rimes.

		Mand.	**MC**	**LHan**	**OCM**	
a	牟 bellow	móu	mjəu	mu	mu	in dialects also 'to love'
bcd	侔眸麰	móu	mjəu	mu	mu	
e	侔	móu	məu < mjəu	mu	mu	

13-78	**= K. 1231**	**Mand.**	**MC**	**LHan**	**OCM**	
a	戊	wù //	məu^{C}	mu^{C} R!	muh	OCB *m(r)jus
f	茂	mào, mòu	məu^{C}	mu^{C} R!	muh R!	

14 OCM rime *-uk Jué bù 覺部

GSR 1016 - 1039

Baxter 1992: 518 ff. (§10.2.14)

See Table 13-1 for OCM rimes *-uŋ, *-uk, *-u in QYS categories; Table 16-1 for comparison of OCM rimes *-auk, *-uk, *-(i)au, *-(i)u, and Table 17-1 for comparison of OCM rimes *-ek, *-ak, *-auk, *-uk. No LHan high vocalic onset need be postulated with the high vowel *u*; however, *i* is inserted after acute initials.

14-1 = K. 1039 In the OB, the element above kǒu 口 is not niú 牛.

		Mand.	MC	LHan	OCM	
a	告	gù,	kuok,	kouk,	kûk,	
		gào	kâu^{C}	kou^{C}	kûkh < kluk(h)	OCB *kuks
	[T] ONW kɑu <> [E] Tai: S. klaau^{B1} < *kl- 'to say, declare' ⋇ lau^{B2} 'to tell, recount'					
e	誥	gào	kâu^{C}	kou^{C}	kûkh < klukh	
f	郜	gù,	kuok,	kouk,	kûk, kûkh	
		gào	kâu^{C}	kou^{C}		
kl	梏牿	gù	kuok	kouk	kûk	
	牿 [E] Also Tai: S. kɔɔk < gɔɔk 'pen, enclosure', kuk^{6} 'prison' <> LB *krok 'jail; pen'					
m	酷	kù	k^{h}uok	k^{h}ouk	khûk	
n	鵠 a bird	hú	ɣuok	gouk	gûk	
	target	gǔ !	kuok	kouk	kûk	'center of target'
o	窖	jiào	kau^{C}	kɔu^{C}	krûkh	= 13-47/1114i
h	皓	gǎo, hào	kâu^{B}	kou^{B}	kûʔ	
	⋇ 13-1/1040g 皞; 13-2/1244c 杲					
i	晧	hào	ɣâu^{B}	gou^{B}	gûʔ	[E] Tai: S. k^{h}aau^{A1} 'white'
j	浩	hào	ɣâu^{B}	gou^{B}	gûʔ	ONW ɣɑu

14-2	**= K. 1017**	**Mand.**	**MC**	**LHan**	**OCM**	
a	匊	jú	kjuk	kuk	kuk	OCB *k(r)juk
cdegfjk	掬椈菊踘蘜鞠簐		= a 匊			
h	鞠	jú	kjuk	kuk	kuk	[E] TB *kuk ~ *guk 'to bend'
i	麴	qū	k^{h}juk	k^{h}uk	khuk	

14-3	**= K. 1038**	**Mand.**	**MC**	**LHan**	**OCM**
a	學	xué	ɣåk	gɔk	grûk
	[T] Sin Sukchu SR ɣjaw (入), LR ɣjawʔ; MGZY (Hȳaw >) Hyaw (入) [ɣjaw]; ONW ɣäk				
d	斆	xiào	ɣau^{C}	gɔu^{C}	grûkh
f	覺 awake	jué	kåk	kɔk	krûk
	覺 awake intr.	jiào	kau^{C}	kɔu^{C}	krûk !

i	攪	jiǎo	kau^B	kɔu^B	krûʔ	
	[E] WT dkrog-pa 'to stir, scare'					
g	嚳	kù	k^{h}uok	k^{h}ouk	khûk	
h	鷽	xué, yuè	ɣåk, ʔåk	gɔuk, ʔɔuk	grûk, ʔrûk	

14-4	= K. 1045	Mand.	MC	LHan	OCM	
a	奧 interior	aò	ʔâu^C	ʔou^C	ʔûkh	
	cove	yù	ʔjuk	ʔuk	ʔuk	
bc	澳隩	aò, yù	ʔâu^C, ʔjuk	ʔou^C, ʔuk	ʔûkh, ʔuk	
	澳 [T] Sin Sukchu SR ʔaw (去); MGZY 'aw (去) [ʔaw]; ONW ʔɑu. [D] Min dial.: Fuzhou o^{C1}-t^{h}au^{A2}, Xiamen u^{C1} <> [E] Viet ao 'pool, pond'					
de	燠薁	yù	ʔjuk	ʔuk	ʔuk	
	燠 'warm' [E] WB uik (i.e. ʔuik) 'feel warm'					

14-5	= K. 1016	Mand.	MC	LHan	OCM	
a	毒 poison n.	dú	duok	douk	dûk	OCB *duk
	[T] ONW douk. MHan 身毒 śin-douk Hinduka <> [D] Yuè tuk^{D2}, Kèjia t^{h}uk^{D2}, Fuzh tøik^{D2} [E] WT gdug-pa 'poison'					
	毒 to poison	dù	dâu^C	dou^C	dûkh	
	[D] Yuè tou^{C2}, Kèjia t^{h}eu^{C1}, Mǐn Fuzh t^{h}au^{C1} 'to poison'					
b	纛	dú, dào	duok, dâu^C	douk, dou^C	dûk, dûkh	
-	裻	dū, dào	tuok	touk	—	SW 3702
-	蓫	dú	duok	douk	—	SW 266

14-6	= K. 1025	Mand.	MC	LHan	OCM	
a	祝 pray	zhù	tśjuk	tśuk	tuk	
	[T] Sin Sukchu SR tʂy (入); MGZY jÿu (入) [tʂy]					
	祝 curse	zhòu	tśjəu^C	tśu^C	tukh	OCB *tjuks
f	柷	chù, zhù	tś(^{h})juk	tś(^{h})uk	tuk, thuk	

14-7	= K. 1026	Mand.	MC	LHan	OCM	
a	孰	shú	źjuk	dźuk	duk	
	[T] ONW dźuk 'Which one, who?'					
b	熟	shóu, shú	źjuk	dźuk	duk	
	[T] Sin Sukchu SR ʐu (入), PR, LR ʐuʔ; MGZY zhÿu (入) [ʐy]; ONW dźuk [E] PKiranti *t^{h}ok ~ t^{h}uk 'ripen'					
c	塾	shú	źjuk	dźuk	duk	

14-8	= K. 1019	Mand.	MC	LHan	OCM	
a	竹	zhú	ṭjuk	ṭuk	truk	
	[T] Sin Sukchu SR tʂy (入), PR tʂuʔ; MGZY jÿu (入) [tʂy]; ONW ṭuk [E] S. tɔɔk^{D1L} < *pr- 'bamboo strip'					
c	筑	zhú	ṭjuk	ṭuk	truk	
de	築 e	zhú	ṭjuk	ṭuk	truk	
	[E] WT rdug 'to strike against'					
fg	竺篤	dǔ	tuok	touk	tûk	OCB *tuk
	[T] Sin Sukchu SR tu (入); MGZY du (入) [tu]. <> [E] WT 'thug-pa 'thick'					

14-9	**= K. 1075**	**Mand.**	**MC**	**LHan**	**OCM**	
a	晝	zhòu	tjəu^{C}	ṭu^{C}	trukh or truh	

[D] PMin *təu^{C} > Xiam, Fu'an tau^{C} 'afternoon'. Ch. -> Tai: S. truu^{B1} 'early morning'
[E] WT gdugs 'midday'

14-10	**= K. 1024**	**Mand.**	**MC**	**LHan**	**OCM**
ab	粥 鬻^{1} gruel	zhōu	tśjuk	tśuk	tuk

粥 [T] ONW tśuk <> [D] PMin *tšyk <> [E] WT t^{h}ug-pa 'soup, broth'

	Mand.	**MC**	**LHan**	**OCM**
鬻^{2} nourish	yù	jiuk	juk	luk

= 14-11/1020a 育; 14-12/1021a 毓. Zhōu was perhaps partially selected for semantic reasons <> [E] JP lu^{31} 'give birth'

14-11	**= K. 1020**	**Mand.**	**MC**	**LHan**	**OCM**	
a	育	yù	jiuk	juk	luk	OCB *ljuk

= 14-11/1024b 鬻^{2}; 14-12/1021a 毓 <> [E] JP lu^{31} 'give birth (to a child)'

14-12	**= K. 1021**	**Mand.**	**MC**	**LHan**	**OCM**	
a	毓	yù	jiuk	juk	luk	= 14-11/1020a 育

14-13 **= K. 1022** The initials could also be OCM *dr-, *d-, *thr-.

		Mand.	**MC**	**LHan**	**OCM**	
a	逐	zhú	ḍjuk	ḍuk	driuk < r-liuk	
d	篴	dí	diek	dek < deuk	liûk	OCB *liwk

= 13-30/1079 笛 <> [T] Sin Sukchu SR di (入); MGZY ti (入) [di]

		Mand.	**MC**	**LHan**	**OCM**
e	蓫	zhú, chù	ṭ^{h}juk, ḍjuk	ṭ^{h}uk, ḍuk	hriuk < r-lhiuk, driuk < r-liuk

OCB hlrjiwk

14-14	**= K. 1023**	**Mand.**	**MC**	**LHan**	**OCM**
ac	賣儥	yù	jiuk	juk	luk
e	覿	dí	diek	dek < deuk	liûk
fgh	匵嬻櫝	dú	duk	dok	lôk
ijk	殰瀆牘	dú	duk	dok	lôk
lno	犢讟遭	dú	duk	dok	lôk
m	讀	dú	duk	dok	lôk

[T] Sin Sukchu SR du (入); MGZY tu (入) [du]; ONW dok

		Mand.	**MC**	**LHan**	**OCM**
qr	韣黷	dú	duk	dok	lôk
s	竇	dòu, dú	dəu^{C}, duk	do^{C}, dok	lôkh, lôk
uv	續藚	xù	zjwok	ziok	s-lok
t	贖	shú	(d)źjwok	źok	m-lok

[E] WT blu-ba 'to buy off, ransom' ≭ blud-pa 'release, ransom' <> PTai *lu^{B2} 'to redeem, tribute', *dl/ru^{B2} 'to donate, ransom' <> AA-OKhmer /lɔk/, Khmer /luk/ ~ /ruk/ 'to sell, to fine'

14-15	**= K. 1018**	**Mand.**	**MC**	**LHan**	**OCM**
a	畜	xù	xjuk	huk	huk

[T] Sin Sukchu SR xy (入); MGZY hȳu (入) [xy]

	Mand.	**MC**	**LHan**	**OCM**
畜	chù	ṭ^{h}juk	ṭ^{h}uk	rhuk

[T] Sin Sukchu SR tṣ'y (入), PR tṣ'u?; MTang ṭ^{h}uk, ONW t^{h}uk
[E] TB *hu 'to rear, raise, nourish'

		Mand.	MC	LHan	OCM	
	畜	chù,	ṭʰjəu^C,	ṭʰu^C,	rhukh,	
		xiù	xjəu^C	hu^C	hukh	
cd	蓄稸	xù, chù	xjəu^C, ṭʰjəu^C	hu^C, ṭʰu^C	hukh, rhukh	
e	慉	xù	xjuk	huk	huk	
f	滀	chù	ṭʰjuk	ṭʰuk	rhuk	

14-16	**= K. 1032**	**Mand.**	**MC**	**LHan**	**OCM**	
a	六	liù	ljuk	liuk	ruk	OCB *C-rjuk
	[T] Sin Sukchu SR lu (入), PR, LR luʔ; MGZY lÿu (入) [ly]; ONW luk.					
	[D] PMin *lhok > NMin Jiànyáng so^{D2} <> [E] TB *d-ruk 'six'					
efh	坴陸稑	lù	ljuk	liuk	ruk	
i	睦	mù	mjuk	muk	mruk	

14-17	**= K. 1033**	**Mand.**	**MC**	**LHan**	**OCM**	
a	肉 flesh	ròu	ńźjuk	ńuk	nuk	
	[T] Sin Sukchu SR ru (入), LR ruʔ; MGZY Zhÿu (入) [ry]; ONW ńuk					
	肉 fleshy	rù	ńźjəu^C	ńu^C	nukh	
-	脜	róu	ńźjəu	ńu	—	

14-18	**= K. 1031**	**Mand.**	**MC**	**LHan**	**OCM**	All -ek < -euk
ag	a 菽	shū	śjuk	śuk	nhuk	OCB *stjiwk
	[E] LB *(s-)nok 'bean'					
b	叔	shū	śjuk	śuk	nhuk	
p	惄	nì	niek	nek < neuk	niûk	[E] WT gñog-pa 'to desire'
fxy	戚慼鏚	qì	tsʰiek	tsʰek	tshiûk < snhiûk	
	[N] Aspirated initials in OC are secondary, one source of tsh- is snh- that, given the phonetic *nhuk, seems to be the source of MC tsʰ- here. Since the nasal disappeared early, the syllable could then be used for words with original affricates.					
v	顣	cù, qì	tsjuk, tsʰiek	tsiuk, tsʰe(u)k	tsiuk, tshiûk	
tu	蹙 u	cù	tsjuk	tsiuk	tsiuk	OCB *Stjiwk
lm	寂家	jì	dziek	dzek	dziûk	
e	掓	cù	tsjuk	tsiuk	tsiuk	
k	踧	cù	tsjuk	tsiuk	tsiuk	
	踧	dí	diek	dek	diûk	
rs	r 蔋	dí	diek	dek	diûk	
j	淑	shū	źjuk	dźuk	diuk	OCB *djiwk
hi	俶諔	chù	tśʰjuk	tśʰuk	thiuk	
no	督裻	dū	tuok	touk	tûk	
q	椒	jiāo	tsjäu, tsieu	tsiau, tseu	—	OCB *tsjiw
	[D] Min *tsiau					

14-19	**= K. 1027**	**Mand.**	**MC**	**LHan**	**OCM**
a	鼀	cù	tsʰjuk	tsʰiuk	tshuk
b	竈	zào	tsâu^C	tsou^C	tsûkh

14-20	**= K. 1029**	**Mand.**	**MC**	**LHan**	**OCM**	
a	宿 pass night	sù	sjuk	siuk	suk	'pass the night'
	[T] ONW suk <> [D] M-Xiam lit. siok^{D1}, col. sik^{D1}					

	宿 mansion	xiù	sjəu^C	siu^C	sukh	ONW su
-	蓿 see 苜蓿 mù-xu 14-24					
c	縮	suō	ṣjuk	ṣuk	sruk	
	[T] ONW ṣuk <> [E] Khmer /cɔɔr/ 'be straight'					
d	蹜	suō	ṣjuk	ṣuk	sruk	

14-21	**= K. 1030**	**Mand.**	**MC**	**LHan**	**OCM**	
a	夙	sù	sjuk	siuk	suk	
	[D] M-Xiam (lit.) siok^{D1} <> [E] LB *C-sok 'morning'					

14-22	**= K. 1028**	**Mand.**	**MC**	**LHan**	**OCM**	
a	肅	sù	sjuk	siuk	siuk	ONW suk
cd	鱐驌	sù,	sjuk,	siuk,	siuk,	
		shōu	ṣjəu	ṣu	sriu	ONW ṣu
e	繡	xiù	sjəu^C	sɪu^C	siuh or siukh	
fg	嘯歗	xiào	sieu^C	seu^C	siûh	
h	簫 panpipe	xiāo	sieu	seu	siû	~ 16-33/1149e'
	[T] MHan sɨu; BTD sėu; ONW sėu; MTang sɨau > siau					
ijk	蕭瀟蟰	xiāo	sieu	seu	siû	

14-23	**= K. 1034**	**Mand.**	**MC**	**LHan**	**OCM**	
a	复	fù	bjuk	buk	buk	
d	復 return	fù	bjuk	buk	buk	OCB *b(r)juk
	[T] Sin Sukchu SR vu (入); MGZY hwu (入) [vu]; MTang bvuk, ONW buk					
	復 repeat	fù	bjəu^C	bu^C	bukh	
g	輹	fù	bjuk	buk	buk	
h	腹	fù	pjuk	puk	puk	[E] TB *pu:k 'cavern'
i	複	fù	pjuk	puk	puk	
j	蝮	fù	p^{h}juk	p^{h}uk	phuk	[E] TB *bu 'insect, snake'
m	覆 turn over	fù	p^{h}juk	p^{h}uk	phuk	
	[T] MTang pfu, ONW p^{h}u <> [E] TB: WT 'bubs 'put on a roof' ¤ spub- 'turn over', PL *pup 'turn over, search for'					
	覆 cover	fù	p^{h}jəu^C	p^{h}u^C	phukh	
l	覆 cover	fù	p^{h}jəu^C	p^{h}u^C	phukh	
k	愎	bì	bjək	bɨk	brək or bruk ?	

14-24	**= K. 1036**	**Mand.**	**MC**	**LHan**	**OCM**	
a	目	mù	mjuk	muk	muk	
	[T] Sin Sukchu SR mu (入); MGZY wu (入) [vu]; ONW muk; BTD 目揵連 muk-gɨan^B-lian Skt. Maudgalyāyana, Pkt. moggallāna <> [D] PMin *mok^{D2} <> [E] TB *mik ~ *myak 'eye'					
-	苜蓿 alfalfa	mù-xu	mjuk-sjuk	muk-siuk (< muk-suk) [SJ]		

14-25	**= K. 1035**	**Mand.**	**MC**	**LHan**	**OCM**	
a	穆	mù	mjuk	muk	muk	

15 OCM rime *-uŋ Dōng bù 冬部

GSR 1002 - 1015

Baxter 1992: 524 ff. (§10.2.15)

See Table 13-1 for OCM rimes *-uŋ, *-uk, *-u in QYS categories.

No LHan high vocalic onset need be postulated with the high vowel *u*; however, *i* is inserted after acute initials.

15-1	= K. 1006	Mand.	MC	LHan	OCM	
a	宫	gōng	kjuŋ	kuŋ	kuŋ	
	[T] ONW kuŋ (also written gōng 公 *kloŋ in Shijing) <> [E] AA-Mon gloŋ 'citadel, palace'					
fe	躬 e	gōng	kjuŋ	kuŋ	kuŋ	[E] TB *guŋ 'body'
hg	窮 g	qióng	gjuŋ	guŋ	guŋ	
	[T] Sin Sukchu SR gjuŋ (平); MGZY kÿung (平) [gjuŋ]					

15-2	= K. 1015	Mand.	MC	LHan	OCM	
-	夅	xiáng	ɣåŋ	gɔŋ	grûŋ	
a	降 go down	jiàng	kåŋ^C	kɔŋ^C	krûŋh	[T] ONW käŋ
	降 submit	xiáng	ɣåŋ	gɔŋ	grûŋ	[T] ONW ɣäŋ
-	絳	jiàng	kåŋ^C	kɔŋ^C		
d	洚	hóng, xiáng, jiàng	ɣuoŋ, guŋ gåŋ, kåŋ^C	go(u)ŋ, g/kɔŋ^C	grûŋ	and many other readings
f	隆 eminent	lóng	ljuŋ	liuŋ	ruŋ	OCB *g-rjuŋ
	[E] Khm ruŋ 'eminent'					
	隆 thunder	lóng	ljuŋ	liuŋ	ruŋ	[E] JP ruŋ^{31} 'rumbling'
g	癃	lóng	ljuŋ	liuŋ	ruŋ	
e	戇	zhuàng, hòng	ṭåŋ^C, xuŋ^C	ṭɔŋ^C, hoŋ^C	trûŋh, hôŋh	

15-3	= K. 1002	Mand.	MC	LHan	OCM	
a	冬	dōng	tuoŋ	touŋ	tûŋ	[T] ONW tauŋ
-	疼	téng	duoŋ	douŋ	dûŋ	[E] WT gduŋ-ba 'feel pain'
e	終	zhōng	tśjuŋ	tśuŋ	tuŋ	
	[T] Sin Sukchu SR tʂjuŋ (平), PR, LR tʂuŋ; MGZY jung (平) [tʂuŋ]; ONW tśuŋ					
	[E] Chepang doŋʔ- 'to end, cease', KN-Lai doŋ / doʔŋ 'to end'					
f	螽	zhōng	tśjuŋ	tśuŋ	tuŋ < tjuŋ ? = 15-4/1010e 蝩	
	[E] WB: kjuiŋ^B 'locust'					

15-4	= K. 1010	Mand.	MC	LHan	OCM	
a	眾	zhòng	tśjuŋ^C	tśuŋ^C	tuŋh = tjuŋh ?	
	[T] Sin Sukchu SR tʂjuŋ (去), PR, LR tʂuŋ; MGZY jung (去) [tʂuŋ]; ONW tśuŋ					
e	蝩	zhōng	tśjuŋ	tśuŋ	tuŋ = tjuŋ ? = 15-3/1002f 螽	

f	潨	zhōng,	tśjuŋ,	tśuŋ,	tuŋ,	
		cóng	dzu(o)ŋ	dzo(u)ŋ	dzûŋ, dzôŋ	

15-5	**= K. 1011**	**Mand.**	**MC**	**LHan**	**OCM**	
a	充	chōng	tś^{h}juŋ	tś^{h}uŋ	thuŋ	
b	統	tǒng !	t^{h}uoŋ^{C}	t^{h}ouŋ^{C}	thûŋh	

15-6	**= K. 1007**	**Mand.**	**MC**	**LHan**	**OCM**	
a	中 middle	zhōng	ṭjuŋ	ṭuŋ	truŋ	OCB *k-ljuŋ

[T] Sin Sukchu SR tʂjuŋ (平), PR, LR tʂuŋ; MGZY jung (平) [tʂuŋ]; MTang ṭuŋ, ONW tuŋ
[E] PMiao *ntrɔŋ^{A}

	中 hit the mid.	zhòng	ṭjuŋ^{C}	ṭuŋ^{C}	truŋh	
f	仲	zhòng	ḍjuŋ^{C}	ḍuŋ^{C}	druŋh	
jl	衷苹	zhōng	ṭjuŋ	ṭuŋ	truŋ	
k	忠	zhōng	ṭjuŋ	ṭuŋ	truŋ	[E] Tai: S. troŋ^{A1} 'faithful, loyal'
n	忡	chōng	ṭ^{h}juŋ	ṭ^{h}uŋ	thruŋ	
o	盅	chōng	ṭ^{h}juŋ,	ṭ^{h}uŋ,	thruŋ,	
			ḍjuŋ	ḍuŋ	druŋ	
p	沖	chōng !	ḍjuŋ	ḍuŋ	druŋ	[E] WT č^{h}uŋ-ba 'young'

15-7	**= K. 1009**	**Mand.**	**MC**	**LHan**	**OCM**	
ca	蟲>虫	chóng	ḍjuŋ	ḍuŋ	druŋ < r-luŋ	

[T] Sin Sukchu SR dʐjuŋ (平), PR dʐuŋ; MGZY cȳung (平) [dʐjuŋ]
虫 also writes 'snake' 28-23/1009. <> [E] TB *d-yuŋ bug

e	融	tóng	duoŋ	douŋ	lûŋ	= 15-8/1008e 彤
f	爞	tóng	duoŋ	douŋ	lûŋ	
d	融	róng	jiuŋ	juŋ	luŋ	

[T] ONW iuŋ <> [E] TB: PL *ʔ-loŋ[1] 'hot'

15-8	**= K. 1008**	**Mand.**	**MC**	**LHan**	**OCM**	
a	肜	róng	jiuŋ	juŋ	luŋ	
e	彤	tóng	duoŋ	douŋ	lûŋ	= 15-7/1009e 融

15-9	**= K. 1005**	**Mand.**	**MC**	**LHan**	**OCM**	
abgh	農 b 噥膿	nóng	nuoŋ	nouŋ	nûŋ	

[T] Sin Sukchu SR nuŋ (平); MGZY ñung (平) [ṇuŋ]; MTang noŋ, ONW nɑuŋ

-	儂	nóng	nuoŋ			
kl	穠禯	nóng	ṇjwoŋ,	ṇioŋ,	nroŋ,	
			ńźjwoŋ	ńoŋ	noŋ	
ij	濃醲	nóng	ṇjwoŋ,	ṇioŋ,	nroŋ,	PTai *hn- > S. nɔɔŋ^{A1} 'pus'
			nuŋ	noŋ	nôŋ	

膿 [T] MTang noŋ, ONW nɑuŋ <> [D] PMin *nhəŋ$^{(C)}$

15-10	**= K. 1013**	**Mand.**	**MC**	**LHan**	**OCM**	
a	戎	róng	ńźjuŋ	ńuŋ	nuŋ	

[T] Sin Sukchu SR rjuŋ (平); PR ruŋ; MGZY Zhȳung (平) [rjuŋ]; ONW ńuŋ

e	茙	róng	ńźjuŋ	ńuŋ	nuŋ	

15-11	**= K. 1012**	**Mand.**	**MC**	**LHan**	**OCM**	
a	嵩	sōng	sjuŋ	siuŋ	suŋ	= 12-13/1190f 崧

15-12	**= K. 1004**	**Mand.**	**MC**	**LHan**	**OCM**
a	宋	sòng	suoŋ^C	souŋ^C	sûŋh

15-13	**= K. 1003**	**Mand.**	**MC**	**LHan**	**OCM**
a	宗	zōng	tsuoŋ	tsouŋ	tsûŋ

[T] Sin Sukchu SR tsuŋ (平); MGZY dzung (平) [tsuŋ]; ONW tsauŋ
[E] WT rdzoŋ(s) 'castle, fortress'

f	綜	zōng, zòng	tsuoŋ^C	tsouŋ^C	tsûŋh
g	琮	cóng	dzuoŋ	dzouŋ	dzûŋ
h	崇	chóng	dẓjuŋ	dẓuŋ	dzruŋ

[T] Sin Sukchu SR dẓuŋ (平); MGZY cung (平) [dẓuŋ]
[E] Khmer /croŋ/ 'to raise up', crūṅa /cròoŋ/ 'be upright'; Riang tsərɔŋ, Khasi jrōŋ 'high'

15-14	**= K. 1014**	**Mand.**	**MC**	**LHan**	**OCM**
a	豐	fēng	pʰjuŋ	pʰuŋ	phuŋ

The phonetic element seems to be GSR 1197

e	豐麥	fēng	pʰjuŋ	pʰuŋ	phuŋ

15-15	**= K. 1253a**	**Mand.**	**MC**	**LHan**	**OCM**
a	賵	fèng	pʰjuŋ^C	pʰuŋ^C	pʰuŋh or pʰəŋh

16 OCM rime *-au Xiāo bù 宵部

GSR 1129 - 1171

Baxter 1992: 526 ff. (§10.2.16)

Table 17-1 compares OCM finals *-ek, *-ak, *-auk, *-uk.

Table 16-1: Comparison of OCM rimes *-auk,. *-uk, *-(i)au, *-(i)u

Div.	*-auk R.17	*-uk R.14	*-au R.16	*-u R.13, *-ukh R.14
I	鶴 ɣâk gɑk *gâuk 樂 lâk lɑk *râuk		高 kâu kɑu *kâu 毛 mâu mɑu *mâu 刀 tâu tɑu *tâu	好 xâu^{B} hou^{B} *hûʔ 寶 pâu^{B} pou^{B} *pûʔ 道 dâu^{B} dou^{B} *lûʔ 誥 kâu^{C} kou^{C} *kûkh
I	隺 ɣuok gouk *gâuk 沃 ʔuok ʔouk *ʔâuk 濼 luok louk *râuk	告 kuok kouk *kûk 毒 duok douk *dûk		
III	虐 ŋjak ŋɨɑk *ŋauk 約 ʔjak ʔɨɑk *ʔiauk 綽 tś^{h}jak tś^{h}ɑk *thauk 雀 tsjak tsiɑk *tsiauk	匊 kjuk kuk *kuk 目 mjuk muk *muk 竹 tjuk ṭuk *truk 六 ljuk liuk *ruk		浮 bjəu bu *bu 覆 p^{h}jəu^{C} p^{h}u^{C} *phukh 舟 tśjəu tśu *tu 祝 tśjəu^{C} tśu^{C} *tukh 劉 ljəu liu *ru
3/3 gr			喬 gjäu3 gɨɑu *gau 夭 ʔjäu^{B}3 ʔɨɑu^{B} *ʔauʔ 表 pjäu^{B}3 pɨɑu^{B} *pauʔ	
III ac			詔 tśjäu^{C} tśɑu^{C} *tauh	
IV	翟 diek deuk *liâuk 櫟 liek leuk *riâuk	惄 niek neuk *niûk 篴 diek deuk *liûk	窔 ʔieu^{C} ʔeu^{C} *ʔiâuh 堯 ŋieu ŋeu *ŋiâu 跳 dieu deu *liâu	梟 kieu keu *kiû 窈 ʔieu^{B} ʔeu^{B} *ʔiûʔ 鳥 tieu^{B} teu^{B} *tiûʔ 寥 lieu leu *riû
3/4			腰 ʔjiäu4 ʔiɑu *ʔiau 票 p^{h}jiäu4 p^{h}iau *phiau	糾 kjieu^{B}4 kiu^{B} *kiuʔ 謬 mjeu^{C}4 miu^{C} *mriuh 鏐 ljeu liu *riu
II	樂 ŋåk ŋɔk *ŋrâuk 卓 ṭåk ṭɔk *trauk 駮 påk pɔk *priâuk	學 ɣåk gɔk *grûk	交 kau kau *krâu 貌 mau^{C} mau^{C} *mrâuh 鐃 ṇau ṇau *nrâu	坳 ʔau ʔɔu *ʔriû 包 pau pɔu *prû 爪 tṣau^{B} tṣɔu^{B} *tsrûʔ 窖 kau^{C} kɔu^{C} *krûkh

16-1	**= K. 1129**	**Mand.**	**MC**	**LHan**	**OCM**	
a	高 high	gāo	kâu	kɑu	kâu	OCB *kaw

[T] Sin Sukchu SR kaw (平); MGZY gaw (平) [kaw]; ONW kɑu. MHan 高附 kɑu-buo^{C} Κάβουρα (Kabul)

	高 height	gāo	kâu^{C}	kɑu^{C}	kâuh
deh	d 暠縞	gǎo	kâu^{B}	kɑu^{B}	kâuʔ

[E] Tai: S. k^{h}au^{A1} 'white, clear, pale'

-fg	稿 fg	gǎo	kâu^B	kɑu^B	kâuʔ	
	[D] PMin *gɔ^{B1} 'rice straw'					
i	膏	gāo	kâu(^{C})	kɑu(^{C})	kâu, kâuh	
jk	槁 k dried	kǎo	k^{h}âu^B	k^{h}ɑu^B	khâuʔ	
	槁 an herb	gǎo	kâu^B	kɑu^B	kâuʔ	
a'	薧 dried fish	kǎo	k^{h}âu^B	k^{h}ɑu^B	khâuʔ	
l	犒	kào	k^{h}âu^C	k^{h}ɑu^C	khâuh	
s	敲	qiāo	k^{h}au(^{C})	k^{h}au(^{C})	khrâu, khrâuh	
mn	毫豪	háo	ɣâu	gɑu	gâu	
yz	壕譹	háo	ɣâu	gɑu	gâu	
o	鎬	hào	ɣâu^B	gɑu^B	gâuʔ	
q	蒿	hāo	xâu	hɑu	hâu	
b'	嚆	hāo !	xau	hau	hâu ?	= 16-9/1168b
v	翯	hè	xåk, ɣåk	hɔk, ɣɔk	hrâuk, grâuk	
u	熇	hè	xuok, xâk	houk, hɑk	hâuk	
t	謞 shout	xiào	xau^C	hau^C	hrâukh or hâuh ?	= x
x	嗃 stern	hè	xâk, xåk	hɑk, hɔk	hrâuk	
	shrill	xiào	xau^C	hau^C	hrâukh or hâuh ?	= t
c'	藃	hào, hè	xâu^C, xåk	hɑu^C, hɔk	hâukh, hrâuk	

16-2	**= K. 1244**	**Mand.**	**MC**	**LHan**	**OCM**
a	羔	gāo	kâu	kɑu	kâu
b	⿰木羔	gǔ, zhuó	kuok, tśjak	kouk, tśak	kâuk ~ kiauk
	[E] TB *kok 'bark, skin' > WB ə-k^{h}ok; WT skog-pa ~ kog-pa 'shell, peel, rind'				
-	⿱大羔	qiāo	k^{h}jiäu 4, k^{h}ieu	k^{h}eu	khiau
-	窯	yáo	jiäu or jiəu	jɑu	jau
-	溔⿰木羔	yǎo	jiäu^B	jɑu	jau

16-3	**= K. 1138**	**Mand.**	**MC**	**LHan**	**OCM**		
ace	喬[1] 僑 鐈	qiáo	gjäu 3	gɨɑu	gau	'high, tall'	OCB *ɦk(r)jaw
a	喬[2] arrogant	jiāo,	kjäu 3,	kɨɑu,	kau,		
		qiāo	k^{h}jäu 3	k^{h}ɨɑu	khau		
i	憍	jiāo	kjäu 3	kɨɑu	kau		
jklm	撟敽矯譑	jiǎo	kjäu^B 3	kɨɑu^B	kauʔ	[T] ONW kau	
d	嶠	jiào	gjäu(^{C}) 3	gɨɑu(^{C})	gau, gauh		
g	橋 bridge	qiáo	gjäu 3	gɨɑu	gau		
	sweep	jiào	kjäu^C 3	kɨɑu^C	kauh		
	energet.	jiǎo	kjäu^B 3	kɨɑu^B	kauʔ	'energetic'	
h	趫	qiáo	gjäu 3	gɨɑu	gau		
n	鷮	jiāo, qiáo	kjäu, gjäu 3	kɨɑu, gɨɑu	kau, gau		
o	驕 high	jiāo	kjäu 3	kɨɑu	kau	OCB *k(r)jaw	
	vigorous	qiāo	k^{h}jäu 3	k^{h}ɨɑu	khau		
	a dog	xiāo	hjäu 3	hɨɑu	hau		
p	繑	qiāo	k^{h}jäu 3	k^{h}ɨɑu	khau		
q	蹻 martial	jiǎo	kjäu^B 3	kɨɑu^B	kauʔ	OCB *k(r)jawʔ	
	蹻 sandal	jué	kjak	kɨɑk	kauk	= r	

	蹻 conceit.	jué	gjak	gɨɑk	gauk	
r	屩	jué	kjak	kɨɑk	kauk	= q

16-4	**= K. 1162**	**Mand.**	**MC**	**LHan**	**OCM**	
ab	敫噭	jiǎo	kieu^B	keu^B	kiâuʔ	= 16-6/1166y 皎
d	徼 seek	jiāo	kieu	keu	kiâu	
	limit	jiào	kieu^C	keu^C	kiâuh	
f	邀	yāo !	kieu	keu	kiâu	
c	噭	jiào	kieu^C, kiek	keu^C, kek	kiâuk, kiâukh	
e	激	jiào, jī	kieu^C, kiek	keu^C, kek	kiâuk, kiâukh	
g	撽	qiào, qī	k^{h}ieu^C, k^{h}iek	k^{h}eu^C, k^{h}ek	khiâuk, khiâukh	
h	竅	qiào	k^{h}ieu^C	k^{h}eu^C	khiâu(k)h	
1258e	繳	zhuó	tśjak	tśɑk	kiauk	

16-5	**= K. 1163**	**Mand.**	**MC**	**LHan**	**OCM**	
a	釗	zhāo, jiāo	kieu, tśjäu	keu, tśɑu	kiâu, kiau	= 16-15/1131r 鉊
		[E] Tai: Lao kiau^{B1} 'to reap, sickle', S. kiau^{B1} 'to cut with a sickle' ⋈ khiau^{A2} < *g- 'a sickle'				

16-6 **= K. 1166** Most or all words in this XS series could have had the OCM rime *-iau.

		Mand.	**MC**	**LHan**	**OCM**	
a	交	jiāo	kau	kau	krâu or kriâu	
		[T] ONW kău <> [E] TB *rjaw > WB ro^B (= rau^B) 'to mix, mingle', Kachin yau 'be mixed' ⋈ kəjau 'to mix, intermix'. <> PYao *klaau^3 'to pay'				
lmo	茭蛟鮫	jiāo	kau	kau	krâu	
n	郊	jiāo	kau	kau	krâu	OCB *kraw
g	咬 cry	jiāo	kau	kau	krâu	
		[E] TB: WB kro 'shout, call out', Lahu kù < *kru				
	咬 cry	yāo	ʔau	ʔau	ʔrâu or ʔau	
		[E] TB *a:w 'cry out'				
	咬 bite	yǎo	ŋau^B	ŋau^B	ŋrâuʔ	
		[D] PMin *ŋ̆au^B: Amoy ka^{C2}, Jiānglè hau^9 <> [E] TB: Chepang ŋaawh 'to bite'				
p	骹	qiāo	k^{h}au	k^{h}au	khrâu	'tibia, spoke of a wheel'
		[D] Min 'foot': *k^{h}au^{A1} > Amoy k^{h}a^{A1}				
c	烄	jiǎo	kau^B	kau^B	krâuʔ	
		[E] TB: WB kro ~ kyo 'to fry', JP krau^{33} 'dry up, overdry' ⋈ kă^{31}-rau^{33} 'dry over a fire'				
k	絞 twist	jiǎo	kau^B	kau^B	krâuʔ	
	a band	xiáo	ɣau	gau	grâu	
j	狡	jiǎo	kau^B	kau^B	krâuʔ	
e	佼 beautiful	jiǎo	kau^B	kau^B	krâuʔ	
f	姣 beautiful	jiāo !	kau^B	kau^B	krâuʔ	
	immoral	xiáo	ɣau	gau	grâu	
h	挍	jiào	kau^C	kau^C	krâuh	
qruv	恔效傚効	xiào	ɣau^C	gau^C	grâuh	
i	校 foot of t.	xiào	ɣau(^{B}/^{C})	gau(^{B}/^{C})	grâu, grâuʔ, grâuh	
	school	xiào	ɣau^C	gau^C	grâuh	⋈ 16-7/1167h
	foot fetters	jiào	kau^C	kau^C	krâuh	
	quickly	jiǎo	kau^B	kau^B	krâuʔ	

xy	晈皎	jiǎo	kieu^{B}	keu^{B}	kiâuʔ	= 16-4/1162b 皦 OCB *kewʔ
b'	較 bars	jué	kåk	kɔk	krâuk	= 16-7/1167m
	compare	jiào	kau^{C}	kau^{C}	krâukh (or krâuh ?)	
z	宎	yǎo	ʔieu^{B}	ʔeu^{B}	ʔiâuʔ	
a'	窔	yào	ʔieu^{C}	ʔeu^{C}	ʔiâuh	= 16-10/1141j 穾
	[E] TB Mru iu (i.e., ʔiu) 'dark'					

16-7 = K. 1167 Most or all words in this XS could have had the OCM rime *-iau.

		Mand.	MC	LHan	OCM	
ade	爻肴殽	yáo	ɣau	gau	grâu	
fhi	[爻支]敎教	jiào	kau^{C}	kau^{C}	krâuh	⪤ 16-6/1166i
	[T] Sin Sukchu SR kjaw (平去); MGZY (gȳaw >) gyaw (平去) [kjaw]; ONW käu					
	[D] Min *kau^{C}; Kejia *kau^{A1}. GSR 1167fg have additional BI forms.					
m	[車爻]	jué	kåk	kɔk	krâuk	= 16-6/1166b' 較

16-8 = K. 1041p-t 13-3/1041a kǎo 丂 OCM khûʔ is semantic and therefore not necessarily phonetic.

		Mand.	MC	LHan	OCM	
p	号	hào	ɣâu^{C}	ɣɑu^{C} [SW]		
q	號 cry out	háo	ɣâu	ɣɑu	ɦâu	OCB *gaw
	[E] TB *gaw ~ *kaw 'shout'					
	號 call	hào	ɣâu^{C}	ɣɑu^{C}	ɦâuh	OCB *gaws
	[T] Sin Sukchu SR ɣaw (去); MGZY Xaw (去) [ɣaw]; ONW ɣɑu					
r	呺 noise	háo	ɣâu	ɣɑu	ɦâu	
	vast	xiāo	xjäu 3	hɨɑu	hau	
s	枵	xiāo	xjäu 3	hɨɑu	hau	
t	鴞	xiāo	jäu 3	wɑu	wau	MC jäu 3 is a unique syllable

16-9 = K. 1168 16-7/1167) is not phonetic, nor is 13-31041 *khûʔ.

		Mand.	MC	LHan	OCM	
a	孝	xiào	xau^{C}	xau^{C}	hrâuh	
b	哮	xiào	xau(^{C})	xau(^{C})	hâu ?	= 16-1/1129b'

16-10 = K. 1141		Mand.	MC	LHan	OCM		
a	夭 bend	yǎo	ʔjäu^{B} 3	ʔɨɑu^{B}	ʔauʔ		
	夭 tender	yāo	ʔjäu 3	ʔɨɑu	ʔau	= c	OCB *ʔ(r)jaw
	[T] ONW ʔau 'delicate, slender'						
	夭 newborn	ǎo	ʔâu^{B}	ʔɑu^{B}	ʔâuʔ	= k	
c	枖 tender	yāo	ʔjäu 3	ʔɨɑu	ʔau	= a	
f	殀	yǎo	ʔjäu^{B} 3	ʔɨɑu^{B}	ʔauʔ		
	[T] ONW ʔau 'break off, die'						
degh	妖媄祅訞	yāo	ʔjäu 3	ʔɨɑu	ʔau	[T] ONW ʔau	
i	宎	yǎo	ʔieu^{B}	ʔeu^{B}	ʔiâuʔ		
j	穾	yǎo, yào	ʔieu($^{B/C}$)	ʔeu($^{B/C}$)	ʔiâu, ʔiâuʔ, ʔiâuh		
	= 16-6/1166a' 窔						
k	䴠	yǎo, ǎo	ʔâu^{B}	ʔɑu^{B}	ʔâuʔ	= a	
l	沃	wò	ʔuok	ʔouk	ʔâuk	OCB *ʔawk	
m	鋈	wù	ʔuok	ʔouk	ʔâuk		

1242a	飫 satiate	yù	ʔjwo^{C}	ʔɨɑ^{C}	ʔah	= 1-28/61e 於

16-11 = K. 1142		Mand.	MC	LHan	OCM	
ab	要[1]腰 waist	yāo	ʔjiäu 4	ʔiɑu	ʔiau	OCB *ʔjew
	[T] ONW ʔiau <> [E] PTai *ʔeu, S. sa-ʔeew 'waist'					
	要[2] import.	yào	ʔjiäu^{C} 4	ʔiɑu^{C}	ʔiauh	
	[T] Sin Sukchu SR ʔjew (平); MGZY ȳaw (平) [ʔjɛw] 'must, have to, want, will'					
cd	喓葽	yāo	ʔjiäu 4	ʔiɑu	ʔiau	

16-12 = K. 1140		Mand.	MC	LHan	OCM
a	囂 clamor	xiāo	xjäu 3	hɨɑu	hâu
	clamor	áo	ŋâu	ŋɑu	ŋâu

16-13 = K. 1130		Mand.	MC	LHan	OCM
ac	敖遨	aó	ŋâu	ŋɑu	ŋâu
efgk	嗷嶅摮鰲	aó	ŋâu	ŋɑu	ŋâu
h	熬	aó	ŋâu	ŋɑu	ŋâu
	[E] ST *ŋau: TB *r-ŋaw (STC no. 270) > WT rŋod-pa, brŋos 'to parch, roast, fry'				
jmo	獒驁鼇	áo	ŋâu	ŋɑu	ŋâu
l	警 reckless	áo, yáo	ŋâu, ŋau	ŋɑu, ŋau	ŋâu, ŋrâu
	jest	ào	ŋâu^{C}	ŋɑu^{C}	ŋâuh
d	傲	aò	ŋâu^{C}	ŋɑu^{C}	ŋâuh
	[T] Sin Sukchu SR ŋaw (去); PR aw; LR aw; MGZY ngaw (去) [ŋaw]				

16-14 = K. 1164		Mand.	MC	LHan	OCM	
-a	垚堯	yáo	ŋieu	ŋeu	ŋiâu	OCB *ŋew
	[T] BTD ŋėu; ONW nŋėu					
b	僥 dwarf	yáo	ŋieu	ŋeu	ŋiâu	
	luck	jiǎo	kieu^{B}	keu^{B}	kiâuʔ	
lno	蕘襓饒	ráo	ńźjäu	ńɑu	ŋiau	
m	蟯	náo, ráo	ńźjäu	ńɑu	ŋiau	
k	繞	rǎo	ńźjäu^{B}	ńɑu^{B}	ŋiauʔ	OCB **ŋjew
	[T] ONW ńau; MTang ńau					
qr	譊鐃	náo	ṇau	ṇau	nrâu or nriâu	
p	橈 oar	ráo	ńźjäu	ńɑu	nau or niau	
	[E] MK: Khmer thnaol 'punting pole'					
	橈 bend	náo !	ṇau^{C}	ṇau^{C}	nrâuh or nriâuh	
t	燒	shāo	śjäu	śɑu, tśʰɑu	ŋhiau or nhiau ?	OCB **hŋjew
	[T] BTD śau; ONW śau; Sin Sukchu SR ʂjew (平), PR ʂjew; MGZY shew (平) [ʂɛw]					
	[D] PWMin *tšhiau, PEMin *šiau 'roast'					
s	撓	náo, hāo	ṇau^{B} !, xâu	ṇau^{B}, hɑu	nrâuʔ, hnâu or hâu	⋇ 16-27/1152a
h	翹	qiáo	gjiäu 4	giau	giau	
c	澆	jiāo	kieu	keu	kiâu	
d	驍	qiāo	kʰieu	kʰeu	khiâu	
ij	磽墝	qiāo, qiǎo	kʰau, kʰieu^{B}	kʰau, kʰeu^{B}	khriâu	
e	曉	xiāo	xieu	heu	hiâu	

		Mand.	MC	LHan	OCM	
f	曉	xiǎo	xieu^B	heu^B	hiâuʔ	
	[T] Sin Sukchu SR xjew (上), PR xjaw; MGZY hyaw (上) [xjɛw]					
	[E] PYao hiu^3 'to know'; MK-Viet. hiểu 'to know'					
g	膮	xiāo	xieu(^{B})	heu(^{B})	hiâu, hiâuʔ	

16-15 = K. 1131/2		**Mand.**	**MC**	**LHan**	**OCM**	
1131a	刀 knife	dāo	tâu	tɑu	tâu	OCB *taw
	[T] ONW tɑu <> [E] ? Area word or CH loan: e.g., TB-Karen *ʔdo 'knife', JP n^{31}-do^{31} 'short knife', Viet. daw 'sword', Stieng taaw. For dāo 舠魛 'small boat', see under 10-2/125a					
	刀刁 flutter	diāo	tieu	teu	tiâu	
c	忉	dāo	tâu	tɑu	tâu	[T] Khot. ttāva
d	叨	tāo	t^{h}âu	t^{h}ɑu	thâu	
1132a	到侄	dào	tâu^C	tɑu^C	tâuh	
	[T] Sin Sukchu SR taw (去); MGZY daw (去) [taw]; ONW tɑu					
c	倒	dǎo	tâu$^{B/C}$	tɑu$^{B/C}$	tâuʔ, tâuh	[T] ONW tɑu
	[E] TB: JP du^{55} 'to pour (from a pot)', PVM *toh 'to pour' <> Tai: S. tok^{D1S} 'to fall down'					
d	菿	dào, zhuō	tâu^C, ṭåk	tɑu^C, ṭɔk	tâukh, trâuk	
1131e	召 call	zhào	ḍjäu^C	ḍiɑu^C	drauh	OCB *drjaws
	[E] Tai: S. rɨak^{A2} 'call'					
	Pl.N.	shào	źjäu^C	dźɑu^C	dauh	
l	招	zhāo	tśjäu	tśɑu	tau	[T] ONW tśɑu
q	詔	zhào	tśjäu^C	tśɑu^C	tauh	
j	超	chāo	ṭ^{h}jäu	ṭ^{h}iɑu	thrau	OCB *thrjaw
	[T] BTD t^{h}au; ONW t^{h}au; MTang ṭ^{h}au					
i	怊	chāo	ṭ^{h}jäu, tś^{h}jäu	ṭ^{h}iɑu, tś^{h}ɑu	thrau, thau	
k	軺	yáo	jiäu	jɑu	lau or jau	
c'	貂	diāo	tieu	teu	tiâu	
d'	苕 a pea	tiáo	dieu	deu	diâu	
	reed	diāo	tieu	teu	tiâu	
e'	鞀	táo	dâu	dɑu	dâu	
m	昭 bright	zhāo	tśjäu	tśɑu	tiau < kiau	OCB *tjaw
	[N] Acc. to SW zhāo 釗 (tśjiäu, kieu) is a loan graph for 昭, therefore the OC stem was prob. *kiau (not *tiau), note also the allofams jiǎo 皎皦 and qiāo 饒)					
	昭 glorious	zhǎo	tśjäu^B	tśɑu^B	tiauʔ < kiauʔ	
	昭 shrined	cháo	źjäu	dźɑu	diau < giau	
no	炤照	zhào	tśjäu^C	tśɑu^C	tiau < kiauh	
	[T] Sin Sukchu SR tʂjew (去); MGZY jew (去) [tʂɛw]; ONW tśɑu					
r	鉊 sickle	zhāo	tśjäu	tśɑu	kiau !	= 16-5/1163a 釗
p	沼 pool	zhǎo	tśjäu^B	tśɑu^B	tauʔ	OCB *tjawʔ
		zhǎo	tśjäu^C	tśɑu^C	tauh	OCB *tjaws
s	弨	chāo	tś^{h}jäu(^{B})	tś^{h}ɑu(^{B})	thau, thauʔ	
t	邵	shào	źjäu^C	dźɑu^C	dauh	
z	紹	shào	źjäu^B	dźɑu^B	dauʔ	
a'b'	韶磬	sháo	źjäu	dźɑu	dau	

16-16 = K. 1133		**Mand.**	**MC**	**LHan**	**OCM**	
a	盜	dào	dâu^C	dɑu^C	dâuh	OCB *daw(k)s

16-17 = K. 1143		**Mand.**	**MC**	**LHan**	**OCM**	
a	朝 morning	zhāo	tjäu	ṭiau	trau	OCB *trjaw

[T] ONW tau <> [E] Tai: S. p^{h}rau^{A2} < *br- 'morning'

	朝 audience	cháo	ḍjäu	ḍiau	drau	OCB *ɦtrjaw
d	潮 tide	cháo	ḍjäu	ḍiau	drau	
1160a	廟	miào	mjäu^C 3	mɨau^C	mrauh	OCB *m(r)jaws

[E] ? MY *prau^2 < *br- 'house'

16-18 = K. 1146		**Mand.**	**MC**	**LHan**	**OCM**
a	肇	zhào	ḍjäu^B	ḍiau^B	drauʔ

16-19 = K. 1147		**Mand.**	**MC**	**LHan**	**OCM**
a	鼂	cháo	ḍjäu	ḍiau	drau

16-20 = K. 1145		**Mand.**	**MC**	**LHan**	**OCM**	
abc	兆垗旐	zhào	ḍjäu^B	ḍiau^B	drauʔ < r-lauʔ	OCB *drjawʔ

[E] TB: Chepang hrawʔ- 'forebode, potend ill fortune, be ill'

dg	姚珧	yáo	jiäu	jau	lau	
u	桃	táo	dâu	dau	lâu	OCB *g-law

[E] MY *glaau^{3A} 'peach'

v	逃	táo	dâu	dau	lâu	
xy	鞉鼗	táo	dâu	dau	lâu	
s	洮 pour	táo !	t^{h}âu	t^{h}au	lhâu	

[T] ONW t^{h}au <> [E] PMiao *ʔleuʔ^A 'to pour'

	洮 Pl.N.	dào	dâu^B	dau^B	lâuʔ	
	洮 a lake	yáo	jiäu [GY]			'name of a lake'
t	咷	táo, tiào	dâu, t^{h}ieu^C	dau, t^{h}eu^C	lâu, lhiâuh	
z	駣	táo, dào	dâu(^{B})	dau(^{B})	lâu(ʔ)	
o	挑 provoke	tiāo	t^{h}ieu	t^{h}eu	lhiâu	

[T] Sin Sukchu SR t'jew (平), PR t'jaw; MGZY thyaw (平) [t'jɛw]. MHan 撲挑 p^{h}ok-deuʔ/-t^{h}eu < *phôk-liâuʔ Puśkalāvati, Πευκελαῶτις

	caper	diào	dieu^B	deu^B	liâuʔ	
	restless	tāo	t^{h}âu	t^{h}au	lhâu	
h	銚 hoe	tiāo, qiāo	t^{h}ieu, ts^{h}jäu	t^{h}eu, ts^{h}iau	lhiâu, slhiâu	
	lance	tiáo	dieu	deu	liâu	
ik	恌祧	tiāo	t^{h}ieu	t^{h}eu	lhiâu	
jlm	眺覜頫	tiào	t^{h}ieu^C	t^{h}eu^C	lhiâuh	
n	佻 usurp	tiāo, tiáo	t^{h}ieu, dieu	t^{h}eu, deu	lhiâu, liâu	
	go/come	tiáo	dieu(^{B})	deu(^{B})	liâu, liâuʔ	
r	誂	diào	dieu^B	deu^B	liâuʔ	
p	跳	tiào !	dieu	deu	liâu	
q	窕[1] perfor.	tiǎo !	dieu^B	deu^B	liâuʔ	'perforate'
	窈窕[2]	yǎo-tiǎo	ʔieu^B-dieu^B	ʔeu^B-deu^B	ʔiûʔ-liûʔ ?	~ 窈糾 'beautiful'
	窕[3] small	tiāo	t^{h}ieu	t^{h}eu	lhiâu	

16-21 = K. 1144		**Mand.**	**MC**	**LHan**	**OCM**
abc	䍃窰窯	yáo	jiäu	jau	jau

		Mand.	MC	LHan	OCM	
defhijkl-	傜傜媱榣瑤謠遙鰩愮 same as a 䍃 yáo					
g	搖	yáo	jiäu	jau	jau	
	[T] Sin Sukchu SR jew (平); MGZY yew (平) [jɛw]; ONW iau <> [D] Min *iau					
	[E] TB: WT g-yo-ba 'to move, shake, change place'					
m	鷂	yào	jiäu^{C}	jau^{C}	jauh	
n	繇 follow	yáo	jiäu	jau	jau	
	OB pron.	zhòu	ḍjəu^{C}	ḍu^{C}	druh < r-luh or r-juh ?	
	'oracle pronouncement'; loan for yóu 13-30/1079 由					
o	櫾	yóu	jiəu	ju	ju	

16-22 = K. 1149e The element 小 is semantic (so SW), not phonetic; MC s- and ś- do not mix in XS.

		Mand.	MC	LHan	OCM	
e	少 few	shǎo	śjäu^{B}	śau^{B}	hjau ?	OCB *h(l)jew?
	[T] ONW śau <> [D] Min-Amoy tsio[53]					
	少 young	shào	śjäu^{C}	śau^{C}	hjauh ?	
	[T] Sin Sukchu SR ʂjew (上), PR ʂjaw; MGZY shew (上) [ʂɛw]; ONW śau					
-	炒	chǎo	tʂʰau^{B}	tʂʰau^{B}	—	[D] M *tšhau^{B}

16-23 = K. 1135		Mand.	MC	LHan	OCM
a	勞 toil	láo	lâu	lau	râu
	[T] Sin Sukchu SR law (平); MGZY law (平) [law]				
	勞 recomp.	lào	lâu^{C}	lau^{C}	râuh
-	癆	lào	lâu^{C}	lau^{C}	—
b	膋	liáo	lieu	leu	riâu
	= 11-24/1151p 膫 <> [T] ONW lėu				

16-24 = K. 1151		Mand.	MC	LHan	OCM	
ab	尞 b	liào	ljäu^{C}	liau^{C}	riauh	
	[T] Sin Sukchu SR ljew (平上), PR ljaw; MGZY lew (上去) [lɛw]					
e	燎	liáo, liào	ljäu(^{C}),lieu^{C}	liau(^{C}), leu^{C}	riau, riauh, riâuh	
h-i	僚嫽寮	liáo	lieu(^{B})	leu(^{B})	riâu, riâuʔ	
g	繚	liǎo, liáo	ljäu^{B}, lieu^{B}	liau^{B}, leu^{B}	riauʔ, riâuʔ	⤧ 16-6/1166k jiǎo 絞
f	療 cure	liào	ljäu^{C}	liau^{C}	riaukh	= 17-8/1125a 樂[4]
	[E] TB: Mru rok / tarok 'to cure'					
o	瞭	liǎo	lieu(^{B})	leu(^{B})	riâu, riâuʔ	
s	橑	lǎo, liáo	lâu^{B}, lieu	lau^{B}, leu	râuʔ, riâu	
t	簝	láo, liáo	lâu, lieu	lau, leu	râu, riâu	
mnqr	憭獠遼鷯	liáo	lieu	leu	riâu	
p	膫	liáo	lieu	leu	riâu	
	= 11-23/1135b 膋 <> [T] ONW lėu					
uv	潦 v	lǎo	lâu^{B}	lau^{B}	râuʔ	

16-25		Mand.	MC	LHan	OCM
-	了	liǎo	lieu^{B}	leu^{B}	

[T] ONW lėu; MTang liau > liau; MGZY lɛw^{B}, ZYYY ljɛwˇ, Sin-SR ljew^{B}, PR ljaw; LMing General and Southern liau <> [E] Viet rồi 'finished', Lang-lo ṣoy; Tai: S. lew[5]

16-26 = K. 1245	**Mand.**	**MC**	**LHan**	**OCM**
c 料	liào	lieu(C)	leu(C)	riâu(h) or riû(h)
d 漖	liáo	lieu	leu	riâu or riû

16-27 = K. 1152 13-14/1071 yōu 憂 looks like the phonetic that includes the drawing of a person that, however, is later interpreted as 'monkey' and hence applied to náo.

	Mand.	**MC**	**LHan**	**OCM**	
b 獿	náo	nâu	nɑu	nâu	
= 13-48/1105g 猱; 13-49 夒 (*nû)					
a 擾	rǎo	ńźjäu^B	ńɑu^B	nauʔ	≍ 16-14/1164s nǎo 撓

16-28 = K. 1244	**Mand.**	**MC**	**LHan**	**OCM**
- 惱	nǎo	nâu^B	nɑu^B	nâuʔ
= 16-14/1164s nǎo 撓 <> [T] ONW nɑu <> [E] WB nok 'dirty, foul, turbid' <> [N] Also related to 25-34/189a 奻 nuán, *nrôn 'to quarrel' [SW]				
f 腦	nǎo	nâu^B	nɑu^B or nou^B	nâuʔ or nûʔ = 16-28A
[T] Sin Sukchu SR naw (上); MGZY naw (上) [naw]. <> [E] TB *nuk 'brain'				

16-28A = K. 1244g	**Mand.**	**MC**	**LHan**	**OCM**
g 㛴	nǎo	nâu^B	nɑu^B or nou^B	nâuʔ or nûʔ = 16-28f

16-29 = K. 1244	**Mand.**	**MC**	**LHan**	**OCM**
ij 呶怓	náo	ṇau	ṇau	nrâu
[N] The 女 element is semantic ('woman' = moral terpitude) and not (primarily) phonetic.				

16-30 = K. 1134	**Mand.**	**MC**	**LHan**	**OCM**	
ac 喿譟	sào	sâu^C	sɑu^C	sâuh	
e 臊	sāo	sâu	sɑu	sâu	
[T] ONW sɑu <> [D] Min-Amoy tsʰo55 <> [E] TB *sa:w					
f 鱢	sāo	sâu	sɑu, S tsʰɑu	sâu ~ C-sâu ?	
[D] PMin *tshɑu 'rank, fishy' <> [E] TB *saw ~ *su 'rot, decay'					
d 燥	zào	sâu$^{B/C}$	sɑu$^{B/C}$	sâuʔ, sâuh	
m 操 grasp	cāo	tsʰâu !	tsʰɑu	tshâu	ONW tsʰɑu
principle	cào	tsʰâu^C	tsʰɑu^C	tshâuh	
l 慅	cǎo	tsʰâu^B	tsʰɑu^B	tshâuʔ < C-sâuʔ	
also written 38-29/647e 慘					
gnhi 澡藻璪繰	zǎo	tsâu^B	tsɑu^B	tsâuʔ	
澡 [T] MHan 護澡 ɣuɑ^C-tsɑuʔ = waxšab <> [E] MY *ntsˡaau3 $^{B/C}$ 'to wash (bathe)'					
jk 趮躁	zào	tsâu^C	tsɑu^C	tsâuh	

16-31 = K. 1148 The OC rime could also be *-iau.

	Mand.	**MC**	**LHan**	**OCM**
a 焦	jiāo	tsjäu	tsiɑu	tsau
[T] Sin Sukchu SR tsjew (平); PR tsjaw; MGZY dzyaw (平) [tsjɛw]				
b 燋 roast	jiāo	tsjäu	tsiɑu	tsau
[E] TB *tsyow > WT 'tsʰod-pa ~ 'tsʰo-ba 'cook in boiling water, bake'				
燋 torch	jué, zhuó	tsjak, tṣåk	tsiɑk, tṣɔk	tsauk, tsrâuk

c	僬 underst.	jiào	tsjäu^{C}	tsiɑu^{C}	tsauh	'understand'
	dwarf	qiáo	dzjäu	dziau	dzau	
df	潐醮	jiào	tsjäu^{C}	tsiɑu^{C}	tsauh	
eg	蕉鷦	jiāo	tsjäu	tsiɑu	tsau	
hj	憔譙	qiáo	dzjäu	dziɑu	dzau	
i	樵	qiáo	dzjäu	dziɑu	dzau	
	[D] PMin*dzhau: Xiam lit. tsʰai^{A2}, col. tsʰa^{A2}					
k	噍 chew	jiào	dzjäu^{C}	dziɑu^{C}	dzauh	
	reduced	jiāo	tsjäu	tsiɑu	tsau	
	cry	jiū	tsjəu	tsiu	tsu	
lm	穛𥻮	zhuō	tṣåk	tṣɔk	tsrâuk	

16-32 = K. 1169		**Mand.**	**MC**	**LHan**	**OCM**	
a	巢	cháo	dẓau	dẓau	dzrâu	
	[T] Sin Sukchu SR dẓaw (平); MGZY caw (平) [dẓaw] <> [E] MY *rau² 'nest'					
b	剿 snatch	chāo	tṣʰau	tṣʰau	tshrâu	
	cut off	jiǎo	tsjäu^{B}	tsiau^{B}	tsauʔ	
c	勦 snatch	chāo	tṣʰau, dẓau	tṣʰau, dẓau	tshrâu, dzrâu	
	weary	jiǎo	tsjäu^{B}	tsiau^{B}	tsauʔ	
d	繅	sāo	sâu	sɑu	sâu	
e	薻	zǎo	tsâu^{B}	tsɑu^{B}	tsâuʔ	= 16-30/1134n

16-33 = K. 1149 In some words, the rime could be OC *-au. See also 16-22/1149e 少.

		Mand.	**MC**	**LHan**	**OCM**	
a	小	xiǎo	sjäu^{B}	siɑu^{B}	siauʔ	OCB *s(l)jewʔ
	[T] Sin Sukchu SR sjew (上), PR sjaw; MGZY sÿaw (上) [sjɛw]; ONW siau					
g	肖 resemble	xiào	sjäu^{C}	siɑu^{C}	siauh	
	disperse	xiāo	sjäu	siɑu	siau	
hjk	宵消痟	xiāo	sjäu	siɑu	siau	[T] ONW siau. OCB *s(l)jew
mno	逍銷霄	xiāo	sjäu	siɑu	siau	
l	綃	xiāo	sjäu, sieu	siɑu, seu	siau, siâu	
x	捎	xiāo	sieu	seu	siâu	
a'b'	筲蛸	shāo	ṣau	ṣau	sriâu	
y	梢	shāo	ṣau	ṣau	sriâu	
z	稍	shào	ṣau^{C}	ṣau^{C}	sriâuh	
c'	削 scrape	xuē, xuè, xiāo	sjak, sjäu^{C}	siɑk, siɑu^{C}	siauk, siaukh	[E] LB *sök 'scrape'
	削 a zone	shào	ṣau^{C}	ṣau^{C}	sriâuh	
d'	揱	xiāo,	sieu,	seu,	siâu,	
		shuò, shāo	ṣåk, ṣau,	ṣɔk, ṣau	sriau, sriauk	
e'	箾 panpipe	xiāo	sieu	seu	siâu	~ 14-22/1028h; ⋈ 17-7/1119a
	箾 a music	shuò	ṣåk	ṣɔk	sriâuk	
pqr	俏哨峭	qiào	tsʰjäu^{C}	tsʰiɑu^{C}	tshiauh < k-siauh ?	
s	悄	qiǎo	tsʰjäu^{B}	tsʰiɑu^{B}	tshiauʔ < k-siauʔ ?	
t	誚	qiào !	dzjäu^{C}	dziɑu^{C}	dziauh	
u	趙 hasten	zhào	ḍjäu^{B}	ḍiɑu^{B}	driauʔ	
	趙 pierce	diào	dieu^{B}	deu^{B}	diâuʔ	

16-34 = K. 1150 Acc. to Shuōwén, the element 夭 is not phonetic.

		Mand.	MC	LHan	OCM	
a	笑	xiào	sjäu^C	siɑu^C, S ts^{h}iɑu^C	sauh or siauh	OCB *sjaws

[D] PMin *tshiau^C

16-35 = K. 1153		Mand.	MC	LHan	OCM
a	表	biǎo	pjäu^B 3	pɨɑu^B	pauʔ

[T] MHan pau; BTD pau; ONW pau; MTang pau

16-36 = K. 1154 髟 biāo — see **13-71**

16-37 = K. 1155		Mand.	MC	LHan	OCM
a	猋	biāo	pjiäu 4	piɑu	piau

16-38 = K. 1156		Mand.	MC	LHan	OCM
a	驫	biāo	pjiäu 4, pjieu 4	piɑu, piu	piau, piu

16-39 = K. 1157			Mand.	MC	LHan	OCM		
ab	㶾票	flames	piāo	p^{h}jiäu	p^{h}iau	phiau		
		dry	piào	p^{h}jiäu^C	p^{h}iau^C	phiauh		
c	熛		biāo	pjiäu 4	piau	piau		

[E] Tai: S. pleeu^{A1} < *pl- 'flame' <> MK: Pearic phlaw ~ phlew 'fire'

d	標		biāo	pjiäu 4	piau	piau		
j	縹		piǎo	p^{h}jiäu^B 4	p^{h}iau^B	phiauʔ		
f	僄		piāo	p^{h}jiäu(^{C}) 4	p^{h}iau(^{C})	phiau, phiauh		
-	慓		piào	p^{h}jiäu^C 4	p^{h}iau^C	phiauh		
g	剽	quick	piào	p^{h}jiäu^C 4	p^{h}iau^C	phiauh		
		tip	piāo,	p^{h}jiäu 4,	p^{h}iau,	phiau,		
			biǎo	pjiäu^B 4	piau^B	piauʔ		
h	嘌		piāo	p^{h}jiäu 4	p^{h}iau	phiau		
i	漂		piāo	p^{h}jiäu 4	p^{h}iau	phiau	OCB *phjew	ONW p^{h}iau
-	薸		piāo	bjiäu 4	biau	biau		

[D] Min: Fúzh p^{h}iu^{A2}, Jiàn'ōu p^{h}iau^{C1}; Hakka p^{h}iau^{A2}, Guǎngzh p^{h}iu^{A2}

[E] MK: Viet bèo 'duckweed', WMon bew 'to ride low on the water'

e	飄	wind n.	piáo,biāo	bjiäu,pjiäu 4	biau, piau	biau, piau

[E] TB *pyaw > WT 'p^{h}yo-ba 'swim, soar, float'. <> ? PTai *pliu^{A1} 'float in the air'

	飄	blow	piāo	p^{h}jiäu 4	p^{h}iau	phiau
k	瓢		piáo	bjiäu 4	biau	biau
l	摽	fall	biào	bjiäu^B 4	biau^B	biauʔ
		crush	piāo, pāo	p^{h}jiäu 4,	p^{h}iau,	phiau,
				p^{h}ieu, p^{h}au	p^{h}eu, p^{h}ɔu	phiâu, phriâu
		lay down	pāo	p^{h}au	p^{h}ɔu	phriâu
		beckon	biāo	pjiäu 4	piau	piau

16-40 = K. 1170			Mand.	MC	LHan	OCM	
a	麃^1	deer	páo	bau	bau	brâu	'kind of deer'
ab	麃^2 儦	run	biāo	pjäu 3	pɨau	pau	'to run' OCB *p(r)jaw
cde	瀌穮鑣		biāo	pjäu 3	pɨau	pau	

fg	皫犥	piǎo	p^{h}jiäu^B 4	p^{h}iau^B	phiauʔ	

16-41 = K. 1137		**Mand.**	**MC**	**LHan**	**OCM**	
aecf	毛髦旄髳	máo	mâu	mɑu	mâu	

毛 [T] Sin Sukchu SR maw (平); MGZY maw (平) [maw]; ONW mɑu
[E] TB *r-maw 'hair', Kachin nmun nmau 'beard', LB *məwʔ 'hair'

g	芼 vegetable	máo	mâu	mɑu	mâu	
	cook	mào	mâu^C	mɑu^C	mâuh	OCB *maw(k)s
h	耄	mào	mâu^C	mɑu^C	mâuh	OCB *maw(k)s
i	眊	mào,	mâu^C,	mɑu^C,	mâukh,	
		mò	mâk, måk	mɔk	mrâuk	
j	秏 diminish	hào	xâu^C	hɑu^C	hmâuh	
	senile	mào	mâu^C	mɑu^C	—	Coblin 1983:218
k	耗	hào	xâu^C	hɑu^C	hmâuh	

16-42 = K. 1171		**Mand.**	**MC**	**LHan**	**OCM**
ab	皃貌	mào	mau^C	mau^C	mrâuh
c	藐 small	miǎo	mjiäu^B 4	miau^B	miauʔ
	far	mò	måk	mɔk	mrâuk
d	邈	miǎo !	måk	mɔk	mrâuk

16-43 = K. 1159		**Mand.**	**MC**	**LHan**	**OCM**	
a	苗	miáo	mjäu 3	mɨɑu	mau	OCB *m(r)jau
b	庿	= 16-17/1160a				
c	貓	māo	mau, mjäu 3	mau	mau	

[T] Sin Sukchu SR maw (平); MGZY maw, mew (平) [maw ~ mɛw]

16-44 = K. 1158 The element 少 is semantic, hence it is only partially phonetic.

		Mand.	**MC**	**LHan**	**OCM**	
acd	眇杪鈔	miǎo	mjiäu^B 4	miɑu^B	miauʔ	
e	渺	miǎo	mjiäu^B 4	miɑu^B	miauʔ	= 16-45/1161a 淼
b	妙	miào	mjiäu^C 4	miɑu^C	miauh	ONW miau

16-45 = K. 1161		**Mand.**	**MC**	**LHan**	**OCM**	
a	淼	miǎo	mjiäu^B 4	miɑu^B	miauʔ	= 16-44/1158e 渺

17 OCM rime *-auk Yào bù 藥部

GSR 1117 - 1128

Baxter 1992: 532 ff. (§10.2.17)

See Table 16-1 for comparison of OCM rimes *-auk, *-uk, *-(i)au, *-(i)u. The rime is mostly *-iauk, rarely *-auk. A diphthong in a short-stopped syllable goes against the structure of the CH language; perhaps the rime was really reduced to *-ɔk, which in LHan had changed to -ɑk, occasionally to *-ouk.

In this OC rime, retroflex initials do not exist in QYS Div. III (tjak < *-auk), they must have shifted into Div. II (QYS ṭɐk); therefore ṭåk derives from OCM *trauk, not trâuk.

Table 17-1: Comparison of OCM rimes *-ek, *-ak, *-auk, *-uk

Div.	*-ek R.8	*-ak R.2	*-auk R.17	*-uk R.14
I		各 kâk kɑk *kâk 郭 kwâk kuɑk *kwâk 落 lâk lɑk *râk 莫 mâk mɑk *mâk	鶴 ɣâk gɑk *gâuk 樂 lâk lɑk *râuk	
I			隺 ɣuok gouk *gâuk 沃 ʔuok ʔouk *ʔâuk 濼 luok louk *râuk	告 kuok kouk *kûk 毒 duok douk *dûk
III		郤 kʰjak kʰɨɑk *khak 攫 kjwak kyɑk *kwak (縛 bjwak buɑk *bak) 著 ḍjak ḍiɑk *drak	虐 ŋjak ŋɨɑk *ŋauk 約 ʔjak ʔɨɑk *ʔiauk 綽 tśʰjak tśʰɑk *thauk 雀 tsjak tsiɑk *tsiauk	匊 kjuk kuk *kuk 目 mjuk muk *muk 竹 ṭjuk ṭuk *truk 六 ljuk liuk *ruk
III ac	刺 tsʰjäk tsʰiek *tshek 易 jiäk jek *lek 役 jiwäk wek *wek	石 źjäk dźak *dak 亦 jiäk jak *jak 射 dźjäk źak *m-lak 夕 zjäk ziak *s-jak		
3/4 gr	益 ʔjiäk4 ʔiek *ʔek 辟 pjiäk4 piek *pek			
IV	擊 kiek kek *kêk 鶪 kiwek kuek *kwêk 厤 liek lek *rêk 覓 miek mek *mêk		翟 diek deuk *liâuk 櫟 liek leuk *riâuk	惄 niek neuk *niûk 篴 diek deuk *liûk
II	搹 kɛk kɛk *krêk 畫 ɣwɛk ɣuɛk *wrêk 脈 mɛk mɛk *mrêk 責 tṣɛk tṣɛk *tsrêk	客 kʰɐk kʰak *khrâk 宅 ḍɐk ḍak *drâk 百 pɐk pak *prâk	樂 ŋåk ŋɔk *ŋrâuk 卓 ṭåk ṭɔk *trauk 駁 påk pɔk *priâuk	學 ɣåk gɔk *grûk
3		戟 kjɐk kɨak *krak 碧 pjäk3 pɨak *prak ?		

This table shows how OC *-auk has merged in MC with reflexes of other OC rimes. It further suggests how in Div. III the rime *-auk > jak has pushed the expected MC Div. III -jak (from *-ak) final over into MC -jäk after acute initials where it merged with finals deriving from OC *-ek.

17 OCM *-auk 藥部 (GSR 1117-1128)

17-1	**= K. 1117**	**Mand.**	**MC**	**LHan**	**OCM**	
a	隺	hè	ɣuok	gouk	gûk or gâuk	
b	鶴	hè	ɣâk	gɑk < gɑuk	gâuk = glauk	
c	搉	què	kåk	kak	krâuk	
d	確	què	k^{h}åk	k^{h}ak	khrâuk	

17-2	**= K. 1118**	**Mand.**	**MC**	**LHan**	**OCM**	
a	虐	nuè	ŋjak	ŋɨɑk <ŋɨɑuk	ŋauk	OCB *ŋ(r)jawk
c	瘧	nuè	ŋjak	ŋɨɑk	ŋauk	

[E] Tai: S. ŋăk-ŋăk 'shivering' ⋊ hŋăk-hŋăk 'shivering' (as from ague)

d	謔	xuè	xjak	hɨɑk	hŋauk	

17-3	**= K. 1165**	**Mand.**	**MC**	**LHan**	**OCM**
a	弔 condol.	diào	tiek, tieu^{C}	tek, teu^{C}	tiâuk, tiâukh
	y. brother	shū 叔	see 14-18b		

[N] In the BI, 弔 writes 叔 shū LHan śuk 'junior brother, younger uncle' (14-18); the graph 叔 originally was designed for *nhiuk 'to harvest'.

d	盄	zhāo, diào	tśjäu	tśau	tiau

17-4 **= K. 1126** The default rime in this series was prob. -iâuk.

		Mand.	**MC**	**LHan**	**OCM**	
a	卓	zhuō	ṭåk	ṭɔk	trâuk	

[T] Sin Sukchu SR tʂwaw, LR tʂwawʔ; MGZY jwaw (入) [tʂwaw]; ONW täk

b	倬	zhuō	ṭåk	ṭɔk	trâuk	
cdf	逴趠踔	chuò	ṭ^{h}åk	ṭ^{h}ɔk	thrâuk	
g	綽	chuò	tś^{h}jak	tś^{h}ɑk	thâuk	OCB *thjawk
i	罩	zhào	ṭau^{C}	ṭau^{C}	trâukh	
j	淖	nào	ṇau^{C}	ṇau^{C}	nrâuh	
m	掉 move	diào	dieu$^{B/C}$	deu$^{B/C}$	diâuʔ, diâuh	
	arrange	nào	ṇåk	ṇɔk	nrâuk	
l	悼	dào	dâu^{C}	dɑu^{C}	dâukh	

17-5 **= K. 1120** This phonetic writes words of the type (C-)jauk. See also 17-16/1244k.

		Mand.	**MC**	**LHan**	**OCM**	
a	勺 ladle	sháo	źjak	dźɑk	diauk < giauk	= b
	勺 to ladle	zhuó	tśjak	tśɑk	tiauk < kiauk	= d
b	杓	sháo	źjak	dźɑk	diauk < giauk	

[E] TB *s-kyok 'ladle' > WT skyogs-pa 'scoop, ladle', WB yok 'ladle', JP tʃo^{31} 'ladle'

d	酌	zhuó	tśjak	tśɑk	tiauk < kiauk	
c	汋 ladle	sháo, zhuó,	tśjak, źjak,	tśɑk, dźɑk,	tiauk, diauk, = kiauk, d/giauk	
		yuè	jiak	jɑk <jɑuk	jauk	
f	灼	zhuó	tśjak	tśɑk	tiauk	⋊ h 的
g	礿	yuè	jiak	jɑk <jɑuk	jauk	
e	妁	zhuó, sháo	tśjak, źjak	tśɑk, źɑk	tiauk, diauk (or *ki-)	
hij	的 i 靮	dí	tiek	tek	tiâuk	
kl	釣魡	diào	tieu^{C}	teu^{C}	tiâukh	

[E] Tai: S. tok^{D1} 'to angle, fish with hook and line'

m	約 bind	yuē	ʔjak	ʔɨɑk < ʔiɑuk	ʔiauk	
	[E] ? TB: WB yok 'wind around, as thread'					
	約 bond	yào	ʔjiäu^{C} 4	ʔiɑu^{C}	ʔiaukh ?	
n	葯	yuè, wò	ʔjak, ʔåk	ʔɨɑk, ʔɔk	ʔiauk, ʔriâuk	

17-6	**= K. 1119**	**Mand.**	**MC**	**LHan**	**OCM**	
ac	龠籥	yuè	jiak	jɑk <jauk	jauk	'flute' OCB *ljewk
	OCM *j- is based on the assumption that yuè is related to 16-33/1149e' siâu 'flute' (= sjâu). For an explanation of the graph's top element, see 38-3.					
fg	爚禴	yuè	jiak	jɑk	jauk	
de	瀹[illegible]	yuè	jiak	jɑk	jauk	
h	龥	yù	jiu^{C}	jo^{C}	jokh	

17-7	**= K. 1124**	**Mand.**	**MC**	**LHan**	**OCM**	
a	翟	dí	diek	dek < deuk	liâuk	OCB *lewk
c	糴	dí	diek	dek	liâuk	
	[D] M-Xiam tiaʔ^{D2}, Y-Guangzh tɛk					
d	籊	tì, dí	tʰiek, diek	tʰek, dek	lhiâuk, liâuk	
f	躍	tì, yuè	tʰiek, jiak	tʰek, jɑk	lhiâuk, liauk	
g	擢	zhuó	ḍåk	ḍɔk	driauk < r-liauk	
mn	m 鑃	diào	dieu^{C}	deu^{C}	liâukh	
l	糶	tiào	tʰieu^{C}	tʰeu^{C}	lhiâukh	
	[D] M-Xiam tʰio^{C1}, Y-Guangzh tʰiu^{C}, K-Meix tʰiau^{C}					
e	趯	tì -tì	tʰiek-tʰiek	tʰek	lhiâuk	
ijk	曜燿耀	yào	jiäu^{C}	jau^{C}	liaukh	OCB *lja/ewk
h	濯	zhuó	ḍåk	ḍɔk	driauk < r-liauk	OCB *lrewk
	濯	zhào	ḍau^{C}	ḍau^{C}	driaukh < r-liaukh	
q	櫂	zhào	ḍau^{C}	ḍau^{C}	draukh < r-laukh	

17-8 **= K. 1125** The phonetic is *lì* 'oak' *riâuk, hence it writes words like *riauk, *rauk and *jauk. See *EDOC* Intr. 7.2.1; this Intro. 9.2.5.

		Mand.	**MC**	**LHan**	**OCM**	
ai	樂[1] > 櫟	lì	liek	lek < leuk	riâuk 'oak'	
a	樂[2] joy	lè	lâk, ŋau^{C}	lɑk, ŋau^{C}	râuk, ŋrâukh	OCB *g-rawk
	[T] Sin Sukchu SR law (入), LR lawʔ; MGZY law (入) [law]; ONW lɑk. See *EDOC* Intro. 5.2.; 5.4.					
	樂[3] music	yuè	ŋåk	ŋɔk	ŋrâuk	[T] ONW ŋäk
	樂[4] cure	liào	ljäu^{C}, lâk	liau^{C}, lɑk	riaukh, râuk ?	= 16-24/1151f
	= 16-24/1151f 療 <> [E] Mru rok / tarok 'to cure'					
j	礫 pebbles	lì	liek, lâk	lek, lɑk	riâuk	= 2-1/766u 珞
k	躒	lì	liek, lâk	lek, lɑk	riâuk	
d	轢	lì, lè	liek, lâk	lek, lɑk	riâuk	
e	讈	lè	lâk	lɑk	râuk	
g	濼	lù	luok	louk	râuk (or rûk ?)	
p	藥	yào	jiak	jɑk	jauk	[T] ONW iak
l	趮	shuò, lì	śjak, liek	śɑk, lek	hjauk, riâuk	
no	爍鑠	shuò	śjak	śɑk	hjauk	[T] ONW śak

17-9	**= K. 1123**	**Mand.**	**MC**	**LHan**	**OCM**	
a	弱	ruò	ńźjak	ńɑk < ńɑuk	niauk	
	[T] Sin Sukchu SR rjaw (入), LR rjawʔ; MGZY Zhew (入) [rɛw]; ONW ńak					
	[E] WT ñog-ñoŋ ‘soft, tender, weak’					
b	蒻	ruò	ńźjak	ńɑk	niauk	
c	愵	nì	niek	nek	niâuk	
d	溺 sink	nì	niek	nek	niâuk	
	[T] Sin Sukchu SR ni (入); MGZY ni (入) [ni]					
	溺 urine	niào	nieu^{C}	neu^{C}	niâu(k)h	= 17-10 尿
e	嫋	niǎo	nieu^{B}	neu^{B}	niâuʔ	

17-10		**Mand.**	**MC**	**LHan**	**OCM**	
-	尿	niào	nieu^{C}	neu^{C}	niâu(k)h	= 17-9/1123d 溺
	[E] PTai *ň- ~ n-: S. jiau^{B2} ‘to urinate’, Saek ɲuu^{B2}					

17-11	**= K. 1128**	**Mand.**	**MC**	**LHan**	**OCM**
a	鑿 to bore	zuò, záo	dzâk	dzɑk	dzâuk
	[E] TB-WB chok ‘chisel’				
	鑿 a hole	zào	dzâu^{C}	dzɑu^{C}	dzâukh
	鑿 rice	zuò	tsâk	tsɑk	tsâuk
b	糳	zuò	tsâk	tsɑk	tsâuk

17-12	**= K. 1121**	**Mand.**	**MC**	**LHan**	**OCM**	
a	爵	jué	tsjak	tsiɑk	tsiauk	OCB *tsjewk
	= 17-13/1122a 雀 <> [T] ONW ts(i)ak					
-	嚼	jiáo	dzjak	dziɑk	dziauk	
	[D] PMin *dzhiak ‘to eat’					
e	爝	jué	dzjak	dziɑk	dziauk	
f	穱	zhuó	tṣåk	tṣɔk	tsrâuk	
gh	灂釂	jiào	tsjäu^{C}	tsiau^{C}	tsiaukh	

17-13	**= K. 1122**	**Mand.**	**MC**	**LHan**	**OCM**	
a	雀 sparrow	què	tsjak	tsiɑk	tsiauk	= 17-12/1121a 爵

17-14	**= K. 1136**	**Mand.**	**MC**	**LHan**	**OCM**		
a	暴[1]	bào	bâu^{C}	bɑu^{C}	bâukh	‘violent’	OCB *bawks
ab	暴[2] 曝	pù	buk	bok	bôk	‘expose to sun’	
	[E] ? TB-Lushai pʰo^{H} ‘to dry or air in sunshine’						
c	瀑	bào	bâu^{C}	bɑu^{C}	bâukh		
d	襮	bú, bó	puok, pâk	pouk, pɑk	pâuk		
e	嚗	bó	påk	pɔk	pâuk	(no *r, onomatopoetic)	

17-15	**= K. 1127**	**Mand.**	**MC**	**LHan**	**OCM**	
ac	駁駮	bó	påk	pɔk	prâuk	OCB *pra/ewk

[E] TB: WB prok ‘be speckled, spotted’ ≭ ə-prok ‘decoration’, Mikir pʰròk ‘speckled’, JP prúʔ, Mru preu ‘of mixed color’. <> [N] 16-6/1166 could be phonetic.

17-16 = K. 1244k			**MC**	**LHan**	**OCM**
k	豹	bào	pau^C	pau^C	prâukh

[N] SW says that 17-5 勺 is phonetic. In GY, this element writes also words of the type *pr(i)auk, piau (always Div. IV, i.e., OC medial *i), hence 17-15 and 17-16 could have had an OC medial *i. Cognate to 17-15/1127 駁.

18 OCM rime *-ai Gē bù 歌部 (1)

GSR 1 - 31; 349 - 360

Baxter 1992: 413 ff. (§10.1.3)

See Table 21-1 for OCM rimes *-an, *-at, *-(t)s, *-ai in QYS categories. See Table 7-1 for a comparison of OC *-i, *-e and *-ai in QYS categories.

The OCM final *-ai 義 (> QYS Div. III -je) still rimes with OCM *-âi 歌 (> Div. I) in Early Han, but has merged with *-e in LHan, when 義 ŋɨe < *ŋai rimes with 帝 te^C < têh.

OC *-âi (gē 歌 MC Div. I) and *-râi (jiā 加 Div. II) have become LHan -ɑ and -a and fallen together with Rime 1 Div. II -a < *-râ (jiā 家), and with Div. III -ia < *-a (shè 舍), while MC OC *-a > MC -jwo (yú 魚) and *-â > MC -uo (tǔ 土) have already become LH -ɔ.

However, in the eastern (Shandong) dialect of Zhèng Xuán OC -âi has survived as *-ɑi; today's Min dialects and 'Old South' still have this final. LHan writes this archaic -ɑi for mainstream -ɑ.

A striking distributional oddity is the near absence of syllables of the type *Tai, while those of the type *(C)Lai abound (see the large phonetic series 18-7 and 18-8).

The OCM coda *-i in diphthongs behaves like a final consonant, hence a strictly phonemic transcription would write it as *-j, as in OCB (*-aj, *-əj, *-uj).

18-1 = K. 1			**Mand.**	**MC**	**LHan -a < -ai**	**OCM**	
-d	X = 柯		kē !	kâ	kɑ < kɑi	kâi	'axe handle'
	X = 丂 without kǒu 口 'mouth' <> [T] ONW kɑ 'axe handle'						
a	可		kě	k^{h}â^B	k^{h}ɑi^B	khâiʔ	
	[T] Sin Sukchu SR, PR, LR k'ɔ (上); MGZY kho (上) [k'ɔ]; ONW k^{h}ɑ [D] Yue-Guangzh ^{35}hɔ^{B1}; Ke-Meix k^{h}ɔ^B. <> [N] Kǒu 'mouth' is occasionally added to early pictographs, as here to the 'axe handle', to indicate that the graph is not used as originally intended but simply borrowed ('mouthed') for its sound or meaning.						
g	河		hé	ɣâ	gɑi	gâi	
i	苛		kē	ɣâ	gɑi	gâi	
f	何	carry	hè	ɣâ^B	gɑi^B	gâiʔ	
	[E] WT 'gel-ba, bkal 'to load, lay on' ⋈ sgal-ba 'to load a beast' ⋈ k^{h}al 'load, burden'						
	何	what	hé	ɣâ	gɑi	gâi	
	[T] Sin Sukchu SR ɣɔ (平), LR ɣɔ; MGZY Xo (平) [ɣɔ]; ONW ɣɑ [D] Y-Guangzh ^{21}hɔ^{A2} <> [E] WT ga-na 'where', ga-ru 'whither'						
o	荷	lotus	hé	ɣâ	gɑi	gâi	
	荷	carry	hè	ɣâ^B	gɑi^B	gâi^B	
-	舸牱		gē	kâ	kɑi	kâi	
-	軻		kē, kě	k^{h}â($^{B/C}$)	k^{h}ɑi	khâi	[T] ONW k^{h}ɑ
e	笴		gě	kâ^B,	kɑi^B,	kâiʔ,	'slender bamboo'
			gǎn	kân^B	kɑn^B	kânʔ	
	= 24-2/140k 簳; 24-1/139j 稈						

pqr 哥歌調 gē kâ kɑi kâi

[T] Sin Sukchu SR kɔ (平), LR kɔ; MGZY go (平) [kɔ]; ONW kɑ <> [D] Yue-Guangzh kɔ^{A1}, Ke-Meix kɔ^{A1}, PMin *kɑi <> [E] ? TB: Lushai kai^{L} / kaiʔ^{L} < kai / kaih 'to play' (a fiddle etc.), TGTM *^{B}gwai 'song', Chepang keʔ- 'sing well', JP kʰai^{31} 'tell' (a story).

m 阿 ā ʔâ ʔɑ < ʔɑi ʔâi

[T] ONW ʔɑ; BTD Skt. ʔa-, e.g. 阿迦貳吒 ʔɑ-ka-ńis-ṭa^{C} Skt. Akaniṣṭa; Han ʔâ-ŋui^{C} 阿魏 Tocharian B ankwaṣ 'asafoetida'; MHan 阿蠻 ʔɑ-man Armenia

jk 呵訶 hē hâ hɑi hâi

s 奇 strange qí gje 3 gɨe < gɨai gai OCB *găj

[T] Sin Sukchu SR gi (平); MGZY ki (平) [gi] <> [E] ? WB kʰai- < kai^{B} 'remarkable'

奇 odd jī kje 3 kɨe < kɨai kai

t 琦 qí gje 3 gɨai gai

v 錡 pot jì, qí, yǐ gje(^{B}), ŋje^{B} gɨai(^{B}), ŋɨai^{B} gai, gaiʔ, ŋaiʔ

chisel qí gje 3 gɨai gai

u 騎 to ride qí gje 3 gɨai gai

[T] Sui-Tang gi < ONW ge <> [D] PMin *ǧhiɑ 'to ride'

騎 rider jì gje^{C} 3 gɨai^{C} gaih

\- 徛 to stand jì gje^{B} 3 gɨai^{B} —

[T] ONW ge^{B} <> [D] PMin *ghiɑ^{B} ~ ǧiɑ 'to stand'.

a' 羇 bridle jī kje 3 kɨai kai = 18-3/1238a 羈 lodge

z 畸 jī kje 3 kɨai kai

y 掎 jǐ kje^{B} 3 kɨai^{B} kaiʔ

c' 踦 one-footed qī kʰje kʰɨai khai

loiter jǐ kje^{B} 3 kɨai^{B} kaiʔ

knock ag. jǐ, yǐ kje^{B} 3, ŋje^{B} kɨai^{B}, ŋɨai^{B} kaiʔ, ŋaiʔ

x 寄 jì kje^{C} 3 kɨai^{C} kaih

[E] WB khai^{C} 'to bring', Lushai kʰai^{L} 'to give a present'

c' 踦 one foot qī kʰje 3 kʰɨai khai

踦 loiter jǐ kje^{B} 3 kɨai^{B} kaiʔ

踦 knock ag. yǐ kje^{B}, ŋje^{B} 3 kɨai^{B}, ŋɨai^{B} kaiʔ, ŋaiʔ

d' 攲 slanting qī, jī kʰje, kje 3 kʰɨai, kɨai khai, kai

[E] WB kai 'oblique, sidewise'

e' 觭 qī kʰje 3 kʰɨai khai

b' 綺 qǐ kʰje^{B} 3 kʰɨai^{B} khaiʔ

g'j' 椅陭 yī ʔje 3 ʔɨai ʔai

i'l' 輢旖 yǐ ʔje^{B} 3 ʔɨai^{B} ʔaiʔ

f' 倚 yǐ ʔje^{B} 3 ʔɨai^{B} ʔaiʔ

[T] Sin Sukchu SR ʔi (上)

h' 猗 particle yī ʔje 3 ʔɨai ʔai

luxuriant yǐ ʔje^{B} 3 ʔɨai^{B} ʔaiʔ

luxuriant ě ʔâ^{B} ʔɑi^{B} ʔâiʔ

n 旑 ě, yǐ ʔâ^{B}, ʔje^{B} ʔɑi^{B}, ʔɨai^{B} ʔâiʔ, ʔaiʔ

18-2 = K. 349 Mand. MC LHan -a < -ai OCM

a 个 tally, item gè kâ^{C} kɑi^{C} kâih

target gàn kân^{B} kɑn^{C} kâns 'side of target'

18-3 = K. 1238a Mand. MC LHan -a < -ai OCM

a 羈 bridle jī kje 3 kɨai kai = 18-1/1a' 羇

18-4 = K. 15 Mand. MC LHan -a < -ai OCM

acd 加枷珈 jiā ka ka < kai krâi

加 [T] BTD Skt. ka- <> [E] WT kral 'to burden, tax' <> [N] For the role of kǒu, see 18-1/1a.

\- 迦 jiā ka, kja ka —

[T] BTD Skt. ka, -kya-: 阿迦貳吒 ʔɑ-ka-ńis-ṭa^{C} Skt. Akaniṣṭa; 釋迦文 śak-kja-mun Skt. śākyamuni

\- 伽 qié ga ga — [T] BTD 僧伽 səŋ-ga Skt. saṃgha

e 駕 jià ka^{C} kai^{C} krâih

[T] ONW kä <> [E] WT bkral-ba 'to impose, place upon' (tax), 'appoint to'

g 嘉 jiā ka kai krâi

[E] ? WT bkra-ba 'beautiful, blooming', bkra-šis 'happiness, prosperity, blessing' (šis 'good luck, fortune, bliss'); Lushai ṭ^{h}a^{L} / ṭ^{h}at^{L} < t^{h}raah / t^{h}rat 'be good'

i 哿 gě kâ^{B} kɑi^{B} kâi

j 賀 hè ɣâ^{C} gɑi^{C} gâih

\- 茄 qié gjâ —

[T] Sin Sukchu SR kje (平) <> [E] PTai *k^{h}ɨe^{A1} > S. k^{h}ɨa^{A1} 'eggplant'

[D] Yue-Guangzh k^{h}ɛ^{A2}, Taish k^{h}iɛ^{A2}; Ke-Meix kj^{h}io^{A2}; PMin *giɔ.

18-5 = K. 2 Mand. MC LHan -ie < -ɨai OCM

ar 我^{1} > 義 yì ŋje^{C} 3 ŋɨe^{C} < ŋɨai^{C} ŋaih

[N] The graph was probably created to write the name of a Shang period people Wǒ (or rather Yì) (often graphs for other ethnic groups include a weapon); 'sheep' was later added, as was done occasionally in ethnic names of nomadic herders, probably to distinguish the name from the conventional use of 我 for 'I'.

rv 義議 yì ŋje^{C} 3 ŋɨai^{C} ŋaih 'consider'

[T] Sin Sukchu SR i, (ŋi) (平), LR ŋi, i; MGZY ngi (平) [ŋi]; ONW ŋe

[E]TB *ŋay > KC-Lushai ŋai^{H} / ŋaiʔ^{L} < *ŋajs 'to think, consider', 'be necessary, have need to', 'be customary'

u 儀 dignity yí ŋje 3 ŋɨai ŋai = 18-6/21a 宜

儀 come yí ŋje 3 ŋɨai ŋai

[E] JP ŋai^{33} 'to come, arrive', NNaga *ŋoj

x 蟻 ant yǐ ŋje^{B} 3 ŋɨai^{B} ŋaiʔ

[T] Sin S. SR i (上); MGZY ngi (上) [ŋi] <> [D] PMin *ŋhiɑi^{B} <> [E] KN-Lai hŋeʔr- 'ant'

yz 羲犧 xī xje 3 hɨai hŋai

a 我^{2} 'I, we' wǒ ŋâ^{B} ŋɑi^{B} ŋâiʔ

[T] Sin Sukchu SR ŋɔ (上), PR, LR ɔ; MGZY ngo (上) [ŋɔ]; ONW ŋɑ

[D] Yue-Foshan ^{13}ŋɔi^{B2}; Ke-Meix ŋa^{B}, PMin *ŋɑi^{B}

[E] TB *ŋai: JP ŋai^{33} 'I', Mikir ne, Chepang ŋi ~ ni 'we', Lushai ŋei^{L} 'self'

h 俄 é ŋâ ŋɑi ŋâi [T] ONW ŋɑ

[D] Yue-Guangzh ŋɔ^{A2}; Min-Xiam go^{A2} <> [E] WB ŋai^{C} 'to lean, be inclined to one side'

i 娥 é ŋâ ŋɑi ŋâi

姮娥 héng-é 'name of the moon goddess': Tai: PTai *hŋai^{A1} 'moonlight', S. dɨan^{A1}-ŋaai^{A1} 'full moon', Po-ai *looŋ^{B2}-haai^{A1} 'moonlight' <> Cf. TB-Tamang ^{3}ŋia 'full moon'

p 鵝 é ŋâ ŋɑi ŋâi

[T] Sin Sukchu SR ŋɔ (平), PR ɔ; LR ɔ, ŋɔ; MGZY ngo (平) [NO]

[D] Yue-Guangzhōu ^{21}ŋɔ^{A2}; Ke-Meixian ŋɔ^{A2}; PMin *ŋiɑi, Xiamen giɑ^{A2}

klmn 峨睋莪誐 é ŋâ ŋɑi ŋâi

q 蛾 silkworm é ŋâ ŋɑi ŋâi Also loan for x 'ant'
o 餓 è ŋâ^C ŋɑi^C ŋâih
[E] TB-Lushai ŋhei^H 'to fast, go without (food, medicine)'

18-6	**= K. 21**	**Mand.**	**MC**	**LHan** -ie < -iai	**OCM**	
a	宜	yí	ŋje 3	ŋie < ŋiai	ŋai	= 18-5/2u 儀
h	誼	yì	ŋje^C 3	ŋiai^C	ŋaih	

18-7	**= K. 22**	**Mand.**	**MC**	**LHan**	**OCM**	
a	虘	xī	xje 3	hɨai	hai	
b	戲	xì	xje^C 3	hɨai^C	haih	

[T] Sin Sukchu SR xi (去); MGZY hi (去) [xi] <> [E] WT 'k^{h}yal-ba 'joke, jest' ⋈ (r)kyal-ka 'joke, jest, trick'; Lushai k^{h}aal^L / k^{h}alʔ^L 'to play with' ⋈ in^L-k^{h}eel^L 'to gamble, play'

- 檥 xī xje 3 hɨai = 桸
[D] Min: PMin *hiɑ 'ladle'

18-8	**= K. 3**	**Mand.**	**MC**	**LHan**	**OCM**	
al	多^1 > 誃	chǐ,	tś^{h}je^B,	tś^{h}e^B < tś^{h}ai^B,	k-hlaiʔ,	'to separate'
		chí	ḍje	ḍe < ḍiai	drai < r-lai	

[T] ONW tś^{h}e, de. <> [E] PL *C-klay$^{1/3}$ 'to separate'; Chepang kləyh-sa 'to break (as sticks)', Lushai hlai^R 'to flay, to skin, split (as cane)'
[N] The original graph shows two pieces of meat next to each other, hence probably 'to separate' (2 x 'meat' = 'many' looks like a folk etymology).
The phonetic *k-hlaiʔ was used to write words with OC *L in the initial; the reading *tlâi 'many' was used to write words that later MC T-like initials; the *(t)R-type initials came about partially for semantic reason, because the phonetic was writing words with the same rime and similar meanings 'separate, open, wide', etc.

i	侈	chǐ	tś^{h}je^B	tś^{h}ai^B	k-lhaiʔ	= q 移^1

[T] 侈哆移 MTang tś^{h}i, ONW tś^{h}e <> [E] OBurm klai, WB kyai 'wide, broad' ⋈ kyai^B 'wide apart' ⋈ k^{h}yai^B ~ k^{h}rai^C 'make wide apart, be diffused'

k	哆	chǐ,	tś^{h}je^B,	tś^{h}ai^B,	k-lhaiʔ
		chě	tś^{h}ja^B	tś^{h}ai^B	
t	痑	chǐ	tś^{h}je^B	tś^{h}ai^B	k-hlaiʔ
h	恀	chǐ !	tśje^B	tśai^B	taiʔ
-	姼	shí, shì,	źje(^{B}),	dźai(^{B}),	dai, daiʔ,
		duò	tâ^B	tɑi^B	tâiʔ

[E] PTai *tai 'maternal grandmother'

j	拸	chǐ	ṭ^{h}je^B	ṭ^{h}iai^B	rhaiʔ

[E] WT 'dral-ba 'to rip up' ⋈ hral-ba 'to rent'

m	趍	chí	ḍje	ḍiai	drai < r-lai	= 18-9/4x
o	陊	zhì	ḍje^B	ḍe^B, ḍiai^B	draiʔ < r-laiʔ	= 18-9/4z 阤

[E] KS *lai^4 'to fall'

q 移^1 change yí jie je < jai lai OCB *ljaj
[T] Sui-Tang i, ONW ie <> [E] TB *laay 'change, exchange'
reach to yì jie^C je^C < jai^C laih
enlarge chǐ tś^{h}je^B tś^{h}ai^B k-lhaiʔ = i 侈
qr 移^{2}迻 yí jie jai lai 'migrate'
[E] Tiddim Chin lal^R / lal^F 'to migrate'

a 多[2] many | duō | tâ | tɑ < tɑi | tâi < tlai

[T] BTD Skt. -t-, -tra <> [E] PTai *hlai^{A1} 'many', PHlai ɬʔooi^{1}

d 㾃 | duò, tuō | tâ^{C}, t^{h}â | tɑi^{C}, t^{h}ɑi | tâih < tlaih, lhâi | = 24-21/147o

[E] WT ldar-ba 'weary, tired, faint'

e 奓 to open | zhā | ṭa | ṭa < ṭai | trâi

⤲ 2-17/795j zhé 磔 *trâk

f f | chà | ṭ^{h}a^{C} ! | ṭ^{h}ai^{C} | thrâih

18-9 = K. 4 | Mand. | MC | LHan -ie < -iai **| OCM**

afl 它[1]f > 蛇 | shé | dźja | źa < źɑi | m-lai 'snake'

f = 施 without 方 <> [T] Sin Sukchu SR ʐje (平); ONW ia (~ źa ?) <> [E] PMin *d̑žiɑi

l 蛇 compliant | yí | jie | jai | lai

h 佗 burden | tuō | t^{h}â^{C} | t^{h}ɑi^{C} | lhâih

compliant | tuó | dâ | dɑi | lâi in wēi-tuó / wēi-yí 委

-- 舵柁 rudder | duò | dâ^{B} | dɑi^{B} | lâiʔ

[D] Yue-Guangzh ^{21}t^{h}ɔ^{A2}, Ke-Meix t^{h}ɔ^{B2}, PMin *dâi^{B}

[E] Tai: S. t^{h}aai^{C2} < *d- 'sternpost'; Old Sino-Viet. (or Viet.?) lai (Pan Wuyun 1987: 29)

jk- 紽沱駝 | tuó | dâ | dɑi | lâi

- 陀 | tuó | dâ | dɑi

[T] BTD 首陀衛 śu^{B}-dɑ-was śuddhavāsa; 和陀波利 ɣuɑ-dɑ-pɑ-li^{C} Skt. vratapari-

m 鉈 | shē | śja | śɑi | lhai

g 也 | yě | jia^{B} | jai^{B} | laiʔ

[T] Sin Sukchu SR je (上); ONW ia

t 池 | chí | ḍie | ḍiai | drai < r-lai

[D] Sui-Tang ḍi < di, ONW de

[E] Lushai dil^{R} 'lake, pond, tank, pool', or Lushai li^{H} < li 'deep pool'

vx 箎馳 | chí | ḍie | ḍiai | drai < r-lai | 馳 = 18-8/3m

b' 地 | dì | di^{C} | di^{C} ? | draih ? < r-laih | OCB *lrjajs (?)

[T] Sin Sukchu SR djej (去), PR, LR di; MGZY ti (去) [di]; ONW dii; BTD Skt. dhi (Yu Min: Coblin 1993: 904)

a' 弛 | shǐ | śje^{B} | śai^{B} | lhaiʔ

[E] PWMiao *klaɨ^{7} 'release, forgive'

y 杝 cleave | chǐ, zhì | ṭ^{h}je^{B}, ḍje^{B} | ṭ^{h}iai^{B}, ḍiai^{B} | thraiʔ < r-lhaiʔ, draiʔ < r-laiʔ | [T] ONW de

杝 poplar | yí | jie | jai | lai

d'f'i 拕拖拸 | tuō | t^{h}â(C), dâ^{B} | t^{h}ɑi(C), dɑi^{B} | lhâi(h), lâiʔ 'to draw'

[D] Mand. archaic colloquialism lā 拉 'to pull'?

e' 髢 | dì see 8-12/850s

c' 他 other | tuō | t^{h}â | t^{h}ɑi | lhâi

他她 he/she | tā | —

[T] Sin SR t'ɔ (平), PR t'a; MGZY tho (平) [t'ɔ] <> [D] Yue-Guangzh ^{55}t^{h}a^{A1}, Ke-Meix t^{h}ɑ^{A1}

z 阤 | zhì, tuó | ḍje^{B} | ḍiai^{B} | draiʔ < r-laiʔ | = 18-8/3o 陊

[E] KS *lai^{4} 'to fall'

nrsk' 匜迆酏酡 | yí | jie | jai | lai

q 訑 conceited | yí | jie | jai | lai

cheat | tuō, tā | t^{h}wâ, t^{h}â | t^{h}(u)ɑi | lhâi (lhôi ?)

i' 迤 turn aside yí jie jai lai

[E] Lushai lei^{H} 'to be on one side, be awry, leaning to one side, rock and roll (as a boat)' ⋇ leiʔ^{L} < leis 'to pour out, upon, water plants'

h'n' 袘椸 yí jie jai lai

l' 施 spreadout shī śje śai lhai

[T] Sin Sukchu SR ʂi (平), PR, LR ʂɿ; MGZY sh^{h}i (平) [ʂɿ]; ONW śe

施 give shì śje^{C} śai^{C} lhaih

施 transfer yí jie jai lai

m' 葹 shī śje śai lhai

j' 弛 shǐ śje^{B} śai^{B} lhaiʔ

g' 胣 evicerate chǐ, yǐ ṭ^{h}je^{B}, jie^{B} ṭ^{h}iai^{B}, jai^{B} t-lhaiʔ (rhaiʔ ?), laiʔ

[T] ONW t^{h}e, ie <> [N] The gloss 'evicerate' has been proposed by a student in a seminar at the U. of WA.

\- 舓 lick shì dźje^{B} źe^{B} (m-leʔ) [Yupian]

= 7-18/1238e 咶 etc.

18-10 = K. 6 Mand. MC LHan -a < -ai OCM

a 羅 luó lâ lɑ < lɑi râi

[T] ONW lɑ; BTD Skt. -la-; rā-. <> [D] Yue-Guangzh ^{21}lɔ^{A2}, Ke-Meix lɔ^{A2}

b 蘿 luó lâ lɑi râi

\- 籮 luó lâ lɑi râi

[T] ONW lɑ <> [D] Yue-Guangzh ^{21}lɔ^{A2}; PMin *lhɑi^{A2}: Jiangle šai^{D3}, Fuzhou lai^{A2}

24a 罹 lí lje liai rai = 18-11/23f 離

18-11 = K. 23 Mand. MC LHan ie< -iai OCM

abc 离魑螭 chī ṭ^{h}je ṭ^{h}ie < ṭ^{h}iai rhai 'a kind of ghost'

[E] WT 'dre < *ɴdre 'goblin, demon, evil spirit' ⋇ gre-bo / -mo 'sp. of demon'; KN *t/s-rai > Tangkhul rai^{H} 'unclean spirit', Bodo ráj 'devil'

de 縭醨 lí lje liai rai

f 離 a bird lí lje liai rai

離 hang d. lí lje liai rai

'To be drooping, hanging down' <> [T] ONW le. MHan 璧流離 piek-liu-liai Skt. vaidurya, Pkt. veluriya <> [E] ? TB: WT brgyal (< b-r(-)yal) 'to sink down (senseless), faint'

離 leave lí lje liai rai = 18-10/24a 罹

[T] 烏弋山離 ʔɑ-jɨk-ṣan-liɑ[i] Alexandria

離 differ from lì lje^{C} liai^{C} raih

[T] ONW le <> [E] ST *ral: Mru ria < ral 'separated from', JP ran^{33} 'be apart, separated, divided' ⋇ mă^{31}-ran^{31} 'to place apart' ⋇ pă^{31}-ran^{31} 'be separate, sort out' ⋇ gă^{31}-ran^{55} 'to divide, distribute' ⋇ ra^{31} 'be parted, separated'

gh 籬灕 lí lje liai rai

18-12 = K. 350 Mand. MC LHan -a < -ai OCM

a 那 pl. name nuó, nà nâ nɑ < nɑi nâi

[T] ONW nɑ; BTD 那替 nɑ-t^{h}es Skt. nadī; 那術 nɑ-źuit Skt. nayuta

那 that nà nâ^{C} nɑ^{C} ?

[T] Sin S. SR nɔ (去), PR, LR na; MGZY no (去) [nɔ]

18-13 = K. 5			**Mand.**	**MC**	**LHan -a < -ai**	**OCM**	
a	左		zuǒ	tsâ^{B}	tsɑ^{B} < tsɑi^{B}	tsâiʔ	
	[D] Yue-Guangzh ^{35}tsɔ^{B1}, Ke-Meix tsɔ^{B}						
	[T] Sin Sukchu SR tsɔ (上), LR tsɔ; MGZY dzo (上) [tsɔ]; ONW tsɑ						
e	佐		zuǒ !	tsâ^{C}	tsɑi^{C}	tsâih	
f	差	choose	chāi	tṣʰaɨ	tṣʰai	tshrâi	
				or tṣʰăi	or tṣʰɛ	or tshrê	
	差	diverge	chā	tṣʰa	tṣʰai	tshrâi	
	[T] Sin Sukchu SR tʂ'a (平); ONW tṣʰä (~ tṣʰëi)						
	差	graduated	cī	tṣʰje	tṣʰiai	tshrai	
	差	to rub	cuō	tsʰâ	tsʰɑi	tshâi	
	差	overseer	shī	ṣje	ṣiai	srai	
h	槎		chá, zhà	dẓa(^{B})	dẓai(^{B})	dzrâi, dzrâiʔ	
i	瑳		cuǒ	tsʰâ^{B}	tsʰɑi^{B}	tshâiʔ	
j	磋	polish	cuō	tsʰâ	tsʰɑi	tshâi	
	[E] AA: Khmer /cnaj/ 'to cut (gems), to polish'						
k	傞		suō, cuō	sâ, tsʰâ	sɑi, tsʰɑi	sâi, tshâi	
l	瘥		cuó, juē	dzâ, tsja	dzɑi, tsiɑi	dzâi, tsai	
m	鹾		cuó	dzâ	dzɑi	dzâi	
	[E] TB *tsa > WT tsʰwa (i.e., tsʰa) 'salt', Kanauri tsa; PL *(t)sa^{2}, WB cʰa^{B}						
n	嗟		jiē	tsja	tsiɑi	tsai ?	
-	齹		cuō, chī	tsʰâ, dzâ			'uneven teeth'
o	髊	[Lüshi ch]	zì	dzje^{C}	dzie^{C}	dzeh	= 7-25/358r 胔 [Liji]

18-14		**Mand.**	**MC**	**LHan**	**OCM**
-	叉	chā	tṣʰaɨ	tṣʰai	tshrâi (or tshrê ?)
	[T] Sin Sukchu SR tʂ'a (平); ONW tṣʰä. <> [N] The MC rime seems to be an irregular development from *-râi, one should expect MC -a. Cf. 8-13f.				
-	杈	chà	tṣʰaɨ^{C}	tṣʰai^{C}	tshrâih (or tshrêh ?)

18-15 = K. 16			**Mand.**	**MC**	**LHan -a < -ai**	**OCM**
ad	沙鯊		shā	ṣa	ṣa < ṣai	srâi
	[T] Sin S. SR ʂa (平); ONW ṣä; BTD Skt. -sāra, -śā[na], śra- <> [D] PMin *sɑi					
	[E] TB *z(l)a-y < **s(l)a-y > WB sai^{B} ~ səlai^{B} 'sand', PL *say^{2} , JP dzai^{31}- 'sand'					
e	娑		suō	sâ	sɑi	sâi
	[T] MHan 劫貝(娑) kɨɑp-pɑs(-sɑ[i]) kārpāsa					
f	莎	a plant	suō	swâ	suɑi	—
		locust	shā	ṣa	ṣai	srâi

18-16 = K. 25			**Mand.**	**MC**	**LHan -ɨe < -ɨɑi**	**OCM**	
a	皮	'hide' n.	pí	bje 3	bɨe < bɨɑi	bai	
	[T] Sin Sukchu SR bi (平); MGZY pue (平) [buɛ]; ONW be <> [D] PMin *phue^{A2}						
	[E] Kachin pʰyi 'skin, bark'						
e	被	be covered	bèi	bje$^{B/C}$ 3	bɨɑi$^{B/C}$	baiʔ, baih	
	[T] Sin Sukchu SR bi (上去), LR bi; MGZY pue (上去) [buɛ]; MTang bi, ONW be						
	被	cover ones.	pī	pʰje 3	pʰɨɑi	phai	'cover oneself with'
	被	cloak	pì	pʰje^{C} 3	pʰɨɑi^{C}	phaih	
f	鞁		bì	bje^{C} 3	bɨɑi^{C}	baih	

i 陂 river bank bēi, bī pje 3 pɨɑi pai

陂 unjust bì pje^{C} 3 pɨɑi^{C} paih

h 詖 bì pje(^{C}) 3 pɨɑi(^{C}) pai, paih

g 彼 bǐ pje^{B} 3 pɨɑi^{B} paiʔ

[T] Sin Sukchu SR pi (上); MGZY bue (上) [puɛ]; ONW pe

d 疲 pí bje 3 bɨɑi bai = 18-17/26a 罷

[T] ONW be <> [E] TB *bal > Bahing bal 'tired, weary'; WB pan^{B} 'tired' ⋇ p^{h}a^{B} 'fatigued', JP ba^{55} ⋇ ban^{31} 'tired' <> Tai: S. p^{h}lia^{A2} < *b- 'weary, exhausted' ⋇ plɨa^{C1} < *p- 'to wear out'

j 披 divide pī p^{h}je 3 p^{h}ɨai phai

[E] PL *bay^{1} 'to separate'; WT dbye-ba 'parting' ⋇ dbyen-pa 'difference', WT 'bye-ba 'to separate, open'

披 supports bì pje^{C} 3 pɨɑi^{C} paih

k 鈹 pī p^{h}je 3 p^{h}ɨɑi phai

p - 頗坡 pō p^{h}wâ p^{h}ɑi phâi [T] ONW p^{h}ɑ

[D] Yue-Guangzh p^{h}ɔ^{A1}, Taishan puɔ^{A1}; Ke-Meix pɔ^{A1}. <> Tai: S. p^{h}lay^{2} 'leaning, sloping'

l 波 bō pwâ pɑi pâi

[T] Sin Sukchu SR pwɔ (平); MGZY bwo (平) [pwɔ]; ONW pɑ; BTD Skt. pā[ri...], -pa-

[E] ? TB: WT dba' (-kloŋ) 'wave'

m 跛 lame bǒ pwâ$^{B/C}$ pɑi$^{B/C}$ pâiʔ, pâih [T] ONW pɑ

[D] Y-Foshan pɐi^{A1}; PMin *pai^{B} <> [E] TB *pay ⋇ *bay 'lame, limp, oblique' ⋇ *bay 'left (side)', Lushai bai^{R} < baʔ 'walk lame'

跛 to lean bì pje^{C} 3 pɨɑi^{C} paih

n 簸 bǒ pwâ$^{B/C}$ pɑi$^{B/C}$ pâiʔ, pâih

[D] Mand. bǒ, K-Meix paː ^{B}, Y-Guangzh pɔ^{C1}, K-Dongguan pɔi^{C} n., vb.; PMin *puɑi^{C}

[E] TB *p^{w}aːy 'chaff, scatter' > PL *pway^{2} 'chaff' > WB phwai^{B} 'husk, chaff', Lushai vai^{H} 'husks of grain'

o 破 pò p^{h}wâ^{C} p^{h}ɑi^{C} phâih

[T] Sin Sukchu SR p'wɔ (去); MGZY phwo (去) [p'wɔ]; ONW p^{h}ɑ <> [D] PMin *phɑi^{C}

[E] WB pai^{C} 'broken off' ⋇ p^{h}ai^{C} 'break off in small pieces'; Lushai peʔ^{L} < pes 'to break, be broken', JP p^{h}jai^{33} 'break'

q 婆 saunter pó bwâ bɑi bâi [T] BTD Skt. -pā-

婆 grandmo. pó —

[T] ONW bɑ <> [E] TB *ba ~ pa 'grandmother'

18-17 = K. 26 Mand. MC LHan OCM

ab 罷^{1} > 羆 bear pí pje 3 pɨe < pɨɑi pai 'a bear' n.

a 罷^{2} exhaust pí bje 3 bɨɑi bai = 18-16/25d 疲

[T] ONW be

罷^{2} stop bà baɨ^{B} bai^{B} or bɛi^{B} brâiʔ or brêʔ

MC -aɨ usually < *rê <> [T] Sin Sukchu SR ba (去); MGZY pay (上) [baj]

[E] WB pri^{B} < pre^{B} 'be done, completed', ? JP p^{h}raʔ^{31} < p^{h}rak^{31} 'to complete'

18-18 = K. 17 Mand. MC LHan -a < -ai OCM

a 麻 hemp má ma ma < mai mrâi

[T] Sin Sukchu SR ma (平); ONW mä

[D] PMin *mai^{A2}: Xiamen muã^{A2}, Jianyang moi^{A2}, Jian'ou muẽ^{C1}, Fuzhou muai^{A2}

ef 摩磨 mó mwâ mɑ < mɑi mâi

[T] Sin Sukchu SR mwɔ (平); MGZY mwo (平) [mwɔ]; ONW mɑ; BTD 楓摩 puəm-mɑ Skt. brahma <> [D] PMin *mɑi <> [E] ? TB: WB hmwa^{C} 'pulverize' ⋇ hmwat 'be fine, smooth', and / or to Lushai mee^{R} < meeʔ 'be sandy and gritty'

c	塺		mò	mwâ[C]	mɑi[C]	mâih
g-	糜糜		mí	mje 3	mɨe < mɨɑi	mai

糜 [D] PMin *m̥ue[A2] 'rice gruel' <> [E] WT dmyal-ba 'to cut up into small pieces'

h	靡	not	mǐ	mje[B] 3	mɨɑi[B]	maiʔ

[T] Sin Sukchu SR mi (平), mjej (上), PR məj (平); MGZY mue (平 上) [muɛ]

	靡	share	mí	mje 3	mɨe < mɨɑi	mai
j	攠		mí	mje	mɨɑi	mai
d	麼		mó	mje[B] 3 (!)	mɨɑi[B]	maiʔ
i	麾		huī	xjwe 3	hye < hyɑi	hmai
442a	糜		mén	muən	mən	mən

18-19 = K. 356			**Mand.**	**MC**	**LHan -ye < -yai**	**OCM**	
a	毀	demolish	huǐ	xjwe[B] 3	hye[B] < hyɑi[B]	hmaiʔ	⋈ 19-9/11ef
b	燬	fire	huǐ	xjwe[B] 3	hyɑi[B]	hmaiʔ	

[E] Tai: S. mai[C1] < *hm- 'to burn'

19 OCM rime *-oi, *-wai Gē bù 歌部 (2)

GSR 1 - 31; 349 - 360

Baxter 1992: 494 ff. (§10.2.8)

See Table 25-1 for OCM rimes *-on / *-wan, *-ot / *-wat, *-oi / *-wai in QYS categories.

After guttural initials the OC rime could be either *-oi or *-wai, but after acute initials only OC *-oi is possible (e.g., only *roi), after labials only *-ai.

In LHan, *-oi* has already broken to *uai* except in old southern dialects. The loss of final *i* in LHan and the merger in Div. III with reflexes of *-e, mentioned in Rime 18, apply here as well. As in 18, I write here conservative southern LHan forms with *i*; the ones encountered in Han literature can be easily deduced by removing the *i*. Occasionally, the literary form has been mentioned as a reminder (kuɑ < kuɑi, etc.). In Div. III one could write either -yai or -ye.

The OCM coda *-i in diphthongs behaves like a final consonant, hence a strictly phonemic transcription would write it as *-j, as in OCB (*-aj, *-əj, *-uj).

19-1	**= K. 7**	**Mand.**	**MC**	**LHan**	**OCM**
a	戈	gē	kwâ	kuɑi	kwâi or kôi
e	划 to punt	huá	ɣwa	ɣuai	gwrâi or grôi
f	𢦏 thrust	huà	ɣwa^{B}	ɣuai^{B}	gwrâiʔ or grôiʔ

19-2	**= K. 351**	**Mand.**	**MC**	**LHan**	**OCM**	
a	果 fruit	guǒ	kwâ^{B}	kuɑi^{B}	kôiʔ or kwâiʔ	
	[T] Sin Sukchu SR kwɔ (上); MGZY gwo (上) [kwɔ]; ONW kuɑ <> [D] PMin *koi^{B}					
	果 satisf.	kuǒ	k^{h}wâ^{B}	k^{h}uɑi^{B}	khôiʔ	
-	餜	guǒ	kwâ^{B}	—		
	[D] PMin *koi^{B1} 'rice cake', also 'dried fruit'					
d	裹	guǒ	kwâ^{B}	kuɑi^{B}	kôiʔ	
ci-	蜾蠃/蠃	guǒ-luǒ	kwâ^{B}-lwâ^{B}	kuɑi^{B}-luɑi^{B}	kôiʔ-rôiʔ	OCB *k(r)ōjʔ-(C)rōjʔ
	[E] TB *k(l)wa-y ≭ g(l)wa-y > WB kwai^{B} 'dammer bee', Chepang kway 'bee'					
ef	堁課	kè	k^{h}wâ^{C}	k^{h}uɑi^{C}	khoih	
l	輠	huà	ɣwa^{B}, ɣwậi^{B}, (ɣwân^{B})	ɣuai^{B}, ɣuəi^{B}, S goi^{C}	grôiʔ, gûiʔ	
j	踝	huái !	ɣwa^{B}	ɣuai^{B}	grôiʔ	
k	髁	kuà !	ɣwa^{B}	ɣuai^{B}	grôiʔ	
-	夥	huǒ	ɣwâ^{B}	ɣuɑi^{B} R!	—	
	[D] PMin *oi^{C} ~ *uai^{B} 'many'					
m	祼	guàn	kwân^{C}	kuɑn^{C}	kôns	= 25-2/158f 灌
gh	倮裸	luǒ	lwâ^{B}	luɑi^{B} / S loi^{B}	rôiʔ	[T] ONW luɑ
n	婐	wǒ	ʔwâ^{B}	ʔuɑi^{B}	ʔôiʔ	

19-3	**= K. 352**	**Mand.**	**MC**	**LHan**	**OCM**	
a	[illegible]	guō	kwâ	kuɑi	kôi or kwâi	
c	[illegible]	guǒ	kwâ^B	kuɑi^B	kôiʔ	= 19-2/351c

19-4 **= K. 18** Some of the words could have the OC rime *-wai.

		Mand.	**MC**	**LHan**	**OCM**	
-	冎	'Scapula' in OB; perh. the s. w. as next: 'cut meat off bones' (> bone cleared of meat)				
-a-	冎咼[1]剮	guǎ	kwa^B	kuai^B	krôiʔ	'cut, bare bone'
a-	咼[2] 喎	kuāi	k^{h}wai (irreg.)	k^{h}uai	khrôi	'wry mouth'
fg	禍 g	huò	ɣwâ^B	ɣuɑi^B	gôiʔ	
e	過 pass by	guō	kwâ	kuɑi	kôi	
	過 trans.	guò	kwâ^C	kuɑi^C	kôih	'transgress' [T] ONW kuɑ
h	薖	kē	k^{h}wâ	k^{h}uɑi	khôi	
-	鍋	guō	kwâ	kuɑi	kôi	
c	蝸	wō, guā, luó	kwa, kwai, lwâ	kuai, S kɔi, loi	krôi, g-rôi	
		[D] PMin *lhɔi <> [E] TB *kroy > WB krwe 'shellfish, cowry', JP k^{h}oi^{33} 'shellfish, shell'				
b	騧	guā	kwa, kwai	kuai	krôi	
d	媧	wā, guā	kwa, kwai	kuai	krôi	

19-5	**= K. 28**	**Mand.**	**MC**	**LHan**	**OCM**
a	虧	kuī	k^{h}jwe 3	k^{h}yai	khwai
		1-23 is perh. also phonetic.			

19-6	**= K. 27**	**Mand.**	**MC**	**LHan**	**OCM**	
a	為 to do	wéi	jwe	wai R!	wai	OCB *w(r)jaj
		[T] Sin Sukchu SR uj (平); MGZY xue (平) [ɦuɛ]; MTang ui, ONW ue				
	為 for	wèi	jwe^C	wai^C	waih	
f	[illegible]	wěi	jwe^B	wai^B	waiʔ	
l	撝	huī	xjwe 3	hyai	hwai	
		[T] TB *way > WB wai^B 'whirlpool, brandish'; Lushai vai^F < *vaiʔ 'to wave' with the hand, arm, or anything horizontally, 'brandish (a sword)' ⋈ hui^F 'to beckon' with hand				
g	嬀	guī	kjwe	kyai	kwai	
m	譌	é	ŋwâ	ŋuɑi	ŋwâi	
k	偽	wèi	ŋjwe^C	ŋyai^C	ŋwaih	

19-7 **= K. 8** MC ɣwâ could derive from OCM *wâi, *gwâi or *gôi; we write *wâi.

		Mand.	**MC**	**LHan**	**OCM**	
a	禾	hé	ɣwâ	ɣuɑi	wâi	
		[T] BTD Skt. vā. <> [D] PWMin *wɔi^{A2}, SMin *g-: Zhangping gue^{A2}				
		[E] Tai: S. k^{h}aa^{A2} < *ɣ- 'straw, thatch grain'				
gk	龢盉	hé	ɣwâ	ɣuɑi	wâi	
e	和 harmo.	hé	ɣwâ	ɣuɑi	wâi	'harmony'
		[T] ONW ɣuɑ; BTD Skt. vā, vra-				
	和 attune	hè	ɣwâ^C	ɣuɑi^C	wâih	
n	科	kē	k^{h}wâ	k^{h}uɑi	khwâi	

19-8 = K. 19 The OCM rime could have been *-wai or *-oi.

		Mand.	MC	LHan	OCM	
a	化	huà	xwa^{C}	hua^{C} < huai^{C}	hŋrôih (or hwâih ?)	

[T] Sin Sukchu SR xwa (去); MGZY hwa (去) [xwa]; ONW huä

-	花	huā	xwa		a late graph for 1-27/44 華 (SW2699)	
de	吪訛	é	ŋwâ	ŋuɑi	ŋôi	
c	貨	huò	xwâ^{C}	huɑi^{C}	hŋôih	[T] ONW huɑ

19-9 = K. 11 The rime could be either *-oi or *-wai. The phonetic also writes 19-16 *duò* 隓 *lôiʔ. Perhaps synonyms for 'shred meat' and/or 'demolish' with similar rimes were written with the same phonetic. Alternatively, MC tʰwâ^{B} < *lhôiʔ 'shred meat' could have had a variant *hoi that then spawned the present group (loss of a discrete initial, with survival of aspiration as *h-, does occur elsewhere).

		Mand.	MC	LHan	OCM	
b	隋	suì,	sjwe^{C},	sye^{C} < syai^{C},	swaih,	'shred sacr. meat'
		huì	xjwe^{C} 3	hyai^{C}	hwaih	See also 19-16.
ef	墮隳	huī	xjwe 3	hyaihwai	'destroy' [Laozi]	

[T] BTD Skt. vai-, Pkt. ve-, e.g., 墮舍利 hyai-śah-lih Skt. Vaiśālī <> [N] Related to 18-19/356 huǐ 毀 *hmaiʔ 'destroy'? See also 19-16.

g	隨	suí	zjwe	zyai	s-wai	

[T] ONW zue; Han BTD Skt. vai- <> [E] TB: LB *s-yuy 'follow'

i	瀡	suǐ !	sjwe^{C}	syai^{C}	swaih	
h	髓	suǐ	sjwe^{B}	syai^{B}, S tsʰyɑi^{B}	swaiʔ	

[T] ONW sue <> [D] M-Xiam col. tsʰe^{B1} <> [E] ST *s(-)wi 'blood'

19-10 = K. 357 The element 委 is occasionally substituted for 19-19 妥.

		Mand.	MC	LHan	OCM	
a	委 compl.	wēi	ʔjwe 3	ʔye < ʔyai	ʔoi-	'compliant'
	委 fall	wěi	ʔjwe^{B} 3	ʔyai^{B}	ʔoiʔ	

[T] ONW ʔue <> [E] ST *yol: WT 'gyel-ba 'to fall, dangle' ⋈ g-yal 'dangling' ⋈ g-yol 'curtain'; WB lway 'suspend from the shoulder'

	委 collect	wěi	ʔjwe$^{B/C}$ 3	ʔyai$^{B/C}$	ʔoiʔ, ʔoih	
bcde	倭痿萎逶	wēi	ʔjwe 3	ʔyai	ʔoi	
f	餧	wèi	ʔjwe^{C} 3	ʔyai^{C}	ʔoih	⋈ 28-9/573 喂餵

[E] TB: Lushai vulʔ^{L} 'to keep or rear (animals), to domesticate'; Mikir wi^{H} 'tend animals'

g	踒	wō	ʔwâ(C)	ʔuɑi(C)	ʔôi(h)	

19-11 = K. 9

		Mand.	MC	LHan	OCM
a	臥	wò	ŋwâ^{C}	ŋuɑ^{C} < ŋuɑi^{C}	ŋôih or ŋwâih

[T] Sin Sukchu SR ŋɔ (去), PR, LR ɔ; MGZY o (去) [ɔ]; ONW ŋuɑ <> [E] TB: Lushai ŋɔi^{H} / ŋɔiʔ^{L} < ŋɔis 'to be quiet, silent, stop, pause', NNaga *C-ŋuaj 'easy, gentle, quiet'

19-12 = K. 29

		Mand.	MC	LHan	OCM
a	危	wéi, wēi	ŋjwe 3	ŋyai	ŋwai (or ŋoi ?)

[T] ONW ŋue <> [E] TB: WB ŋwa 'large, high, project'

bcde	詭佹垝恑	guǐ	kjwie^{B} 3	kyai^{B}	kwaiʔ
f	跪	guì,	gjwe^{B},	gyai^{B},	gwaiʔ,
		kuǐ	kʰjwe^{B} 3	kʰyai^{B}	khwaiʔ

19-13 = K. 20		**Mand.**	**MC**	**LHan**	**OCM**
a	瓦	wǎ	ŋwa^{B}	ŋuai^{B}, ŋɔi^{B}	ŋrôiʔ (or ŋwâiʔ ?)
	[T] Sin Sukchu SR ŋwa (上), PR, LR wa; MGZY xwa (上) [ɦwa] <> [D] PMin *ŋhiɑi^{B}				

19-14 = K. 10		**Mand.**	**MC**	**LHan**	**OCM**
a	朵	duǒ	twâ^{B}	tuɑi^{B}	tôiʔ 'hang on a tree' = 19-17/31L
	[T] Sin Sukchu SR tɔ (上), LR tɔ, twɔ; MGZY dwo (上) [twɔ]; ONW tuɑ^{B}				
-	剁	duò	twâ^{C}	tuɑi^{C}	tôih

19-15 = K. 30		**Mand.**	**MC**	**LHan**	**OCM**
a	吹 blow	chuī	tśʰjwe	tśʰuai	k-hloi or thoi
	[T] Sin Sukchu SR tʂ'uj (平); MGZY chue (平) [tʂ'uɛ]; ONW tśʰue				
	吹 concert	chuì	tśʰjwe^{C}	tśʰuai^{C}	k-hloih or thoih
	[D] PMin *tšhue <> [E] AA: Khmer khloy n. 'flute'				
b	炊 cook	chuī	tśʰjwe	tśʰuai	k-hloi or thoi

19-16 = K. 11 The phonetic also writes syllables of a different type, see 19-9.

		Mand.	**MC**	**LHan**	**OCM**
ae	陊墮	duò	dwâ^{B}	duɑ^{B} < duɑi^{B}	lôiʔ 'destroy' See also 19-9.
b	隋	tuǒ	tʰwâ^{B}	tʰuɑi^{B}	lhôiʔ 'shred sacrif. meat'
	[E] ? TB: Lushai hlɔi^{F} 'cut off, slash off' (in lengthwise motion). See also 19-9.				
d	隓	duò	dwâ^{B}	duɑi^{B}	lôiʔ 'long and narrow'
	'Long and narrow' (mountain) <> [E] TB: JP diŋ^{31}-loi^{33} 'long and narrow' ⋇ 22-9/274				
c	橢 oval	tuǒ	tʰwâ^{B}	tʰuɑi^{B}	lhôiʔ
j	鬌	duǒ, duò	twâ^{B}, dwâ^{B}	tuɑi^{B}, duɑi^{B}	tlôiʔ, lôiʔ
		chuí	ḍjwe	ḍyai	droiʔ or r-loiʔ
	[E] ? TB: WB lwai 'suspend from shoulder'				
k	媠	tuǒ,	tʰwâ^{B},	tʰuɑi^{B},	lhôiʔ,
		duò	dwâ^{C}	duɑi^{C}	lôih
l	惰	duò	dwâ$^{B/C}$	duɑi$^{B/C}$	lôiʔ, lôih ⋇ 22-13/324a 兌 *lôts

19-17 = K. 31		**Mand.**	**MC**	**LHan**	**OCM**
ab	垂陲	chuí	źjwe	dźye < dźuai	doi (= djoi ?)
	[E] TB *dzywal > WT 'jol-ba 'to hang down' ⋇ yol 'curtain'; Lushai fual^{R} 'sag, hang low'				
d	睡	shuì	źjwe^{C}	dźuai^{C}	doih (= djoih ?)
	[T] ONW dźue <> [E] TB: WT yur-ba 'to slumber' ⋇ g-yur 'sleep'				
e	菙	shuì	źjwe^{B}	dźuai^{B}	doiʔ
ij	捶箠	chuí !	tśjwe^{B}	tśuai^{B}	toiʔ
k	諈	zhuì	tjwe^{C}	ṭyai^{C}	troih
h	硾	zhuì	ḍjwe^{C}	ḍyai^{C}	droih = drjoih or r-djoih
fg	甀鎚	chuí, zhuì	ḍjwe(^{C})	ḍyai(^{C})	droi, droih
	甀 [E] WT yol-go 'earthenware, crockery' <> [D] 鎚 PMin *dhui				
l	埵	duǒ	twâ^{B}	tuɑi^{B}	tôiʔ = 19-14
m	唾	tuò	tʰwâ^{C}	tʰuɑi^{C}	thôih
	[D] PMin *thoi^{C}; some dialects in the Yue area have aberrant forms: Guangzh col. tʰœ^{C1} beside tʰɔ^{C1}, Zengcheng sœy^{C2}, Bao'an sui^{B2}, Enping tsʰui^{A2}; Ke-Dongguan sui^{B}				
	[E] ST *tol > WT tʰo-le (i.e., *tol-e) 'debs-pa 'to spit' ('debs-pa 'to throw'); WB tʰwe^{B} 'spit'				

19-18 = K. 14		**Mand.**	**MC**	**LHan**	**OCM**	
b	蠃: 蜾蠃	guǒ-luǒ	kwâ^B-lwâ^B	kuɑi^B-luɑi^B,	kôiʔ-rôiʔ	See 19-2.
c	羸	léi	ljwe	lyai	roi	

19-18A = K. 1236b			**MC**	**LHan**	**OCM**
	蓏	luǒ	lwâ^B	luɑi^B	rôiʔ

19-19 = K. 354 The element 19-10 委 is in some graphs substituted for 妥.

		Mand.	**MC**	**LHan**	**OCM**	
a	妥	tuǒ	tʰwâ^B	tʰuɑ^B < tʰuɑi^B	nhôiʔ	OCB *nhojʔ
	[E] ST *C-nwal: WT rnal 'rest, tranquility of mind'					
f	諉	wěi !	n̥wie^C	n̥yai^C	nroih	
-	胡荽	hú-suī	ɣuo-swi	gɑ-sui	'coriander' Iranian gošniz (ca. 300 AD)	
g	綏 strap	suí	swi	sui	snui	OCB *snjuj
	[T] ONW sui					
	綏 sacrif.	suī, huī	sjwe, xjwie	syai	snoi	'a sacrifice'
	綏 level	tuǒ	tʰwâ^B	tʰuɑi^B	nhôiʔ	'keep level...'
d	餒	něi	nwậi^B	nuəi^B	nûiʔ	OCB *nujʔ
e	緌	ruí	ńźwi	ńui	nui	= 28-18/1237v 蕤

19-20 = K. 1238jk			**MC**	**LHan**	**OCM**	
-	惢	suǒ	swâ^B	suɑi^B	snôiʔ	SW 4791
jk	繠蕊	ruǐ	ńźwi^B, ńźjwe^B	ńui^B, ńuai^B	nuiʔ, noiʔ	⋊ 19-19/354g 緌
	[E] AA: OMon jnor ~ jnow 'hanging banner'					

19-21 = K. 12		**Mand.**	**MC**	**LHan**	**OCM**
a	坐 sit	zuò	dzwâ^B	dzuɑi^B	dzôiʔ
	[T] Sin Sukchu SR dzwɔ (上); MGZY tswo (上) [dzwɔ]; ONW dzuɑ [D] PMin *dzoi^B				
	坐 seat	zuò	dzwâ^C	dzuɑi^C	dzôih
b	痤	cuó	dzwâ	dzuɑi	dzôi
c	挫	cuò !	tswâ^C	tsuɑi^C	tsôih
-	夎	zuò	tswâ^C, tswậi^C	tsuɑi^C, tsuəi^C	tsôih, tsûih
d	蓌	zuò	tswâ^C, tṣa^C	tsuɑi^C, tṣai^C	tsrôih
- e	莝剉	cuò	tsʰwâ^C, tswâ^C	ts(ʰ)uɑi^C	tshôih < k-sôih ?
	[E] AA: PMon *ksɔɔy 'useless fibre, hay', PWa *sɔh 'cut grass'				
f -	脞 䂳	cuǒ	tsʰwâ^B	tsʰuɑi^B	tshôiʔ
g	髽	zhuā	tṣwa	tṣuai	tsrôi

19-22 = K. 13		**Mand.**	**MC**	**LHan**	**OCM**
ab	貨瑣	suǒ	swâ^B	suɑi^B	sôiʔ
	[T] Sin Sukchu SR swɔ (上); MGZY swo (上) [swɔ]				

19-23 = K. 355		**Mand.**	**MC**	**LHan**	**OCM**	
abc	衰[1] > 蓑簑	suō	swâ	sua < suai	sôi 'raincoat'	
a	衰[2]	shuāi	ṣwi	ṣui	srui	'diminish'
	[T] Sin Sukchu SR ʂuj (平), PR ʂwaj; MGZY (zhway >) shway (平) [ʂwaj]					
	衰	chuī	tṣʰjwe	tṣʰyai	tshroi < k-sroi	'reduce'
ae	衰[3] 縗	cuī	tsʰwậi	tsʰuəi	tshûi < k-sûi	'mourning clothes'
d	榱	cuī	ṣwi	ṣui	srui	'rafter'

20 OCM rime *-et, *-ets, *-es Yuè- Jì bù 月祭部 (1)

GSR 268 - 348

Baxter 1992: 389 ff. (§10.1.2)

Table 20-1: OCM rimes *-en, *-et, *-e(t)s in QYS categories

Div.	*-en R.23	*-et R.20	*-e(t)s R.20
IV	見 kien^C ken^C *kêns 縣 ɣiwen^C ɣuen^C *gwêns 獧 kiwen^C kuen^C *kwêns 片 p^{h}ien^C p^{h}en^C *phêns 前 dzien dzen *dzên	鍥 k^{h}iet k^{h}et *khêt 蔑 miet met *mêt	契 k^{h}iei^C k^{h}es *khêts
3/3 gr	辨 bjän^{B}3 bɨan^B *brenʔ	別 pjät3 pɨat *pret	劓 ŋjäi^{C}3 ŋɨas *ŋrets
3/4 gr	遣 k^{h}jiän^{B}4 k^{h}ian^B *khenʔ 面 mjiän^{C}4 mian^C *mens	滅 mjiät4 miat *met	瘈 kjiäi^{C}4 kias *kets 埶 ŋjiäi^{C}4 ŋias *ŋets 敝 bjiäi^{C}4 bias *bets
III ac	difficult to distinguish from *-an	設 śjät śat *nhet 熱 ńźjät ńat *net difficult to distinguish from *-at	difficult to distinguish from *-a(t)s
III w	圜 jwän3 wen *wen 還 zjwän zyan *s-wen		
II	環 ɣwan ɣuan *wên		快 k^{h}wai^C k^{h}uas *khwêts
II	閒 kăn kɛn *krên 幻 ɣwăn^C ɣuɛn^C *gwrêns 辦 băn^C bɛn^C *brêns	八 păt pɛt *prêt	介 kăi^C kɛs *krêts 拜 păi^C pɛs *prêts

The OC vowel in rime *-et,*-es left only traces in MC Div. IV -iet, -iei^C, and chongniu Div. 3/4 finals (which occur only after grave initials). After acute initials, reflexes of OC *-et and *-at have merged in Div. III, therefore some of the series under rime no. 21 *-at may have been OC *-et. MC -ăt, -ăi^C normally derive from *-rêt, *-rê(t)s, but can also derive from OC *-rât, *-râ(t)s due to a convergence tendency in the QYS.

For LHan, *chóngniǔ* Div. 3/4 items (QYS -jiät 3/4) could be written *-iet* or *-iat*; I write *-iat* because this is parallel to the breaking of *-ot to LHan *-uat.

20-1	**= K. 279**	**Mand.**	**MC**	**LHan**	**OCM**	
a	丰刀	qiè	kʰăt	kʰɛt	khrêt	
b	契[1]	qì	kʰiei^{C}	kʰes	khêts < s-kêts ?	OCB khets

[T] ONW kʰėi <> [N] See §5.8.1 for *s-k... > *kh...

	契[2]闊	qiè-kuò	kʰiet-kʰuât	kʰet--kʰuɑt	khêt-khôt	
c	挈	qiè	kʰiet	kʰet	khêt	
f	鍥	qiè	kʰiet	kʰet	khêt	
g	瘈	jì	kjiäi^{C} 4	kias	kets	
d	絜	jié	kiet, ɣiet	ket, get	kêt, gêt	
j	潔	jié	kiet	ket	kêt	
k	廮	qiè, xié	kʰiet, ɣiet	kʰet, get	khêt, gêt	

[E] ST *ke(t): WT rked-pa 'the waist, loins, middle', JP ʃiŋ^{31}-kjit^{55} 'waist', Tamang (^{1})ke: 'belt'

h	喫 energet.	qiè	kʰai^{C}	kʰas	khrâs (or khrês ?)	
	喫 eat	qiè	kʰiek	—		[T] MTang kʰɨk, ONW kʰėk
e	齧	niè	ŋiet	ŋet	ŋêt	
b-	契[3]偰 NP	xiè	sjät	siat	set	= 20-11/309-卨
i	楔	xiē	siet	set	sêt	

[E] AA: Khmer sniata /snìiət/ 'peg, pin, ... wedge, ...'

20-2	**= K. 327**	**Mand.**	**MC**	**LHan**	**OCM**	
a	介 scale	jiè	kăi^{C}	kɛs	krêts	

[E] TB-WB ə-kre^{B} 'scales of a fish' <> PTai *klet^{D1}S 'fish scales'

	介 sudden	jiā	kăt	kɛt	krêt	
df	价疥	jiè	kăi^{C}	kɛs	krêts	
e	界	jiè	kăi^{C}	kɛs	krê(t)s	~ 29-4/510b 届 *krîs
j	芥 musta.	jiè	kăi^{C}	kɛs	krêts	

[E] PTai *kat: S. kaat^{D1L} 'mustard plant'

	芥 grass	jiè	kăi^{C}	kɛs	krêts	

[N] GSR has MC kai^{C} with this meaning

k	紒	jì	kiei^{C}	kes	kêts	
h	齘	xiè	ɣăi^{C}	gɛs	grêts	
i	忦	xiè	xăi^{C}	hɛs	hrêts	

20-3	**= K. 312**	**Mand.**	**MC**	**LHan**	**OCM**
a	夬 thimble	jué	kiwet	kuet	kwêt
	夬 divide	guài	kwai^{C}	kuas	kwêts

[N] For Div. II -wai^{C} from *kwêts (not *kwrâts), see Introduction 5.2.3 <> [E] TB: WB kyui^{B} 'be broken' ⋇ kʰyui^{B} 'to break in two'

k	快	kuài	kʰwai^{C}	kʰuas	khwêts

[T] Sin Sukchu SR k'waj (去); MGZY khway (去) [k'waj]; ONW kʰuëi

b	決 open	jué	kiwet	kuet	kwêt

[T] Sin Sukchu SR kye (入); MGZY gwÿa (入) [kyɛ]; ONW kuėt. LHan 句決 kuo^{C} (or kɨo^{C}) -kuet 'a kind of hat', cf. Mongol kökül (Pulleyblank 1983: 453)

	決 quick	xuè	xiwet	huet	hwêt
c	玦	jué	kiwet	kuet	kwêt
efg	訣趹駃	jué	kiwet	kuet	kwêt

-	駃騠	jué-tí	kiwet-diei	kuet-dei	—	
-	昳	jué	kiwet [GY], ɣiwet [JY]	kuet, guet	kwêt, gwêt	

[E] AA: Central Sakai gawet, giwet, Khasi k^hawoit 'beckon with hand'

d	袂	jué	kiwet,	kuet,	kwêt,	
	袂	mèi,	mjiäi^C 4	mias	me(t)s	
h	缺	quē	k^hiwet, k^hjwät	k^huet, k^hyat	khwet	
i	吷	xuè	xiwet	huet	hwêt	
j	抉	jué	ʔiwet	ʔuet	ʔwêt	

20-4	= K. 280	Mand.	MC	LHan	OCM	
a	軋	yà	ʔăt	ʔɛt	ʔrêt	
b	札	zhá	tṣăt	tṣɛt	tsrêt	

20-5	= K. 1256a	Mand.	MC	LHan	OCM	
a	隉	niè	ŋiet	ŋet	ŋêt	= 20-7/285d 臲

20-6	= K. 331	Mand.	MC	LHan	OCM	
a	帠	yì	ŋjiäi^C 4	ŋias	ŋets	OCB *ŋJets

= 20-13/330 埶蓺藝

20-7	= K. 285	Mand.	MC	LHan	OCM	
a	臬	niè	ŋiet [GY], ŋjät 3	ŋet	ŋêt	

[E] TB: KN-Lai ŋiat 'to aim at', middle voice 'spy, watch'

d	臲	niè	ŋiet	ŋet	ŋêt	= 20-5/1256a 隉
c	闑	niè	ŋjät 3, ŋiet	ŋɨat, ŋet	ŋret, ŋêt	= 20-13/330h 槷
e	劓	yì	ŋjäi^C 3	ŋɨas	ŋrets	

20-8	= K. 290	Mand.	MC	LHan	OCM	
a	設	shè	śjät	śat	nhet < *ŋhet ?	OCB *h(l)jet

[T] ONW śat <> [E] TB: Lushai ŋhet^L / ŋheʔ^L (< ŋhets) 'be firm, establish' ⋈ ŋheet^F intr. 'to settle or get firm (as earth, cooked rice)', Limbu nɛma < nɛss- 'to lie (including of geographical features, fields, etc.)'. ⋈ 20-13/330l 勢

20-9	= K. 1256	Mand.	MC	LHan	OCM	
b	鐵	tiě	t^hiet	t^het	lhêt	[T] ONW t^hėt
c	驖	tiě	t^hiet, diet	t^het, det	lhêt, lêt	

The OC rime could also have been *-it <> [E] TB: WT lčags < *lhjaks 'iron'. Tai: S. lek^{D1}S < *hl- 'iron', KS *k^hlit^7; PVM *khăc 'iron'

20-10	= K. 288	Mand.	MC	LHan	OCM	
a	舌	shé	dźjät	źat	m-let (or m-lat?0	OCB *mlăt

[T] Sin Sukchu SR zje (入); ONW źat <> [D] PMin *d̯žiat < *m-l- <> [E] MY *nbret (< *mlet ?) < TB-Magari milet (or me-leṭ), let, Newari meč 'tongue', JP ʃiŋ^{31}-let^{31}

20-11	**= K. 309**	**Mand.**	**MC**	**LHan**	**OCM**	
-	禼 insect	xiè	sjät	siat	set	'some kind of insect' [SW]
	禼 NP	xiè	sjät	siat	set	= 20-1/279b 契[3]

name of a Yin dynasty ancestor

a	竊	qiè	ts^{h}iet	ts^{h}et	tshêt < k-sêt

[N] For *k-s- > *tsh-, see EDOC §5.9.1

20-12	**= K. 310**	**Mand.**	**MC**	**LHan**	**OCM**
a	截	jié	dziet	dzet	dzêt

20-13	**= K. 330**	**Mand.**	**MC**	**LHan**	**OCM**		
a	埶 sow	yì	ŋjiäi^C 4	ŋias	ŋets		
		shì	śjäi^C	śas	nhets < hŋets		
e	蓺 sow	yì	ŋjiäi^C 4	ŋias	ŋets		
f	藝 method	yì	ŋjiäi^C 4	ŋias	ŋets	= 20-6/331 臬	OCB *ŋJets

[T] Sin Sukchu SR i (去); MGZY yi (去) [ji]; ONW ŋiei

[E] Tai: S. kra^4-net^4 'tactics, methods, strategy'

i	囈	yì	ŋjiäi^C 4	ŋias	ŋets	
g	摰	niè	ŋiet	ŋet	ŋêt	
h	槷	niè	ŋiet	ŋet	ŋêt	= 20-7/285c 闑
l	勢 force	shì	śjäi^C	śas	nhets < hŋets	

[T] ONW śei <> [E] TB *ŋeis > WT ŋes-pa 'certain, true, firm', Lushai ŋei^L < ŋeih (< ŋes) 'really, truly, verily', Tiddim ŋɛːi^F < ŋɛːih < *ŋeːis 'certainly, be sure'

j	熱	rè	ńźjät	ńat	net or ŋet	OCB *ŋjet

[T] Sin Sukchu SR rje (入); MGZY Zhya (入) [rje]; ONW ńat <> [D] PMin *niɑt ~ *jiat

k	爇	ruò	ńźjwät	ńuat	niot
m	暬 familiar	xiè	sjät	siat	snet
n	褻	xiè	sjät	siat	snet

[E] TB: WT sñed 'about, near (after round sums)'

20-14	**= K. 281**	**Mand.**	**MC**	**LHan**	**OCM**
a	八	bā	păt	pɛt	prêt

[T] MTang pär, ONW pät <> [D] PMin *pet, K-Meix pat <> [E] ST *priat ~ *pret: TB *b-r-yat

20-15	**= K. 292**	**Mand.**	**MC**	**LHan**	**OCM**	
a	別 divide	bié	pjät 3	pɨat	pret	OCB *prjet

[T] Sin Sukchu SR pje, bje (入); MGZY bya (入) [pjɛ]; ONW pat

[E] TB: LB *brat 'split, crack' > WB prat 'be cut in two'

	別 differ.	bié	bjät 3	bɨat	bret	'different'	OCB *brjet

20-16	**= K. 341**	**Mand.**	**MC**	**LHan**	**OCM**
a	敝	bì	bjiäi^C 4	bias	bets or bes

[T] Sin Sukchu SR bi (去); MGZY pi (去) [bi]; ONW biei

[E] TB: Lushai p^{h}uai^H < p^{h}uai 'be worn, worn out, frayed', JP p^{h}je^{31} 'to ruin'. Also Lushai paiʔ^L < *pais 'to throw away, discard, annul'

defg	幣弊斃獘	bì	bjiäi^C 4	bias	bets	[T] ONW biei
h	蔽	bì	pjiäi^C 4	pias	pets	[T] ONW piei^C
i	鷩	bì, biē	pjiäi^C, pjiät	pias, piat	pet, pets	
jk	鼈鱉	biē	pjiät 4	piat	pet	

l	憋	biē	pʰjiät ?	pʰiat	phet	
m	鱉	bié	biet	bet	bêt	

20-17 = K. 328		**Mand.**	**MC**	**LHan**	**OCM**	
a	拜	bài	păiC	pɛs	prêts	OCB *prots

20-18 = K. 311		**Mand.**	**MC**	**LHan**	**OCM**	
agh	蔑懱蠛	miè	miet	met	mêt	[T] ONW mėt
-	衊	miè	miet	met		
f	幭 cover	miè	miet, miek	met, mek	mêt, mêk	
	MC miek = 8-21/859 鼏; on *-ek ~ *et, see Baxter 1992: 300; 484					
ik	穖篾	miè	miet	met	mêt	
lm -	韤韈襪	wà	mjwɐt	muɑt	mat	

20-19 = K. 294		**Mand.**	**MC**	**LHan**	**OCM**	
a	威	xuè	xjwät 3	hyat	hmet (or hmat ?)	OCB *hmjet
	[E] ? TB *mit					
bc	滅搣	miè	mjiät 4	miat	met	OCB *mjet
	[T] ONW miat					

21 OCM rime *-at, *-ats, *-as Yuè- Jì bù 月祭部 (2)

GSR 267 - 348

Baxter 1992: 389 ff. (§10.1.2)

Table 21-1: OCM rimes *-an, *-at, *-a(t)s, *-ai in QYS categories

Div.	*-an R.24	*-at R.21	*-a(t)s R.21	*-ai R.18
I	干 kân kɑn *kân 彈 dân dɑn *dân 半 pwân^{C} pɑn^{C} *pâns	割 kât kɑt *kât 達 dât dɑt *dât 犮 bwât bɑt *bât	害 ɣâi^{C} gɑs *gâts 太 tʰâi^{C} tʰɑs *tʰâs 貝 pwâi^{C} pɑs *pâts	何 ɣâ gɑi *gâi 跛 pwâ pɑi^{B}*pâiʔ 多 tâ tɑi *tâi
III gr	建 kjɐn^{C} kɨɑn^{C} *kans 反 pjwɐn^{B} puɑn^{B} *panʔ 勸 kʰjwɐn^{C} kʰyɑn^{C} *khwans 遠 jwɐn^{B} wɑn^{B} *wanʔ	猲 xjɐt hɨɑt *hat 發 pjwɐt puɑt *pat 越 jwɐt wɑt *wat	艾 ŋjɐi^{C} ŋɨɑs *ŋas 吠 bjwɐi^{C} buɑs *bas 顪 xjwɐi^{C} hyɑs *hwats	
3/3 gr	搴 kjän^{B}3 kɨan^{B} *krianʔ 拚 bjän^{C}3 bɨan^{C} *brans	桀 gjät3 gɨat *gat	揭 kʰjäi^{C}3 kʰɨas *khats	騎 gje3 gɨɑi *gai 皮 bje3 bɨɑi *bai
III ac	戰 tśjän^{C} tśan^{C} *tans 延 jiän jan *lan	紲 sjät siat *slat	世 śjäi^{C} śas *lhats 曳 jiäi^{C} jas *lats	離 lje liɑi *rai
III ac				蛇 dźja źai *m-lai
II	姦 kan kan *krân 山 ṣan ṣan *srân		邁 mai^{C} mas *mrâts 敗 pai^{C} pas *prâts	加 ka kai *krâi 麻 ma mai *mrâi 沙 ṣa ṣai *srâi

Finals in *-wat/s are under rime 22 *-ot/s, rimes in *-et/s under rime 20.

After acute initials in Div. III, OC *-at and *-et have merged into MC -jät, these OC rimes are therefore difficult to untangle; they are included in this rime group. See Table 20-1.

After gutturals in Div. III occur two MC finals, Kjɐt and *chóngmiŭ* 3/3 Kjät. Baxter reconstructs all MC Kjät with OC medial *r. However, after *ʔ, x* and *ŋ* only *-jɐt* occurs, and -*jät* as a rare doublet. Tone C words tend to belong to Div. 3/3 (-jäi^{C} 3), but the closed counterpart to belong to Div. III (-jɐt). Therefore Div. 3/3 Kjät(s) and Div. III Kjɐt are nearly in complementary distribution, both are the regular reflexes of OCM *kat (without medial *r). See Intro. 5.2.3 for more about the removal of OCB medial *r in MC Div. 3/3 syllables.

21-1	**= K. 313**	**Mand.**	**MC**	**LHan**	**OCM**
a	匄	gài	kâi^{C}, kât	kɑs, kɑt	kâst, kât
i	葛	gé	kât	kɑt	kât
-	擖	gè	kat 2, kăt 2	kat, kɛt	krât or krêt

[E] TB: Lepcha hrit 'to comb', LB *kret 'scrape' > WB kʰrac 'to scrape', Kachin kʰrèt 'rasp, grate' <> Tai: S. kʰraat^{D2} < *g- 'to scrape, rake' ⪤ kraat^{D1} 'metal scraper or grater'

def	曷髷蝎	hé	ɣât	gɑt	gât

			MC	LHan	OCM	
g	褐	hè	ɣât	gɑt	gât	
h	鶡 bird A	hé	ɣât	gɑt	gât	
	bird B	kě	kʰât	kʰɑt	khât	
jz	渴¹㵣	kě	kʰât	kʰɑt	khât	'thirst'
j	渴² dried	jié	gjät 3	gɨat	gat	
	[T] Sin Sukchu SR gje (入)					
o	楬 pole	jié	gjät 3	gɨat	gat	
	mus. in.	qià	kʰat	kʰat	khrât	'musical instrument'
p	偈 robust	jié	gjät 3, kjɐt	gɨat, kɨɑt	gat, kat	[T] Indic gāthā, gadha
	go away	qiè	kʰjät 3	kʰɨat	khat	= m
qr	碣竭	jié	gjät 3	gɨat	gat	
-	羯	jié	kjät 3	kɨat	kat	
	[T] MTang kar, ONW kat <> [E] ? TB: Kanauri kʰas 'sheep'					
m	朅	qiè	kʰjät 3, kʰjɐt	kʰɨat	khat	
n	揭 lift	jiē, qì	kʰjäi^C 3	kʰɨas	khats	'lift one's clothes'
	lift	jié, jiē, qiè	gjät, kjät 3, kʰjät	gɨat, kɨat, kʰɨat	gat, kat, khat	'lift on shoulder' OCB *khrjats
	The graph has additional MC readings, see GSR 313n.					
s	愒 to rest	qì, qiè	kʰjäi^C 3, kʰjät	kʰɨas, kʰɨat	khats, khat	= 21-6/329 憩
	desire	kài	kʰâi^C	kʰɑs	khâts	
t	猲	xiè, xié	xjɐt	hɨɑt	hat	
u	歇	xiē	xjɐt	hɨɑt	hat	
k	喝 shout	hē	xât	hɑt	hât	
	choke	ài	ʔai^C	ʔas	ʔâts	
	[N] It seems that after *ʔ-, tone C counterparts to Div. I *ʔât appear in QYS Div. II					
l	遏	è	ʔât	ʔɑt	ʔât	= 1-28/270a 閼
v	暍	yē	ʔjɐt	ʔɨɑt	ʔat	
x	謁	yè	ʔjɐt	ʔɨɑt	ʔat	
a'	藹	ǎi	ʔâi^C	ʔɑs	ʔâts	
y	餲	yì, ài	ʔjäi^C 3, ʔai^C, ʔât	ʔɨas, ʔas, ʔɑt	ʔats, ʔât(s)	

21-2	**= K. 314**	**Mand.**	**MC**	**LHan**	**OCM**	
a	害	hài	ɣâi^C	gɑs	gâts	OCB *ɦkat(s)
	[T] ONW ɣɑC					
d	割	gē	kât	kɑt	kât	
	[T] Sin Sukchu SR kɔ (入); MGZY go (入) [kɔ] <> [D] *k̥ɑt					
	[E] ST and area: TB *(s-)kat 'cut', WT 'gas-pa 'to split, break'					
c	犗	jiè	kai^C	kas	krâts	
f	轄	xiá	ɣat	gat	grât	= 21-3/282 舝
g	豁	huò	xwât	huɑt	hwât	

21-3	**= K. 282**	**Mand.**	**MC**	**LHan**	**OCM**	
a	舝	xiá	ɣat	gat	grât	= 21-2/314f 轄

21-4	= K. 283	Mand.	MC	LHan	OCM	
a	孑	jié	kjät 3	kɨat	kat	

21-5	= K. 284	Mand.	MC	LHan	OCM	
a	桀 hero	jié	gjät 3	gɨat	gat	OCB *grjat
	[E] ? TB: WT gyad 'champion, athlete'; or Lushai hrat[F] < hraat 'brave, resolute'					
	lift	jiē	kjät 3	kɨat	kat	
b	傑	jié	gjät 3	gɨat	gat	OCB *grjat

21-5A		Mand.	MC	LHan	OCM
-	彑	jì	kjäi[C] 3	kɨas	kats

21-5B		Mand.	MC	LHan	OCM
-	罽[illegible]蘮瀱	jì	kjäi[C] 3	kɨas	kats
	罽 [T] MHan Indic kāth; 罽賓 kɨas-pin Kashmir				

21-6	= K. 329	Mand.	MC	LHan	OCM		
a	憩	qì	kʰjäi[C] 3	kʰɨas	khats	= 21-1/313s 愒	OCB *khrjats

21-7	= K. 332	Mand.	MC	LHan	OCM
a	瘞	yì	ʔjäi[C] 3	ʔɨas	ʔats or ʔas

21-8	= K. 268	Mand.	MC	LHan	OCM
a	枿	è	ŋât	ŋɑt	ŋât
	= 21-9/269 歹, = 24-17/252j 欁, 21-11/289j 糱				

21-9	= K. 269	Mand.	MC	LHan	OCM	
a	歹	è	ŋât	ŋɑt	ŋât	= see 21-8/268

21-10	= K. 347	Mand.	MC	LHan	OCM	
a	乂	yì	ŋjɐi[C]	ŋɨɑs	ŋas	
cb	艾[1]刈	yì	ŋjɐi[C]	ŋɨɑs	ŋas	'to mow'
	[E] TB: WT rŋa-ba, brŋas 'to mow, cut, reap', West Tib. col. rŋab-pa					
c	艾[2] artem.	ài	ŋâi[C]	ŋɑs	ŋâs	'artemisia'
	[T] Sin Sukchu SR ŋaj (去); MGZY ŋay (去) [ŋaj]					

21-11 = K. 289 There is only one syllable of the type ŋjɐt in SSYP, hence ŋjät 3 probably represents OCM ŋat, not ŋrat.

		Mand.	MC	LHan	OCM	
a	辥	xiē	sjät	siat	sŋat	
ed	薛 d	xuē	sjät	siat	sŋat	
f	躠	sà, xiē	sât, siet	sɑt, set	sât, sêt	
g	孽	niè	ŋjät 3	ŋɨat	ŋat	[T] ONW ŋat
h	蠥	niè	ŋjät 3	ŋɨat	ŋat	
	[E] ST *ŋja(t) or *ŋje(t): WT ñes-pa 'evil, calamity, crime', Kachin nye 'punish, cause woe'					
i	糱 malt	niè	ŋjät 3	ŋɨat	ŋat	[T] ONW ŋat
	[E] TB: Lushai ŋaan[H] < ŋaan 'malt'					

j	檗	è,	ŋât,	ŋɑt,	ŋât,	
		niè	ŋjät 3	ŋɨat	ŋat	
	= 21-8/268a 枿; 24-17/252j 巘					

21-12 = K. 317		**Mand.**	**MC**	**LHan**	**OCM**	
a	大	dà, dài,	dâi^{C},	dɑs, dɑh,	dâs,	OCB *lāts
		tài	t^{h}âi^{C}	t^{h}ɑs	thâs	
	[T] Sin Sukchu SR daj (去), PR, LR da; MGZY tay (去) [daj]; Sui-Tang dɑ(i)^{C}, ONW dɑC/^{C}					
	[D] Y-Guangzh tai^{C2}, Taishan ai^{C}; K-Meix t^{h}a^{C}					
d	太	tài	t^{h}âi^{C}	t^{h}ɑs	thâs	OCB *hlāts
	= 21-13/316a 泰 <> [T] ONW t^{h}ɑC <> [E] ? TB *tay 'big' > WT mt^{h}e-bo 'thumb', Nung t^{h}ɛ 'big, large, great', Mikir t^{h}è, ket^{h}è 'id.'; WB tay 'very'; Abor-Miri ta 'large'					
fg	汏汰 wave	dài	dâi^{C}	dɑs	dâts (< lâts ?)	
	[E] TB: WT rlabs 'wave'					
	汏 penetr.	tài	t^{h}âi^{C}	t^{h}ɑs	thâts	⋈ 21-14/271b 達
	汏 pass o.	tà	t^{h}ât	t^{h}ɑt	thât	
hl	軑鈦	dài, dì	diei^{C}, dâi^{C}	des, dɑs	dês, dâs	
	[E] TB: WB t^{h}it 'stocks for confinement'					
j	杕	dì	diei^{C}	des	dês	
i	忕	shì	źjäi^{C}	dźas	das or des	

21-13 = K. 316		**Mand.**	**MC**	**LHan**	**OCM**	
a	泰	tài	t^{h}âi^{C}	t^{h}ɑs	thâs	= 21-12/317a 大

21-14 = K. 271		**Mand.**	**MC**	**LHan**	**OCM**	
a	羍 lamb	tà	t^{h}ât	t^{h}ɑt	thât	
	The graph shows a sheep between the legs of a standing person.					
b	達 reach	dá	dât	dɑt	dât	⋈ 21-12/317f 汏
	[T] Sin Sukchu SR da (入); ONW dɑt <> [E] TB: LB *dat 'alive, to be'; Lushai dɔɔt^{F} / dɔʔ^{L} 'to pierce, stick in, sprout up'					
	達 to a. fro	tà	t^{h}ât	t^{h}ɑt	thât	'go to and fro'
de	撻闥	tà	t^{h}ât	t^{h}ɑt	thât	

21-15 = K. 315		**Mand.**	**MC**	**LHan**	**OCM**	
a	帶	dài	tâi^{C}	tɑs	tâs R!	OCB *tats
	[T] Sin Sukchu SR taj (去); MGZY day (去) [taj]; ONW tɑC <> [E] TB *ta:y, Lushai tai^{R} 'waist'					
-	蹛	dài	tâi^{C}	tɑs		
c	蔕	dì	tiei^{C}	tes	tês	
-	螮	dì	tiei^{C}	tes		[T] BTD Skt. darś-,dr̥ś
d	墆 screen	dì	diei^{C}	des	dêts	
	hoard	dié	diet	det	dêt	
e	遰 go away	dì	diei^{C}	des	dês	
	sheath	shì	źjäi^{C}	dźes	des	
b	滯	zhì	ḍjäi^{C}	ḍes	dres	
f	懘	chì, zhǐ	tś^{h}jäi^{C}, tśje^{B}	tś^{h}as, tśe^{B} ?	thes, teʔ	

21-16 = K. 336		**Mand.**	**MC**	**LHan**	**OCM**	
ab	筮 b	shì	źjäi^C	dźas	dats	
cd	噬澨	shì	źjäi^C	dźas	dats	

21-17 = K. 335		**Mand.**	**MC**	**LHan**	**OCM**	
ab	制製	zhì	tśjäi^C	tśas	tats or kets ?	

[T] Sin Sukchu SR tʂi (去); MGZY ji (去) [tʂi]; ONW tśei

c	掣	chè	tśʰjät, tśʰjäi^C	tśʰiat, tśʰias	that(s) or *e?	
d	猘	zhì	kjäi^C 3	kɨas	kats or krets ?	

21-18 = K. 334		**Mand.**	**MC**	**LHan**	**OCM**	
a	彘	zhì	ḍjäi^C	ḍias	drats < r-lats	

[E] KT: KS *ʔdlaai^B 'wild pig', PHlai *lat

21-19 = K. 287		**Mand.**	**MC**	**LHan**	**OCM**	
a	折 break	zhé	tśjät	tśat	tet (or tat)	

OCB *tjats (1992: 393), *tjet (1998) <> [T] ONW tśat

	折 bend	shé	źjät	dźat	det	OCB *N-tjet

[T] ONW dźat <> [E] TB *tsyat, or rather *tyat: LB *tsat ~ C-tsat 'break in two, conclude'; WT 'cʰad-pa, čʰad 'to cut, explain'

	折 slow	tí	diei	de	dê	
h	硩	chè, tì	ṭʰjät, tʰiek	ṭʰiat, tʰek	thret, thêk	
cdg	哲悊蜇	zhé	ṭjät	ṭiat	trat	[T] ONW tat
ij	晣晢	zhé, zhì	tśjät, tśjäi^C	tśat, tśas	tat, tats	OCB *tjats
km	誓逝	shì	źjäi^C	dźas	dats	OCB *djats
n	哳	zhā	ṭat	ṭat	trât	

21-19A	心	jí	tśjät	tśat	tat or tet	SW 490

21-20 = K. 286		**Mand.**	**MC**	**LHan**	**OCM**	
a	㪿	?				
bc	撤徹	chè	ḍjät, ṭʰjät	ṭʰiat	thret R!	OCB *thrjet, *ɦthrjet

徹 [T] ONW tʰat <> [E] ? TB: WB tat 'to know, be skilled in', Tani *tas 'to listen / hear', WT tʰos-pa 'to hear'

d	澈	chè	ḍjät	ḍiat	dret	
ef	轍[illegible]	ché	ḍjät	ḍiat	dret	

[E] TB: WT rǰes < rjes 'trace, track'

21-21 = K. 338		**Mand.**	**MC**	**LHan**	**OCM**	
a	曳	yì	jiäi^C	jas	lats	
b	洩 leak	xiè	sjät	siat	slat	= 21-23/339h 泄

[E] TB: Mru yat 'to leak, ooze'

	洩 dispers.	yì	jiäi^C	jas	lats	
c	絏	xiè	sjät	siat	slat	= 21-23/339 紲緤 緤

21-22 = K. 333		**Mand.**	**MC**	**LHan**	**OCM**	
a	裔	yì	jiäi^C	jas	lats	

21-23 = K. 339 The OC vowel could have been either *a or *e. The PCH final consonant was probably *-p in some of the words; 339a is only partially phonetic in 35-10/633 because of the transparent semantic connection.

		Mand.	MC	LHan	OCM	
a	世	shì	śjäi^{C}	śas	lhats < *-ps	

[T] Sin Sukchu SR ṣi (去); MGZY shi (去) [ṣi]; ONW śei; BTD Skt. -śatru

		Mand.	MC	LHan	OCM	
d	貰	shì	śjäi^{C}, (d)źja^{C}	śas, (d)źa^{C}	lhas, m-lah	
k	勩 toil	yì	jiäi^{C}	jas	lat, lats	

[E] TB: WT las, OTib. blas 'work, toil', TGTM *gjat < *gl-

		Mand.	MC	LHan	OCM	
e	抴	yì	jiäi^{C}, jiät	jas, jat	lat, lats	
fg	枻詍	yì	jiäi^{C}	jas	lats < laps	
h	泄	xiè, yì	sjät, jiäi^{C}	siat, jas	slat, lats	= 21-21/338b 洩
ijl	紲靾渫	xiè	sjät	siat	slat	
m	緤	xiè	sjät	siat	slat	= 21-21/338c 絏

21-24 = K. 272		Mand.	MC	LHan	OCM	
a	剌	là	lât	lɑt	rât	

[E] TB *(g-)ra-t ≭ *(g-)rya-t > WT dra-ba 'cut, clip, lop, prune, pare', Lepcha hra 'cut', Nung rat 'sever', WB hra^{C} 'wound, slightly cut'

		Mand.	MC	LHan	OCM	
-	辣	là	lât			

[D] Min: Amoy loáh [loaʔ^{D2}], lit. loát 'pungent' <> [E] Tai: Saek thaat < d- 'peppers, spicy, hot', Po-ai šaat^{D2L} < ǰ-, 'hot, peppery', Dioi śat[1] (< *b-lat[1])

		Mand.	MC	LHan	OCM	
e	賴	lài	lâi^{C}	lɑs	râts	

[T] Indic raś, rāṣ (Coblin 1983: 83). MHan 都賴 tɑ-lɑs Talas

		Mand.	MC	LHan	OCM	
fg	瀨籟	lài	lâi^{C}	lɑs	râts	

瀨 [E] AA: Wa-Lawa-Bulang *rah 'rapids, waterfall' ≭ OKhmer rat /rɔt/ 'to move swiftly, run' <> PTai *hlaai^{B1} 'rapids in a river'

		Mand.	MC	LHan	OCM	
h	藾 artem.	lài,là	lâi^{C}, lât	lɑs, lɑt	râts	'artemisia'
	shade	lài	lâi^{C}	lɑs	râts	
-	懶	lǎn	lân^{B}	—	[T] ONW lɑn^{B} <> [D] PMin *diɑn^{B}	
i	獺	tǎ, chǎ	tʰât, ṭʰat	tʰɑt, ṭʰat	rhât	

21-25 = K. 291 Some OC syllables in this series may have the vowel *e rather than *a.

		Mand.	MC	LHan	OCM	
a	列	liè	ljät	liat	rat	
bcd-	冽洌烈	liè	ljät	liat	rat R!	OCB *C-rjat
-ef	颲茢裂	liè	ljät	liat	rat or ret ?	

[T] Sin Sukchu 裂 SR lje (入); MGZY 裂 lÿa (入) [ljɛ]

[E] TB: WT dres-ma, dred-ma 'grass for ropes and shoes', WB krit 'a kind of grass'

		Mand.	MC	LHan	OCM	
g	栵	lì, liè	ljäi^{C}, ljät	lias, liat	rats or rets ?	OCB *C-rjets (?)
hi	例痢	lì	ljäi^{C}	lias	rats	

21-26 = K. 326, 340, 267		MC	LHan	OCM	
326a	萬[1] > 蠆 chài	ṭʰăi^{C}	ṭʰas	rhâts	OCB *hrjats
267cd	萬[2] > 勱邁 mài	mai^{C}	mas	mrâts	OCB *mrats
267a	萬[3] wàn	mjwɐn^{C}	muɑn^{C}	mâns	'10000'

[T] Sin Sukchu SR vwan (去), LR vwan; MGZY (khan >) wan (去) [van]; ONW muan

340a 厲[1] hedge lì ljäi^{C} lias rats
[E] TB: Tiddim gɔɔl^{F} < *rɔɔls 'fence' <> rua^{C2} < *r- 'fence'

a 厲[2] drag lì ljäi^{C} lias rats OCB *C-rjats

ac 厲[3]勵 lì ljäi^{C} lias rats 'cruel' OCB *C-rets
~ 29-25/532a 戾 <>[E] TB: WT hrad-pa 'exert oneself, push violently, stem tide'
[T] BTD Skt. re (Coblin 1993: 912)

a 厲[4] ford lì ljäi^{C} lias rats
[E] TB: WT rab(s) 'ford'; JP rap^{55} 'to ford, cross a river'

ab 厲[5]礪 lì ljäi^{C} lias rats 'grind'

d 癘 lì ljäi^{C} lias rats
(Baxter 1992: 404) <> [E] KT: PTai *tr-: S. taai^{A1} 'to die', Saek praai^{1}

ef 蠣蠆 lì ljäi^{C} lias rats
[T] MGZY li (去) [li] <> [E]-> PTai *nl/r-: S. (lek-)nai^{A2}, Po-ai lai^{A2} 'bee's sting'

g 糲 lài, là, lì lâi^{C}, lât, ljäi^{C} lɑt/s, lias rât, râts, rats
[E] Cf. TB: WT 'bras 'rice' ⋊ 'bras-bu 'fruit', Lushai raʔ^{L} < *raʔ or *rah (< *-s) 'fruit'

21-27 = K. 318 **Mand.** **MC** **LHan** **OCM**

ab 奈[1]柰 nài nâi^{C} nɑs nâs or nâts
Cf. Japanese (kara)nashi 梨. <> [T] BTD Skt. [Vārā]ṇasī

a 奈[2] nài nâi^{C} nɑs nâs
Starting with a few occurrences in Zuozhuang, *nâs replaces rú 如 *nah < *naas in the Zhanguo period in the expression 如何 rú hé (Unger *Hao-ku* 22, 1983).

21-28 = K. 337 The MC finals are ambiguous; in some words, the OC rime could have been *-at, in others *-et.

Mand. **MC** **LHan** **OCM**

a 祭 sacrif. jì tsjäi^{C} tsias tsats or tsets
祭 a state zhài tṣăi^{C} tṣɛs tsrâts or tsrêts

e 穄 jì tsjäi^{C} tsias tsats
[E] WB c^{h}ap 'millet'

f 際 jì tsjäi^{C} tsias tsats OCB *tsjats < *tsjaps
[T] Sin Sukchu SR tsjej (去), PR, LR tsi; MGZY dzi (去) [tsi] <> [E] TB: WT č^{h}abs 'together'; Garo tsap-tsap 'adjacent'; WB cap 'to join, unite', Kachin tśyap 'adhere'

i 蔡 sacrif. cài ts^{h}âi^{C} ts^{h}ɑs, sɑs, sɑ^{C} tshâts < k-sâts, sâts OCB srats
= 21-29/319a 杀. <> [T] Han BTD Pkt. sā-
蔡 a state zhài tṣăi^{C} tṣɛs tsrets

h 瘵 zhài tṣăi^{C} tṣɛs tsrêts OCB *tsr(j)ets
[E] AA: PVM *k-ceːt > Viet. chêt 'to die'; PMonic kcət 'to die' ⋊ k-r-cet 'to kill'

j 察 chá tṣ^{h}ăt tṣ^{h}ɛt tshrêt R! OCB tshrjet (1992: 412)
[T] Sin Sukchu SR tʂ'a (入)

g 傺 chì ṭ^{h}jäi^{C} ṭ^{h}ias thrats

21-29 = K. 319 The MC finals are ambiguous; in some words, the OC rime could have been either *-at or *-et.

Mand. **MC** **LHan** **OCM**

a 杀 cài ts^{h}âi^{C} ts^{h}ɑs tshâts < k-sât = 21-28/337i 蔡

de 殺 kill shā ṣăt ṣat R! srât OCB *srjet < *srjat
[T] Sin Sukchu SR ṣa (入); ONW ṣät <> [E] TB *g-sat 'to kill' > WT gsod-pa, bsad, Chepang sat-sa, WB sat, PL *C-sat, JP sat^{31} ≭ gă^{31}-sat^{55} 'attack'
殺 reduce shài ṣăi^{C} ṣas srâts 'to diminish, reduce'
\- 刹 chà tṣʰat tṣʰat —
[T] ONW tṣʰät. BTD Skt. kṣat-; Skt. kṣetra 'place, seat, sphere of activity'
g 摋 sà sât sɑt sât
f 榝 shā, shè ṣăt, ṣjät ṣɛt, ṣet srat or sret

21-30 = K. 275 **Mand.** **MC** **LHan** **OCM**
ade 癶撥襏 bō pwât pɑt pât
b 癹 bó bwât bɑt bât
GSR writes the lower element as gōng 弓.
c 發 shoot fā pjwɐt puɑt pat
[T] Sin Sukchu SR fwa (入), PR, LR faʔ; MTang pfar < pfuar, ONW puat <> [D] Min: Xiam col. puʔ^{D1}, lit. huat^{D1} <> [E] Area word: TB-LB *C-pat 'vomit', WB pʰat, JP n^{31}-pʰat^{31}. <> AA: Mon pnoh 'bow' ≭ poh 'to shoot with a pellet-bow'
發 splash bō pwât pɑt pât
f 廢 neglect fèi pjwɐi^{C} puɑs pats = 21-31/276o 祓
[E] Tai: S. bap4 'exhausted, worn out'
廢 great fā pjwɐt puɑt pat

21-31 = K. 276 **Mand.** **MC** **LHan** **OCM**
a 犮 bá bwât bɑt bât
bc 跋魃 bá bwât bɑt bât
h 拔 bèi bwâi^{C} bɑs bâts 'thinned' OCB *bots R!
= 30-18/501f pèi 沛
拔 bá bwât bɑt bât 'rise'
拔 bá băt bɛt or bat brât ? 'pull out'
[T] MTang bär, ONW bät <> [E] TB: Lushai pɔt^{L} / pɔʔ^{L} 'to pull, pull up, out'
g 茇 halt bá bwât bɑt bât
茇 roots bá pwât pɑt pât
[E] JP (n^{31}-/niŋ^{31}-) pot^{31} 'root, origin'
f 胈 bá pwât pɑt pât
d 坺 bá, fá bwât, bjwɐt bɑt, buɑt bât, bat
e 軷 bá, bèi bwât, bwâi^{C} bɑt, bɑs bât, bâts
o 祓 fèi pjwɐi^{C} puɑs pats = 21-30/275f 廢
i 髮 fā pjwɐt puɑt pat OCB *pjot R!
[E] ? TB: WT pʰud 'hair knot, tuft of hair'
j j fá bjwɐt buɑt bat
klm 紱韍黻 fú pjwət put pət
= 30-18/501c 芾; = 30-17/500k 茀
n 帗 wand fú pʰjwət pʰut pʰət
o 祓 purify fú pʰjwət pʰut pʰət
fèi pjwɐi^{C} puɑs pats

21-32 **Mand.** **MC** **LHan** **OCM**
\- 鉢 bō pwât pɑt < Skt. pātra [T] ONW pɑt

21-33 = K. 307		**Mand.**	**MC**	**LHan**	**OCM**	
a-	伐筏	fá	bjwɐt	buɑt	bat	≍ 21-31/276d 坺茷
	伐 [T] MTang bvar < bvuar, ONW buat					
f	茷 lush	fá	bjwɐt	buɑt	bat	
	flutter	pèi, péi !	bwâi^C	bɑs	bâts	= 30-18 / 501 旆

21-34 = K. 308		**Mand.**	**MC**	**LHan**	**OCM**	
a	罰	fá	bjwɐt	buɑt	bat	= 21-33/307a 伐
	[T] MTang bvar < bvuar, ONW buat					

21-35 = K. 320		**Mand.**	**MC**	**LHan**	**OCM**	
a	貝	bèi	pwâi^C	pɑs	pâts	
	[T] Sin Sukchu SR puj (去), PR pəj, LR pəj; MGZY bay (去) [paj]; BTD Skt. pat[tra]. MHan 劫貝(娑) kɨɑp-pɑs(-sɑ[i]) Skt. kārpāsa					
	[E] ST *pop (?): TB Chepang bop 'snail', JP lă^{55}-pop^{55} 'snail'					
-	垻	bà	pa^C	<- Tai loan: S. paa^{B1} < pa^B 'meadow'		
f	敗 ruin	bài	pai^C	pɑs	prâts	OCB *prats
	[T] Sin Sukchu SR pai, bai (去); MGZY bay, pay (去) [paj ~ bɑj]					
	敗 be ru.	bài	bai^C	bɑs	brâts	'be ruined' OCB *fiprats
-	唄	bài	bai^C	bɑs	—	[T] BTD Skt. paṭh

21-36 = K. 348		**Mand.**	**MC**	**LHan**	**OCM**	
a	吠	fèi	bjwɐi^C	buɑs	bas < *bos	OCB *bjots
	[T] ONW bei <> [E] ST *baus: KN-Lushai bauʔ < *baus 'to bark'					

21-37 = K. 277		**Mand.**	**MC**	**LHan**	**OCM**	
ac	末秣	mò	mwât	mɑt	mât	
	[T] ONW mɑt. MHan 且末 tsʰia^B-mɑt = Calmadana					
b	沫 foam	mò	mwât	mɑt	mât	
	finish	mèi	mwâi^C	mɑs	mâts	
-	茉莉	mò-lì	mwât-lji^C	—	'Jasmine or moly' < Skt. mallikā	

21-38 = K. 293		**Mand.**	**MC**	**LHan**	**OCM**	
a	罿	xuè	xjwät 3	hyat	hmat	

22 OCM rime *-ot, *-wat, *-o(t)s,*-wa(t)s Yuè- Jì bù 月祭部 (3)

GSR 268 - 348

Baxter 1992: 389 ff. (§10.1.2)

See Table 25-1 for OCM rimes *-on / *-wan, *-ot / *-wat, *-oi / *-wai in QYS categories. See Table 28-1 for MC Div. 3/3 without OC medial *r; see also Intro. 5.2.3 for more about the removal of OCB medial *r in MC Div. 3/3 syllables.

After grave initials in Div. III, the QYS distinguishes the finals -jwɐt / -jwɐi^C and -jwät / -jwäi^C. Only the latter occur after acute initials, but also after grave initials in tone C (-jwäi^C), while the final *t* counterparts have the final -jwɐt. We assume a single LHan and OC source for both rimes. In OCB system, MC -jwät / -jwäi^C would go back to a medial *r. This distributional pattern is parallel to *-at*, rime 21.

22-1 **= K. 302** The OC rime of some syllables is not certain.

		Mand.	MC	LHan	OCM		
a	𠯑	jué	kjwɐt	kyɑt	kwat		
ef	𠯑舌	guō	kwât	kuɑt	kwât		
h	括	kuò	kwât	kuɑt	kwât	⋈ 佸	OCB *kʷat
	[E] TB: Lushai kuaʔ^L < kuas 'put arm(s) around (tree, neck, waist, etc.)'						
i	栝	kuò	kwât	kuɑt	kwât		
j	聒	kuò	kwât	kuɑt	kwât		
k	髺	kuò	kwât	kuɑt	kwât		
l	佸	huó	ɣwât, kwât	ɣuɑt, kuɑt	gwât, kwât	⋈ 括	
m	活 purl	guō	kwât	kuɑt	kwât		OCB *kʷat
	'to purl (as running water)'						
	活 alive	huó	ɣwât	ɣuɑt	gwât R!		OCB *gʷat
	[T] BTD Skt. vat						
n	刮	guā	kwat	kuat	kwrât or krôt		
	[T] Sin Sukchu SR kwa (入); MGZY gwa (入) [kwa] <> [D] PMin *kuot						
o	話	huà	ɣwai^C	ɣuas	gwrâts or grôts		
	[T] Sin Sukchu SR ɣwa (去); MGZY Xway (去) [ɣwaj] <> [D] PMin *hua^C						
p	銛	guō	kwât	kuɑt	kwât		
q	闊 far	kuò	kʰwât	kʰuɑt	khwât		
	OCB *khot (Baxter 1992: 409) <> [T] Sin Sukchu SR k'wɔ (入); MGZY khwo (入) [k'wɔ]						
	契闊	qiè-kuò	kʰwât	kʰuɑt	khêt-khôt 'bound together'		
	See Baxter 1992: 409-410.						

22-2 **= K. 301** With some syllables the OC rime is not certain. The MC rime Kjwɐt has the tone C counterpart Kjwäi^C 3 (Kjwɐi^C is extremely rare), hence these syllables had no OC medial r.

		Mand.	MC	LHan	OCM	
a	欮	jué	kjwɐt	kyɑt	kot	
c	厥	jué	kjwɐt	kyɑt	kot	[T] ONW kuat
-	[illegible]	jué	kjwɐt	kyɑt	kot	
d	蕨	jué	kjwɐt	kyɑt	kot	OCB *kjot
	[D] PMin *k̑iot 'bracken' <> [E] TB: WT skyas-ma, skyes-ma 'fern'					
e	蟩	jué	kjwɐt	kyɑt	kot	
jk	橛 k	jué	gjwɐt	gyɑt	got	
fg	f 蹶 agile	guì	kjwäi^C 3	kyɑs	gots	OCB *g^{w}rjats
	stumble	jué	k/gjwɐt	k/gyɑt	kot, got	
h	闕 gate	què	k^{h}jwɐt	k^{h}yɑt	khot	OCB *k^{w}hjat
	闕 excava.	jué	gjwɐt	gyɑt	got	
	[E] ST *(k)wa- 'passage through': Lushai kua^L 'a hole, burrow, cavity' ⪤ kua^L / kuakF 'be open or clear'; WB ə-wa^C 'opening of door, hole'					
i	撅 dig out	jué	gjwɐt	gyɑt	got	
	[E] ST: *r-ko-t > WT rkod-pa 'excavate, dig' ⪤ rko-ba 'to dig'; JP got[31] 'dig'					
	撅 lift	guì	kjwäi^C 3	kyɑs	kots	⪤ kōu 摳 *kho
l	嶡	guì	kjwäi^C 3	kyɑs	gots	

22-3	**= K. 321**	**Mand.**	**MC**	**LHan**	**OCM**	
a	會 unite	huì	ɣwâi^C	ɣuɑs	gôts	
	⪤ 22-1/302l 括 *kwât <> [T] Sin Sukchu SR ɣuj (去); MGZY Xue (去) [ɣuɛ]; MTang guɑi, ONW ɣuɑC; BTD Skt. vāsa, bhas. OCB *gots < *gops; OCB rime *-ops is based on etymological assumptions and is not borne out by actual rimes					
	會 calcul.	kuài	kwâi^C	kuɑs	kôts	'calculation'
def	廥旝澮	kuài	kwâi^C	kuɑs	kôts	
gh	膾襘	kuài	kwâi^C	kuɑs	kôts	
i	檜	guì, guō	kwâi^C, kwât	kuɑs, kuɑt	kôt, kôts	
j	禬	guì, huì	kwâi^C, ɣwâi^C	kuɑs, ɣuɑs	kôts, gôts	
k	繪	huì	ɣwâi^C	ɣuɑs	gôts	
l	噲 comf.	kuài	k^{h}wai^C	k^{h}uɑs	khrôts	'comfortable'
	faded		kwâi^C, kwât	kuɑs, kuɑt	kôt, kôts	
m	鬠	guì	kwâi^C, ɣwât	kuɑs, ɣuɑt	kôts, gôt	
n	薈	huì	ʔwâi^C	ʔuɑs	ʔôts	OCB *ʔops

22-4	**= K. 304**	**Mand.**	**MC**	**LHan**	**OCM**	
a	曰	yuē	jwɐt	wɑt	wat	
	[T] Sin Sukchu SR ŋye (入); MGZY xwÿa (入) [ɦyɛ]; MTang uar, ONW uat < wat					
e	抇	hú	ɣwət	ɣuət	(g)wə̂t	
f	汩 bubble	hú	ɣwət	ɣuət	gwə̂t	
	regulate	gǔ	kwət	kuət	kwə̂t	
	flow	yù	kiwet, juet	kuet, wit	kwît, wit	= 29-11/507o 潏

22-5	**= K. 303, 346**		**MC**	**LHan**	**OCM**	
ad	戉鉞	yuè	jwɐt	wɑt	wat	
e	越 transgr.	yuè	jwɐt	wɑt	wat	OCB *wjat
	[T] ONW wat; Han BTD *wat: Skt. -pati, -vatī, vata					
	越 plait	huó	ɣwât	ɣuɑt	wât	
f	狘	xuè	xjwɐt	hyɑt	hwat	
346a	歲	suì	sjwäi^C	syas	swats	
	[T] Sin Sukchu SR suj (去); MGZY sue (去) [suɛ]; ONW suei <> [D] PMin *hue^C					
f	顪	huì	xjwɐi^C	hyɑs	hwats	= 25-28/171o 喙
	[T] ONW huei^C <> [E] KT: S. nuat^DIL < *hn- 'beard'					
g	翽	huì	xwâi^C	huɑs	hwâts	
h	濊	huò	xwât	huɑt	hwât	
i	穢	huì	ʔjwɐi^C	ʔyɑs	ʔwats	
j	噦 vomit	yuě	ʔjwɐt, ʔjwät	ʔyɑt	ʔwat	
	[E] TB: LB *ut (not ʔut) 'to belch'					
	噦 tinkle	huì	xwâi^C	huɑs	hwâts	OCB *hwats
k	劌	guì	kjwäi^C	kyɑs	kwats or kots	

22-6	**= K. 305**	**Mand.**	**MC**	**LHan**	**OCM**	
a	粵	yuè	jwɐt	wɑt	wat	

22-7	**= K. 273**	**Mand.**	**MC**	**LHan**	**OCM**	
a	叞	wò	ʔwât	ʔuɑt	ʔwât	
b	掔	wàn	ʔwân^C	ʔuɑn^C	ʔwâns	= 25-17/260m 腕

22-8	**= K. 306, 322**		**MC**	**LHan**	**OCM**	
ag	月抈	yuè	ŋjwɐt	ŋyɑt, S ŋɨot	ŋwat	OCB *ŋʷjat
	[T] Sin Sukchu SR ŋye (入); MGZY xwŷa (入) [ɦyɛ]; MTang ŋuar, ONW ŋuat					
hj	刖跀	yuè	ŋjwɐt, ŋwat	ŋyɑt, ŋuat	ŋwat, ŋrwât	
322a	外	wài	ŋwâi^C	ŋuɑs	ŋwâts	
	[T] Sin Sukchu SR ŋwaj (去), PR ŋwaj, waj; LR waj; MGZY xue (去) [ɦuɛ]; ONW ŋuɑC. The OB graph is identical with bǔ 卜, but here a stroke marks the outside of something symbolized by a vertical line; 'moon' was later added as phonetic.					

22-9	**= K. 274**	**Mand.**	**MC**	**LHan**	**OCM**	
a	奪 rob	duó	dwât	duɑt	lôt	= 22-13/324j
	奪 narrow	duì	dwâi^C	duɑs	lôts	⋈ 19-16/11d

22-10	**= K. 295**	**Mand.**	**MC**	**LHan**	**OCM**	
a	叕	zhuó	tjwät	ṭyat	trot	
de	惙輟	chuò	tjwät	ṭyat	trot	
bf	綴畷	zhuó, zhuì	tjwät, tjwäi^C	ṭyat, ṭyas	trot, trots	
j	錣 point	zhuā, zhuó	ṭwat	ṭuat	trôt	'sharp point at end of whip'
	tallies	zhuì	tjwäi^C	ṭyas	trots	
c	啜 gulp	zhuó	tjwät	ṭyat	trot	
	啜 eat	chuò, shuì	tśʰjwät, źjwäi^C	tśʰuat, dźuas	thot, dots	

i	歠	chuò	tśʰjwät	tśʰuat	thot	
	[D] Ke-Meix tsʰɔt^{11}, Min-Fuzh tsʰuɔʔ^{43}, Jian'ou tsʰyɛ^{34}, Xiamen tsʰeʔ^{32} 'drink'					
g	剟	zhuó, duō, duó	tjwät, twât	tyat, tuɑt	trot, tôt	
h	掇	duō, zhuó	twât, tjwat	tuɑt, tyat	tôt, trot	cf. 22-14/299e
k	蝃蝀	dì-dōng	tiei^C-tuŋ	tes-toŋ	tês-tôŋ	

22-11 = K. 343		Mand.	MC	LHan	OCM	
a	贅	zhuì	tśjwäi^C	tśuas	tots	⋈ 22-10/295b
	[E] TB: WT: gtod-pa, btod-pa 'to tether, tie up, stake' ⋈ rtod-pa 'to tether, a stake or peg'					

22-12 = K. 344		Mand.	MC	LHan	OCM
a	睿叡	ruì	jiwäi^C	juas	los or lots

22-13 = K. 324		Mand.	MC	LHan	OCM	
a	兑 open	duì	dwâi^C, tʰwâi^C	duɑs, tʰuɑs	lôts, lhôts	
	[E] Tai: S. lɔɔt^{D2}L < *dl- 'to slip through a hole or tunnel'					
	兑 glad	duì	dwâi^C	duɑs	lôts	
l	捝 take	tuō, duó	tʰwât, dwât	tʰuɑt, duɑt	lhôt, lôt	'take away'
	[T] ONW tʰuɑt, duɑt <> [D] M-Amoy col. teʔ^{D2}, lit. toat^{D2}, Jiēyáng toʔ^{D2} 'take away forcibly'; Amoy col. tʰuɑʔ^{D1}, lit. tʰuɑt^{D1} 'escape'					
	wipe	shuì	śjwäi^C	śuai^C	lhots	
m	脱 peel o.	tuō, duó	tʰwât, dwât	tʰuɑt, duɑt	lhôt, lôt	[T] ONW tʰuɑt, duɑt
	easy	tuì	tʰwâi^C	tʰuɑs	lhôts	⋈ 19-16/11L
d	駾	tuì, duì	dwâi^C, tʰwâi^C	duɑs, tʰuɑs	lôts, lhôts	
	[E] TB *g-lwat 'loose, relax'					
e	蜕	tuì, tuò, shuì, yuè	tʰwâi^C, tʰwâ^C, śjwäi^C, jiwät	tʰuɑs, tʰuɑi^C, śuai^C, juat	lhôts, lhôih, lhots, lot	
f	鋭 sharp	ruì	jiwäi^C	juas	lots	
	lance	duì	dwâi^C	duɑs	lôts	
gh	帨涚	shuì, cuì	śjwäi^C, tsʰjwäi^C	śuas, tsʰyas	lhots, tshots < s-lhots	
j	敓	duó	dwât	duɑt	lôt	= 22-9/274
op	悦閲	yuè	jiwät	juat	lot	[T] ONW iuat
n	棁	zhuó	tśjwät	tśuat	tot	
	[E] TB: WT rtod-pa 'a post'					
i	税 tax	shuì	śjwäi^C	śuas	lhots	[T] ONW śuei
	mourn.	tuì	tʰwâi^C	tʰuɑs	lhôts	
	dress	tuàn	tʰwân^C !	tʰuɑn^C	lhôns	
q	説 speak	shuō	śjwät	śuat	lhot	
	[T] Sin Sukchu SR ʂye (入); MGZY shwÿe (入) [ʂyɛ]; ONW śuat					
	説 exhort	shuì	śjwäi^C	śuas	lhots	
	[E] shuì 'rest over night': KS: *s-lwa^B 'to rest'					

22-14 = K. 299		**Mand.**	**MC**	**LHan**	**OCM**	
ac	a 鋝	luè	ljwät	lyat	rot	
d	埒	liè	ljwät	lyat	rot	
e	捋	luō	lwât	luɑt	rôt	

[E] PTai ruut^D2 'to scrape off (mud from limbs), strip off (grains from stalk)'

-	酹	lèi	lwâi^C	luɑs	rôts < g-rots

[E] Tai: S. kruat^D1 'to make a libation' ⋇ S. rot^D2 'to sprinkle (water), to water (plants)'

22-15		**Mand.**	**MC**	**LHan**	**OCM**
-	劣	liè	ljwät	lyat	rot (rjot ?)

[T] ONW luat <> [E] TB *ryut > JP yut^31 'become worse (illness)', WB yut < rut 'inferior, mean' ⋇ hrut 'put down'

22-16 = K. 296		**Mand.**	**MC**	**LHan**	**OCM**	
a	絕	jué	dzjwät	dzyat	dzot	
b	蕝	jué,	tsjwät,	tsyat,	tsot,	
		zuì	tsjwäi^C	tsyas	tsots	
cd	脃脆	cuì	tsʰjwäi^C	tsʰyas	tshots	⋇ 22-17/345c 臎

22-17 = K. 345		**Mand.**	**MC**	**LHan**	**OCM**	
a	毳	cuì	tsʰjwäi^C,	tsʰyas,	tshots (< k-sots?),	
			tṣʰjwäi^C	tṣʰyas	tshrots	
c	臎	cuì, quē	tsʰjwät	tsʰyat	tshot	⋇ 22-16/296cd 脆
b	竁	cuì	tsʰjwäi^C	tsʰyas	tshots	OCB *tshjots < *-ops?
	竁	chuì,	tśʰjwäi^C,	tśʰuas,	thots (or k-hlots?),	
		chuàn	tśʰjwän^C	tśʰuan^C	thons	

22-18 = K. 297		**Mand.**	**MC**	**LHan**	**OCM**
a	雪	xuě	sjwät	syat	sot

[T] ONW suat <> [E] KT: Tai-Po'ai nwai^A1 < *hn- 'snow'; KS *ʔnu:i 'snow'

22-19 = K. 298		**Mand.**	**MC**	**LHan**	**OCM**
a	刷	shuā	ṣjwät, ṣwat	ṣuat	srot

[T] Sin Sukchu SR ṣwa (入); MGZY (zhwa >) shwa (入) [ṣwa]

[E] TB: Mru charüt 'comb'; Lushai hru / hruuk 'to rub (off), wipe (off)', JP brut^2 'a brush' (shuāzi) ⋇ lă^55-rut^55 'a brush (shuāzi)', WT šud-pa, bšud < *rhjut 'to rub, get scratched'

23 OCM rime *-en Yuán bù 元部 (1)

GSR 139 - 266

Baxter 1992: 370 ff. (§10.1.1)

See Table 20-1 for OCM rimes *-en, *et in QYS categories.

For LHan, *chongniu* Div. 3/4 items (QYS -jiän 3/4) could be written -ien or -ian; I write -ian because this agrees with the treatment of this final after acute initials, and it is parallel to the breaking of *-on to LHan -uan.

There are no Div. 3/4 (i.e., MC medial yod) counterparts to Div. IV types like MC kien, i.e., no syllable reconstructable as *ken (except after aspiration and labiovelar kw- that block palatalization, see 23-4, 23-17). Therefore velars appear to have palatalized (?) and completely merged with initial dentals by the time phonetic series reached their traditional composition. A velar survives only in 24-29c.

23-1	**= K. 240**	**Mand.**	**MC**	**LHan**	**OCM**	
a	肩 shoulder	jiān	kien	ken	kên	
	[T] MTang kian < kɨan, ONW kėn					
	肩 thin	xián, hén	ɣien, ɣən	gen, gən	gên (and gən ?)	
bc	b 猏	jiān	kien	ken	kên	= 23-3/239b
e	顅	qiān	kʰien, kʰan	kʰen, kʰan or kʰɛn	khên, khrên	

23-2	**= K. 241**	**Mand.**	**MC**	**LHan**	**OCM**	
a	見[1] see	jiàn	kienᶜ	kenᶜ	kêns	
	[T] Sin Sukchu SR kjen (去); MGZY gyan (去) [kjɛn]; MTang kian < kɨan, ONW kėn					
	[E] TB *m-kyen (STC no. 223) > WT mkʰyen-pa 'to know', PTani *ken 'know', NN *C-kʰyeŋ					
	見 covering	jiàn	kănᶜ	kɛnᶜ	krêns	
ae	見[2] 現	xiàn	ɣienᶜ	genᶜ	gêns	'appear'
	[T] MTang ɣian < ɣɨan, ONW ɣėn					
f	俔	qiàn,xiàn	kʰienᶜ,ɣienᴮ	kʰenᶜ, genᴮ	khêns, gênʔ	
g	睍	xiàn	ɣienᴮ	genᴮ	gênʔ	
h	莧 a plant	xiàn	ɣănᶜ	gɛnᶜ	grêns	cf. 25-14
	smile	huàn	see 25-7			
-	硯	yàn	ŋienᶜ	ŋenᶜ	ŋêns	OCB *ŋens
	[D] PMin *ŋhianᶜ					
-	霰 hail	xiàn	sienᶜ	senᶜ	sêns	OCB *s(k)ens
	Alternative graph of 霰 <> [T] TB: WT ser-ba 'hail', JP sin³³					

23-3	**= K. 239**	**Mand.**	**MC**	**LHan**	**OCM**	
ab	幵豣	jiān	kien	ken	kên	豣 = 23-1/240bc
c	趼	jiǎn	kienᴮ	kenᴮ	kênʔ	

d	汧	qiān	k^{h}ien(C)	k^{h}en(C)	khên, khêns	
f	蚈	qiān	k^{h}ien	k^{h}en	khên	
gh	g 研	yán	ŋien	ŋen	ŋên	OCB *ŋen
i	枅	jī	kiei, kien	ke, ken	kê, kên	

23-4	**= K. 196**	**Mand.**	**MC**	**LHan**	**OCM**	
a	a	qiǎn	k^{h}jiän^B 4	k^{h}ien^B	khenʔ	
b	遣 send	qiǎn	k^{h}jiän^B 4	k^{h}ien^B	khenʔ	
	[T] ONW k^{h}ian; Han BTD khian <> [E] TB: WT skyel-ba 'send'					
	遣 s. to grave	qiàn	k^{h}jiän^C 4	k^{h}ien^C	khens	
e	繾	qiǎn	k^{h}jiän^B 4	k^{h}ien^B	khenʔ	
f	譴	qiǎn !	k^{h}jiän^C 4	k^{h}ien^C	khens	

23-5	**= K. 191**	**Mand.**	**MC**	**LHan**	**OCM**	
ab	閒間	jiān	kǎn	kɛn	krên	OCB *kren 'interstice'
	[T] Sin Sukchu SR kjan (平); MGZY (gȳan >) gyan (平) [kjan]; ONW kän					
	閒間	jiàn	kǎn^C	kɛn^C	krêns	'separate'
	[E] TB: Lushai in^L-kaar^L 'the space, interval or distance between, difference' ≭ in^L-kaar^H-aʔ^L 'to come between'; LB *gra^2 > WB kra^B 'have space between, be apart'					
	閒	xián	ɣǎn	gɛn	grên	OCB *ɦkren 'leisure'
f	蕑	jiān	kǎn	kɛn	krên	OCB *kren
	[E] Vietnamese sen 'lotus'					
d	簡	jiǎn	kǎn^B	kɛn^B	krênʔ	
g	僩	xiàn	ɣǎn^B	gɛn^B	grênʔ	
h	瞯	xián	ɣǎn	gɛn	grên	
i	澗	jiàn	kan^C	kan^C	krâns	
j	撊	xiàn	ɣan^B	gan^B	grânʔ	

23-6	**= K. 192**	**Mand.**	**MC**	**LHan**	**OCM**	
a	閑 leisure	xián	ɣǎn	gɛn	grên	OCB *ɦkren
	[T] Sin Sukchu SR ɣjan (平); MGZY (Xȳan >) Xyan (平) [ɣjan]; ONW ɣän, n -/- 'lazy'					
	[E] Tai: PTai *gran^{C2} 'lazy'					
	閑 train	xián	ɣǎn	gɛn	grân	OCB *gran
-	嫻 refined	xián	ɣǎn	gɛn	grên	

23-7	**= K. 185**	**Mand.**	**MC**	**LHan**	**OCM**	
a	柬	jiǎn	kǎn^B	kɛn^B	krênʔ	
e	揀	jiǎn	kǎn^B	kɛn^B	krênʔ	
	[E] Tai: S. klan^{B1} 'select' (as jewels)					
-	楝	liàn	lien^C	len^C	rêns	
	[E] Tai: S. krian^{A1}					
hij	湅練鍊	liàn	lien^C	len^C	rêns	練 [T] ONW lėn
b	諫	jiàn	kan^C	kan^C	krâns	
f	闌 barrier	lán	lân	lɑn	rân	
	[E] ? TB: WB ran^B 'make a barrier on one side'					
q	欄 barrier	lán	lân	lɑn	rân	
	欄 a tree	liàn	lien^C	len^C	rêns	
-	攔	lán	lân	lɑn	rân	

n	蘭	lán	lân	lɑn	rân	OCB *g-ran
	[T] ONW lɑn. MHan 樓蘭 Krorayina					
-	韊	lán	lân	lɑn	rân	
k	瀾	lán	lân(^{C})	lɑn(^{C})	rân, râns	
lm	爛爤	làn	lân^{C}	lɑn^{C}	râns	
o	讕	lán	lân(^{B})	lɑn(^{B})	rân, rânʔ	

23-8	**= K. 1250f**	**Mand.**	**MC**	**LHan**	**OCM**	
f	蠲	juān	kiwen	kuen	kwên	= 23-17/228h 涓

23-9	**= K. 248**	**Mand.**	**MC**	**LHan**	**OCM**	
ab	縣[1] 懸	xuán	ɣiwen	ɣuen	gwên	'suspend'
	[T] MTang ɣuian(?), ONW ɣuėn <> [D] PMin *guen > Fúzh keiŋ^{A2} 'high' ≭ heiŋ^{A2} 'hanging down' <> Tai 'suspend': S. kʰwɛɛn^{A1} < *xw-					
a	縣[2]	xiàn	ɣiwen^{C}	ɣuen^{C}	gwêns	'district' = 23-11/256s
	[T] Sin Sukchu SR ɣjen (去); MGZY Xwŷan (去) [ɣyɛn]					

23-10	**= K. 227**	**Mand.**	**MC**	**LHan**	**OCM**		
ac	員[1] > 圓	yuán	jwän 3	wan	wen	'circle'	
	[T] Sin Sukchu SR yen (平); MGZY xwŷan (平) [ɦyɛn]; ONW uan						
a	員[2] a part.	yún	jwən	wun	wən		OCB *wjən
f	緷	yún	jwen	wɨn	wrən		
eghi	殞隕磒霣	yǔn	jwen^{B} 3	wɨn^{B}	wrənʔ R!		OCB *wrjən(ʔ)
d	塤	xūn !	xjwen	hyɑn	hwan		
j	嫄	yún	jwən	wun	wən		= 34-14/460c 妘
-	韻	yùn	jwən^{C}	—	—		
435a	損	sǔn	swən^{B}	suən^{B}	swənʔ		[T] ONW son

23-11 = K. 829, 256h-c' The blocks GSR 256a-g and h-c' are graphically and phonologically distinct and form separate phonetic series (23-11 and 25-15). GSR 829a was probably originally intended for 'scared and alone...' because prominent eyes tend to be associated with the meaning 'fear'. Since all other words written with this graph rime in *-wen, the series is entered in this rime group.

MC ɣwan II occurs frequently (from OCM *wrân and *wrên), MC ɣiwen < *gwên is rare and tends to be a doublet of MC ɣwan. I suspect that MC ɣwan goes back to simple OCM *wên rather than *wrên (or *wrân), and that the rare MC ɣwǎn derives from OCM *gwrên.

		Mand.	**MC**	**LHan**	**OCM**	
829ab	睘[1] = 嬛	qióng	gjiwäŋ 4	gyeŋ	gweŋ	OCB *gʷjeŋ
	= 32-8/830a 惸, 9-9/843g 煢					
256b'	獧	juàn	kiwen^{C} GY	kuen^{C}	kwêns	
y	圜	yuán	jwän 3	wan	wen	= 23-10/277ac 員圓
	[T] Sin Sukchu SR yen (平); MGZY xwŷan (平) [ɦyɛn]; ONW uan					
za'	儇翾	xuān	xjiwän 4	hyan	hwen	OCB *hwjen
q	繯	huán	ɣiwen^{B}, ɣwan^{C}	ɣuen^{B}, ɣuan^{C}	gwênʔ, wêns	
256hk	睘[2] > 還[1]	huán	ɣwan	ɣuan	wên	
	[T] Sin Sukchu SR ɣwan (平); MGZY Xwan (平) [ɣwan]; ONW ɣuan					

k	還[2]	xuán	zjwän	zyan	s-wen	OCB *ɦswjen
	= 23-13/236a 旋					
n	環	huán	ɣwan	ɣuan	wên	OCB *wren
	[T] Sin Sukchu SR ɣwan (平); MGZY Xwan (平) [ɣwan]; ONW ɣuan					
r	鐶	huán	ɣwan	ɣuan	wên	
s	寰 r. domain	huán	ɣwan	ɣuan	wên	
	district		ɣiwen^{C}	ɣuen^{C}	gwêns	= 23-9/248a 縣
x	懁	huán,	ɣwan,	ɣuan,	gwên,	
		xuān	xjwän,	hyan	hwen	
			kiwen^{C} GY			
uv	擐轘	huàn	ɣwan^{C}	ɣuan^{C}	wên	
c'	噮	yuàn	ʔiwen^{C}	ʔuen^{C}	ʔwêns	

23-12 = K. 167 *GSR* treats this group as part of 25-13/167 奐. Although the graphic elements and rimes are different, 167 奐 (25-13) is perhaps partially phonetic.

		Mand.	MC	LHan	OCM
g	敻	xuàn,	xiwen^{C},	huen^{C},	hwêns
		xiòng	xjwäŋ^{C}	hyeŋ^{C}	hweŋh
h	讂	xuàn	xiwen^{C}	huen^{C}	hwêns
i	瓊	qióng	gjwäŋ	gyeŋ	gweŋ
1256f	觼	jué	kiwet	kuet	kwêt

23-13 = K. 1248c		**Mand.**	**MC**	**LHan**	**OCM**
c	幻	huàn	ɣwăn^{C}	ɣuɛn^{C}	gwrêns or gwrîns
	[T] ONW ɣuän. The old graph was said to be yú 予 inverted (SW 1684).				

23-14 = K. 236		**Mand.**	**MC**	**LHan**	**OCM**	
a	旋	xuán	zjwän	zyan	s-wen	= 23-11/256k 還
cde	嫙璇琁	xuán	zjwän	zyan	s-wen	

23-15 = K. 243		**Mand.**	**MC**	**LHan**	**OCM**	
a	燕 swallow	yàn	ʔien^{C}	ʔen^{C}	ʔêns	'a swallow (bird)'
	[T] ONW ʔėn <> [D] X-Changsha iɛn^{B}, W-Wenzh I^{B}(tone!)					
	[E] Tai: Saek ʔeen^{C2} ~ ʔɛɛn^{C2} 'swallow', S. ʔɛɛn^{B1}					
	燕 rest	yàn	ʔien^{C}	ʔen^{C}	ʔêns	= 24-12/253b 宴
	燕 Pl.N.	yān	ʔien	ʔen	ʔên	
c	嚥 gullet	yàn	ʔien^{C}	ʔen^{C}	ʔêns	~ 32-9/370h 咽
de	曣讌	yàn	ʔien^{C}	ʔen^{C}	ʔêns	

23-16 = K. 242		**Mand.**	**MC**	**LHan**	**OCM**
ac	顯韅	xiǎn	xien^{B}	hen^{B}	hênʔ
	[T] MTang hian < hɨan, ONW hėn				

23-17 = K. 228		**Mand.**	**MC**	**LHan**	**OCM**
a	肙	yuān	ʔiwen	ʔuen	ʔwên

b	蜎	yuān,	ʔiwen,	ʔuen,	ʔwên,	
			ʔjiwän(^{B}) 4,	ʔyen(^{B})	ʔwen, ʔwenʔ	
		juàn	gjiwän^{B} 4	gyen^{B}	gwenʔ	
cd	悁痟	yuān	ʔjiwän 4	ʔyen	ʔwen	
ef	狷絹	juàn	kjiwän^{C} 4	kyen^{C}	kwens	
h	涓	juān	kiwen	kuen	kwên	= 23-8/1250f 蠲
i	睊	juàn	kiwen(^{C})	kuen(^{C})	kwên, kwêns	
j	鞙	xuàn	ɣiwen^{B}	ɣuen^{B}	gwênʔ	
k	駽	xuān	xiwen(^{C})	huen(^{C})	hwên, hwêns	
g	捐	juān !	jiwän 4	wen	wen	

MC Div. 3/4 initial ji- is perhaps a mistake for jwän 3, hence OCM *wen?

23-18 = K. 244		**Mand.**	**MC**	**LHan**	**OCM**
a	靦	tiǎn	tʰien^{B}	tʰen^{B}	thênʔ

23-19 = K. 1250e		**Mand.**	**MC**	**LHan**	**OCM**
e	晛	niàn	nien^{C}	nen^{C}	nêns

The MC alternate reading ɣienʔ has perhaps been transferred from 23-2/241g.

23-20 = K. 245		**Mand.**	**MC**	**LHan**	**OCM**	
a	前	qián	dzien	dzen	dzên	

[T] Sin Sukchu SR dzjen (平); MGZY tsen (平) [dzɛn]; ONW dzėn

fg	湔煎	jiān	tsjän	tsian	tsen	
eij	揃翦剪	jiǎn	tsjän^{B}	tsian^{B}	tsenʔ	
h	箭 arrow	jiàn	tsjän^{C}	tsian^{C}	tsens	[E] Toch.B tsain
k	鬋 hair tuft	jiān	tsjän(^{C})	tsian(^{C})	tsen, tsens	
	鬋 cut hair	jiǎn	tsjän^{B}	tsian^{B}	tsenʔ	

23-21 = K. 209		**Mand.**	**MC**	**LHan**	**OCM**	
a	鮮 fresh	xiān	sjän	sian	sen or san	= 23-22/211a 鱻

[T] Sin Sukchu SR sjen (平); MGZY sy̆an (平) [sjɛn]. LHan 鮮卑 sian-pie *Särbi

[E] TB *sar > WT gsar-ba 'new, fresh'; WB sa^{C} 'make anew'; Lushai tʰar^{H} 'new'

	鮮 rare	xiǎn	sjän^{B}	sian^{B}	senʔ	OCB *sjenʔ (Baxter 1992: 385)

= 23-23/210a 尟

d	癬	xiǎn	sjän^{B}	sian^{B}, S tsʰiɑn^{B}	senʔ	OCB *sjenʔ

[D] PMin *tshiɑn^{B} ~ siɑn^{B}

e	蹮	xiān	sien	sen	sên	= 24-42/206 躚

23-22 = K. 211		**Mand.**	**MC**	**LHan**	**OCM**
a	鱻	xiān	sjän	sian	sen or san

= 23-21/209a 鮮 'fresh'

23-23 = K. 210		**Mand.**	**MC**	**LHan**	**OCM**	
a	尟	xiǎn	sjän^{B}	sian^{B}	senʔ	OCB *sjenʔ

= 23-21/209a 鮮 'rare'

23-24 = K. 218		Mand.	MC	LHan	OCM	
a	片 partial	piàn	p^{h}ien^C	p^{h}en^C	phêns	
	片 half	pàn	p^{h}wân^C	p^{h}ɑn^C	phâns	
	= 24-47/181df 判泮					

23-25 = K. 221		Mand.	MC	LHan	OCM	
a	便 eloquent	pián	bjiän 4	bian	ben	
	便 comfort	biàn	bjiän^C 4	bian^C	bens	
	[E] Sin Sukchu SR bjen (去); MGZY pen (去) [bɛn]; ONW bian					
b	楩	pián	bjiän(^{C}) 4	bian(^{C})	ben, bens	
c	鞭	biān	pjiän 4	pian	pen	
745f	緶	bǐng	pjiäŋ^B 4?	pieŋ^B	peŋʔ	'wheel rim'
	[N] The readings bǐng MC pjiäŋ^B and bǎn MC pwân^B may reflect the dialects of different commentators (Coblin 1983: 153). Karlgren considers bǐng to belong to 3-11/ 745f.					

23-26 = K. 224		Mand.	MC	LHan	OCM
ab	臱櫋	mián	mjiän 4	mian	men
-	[illegible]	mián	mien	men	mên
cf	邊籩	biān	pien	pen	pên
	邊 [T] Sin Sukchu SR pjen (平); MGZY bỹan (平) [pjɛn]; ONW pėn				
	[E] ST *pel: Lushai beel^H 'pot, utensil, vessel'				

23-27 = K. 246		Mand.	MC	LHan	OCM	
a	扁 district	biǎn	pien^B	pen^B	pênʔ	
	[E] TB: Lushai bial^H < bial 'a circle'					
	扁 thin	biǎn	pien^B	pen^B	pênʔ	
	[E] ST *per: TB *pe:r > Lushai peer^L / perʔ^L; NNaga pwe:r 'thin'					
bc	徧遍	biàn	pien^C	pen^C	pêns	
	[E] ? TB: Lushai p^{h}iar^R < p^{h}iarʔ (< -ʔ) 'all, completely'					
-	蝙蝠	biān-fú	pien-pjuk	pen-puk		
d	楄	pián	bien	ben	bên	
e	編 weave	biān	pien, pjiän4	pen, pian	pên, pen	⋈ 23-28/219
	[E] TB *pyar ~ byar > WT 'byor-ba ~ 'byar-ba 'stick to, adhere to'; Bahing p^{h}jer 'to sew'; Lushai p^{h}iar^H < p^{h}iar 'to knit, plait'; LB *pan^2 'to braid, plait'					
	編 arrange	biàn	bien^B	ben^B	bênʔ	
i	猵 otter	biān	pien	pen	pên	
	[T] ONW pėn <> [E] WB p^{h}yam 'otter'					
	猵 an animal	piàn	p^{h}jiän^C 4	p^{h}ian^C	phens	
fg	惼褊	biǎn	pjiän^B 4	pian^B	penʔ	
	[T] MGZY bỹan (上) [pjɛn]					
hjk	偏篇翩	piān	p^{h}jiän 4	p^{h}ian	phen	
	翩 OCB *phin. <> 篇 [T] ONW p^{h}ian					
l	萹	piān, biǎn	p^{h}jiän 4, pien(^{B})	p^{h}ian, pen(^{B})	phen, pên, pênʔ	
m	諞	pián	bjiän(^{B}) 4	bian(^{B})	ben, benʔ	

23-28 = K. 219		**Mand.**	**MC**	**LHan**	**OCM**	
a	辡	biǎn	pjän^B 3	pɨan^B	pren?	
bc	辨	biàn,	bjän^B 3,	bɨan^B,	bren?,	
		[T] Sin Sukchu SR bjen (上); MGZY pen (上) [bɛn]; ONW ban				
		bàn	bǎn^C	bɛn^C	brêns	
e	辯	biàn	bjän^B 3	bɨan^B	bren?	
f	辦	bàn	bǎn^C	bɛn^C	brêns	
		[T] Sin Sukchu SR ban (去); MGZY pan (去) [ban] <> [E] ST *brel: WT brel-ba 'be employed'				
-	辮	biàn	bien^B	ben^C	bêns	⋈ 23-27/246e
-	瓣	bàn	bǎn^C	bɛn^C		

23-29 = K. 225		**Mand.**	**MC**	**LHan**	**OCM**	
-	𦁧	mián	mjiän 4	mian	men	
ab -	綿緜棉	mián	mjiän 4	mian	—	= 23-32/223d

23-30		**Mand.**	**MC**	**LHan**	**OCM**
-	宀 roof	mián	mjiän 4	mian	—

23-31 = K. 223		**Mand.**	**MC**	**LHan**	**OCM**	
a	面	miàn	mjiän^C 4	mian^C	mens	
		[T] Sin Sukchu SR mjen (去); MGZY men (去) [mɛn]; ONW mian <> [D] M-Xiam bĩ^{C2}, Y-Guangzh min^C, K-Meix mian^C				
		[E] TB *s-mel > Lushai hmeel^H 'face' ~ hmai^R < hmai?, JP man^{33} 'face'				
bcd	偭湎緬	miǎn	mjiän^B 4	mian^B	men?	緬 = 23-30/225a

23-32 = K. 247		**Mand.**	**MC**	**LHan**	**OCM**	
a	丏	miǎn	mien^B	men^B	mên?	
-	麪	miǎn	mien^C	men^C	—	SW ~ 麵 miàn
-	宀	miàn	mien^C	men^C	—	
b	眄	miǎn	mien$^{B/C}$	men$^{B/C}$	mên?, mêns	
-	蚵	miān	mjiän 4	mian	—	SW
c	沔	miǎn	mjiän^B 4	mian^B	men?	

24 OCM rime *-an Yuán bù 元部 (2)

GSR 139 - 266

Baxter 1992: 370 ff. (§10.1.1)

The rime *-wan is combined with *-on in rime 25. See Table 21-1 for OCM rimes *-an, *-at, *-ai in QYS categories. After acute initials, MC Div. III -jän has resulted from a merger of OC *-an and *-en, which are difficult to untangle.

See Table 34-2 for MC Div. 3/3 without OC medial *r.

24-1	**= K. 139**	**Mand.**	**MC**	**LHan**	**OCM**	
ae	干忓	gān	kân	kɑn	kân	[T] ONW kɑn
gkl	玕竿肝	gān	kân	kɑn	kân	
i	丹矸	dān-gān	tân-kân	tɑn-kɑn	tân-kân	
cd	奸豻	jiān !	kân	kɑn	kân	
	Mand. jiān has been transferred from the syn. jiān 姦, unless MC kân is an *r-less variant.					
m	飦	gān, jiān	kân, kjɐn	kɑn, kɨɑn	kân, kan	
	24-29c 餰 *kian(?) ~ 24-23m 饘 *tan(?) ~ 24-1m 飦 *kân, *kan 'rice gruel'					
j -	秆稈	gǎn	kân^B	kɑn^B	kânʔ	
	= 18-1/1e 笴; 24-2/140k 簳					
h	皯	gǎn	kân^B	kɑn^B	kânʔ	
f	盰	gàn	kân^C	kɑn^C	kâns	
no	刊栞	kān	kʰân	kʰɑn	khân	
p	衎	kàn	kʰân^C	kʰɑn^C	khâns	OCB *khans
-	靬	jiān	kan,kjɐn,kʰân^C	kan ?	—	name of a foreign country
uv	虷邗	hán	ɣân	gɑn	gân	
qz	扞閈	hàn	ɣân^C	gɑn^C	gâns	
	[E] WT 'gal-ba 'to oppose'; WB ka 'a shield, to ward off'; Lushai in^L-kalʔ^L < -kalʔ/h 'to withstand, oppose'					
tb'	汗馯	hàn	ɣân^C	gɑn^C	gâns	
	汗 [D] PMin *gan^{C2} <> [E] ? TB: PKiranti *gʰàl 'sweat'					
y	釬 cuff	hàn	ɣân^C	gɑn^C	gâns	
	brisk	gān	kân	kɑn	kân	
s	旱	hàn	ɣân^B	gɑn^B	gânʔ	
j'	睅	huàn	ɣwan^B	guan^B	gwrânʔ	= 25-19 睆
h'i'	悍捍	hàn	ɣân^C	gɑn^C	gâns	
-	趕	gǎn	—			'pursue, overtake'
c'd'	犴豻	àn	ŋân^C	ŋɑn^C	ŋâns	
e'	岸	àn	ŋân^C	ŋɑn^C	ŋâns	See also 24-15.
	[T] Sin Sukchu SR ŋɔn (去); PR ʔan; LR ʔan; MGZY ngan (去) [ŋan]; ONW ŋɑn					
f'	罕	hǎn	xân^B	hɑn^B	hŋânʔ	
g'	軒	xuān !	xjɐn	hɨɑn	hŋan	= 24-17/252

-	鼾		hān	xân	—	

[E] WT hal-ba 'to pant, wheeze, snort'

300a	訐		jié	kjɐt, kjät 3, kjäi^{C}	kɨɑt, kɨas	kat, kats

The element 干 is also semantic.

24-2	**= K. 140**		**Mand.**	**MC**	**LHan**	**OCM**	
a	馯		gàn	kân^{C}	kɑn^{C}	kâns	
c	乾	stem	gān	kân	kɑn	kân	

[T] Sin Sukchu SR kɔn (平), PR, LR kan; MGZY gan (平) [kan]; ONW kɑn.
[E] ST *kar: TB *kan > WB kʰan^{B} 'dry up'; JP kan^{31} 'solidify, dry up'; Atsi kʔan 'dry up'

	乾	heaven	qián	gjän 3	gɨɑn	gan	
de	幹榦		gàn	kân^{C}	kɑn^{C}	kâns	

幹 [T] Sin Sukchu SR kɔn (去ɔ, PR, LR kan; MGZY gan (去) [kan]

k	簳		gǎn	kân^{B}	kɑn^{B}	kânʔ	

= 18-1/1e 笴; 24-1/139j 稈

hij	韓韓鶾		hán	ɣân	gɑn	gân	
f	翰		hàn	ɣân^{C}	gɑn^{C}	gân^{A} !	OCB *gans
m	澣		huàn	ɣwân^{B}	guɑn^{B}	gwânʔ	

= 25-19/257o 浣 'wash clothes'; ≍ 25-5/161 盥 'wash the hands'

l	斡	axle cap	guǎn	kwân$^{B/C}$	kuɑn$^{B/C}$	kwânʔ, kwâns	= 25-1/157j 錧
	斡	turn around		ʔwât	ʔuɑt	—	

The OC rime of these last words could be either *-wân or *-ôn, but an interchange in phonetic series between *-ân and *-wân is more likely than with *-ôn because of parallel instances *-aŋ ~ *waŋ, while there is no interchange between *-aŋ and *-oŋ.

24-3	**= K. 141**	**Mand.**	**MC**	**LHan**	**OCM**
a	侃	kǎn	kʰân$^{B/C}$	kʰɑn$^{B/C}$	khânʔ, khâns
d	諐	qiān	kʰjän 3	kʰɨɑn	khan

24-4	**= K. 142**	**Mand.**	**MC**	**LHan**	**OCM**
a	看	kàn	kʰân^{C}	kʰɑn^{C}	khâns

[T] Sin Sukchu SR k'ɔn (去), PR, LR k'an; MGZY khan (去) [k'an]
[E] ? TB: WT mkʰan-po 'professor, abbot'

24-5	**= K. 143**	**Mand.**	**MC**	**LHan**	**OCM**	
a	寒	hán	ɣân	gɑn	gân	[T] ONW ɣɑn
fi	蹇攓	jiǎn	kjɐn^{B}, kjän^{B} 3	kɨɑn^{B}	kanʔ	
e	謇	jiǎn	kjän^{B} 3	kɨɑn^{B}	kanʔ	
d	搴	qiān !	kjän^{B} 3	kɨɑn^{B}	kranʔ or krianʔ	

[E] ? TB: WT 'kʰyer-ba 'to take, bring, carry'

g	褰	qiān	kʰjän 3	kʰɨɑn	khran	
h	騫	qiān	kʰjän 3	kʰɨɑn	khran or krian	

= 24-29/197b 愆 <> [E] ? TB: WT 'kʰyar-ba 'to err, go astray, deviate'

24-6		**Mand.**	**MC**	**LHan**	**OCM**
-	囝	jiǎn	kjɐn^{B}, kjän^{B} 3	kɨɑn^{B}	kanʔ

[D] PMin *kiɑn^{B}: Jian'ou kyeŋ^{B1}, Fuzh kiaŋ^{B1}, Xiam kiã^{B1}
[E] AA: PVM *kɔːn 'son'; Mon kon 'child'

24-7	**= K. 198**		**Mand.**	**MC**	**LHan**	**OCM**	
a	虔		qián	gjän 3	gɨan	gan	OCB *grjan

24-7A			**Mand.**	**MC**	**LHan**	**OCM**	
-	䇂		qiān	kʰjän 3	kʰɨan	khran or khrian	= 24-29/197 愆

24-8	**= K. 249**		**Mand.**	**MC**	**LHan**	**OCM**	
a	建		jiàn	kjɐn^C	kɨɑn^C	kans	
	[T] Sin Sukchu SR kjen (去); MGZY gen (去) [kɛn]						
c-	鞬犍		jiān	kjɐn	kɨɑn	kan	
	鞬 [E] ? TB: WT rkyal-pa 'leather sack, bag'						
d	騝		jiān, qián	kjɐn, gjän 3	kɨɑn, gɨan	kan, gan	
f	腱	sinew	jiàn	kjɐn, gjɐn^C	kɨɑn, gɨɑn^C	kan, gans	
b	揵		jiǎn, jiàn	kjɐn^B, gjɐn^B	kɨɑn^B, gɨɑn^B	kanʔ, ganʔ	
	[T] BTD 目揵連 mɨuk-gɨan^B-lian Skt. Maudgalyāyana, Pkt. moggallāna						
g	健		jiàn	gjɐn^C	gɨɑn^C	gans	
	[E] TB: WT gar-ba 'strong', gar-bu 'solid'						
h	楗	lock	jiàn	gjɐn^B	gɨɑn^B	ganʔ	= 鍵
	[E] ? TB: Lushai kalʔ^L 'to wrench, plait, lock' ⋈ kalʔ^L-na^H 'a lock'						
	楗	weary	jiǎn	kjɐn^B	kɨɑn^B	kanʔ	
i	鍵		jiàn	gjän^B 3	gɨan^B	ganʔ	= 楗

24-9	**= K. 184**		**Mand.**	**MC**	**LHan**	**OCM**	
a	姦		jiān	kan	kan	krân	

24-10	**= K. 144**		**Mand.**	**MC**	**LHan**	**OCM**	
a	暵		hàn	xân$^{B/C}$	hɑn$^{B/C}$	hânʔ, hâns	
	[N] Acc. to GSR 144 the graph is a semantic composit of rì 'sun' and jiān 33-5/480 'calamity' (contra SW that considers jiān phonetic). Since in the early development of the script elements were also chosen for their meaning, I follow Karlgren.						
b	熯	burn	hàn	xân^B	hɑn^B	hânʔ	
		respectful	rǎn	ńźjän^B	ńan^B	nanʔ	OCB *njanʔ
	This is a loan application of the graph through confusion with 24-35/152.						
c	漢		hàn	xân^C	hɑn^C	hâns	
	[N] The old type graph (gǔwén) consisted of 水+或+大, the element that looks like a phonetic today (as in hàn 暵) appears in the seal script (Shuowen) <> [T] BTD Skt. (ar)hant						

24-11	**= K. 146**		**Mand.**	**MC**	**LHan**	**OCM**	
a	安		ān	ʔân	ʔɑn	ʔân	
	[T] Sin S. SR ʔɔn (平); PR ʔan; LR ʔan; MGZY 'an (平) [ʔan]; ONW ʔɑn. MHan 安息 Arśak; 安敦 ʔɑn-tuən Antonius						
-	鞍		ān	ʔân	ʔɑn	ʔân	
de	按案		àn	ʔân^C	ʔɑn^C	ʔâns	
gi	鴳鷃		yàn	ʔan^C	ʔan^C	ʔrâns	
	[E] TB: KN-Lushai ʔaar^H 'fowl', Tiddim ʔaak^M 'fowl' < *ʔaar						
f	晏	late	yàn	ʔân^C, ʔan^C	ʔɑn^C, ʔan^C	ʔâns or ʔrâns	
		bright	yàn	ʔan^C	ʔan^C	ʔrâns	
		rest	yàn	ʔien^C, ʔan^C	ʔen^C, ʔan^C	ʔêns, ʔrâns	= 24-12/253b 宴
h	頞		è	ʔât	ʔɑt	ʔât	

24-12 = K. 253		**Mand.**	**MC**	**LHan**	**OCM**	
a	晏 tranquil	yàn	ʔan^{C}	ʔan^{C}	ʔrâns	= 24-11/146f 晏
b	宴 rest	yàn	ʔien^{C}	ʔen^{C}	ʔêns	
	= 23-15/243a 燕; 24-11/146f 晏 <> [T] ONW ʔèn					
d	匽	yǎn	ʔjɐn$^{B/C}$	ʔɨɑn$^{B/C}$	ʔanʔ, ʔans	
	[E] ? TB: Lushai zaal^{H} < jaal 'to lie down, recline' ⋈ zalʔ^{L} < jalʔ/h 'lay on the back'					
gj	偃鰋	yǎn	ʔjɐn^{B}	ʔɨɑn^{B}	ʔanʔ	
h	鄢	yàn	ʔjɐn^{C}	ʔɨɑn^{C}	ʔans	
l	蝘	yǎn	ʔien^{B}	ʔen^{B}	ʔênʔ	
m	揠	yà	ʔat	ʔat	ʔrât	

24-13 = K. 254		**Mand.**	**MC**	**LHan**	**OCM**
a	㫃	yǎn	ʔjɐn^{B}	ʔɨɑn^{B}	ʔanʔ

24-14 = K. 200		**Mand.**	**MC**	**LHan**	**OCM**	
a	焉 suffix	yān	jän 3 !	ɨɑn	ʔan > an	[T] ONW ʔan, -an
	焉 how	yān	ʔjän 3	ʔɨɑn	ʔan	
	[T] Sin Sukchu SR ʔjen, jen (平); ONW ʔan					
-	蔫	yān	ʔjän 3	ʔɨɑn	ʔan	
b	嗎	xiān	xjän 3	hɨɑn	han	

24-15 = K. 145, 186			MC	LHan	OCM	
145a	厂	hàn	xân^{C}	hɑn^{C}	hŋans	
139e'	岸	àn	ŋân^{C}	ŋɑn^{C}	ŋâns	See also 24-1.
	[T] Sin Sukchu SR ŋɔn (去); PR ʔan; LR ʔan; MGZY ngan (去) [ŋan]; ONW ŋɑn					
186a	雁	yàn	ŋan^{C}	ŋan^{C}	ŋrâns	
	[T] ONW ŋän <> [E] TB: WT ŋaŋ-pa 'goose', WB ŋan^{B} <> PTai *han^{B1} < *hŋ- 'goose'					

24-16 = K. 251		**Mand.**	**MC**	**LHan**	**OCM**
a	言 speak	yán	ŋjɐn	ŋɨɑn	ŋan
	[T] Sin Sukchu SR jen (平); MGZY ngen (平) [ŋɛn]; ONW ŋan; Han BTD ŋan				
	言 content	yín	ŋjən	ŋɨən	ŋən
e	唁	yàn	ŋjän^{C} 3	ŋɨan^{C}	ŋans or ŋrans
f	誾	yín	ŋjen 3	ŋɨn	ŋrən
g	狺	yín	ŋjən, ŋjen 3	ŋɨn	ŋən

24-17 = K. 252		**Mand.**	**MC**	**LHan**	**OCM**	
a	甗	yàn	ŋjɐn^{C}	ŋɨɑn^{C}	ŋans	
d	甗	yàn, yǎn	ŋjɐn	ŋɨɑn	ŋan, ŋanʔ, ŋans	
			ŋjän$^{B/C}$	ŋɨan$^{B/C}$		
e	獻	xiàn	xjɐn^{C}	hɨɑn^{C}	hŋans	OCB *hŋjans
	= 24-18/250a 憲					
h	巘	yǎn	ŋjɐn^{B}, ŋjän^{B} 3	ŋɨɑn^{B}	ŋanʔ 'hilltop'	
i	讞	yàn (!)	ŋjät 3	ŋɨat	ŋat	
j	櫱	è	ŋât	ŋɑt	ŋât	
	= 21-11/289j; see GSR 268					

24-18 = K. 250		**Mand.**	**MC**	**LHan**	**OCM**	
a	憲	xiàn	xjɐn^{C}	hɨɑn^{C}	hŋans	OCB *hjans
	= 24-17/252e 獻					
c	瀗	xiàn	xjɐn^{C}	hɨɑn^{C}	hŋans	

24-19 = K. 199		**Mand.**	**MC**	**LHan**	**OCM**	
ab	彥諺	yàn	ŋjän^{C} 3	ŋɨan^{C}	ŋans or ŋrans	OCB *ŋrjans
c	顏	yán	ŋan	ŋan	ŋrân	
d	喭	yàn	ŋân^{C}	ŋɑn^{C}	ŋâns	

24-20 = K. 150		**Mand.**	**MC**	**LHan**	**OCM**	
a	丹	dān	tân	tɑn	tân	OCB *tan
	[E] KT: KS *h-lan^{C} 'red' (Edmondson/Yang)					
c	旃	zhān	tśjän	tśan	tan	[T] ONW tśan

24-21 = K. 147		**Mand.**	**MC**	**LHan**	**OCM**	
az	單[1] > 蟬	chán	źjän	dźan	dan 'cicada'	
a	單[2] simple	dān	tân	tɑn	tân	
	[T] Sin Sukchu SR tan (平); MGZY dan (平) [tan]; ONW tɑn; BTD Skt. tar					
y	嬋	chán	źjän	dźan	dan	
a'	墠	shàn	źjän^{B}	dźan^{B}	danʔ	
b'	禪 cede	shàn	źjän^{C}	dźan^{C}	dans	
	Zen	shàn	źjän^{C}	dźan^{C}	—	[T] BTD Skt. dhyāna
r	戰	zhàn	tśjän^{C}	tśan^{C}	tans	= 24-23/148s 顫
	[T] Sin Sukchu SR tʂjen (去); MGZY jyan (去) [tʂjɛn]; ONW tśan; Han BTD tśan					
	[E] TB: WT 'dar-ba 'tremble, shudder, shiver with fear or cold' ⋇ sdar-ma 'trembling'					
s	樿 a tree	zhǎn	tśjän^{B}	tśan^{B}	tanʔ	
	coffin	shàn	źjän^{C}	dźan^{C}	dans	
t	燀	chǎn, zhǎn	tś(ʰ)jän^{B}	tś(ʰ)an^{B}	tanʔ, thanʔ	
m	嘽 slow	chǎn	tśʰjän^{B}	tśʰan^{B}	thanʔ	
	嘽 exhaust.	tān	tʰân	tʰɑn	thân	
uvx	幝繟闡	chǎn	tśʰjän^{B}	tśʰan^{B}	thanʔ	
g	殫	dān	tân	tɑn	tân	
fhij	匰簞襌鄲	dān	tân	tɑn	tân	
e	僤	dǎn	tân^{B}	tɑn^{B}	tânʔ	
l	癉	dǎn, duò	tân^{B} !, tâ^{C}	tɑn^{B}, tɑi^{C}	tânʔ, tâih	
n	彈 shoot	tán	dân	dɑn	dân	
	[T] ONW dɑn <> [D] PMin *d̯ɑn ~ *dɑn^{C} 'to pluck (a lute)'					
	彈 pellet	dàn	dân^{C}	dɑn^{C}	dâns	
	[E] TB *m-dan or rather *tal > JP n^{31}-dan^{33} 'crossbow', Tiddim tʰal^{R} < tʰalʔ 'a bow'; Lushai tʰal^{R} < tʰalʔ 'arrow, dart'					
o	憚 fear	dàn	dân^{C}	dɑn^{C}	dâns	
	憚 exhausted	duò	tâ^{C}	tɑi^{C}	tâih	= 18-8/3d
e'h'	鼉鱓	tuó, tán	dâ, dân	dɑi, dɑn	dâi, dân	
d'	驒	tuó, tán	dâ, dân, tien	dɑi, dɑn, ten	dâi, dân, tên	
-	磾	dī	tiei	te	tê	

		Mand.	MC	LHan	OCM	
c’	觶	zhī	tśje(C)	tśai(C)	tai, taih	
p	⿰犭單	chān	ṭʰăn	ṭʰɛn	thrên	
-	撣	tán, chán	dân, źjän	dɑn, dźan	dân, dan	

24-22 = K. 149		Mand.	MC	LHan	OCM	
ac	旦鴠	dàn	tânC	tɑnC	tâns	

旦 [E] TB: Chepang darʔ-do (place) ‘of sunrise, in east’

e	但	dàn	dânB	dɑnB	dânʔ	

[T] Sin Sukchu SR dan (上); MGZY tan (上去) [dan]; ONW dɑn
[E] ST *twar ? : TB *t(w)ar > WT tʰor-bu ‘single, separate’

f	袒	tǎn !	dânB	dɑnB	dânʔ	= 24-23/148g
d	坦	tǎn	tʰânB	tʰɑnB	thânʔ	
g	怛	dá	tât	tɑt	tât	

24-23 = K. 148		Mand.	MC	LHan	OCM	
ab	亶⿸疒亶	dǎn	tânB	tɑnB	tânʔ	
c	儃	tǎn	tʰânB	tʰɑnB	thânʔ	
	儃	chán	źjän	dźan	dan	
d	壇	tán	dân	dɑn	dân	
e	檀 a tree	tán	dân	dɑn	dân	[T] BTD Skt. dana
	栴檀	zhān-tán	tśjän-dân	tśan-dɑn	dân	< Indic candana
f	澶	dàn	dânC	dɑnC	dâns	
g	襢 bare	tǎn	dânB	dɑnB	dânʔ	[T] ONW dɑn
	襢 single	zhǎn	ṭjänB	ṭianB	tranʔ	
	襢 bare	zhàn	ṭjänC	ṭianC	trans	
-	繵	dàn	tânB, dânB	tɑnC, dɑnB	tâns, dânʔ	

[E] TB: WT star-ba ‘tie, fasten’ ⋇ dar ‘silk, piece of cloth, scarf’

h	皽	zhǎn	ṭjänB, tśjänB	ṭianB, tśanB	tranʔ, tanʔ	
j	鱣	zhān	ṭjän	ṭian	tran	
i	邅 difficult	zhān	ṭjän	ṭian	tran	
	turn	zhàn	ḍjänB	ḍianB	dranʔ	
kln	旜氈鸇	zhān	tśjän	tśan	tan	
m	饘	zhān	tśjän(B)	tśan(B)	tan(ʔ) or tian(ʔ) < kian(ʔ) ?	

24-29c ⿰飠衍 *kian(ʔ) ~ 24-23m 饘 *tan(ʔ) ~ 24-1m 飦 *kân, *kan ‘rice gruel’

o	擅	shàn	źjänC	dźanC	dans	
p	蟺	shàn	źjänB	dźanB	danʔ	
qrs	羶膻顫	shān	śjän	śan	lhan ?	

24-24 = K. 151		Mand.	MC	LHan	OCM
a	炭	tàn	tʰânC	tʰɑnC	thâns

[E] WT tʰal-ba ‘dust, ashes’, Lushai taalR < taalʔ ‘wood ashes, dust’

24-25 = K. 205		Mand.	MC	LHan	OCM
a	善	shàn	źjänB	dźanB	danʔ

[T] Sin Sukchu SR zjen (上), LR zjen (上); MGZY zhen (上) [zɛn]; ONW dźan
[E] ? TB: Chepang dyanh- ‘be good’

df 膳繕 shàn zjän^C dźan^C dans

[T] Sin Sukchu SR zjen (去); ONW dźan

\- 鄯 shàn źjän^C dźan^C dans

[T] MHan 鄯善 dźan^C-dźan^B Cherchen (*Jarjan)

24-26 = K. 201 **Mand.** **MC** **LHan** **OCM**

a 展 unfold zhǎn tjän^B ṭian^B trenʔ or tranʔ OCB *trjenʔ

展 robe zhàn tjän^C ṭian^C trens or trans

[T] Han BTD tan <> [E] WT rdal-ba, brdal 'to spread, unfold, extend over', WB tan^B 'extend in a line, stretch out straight' ⋈ ə-tan^B 'line, row, duration, length'

b 輾 zhǎn tjän^B ṭian^B trenʔ ! (Baxter 1992: 386)

c 蹍 niǎn ṇjän^B ṇian^B nrenʔ or nranʔ

24-27 = K. 202 **Mand.** **MC** **LHan** **OCM**

a 蕆 chǎn ṭʰjän^B ṭʰian^B , thranʔ

24-28 = K. 204 **Mand.** **MC** **LHan** **OCM**

a 廛 chán ḍjän ḍian dran

[E] Tai: S. rɨan^{A2} < *rɨan^A 'house'; KS *hraːn^1 'house'; PHlai *rʔuun^1 'house'

b 躔 chán ḍjän ḍian dran

c 纏 chán ḍjän(^{C}) ḍian(^{C}) dran, drans

24-29 = K. 197 **Mand.** **MC** **LHan** **OCM**

a 衍 yǎn, yàn jiän$^{B/C}$ jan$^{B/C}$ janʔ, jans ~ 33-19/450k 演

[T] ONW ian; Han BTD jan <> [E] TB: WT yar-ba 'to disperse, ramble, stray'

b 愆 qiān kʰjän 3 kʰɨan khrian OCB khrjan

= 24-5/143hg 騫

c 餰 zhān tśjän(^{B}) tśan(^{B}) kian, kianʔ [Xun]

24-29c 餰 *kian(ʔ) ~ 24-23m 饘 *tan(ʔ) ~ 24-1m 飦 *kân, *kan 'rice gruel'

24-30 = K. 203 **Mand.** **MC** **LHan** **OCM**

abc 延筵綖 yán jiän jan lan

延 [T] ONW ian, BTD Skt. jina <> [E] Old Sino-Viet. lan <> Tai: S. lɨan^{B2} 'delay, extend'

ef 埏挻 shān śjän śan lhan

g 誕 dàn dân^B dɑn^B lânʔ

\- 涎 saliva xián zjän, zian, s-lan,

jiän^C jan^C, S lan^B lans, lanʔ

[T] Sin Sukchu SR zjen (平); MGZY zen (平) [zɛn] <> [D] Old South *lɑn^B: PMin *lɑn^B, Meix. lan^{A2}, Yue: Zhongshan hɐu^B-nan^B 口涎 <> [E] ? TB: WT zlan 'moisture'

d 梴 chān ṭʰjän ṭʰian rhan

24-31 = K. 207 **Mand.** **MC** **LHan** **OCM**

a 羨 desire xiàn zjän^C, dzjän^C zian^C s-lans

oblong yán jiän jan lan

24-32 = K. 213 **Mand.** **MC** **LHan** **OCM**

a 連 carriage liǎn ljän^B lian^B ranʔ or renʔ ? = 24-34/215a 輦

			Mand.	MC	LHan	OCM	
	連	connect	lián	ljän	lian	ran or ren ?	= 24-33/214a 聯

[T] Sin Sukchu SR ljen (平); MGZY len (平) [lɛn]; ONW lian; Han BTD 目揵連 muk-gɨan^{B}-lian Skt. Maudgalyāyana, Pkt. moggallāna

			Mand.	MC	LHan	OCM	
c	璉		liǎn	ljän^{B}	lian^{B}	ranʔ or renʔ ?	
b	漣		lián	ljän	lian	ran or ren ?	
d	蓮		lián	lien ! [GY]	len	rên	OCB *g-ren

[T] ONW lėn

			Mand.	MC	LHan	OCM	
-	健		lián, liàn	ljän^{A2}	lian(^{C})	—	'young female chicken'

[D] PMin *lhɑn^{C1}: Jiēyáng nuã^{C1}, Jiānglè šuai^{C1}; Kejia kai^{A1}-lon^{C1} (kai^{1} 'chicken')

24-33 = K. 214		**Mand.**	**MC**	**LHan**	**OCM**	
a	聯	lián	ljän	lian	ran or ren ?	= 24-32/213a 連

[T] Sin Sukchu SR ljen (平); MGZY len (平) [lɛn]; ONW lian

[E] TB *ren: *m-ren 'line up, be equal': JP ren^{31} 'place in a long, even row'; WB rañ-tu 'be equal', hrañ 'put together, side by side'; Mikir ren 'line, range, row'

24-34 = K. 215		**Mand.**	**MC**	**LHan**	**OCM**	
a	輦	niǎn	ljän^{B}	lian^{B}	ranʔ or renʔ ?	= 24-32/213a 連

[T] Sin Sukchu SR ljen (上); MGZY len (上) [lɛn]; ONW (l)ian

24-35 = K. 152			**Mand.**	**MC**	**LHan**	**OCM**	
ac	嘆歎		tān	t^{h}ân(^{C})	t^{h}ɑn(^{C})	nhân, nhâns	

[N] Following GSR 152, I consider the graph 嘆 a semantic composit of *kǒu* 'mouth' and *jiān* 33-5/480 'distress' (contra SW that considers *nán* 難 an abbreviated phonetic in 歎, and 歎 the abbreviated phonetic in 嘆), since in the early development of the script, elements were also chosen for their meaning. Thus the element *jiān* spawned a phonetic series *nân.

			Mand.	MC	LHan	OCM	
dg	難鸌	diff.	nán	nân	nɑn	nân	'difficult'

[T] Sin Sukchu SR nan (平); MGZY nan (平) [nan]; ONW nɑn. BTD nán-dài 難待 Skt. nanda

			Mand.	MC	LHan	OCM	
	難	difficulty	nàn	nân^{C}	nɑn^{C}	nâns	[T] BTD Skt. nan[da]
h	戁		nǎn, rǎn	ṇan^{B}, ńźjän^{B}	ṇan^{B}, ńan^{B}	nrânʔ, nanʔ	
i	熯		rán	ńźjän	ńan	nan	= 24-36/217a 然
k	儺	expel	nuó	nâ	nɑi	nâi	

[E] TB *na ~ *nat 'ill', WB na 'be ill, be in pain' ⋈ nat 'demon, spirit' < *LB *nat

			Mand.	MC	LHan	OCM
	儺	rich	nuó	nâ(^{B})	nɑi(^{B})	nâi, nâiʔ
l	臡		ní, nuó	niei, nâ	nei, nɑi	nə̂i (?), nâi
m	灘灘		tān	t^{h}ân	t^{h}ɑn	—

'To dry up (of a river)' [SW], later 'beach'. The graph suggests an OC initial *nh-. However, tān could be compared to TB *tan > WT t^{h}an-pa 'dry weather, heat, drought', WB t^{h}an^{C}-t^{h}an^{C} 'nearly dry', if we assume that the word was written with this phonetic only during the Han period (note its first attestation in SW) when OC *nh- had merged with *th-.

24-36 = K. 217			**Mand.**	**MC**	**LHan**	**OCM**
-	肰	dog meat	rán	ńźjän	ńan	nan

[N] This is the phonetic to the following (Baxter 1992: 380; SW 4454).

			Mand.	MC	LHan	OCM
ab	然燃		rán	ńźjän	ńan	nan

[T] Sin Suk. SR rjen (平); MGZY Zhen (平) [rɛn]; ONW ńan <> [D] Min: Dongan nã^{A2} 'to take fire accidentally' ⋈ Amoy nã$^{C1/C2}$ 'to singe or burn slightly' (Douglas), hiã^{A2} 'to burn'

24-37 = K. 216		**Mand.**	**MC**	**LHan**	**OCM**	
a	㞋	niǎn	ṇiän^{B}	ṇian^{B}	nranʔ	
	[E] WT mñel-ba, gñel-ba 'to tan or dress hide', ñer-ba 'to tan, dress, soften'					
b	赧	nǎn	ṇan^{B}	ṇan^{B}	nrânʔ	[T] ONW ṇän < nän

24-38 = K. 212		**Mand.**	**MC**	**LHan**	**OCM**	
a	扇	shàn	śjän^{C}	śan^{C}	nhans	
	[T] Sin Sukchu SR ṣjen (去); MGZY (zhy̅an >) shy̅an (去) [ṣjɛn]					[T] ONW śan
b	傓	shàn	śjän^{C}	śan^{C}	nhans	
c	煽	shàn	śjän^{C}	śan^{C}	nhans (*nh- !) ※ 24-36/217a 然	
	[E] TB: JP ʃa^{33}-nan^{33} 'torch' (CVST 2: 24). An allofam might possibly be → rè 熱 'hot'.					

24-39 = K. 153		**Mand.**	**MC**	**LHan**	**OCM**
ab	贊 b	zàn	tsân^{C}	tsɑn^{C}	tsâns
c	讚	zàn	tsân^{C}	tsɑn^{C}	tsâns
de	瓚 e	zàn	dzân^{B}	dzɑn^{B}	dzânʔ
fg	纘酇	zuǎn	tswân^{B}	tsuɑn^{B}	tsônʔ
hi	鑽 i	zuān	tswân	tsuɑn	tsôn
jk	欑 k	cuán	dzwân	dzuɑn	dzôn
l	攢	cuán !	dzwân^{C}	dzuɑn^{C}	dzôns

24-40 = K. 154		**Mand.**	**MC**	**LHan**	**OCM**
a	𣦼	cán	dzân	dzɑn	dzân
c	餐	cān	tsʰân	tsʰɑn	tshân
	[T] Sin Sukchu SR ts'an (平); MGZY tshan (平) [ts'an]				
b -	粲燦	càn	tsʰân^{C}	tsʰɑn^{C}	tshâns
	粲 [E] ? TB *dza 'to eat' > WT bzan 'food', gzan-pa 'to eat'				

24-41 = K. 155 Most words may have had OC *e rather than the default Div. III *a.

		Mand.	**MC**	**LHan**	**OCM**	
a	戔 damage	cán	dzân	dzɑn	dzân	
	戔 accumul.	qián	dzien	dzen	dzên	
c	殘	cán	dzân	dzɑn	dzân	
d	棧	zhàn	dẓan$^{B/C}$,	dẓan$^{B/C}$?,	dzrânʔ, dzrâns or	
			dẓăn^{B}	dẓɛn^{B}	dzrênʔ	
	[E] ? Tai: S. raan^{C2} 'machan, booth, stall, shop'					
ef	琖盞	zhǎn	tṣăn^{B}	tṣɛn^{B}	tsrênʔ	
h	醆	zhǎn	tṣăn^{B}, tsjän^{B}	tṣɛn^{B}, tṣian	tsrênʔ	
i	剗	chǎn	tṣʰăn^{B}	tṣʰɛn^{B}	tshrênʔ	
j	錢 hoe	jiǎn	tsjän^{B}	tsian^{B}	tsanʔ	
	錢 coin	qián	dzjän	dzian	dzan	
	[T] Sin Sukchu SR dzjen (平); MGZY tsen (平) [dzɛn]; ONW dzian					
k	淺 shallow	qiǎn	tsʰjän^{B}	tsʰian^{B}	tshenʔ	
	[T] Han BTD tsh(i)an <> [D] PMin *tshiem^{B}					
	淺 flow	jiān	tsien	tsen	tsên	'flow rapidly'
l	俴	jiàn	dzjän^{B}	dzian^{B}	dzanʔ	
o	踐	jiàn	dzjän^{B}	dzian^{B}	dzanʔ	OCB *dzjanʔ

p	餞	jiàn	dzjän$^{B/C}$	dzian$^{B/C}$	dzanʔ, dzans	
q	帴	jiǎn, jiān	dzjän^{B}, tsjän	dzian^{B}, tsian	dzanʔ, tsan	
m	諓	jiàn	dzjän$^{B/C}$	dzian$^{B/C}$	dzanʔ, dzans	[T] ONW dzian
n	賤	jiàn	dzjän^{C}	dzian^{C}	dzans	[T] ONW dzian
s	濺	jiàn, jiān	tsjän^{C}, tsien	tsian^{C}, tsen	tsens, tsên	
r	綫	xiàn	sjän^{C}	sian^{C}	sans	= 25-40/237e 線

24-42 = K. 206		**Mand.**	**MC**	**LHan**	**OCM**	
a	a	qiān	tsʰjän	tsʰian	tshan	
c	遷	qiān	tsʰjän	tsʰian	tshan < k-san or tshen < k-	
b	僊	xiān	sjän	sian	san or sen	= 24-45/193f 仙
-	蹮	xiān	sien, sjän	sen, sian	sên, sen	= 23-21/209e

24-43 = K. 208		**Mand.**	**MC**	**LHan**	**OCM**
a	孱	chán	dẓjän, dẓăn	dẓian	dzren or dzran
b	潺	chán	dẓjän	dẓian	dzran
cd	僝 d	zhàn, zhuàn	dẓăn^{B}, dẓjwän^{C}	dẓan^{B}, dẓyan^{C}	dzrânʔ, or dzrênʔ, dzrons
e	轏	zhàn	dẓăn^{C}, dẓan^{B}	dẓan^{B}	dzrânʔ

24-44 = K. 156		**Mand.**	**MC**	**LHan**	**OCM**	
a	散 scatter	sǎn	sân^{B}	sɑn^{B}	sânʔ	
	[T] ONW sɑn <> [E] TB: LB *šan 'sow, scatter seeds' > WB swan^{B} 'pour upon, cast out by pouring' ≭ swan 'pour out, spill, shed'					
	散 disperse	sàn	sân^{C}	sɑn^{C}	sâns	
	[T] MHan 澤散 ḍak-sɑn^{C} Alexandria					
-	撒	sā, sǎ	sât	sɑt	sât	
	[E] TB: LB *šat 'pour, spill', BV-Limbu sɛs- 'scatter, be split'					
d	霰	xiàn	sien^{C}	sen^{C}	sêns	OCB *s(k)ens
	Alternative graph 䨘 <> [T] TB: WT ser-ba 'hail', JP sin[33]					
c	潸	shān	ṣan(^{B}), ṣăn	ṣan(^{B})	srân, srânʔ	

24-44A		**Mand.**	**MC**	**LHan**	**OCM**
-	珊瑚	s(h)ān-hú	sân-ɣuo	sɑn-gɑ	—
	[T] MHan: Iranian sanga 'stone'				
-	删	shān	ṣan	ṣan	
-	狦	sān	sân, ṣan	sɑn, ṣan	—

24-45 = K. 193		**Mand.**	**MC**	**LHan**	**OCM**	
a	山	shān	ṣan, ṣăn	ṣan, ṣɛn	srân	OCB *srjan
	[T] Sin Sukchu SR ṣan (平); MGZY (zhan >) shan (平) [ṣan]. MHan 烏弋山離 ʔɑ-jik-ṣan-liɑi Alexandria					
d	汕	shàn	ṣan^{C}	ṣan^{C}	srâns	OCB *s(C)r(j)ans
e	訕	shàn	ṣan(^{C})	ṣan(^{C})	srân, srâns	
f	仙	xiān	sjän	sian	san or sen	= 24-42/206 僊
-	秈	xiān	sjän	sian	san	
	[E] PTai *s- : S. saan^{A1} 'husked rice'					

24-46 = K. 194		**Mand.**	**MC**	**LHan**	**OCM**
a	產	chǎn	ṣǎn^B	ṣan^B or ṣɛn^B	srânʔ or srênʔ (?)
	[T] Sin Sukchu SR tʂ'an (上); MGZY shan (上) [ṣan]; ONW ṣän; BTD Skt. ṣadya. OCB *sŋrjanʔ <> [E] WT srel-ba 'to bring up, rear'				
-	薩	sà	sât	sat	—
	[T] 菩薩 bo-sat Bodhisattva				

24-47 = K. 181		**Mand.**	**MC**	**LHan**	**OCM**	
ab - -	半靽絆姅	bàn	pwân^C	pan^C	pâns	
	[T] Sin Sukchu SR pwɔn (去), PR pɔn, LR pɔn; MGZY bon (去) [pɔn]; ONW pan					
e	拌	pān, pàn	p^{h}wân	p^{h}an	phân	
c	伴 relaxed	pàn	p^{h}wân^C	p^{h}an^C	phâns	
	comrade	bàn	bwân^B	ban^B	bânʔ	
dfgi	判泮牉頖	pàn	p^{h}wân^C	p^{h}an^C	phâns	= 23-24/218a 片
k	畔	pàn	bwân^C	ban^C	bâns	
	[E] ST *par: WT bar 'intermediate space', NNaga p^{h}ar 'divide'; JP ban 'division, part'					
l	叛	pàn	bwân^C	ban^C	bâns	
h	胖 big, fat	pán, pàng	bwân	ban	bân	
	[E] TB *bwam > WT sbom 'thick, stout'; LB *C-pwam					
	胖 meat	pàn	p^{h}wân^C	p^{h}an^C	phâns	
j	柈	pán	bwân	ban	bân	
m	袢	fán	bjwɐn	buan	ban	

24-48 = K. 182		**Mand.**	**MC**	**LHan**	**OCM**
ade	般[1] 槃盤	pán	bwân	ban	bân
	盤 [T] Sin Sukchu SR bwɔn (平), PR, LR bɔn; MGZY pon (平) [bɔn]				
	[E] ? TB: Perh. cognate to WB pran 'return, repeat', Mru plan 'turn'				
a -	般[2] 搬	bān	pwân	pan	pân
	般 [T] MGZY bon (平) [pɔn]; BTD Skt. -pāna <> 搬 [T] Sin S. SR pwɔn (平), PR pɔn, LR pɔn				
ghi	磐縏鞶	pán	bwân	ban	bân

24-49 = K. 262		**Mand.**	**MC**	**LHan**	**OCM**
ae	反返	fǎn	pjwɐn^B	puan^B	panʔ
	[T] Sin Sukchu SR fwan (上), PR fan; MGZY h(w)an (上) [fan]				
f	販	fàn	pjwɐn^C	puan^C	pans
g	阪	fǎn, bǎn	pjwɐn^B, ban^B	puan^B, ban^B	panʔ, brânʔ
i	飯 rice	fàn	bjwɐn^C	buan^C	bans
	[T] Sin Sukchu SR vwan (去), PR, LR van; MGZY H(w)an (去) [van]; ONW buan				
	飯 eat	fàn	bjwɐn^B	buan^B	banʔ
	[E] AA: PMonic *pooŋ 'cooked rice', SBahn. piaŋ ~ pieŋ				
jkl	板版鈑	bǎn	pan^B	pan^B	prânʔ
	[E] ST *par: WT 'p^{h}ar 'small plank'				
m	扳	pān	p(^{h})an	p(^{h})an	prân, phrân
n	昄	bǎn	pan^B, ban^B	pan^B, ban^B	prânʔ, brânʔ
	[E] WT 'p^{h}ar-ba 'raised, elevated'				

24-50 = K. 263		**Mand.**	**MC**	**LHan**	**OCM**
ab	棥樊[1]	fán	bjwɐn	buan	ban
	[E] TB: Lepcha tuk-pól 'hedge, fence' ⋇ pól 'magic circle', Lushai pal^H 'hedge, fence'				

b	樊[2] belt	pán	bwân	bɑn	bân	= 24-55/265b
d	攀	pān	p^han	p^han	phrân	

24-51 = K. 264		Mand.	MC	LHan	OCM	
ab	煩蹞	fán	bjwɐn	buɑn	ban	= 24-51/195l 蹞

24-52 = K. 265		Mand.	MC	LHan	OCM	
ab	a 繁 belt	pán	bwân	bɑn	bân	= 24-53/263b
	繁 abundant	fán	bjwɐn	buɑn	ban	= 24-51/195m 蕃
d	蘩	fán	bjwɐn	buɑn	ban	

24-53 = K. 190		Mand.	MC	LHan	OCM	
ac	班斑	bān	pan	pan	prân	
	班 [T] Sin Sukchu SR pan (平); MGZY ban (平) [pan] <> WT 'p^hral-ba 'to separate, part'					

24-54 = K. 195		Mand.	MC	LHan	OCM	
a	釆	bàn, biàn	bǎn^C, bjän^C 3	bɛn^C	brêns, brens	
b	番 a turn	fān	p^hjwɐn	p^huɑn	phan	
	番 [E] TB: WT p^har 'interest (on money)', 'exchange', Lepcha far 'price' × par 'buy'					
	番 martial	bō	puâ	pɑi	pâi	
de	幡旛	fān	p^hjwɐn	p^huɑn	phan	
gs	轓藩	fān	pjwɐn	puɑn	pan	
h	緐	fán	p^h/bjwɐn	p^huɑn, buɑn	phan, ban	
ijk	燔璠膰	fán	bjwɐn	buɑn	ban	
	[E] TB *bar ~ *par > WT 'bar-ba 'to burn, to bloom' × sbar-ba ~ sbor-ba 'light, kindle'					
l	蹯	fán	bjwɐn	buɑn	ban	= 24-54/264b
	[E] TB: WT sbal 'soft muscles or parts of inner hand or paw'					
-	鱕	fán	bjwɐn	buɑn	—	SW
m	蕃 luxur.	fán	bjwɐn	buɑn	ban	= 24-55/265d 繁
	[E] ? ST *pom<> PTai *b- : S. p^huun^{A2} 'increase, flourishing'					
	蕃 hedge	fān	pjwɐn	puɑn	pan	
-	翻	fān	p^hjwɐn	p^huɑn	phan	
	= 24-52/220 弁拚 <> [E] TB: WB p^hran^C 'spread out, spread wings' × pran^C 'expanded, spread out'; JP p^hyan^{55} 'spread the wings'					
n	潘	pān	p^hwân	p^hɑn	phân	[D] PEMin *p^hon^{A1}
o	蟠	pán	bwân	bɑn	bân	
	[E] TB *boy > WB bhwe 'curl in hair of animal'; Kachin boi 'have a cowlick'					
p	播 winnow	bò	pwâ^C	pɑi^C	pâih	
	= 18-16/25n bò 簸 <> [T] ONW pɑ					
pq	播譒	bò	pwâ^C	pɑi^C	pâih	'spread, sow'
	[E] TB *b^wâr > WT 'bor-ba 'to throw, cast', Chepang wa:r 'sow'					
r	皤	pó	bwâ, pwâ	bɑi	bâi	[E] TB *pwa:r, *poj 'white'

24-55 = K. 220		Mand.	MC	LHan	OCM	
abc	弁卞拚	biàn	bjän^C 3	bian^C	brans	OCB *brjons
d	拚 = 抃	biàn	bjän^C 3	bian^C	brans	
	拚 to fly	fān	p^hjwɐn	p^huɑn	phan 'fly up'	= 24-51/195 翻
	拚 to dust	fèn	pjwən^C	pun^C	pəns	

e	犿	fān	p^{h}jwɐn	p^{h}uɑn	phan	
f	笲	fán, biàn	bjwɐn, bjän^C 3	buɑn, bɨɑn^C	ban	

24-56 = K. 266		**Mand.**	**MC**	**LHan**	**OCM**	
a	曼[1]	màn	mwân^C	mɑn^C	mâns	[T] ONW mɑn
	頭曼	tóu-mán	dəu-mwân !	do-mɑn	—	a Xiongnu ruler
ad	曼[2] 蔓	wàn	mjwɐn^C	muɑn^C	mans	
egh	嫚僈慢	màn	man^C	man^C	mrâns	
	[T] Sin Sukchu SR man (去); MGZY man (去) [man]					
i	墁	mán	mwân	mɑn	mân	
jkln	幔縵鄤 漫	màn	mwân^C	mɑn^C	mâns	
	漫 [T] BTD Skt. mai[tra...]					
o	謾 excessive	màn	mwân^C	mɑn^C	mâns	
	謾 deceive	mán,	mwân,	mɑn,	mân,	
		màn,	mwân^C, man^C,	mɑn^C, man^C,	mâns, mrâns,	
		mián	mjän 3	mɨan	mran	
	謾 reckless	màn	mwân^C	mɑn^C	mâns	

24-57 = K. 183		**Mand.**	**MC**	**LHan**	**OCM**
ad	㒼瞞	mán	mwân	mɑn	mân
c	滿	mǎn	mwân^B	mɑn^B	mânʔ
g	懣	mǎn,	mwân^B,	mɑn^B,	mânʔ,
		mèn	mwən$^{B/C}$	mən$^{B/C}$	mə̂nʔ, mə̂ns
f	璊	mén	mwən	mən	mə̂n
e	樠 elm	mén,	mwən,	mən,	mə̂n,
		wán	mjwɐn	muɑn	man
	樠 resin	wán,	mjwɐn,	muɑn,	man,
		mán	mwân(^{C})	mɑn(^{C})	mân, mâns

24-58 = K. 222		**Mand.**	**MC**	**LHan**	**OCM**
a	免[1]	miǎn	mjän^B 3	mɨan^B	mranʔ
	[T] ONW man; Han BTD man				
ak	免[2] 絻	wèn	mjwən^C	mun^C	məns
bcd	俛勉冕	miǎn	mjän^B 3	mɨan^B	mranʔ
g	娩	wǎn, miǎn	mjwɐn^B, mjän^{B}3	muɑn^B, mɨan^B	mânʔ, mranʔ
hij	晚脕輓	wǎn	mjwɐn^B	muɑn^B	manʔ
e	悗	mán, mèn	mwân, mwən^B	mɑn, mən^B	mân, mə̂nʔ
f	鞔	mán	mwân	mɑn	mân
l	浼	měi	mwậi^B	məi^B	mə̂iʔ

25 OCM rime *-on, *-wan Yuán bù 元部 (3)

GSR 157 - 266

Baxter 1992: 370 ff. (§10.1.1)

The MC rimes with guttural initials can derive either from OC *-ôn or *-wân; they are difficult if not impossible to distinguish. Baxter 1992: 381-389 tries to determine the final of some words through *Shijing* rimes and loan graphs. By default, we tentatively assume *Kôn in large XS without initial *w-, but *Kwân in XS that include initial *w-. Accordingly, MC Div. III syllables of the type Kjwɐn seem to derive from OC *Kwan, syllables Kjwän from OC *Kon. After *ʔ* and *ŋ* occurs only -jwɐn. The situation is somewhat parallel to rimes in *-un / *-wən, see rime 28.

See Intro. 5.2.3 for more about the removal of OCB medial *r in MC Div. 3/3 syllables.

Table 25-1: OCM rimes *-on / *-wan, *-ot / *-wat, *-oi / *-wai in QYS categories

Div.	*-on / *-wan R.25	*-ot / *-wat R.22	*-o(t)s / *-wa(t)s R.22	*-oi / *-wai R.19
I	冠 kwân kuɑn *kôn 斷 twân^{C} tuɑn^{C} *tôns	奪 dwât duɑt *lôt	會 kwâi^{C} kuɑs *kôts 兑 dwâi^{C} duɑs *lôts	果 kwâ^{B} kuɑi^{B} *kôiʔ 坐 dzwâ^{B} dzuɑi^{B} *dzôiʔ
I gr	官 kwân kuɑn *kwân	括 kwât kuɑt *kwât	翽 xwâi^{C} huɑs *hwâts	禾 ɣwâ ɣuɑi *wâi
III gr	勸 kʰjwɐn^{C} kʰyɑn^{C} *khwans 遠 jwɐn^{B} wɑn^{B} *wanʔ	越 jwɐt wɑt *wat	顪 xjwɐi^{C} hyɑs *hwats	虧 kʰjwe3 kʰyai *khwai 為 jwe wai *wai
III gr	元 ŋjwɐn ŋyɑn *ŋon 怨 ʔjwɐn^{C} ʔyɑn^{C} *ʔons	月 ŋjwɐt ŋyɑt *ŋot or *ŋwat		
III gr	—	蕨 kjwɐt kyɑt *kot	—	
3/3	卷 kjwän^{B}3 kyan^{B} *konʔ	—	撅 kjwäi^{C}3 kyas *kots	危 ŋjwe3 ŋyai *ŋoi
III ac	傳 ḍjwän ḍyan *dron 沿 jiwän4 juan *lon	説 śjwät śuat *lhot	税 śjuäi^{C} śuas *lhots	垂 źjwe dźye <dźuai *doi
II	關 kwan kuan *krôn 蠻 man man *mrôn	刮 kwat kuat *kwrât or *krôt	話 ɣwai^{C} guas *gwrâts or *grôts	蝸 kwa kuai *krôi 髽 tṣwa tṣuai *tsrôi
II	鍰 ɣwan ɣwan *wrân			

25 OCM *-on, *-wan 元部 (3) (GSR 157-266)

25-1	= K. 157	Mand.	MC	LHan	OCM	
a	官	guān	kwân	kuɑn	kwân	OCB kʷan ?

[T] Sin Sukchu SR kwɔn (平); MGZY gon (平) [kɔn]; ONW kuɑn

l	倌 servant	guān,	kwân,	kuɑn,	kôn,	
		guàn	kwan^{C}	kuɑn^{C}	krôns	

⋈ 25-10/188 宦 *grôns 'servant' <> [E] WT kʰol-po 'servant, vassal'

m	逭	huàn	ɣwân^{C}	ɣuɑn^{C}	gôns	
e	棺 coffin	guān	kwân	kuɑn	kôn	
	put in c.	guàn	kwân^{C}	kuɑn^{C}	kôns	
f	涫	guàn	kwân^{C}	kuɑn^{C}	kôns	

[E] ST *kol > WT 'kʰol-ba, kʰol 'to boil' ⋈ skol-ba 'to cause to boil'

k	館	guǎn !	kwân^{C} !	kuɑn^{C}	kôns	OCB *kons
hi	管琯 flute	guǎn	kwân^{B}	kuɑn^{B}	kônʔ !	筦 OCB *konʔ
	= 25-19/257r					
g	痯 exhausted	guǎn	kwân^{B}	kuɑn^{B}	kwânʔ !	OCB *kʷanʔ
j	錧 axle cap	guǎn	kwân$^{B/C}$	kuɑn$^{B/C}$	kwânʔ/s ?	≈ 24-2/140l 幹
n	菅	jiān	kan	kan	krân	

25-2	= K. 158	Mand.	MC	LHan	OCM	
ae	雚鸛	guàn	kwân^{C}	kuɑn^{C}	kwâns	
gh	爟瓘	guàn	kwân^{C}	kuɑn^{C}	kwâns	
f	灌	guàn	kwân^{C}	kuɑn^{C}	kwâns	= 19-2/351m 祼

[E] TB: Chepang kʰur, Boro kur 'to scrape', Mikir hòr 'to ladle out'

i	觀 look	guān	kwân	kuɑn	kwân	

[T] Sin Sukchu SR kwɔn (平); MGZY gon (平) [kɔn]; ONW kuɑn

	觀 show	guàn	kwân^{C}	kuɑn^{C}	kwâns	OCB kwans
opq	權蠸趯	quán	gjwän 3	gyɑn	gon	

See comment under 25-11/226.

s	勸	quàn	kʰjwɐn^{C}	kʰyɑn^{C}	khwans	
n	讙	huān, xuān	xwân,xjwɐn	huɑn, hyɑn	hwân, hwan	
jkl	歡懽驩	huān	xwân	huɑn	hwân	

[T] MHan 驩泥 huɑn-nei kuhani or khvani

m	嚾	huān !	xwân^{C}	huɑn^{C}	hwâns	

The last three rows could also have been OCM *hôn, but *hwân is a more common syllable.

25-3	= K. 159	Mand.	MC	LHan	OCM	
-	毌	guān	kwân	kuɑn	—	SW
a	貫 perfor.	guàn	kwân(^{C})	kuɑn(^{C})	kôns !	OCB *kons
acde	貫摜慣串	guàn	kwan^{C}	kuɑn^{C}	krôns	'familiar, custom'
f	患	huàn	ɣwan^{C}	ɣuɑn^{C}	grôns	

25-4	= K. 160	Mand.	MC	LHan	OCM	
a	冠 cap	guān	kwân	kuɑn	kôn	OCB *kon
	冠 vb.	guàn	kwân^{C}	kuɑn^{C}	kôns	OCB *kons

[N] Acc. to SW 3357, 25-19 yuán 元 *ŋwan 'head' is "also phonetic" <> [T] ONW kuɑn
[E] TB *gwa ~ *kwa:n > WT bgo-ba, bgos 'clothes, put on clothes' ⋈ gon-pa 'to put on, dress'

25-5	**= K. 161**		**Mand.**	**MC**	**LHan**	**OCM**	
a	盥		guàn	kwân$^{B/C}$	kuɑn^{B}, kuɑn^{C}	kwânʔ, kwâns	

≭ 24-2/140m 澣 'wash'; ≭ 25-19/257o 浣 'wash clothes'

25-6	**= K. 162**		**Mand.**	**MC**	**LHan**	**OCM**	
a	款		kuǎn	kʰwân^{B}	kʰuɑn^{B}	khwânʔ	
b	窾		kuǎn	kʰwân^{B}	kʰuɑn^{B}	khwânʔ	

[E] TB *kwar > Lushai kʰur^{H} 'a hole, pit, cavity' ≭ kʰuar^{H} id., Tangkhul Naga kʰur 'hole'

25-7	**= K. 165**		**Mand.**	**MC**	**LHan**	**OCM**	
165a	莧	sheep	huán	ɣwân	ɣuɑn	gwân	cf. 23-2
241h	莧	smile	huàn	ɣwan^{B}	ɣuan^{B}	gwrânʔ	

23-2/241h; ~ 25-19/257q

165b	寬		kuān	kʰwân	kʰuɑn	khwân	OCB *kʷhan

25-8	**= K. 166**		**Mand.**	**MC**	**LHan**	**OCM**	
a	萑		huán	ɣwân	ɣuɑn	gwân ?	

25-9	**= K. 187**		**Mand.**	**MC**	**LHan**	**OCM**	
a	丱		guàn	kwan	kuan^{C}	krôns	OCB *krons
b	關	bar	guān	kwan	kuan	krôn	OCB *kron

[T] Sin Sukchu SR kwan (平), LR kwɔn; MGZY gwan (平) [kwan]; ONW kuän

[E] -> PTai *klɔn^{A1} 'rafter, latch on door'

	關	bend	wān	ʔwan	ʔuan	ʔrôn	

25-10	**= K. 188**		**Mand.**	**MC**	**LHan**	**OCM**	
a	宦		huàn	ɣwan^{C}	ɣuan^{C}	grôns	≭ 25-1157l 倌

[E] TB: LB *gywan[1] > WB kywan 'slave, servant'

25-11 = K. 226 The rime MC -jwän 3 occurs also after acute initials, therefore I tentatively consider MC Kjwän to derive from *Kon, Kjwen from *Kwan.

			Mand.	**MC**	**LHan**	**OCM**	
a	卷	roll	juǎn	kjwän^{B} 3	kyan^{B}	konʔ	OCB *krjonʔ 'a roll'

[T] Sin Sukchu SR kyen (上); MGZY gyon (上) [kyɔn]

[E] TB: Lushai hrual^{H} 'roll up in the hand, twist'

	卷	bend	quán	gjwän 3	gyan	gon	
	卷 = e 鬈		quán	gjwän 3	gyan	gwren	OCB *gʷrjen 'handsome'
e	鬈		quān,	kʰjwän 3,	kʰyan,	khon,	
			quán	gjwän 3	gyan	gon	OCB *gʷrjen 'handsome'
bc	睠眷		juàn	kjwän^{C} 3	kyan^{C}	kons	
d	棬	crooked	quān	kʰjwän 3	kʰyan	khon	
		ring	juàn	kjwän^{C} 3	kyan^{C}	kons	
fgh	捲拳蜷		quán	gjwän 3	gyan	gon	

拳 [E] Tai: Wu-ming klian^{C1} 'roll, scroll', Mun gluan^{C2} 'roll up'

ij	倦勌		juàn	gjwän^{C} 3	gyan^{C}	gons	

[T] Sin Sukchu SR gyen (去); MGZY kwyan (去) [gyɛn]

op	豢犧		huàn	ɣwan^{C}	ɣuan^{C}	grôns	

k	圈 pig sty	juàn	gjwɐn^{B},	gyɑn^{B},	gwanʔ,	
			gjwän^{B} 3,	gyan^{B},	gonʔ,	(SSYP 307)
			gjiwän^{B} 4	gyen^{B}	gwenʔ	(GYSX 409)
	圈 turn ar.	quǎn	k(ʰ)jwɐn^{B}	k(ʰ)yɑn^{B}	kwanʔ, khwanʔ	
m	綣	quǎn	kʰjwɐn$^{B/C}$	kyɑn^{B}	khwanʔ R!	OCB *khjonʔ
n	卷	quǎn	kʰjwɐn^{B},	kyɑn^{B},	khwanʔ,	
		yuān	ʔjwɐn^{A} !	ʔyɑn	ʔwan	= 25-18/ 261 冤
l	券	quàn	kʰjwɐn^{C}	kyɑn^{C}	khwans	

25-11A		Mand.	MC	LHan	OCM	
-	㗊	juàn	kjwän^{C} 3	kyan^{C}	kons	SW

25-11B		Mand.	MC	LHan	OCM	
-	巻	juàn	kjwän^{C} 3	kyan^{C}	kons	SW

25-12 = K. 164		Mand.	MC	LHan	OCM	
a	亘	xuān	sjwän	syan	swan	[T] BTD Skt. svāra
fgjk	桓洹狟荁	huán	ɣwân	ɣuɑn	wân	桓 = 25-19/257n 垸
	洹 [T] ONW ɣuɑn; BTD Skt. (nir)vāṇa; -varṇa; -panna; 桓 Skt. vana; 烏桓 ʔɑ-ɣuɑn *Awar					
l	貆	huán	x/ɣwân,	huɑn, ɣuɑn,	hwân, wân,	
			xjwɐn	hyɑn	hwan	
mn	垣趄	yuán	jwɐn	wɑn	wan	
qr	咺晅	xuǎn	xjwɐn^{B}	hyɑn^{B}	hwanʔ	
xy	喧愃	xuān !	xjwɐn^{B}	hyɑn^{B}	hwanʔ	
s	烜	xuǎn, xuān	xjwɐn(^{B})	hyɑn(^{B})	hwan, hwanʔ	
	[N] huǐ is a ghost reading.					
z	諠	xuān	xjwɐn	hyɑn	hwan	
t	宣	xuān	sjwän	syan	swan	
	[E] TB: LB *swan² > Lahu šē 'sow, broadcast', WB swan^{B} 'pour upon, cast by pouring'.					

25-13 = K. 167 GSR 167 includes 23-12 in this group, even though the graphs and rimes are distinct.

		Mand.	MC	LHan	OCM	
abc	奐渙煥	huàn	xwân^{C}	huɑn^{C}	hwâns	渙 OCB *hwans
f	換	huàn	ɣwân^{C}	ɣuɑn^{C}	wâns	= 25-19/257p 睆
	[T] Sin Sukchu SR ɣwɔn (去); MGZY Xon (去) [ɣɔn]; ONW ɣuɑn					
d	寏	huán	ɣwân	ɣuɑn	wân	'encircling wall'
	※ 25-12/164m 垣					

25-14 = K. 255		Mand.	MC	LHan	OCM
ad	爰猨	yuán	jwɐn	wɑn	wan
l	緩	huǎn	ɣwân^{B}	ɣuɑn^{B}	wânʔ
j	暖[1]	xuān	xjwɐn(^{B})	hyɑn(^{B})	hwan, hwanʔ
	[E] ? TB: WT hol-hol 'soft, loose, light'				
ik	煖[1] 諼	xuān	xjwɐn	hyɑn	hwan
h	湲	yuán	jwän	wɑn	wen

		Mand.	MC	LHan	OCM	
f	瑗 ring	yuàn	jwän^{C}, jwɐn^{C}	wan^{C}, wan^{C}	wens, wans	
	= 25-19/257u 院; 23-11/256u 擐					
g	媛 beauty	yuàn	jwän^{C}	wan^{C}	wens	
	embarr.	yuán	jwɐn	wan	wan	
e	援 pull	yuán	jwɐn	wan	wan	
	succour	yuàn	jwɐn^{C}	wan^{C}	wans	
m	鍰	huán	ɣwan	ɣuan	wên or gwrân	
ij	煖² 暖²	nuǎn	nwân^{B}	nuan^{B}	nônʔ	[T] ONW nuan

25-15 = K. 256 GSR 829 and items starting with 256h belong to phonetic series 23-12.

		Mand.	MC	LHan	OCM	
abde	袁園榬轅	yuán	jwɐn	wan	wan	園 OCB *wjan
c	猿	yuán	jwɐn	wan	wan	
	[E] TB *woy ~ (b)woy, JP woi^{33}					
f	遠 far	yuǎn	jwɐn^{B}	wan^{B}	wanʔ	OCB *wjanʔ
	[T] Sin Sukchu SR yen (上); MGZY xwÿan (上) [ɦyɛn]; ONW uan					
	遠 leave	yuàn	jwɐn^{C}	wan^{C}	wans	

25-15A		Mand.	MC	LHan	OCM	
-	吅	xuān	xjwɐn	hyan	hwan	SW

25-16 = K. 163		Mand.	MC	LHan	OCM	
ad	丸芄	wán	ɣwân	ɣuan	wân	
c	紈	huán	ɣwân	ɣuan	wân	
b	疣	huàn	ɣwân^{C}	ɣuan^{C}	wâns	
e	骫 bent	wěi	ʔjwe 3	ʔye < ʔyai	ʔoi-	= 19-10/357a

25-17 = K. 260 Provisionally I assume OC *ʔon because this syllable is probably more common than *ʔwan.

		Mand.	MC	LHan	OCM	
a	夗	yuǎn	ʔjwɐn^{B}	ʔyan^{B}	ʔonʔ	
i	晩	wǎn	ʔjwɐn^{B}	ʔyan^{B}	ʔonʔ	
d	苑 rich fol.	yuàn	ʔjwɐn^{B}	ʔyan^{B}	ʔonʔ	OCB *ʔjon
	[T] Sin Sukchu SR ʔyen (上); MGZY 'wÿan (上) [ʔyɛn]					
	苑 obstruct	yǔn	jwən^{B}	wun^{B}	wənʔ	
	苑 pent up	yù	ʔjwət	ʔut	ʔut	
	= 31-4/495 鬱 [T] ONW ʔut					
c	怨 resent	yuàn	ʔjwɐn^{C}	ʔyan^{C}	ʔons	OCB *ʔjons
	怨 enemy	yuàn	ʔjwɐn(^{C})	ʔyan(^{C})	ʔon, ʔons	
ek	鴛鵷	yuān	ʔjwɐn	ʔyan	ʔon	
f	智	wān	ʔwân	ʔuan	ʔôn	
bgj	宛婉畹	wǎn	ʔjwɐn^{B}	ʔyan^{B}	ʔonʔ	OCB *ʔjonʔ
	[T] MHan 大宛 da^{C}-ʔyan or -ʔion perhaps Great Yavana = Ἰάονες (Ferghana)					
h	怨	yuān !	ʔjwɐn^{B}	ʔyan^{B}	ʔonʔ	
-	裷	yuǎn	ʔjwɐn^{B}	ʔyan^{B}	ʔonʔ	
	[D] PMin *ʔyon^{B}: Fú'ān un^{B1}, Fúzh uoŋ^{B1}, Xiamen ŋ^{B}, Jiànyáng yeŋ^{B1}					

l	琬	yuǎn,	ʔjwɐn^B,	ʔyɑn^B,	ʔonʔ,	
		wǎn	ʔwân^C	ʔuɑn^C	ʔôns	
mn	捥腕	wàn	ʔwân^C	ʔuɑn^C	ʔôns	= 22-7/273b 掔
o	椀	wǎn	ʔwân^B	ʔuɑn^B	ʔônʔ	
-	碗	wǎn	ʔwân^B	ʔuɑn^B	ʔônʔ	
p	輐	yuān,	ʔjwɐn,	ʔyɑn,	ʔon,	
		yūn	ʔjwən	ʔun	ʔun	
q	菀	yuàn,	ʔjwɐn^B,	ʔyɑn^B,	ʔonʔ,	
		yù	ʔjwət	ʔut	ʔut	
r	餇	yuè,	ʔjwɐt,	ʔyɑt,	ʔot,	
		yù	ʔjwət	ʔut	ʔut	

25-18 = K. 261		**Mand.**	**MC**	**LHan**	**OCM**
a	冤	yuān	ʔjwɐn	ʔyɑn	ʔon

[T] Sin Sukchu SR ʔyen (平); MGZY 'wȳan (平) [ʔyɛn]

25-19 = K. 257 After initials ʔ and ŋ the MC rime *-jwän* does not occur, therefore *ŋjwɐn* can derive from OC *-on or *-wan. It is not clear which syllables represent OC *ŋon, which ŋwan. The OCM origin of the many MC ɣwân could be *wân, *gwân or *gôn.

		Mand.	**MC**	**LHan**	**OCM**	
a	元	yuán	ŋjwɐn	ŋyɑn	ŋon	OCB *Nkjon

[T] Sin Sukchu SR ŋyen (平); MGZY xwȳan (平) [ɦyɛn]; ONW ŋuan

This is probably the same word as 25-20/258 *ŋwan 原 'source', hence the OCM reading.

d	芫	yuán	ŋjwɐn	ŋyɑn	ŋwan	
ef	黿魭	yuán	ŋjwɐn, ŋwân	ŋyɑn	ŋwan	
g	頑	wán	ŋwan, ŋwăn	ŋuan	ŋrôn	⋈ 10-11/124g *ŋo
hi	刓园	wán	ŋwân	ŋuɑn	ŋwân	
j	忨	wàn	ŋwân(C)	ŋuɑn(C)	ŋwân, ŋwâns	
kl	玩翫	wán !	ŋwân^C	ŋuɑn^C	ŋwâns	
m	完	wán !	ɣwân	ɣuɑn	gôn	OCB *ɦkon

Possibly phonetic in 10-4/111a 寇 *khôh

r	筦	guǎn	kwân^B	kuɑn^B	kônʔ !	= 25-1/157h 管
n	垸	huán	ɣwân	ɣuɑn	gwân !	

⋈ 25-12/164f 桓 huán! [T] ONW ɣuɑn, QY also ŋwân$^{B/C}$

o	浣 wash clo.	huàn	ɣwân^B	ɣuɑn^B	gwânʔ	

= 24-2/140m 澣 'wash'; ⋈ 25-5/161 盥 'wash the hands'

[E] TB: KN-Lai khoʔl 'to clean (with water)'

p	睆	huàn,	ɣwân^C,	ɣuɑn^C,	gwâns, !	= 25-13/167f 換

[T] Sin Sukchu SR ɣwɔn (去); MGZY Xon (去) [ɣɔn]; ONW ɣuɑn

		wàn	ŋwân$^{B/C}$	ŋuɑn$^{B/C}$	ŋwânʔ, ŋwâns	
q	莞 Cyperus	huán, guān	ɣwân, kwân	ɣuɑn, kuɑn	gwân, kwân	
	smile	wǎn !	ɣwân^B	ɣuɑn^B	gwânʔ	~ 23-2/241h
u	院	yuàn	jwän^C	wan^C	wens	

= 25-14/255f 瑗; 23-12/256u 擐

s	梡	kuǎn	k^{h}wân^B	k^{h}uɑn^B	khwânʔ	
t	睆	huǎn	ɣwan^B	ɣuan^B	gwrânʔ ?	= 24-1/139j' 睅

25-20 = K. 258		**Mand.**	**MC**	**LHan**	**OCM**	
ac	原 > 源	yuán	ŋjwɐn	ŋyɑn	ŋwan 'source'	
	原 a plain	yuán	ŋjwɐn	ŋyɑn	ŋwan !	OCB *ŋʷjan

This is a later substitution for 25-21/259 邍 'high plain', q.v. <> [T] ONW ŋuan

e	謜	yuán	ŋjwɐn	ŋyɑn	ŋwan	
g	騵	yuán	ŋjwɐn	ŋyɑn	ŋwan	
df	愿願	yuàn	ŋjwɐn^{C}	ŋyɑn^{C}	ŋons	OCB *ŋjons
h-	豲獂	huán	ɣwân	ɣuɑn	gwân	

25-21 = K. 259		**Mand.**	**MC**	**LHan**	**OCM**
a	邍	yuán	ŋjwɐn	ŋyɑn	ŋwan

This is the original graph for 25-20/258 原 'high plain' (Duan SW 5152).

25-22 = K. 170		**Mand.**	**MC**	**LHan**	**OCM**	
a	斷	duàn	twân$^{B/C}$,	tuɑn$^{B/C}$,	tônʔ, tôns,	OCB *tonʔ/s
			dwân^{B}	duɑn^{B}	dônʔ	OCB *ɦtonʔ

25-23 = K. 172		**Mand.**	**MC**	**LHan**	**OCM**
a	段 hammer	duàn	twân^{C}	tuɑn^{C}	tôns
	torn	duàn	dwân^{C}	duɑn^{C}	dôns
cd	鍛腶	duàn	twân^{C}	tuɑn^{C}	tôns

[E] TB *tow (STC no. 317) > WT t^{h}o-ba ~ mt^{h}o-ba 'hammer (large)'

25-24 = K. 168		**Mand.**	**MC**	**LHan**	**OCM**	
ad	耑端	duān	twân	tuɑn	tôn	[T] ONW tuɑn

[E] TB: WT rdol-ba, brtol 'to come out, break out, sprout'

e	剬	duān	twân, tśjwän^{B}	tuɑn, tśuan^{B}	tôn, tonʔ	= 25-25/231c 剸
fg	褍鍴	duān	twân	tuɑn	tôn	
i	湍	tuān	t^{h}wân	t^{h}uɑn	thôn	
-	貒 pig EY	tuān	t^{h}wân(C)	t^{h}uɑn(C)	thôn(s)	~ 25-28/171 彖
j	喘 to pant	chuǎn	tś^{h}jwän^{B}	tś^{h}uan^{B}	thonʔ	
k	諯	chuán,	źjwän,	dźuan,	don,	
		chuàn	tś^{h}jwän^{C}	tś^{h}uan^{C}	thons	
lm	輲遄	chuán	źjwän	dźuan	don	
o	惴 wriggle	chuǎn	tś^{h}jwän^{B}	tś^{h}uan^{B}	thonʔ	
	anxious	zhuì	tśjwe^{C}	tśuai^{C}	toih	
p	瑞	ruì !	źjwe^{C}	dźuai^{C}	doih	
q	揣	chuǎn,	tś^{h}jwän^{B},	tś^{h}uan^{B},	thonʔ,	
		chuǎi,	tṣ^{h}jwe^{B},	tṣ^{h}yai^{B},	tshroiʔ,	
		duǒ	twâ^{B}	tuɑi^{B}	tôiʔ	
-	圌	chuí	źjwe,	dźuai,	doi,	
			źjwän	dźuan	don	
-	顓	zhuān	tśjwän	tśuan	ton	

25-25 = K. 231		**Mand.**	**MC**	**LHan**	**OCM**	
a	專 locust ?	yuán	jiwän 4	juan	lon	= 25-28/171c

		Mand.	MC	LHan	OCM	
	專 alone	zhuān	tśjwän	tśuan	ton	

[E] MK: Khmer -tola /-taaol/ 'be alone, single'

c	剸	zhuān,	tśjwän^{B},	tśuan^{B},	tonʔ,	= 25-24/168e 剬
		tuán	dwân	duɑn	dôn	
d	篿	zhuān	tśjwän	tśuan	ton	
e	轉	zhuǎn	ṭjwän^{B}	ṭyan^{B}	tron	[T] MTang ṭuan, ONW tuan
f	傳 transmit	chuán	ḍjwän	ḍyan	dron	

[T] Sin Sukchu SR dẓyen (平); MGZY cwyan (平) [dẓyɛn]; MTang ḍuan, ONW duan

	傳 a record	zhuàn	ḍjwän^{C}	ḍyan^{C}	drons	

[E] TB: Old Tib. 'drul 'to transmit, communicate'

	傳 relay post	zhuàn	ṭjwän^{C}	ṭyan^{C}	trons	
nopq	團慱摶漙	tuán	dwân	duɑn	dôn	

[T] Sin Sukchu SR dwɔn (平); MGZY ton (平) [dɔn]

j	縳	zhuàn	ḍjwän^{B}	ḍyan^{B}	dronʔ	
k	膞 cut meat	shuàn,	źjwän^{B},	dźuan^{B},	donʔ,	cf. 25-31/178i
		zhuǎn	tśjwän^{B}	tśuan^{B}	tonʔ	
	turning m.	chuán	źjwän	dźuan	don	
	femur	chún,	źjwen,	dźuin,	dun,	
		zhǔn	tśjwen^{B}	tśuin^{B}	tunʔ	
l	鱄 a fish A	shuàn	źjwän^{B}	dźuan^{B}	donʔ	
	鱄 a fish B	shuàn	tśjwän(^{B})	tśuan(^{B})	ton, tonʔ	
m	竱	duān,	twân,	tuɑn,	tôn,	
		zhuǎn	tśjwän^{B}	tśuan^{B}	tonʔ	

25-26 = K. 232		**Mand.**	**MC**	**LHan**	**OCM**
a	穿	chuān	tśʰjwän	tśʰuan	thon

[T] Sin Sukchu SR tṣ'yen (平); MGZY chwyan (平) [tṣ'yɛn]; ONW tśʰuan
[E] TB: WT rtol-ba 'to bore, pierce, perforate'

25-27 = K. 233		**Mand.**	**MC**	**LHan**	**OCM**
a	舛	chuǎn	tśʰjwän^{B}	tśʰuan^{B}	thonʔ

25-28 = K. 171 The initials of some words are not certain.

		Mand.	**MC**	**LHan**	**OCM**	
a	彖 pig SW	tuàn	tʰwân^{C}	thuɑns	—	~ 25-24/168 tuān 貒
b	褖	tuàn	tʰwân^{C}	thuɑns	lhôns	
e	椽 rafter	chuán	ḍjwän	ḍyan	dron	⋇ 10-19/129e *troʔ
fg	瑑篆 carved	zhuàn	ḍjwän^{B}	ḍyan^{B}	dronʔ	⋇ 10-29/123m *rôh
h	腞 carved	zhuàn,	ḍjwän^{B},	ḍyan^{B},	dronʔ,	
		chuǎn	ṭʰjwän^{B}	ṭʰyan^{B}	thronʔ	
i	喙 to pant	chuì	tśʰjwäi^{C}	tśʰuas	thos	⋇ 25-24/168 喘
	喙 snout	huì	xjwɐi^{C}	hyɑs	hwats	= 22-5/346 顪

[T] ONW hueiC <> [E] ? TB: WB hnut 'mouth, womb'

c	蝝 locust	yuán	jiwän 4	juan	lon	= 25-25/231a
d	緣 hem	yuàn	jiwän^{C} 4	juan^{C}	lons	⋇ 25-29/229b 沿

[T] Sin Sukchu SR, LR yen (平); MGZY ywyan (平) [jyɛn]

	緣 follow	yuán	jiwän 4	juan	lon	= 25-29/c

25-29 = K. 229		**Mand.**	**MC**	**LHan**	**OCM**	
a	㕣	yuán	jiwän^B 4	juan^B	lonʔ	

[E] Tai: S. leen^{A2} 'marsh, mire'

b	沿	yán	jiwän 4	juan	lon	⋈ 25-28/171 緣
c	鉛	qiān //	jiwän 4	juan	lon	

[T] Sin Sukchu SR jen (平); MGZY ywȳan (平) [jyɛn] <> [D] M-Xiamen iɛn^{35}

d	兖	yǎn	jiwän^B	juan^B	lonʔ	
e	船	chuán	dźjwän	źuan	m-lon	

[T] Sin Sukchu SR dʐyen (平); MGZY cwȳan (平) [dʐyɛn] <> [D] PMin *d̂žiun ~ *d̂žion
[E] TB *(m-)loŋ > WB loŋ^B 'canoe, long boat'; Lushai lɔŋ^L 'boat', S. Khâmi mlauŋ

25-30 = K. 230		**Mand.**	**MC**	**LHan**	**OCM**	
a	鳶	yuān	jiwän	juan	jon ?	

[E] TB: PL *(k-)dzwan^1 'hawk'

25-31 = K. 178		**Mand.**	**MC**	**LHan**	**OCM**	
af	䜌 > 鑾	luán	lwân	luɑn	rôn	OCB *b-ron

[E] Tai: S. p^{h}ruan^{A2} < *br- 'neck bells (for domestic animals)'

cdeh	巒欒灓鸞	luán	lwân	luɑn	rôn	欒 OCB *b-ron
i	臠 emaciated	luán	lwân	luɑn	rôn	

[E] TB: WB prun^B 'worn away, exhausted, spent (as property)' ⋈ p^{h}run^B 'wear away, exhaust'

	cut meat	lüán	ljwän^B	lyan^B	ronʔ	cf. 25-25/231k
k	孌	luán	ljwän$^{B/C}$	lyan$^{B/C}$	ronʔ	OCB *b-rjonʔ
m	戀	liàn !	ljwän^C	lyan^C	rons	
n	攣	luán !	ljwän	lyan	ron	
o	變	biàn	pjän^C 3	pɨɑn^C	prons	OCB *prjons

[T] Sin Sukchu SR pjen (去); MGZY bȳan (去) [pjɛn]; ONW pan

p	蠻	mán	man	man	mrôn	

[T] MHan 阿蠻 ʔɑ-man Armenia

q	孿	lüán, shuàn	ṣwan^C, ṣjwän^C	ṣuan^C	srôns	

[E] TB: JP mǎ^{31}-run^{55} 'twin'

--	彎灣	wān	ʔwan	ʔuan	ʔrôn	

25-32 = K. 179		**Mand.**	**MC**	**LHan**	**OCM**	
a	卵	luǎn	lwân^B	luɑn^B	rônʔ	OCB *C-ronʔ

[T] ONW luɑn <> [D] Min: Jiànōu se^{C2}
[E] TB *(s-)rwa 'nit' > WT sro-ma 'eggs of louse, nit', JP tsiʔ-ru 'louse eggs'

25-33 = K. 180		**Mand.**	**MC**	**LHan**	**OCM**	
ac	a 亂	luàn	lwân^C	luɑn^C	rôns	OCB *C-rons

[T] Sin Sukchu SR lwɔn (去); MGZY lon (去) [lɔn]; ONW luɑn.

25-34 = K. 189		**Mand.**	**MC**	**LHan**	**OCM**	
a	奻	nuán	nwan$^{(C)}$	nuan$^{(C)}$	nrôn, nrôns	⋈ 16-28/1244 nǎo 惱

25-35 = K. 238 The elements 耎 and 10-31/134 需 are occasionally substituted for each other.

		Mand.	MC	LHan	OCM
a-	耎輭軟	ruǎn	ńźjwän^B	ńuan^B	nonʔ

[T] Sin Sukchu SR ryen (上); MGZY Zhwȳan (上) [ryɛn]
[E] TB: WB nwai 'stretch along' ⋇ nwai^C 'bend flexibly'

		Mand.	MC	LHan	OCM
cd	蝡蝡	ruǎn	ńźjwän^B	ńuan^B	nonʔ
ef	瑌瓀	ruǎn	ńźjwän(^{B})	ńuan(^{B})	non, nonʔ
g	偄	nuàn	nwân^C	nuɑn^C	nôns
h	渜	nuǎn	nwân$^{B/C}$	nuɑn$^{B/C}$	nônʔ, nôns
i	煗	nuǎn	nwân^B	nuɑn^B	nônʔ
jk	抨擩	ruán !	ńźjwät	ńuat	not

25-36 = K. 176		**Mand.**	**MC**	**LHan**	**OCM**
a	竄	cuàn	tsʰwân^C	tsʰuɑn^C	tshôns

25-37 = K. 177		**Mand.**	**MC**	**LHan**	**OCM**
a	爨	cuàn	tsʰwân^C	tsʰuɑn^C	tshôns

25-38 = K. 234		**Mand.**	**MC**	**LHan**	**OCM**
ac	全牷	quán	dzjwän	dzyan	dzon

[T] Sin Sukchu SR dzyen (平); MGZY tswȳan (平) [dzyɛn]

		Mand.	MC	LHan	OCM
defg	痊筌荃銓	quán	tsʰjwän	tsʰyan	tshon
h	輇 measure	quān	tsʰjwän	tsʰyan	tshon
	輇 a car	chuán	źjwän	dźuan	—

25-39 = K. 235		**Mand.**	**MC**	**LHan**	**OCM**
a	雋	juàn	dzjwän^B	dzyan^B	dzonʔ
b	臇	juǎn	tsjwän^B	tsyan^B	tsonʔ

[E] TB *tsow > WT tsʰo-ba 'fat, greasy', WB cʰu 'be fat, obese'

		Mand.	MC	LHan	OCM
c	鐫	juān	tsjwän	tsyan	tson

[E] TB *tsow 'thorn' > Chepang cuʔ, Boro suʔ, WT mtsʰon 'any pointed or cutting instrument'

		Mand.	MC	LHan	OCM
d	儁	jùn	tsjwen^C	tsuin^C	tsuns

25-40 = K. 237		**Mand.**	**MC**	**LHan**	**OCM**	
a	泉	quán	dzjwän	dzyan	dzwan R!	OCB *Sgʷjan

[T] Sin Sukchu SR dzyen (平); MGZY tswȳan (平) [dzyɛn]
[E] The word rimes in *-an, not the expected *-on. TB *tso 'bubble, boil': WT 'tsʰo-ba, 'tsʰod-pa 'cook in boiling water'; WB tshu 'to boil, bubble'

		Mand.	MC	LHan	OCM	
e	線	xiàn	sjän^C	sian^C	sans	= 24-41/155r 綫

線 is a late [Zhouli] loan graph for 綫, perh. due to confusion with some other graph (SW 5877) <> [D] PMin *siɑn^C

25-41 = K. 1249a		**Mand.**	**MC**	**LHan**	**OCM**
a	縓	quàn	tsʰjwän^C	tsʰyan^C	tshons

Acc. to SW (5845) 原 is phonetic, meant as perhaps just the rime; or rather the phonetic seems to be 25-40/237 quán 泉.

25-42 = K. 173		**Mand.**	**MC**	**LHan**	**OCM**
a	筭	suàn	swân^{C}	suɑn^{C}	sôns

25-43 = K. 174		**Mand.**	**MC**	**LHan**	**OCM**
a	算	suàn	swân$^{B/C}$	suɑn$^{B/C}$	sônʔ, sôns
	[T] Sin Sukchu SR swɔn (去); MGZY son (去) [sɔn]; ONW suɑn				
bc	匴篹	suǎn	swân^{B}	suɑn^{B}	sônʔ
d	纂	zuǎn	tswân^{B}	tsuɑn^{B}	tsônʔ
e	篡	cuàn	tṣ^{h}wan^{C}	tṣ^{h}uan^{C}	tshrôns

25-44 = K. 175		**Mand.**	**MC**	**LHan**	**OCM**
ab	祘蒜	suàn	swân^{C}	suɑn^{C}	sôns
	[E] TB: PL *swan$^{1/2}$ 'onion', WB krak-swan				

26 OCM rime *-i, *-əi Zhī bù 脂部

GSR 547 - 605

Baxter 1992: 446 ff. (§10.1.8)

See Table 7-1 for a comparison of OC *-i, *-e and *-ai in QYS categories. See Table 32-1 for OC rimes *-in, *-it, *-(t)s, *-i.

Table 26-1: OCM rimes *-i, *-əi, *-ui and *-ə in QYS categories

Div.	*-i R.26	*-əi R.27	*-ui R.28	*-ə R.4
I gr		開 kʰậi kʰəi *khə̂i 回 ɣwậi ɣuəi *wə̂i 枚 mwậi məi *mə̂i	偎 ʔwậi ʔuəi *ʔûi	改 kậi^{B} kə^{B} *kə̂ʔ 恢 kʰwậi kʰuə *khwə̂ 每 mwậi^{B} mə^{B} *mə̂ʔ
I ac			堆 twậi tuəi *tûi	在 dzậi^{B} dzə^{B} *dzə̂ʔ
IV gr	啟 kʰiei^{B} kʰei^{B} *khîʔ 米 miei^{B} mei^{B} *mîʔ 睽 kʰiwei kʰuei *khwî			
IV ac	氐 tiei^{B} tei^{B} *tîʔ	妻 tsʰiei tsʰei *tshə̂i		
III gr		幾 kjei^{B} kɨi^{B} *kəiʔ 歸 kjwei kui *kwəi 圍 jwei wui *wəi 飛 pjwei pui *pəi		III *-ə merged with *-u after labial and labiovelar initials
3/3	耆 gji3 gɨ *gri 戣 gjwi3 gwɨ *gwri	冀 kji^{C}3 kɨ^{C} *krəih 美 mji^{B}3 mɨ^{B} *mrəiʔ	夔 gjwi 3 guɨ *gui	龜 kjwɨ3 kuɨ<kwɨə *kwrə 鄙 pjɨ^{B}3 pɨ^{B}< pɨə^{B} *prəʔ
3/4	伊 ʔi4 ʔi *ʔi 比 pi^{B}4 pi^{B} *piʔ 癸 kwi^{B}4 kwi^{B}*kwiʔ 維 jiwi4 wi *wi			
III ac	死 si^{B} si^{B} *siʔ	(*təi merged w. *ti)	誰 źwi dźui *dui	
II	階 kăi kɛi *krî	(*-rə̂i merged w. *rî)	褢 ɣwăi guɛi *grûi	戒 kăi^{C} kɛ^{C} *krə̂h 怪 kwăi^{C} kuɛ^{C} *kwrə̂h

The Table shows the MC mergers of OC finals (MC homophones in boxes). After acute initials, the later reflexes of OC rimes *-i and *-əi have merged so that it is difficult or impossible to untangle them. Most XS with acute initials are listed here, written with the OCM default rime *-i. Baxter has tried to identify the rimes of individual words with the *Shijing*, with the result that the traditional phonetic series at our disposal appear to mix the two OC rimes. This approach presumes that the rimes in poetry keep *-i and *-əi strictly separate. On the other hand, frequently riming words like *dì* 弟 'younger brother' rime with both *-i and *-ə i, thereby calling a reliable distinction into question. But OCM follows Baxter for the most part.

26-1	**= K. 586**	**Mand.**	**MC**	**LHan**	**OCM**	
a	笄	jī	kiei	kei	kî	

26-2	**= K. 587**	**Mand.**	**MC**	**LHan**	**OCM**	
a	卟	jī	kiei(^{B})	kei(^{B})	kî, kîʔ	

26-3	**= K. 1241a**	**Mand.**	**MC**	**LHan**	**OCM**	
a	計 calculate	jì	kiei^{C}	kei^{C}	kîh	⋇ 26-6/552o jī 稽
	[T] ONW kėi; OCB *keps (1992: 546), but see Intro. 9.2.9.					

26-4	**= K. 588**	**Mand.**	**MC**	**LHan**	**OCM**	
ac	启啟	qǐ	k^{h}iei^{B}	k^{h}ei^{B}	khîʔ	[T] ONW k^{h}ėi
h	棨	qǐ,	k^{h}iei^{B}	k^{h}ei^{B}	khîʔ	'joint (in the body)'
		qǐng	~ k^{h}ieŋ^{B}	~ k^{h}eŋ^{B}	~ khêŋʔ	⋇ 26-6i,o
j	晵	qǐ	k^{h}iei^{B}	k^{h}ei^{B}	khîʔ	

26-5 **= K. 1241** OCM is based on the assumption that 兮 is phonetic in 諡 and that the MC affrication in dźi^{C} is irregular as in the homophone shì 示 26-7/553a.

		Mand.	**MC**	**LHan**	**OCM**	
d	兮	xī	ɣiei	ɣei	gî	
h	盻	xì	ɣiei^{C},	ɣei^{C},	gîh,	
			ŋiei^{C}	ŋei^{C}	ŋîh	
-	肹	xī	xjet 3, xjət	hɨt	—	= 肸
1237l	諡	shì	dźi^{C}	źi^{C} < gi^{C} ?	gih	

26-6	**= K. 552**	**Mand.**	**MC**	**LHan**	**OCM**	
a	旨	zhǐ	tśi^{B}	tśi^{B} < ki^{B}	kiʔ	OCB *kjijʔ
	[T] Sin Sukchu SR tʂi (上), PR, LR tʂɿ; MGZY ji (上) [tʂi]; ONW tśi					
f	指	zhǐ	tśi^{B}	tśi^{B} < ki^{B}	kiʔ	
	[T] Sin Sukchu SR tʂi (上), PR, LR tʂɿ; MGZY ji (上) [tʂi]; ONW tśi <> [D] M-Amoy ki^{B}					
g	脂	zhī	tśi	tśi < ki	ki	OCB *kjij
p	嗜	shì	źi^{C}	dźi^{C} b< gi^{C}	gih	OCB *gjijs
	[T] ONW dźi^{C} <> [E] WT dgyes-pa 'rejoice' ⋇ dge-ba 'happiness, virtue'					
h	鮨	qí	gji 3	gɨ	gri	
-	[illegible]	jǐ	kji^{B} 3	kɨ^{B}	kriʔ	= 26-8/602 麂
l	耆 old	qí	gji 3	gɨ	gri	
	[T] ONW gi; BTD Skt. gṛ-, Pkt. gi (Coblin 1982: 129) <> [E] WT bgre-ba 'to grow old'					
	耆 settle	zhǐ	tśi^{B}	tśi^{B} < ki^{B}	kiʔ	
mn	鰭鬐	qí	gji 3	gɨ	gri	
i	䭫	qǐ	k^{h}iei^{B}	k^{h}ei^{B}	khîʔ	= o; ⋇ 26-4h
o	稽	qǐ	k^{h}iei^{B}	k^{h}ei^{B}	khîʔ	= i; ⋇ 26-4h
	'to bow down (the head) to the ground'					
	稽 calculate	jī	kiei	kei	kî	
	⋇ 26-3/1241a 計 <> [T] ONW k^{h}ėi					
k	詣	yì	ŋiei^{C}	ŋei^{C}	ŋîh	
q	蓍	shī	śi	śi	hji	OCB xjij

26-7	**= K. 553**	**Mand.**	**MC**	**LHan**	**OCM**	
a	示	shì	dźi^{C}	dźi^{C} < gi^{C} !	gih	

[T] Sin Sukchu SR ʐi (去), PR ʐɿ; MGZY ci (去) [dʐi]; ONW dźi (transcriptional material indicates that 示 had the same initial as 視)

h	視	shì	źi^{B}, źi^{C}	gi^{B}, gi^{C}	giʔ R!	=26-14/590q

[T] Sin Sukchu SR ʐi (去), PR ʐɿ; MGZY zhi (上去) [ʐi]; MTang dźi > źi, ONW dźi

i	祁	qí	gji 3	gɨ	gri	OCB grjəj

[E] ? TB: WB kri^{B} 'great, big'

26-8	**= K. 602**	**Mand.**	**MC**	**LHan**	**OCM**	
ac	几机	jǐ	kji^{B} 3	kɨ^{B}	kriʔ	OCB *krjəj

[E] TB *kriy > PL *kre^{1} > WB k^{h}re 'foot, leg' ⋇ ə-k^{h}re 'foundation, foot', WT k^{h}ri 'seat, chair', Lepcha hri 'chair'

f	飢	jī	kji 3	kɨ	kri	OCB *krjəj

[T] ONW ki

de	肌[illegible]	jī	kji 3	kɨ	kri	
-	麂	jǐ	kji^{B} 3	kɨ^{B}	kriʔ	=26-6/552 [illegible]

[E] TB *d-kiy: PL *kye' 'barking deer'; WB khye, gyi^{A} 'barking deer', JP tʃǎ^{33}-k^{h}ji^{33} 'muntjac', k^{h}yi^{1}-maʔ^{1} 'a kind of muntjac', Lushai sa^{H}-khi^{L} < -k^{h}iʔ/h 'barking deer'

26-9	**= K. 599**	**Mand.**	**MC**	**LHan**	**OCM**	
ad	皆階	jiē	kǎi	kɛi	krî	OCB *krij

[T] ONW këi

b	偕	xié	kǎi	kɛi	krîʔ !	OCB *krij(ʔ)
c	喈	jiē	kǎi	kɛi	krî	OCB *krəj
e	楷	kǎi	k^{h}ǎi^{B}	k^{h}ɛi^{B}	khrîʔ	
-	稭	jiē	kǎi	kɛi	krî	
g	諧	xié	ɣǎi	gɛi	grî	[T] ONW ɣëi
f	湝	xié, jiē	ɣǎi, kǎi	gɛi, kɛi	grî	OCB *grəj
h	揩	jiā	kǎt	kɛt	krə̂t or krît	= 30-5/504a 戛

'Musical box'; MC kǎt can derive from *krə̂t and *krît.

26-10 = K. 605 Here the main vowel is i, therefore LHan -wi in Div. 3/4 and 3/3; this contrasts with the rime 28 (e.g., 28-1/569 鬼) where i is part of the diphthong -ui (i.e., -uj).

		Mand.	**MC**	**LHan**	**OCM**	
a	癸	guǐ	kwi^{B} 4	kwi^{B}	kwiʔ	
e	揆	kuǐ	gwi^{B} 4	gwi^{B}	gwiʔ	
g	葵	kuí	gwi 4	gwi	gwi R!	OCB *g^{w}jij
f	戣	kuí	gjwi 3	gwɨ	gwri	
h	騤 sturdy	kuí	gjwi 3	gwɨ	gwrəi R!	OCB *g^{w}rjəj
	a horse	què	k^{h}iwet	k^{h}uet	khwît	'kind of horse'
i	睽	kuí	k^{h}iwei	k^{h}uei	khwî	
k	闋	què	k^{h}iwet	k^{h}uet	khwît	

[N] Li writes syllables like a to g as MC kwi, gwi; I write kjiwi 4, gjiwi 4 in order to make them parallel with rimes *-it and *-in. Li does not provide an example for kjwi 3; he may have considered the 3/3 ~ 3/4 distinction spurious.

26-11	= K. 1241i	Mand.	MC	LHan	OCM
i	醯	xī	xiwei	hue(i)	hwî / hwê ?

26-12	= K. 589	Mand.	MC	LHan	OCM
ab	医殹	yì	ʔiei^{C}	ʔei^{C}	ʔîh
f	翳	yì	ʔiei(^{C})	ʔei(^{C})	ʔî, ʔîh
eg	緊鷖	yī	ʔiei	ʔei	ʔî

26-13	= K. 604	Mand.	MC	LHan	OCM
ad	伊咿	yī	ʔi 4	ʔi	ʔi

伊 [T] Sin Sukchu SR ʔi (平); MGZY Yi (平) [ʔji]; STCA ʔɨ, ONW ʔii; BTD Skt. ī-. MHan 伊循 ʔi-zuin < -s-jun (< *s-lun) Ἰσσηδόνες (Issedones)

[E] TB: Lushai ʔi^{L} 'this, that', Chepang ʔiʔ 'he', WB i 'this'

26-14	= K. 590	Mand.	MC	LHan	OCM	
a	氐 base	dǐ	tiei^{B}	tei^{B}	tîʔ	OCB *tijʔ

[D] PMin *tie^{B} <> [E] WT mt^{h}il, OTib. t^{h}ild < *m-tild 'bottom, floor', Tamang ^{3}ti: 'below'

		Mand.	MC	LHan	OCM	
	氐 a tribe	dī	tiei	tei	tî	
c	底 bottom	dǐ	tiei^{B}	tei^{B}	tîʔ	
	come to	zhǐ	tśi^{B}	tśi^{B}	tiʔ	
d	柢	dǐ	tiei($^{B/C}$)	tei($^{B/C}$)	tî, tîʔ, tîh	
fgi	弤抵邸	dǐ	tiei^{B}	tei^{B}	tîʔ	
eh	低羝	dī	tiei	tei	tî	

低 [T] Sin Sukchu SR tjej (平), PR ti; MGZY di (平) [ti]; ONW tėi

		Mand.	MC	LHan	OCM	
j	詆	tí, dǐ	diei, tiei^{B}	dei, tei^{B}	dî, tîʔ	
no	厎砥	zhǐ	tśi^{B}	tśi^{B}	tiʔ	OCB *tjijʔ
p	祗	zhī	tśi	tśi	ti	OCB *tjəj
s	鴟	chī	tś^{h}i	tś^{h}i	thi	OCB *thjij
qr	q 眡	shì	źi$^{B/C}$	dźi$^{B/C}$	(giʔ/h)	= 26-7/553h 視
k	胝	zhī	ṭi	ṭi	tri	
l	坻	chí	ḍi	ḍi	dri	= 26-16/596c 墀
m	蚳	chí	ḍi	ḍi	dri	
867h	疷 illness	dǐ	tiei^{B}	tei^{B}	tîʔ	

[N] There is some confusion with 7-6/GSR 867.

26-15	= K. 591	Mand.	MC	LHan	OCM	
a	弟 y. bro.	dì	diei^{B}	dei^{B}	dîʔ	OCB *dəjʔ / *dijʔ < *dujʔ ?

[T] Sin Sukchu SR djej (上), PR, LR di; MGZY ti (上) [di]; ONW dėi <> [D] PMin *die^{B}

[E] ST *dwi: TB *doy 'younger brother' > WB t^{h}we^{B} 'be youngest', JP šədói 'last born child'

		Mand.	MC	LHan	OCM	
	弟 fraternal	dì	diei^{C}	dei^{C}	dîh	
d	娣	dì	diei$^{B/C}$	dei$^{B/C}$	dîʔ, dîh	
f	悌	tì	diei^{C}	dei^{C}	dîh	
e	第	dì	diei^{C}	dei^{C}	dîh	
g	稊 sprout	tí	diei	dei	dî	= 26-17/551k
i	苐 a grain	tí	diei	dei	dî	= 26-17/551k
hj	綈鵜	tí	diei	dei	dî	

k 睇 dì diei^{C}, t^{h}iei dei^{C}, t^{h}ei dîh, thî

[E] TB: Chepang d^{h}əy- 'concentrate, look at (esp. when aiming), be watchful, alert' ⋈ d^{h}es- 'see clearly, sight clearly (when aiming)'

m 涕 tì t^{h}iei$^{B/C}$ t^{h}ei^{B}, t^{h}ei^{C} thîʔ, thîh OCB *thijʔ

= 26-17/551f 洟 (late graph) <> [E] TB *ti / *tui 'water' > Chepang tiʔ 'water', WT mč^{h}i-ma 'a tear', Chepang ma-tiʔ 'river', Kanauri *ti 'water'; Dhimal hna-thi 'snot'

l 梯 tī t^{h}iei t^{h}ei thî

[D] PMin *thəi ~ *thuəi <> [E] WB hle-ka^{B} 'stairs, ladder', TGTM *^{A}hli, Chepang hləyʔ

- 剃 tì t^{h}iei^{C} — — See 8-12/850hr 鬄鬄.

[T] ONW t^{h}ėi <> [D] PMin *thie^{C} = tī 鬄 (t^{h}iei^{C})

n 鬀 zhì ḍjet ḍit drit

26-16 = K. 595, 596 See comment under 26-33.

	Mand.	MC	LHan	OCM	
595g 稺, 596e 稚	zhì	ḍi^{C}	ḍi^{C}	drih	OCB *drjəjs
595h 緻 sew BI	zhì	ḍi^{C}	ḍi^{C} or ḍis	drih or drəts	= 29-15/413 緻

⋈ 29-17/402 紩 *drit

	Mand.	MC	LHan	OCM	
596d 遲, 595d 遟	chí	ḍi	ḍi	dri 'tarry'	OCB *drjəj

[T] ONW di

	Mand.	MC	LHan	OCM	
遲	zhì	ḍi^{C}	ḍi^{C}	drih 'wait'	
596c 墀	chí	ḍi	ḍi	dri	= 26-14/590l 坻

26-17 = K. 551 In some graphs 夷 seems to have been confused with 弟. *-i is the default final.

		Mand.	MC	LHan	OCM	
ade	夷侇姨	yí	ji	ji	ləi	夷 OCB ljəj

夷 = 26-18/1237c 彝

		Mand.	MC	LHan	OCM	
gh	痍陝	yí	ji	ji	li	
j	桋 a tree	yí	ji	ji	li	OCB ljəj
f	洟	tì, yí	t^{h}iei$^{B/C}$, ji	t^{h}ei$^{B/C}$	thîʔ, thîh !	OCB *thijʔ

= 26-15/591m 涕

		Mand.	MC	LHan	OCM	
k	荑 sprout	tí	diei	dei	dî	= 26-15/591g
	a grain	tí	diei	dei	dî	= 26-15/591i
	mow	yí	ji	ji	li	

26-18 = K. 1237c

		Mand.	MC	LHan	OCM	
c	彝	yí	ji	ji	ləi	OCB ljəj = 26-17/551a 夷

[T] ONW i < ji

26-18A

		Mand.	MC	LHan	OCM
-	希	dì, yì	diei^{C}, ji^{C}	dei^{C}, ji^{C}	lîh, lih ?

SW: 'a long-haired animal'. The OC final could also have been lôih, ləih, or lî(t)s, li(t)s. The OB form of this graph is thought to write 21-29K. 319d 殺 (K. Takashima).

26-19 = K. 560

		Mand.	MC	LHan	OCM	
a	矢	shǐ	śi^{B}	śi^{B}	lhiʔ !	OCB *hljijʔ [T] ONW śi

[E] ? TB *d-liy 'bow' > Bahing li, Limbu li 'bow', Lepcha să-lí, Nung t^{h}əli, WB le^{B}

e 雉 zhì ḍi^B ḍi^B driʔ !

[E] WB rac 'pheasant', WT sreg-pa 'partridge', Lushai va^L-hrit^L, SChin-Areng tari', Mru rik, Garo grit 'pheasant'

m 薙 tì, t^{h}iei^C, t^{h}ei^C, lhîh,

zhì, sì ḍi^B, zi^B ḍi^B, zi^B driʔ < r-liʔ, s-liʔ

ij 矧弞 more shěn śjen^B śin^B lhinʔ 'how much the more'

矧弞 gums shěn śjen^B śin^B hinʔ or nhinʔ ⌘ 26-32/594i 哂

[E] WT rñil ~ sñil 'gums' <> [N] The original phonetic is probably 32-20.

k 眣 blink shùn śjwen^C śuin^C hwins

= 32-24/469c 瞬; 33-19/450[m] 瞚

26-20 = K. 561 **Mand.** **MC** **LHan** **OCM**

a 尸 shī śi śi lhi OCB *hljij

[T] ONW śi; BTD Skt. śila

ce 屍鳲 shī śi śi lhi

d 屎 excrem. shǐ śi^B śi^B lhiʔ !

[T] Sin Sukchu SR ʂi (上); PR ʂʅ <> [E] ST *kliʔ

屎 groan xī xi 4 hi həi !

[N] An OCM hi would have yielded MC śi.

26-21 = K. 556 **Mand.** **MC** **LHan** **OCM**

a 兕𤉡 (SW) sì zi^B zi^B s-jəiʔ OCB *zjijʔ

'Wild water buffalo' (not 'rhinoceros') <> [E] ST *s-jəl: TB-Lushai sial^H< sial 'domestic buffalo'

26-22 = K. 562 **Mand.** **MC** **LHan** **OCM**

a 履 lǚ li^B li^B riʔ OCB *C-rjijʔ

This graph transcribes Indic syllables ri, ḍi, mi, me, vi (Pulleyblank 1983: 100)

26-23 = K. 597 **Mand.** **MC** **LHan** **OCM**

a 豊 lǐ liei^B lei^B rîʔ

dh 禮鱧 lǐ liei^B lei^B rîʔ [T] ONW lėi

e 醴 lǐ liei^B lei^B rîʔ OCB *C-rijʔ

i 體 tǐ t^{h}iei^B t^{h}ei^B rhîʔ OCB *hrijʔ

[T] ONW t^{h}ėi <> [E] ST *sri 'to exist' > TB *sri(-t) > WT srid-pa 'existence, life, things existing, the world, a single being', WB hri^C 'to be (in some place)'. WT gšis < *g-rhjis (?) 'person, body, natural disposition'

26-24 = K. 519 **Mand.** **MC** **LHan** **OCM**

ab 利 lì li^C li^C rih ! OCB *C-rjij/ts

[T] Sin Sukchu SR ljej (去), PR, LR li; MGZY li (去) [li]; ONW li; Han BTD Indic -rī, -riya, -li, e.g., 墮舍利 hyai-śah-lih Skt. Vaiśālī; this shows that *lì* was an open syllable, it did not end in -ts <> [E] TB *riːt 'reap, cut' > LB *riːt > WB rit 'to reap, mow, shave'; Lushai riit^F / riʔ^L 'cut, dig or scrape with a hoe'; Mikir rè- 'be sharp'

\- 莉 lì li^C See 21-37.

hi 梨 lí li li ri

[T] Sin Sukchu SR ljej (平), PR, LR li; MGZY li (平) [li]; ONW li

[D] PMin *li ~ *ləi <> MY: *rai^1

l 蔾 lí li li ri

g 犁犂 lí liei, li lei, li rî, ri [T]

[T] ONW lėi. 薪犁 xīn-lí LH sin-li Turk. Syr (Pulleyblank 1983: 455) <> [D] PMin *le

[E] KT: PTai *t^{h}ləi^{A1} 'to plow', Kam k^{h}aj 'plow' <> PMY *l^{2}ai^{3A}

jkm 黧黎藜 lí liei lei rî

26-25 = K. 563 **Mand.** **MC** **LHan** **OCM**

a 尼 near ní ṇi ṇi nri

[T] Sin Sukchu SR njej (平), PR ni; MGZY ñi (平) [ṇi]; ONW ni; Han BTD Skt. nir-, ṇi

尼 stop nì niei^{C} nei^{C} nîh

b 怩 ní ṇi ṇi nri

[E] TB *(r-)ni : JR kəwurni < *g-rni 'red', tərni 'gold', Qiang ńhi 'red'; WB ni 'red', Lahu ní ~ ni 'red, bare, naked'

c 柅 nǐ ṇi$^{B/C}$ ṇi$^{B/C}$ nriʔ, nrih

e 旎 nǐ ṇje^{B} ṇe^{B} nreʔ

d 泥 mud ní niei nei nî

[T] Sin Sukchu SR njej (平), PR ni; MGZY ni (平) [ni]; ONW nėi. MHan 驩泥 huan-nei kuhani or khvani <> [D] In many dialects, the word means 'earth' tǔ 土, e.g., K-Meix nɐi^{11} 'soil, earth'.

泥 moisten nǐ niei^{B} nei^{B} nîʔ OCB *nəjʔ

泥 obstruct. nì niei^{C} nei^{C} nîh

f 昵 ní ṇjet, niei^{B} ṇit, nei^{B} nrit, nîʔ = 29-26/404 衵 䵒 glue

[N] For MC niei^{B}, see Coblin 1983: 239. <> [E] Prob. MK: Khmu klɲaʔ 'resin', the prefix kl- derives from kə̆l 'tree'.

26-26 = K. 592 **Mand.** **MC** **LHan** **OCM**

a 妻 wife qī ts^{h}iei ts^{h}ei tshə̂i ! OCB *tshəj

[T] Sin Sukchu SR ts'jej (平), PR ts'i; MGZY tshi (平) [ts'i]; ONW ts^{h}ėi

[E] MK: Khmer *-sai: khsai /ksaj/ 'be female' ⋈ Mid. Khmer kansai /kənsay/ 'wife'

妻 give wife qì ts^{h}iei^{C} ts^{h}ei^{C} tshə̂ih

ef 悽淒 qī ts^{h}iei ts^{h}ei tshî < *k-sî OCB *tshəj

淒 [E] ? TB-WT bsil-ba 'cool', JP gă^{31}-tsi^{33} 'cold'. Or ? WT (b)ser, gser-bu 'a fresh cold breeze, feeling cold', WB chi^{B} (< *-e) 'frost, hoarfrost'

gi 萋緀 qī ts^{h}iei ts^{h}ei tshî OCB *tshəj

j 陵 jī tsiei(^{C}) tsei(^{C}) tsî, tsîh = 26-27/593

l 棲 xī siei sei sî OCB *səj = 26-32/594f 栖

[T] Sin Sukchu SR sjej (平), PR, LR si; 'Phags-pa: MGZY si (平) [si]; ONW sėi

26-27 = K. 593 **Mand.** **MC** **LHan** **OCM**

a 齊 equal qí dziei dzei dzî OCB *fits(h)əj

[T] Sin Sukchu SR dzjej (平), PR dzi; MGZY tsi (平) [dzi]; ONW dzėi <> [D] PMin *dze

齊 edge zī tsi tsi tsi

- 艩 qí dziei dzei dzî

f 臍 qí dziei dzei dzî

[D] PMin *dzəi ~ *dzhəi <> [E] ? TB *lay, *s-tay > JP dai^{31}, ʃa^{31}-dai^{33} 'navel'

g 蠐 qí dziei dzei dzî

h 劑 cut jì dziei^{C} dzei^{C} dzîh

bond jī tsje tsie tse or tsai

i 嚌 jì dziei^{C} dzei^{C} dzîh

l	薺	jì	dziei^{B}	dzei^{B}	dzîʔ	
k	癠	jì	dziei($^{B/C}$)	dzei($^{B/C}$)	dzî, dzîʔ, dzîh	
j	懠	jì	dziei(^{C})	dzei(^{C})	dzîh	

OCB *dzəjs, but all rimes in Shijing 254.5 are *-i.

m	穧	jì	dziei^{C}, tsiei^{C}	dzei^{C}, tsei^{C}	dzîh, tsîh	OCB *dzəjs
t	齏	jī	tsiei	tsei	tsî	= 26-29/554j; 26-30/555k
u	齎	jī, zī	tsiei, tsi	tsei, tsi	tsî, tsi	
r	隮	jī	tsiei(^{C})	tsei(^{C})	tsî, tsîh	OCB *tsəj
s	霽	jì	tsiei^{C}	tsei^{C}	tsîh	
p	躋	jī	tsiei	tsei	tsî	OCB *tsəj
n	擠	jǐ	tsiei($^{B/C}$)	tsei($^{B/C}$)	tsî, tsîʔ, tsîh	

[E] TB: WT 'tsʰir-ba 'to press, press out'

o	濟 ford	jì	tsiei^{C}	tsei^{C}	tsîh	OCB *tsəjs

[E] MK: Mon inscr. cnis [cnøs] > cnih 'a ghat, place of access to river..., landing place'

	濟 beautiful	jì	tsiei^{B}	tsei^{B}	tsîʔ	OCB *tsijʔ
v	齍	zī	tsi	tsi	tsi	
y	齋	zhāi	tṣăi	tṣɛi	tsrî	
z	儕	chái	dẓăi	dẓɛi	dzrî	

[E] Tai: S. raai^{A2} 'set, category, list'

26-28 = K. 554		**Mand.**	**MC**	**LHan**	**OCM**	
abc	𠂔姊姉	zǐ	tsi^{B}	tsi^{B}	tsiʔ	

[E] TB *dzar > JP dʒan^{33}, Lushai farR-nu^{L}, Tangkhul əzăr-vă 'sister (man speaking)'

d	秭	zǐ	tsi^{B}	tsi^{B}	tsiʔ	OCB *tsjijʔ
fg	笫胏	zǐ	tṣi^{B}	tṣi^{B}	tsriʔ	
hi	柹柿	shì	dẓi^{C}	dẓi^{C}	dzrih	
j	韰	jī	tsiei	tsei	tsî	See 26-28/593t.
-	泲	jǐ	tsiei^{B}	tsei^{B}	tsîʔ	

26-29 = K. 555		**Mand.**	**MC**	**LHan**	**OCM**	
acd	次佽欳	cì	tsʰi^{C}	tsʰi^{C}	tshih < *s-nhis ? OCB *tshjijs	

[T] Sin Sukchu SR ts'ɿ (去); MGZY tshʰi (去) [ts'ɿ]; ONW tsʰi

ij	茨瓷	cí	dzi	dzi	dzi	OCB *dzjij
e	咨	zī	tsi	tsi	tsi	
l	諮	zī	tsi	tsi	tsi	
h	資	zī	tsi	tsi	tsi	
mn	穦薋	zī !	dzi	dzi	dzi	
-	積	zī	dzi	dzi	dzi	
f	恣	zì	tsi^{C}	tsi^{C}	tsih	
g	粢 grain	zī	tsi	tsi	tsi	
	liquor	jì	dziei^{C}	dzei^{C}	dzîh	
k	韰	jī	tsiei	tsei	tsî	See 26-28/593t.
-	瓷	cí	dzi	dzi		

26-30 = K. 1237m **Mand.** **MC** **LHan** **OCM**
m 自 zì dzi^{C} dzi^{C} dzih
[T] Sin Sukchu SR dzɿ (去); MGZY ts^{h}i (去) [dzɿ]; ONW dzi
This is the original OB graph for 'nose' 29-39 > bì 鼻 29-38/521c. See Intro. 6.2.1.

26-31 = K. 594 **Mand.** **MC** **LHan** **OCM**
af 西栖 xī siei sei sî (< snî ?) OCB *səj = 26-26/592l 棲
[T] Sin Sukchu SR sjej (平), PR, LR si; 'Phags-pa: MGZY si (平) [si]; ONW sėi
[N] xī is sometimes thought to be phonetic in 迺 *nə 4-39/946
g 洒 sprinkle sǎ, shǎi ṣǎi^{B} ṣɛi^{B} srîʔ
[T] ST *sri: Lushai hri^{L} / hrik^{F} < hriih / hriik 'to sift, screen'
洒 wash xiǎn, xǐ siei^{B}, sien^{B} sei^{B}, sen^{B} sîʔ, sînʔ = 33-25/478j 洗
[T] ONW sėi <> [E] ST *sil: TB *(m-)sil ~ *(m-)syal > WT bsil-ba 'to wash', Lushai sil^{R}, WB ts^{h}e^{B} 'to wash', Mikir iŋt^{h}ī(?), JP ^{1}gə-^{1}šin 'wash'
i 哂 shěn śjen^{B} śin^{B} nhinʔ ! ⋇ 26-19/560i 矧

26-32 = K. 595 **Mand.** **MC** **LHan** **OCM**
a 屖 xī siei sei sî
Acc. to SW 3787, this graph means 'to wait' and shows a person sitting 尸 on the phonetic xīn 辛 *sin; the word is a semantic extension of xī 栖 *sâi 26-31/594f 'roost, keep still'. Because of its meaning, the graph 屖 was then borrowed for a synonym chí 遲 *dri 'to wait'. 屖 xī is therefore not phonetic in 遲.
屖 (SW 3787) and the homophone xī 犀 *sî 26-33/596a 'rhinoceros' (SW 540) look nearly identical in the seal script, so that these two graphic elements are used almost indiscriminately to write the words of GSR 595 and 596, which are here combined into 26-16.

26-33 = K. 596 **Mand.** **MC** **LHan** **OCM**
a 犀 xī siei sei sə̂i OCB *səj
See Intro. 9.2.2 <> [T] ONW sėi <> [E] ST *səj: WT bse 'rhinoceros'
For the remaining items written with this element in GSR 596, see 26-16.

26-34 = K. 557 **Mand.** **MC** **LHan** **OCM**
ab 厶私 sī si si si OCB *sjəj
[T] Sin Sukchu SR sɿ (平); MGZY s^{h}i (平) [sɿ]; ONW si
[E] ? TB: Lushai teei^{L} < teeis 'myself, thyself...'

26-35 = K. 558 **Mand.** **MC** **LHan** **OCM**
a 死 sǐ si^{B} si^{B} siʔ !
[T] Sin Sukchu SR sɿ (上); MGZY s^{h}i (上) [sɿ]; ONW si
[E] TB *siy 'to die' > WT 'č^{h}i-ba < *ɴsi, ši

26-36 = K. 559 **Mand.** **MC** **LHan** **OCM**
a 師 shī ṣi ṣi sri OCB *srjij
[T] Sin S. SR ṣi (平), PR, LR ṣʅ; MGZY sh^{h}i (平) [ṣʅ]; BTD 師利 Skt. śrī; MHan 貳師 ńis-ṣi Nesef
\- 獅子 shī-zǐ ṣi-tsɨ^{B} ṣi-tsiə^{B} [E] Tocharian A śiśäk, B ṣecake 'lion'
\- 篩 shāi, shī ṣi ṣi —
[T] Sin Sukchu SR ṣi, ṣaj (平), PR ṣʅ; MGZY 簁 sh^{h}i (平) [ṣʅ] <> [D] M-Amoy thai^{A1}

26-37	**= K. 565**	**Mand.**	**MC**	**LHan**	**OCM**	
ab	匕朼	bǐ	pi^B 4	pi^B	piʔ	'spoon'

The old form of this graph is distinct from 26-38/566.

26-38	**= K. 566**	**Mand.**	**MC**	**LHan**	**OCM**	
an	匕 > 妣	bǐ	$pi^{B/C}$ 4	$pi^{B/C}$	piʔ, pih	OCB *pjijʔ
	The old form of this graph is distinct from 26-37/565.					
	[E] ST *pi: TB *pəy or *piy > WT ʔa-p^hyi, p^hyi-mo 'grandmother'					
i	牝	pìn,	bjien^B 4,	bin^B,	binʔ,	ONW biin
		bì	bi^B 4	bi^B	biʔ	
	[E] TB *pwi(y) 'female' > Lushai pui^R < puiʔ 'a grown female'					
l	疕	bǐ	p^hji^B 3, pji^B 3	$p^hɨ^B$,	p(h)riʔ ?,	
			p^hje^B 3	$p^hɨe^B$	phaiʔ or phreʔ ?	
	[E] ? TB: WB ə-p^he^B 'scab over (head)'					
k	庀	pǐ	p^hi^B 4,	p^hi^B,	phiʔ,	[E] TB: Lushai peiʔ^L 'to finish'
			p^hjie^B 4	p^hie^B	pheʔ	
g	比 compare	bǐ	pi^B 4	pi^B	piʔ	
	[T] Sin S. SR pi (上), PR pəj, LR pi; MGZY bi (上) [pi]; MTang pɨ, ONW pii; BTD Skt. bhi					
	比 combine	bì	pi^C 4, bi^C 4	pi^C, bi^C	pih, bih	
	[E] ? ST *prel: WT 'brel-ba 'to come together, join, hang together'					
	比 tiger skin	pí	bi 4	bi	bi	
qr	秕[1]粃 grain	bǐ	pi^B 4	pi^B	piʔ	
	[E] ? ST *pi(ʔ): Lushai pi^H < pii 'short and small for one's age, stunted growth'					
q	秕[2] comb	bì	bi^C 4			
	[E] ? ST: WB p^hri^B ~ p^hi^B 'to comb, brush'					
m	枇 spoon	bǐ	pi^B 4	pi^B	piʔ	= 26-37/565ab
p	庇	bì	pi^C 4	pi^C	pih	
t	紕 silk	pǐ	p^hi^B 4	p^hi^B	phiʔ	
	error	pī,	p^hi 4, p^hjie,	p^hi, p^hie,	phi, phe,	
		bī	piei	pei	pî	
	braid	pí	bjie, bi^C 4	bie, bi^C	bih R!	
v	釓	pí	bi 4	bi	bi	
z	芘 herb	pí	bi 4	bi	bi	
	cover	bì	$pi^{(C)}$ 4?	$pi^{(C)}$	pi, pih	OCB *bjijs
a'	批 slap	pī	p^hiei	p^hei	phî	
	knock ag.	piē	biet	bet	bît	
d'	吡	pǐ	p^hjie^B 4	p^hie^B	pheʔ	
-	屁	pì	p^hi^C 4	p^hi^C	phih	
	[E] TB *pwe ?: Limbu p^he-ma, Mikir kep^{h}é, Naga *b-woy[3], Chin *woy-s[4], Lushai voiʔ					
-	蚍蜉	pí-fú	bj 4-bjəu	bi-bu	bi-bu	'large ant'
s	仳 separated	pǐ	p^hi^B, bi^B 3	$p^hɨ^B$, $bɨ^B$	briʔ	
	ugly	pí	bi 4	bi	bi	
u	毗	pí	bi 4	bi	bi	OCB *bjij
	[E] WT 'p^hel-ba, p^hel (OTib p^held) 'to increase, augment, enlarge, improve, develop'					
y	坒	bì	bi^C 4	bi^C	bih	
b'c'	梐陛	bì	$biei^B$	bei^B	bîʔ	

e' 毘 navel pí bi 4 bi bi < bli ?

[T] BTD Skt. -mi, -pita. <> [E] KT: PKS * lwa^{1} 'navel', Mak ʔdaai^{6}, PT *ʔbl/r-: S. sa-dɨɨ^{A1}

f'g' 膍 g' stom. pí bi 4 bi bi < bli ? 'stomach' [T] ONW bėi

膍 navel pí biei bei bî < bli ?

h' 貔 pí bi 4 bi bi [E] TB: WT dbyi 'lynx'

26-39 = K. 598 **Mand.** **MC** **LHan** **OCM**

a 米 mǐ miei^{B} mei^{B} mîʔ OCB *mijʔ

[T] Sin Sukchu SR mjej (上); MGZY mi (上) [mi]

[D] PMin *m̥i^{B2} 'husked rice' < ? TB *ma-y

d 眯 mǐ miei^{B} mei^{B} mîʔ

e 迷 mí miei mei mî OCB *mij

[E] TB: Lushai hmaiʔ^{L} < hmaih 'to overlook, miss, forget' < TB *maay, WB me^{C} 'forget'

[T] ONW mėi

\- 謎 mí miei^{C} mei^{C} mîh [T] ONW mėi

f 麋 mí mji 3 mɨ mri OCB *mrjij

[E] ? TB: Chepaŋ maiʔ 'meat', Boro mʏiʔ 'deer', Liangmei ka-mî 'meat'; NNaga *meːy 'meat, flesh'

m 蘪 mí mji 3 mɨ mri

hi 敉侎 mǐ mjie^{B} 4 mie^{B} meʔ = 7-31/360a 弭

[T] MTang mi, ONW me [i.e., QYS Div. 3])

kl 冞罙罧 mí mjie 4 mie me = 7-20/359m 彌

27 OCM rime *-əi Wēi bù 微部 (1)

GSR 541 - 605
Baxter 1992: 446 ff. (§10.1.8)

See Table 30-1 for OCM rimes *-ən, *-ət, *-ə(t)s, *-əi in QYS categories. See Table 26-1 for a comparison of OC rimes *-i, *-əi, *-ui and *-ə.

OC rimes *-əi and *-i are distinguished in MC only after grave initials, they have merged after acute initials, they are inlcuded in Rime 26 by default. OC *-əi and *-ui have merged after labial initials, they are included in this Rime 27. The OCM coda *-i in diphthongs behaves like a final dental consonant, hence a strictly phonemic transcription would write it as *-j, as in OCB (*-aj, *-əj, *-uj).

27-1	= K. 541	Mand.	MC	LHan	OCM	
a	開	kāi	kʰâi	kʰəi	khə̂i	= 27-2/548f 闓

[T] Sin Sukchu SR k'aj (平); MGZY khay (平) [k'aj]; ONW kʰɑ <> [E] MY: Yao khai¹ (< *kh-) 'to open' tr. ⪤ gai¹ (< *ŋkh-) 'to open' intr.: 'be happy, to blossom' <> Tai: S. kʰaiᴬ¹ 'to open'

27-2	= K. 548	Mand.	MC	LHan	OCM	
a	豈 happy	kǎi	kʰâiᴮ	kʰəiᴮ	khə̂iʔ	
	how	qǐ	kʰjeiᴮ	kʰɨiᴮ	khəiʔ	
bcd	凱愷塏	kǎi	kʰâiᴮ	kʰəiᴮ	khə̂iʔ	
f	闓	kǎi	kʰâi(ᴮ)	kʰəi(ᴮ)	khə̂i, khə̂iʔ	= 27-1/541a 開
e	鎧	kǎi	kʰâiᴮ/ᶜ	kʰəiᴮ/ᶜ	khə̂iʔ, khə̂ih	
g	豈	hái	ɣâi	gəi	gə̂i	
j	覬	jì	kjiᶜ 3	kɨᶜ	krəih	= 27-3/603 冀
i	螘	yǐ	ŋjeiᴮ	ŋɨiᴮ	ŋəiʔ	TB: KN-Lai hŋeʔr-tee 'ant'

27-3	= K. 603	Mand.	MC	LHan	OCM	
ac	冀驥	jì	kjiᶜ 3	kɨᶜ	krəih	= 27-2/548j 覬

27-4	= K. 547	Mand.	MC	LHan	OCM
a	幾 few	jǐ	kjeiᴮ	kɨiᴮ	kəiʔ

[T] Sin Sukchu SR kjej (上), PR, LR ki; MGZY gi (上) [ki]; ONW ki
[E] -> PTai *kiiᶜ 'several, how many' > S. kiiᴮ¹, Saek kii³

	幾 small	jī	kjei	kɨi	kəi
	幾 hem	qí	gjei	gɨi	gəi
cde	機璣磯	jī	kjei	kɨi	kəi
f	禨 auspic.	jī	kjei	kɨi	kəi
	a drink	jì	kjeiᶜ	kɨiᶜ	kəih
g	機	jǐ	kjeiᴮ	kɨiᴮ	kəiʔ

		Mand.	MC	LHan	OCM	
h	蟣 louse	jǐ	kjei^{B}	kɨi^{B}	kəiʔ	[E] ? TB-KN *m-kei 'to bite'
	leech	qí	gjei	gɨi	—	
	[D] PMin *ghi > Fúzh ma^{A2}-k^{h}i^{A2}, Xiamen gɔ^{A2}-k^{h}i^{A2}; Yue Guǎngzh k^{h}ei^{A2}-na^{B}					
ij	譏機	jī	kjei	kɨi	kəi	
k	饑	jī	kjei	kɨi	kəi	
	[E] TB: WT bkres 'be hungry', JP kyet^{31} 'hungry', Chepang kray- vb. 'hunger', Mru krai					
l	畿	jī !	gjei	gɨi	gəi	

27-5	**= K. 550**	**Mand.**	**MC**	**LHan**	**OCM**	
a	衣 clothes	yī	ʔjei	ʔɨi	ʔəi	OCB *ʔjəj
	[T] Sin Sukchu SR ʔi (平); MGZY ʔi (平) [ʔi]; ONW ʔi					
	衣 wear	yì	ʔjei^{C}	ʔɨi^{C}	ʔəih	OCB *ʔjəjs
f	依 lean on	yī	ʔjei	ʔɨi	ʔəi	
	metaphor	yǐ	ʔjei^{B}	ʔɨi^{B}	ʔəiʔ	
g	扆	yǐ	ʔjei^{B}	ʔɨi^{B}	ʔəiʔ	
j	偯	yǐ	ʔjei^{B}	ʔɨi^{B}	ʔəiʔ	
h	哀	āi	ʔậi	ʔəi	ʔə̂i	OCB *ʔəj

27-6	**= K. 549**	**Mand.**	**MC**	**LHan**	**OCM**	
ag	希睎	xī	xjei	hɨi	həi	
	[T] Sin Sukchu SR xi (平); MGZY hi (平) [xi]					
bcd	悕晞欷	xī	xjei	hɨi	həi	OCB *xjəj
ef	狶豨	xī, xǐ	xjei(^{B})	hɨi(^{B})	həi, həiʔ	
1237k	絺 fine cloth	chī	ṭ^{h}i	ṭ^{h}i	thrəi	? ≍ 27-7/1237i 黹

27-7	**= K. 1237i**	**Mand.**	**MC**	**LHan**	**OCM**
i	黹 embroid.	zhǐ	ṭi^{B}	ṭi^{B}	triʔ (or trəiʔ ?)
	? ≍ 27-6/1237k 絺; ≍ 26-16/595h 緀; ≍ 29-15/413 黻				

27-8	**= K. 579**	**Mand.**	**MC**	**LHan**	**OCM**	
ad	非扉	fēi	pjwei	pui	pəi	
	[T] Sin Sukchu SR fi (平), LR fi; MGZY h(w)i (平) [fi]; ONW pui					
g	誹	fěi	pjwei(^{C})	pui(^{C})	pəi, pəih	
	[E] ? TB: WT p^{h}yar-k^{h}a 'blame, affront, insult'					
e	棐	fěi	pjwei^{B}	pui^{B}	pəiʔ	
cf	匪篚	fěi	pjwei^{B}	pui^{B}	pəiʔ	
hi	悱斐	fěi	p^{h}jwei^{B}	p^{h}ui^{B}	phəiʔ	
j	霏	fēi	p^{h}jwei	p^{h}ui	phəi	OCB *phjəj
k	騑 run	fēi	p^{h}jwei	p^{h}ui	phəi	
	horse	fēi	pjwei	pui	pəi	
l	菲 a plant	fěi	p^{h}jwei^{B}	p^{h}ui^{B}	phəiʔ	
	fragrant	fēi	p^{h}jwei	p^{h}ui	phəi	
	sandal	fèi	bjwei^{C}	bui^{C}	bəih	
mno	剕屝屝	fèi	bjwei^{C}	bui^{C}	bəih	
p	翡	fèi !	bjwei^{C}	bui^{C}	bəih	
q	腓	féi	bjwei	bui	bəi	OCB *bjəj

r	蜚	fèi,	bjwei^{C},	bui^{C},	bəih,	
		fěi	pjwei^{B}	pui^{B}	pəiʔ	
s	陫	fěi	bjwei$^{B/C}$	bui$^{B/C}$	bəiʔ, bəih	
u	悲	bēi	pji 3	pɨ	prəi	OCB *prjəj

[T] Sin Sukchu SR pi (平); PR pəj; MGZY bue (平) [puɛ]

t	徘	pái	bwậi	bəi	bə̂i	
vx	俳排	pái	bǎi	bɛi	brə̂i	

27-9 = K. 580

		Mand.	MC	LHan	OCM	
a	飛	fēi	pjwei	pui	pəi	OCB *pjəj

[T] Area word: TB *pur ~ *pir > WT ’p^{h}ur-ba ‘to fly’

27-10 = K. 581

		Mand.	MC	LHan	OCM
a	妃 wife	fēi	p^{h}jwəi	p^{h}ui	phəi
	match	pèi	p^{h}wậi^{C}	p^{h}uəi^{C}	phə̂ih or phə̂s

[N] Pèi ‘match’ is transferred from a partial syn. pèi 配 30-12/514

27-11 = K. 582

		Mand.	MC	LHan	OCM
a	肥	féi,	bjwei,	bui,	bəi,

[T] Sin Sukchu SR vi (平), LR vi; MGZY H(w)i (平) [vi]; ONW bui

[D] PMin *byi. <> ? Tai *bii^{A} ‘fat’ (CH loan?)

27-12 = K. 353

		Mand.	MC	LHan	OCM	
a	火	huǒ	xuâ^{B}	huɑi^{B}	hmə̂iʔ R!	OCB hməjʔ

[T] Sin Sukchu SR xwɔ (上); MGZY hwo (上) [xwɔ]; ONW huɑ <> [D] PMin *hoi^{B}

[E] TB *mey > WT me, OTib. smye; Chepang hmeʔ; LB *ʔmey² [Matisoff], WB mi^{B}, Lushai mei^{R} < meiʔ. See Intro. 4.1.

27-13 = K. 546

		Mand.	MC	LHan	OCM	
ab	枚玫	méi	mwậi	məi	mə̂i	OCB *məj

枚 [T] MK: OKhmer mēk [mɛɛk] ‘branch, bow, limb, twig’

27-14 = K. 567 See Intro. 5.2.3 and Rime 28 for the Div. 3/3 OC *u* for OCB medial *r.

		Mand.	MC	LHan	OCM	
a	眉 eyebrow	méi	mji 3	mɨ	mui	OCB *mrjəj [T] ONW mi
	眉 vigorous	měi	mjwei^{B}	muiʔ	məiʔ	OCB *mjəjʔ

= 27-15/585a 亹

gf-	湄楣郿	méi	mji 3	mɨ	mui	OCB *mrjəj
d	媚	mèi	mji^{C} 3	mɨ^{C}	muih	

27-15 = K. 585

		Mand.	MC	LHan	OCM	
a	亹 vigorous	wěi	mjwei^{B}	mui^{B}	məiʔ	= 27-14/567a 眉

See Intro. 5.2.3 and Rime 28 for the Div. 3/3 OC *u* for OCB medial *r.

	亹 a gorge	mén	muən	mən	mə̂n	OCB *mən

27-16 = K. 568

		Mand.	MC	LHan	OCM	
a	美	měi	mji^{B} 3	mɨ^{B}	muiʔ	OCB *mrjəjʔ

[T] Sin Sukchu SR muj (上), PR, LR məj; MGZY mue (上) [muɛ]; ONW mi

[E] TB *moy > Lushai mɔi^{H}, Kachin moi

27-17 = K. 583		**Mand.**	**MC**	**LHan**	**OCM**	
a	尾	wěi	mjwei^B	mui^B	məiʔ	OCB *mjəjʔ

[T] Sin Sukchu SR vi (上); MGZY wi (上) [vi]; ONW mui^B <> [D] PMin *mye^B

[E] TB *r-may 'tail' > PL *ʔ-mri², WB mri^B; KN-Aimol rəmai; Lushai mei^R < meiʔ

cd	娓浘	wěi	mjwei^B	mui^B	məiʔ	
e	焜	huǐ	xjwei^B	hui^B	hməiʔ	

27-18 = K. 584		**Mand.**	**MC**	**LHan**	**OCM**	
a	散	wēi	mjwei !	mui	məi	
dfg	微薇	wēi	mjwei	mui	məi	OCB *mjəj

微 [T] Sin Sukchu SR vi (平); MGZY wi (平) [vi]; ONW mui

g	媺	měi	mji^B 3	mɨ^B	muiʔ	= 27-16 美

See Intro. 5.2.3 and Rime 28 for the Div. 3/3 OC *u* for OCB medial *r.

h	徽 rope	huī	xjwei	hui	hməi	

[E] Tai: S. mai^A1 < *hm- 'thead, silk'

	徽 signal	huī	xjwei	hui	hməi	

[E] TB: WB hmwe^C 'whirl about, twirl', Lushai hmui^R < hmuiʔ 'spinning wheel'

27-19 = K. 572		**Mand.**	**MC**	**LHan**	**OCM**	
a	虺 snake	huǐ	xjwei^B	hui^B	(hməiʔ)	= 27-20/1009 虫
	thunder	huǐ	xjwei^B	hui^B	hwəiʔ	OCB *huj
	exhausted	huī	xwậi, xwăi	huəi, huɛi	hrûi	

The graph was probably borrowed later for 虫 'snake' and replaced it.

27-20 = K. 1009		**Mand.**	**MC**	**LHan**	**OCM**	
a	虫 snake	huǐ	xjwei^B	hui^B	hməiʔ	= 27-19/572 虺

[E] TB *m/b-ru:l > WT sbrul < s-mrulʔ, LB *m-r-wiy¹, KN *m-ruul, Lushai ruul^H < ruul

28 OCM rime *-ui, *-wəi Wēi bù 微部 (2)

GSR 541 - 605

Baxter 1992: 446 ff. (§10.1.8)

See Table 26-1 for OC rimes *-i, *-əi, *-ui and *-ə in QYS categories. See Table 31-1 for a comparison of OCM *-ut, *-wət, *-wit, *-ui, *-u(t)s, *-wəi, *-wə(t)s, *-wi(t)s. See Intro. 5.2.3 for more about the removal of OCB medial *r in MC Div. 3/3 syllables.

The OCM coda *-i in diphthongs behaves like a final dental consonant, hence a strictly phonemic transcription would write it as *-j, as in OCB (*-aj, *-əj, *-uj).

Table 28-1: OCM rimes *-un / -wən, *-ut and *-ui / -wəi

MC	*-un / *-wən R.34	*-ut R.31	*-ui, *-u(t)s / *-wəi R.28, 31
III gr	君 kjwən kun *kwən 雲 jwən wun *wən	—	歸 kjwei kui *kwəi 貴 kjwei^C kus *kwəs 謂 jwei^C wus *wəs
III gr	—	屈 kʰjwət kʰut *khut	—
3/3 gr	菌 gjwen^{B}3 guɨn^B *gunʔ	—	夔 gjwi3 guɨ *gui 匱 gjwi^{C}3 guɨs *gus
III ac	春 tśʰjwen tśʰuin *thun 允 jiwen^B juin^B *junʔ	出 tśʰjwet tśʰuit *k-hlut	誰 źwi dźui *dui

Note to Table: (1) Acc. to Gāo Yòu, the reading of *jùn* 菌 gjuen^B was similar to *lún* 綸 ljuen (see Coblin 1983: 232). This can confirm either Baxter's medial *r hypothesis (*jùn* < *grunʔ); or it could mean that the *final* of *jùn* was similar to *lún* (MC -juen, not -juən). All else being equal, the second interpretation is less complex (i.e., adds no phoneme in OC) and is therefore preferable for OCM for the time being. Incidentally, this comment by Gāo Yòu illustrates the frequent ambiguities of such glosses and their doubtful value for a firm basis for reconstruction.

(2) *Wèi* 位 jwi 3 derives from OCB *(w)rəps as Baxter explains the MC chóngniǔ Div. 3/3 by loss of an OC medial *r. However, if, according to my interpretation (see main text), *guì* 匱 MC gjwi^C 3, LH guɨs derives from OCM *gus, then *wèi* 位 MC jwi 3 should derive from LH wɨs < wuɨs, < OCM *wus. Similarly, as *kuí* 夔 gjwi 3 derives from LH guɨ, < OCM *gui, so *wéi* 帷 jwi 3 should derive from LH wɨ < wuɨ, < OCM *wui, in contrast to wéi 惟 MC jiwi 4 < OCM *wi; and wéi 違 jwei, LH wui < OCM *wəi.

In some syllables with initial velars and the assumed OC rimes -ui, -ut/s, -un, Div. 3/3 abounds, it is almost exclusive. According to Baxter, these had all medial *r. Thus he has seven syllables of the type *kruts, but only one *kuts. This is rather odd. As Div. 3/3 also can derive from OC vowels (-je 3/3 < *ai, jau 3/3 < *au), I suggest that this is the case in these rimes as well:

28 OCM *-ui, *-wəi 微部 (2) (GSR 541-605)

Div. III		Div. 3/3	
MC jwən	< OCM *wən	—	
MC kjwən	< OCM *kwən	MC kjwen 3	< OCM *kun
MC kjwei^{C}	< OCM *kwə(t)s	MC kjwi^{C} 3	< OCM *ku(t)s
MC kjwei	< OCM *kwəi	MC kjwi 3	< OCM *kui

Thus MC kjwen 3 behaves in a way that is parallel to MC kjwän < *kon (Rime 25). Also, the syllables *wən tend to occur with MC final -juən (< *-wən), not with MC -jwen 3 (< *-un). In a short-stopped syllable with final *-t, and in syllables with initial ʔ-, there is no III ~ 3/3 contrast, only Div. III. Therefore I assume OC *-ut rather than *-wət:

	MC kjwət	< OCM *kut
cf.	MC tśjwet	< OCM *tut
	MC ʔjwət	< OCM *ʔut
	MC ʔjwən	< OCM *ʔun
	MC ʔjwei	< OCM *ʔui

28-1 = K. 569 See Intro. 5.2.3 and comment above for the Div. 3/3 OCM *u* for OCB medial *r.

		Mand.	MC	LHan	OCM	
a	鬼	guǐ	kjwei^{B}	kui^{B}	kwəiʔ	
	[T] Sin Sukchu SR kuj (上); MGZY gue (上) [kuɛ]; ONW kui <> [D] PMin *kyi^{B}					
g	塊	kuì,	k^{h}wə̑i^{C},	k^{h}uəi^{C},	khwə̂ih,	~ 31-3/510a
		kuài	k^{h}wăi^{C}	k^{h}uɛi^{C}	khrwə̂ih	
	[T] Sin Sukchu SR k'waj, k'uj (去), LR k'waj; MGZY khue (去) [k'uɛ]					
de	傀瑰	guī	kwə̑i	kuəi	kûi	= 28-6/600e 瓌
f	魁	kuí	k^{h}wə̑i	k^{h}uəi	khûi	
h	瘣	huì	ɣwə̑i^{B}	ɣuəi^{B}	gûiʔ	
q	螝	guī,	kjwi$^{(C)}$ 3,	kuɨ$^{(C)}$,	kui, kuih	
		huì	ɣwə̑i^{C}	ɣuəi^{C}	gûih	
i	槐	huái	ɣwə̑i, ɣwăi	ɣuəi, ɣuɛi	grûi	
ln	愧媿	kuì	kjwi^{C} 3	kuɨ^{C}	kuih	
r	餽	kuì	gjwi^{C} 3	guɨ^{C}	guih [Meng]	
	= 31-2/540l 饋 [Shu]					
j	嵬	wěi	ŋwə̑i$^{(B)}$	ŋuəi$^{(B)}$	ŋûi	OCB *ŋuj
k	魏	wèi	ŋjwei$^{(C)}$	ŋui$^{(C)}$	ŋwəi, ŋwəih or ŋwəs	
	[T] MHan ʔâ-ŋui^{C} < ʔâi-ŋwəis (?) 阿魏 Tocharian B ankwaṣ 'asafoetida'					
s	巍	wéi, wēi	ŋjwei	ŋui	ŋwəi	
-	犩	wéi	ŋjwi 3	ŋuɨ	—	⌘ 28-3/1237s 犪
	'Buffalo' [Erya] <> [E] ? TB: *lwaay 'buffalo', JP ʔu^{33}-loi^{33}, ŋa^{33}-loi^{33} (ŋa^{33} 'bovine')					

28-2	**= K. 570**	**Mand.**	**MC**	**LHan**	**OCM**	
a	歸	guī	kjwei	kui	kwəi	OCB *k^{w}jəj (1992: 459ff)
	[T] ONW kui. Guī generally rimes with *-wəi in Shijing.					
g	巋	kuī	k^{h}jwi$^{(B)}$ 3	k^{h}uɨ$^{(B)}$	khui, khuiʔ	

28-3	**= K. 1237s**	See Intro. 5.2.3 and the comment above on the Div. 3/3 OCM *u* for OCB *-r-.				
		Mand.	**MC**	**LHan**	**OCM**	
s	夔	kuí	gjwi 3	guɨ	gui	
	犪	kuí	gjwi 3	guɨ	—	⋇ 28-1/569 犩
		[E] Area word: PTai *ɣwai^{A} 'buffalo'; Sui kwi^{A2} < *gwi^{A} 'buffalo'				

28-4	**= K. 542**	**Mand.**	**MC**	**LHan**	**OCM**	
abcd	回迴廻佪	huí	ɣwậi	ɣuəi	wə̂i	OCB *wəj [T] ONW ɣuɑi
ef	洄蛔	huí	ɣwậi	ɣuəi	wə̂i	

28-5	**= K. 571, 342**		**MC**	**LHan**	**OCM**	
ag	韋圍	wéi	jwei	wui	wəi	OCB *wjəj
		[T] BTD Skt. ve- (Coblin 1993: 907) <> [E] TB: Lushai veel^{F} 'go around, surround'; Siyin vil 'watch' <> AA. MK *wìəl: Khmer viala /wíiəl/ 'to turn, move around'				
d	違	wéi	jwei	wui	wəi	OCB *wjəj
		[T] ONW ui; BTD Indic ve-				
ho	幃闈	wéi	jwei	wui	wəi	
fjkp	偉煒瑋韙	wěi	jwei^{B}	wui^{B}	wəiʔ	
q	韡	wěi	jwei^{B}	wui^{B}	wəiʔ	OCB *wjəjʔ
		[E] TB *hwa-t > WT 'od				
n	葦	wěi	jwei^{B}	wui^{B}	wəiʔ	OCB *wjəjʔ
m	緯 bind	wěi	jwei^{B}	wui^{B}	wəiʔ	
	weave	wěi	jwei^{C}	wui^{C}	wəih	
l	禕	yī	ʔje 3	ʔɨai	ʔai	
r	褘	huī	xjwei	hui	hwəi	
s	諱	huì	xjwei^{C}	hui^{C}	hwəih	
		[E] TB: Lushai ui^{H} < ʔui 'to regret, dissuade, forbid' <> MK: Khmer veḥ /wéh/ 'to quit, leave, avoid, shun...'				
342a	衛	wèi	jwäi^{C}	was	wes	OCB *wrjats
		The element 韋 is partially semantic. <> [T] ONW uei; BTD Skt. -vas(ti), -vas[tu], -vāsa, -paś(yin), vatāra				
f	讆	wèi	jwäi^{C}	was	wes	
g	躛	wèi	ɣwai^{C}	ɣwas	wês	

28-6	**= K. 600**	**Mand.**	**MC**	**LHan**	**OCM**	
a	褱	huái	ɣwǎi	ɣuɛi	grûi	
d	壞	huài,	ɣwǎi^{C},	ɣuɛi^{C},	grûih,	OCB *ɦkrujs [T] ONW ɣuëi
		guài,	kwǎi^{C},	kuɛi^{C},	krûih,	OCB *krujs
		huài	ɣwậi^{B}	ɣuəi^{B}	gûiʔ	
c	懷	huái	ɣwǎi	ɣuɛi	grûi	OCB *gruj
e	瓌	guī	kwậi	kuəi	kûi	= 28-1/569de 傀瑰

28-7	**= K. 1240h**	**Mand.**	**MC**	**LHan**	**OCM**
h	乖	guāi	kwǎi	kuɛi	krûi

28-8	**= K. 1239a**	**Mand.**	**MC**	**LHan**	**OCM**	
a	卉	huì	xjwei$^{B/C}$	hui$^{B/C}$	hwəiʔ, hwəih ?	

The OC initial could also be *hm-.

28-9	**= K. 573**	**Mand.**	**MC**	**LHan**	**OCM**	
a	畏	wèi	ʔjwei^{C}	ʔui^{C}	ʔuih	OCB *ʔjuj(s) [T] ONW ʔui
- -	喂餵	wèi	ʔjwei^{C}	ʔui^{C}	ʔuih	⤱ 19-10/357f 餧
d	崼	wěi	ʔjwei^{B}, ʔwậi^{B}	ʔui^{B}, ʔuəi^{B}	ʔuiʔ, ʔûiʔ	
efh	偎煨隈	wēi	ʔwậi	ʔuəi	ʔûi	
g	猥	wěi	ʔwậi^{B}	ʔuəi^{B}	ʔûiʔ	

28-10	**= K. 574**	**Mand.**	**MC**	**LHan**	**OCM**	
a	威	wēi	ʔjwei	ʔui	ʔui	OCB **ʔjuj [T] ONW ʔui
d	崴	wēi	ʔwăi	ʔuɛi	ʔrûi	

28-11	**= K. 575**	**Mand.**	**MC**	**LHan**	**OCM**	See Intro. 9.2.6.
aef	隹[1] > 騅鵻	zhuī	tświ	tśui	tui	

[E] ST *twil (?): WT mčʰil-ba 'a little bird'. See Intro. 9.2.6.

gh-	錐騅萑	zhuī	tświ	tśui	tui	
u	誰	shuí, shéi	źwi	dźui	dui	
rs	椎顀	chuí	ḍwi	ḍui	drui	
y	稚	zhì	ḍi^{C}	ḍi^{C}	drih	
z	堆	duī	twậi	tuəi	tûi	= 28-12/543a 𠂤

[E] PTai *ʔdl/rɔi^{A}: S. dɔɔi^{A1} 'mountain', Saek rɔɔy^{A1}

-	碓	duì	twậi^{C}	tuəi^{C}	tûih	[E] PY *tui 'pestle'
a'i'	推蓷	tuī, chuī	tʰwậi, tśʰwi	tʰuəi, tśʰui	thûi, thui	OCB *thuj
b'	隓	duì	dwậi^{B}	duəi^{B}	dûiʔ	OCB *dujʔ
an	隹[2] 惟	wéi	jiwi 4	wi	wi	OCB *wjij

See Intro. 9.2.6. [T] Sin Sukchu SR vi (平); MGZY ywi (平) [yi]; ONW iui; Han BTD Skt vi

[E] TB *wəy > LB *wəy 'to be'

o	維	wéi	jiwi 4	wi	wi	[T] BTD Skt. vi, pi
i	唯 only	wéi	jiwi 4	wi	wi	OCB *wjij
	yes	wěi	jiwi^{B}	wi^{B}	wiʔ	
	out and in	cuǐ	tsʰwi^{B}	tsʰui^{B}	tshuiʔ	= e'
g'	鷕	wěi (yǎo)	jiwi^{B} 4	wi^{B}	wiʔ	
v	雖	suī	swi	sui	swi	
h'	蠵	wèi	jiwi^{C} 4	wi^{C}	wih	

[E] AA: PAA *ruwaj > PVM *m-rɔːj 'a fly', PMon *ruuy 'housefly', Khmer /ruj/ 'a fly' ⤱ /roj/ 'dart here and there...'

q	蜼 monkey	wèi, wěi, lěi, yòu	jiwi^{C} 4, ljwi^{B}, jiəu^{C}	wi^{C}, lui^{B}, ju^{C}	wih < r-wih ?, ruiʔ, juh < wuh	OCB *lŭjs = 13-37/1246c
m	帷	wéi	jwi 3	wɨ	wri or wui ?	
601a	淮	huái	ɣwăi	ɣuɛi	wî	
d	匯	huì	ɣwậi^{B}	ɣuəi^{B}	gwîʔ	
1237u	睢倠婎	huī	xjiwi 4	hui	hwi	
575e'	趡	cuǐ	tsʰwi^{B}	tsʰui^{B}	tshuiʔ	= i

d'l'	崔摧	cuī	dzwâi	dzuəi	dzûi	OCB *dzuj (< *Sduj?)
j'	催	cuī	tsʰwâi	tsʰuəi	tshûi	OCB *tsʰuj (< *Sthuj ?)
k'	漼	cuǐ	tsʰwâiᴮ	tsʰuəiᴮ	tshûiʔ	

28-12 = K. 543		Mand.	MC	LHan	OCM	
a	𠂤	duī	twâi	tuəi	tûi	= 28-11/575z 堆
d	追 pursue	zhuī	ṭwi	ṭui	trui	
	[E] ? TB-Lushai čʰuiᴴ < chui 'to track, follow a trail', Chepang dyul- 'follow a trail...'					
	追 carve	duī	twâi	tuəi	tûi	
-	槌	chuí	ḍwi	ḍui	drui	'pestle' [SW]
hi	縋膇	zhuì	ḍjweᶜ	ḍuɑiᶜ	droih	

28-13 = K. 544		Mand.	MC	LHan	OCM
abc	隤積頹	tuí	dwâi	duəi	dûi
	31-2/540 may be partially phonetic. Cf. 11-11/1205a				

28-14 = K. 576		Mand.	MC	LHan	OCM	
a	水	shuǐ	świᴮ	śuiᴮ, S tśuiᴮ	lhuiʔ ?	OCB h[l]jujʔ ?
	[T] Sin Sukchu SR ʂuj, ʂi (上), PR ʂi, LR ʂuj; MGZY shue (上) [ʂuɛ]; ONW śui					
	[D] PMin *tšuiᴮ <> [E] TB *lwi(y) > Lushai luiᴸ < luih, Tiddim luuiᶠ < luuih 'stream, river'					

28-15 = K. 577		Mand.	MC	LHan	OCM	
a	畾	lěi, léi	ljwiᴮ, lwâi	luiᴮ, luəi	ruiʔ, rûi	
d	壘	lěi	ljwiᴮ	luiᴮ	ruiʔ	
eg	櫐藟	lěi	ljwiᴮ	luiᴮ	ruiʔ	
	[E] TB *(s-)rwey 'cane, creeper', Lushai hruiᴿ 'a creeper, cane, rope, cord, string'; OKuki *hrui (Kom) 'rope', WB ruiᴮ- 'kind of creeper, tree', Mru rui 'rope'					
hik	讄讄轠	lěi	ljwiᴮ	luiᴮ	ruiʔ	
-	磥	lěi	lwâiᴮ	luəiᴮ	rûiʔ	= 28-16/545a 磊
j	傫	lěi	lwâi(ᴮ)	luəi(ᴮ)	rûi, rûiʔ	
l	罍	léi	lwâi	luəi	rûi	
no	靁雷	léi	lwâi	luəi	rûi	OCB *C-ruj
	[T] Sin Sukchu SR lɔ (平); MGZY lwo (平) [lwɔ]) <> [D] Mand. Jinan luei³²; Y-Guangzhou løy²¹; K-Meix lui¹¹, PMin *lh(u)əi: Jiànōu soᶜ¹					
p	儽	lěi !	lwâiᶜ, ljwi	luəiᶜ, lui	rûih, rui	
	[E] TB-Lushai rɔiʔᴸ < *rɔis 'be weak, worn out, fade, diminish'					
sf	縲纍	léi	ljwi	lui	rui	
	縲 [E] MTang lui, ONW lue					
r	累 bind	léi	ljwi	lui	rui	
	accumul.	lěi	ljweᴮ	lyaiᴮ	roiʔ	
	implicate	lèi	ljweᶜ	lyaiᶜ	roih	
	naked	luǒ	lwâᴮ	luɑiᴮ	rôiʔ	
q-	蘽蔂	luó	lwâ	luɑi	rôi	
t	騾	luó	lwâ	luɑi	rôi	
-	螺	luó	lwâ	luɑi / S loi	rôi	[D] PMin *lhoi

28-16 = K. 545	**Mand.**	**MC**	**LHan**	**OCM**	
a 磊	lěi	lwậi^B	luəi^B	rûiʔ	= 28-15/577- 礧

28-17 = K. 578	**Mand.**	**MC**	**LHan**	**OCM**
a 耒	lěi, lèi	ljwi^B, lwậi^C	lui^B, luəi^C	ruiʔ, rûih
b 誄	lěi	ljwi^B	lui^B	ruiʔ

28-18 = K. 1237v	**Mand.**	**MC**	**LHan**	**OCM**	
v 蕤	ruí	ńźwi	ńui	nui	= 19-19/354e 緌

28-19 = K. 1237x	**Mand.**	**MC**	**LHan**	**OCM**	
x 夊	suī	swi	sui	snui	= 19-19/354g

28-20 = K. 513	**Mand.**	**MC**	**LHan**	**OCM**
ab 罪辠	zuì	dzwậi^B	dzuəi^B	dzûiʔ

[N] fēi 非 is not phonetic, see Intro. 9.2.3 <> [T] ONW dzuɑi <> [E] ? TB: Lushai sual^R 'bad, wicked, evil, wrong, to misbehave, sin' ⋈ sual^H 'to rape'

29 OCM rime *-it, *-its, *-is Zhì bù 質部

GSR 393 - 415

Baxter 1992: 434 ff. (§10.1.6)

Shijing rimes *(-)wit and *-ut tended to mix (Baxter 1992: 444ff). By Han time both had become > *-uit. The Div. 3/3 items could also have been OCM *gət instead of *grit.

See Table 33-1 for a comparison of OC rimes *-in, *-ən, *-it, *-ət. See Table 32-1 for OC rimes *-in, *-it, *-(t)s, *-i in QYS categories.

29-1 = K. 393 With one exception MC gjet 3 syllables are doublets of Div. 3/4.

		Mand.	**MC**	**LHan**	**OCM**	
a	吉	jí	kjiet 4	kit	kit	
	[T] ONW kiit <> [E] WT skyid-pa 'happy'					
ij	蛣詰	jié !	k^hjiet 4	k^hit	khit	
n	拮	jí	kjiet 4,	kit,	kit,	
		jié	kiet	ket	kît	
k	佶[1]	jí	gjiet 4,	git	git	
		jí	gjet 3			
l	姞	jí	gjet 3	gɨt	grit	
-	狤	jí	kjiet 4,	kit	kit	
		jí	gjet 3			
-	趌	jí, jié	k(^{h})jiet 4	k(^{h})it	k(h)it	
	洁	jí	kjiet 4	kit	kit	
-	鮚	jí	gjiet 4,	git	git	
			gjet 3			
-	咭	jié	gjiet 4	git	git	
ryz	頡襭擷	xié	ɣiet	get	gît	
p	結	jié	kiet	ket	kît	
	[T] MTang kiar < kɨar, ONW kėt <> [E] TB *kik > WT 'k^{h}yig-pa, bkyigs 'to bind', JP gyit^{31} 'to tie, bind'; Kuki *d-k^{h}ik					
o	桔	jié	kiet	ket	kît	
q	袺	jié	kiet	ket	kît	
		jiá	kǎt	kɛt	krît	
t	髻 hair knot	jì	kiei^C	kes	kîts	
	a god	jié	kiet	ket	kît	
x	劼	jié	k^hǎt	k^hɛt	khrît	
u	秸	jiē	kǎt	kɛt	krît	= 29-2/278a 鞂
v	黠	xiá	ɣǎt	gɛt	grît	

29-2	**= K. 278**	**Mand.**	**MC**	**LHan**	**OCM**	
a	鞂	jiē	kǎt	kɛt	krît	= 29-1/393u 秸

29-3	**= K. 535**	**Mand.**	**MC**	**LHan**	**OCM**	
a	棄	qì	k^hi^C 4	k^his	khis or khits	

29-4	**= K. 510b**	**Mand.**	**MC**	**LHan**	**OCM**	
b	屆	jiè	$kăi^C$	kɛs	krîs R!	OCB *krets

~ 20-2/327e 界 *krêts. Unambiguous Shijing rimes indicate *-its. 31-3/510a 凷 is thought to be phonetic.

29-5 = K. 538 For the LHan medial w (rather than u), see comment under 26-10/605.

		Mand.	**MC**	**LHan**	**OCM**	
a	季	jì	kwi^C 4	kuis	kwis	OCB $*k^wjits$
e	悸	jì	gwi^C 4	guis	gwis	

(a) [D] PMin $*kie^C$ ~ $*kyi^C$

29-6	**= K. 409**	**Mand.**	**MC**	**LHan**	**OCM**		
a	穴	xué	ɣiwet	ɣuet	wı̂t		OCB *wit
c	泬	xuè	xiwet	huet	hwı̂t		
d	⿰馬穴	yù	jiwet	wit	wit	'awry'	= 29-11/507b 矞

29-7 = K. 410 GSR 930 (5-7) may have 血 as phonetic.

		Mand.	**MC**	**LHan**	**OCM**	
a	血	xuè	xiwet	huet	hwı̂t	OCB *hwit

[T] ONW huet <> [D] PMin *huet: Xiam $hui?^{D1}$; K-Meix $šiæt^B$; Y-Guangzh hyt^{C1}; G-Nanchang ɕyɔt, K-Ruijin ɕiot
[E] ST *s-wiʔ ~ *swiʔ: TB *s-hywəy or *s(-)wiʔ > Kanauri šui, PL $*swiy^2$, WB swe^B; Chepang wəyʔ ~ huy 'blood', Magari hyu < hwi

		Mand.	**MC**	**LHan**	**OCM**	
d	洫	xù	—	huit	hwit	OCB *hwjit

'water channel' > 'moat', perh. ≍ 潏 *wit 'to flow'; same graph used for the syn. 5-7/930a

		Mand.	**MC**	**LHan**	**OCM**	
e	恤 care abt.	xù	sjwet	suit	swit	OCB *swjit
f	卹 care abt.	xù	sjwet	suit	swit	
	卹 rub	xù	suət	suət	sût	

[E] TB: LB *sut 'wipe, sweep' > WB sut 'wipe', Lahu šiʔ < *sit

29-8	**= K. 533**	**Mand.**	**MC**	**LHan**	**OCM**	
-e	叀 > 蟪	huì	$ɣiwei^C$	ɣues	wı̂s	
afg	惠蕙譓	huì	$ɣiwei^C$	ɣues	wı̂s R!	OCB *wets
h	穗	suì	zwi^C	zuis	s-wis	OCB *ɦswjits (?)
i	繐	suì	$sjwäi^C$	sues	swes	

(h) = 29-9/526k 穟. Rimes *-uts in Shi 65.2, -its in 212.3 <> [E] TB: Lushai vui^L /$vuiʔ^L$ < vuis 'to ear (as grain, grass), come into ear', Kuki-Chin *vui

29-9 = K. 526 The rime could be either *-jus or *-wis. 526k was certainly *s-wis, whereas 526fg can only have been *-us. Although this looks like a pure *-s series, the finals could in some or all items have been *-ts.

		Mand.	**MC**	**LHan**	**OCM**
a	a	suì	zwi^C	zuis	s-wis

d 遂 suì zwi^{C} zuis s-wis ~ s-jus OCB *zjuts
Rimes in Shi 60.1, 2 -its; 194.4 -uts <> [T] ONW zue <> [E] LB *s-yuy; Kamarupan *s-yuy ~ *m-yuy 'to follow', Kuki-Naga *jwi 'follow' > Lushai zui^{F}, Siyin jui

k 穟 suì zwi^{C} zuis s-wis ! OCB *zjuts
= 29-8/533h 穗 — No rime in Shi 245.4. <> [E] TB: Lushai vui^{L} / vuiʔ^{L} < vuis 'to ear (as grain, grass), come into ear', Kuki-Chin *vui

h 檖 suì zwi^{C} zuis s-jus OCB *zjuts

ijln 燧璲襚旞 suì zwi^{C} zuis s-jus

o 邃 suì swi^{C} suis swis

m 隧 suì zwi^{C} zuis s-jus OCB *zjuts
Rimes -uts in Shi 132.3

f 隊 troops duì duậi^{C} duəs dûs
fall down zhuì ḍwi^{C} ḍus drus

g 墜 fall zhuì ḍwi^{C} ḍus drus
[E] AA: Khmer OKhmer ruḥ /ruh/ 'to fall, drop' ⋈ jruḥ /cruh/ 'to fall, drop, come off...'; PVM *ruh 'to fall'

29-10 = K. 527 Mand. MC LHan OCM

ab- 彗篲箒 suì zwi^{C}, zuis, s-wis, 'broom'
zjwäi^{C} zyas s-wes

c 嘒 huì xiwei^{C} hues hwîs R! OCB *hwets

de 慧譓 huì ɣiwei^{C} ɣues wîs

29-11 = K. 507 None of these graphs rime in Shijing.

Mand. MC LHan OCM

a 矞 yù jiwet wit wit

b 遹 awry yù jiwet wit wit = 29-6/409d 鴥
回遹 huí - yù ɣuậi-jiwet ɣuəi-wit wûi-wit

ef 驈鷸 yù jiwet wit wit

ij 僪獝 jú gjwet 3,4 guit gwit

h 繘 jú, yù kjiwet, jiwet kuit, wit kwit, wit or kjut, jut
Relatively late word [Liji] <> [E] TB: WT: rgyud < *r-jut 'string, cord'

g 橘 jú kjiwet 4 kuit kwit OCB *k^{w}jit
[T] ONW kuit <> [E] MK-Khmer kwic 'tangerine'

k 劀 guā kwăt kuɛt kwrît

lmn 譎憰鐍 jué kiwet kuet kwît

o 潏 jué, yù kiwet, jiwet kuet, wit kwît ~ wit = 22-4/304f 汩
[E] ? Old Sino-Viet. lut

p 瞲 huì, xjiwi^{C} 4, huis, hwits,
xuè xiwet huet hwît

29-12 = K. 394 Mand. MC LHan OCM

a 一 yī ʔjiet 4 ʔit ʔit = 29-13/395a 壹
[T] Sin Sukchu SR ʔi (入); MGZY Yi (入) [ʔji]; MTang ʔir, ONW ʔiit
[E] TB *ʔit: Chepang yat 'one', Kanauri ʔit 'one', WB ac

29-13 = K. 395		**Mand.**	**MC**	**LHan**	**OCM**	
a	壹	yī	ʔjiet 4	ʔit	ʔit	= 29-12/394a 一
b	噎	yē	ʔiet	ʔet	ʔît	[T] ONW ʔėt
cdh	懿懿饐	yì	ʔi^{C}	ʔis	ʔits	
ijk	曀墤殪	yì	ʔiei^{C}	ʔes	ʔîts	

29-14 = K. 1241j		**Mand.**	**MC**	**LHan**	**OCM**	
j	替	tì	t^{h}iei^{C}	t^{h}es	thîts ot thîh	OCB *thij/ts

[T] BTD 那替 na-t^{h}es Skt. nadī; 優波替 ʔu-pa-t^{h}es Skt. upatiṣya

29-15 = K. 413		**Mand.**	**MC**	**LHan**	**OCM** See *EDOC* Indro. §8.1.5	
a	至	zhì	tśi^{C}	tśis	tits	OCB *tjits

[T] Sin Sukchu SR tṣi (去), PR, LR tṣɿ; MGZY ji (去) [tṣi]; ONW tśi

[E] TB: WT mčʰi-ba, mčʰis 'come, go, exist', WB ce^{C} 'to complete'

d	致	zhì	ṭi^{C}	ṭis	trits	

[T] Sin Sukchu SR tṣi (去), PR, LR tṣɿ; MGZY ji (去) [tṣi]; ONW ti

-	緻	zhì	ḍi^{C}	ḍis	(drits)	⋈ 29-17/402 紩

= 26-16/595h <> [T] ONW di <> [E] ST *C-rwi: Lushai tʰui^{H} 'to sew', JP ri^{31} 'thread'

-	蛭	zhì	tśjet, ṭjet,	tet ? tśit ?	tit...	OCB *tjit, tit
			tiet, ṭjäi^{C}	ṭit ?		PCH *m-lhit ?

[E] TB *m-liit 'water leech', KN *m-hliit > Lushai hliit < *hl-< *C-lit

e	輊	zhì	ṭi^{C}	ṭis	trits	OCB *trjits

[T] ONW ti <> [E] TB *s-liy > KN *rit > Lushai rit^{L} / riʔ^{L} < rit / rih 'be heavy'; TB *s-ləy 'heavy' > WT lči-ba < *lhji, lǰi-ba < *lji; Kanauri li-ko 'heavy', Lepcha lí, lím, PL *C-li^{2} > WB le^{B}, JP li^{33}

f	挃	zhì	ṭjet	ṭit	trit	OCB *trjit
g	銍	zhì	ṭjet	ṭit	trit	

[E] ? TB: WT gri 'knife', WB kre^{B} 'copper', JP mă^{31}-gri^{33} 'brass', Lushai hrei^{L} < hreih 'axe, hatchet'

h	窒	stop up zhì	ṭjet, tiet	ṭit, tet	trit, tît	OCB *trjit

[T] ONW tit <> WT 'dig-pa 'to stop up'

		threshold dié	diet	det	dît	
i-	桎郅	zhì	tśjet	tśit	tit	[T] ONW tśit
o	姪	zhí	diet, ḍjet	det, ḍie	dît, drit or lît, r-lit	OCB *dīt

[T] ONW dėt <> TB *b-ləy 'nephew, grandchild', OBurm. mliy, WT mre^{B} 'grandchild'

-	膣	zhì	ṭjet, tiet			

[Yupian, 6th cent. AD] (the reading may simply be the one of the phonetic)

[E] ST *tey: TB *tey^{B}, PKaren *ʔte^{B}

n	垤	dié	diet	det	dît or lît	OCB *dit

[E] TB: KN *m-hliŋ, Sabeu pa̤-lait 'ant'

m	咥	dié	diet	det	dît or lît	
qr	絰耋	dié	diet	det	dît or lît	
j	室	shì	śjet	śit	lhit	OCB *stjit

[T] Sin Sukchu SR ṣi (入); MGZY shi (入) [ṣi]; ONW śit

[E] ST *k-li(s) > WT gži 'ground, foundation, cause; residence, abode' ⋈ gžis 'native place', yul-gžis 'house, estate, property'; Lepcha lí 'house'; WB mre 'earth, ground', Nung məli 'ground, mountain', Dulong mə̆lì 'place'

29-16 = K. 415		**Mand.**	**MC**	**LHan**	**OCM**	
a	疐 stem	dì	tiei^{C}	tes	tîts	
	疐 to slip	zhì	ṭi^{C}	ṭis	trits	~ 30-10/493c 躓
d	懥 angry	zhì	tśi^{C}, ṭʰi^{C}	tśis, ṭʰis	tits, thrits	~ 30-10/493d 懫
e	嚔	tì !	tiei^{C}	tes	tîts	

29-17 = K. 402		**Mand.**	**MC**	**LHan**	**OCM**	
a	失	shī	śjet	śit	lhit	[T] ONW śit
b	佚	yì	jiet	jit	lit	= 29-19/396a 逸
	[T] ONW it <> [E] Note Tai: S. let^{D2}-lɔɔt^{D2} 'escape artfully or adroitly'					
cd	泆軼	yì, dié	jiet, diet	jit, det	lit, lît	
i	瓞	dié	diet	det	lît OCB *lit	⤨ 29-16/415a
j	跌	dié	diet	det	lît	
	[T] ONW dėt <> [E] TB *ble or *blai 'to slip', Mikir -iŋlìt < *m-lìt 'be slippery'; WT 'byid-pa 'to slip' < *mlit?					
k	迭	dié	diet	det	lît	
	[T] MTang diar < dɨar, ONW dėt					
-	紩	zhì	ḍjet GY	ḍit FY	— (drit)	⤨ 29-15/413 緻
fgh	秩袠秩	zhì	ḍjet	ḍit	drit < r-lit	OCB *lrjit
e	抶	chì	ṭʰjet	ṭʰit	rhit < r-lhit ?	
l	眣	dié, chì	diet, ṭʰjet	det, ṭʰit	lît, rhit < r-lhit ?	

29-18 = K. 398		**Mand.**	**MC**	**LHan**	**OCM**	
a	實 fruit	shí	dźjet	źit (dźit ?)	m-lit	OCB *Ljit
	[T] Sin Sukchu SR ʂi (入); MGZY ci (入) [dẓi]; ONW źit <> [E] TB: Lepcha lí, lí-m 'be ripe', lí, a-lí 'seed'; Mikir lík 'pick, pluck'					
	實 real	shí				~ 7-14/866s 寔

29-19 = K. 396		**Mand.**	**MC**	**LHan**	**OCM**	
a	逸	yì	jiet	jit	lit	
	= 29-17/402b 佚 <> [T] ONW it					

29-20 = K. 1257ab			MC	LHan	OCM	
ab	溢鎰	yì	jiet	jit	lit	⤨ 29-17/402c 泆
	[E] Lepcha lyit / lít 'to overflow'. The graph 益 849a *ʔek has been chosen in part for its meaning.					

29-21 = K. 397		**Mand.**	**MC**	**LHan**	**OCM**	
a	佾	yì	jiet	jit	lit	
1256d	屑 reckless	yì	jiet	jit	lit	= 29-17/402c
	屑 pure	xiè	sjet	sit	slit	

29-22 = K. 1257c		**Mand.**	**MC**	**LHan**	**OCM**
c	欥	yì	jiet	jit	jit or lit

29-23 = K. 403		**Mand.**	**MC**	**LHan**	**OCM**	
a	栗	lì	ljet	lit	rit	OCB *C-rjit
	[T] ONW lit <> [E] KS-Ten lik^{31} 'chestnut'					

d 慄 lì ljet lit rit
[E] TB: WT žed-pa < *rjet < *ret 'to fear, be afraid', bred-pa < *b-ret 'be frightened'
e 瑮 lì ljet lit rit

29-24 = K. 1241n **Mand.** **MC** **LHan** **OCM**
n 盭 lì lieiC, liet les, let rîts, rît
The OC form could also have been *rêt(s); = 29-25 綟

29-25 = K. 532 **Mand.** **MC** **LHan** **OCM**
a 戾 evil lì, liè lieiC, liet les, let rîts, rît
come to lì lieiC les rîts R! OCB *C-rets
Unambiguous Shijing rimes are with *-it, *-i (see Baxter 1992).
b 悷 lì lieiC les rîts
c 淚 lèi ljwiC lus ruts = rjuts ?
[T] Sin Sukchu SR luj (去); MGZY lue (去) [luɛ]
\- 綟 lì lieiC les rîts [SW] = 29-24 盭

29-26 = K. 404 **Mand.** **MC** **LHan** **OCM**
a 日 rì ńźjet ńit nit
[T] Sin Sukchu SR ri (入); MGZY Zhi (入) [ri]; ONW ńit.
[E] TB *nyiy > OTib. gñi, WT ñi-ma 'sun', ñin (-mo) 'day'
eg- 衵 g 䵒 nì ṇjet ṇit nrit
= 26-24/563f 昵; ≠ 33-20/456i 刹 <> [T] ONW nit
f 馹 rì ńźjet ńit nit
hj 圼涅 niè niet net nît
[T] MTang niar < nɨar, ONW nėt
[E] TB: WB ə-nañ ~ ə-nac < *nik., WT sñigs-pa 'impure sediment'

29-27 = K. 414 **Mand.** **MC** **LHan** **OCM**
a 衵 rì ńźjet ńit nit

29-28 = K. 564 **Mand.** **MC** **LHan** **OCM**
agi 二貳樲 èr ńźiC ńis nis
二 [T] Sin Sukchu SR ri (去), PR, LR rɿ; MGZY Zhi (去) [ri]; ONW ńi
貳 [T] Han BTD 阿迦貳吒 ʔɑ-ka-ńis-ṭaC Skt. akaniṣṭa. MHan 貳師 ńis-ṣi Nesef
[E] TB *g-nis > WT gñis
j 膩 nì ṇiC ṇis nris
838a 佞 nìng nieŋ neŋC nêŋh < nêŋs

29-29 = K. 494 **Mand.** **MC** **LHan** **OCM**
a 疾 jí dzjet dzit dzit = 29-29/923c 堲 'detest'
[T] Sin Sukchu SR dzi (入); MGZY tsi (入) [dzi]; ONW dzit.
[E] ? TB: Chepang ɟik- 'be sick, injured, hurt'
d 蒺 jí dzjet dzit dzit
e 嫉 jí dzjet, dziC dzit, dziC dzit, dzits

29-30 = K. 399, 923 The graph is also phonetic in 5-26/923.

		Mand.	MC	LHan	OCM	
399a	即	jí (?)	tsjet	tsit	tsit R!	

[T] Sin Sukchu SR tsi (入); MGZY dzi (入) [tsi] <> [E] MK: Khmer jita /cit/, OKhmer jit /ɟit/ 'to be near to, to the point of, be close'

		Mand.	MC	LHan	OCM	
e	節 knots	jié	tsiet	tset	tsît	

節 [T] Sin Sukchu SR tsje (入); MGZY dzȳa (入) [tsjɛ]; MTang tsiar < tsɨar, ONW tsėt
[E] ST *tsik: TB *tsik: WT 'tsʰigs 'joint, knot, knee'; LB *ʔdzik > WB cʰac 'a joint'

		Mand.	MC	LHan	OCM	
	crest-like	jié	tsiet, dziet	tset, dzet	tsît, dzît	
dg-	楖櫛榔	zhì	tṣjɛt	tṣit	tsrit	OCB *tsrjit
923c	堲 detest	jí	dzjet	dzit	dzit	= 29-28/494a 疾

[T] Sin Sukchu SR dzi (入); MGZY tsi (入) [dzi]; ONW dzit.
[E] TB: WT tsʰig-pa 'anger, indignation'.

		Mand.	MC	LHan	OCM	
	堲 masonry	jí	tsjet	tsit	tsit	OCB *tsjit < *tsjik

'Masonry' <> [E] WT rtsig-pa 'a wall, masonry'

		Mand.	MC	LHan	OCM	
	堲 coaled	jí	tsjet	tsit	tsit	OCB *tsjit < *tsjik

'Coaled part' <> [E] WT 'tsʰig-pa 'to burn'

29-31 = K. 400

		Mand.	MC	LHan	OCM	
a	七	qī	tsʰjet	tsʰit	tshit < snhit ?	

[T] Sin Sukchu SR ts'i (入); MGZY tshi (入) [ts'i]; ONW tsʰit <> [D] PMin *tshit
[E] TB *snis > Himalayan lgs. *snis; Jiarong kĕsnĕs; LB *snit; JP să^{31}-nit^{31}; Trung snit

		Mand.	MC	LHan	OCM	
f	切 to cut	qiè	tsʰiet	tsʰet	tshît	⋈ 29-29/399e 節
	close to	qiè	tsʰiet	tsʰet	tshît	⋈ 29-29/399a 即

[T] MTang tsʰiar < tsʰɨar, ONW tsʰėt

		Mand.	MC	LHan	OCM	
e	叱	chì	tśʰjet	tśʰit	thit	

29-32 = K. 401

		Mand.	MC	LHan	OCM	
ab	桼漆	qī	tsʰjet	tsʰit	tshit	OCB *tshjit

[E] TB *tsiy > WT tsʰi-ba 'tough, sticky matter'; LB *dziy^{2} 'sap, juice' > WB ce^{B} 'sticky, adhesive'

		Mand.	MC	LHan	OCM	
c	膝 knee	xī	sjet	sit	sit	

[T] MTang sir, ONW sit

29-33 = K. 1257

		Mand.	MC	LHan	OCM	
e	悉	xī	sjet	sit	sit	

[T] MTang sir, ONW sit <> [E] TB *syey 'know' > WT šes-pa, Vayu ses; Lushai tʰei^{L} / tʰeiʔ^{L} (<*sei/s) 'can, be able', PL*si^{2}

		Mand.	MC	LHan	OCM	
f	蟋蟀	xī-shuò	sjɛt-ṣjuət	ṣit-ṣuit	srit-srut	

OCM *it (not *-ət) because xī in xī-shuò must have been -it to contrast with -ut

29-34 = K. 518

		Mand.	MC	LHan	OCM	
ae	四駟	sì	si^{C}	sis	sis or slis	OCB *splĭts = 30-11/509h 肆

[T] Sin Sukchu SR sɿ (去); MGZY sʰi (去) [sɿ]; Sui-Tang si^{C}, sit?, ONW si^{C}
[E] ? TB *b-ləy 'four' > WT bži < *bli

		Mand.	MC	LHan	OCM	
fg	柶泗	sì	si^{C}	sis	sis	

29-35 = K. 506		**Mand.**	**MC**	**LHan**	**OCM**	
a	虱	shī	ṣjɛt	ṣit	srit < srik	

[D] PMin *šət <> [E] TB *s-rik > WT šig < *hrjik 'louse', Bunan śrig, Chepang srəyk 'head louse', Lushai hrik^{L}

29-36 = K. 411		**Mand.**	**MC**	**LHan**	**OCM**	
a	瑟	sè	ṣjɛt	ṣit	srit	OCB *sprjit

29-37 = K. 412		**Mand.**	**MC**	**LHan**	**OCM**	
a	閉	bì	piei^{C}, piet	pes, pet	pît(s)	[T] ONW pėi

29-38 = K. 408		**Mand.**	**MC**	**LHan**	**OCM**	
ad	匹疋	pǐ	p^{h}jiet 4	p^{h}it	phit	OCB *phjit
-	鵯	pǐ	p^{h}jiet 4	p^{h}it	phit	

[E] Area word: Tai: S. and Tai lgs in general pet^{D1} 'duck'; MK: Viet. vit, NBahn. pĕt'; TB: Lolo-Zaiwa et al. pj̱et^{55} 'duck', Geman Deng kɹɑi^{35}-pit^{55}

29-39 = K. 521		**Mand.**	**MC**	**LHan**	**OCM**	
a	畀	bì	pi^{C} 4	pis	pis	OCB *pjits

[T] Sui-Tang pɨ, ONW pii <> [D] Y-Guǎngzh pei^{B1}, Zhōngsh pi^{B1}, Táish i^{B1} < *pi^{B}, Téngxian ʔbi^{B1} (MC pi^{B}) <> [E] ST *pi(s): TB *pəy: Lepcha byi ⋈ byi-n 'to give'; LB: WB pe^{B} ⋈ p^{h}it 'invite, offer to give'

c	鼻 nose	bí	bjiet 4	bit	bit	

[T] Tang period: col. Shāzhōu *bir, *bit. See Intro. 6.2.1.

	鼻 nose	bì	bi^{C} 4	bis	bits	

[T] Sin Sukchu SR bi (去); MGZY pi (去) [bi]
[D] Min *bhi^{C}: Jian'ou p^{h}i^{C2}, Fuzh p^{h}ei^{C}, Xiam p^{h}ĩ^{C2}; Kejia: Meix p^{h}i^{C1}

d	淠 float	pì	p^{h}iei^{C}, p^{h}jäi^{C}	p^{h}es, p^{h}ias	phîts, phêts	
	淠 in crowds	pì	p^{h}iei^{C}	p^{h}es	phîts	OCB *phits

29-40 = K. (1237m)			**MC**	**LHan**	**OCM**	
-	自 nose	bì	bi^{C} 4	bis	bits	

This is the original OB graph for 'nose' > 鼻 29-38/521c; the reading *bì* survives in the next graph for 'first-born'. This graph also writes a different word zì 自 26-31/1237m 'self'. See Intro. 6.2.1.

-	自 > 鼻鼻	bì	bi^{C} 4	bis	bits	'the first-born' [SW 109]

29-41 = K. 405 Most graphs ending in -it are in Div. 3/4, but all tone C counterparts fall into chóngniǔ Div. 3/3 so that these may include original OC rimes in *-its (rather than only *-rits). In fact, except for words in 29-39/521 above, all MC -i^{C} 3/4 words in tone C derive from OC open syllables *-ih (Rime 26), and all MC -i^{C} 3/3 derive from OC closed syllables *-ts (see SSYP).

		Mand.	**MC**	**LHan**	**OCM**	
a	必	bì	pjiet 4	pit	pit	

[T] Sin Sukchu SR pi (入); MGZY bi (入) [pi]

c	珌	bì	pjiet 4	pit	pit	OCB *pjit
def	怭柲駜	bì	bjiet 4	bit	bit	
gh	苾飶	bì	bjiet 4, biet	bit, bet	bit, bît	OCB *bjit

j	柲	bì	pj(i)et 3,4	pɨt !,	prit !,	= 29-43/406a 弜
			pji^{C} 3	pɨs	prits	
	[T] ? TB: Chepang pit- 'grip (as with pincers), hold between knees or under the arm'					
i	覕	bié	biet, miet	bet, met	bît, mît	
k	毖	bì	pji^{C} 3	pɨs	pits	OCB *prjits
l	泌	bì	bjiet 4,	bit,	bit,	OCB *bjit
			pji^{C} 3	pɨs	pits !	
m	祕	mì !	pji^{C} 3	pɨs	pits	
n	閟	bì	pji^{C} 3	pɨs	pits	
	[T] TB-PL *pi^{2} 'to close', Mru pit 'shut, close'					
o	宓	mì	mjet 3	mɨt	mrit	
p	密 silence	mì	mjet 3	mɨt	mrit	[E] Tai: Saek mit 'quiet'
	密 near	mì	mjet 3	mɨt	mrit	OCB *mrjit
	[T] ONW mit. MHan 都密 tâ-mɨt (*tâ-mrit) Tarmita, Termes					
r	蜜	mì	mjiet 4	mit	mit	
	[T] MTang mir < mɨr, ONW miit; BTD Skt. -mitā <> [D] PMin *mit					
s	監	mì	mjiet 4	mit	mit	OCB *Npjit
t	謐	mì	mjiet 4	mit	mit	

29-42 = K. 407		**Mand.**	**MC**	**LHan**	**OCM**
ade	畢罼韠	bì	pjiet 4	pit	pit
	[T] Sin Sukchu SR pi (入); MGZY bi (入) [pi]; MTang pir < pɨr, ONW piit 'finish'				
	[E] TB: Lushai peiʔ^{L} < peih < *-s 'to complete'; WT dpyis p^{h}yin-pa 'to come to the last'				
ijkl	彃篳縪蹕	bì	pjiet 4	pit	pit
m	韠	bì	pjiet 4	pit	pit
	[E] TB: PTib *pis-mo; Nung p^{h}aŋ-p^{h}it 'knee'				

29-43 = K. 1257g		**Mand.**	**MC**	**LHan**	**OCM**
g	鷩	bì	pjiet 4	pit	pit

29-44 = K. 406		**Mand.**	**MC**	**LHan**	**OCM**	
a	弜	bì	pjet 3	pɨt	prit	= 29-40/405j 柲
e	弼	bì	bjet 3	bɨt	brit	

30 OCM rime *-ət, *-əts, *-əs Wù bù 物部 (1)

GSR 486 - 540

Baxter 1992: 437 ff. (§10.1.7)

Table 30-1: OCM rimes *-ən, *-ət, *-ə(t)s, *-əi in QYS categories

Div.	*-ən R.33	*-ət R.30	*-ə(t)s R.30	*-əi R. 27
I gr	根 kən kən *kən̂ 本 pwən^{B} pən^{B} *pən̂ʔ	勃 bwət bət *bət̂	愛 ʔậi^{C} ʔəs *ʔəŝ 配 p^{h}wậi^{C} p^{h}əs *phəŝ	開 k^{h}ậi k^{h}əi *khəî 回 ɣwậi ɣuəi *wəî 枚 mwậi məi *məî
IV ac	典 tien^{B} ten^{B} *tən̂ʔ			妻 ts^{h}iei ts^{h}ei *tshəî
III gr	近 gjən^{B} giən^{B} *gənʔ 分 pjwən pun *pən	乞 k^{h}jət k^{h}iət *khət 物 mjwət mut *mət	氣 k^{h}jei^{C} k^{h}iəs *khəs 謂 jwei^{C} wus *wəs	幾 kjei^{B} kɨi^{B} *kəiʔ 歸 kjwei kui *kwəi 圍 jwei wui *wəi 飛 pjwei pui *pəi
III ac	刃 ńźjen^{C} ńɨn^{C} *nəns	質 tśjet tśit *tət		
3/3	巾 kjen3 kɨn *krən 貧 bjen3 bɨn *brən	乙 ʔjet3 ʔɨt *ʔrət ?	器 k^{h}ji^{C}3 k^{h}ɨs *khrəs	冀 kji^{C}3 kɨ^{C} *krəih 美 mji^{B}3 mɨ^{B} *mrəiʔ

See Table 33-1 for a comparison of OC rimes *-in, *-ən, *-it, *-ət.

30-1 = K. 517 Some or all OC finals *-s could have been *-ts.

		Mand.	**MC**	**LHan**	**OCM**	
ac	气氣[1] air	qì	k^{h}jei^{C}	k^{h}ɨəs	khəs	
	[T] Sin Sukchu SR k'jej (去), PR k'i; MGZY khi (去) [k'i]; ONW k^{h}i^{C}					
ce	氣[2] 餼 gift	xì	xjei^{C}	hɨəs	həs	
d	愾 angry	kài	k^{h}ậi^{C}	k^{h}əs	khəŝ	
	[T] ONW k^{h}ɑi^{C} <> [E] AA: Kharia k^{h}is 'anger', Sora kissa 'move with great effort', Khm k^{h}ɛs 'strive after' <> TB-JR khɐs 'anger'					
	愾 sigh	kài,	k^{h}ậi^{C},	k^{h}əs,	khəŝ,	= 30-2/515m
		xì	xjei^{C}	hɨəs	həs	
f	乞 pray	qǐ	k^{h}jət	k^{h}ɨət	khət	[T] ONW khit
g	吃 stutter	jī, jí	kjət	kɨət	kət	
	吃 to eat	chī	—	—		
	[T] Sin Sukchu SR k'i (入), LR tʂ'iʔ; MGZY khi (入) [k'i]					
h	訖	qì	kjət	kɨət	kət	[T] ONW kit
jk	汔迄	qì !	xjət	hɨət	hət or hŋət ?	
i	扢	xì	xjət	hɨət	hət or hŋət ?	
mn	仡圪	yì, xì	ŋjət, xjət	ŋɨət, hɨət	ŋət, hŋət	
o	齕	hé, xié	ɣwət, ɣiet	guət, get	gût, gît	
p	刉	jī	kjei	kɨi	kəi	

30-2 = K. 515 Some or all OC finals *-s could have been *-ts.

		Mand.	MC	LHan	OCM	
ac	旡既	jì	kjei^C	kɨəs	kəs	
	[T] Sin Sukchu SR kjej (去), PR, LR ki; MGZY gi (去) [ki]; ONW ki					
g	蔇 vegetat.	jì	kjei^C	kɨəs	kəs	
	to come	jì	gji^C 3	gɨs	gəs	
o	暨	jì	gji^C 3	gɨs	grəts	OCB *grjəts < *grjəps
	= 洎 30-4/1237a <> [T] MGZY ki (去) [gi]					
jkl	j 概溉	gài	kâi^C	kəs	kə̂s	OCB *kəts
mn	嘅慨	kài	k^{h}âi^C	k^{h}əs	khə̂s	= 30-1/517d
h	塈	xì,	xjei^C, xji^C,	hɨs	həs	OCB *xjəts
		jì	gji^C			
i	摡	xì,	xjei^C,	hɨəs,	həs,	
		gài	kâi^C	kəs	kə̂s	

30-3 = K. 536

		Mand.	MC	LHan	OCM
a	器	qì	k^{h}ji^C 3	k^{h}ɨs	khrəs or khrəts

30-4 = K. 1237a

		Mand.	MC	LHan	OCM	
a	洎 pour out	jì	kji^C, gji^C 3	kɨs, gɨs	krəts, grəts	
	洎 together	jì	gji^C 3	gɨs	grəts	= 30-2/515o 暨
-	垍	jì	gji^C 3	gɨs	grəts ?	
-	郋	xī	ɣiei	gei	—	

30-5 = K. 504

		Mand.	MC	LHan	OCM	
a	戛	jiá	kăt	kɛt	krə̂t or krît	= 26-9/599h

30-6 = K. 508 Some or all OC finals in *-s could have been *-ts.

		Mand.	MC	LHan	OCM	
a	愛	ài	ʔâi^C	ʔəs	ʔə̂s	
	[T] Sin Sukchu SR ʔaj (去); MGZY 'ay (去) [ʔaj]; ONW ʔɑi^C					
	[D] PMin *ʔuəi^C <> [E] TB-PKaren *ʔai					
bc	曖薆	ài	ʔâi^C	ʔəs	ʔə̂s	
d	僾 indist.	ài	ʔâi^C,	ʔəs,	ʔə̂s,	'indistinct'
			ʔjei^B	ʔɨi^B	ʔəʔ	
	to pant	ài	ʔâi^C	ʔəs	ʔə̂s	

30-7 = K. 505

		Mand.	MC	LHan	OCM
a	乙	yǐ	ʔjet 3	ʔɨt	ʔrət ?

30-8 = K. 537

		Mand.	MC	LHan	OCM
a	劓	yì	ŋji^C 3	ŋɨs	ŋrəts

30-9 = K. 516

		Mand.	MC	LHan	OCM
ac	豙毅	yì	ŋjei^C	ŋɨəs or ŋɨih	ŋəs or ŋəih (< *ŋəls) ?
	[T] Sin Sukchu SR i (去); MGZY ngi (去) [ŋi] <> [E] TB: Lushai (sa^L-)ŋhàl^L < ŋhalh < ŋhals 'wild pig' ⋇ ŋhal^R < ŋhalʔ 'ill-behaved, unruly, over-bold'; Paang. maŋàl ~ raŋàl 'wild boar'				
d	藙	yì	ŋjei^C	ŋɨəs or ŋɨih	ŋəs or ŋəih

30-10 = K. 493	**Mand.**	**MC**	**LHan**	**OCM**	
a 質 solid	zhì	tśjet	tśit	tət	
hostage	zhì	tśi^C	tśis	təts	
b 鑕	zhì	tśjet	tśit	tət	
c 躓	zhì	ṭi^C	ṭis	trəts	~ 29-16/415a 疐
[E] TB: WT 'dred-pa 'to slip, slide, glide'; Kanauri *bret					
d 懫	zhì	tśi^C, ṭi^C	tśis, ṭ^{h}is	təts, thrəts	~ 29-16/415d 懥

30-11 = K. 509 Some or all OC finals could have been -ts.

	Mand.	**MC**	**LHan**	**OCM**	
a 隶 come to	dài, lì	dâi^C, i^C	dəs, jis	lə̂s	
c 逮 come to	dài, dì, lì	dâi^C, i^C	dəs, jis	lə̂s	OCB *(g-)ləps
peaceful	dì	diei^C	des	lî̂s	
e 嚃	dài	t^{h}âi^C	t^{h}əs	lhə̂s	
f 棣 cherry	dì	diei^C	des	lî̂s	
perfect	dì, dài	diei^C, dâi^C	des, dəs	lî̂s, lə̂s	
g 肄	yì	i^C	jis	lis	
h 肆	sì	si^C	sis	sis < slis	= 29-33/518a 四
[T] Sin Sukchu SR sɿ (去); MGZY s^{h}i (去) [sɿ]; Sui-Tang si^C, sit?, ONW si^C. OCB sljəps					
n 蕼	sì	si^C	sis	sis < slis ?	
m 緣	sì	si^C	sis	sis < slis ?	
op 殔	sì, yì	si^C, ji^C	sis, jis	slis, lis	
1241m 隸	lì	liei^C	les	rî̂s or lî̂s	

30-12 = K. 514	**Mand.**	**MC**	**LHan**	**OCM**
a 配	pèi	p^{h}wâi^C	p^{h}əs	phə̂s or phə̂ih = 27-10

30-13 = K. 491	**Mand.**	**MC**	**LHan**	**OCM**	
a 孛	bó, bèi	bwət, bwâi^C	bət, bəs	bə̂t, bə̂ts	
b 勃	bó	bwət	bət	bə̂t	
'Powdery' [E] ST *put: WB p^{h}ut 'dust', Lushai p^{h}ut^L 'flowery, powdery'					
'Sudden' [E] TB: Lushai p^{h}uut^H 'suddenly'					
- 脖	bó	bwət	bət	—	
c 浡	pó	bwət	bət	bə̂t	OCB *buts
[E] ? TB: WT 'bu-ba, 'bus 'to open, unfold (flower)', 'be lighted, kindled'					
d 悖 discord	bó, bèi	bwət, bwâi^C	bət, bəs	bə̂t, bə̂ts	
abundant	pó	bwət	bət	bə̂t	
e 誖	pó	bwət, bwâi^C	bət, bəs	bə̂t, bə̂ts	
f 綍	fú	pjwət	put	pət	

30-14 = K. 500	**Mand.**	**MC**	**LHan**	**OCM**	
a 弗 not	fú	pjwət	put	pət	
[T] MTang pfur, ONW put; BTD Skt. putra					
弗 gust	fú	pjwət	put	pət	OCB *pjut
[E] TB: WT 'bud-pa, bus 'to blow' intr.					

de 第紼 fú pjwət put pət

fij 刜佛髴 fú pʰjwət pʰut phət

h 拂 fú pʰjwət pʰut phət

[E] PYao *pʰwot 'sweep, clear away'

k 茀 dense fú pʰjwət pʰut phət

茀 elimin. fú pjwət put pət OCB *pjut

q 沸 gush fú pjwət put pət

[T] ONW put <> [E] TB *brup ~ *prup 'to gush forth': WT 'brup-pa 'gush, spout forth', JP 'pʰrup^{31} 'to squirt' (as water from mouth).

沸 bubble fèi pjwei^{C} pus pəts

[D] *pyi^{C}. <> [E] MY *npwei^{1C} . TB: JP prut^{31} 'to boil'

l 佛 resist fú bjwət but bət

佛 Buddha fó bjwət but --

[T] Sin Sukchu SR vu (入); MGZY hwu (入) [vu]; BTD Skr. buddha

mn 咈岪 fú bjwət but bət

o 怫 fú, fèi bjwət, bjwei^{C} but, bus bət, bəts

p 艴 bó, fú bwət, pʰjwət bət, pʰut bət, phət

rs 昲費 fèi pʰjwei^{C} pʰus phəts

費 [T] Sin Sukchu SR fi (去) ; LR fi; MGZY h(w)i (去) [fi]

\- 疿 fèi pjwei^{C} pus

[T] ONW pui^{C} <> [E] WT 'bos 'boil, bump, tumor' ⋈ 'bo-ba, bos 'to swell, rise, sprout'. <> Tai: S. pʰot^{D1} 'prickly heat'.

30-15 **Mand.** **MC** **LHan** **OCM**

\- 乀 fú pʰjwət pʰut — SW5660

30-16 = K. 501 **Mand.** **MC** **LHan** **OCM**

a 市 fú pjwət put pət

c 芾 knee cov. fú pjwət put pət < put OCB *pjut

= 21-31/276l 韍 <> [E] TB *put > WT pus-mo 'knee', PTib *pus-mo, *puks-mo; Nung ur-pʰut 'elbow'; JP pʰut^{31} 'to kneel', lă^{31}-pʰut^{31} 'knee'

芾 covering fèi, pjwei^{C}, pus, pəts,

bèi pwâi^{C} pɑs pâts

d 旆 pèi ! bwâi^{C} bɑs bâts

e 怖 pèi pʰwâi^{C} pʰɑs phâts

f 沛 abundant pèi pʰwâi^{C} pʰɑs phâts

沛 uprooted bèi pwâi^{C} pɑs pâts = 21-31/276h 拔

沛 marshy bèi pwâi^{C} pɑs pâts

g 肺 lung fèi pʰjwɐi^{C} pʰuɑs phats

[T] ONW pʰei > pʰuei <> [E] AA-PVM *p-sɔːs > p-hɔːc > pɔːc / pʰɔːc 'lungs', Tai: S. pɔɔt^{D1L} < *pɨɔt 'lung' ⋈ S. pʰɔɔt^{D1} 'breathe, inhale'

肺 dense pèi pʰwâi^{C}, pʰɑs, phâts,

bwâi^{C} bɑs bâts

30-17 = K. 530 **Mand.** **MC** **LHan** **OCM**

a 朏 fěi pʰjwei^{B}, pʰwət pʰui^{B}, pʰət phəiʔ, phə̂t < phuiʔ, phût

The element chū 出 'come out' is partially semantic. Cf. 31-16/496t

30-18 = K. 492 **Mand.** **MC** **LHan** **OCM**

a 𠬛 mò mwət mət mə̂t

b 沒 dive mò mwət mət mə̂t, prob. mût R OCB *mut

[T] Sin Sukchu SR mu (入); MGZY mu (入) [mu]; ONW mot <> [E] Tai: S. mut[D2] 'to dive'

沒 covet mò mwət mət mə̂t

[E] TB: WT mod-pa, mos-pa 'be pleased, wish', smon-pa 'to wish, desire'

沒 not have méi < wú yǒu 無有

c 歿 mò mwət mət mə̂t = 30-20/503k

d [illegible] mò mwət mət mə̂t

30-19 = K. 503 In the OB the graph for this word 'don't' is different from 30-20.

Mand. **MC** **LHan** **OCM**

a 勿 don't! wù mjwət mut mət

30-20 = K. 503 **Mand.** **MC** **LHan** **OCM**

ah 勿 > 物 wù mjwət mut mət, probably mut

[T] Sin Sukchu SR vu (入), PR, LR vuʔ; MGZY wu (入) [vu]; MTang mvur, ONW mut

[E] TB *mruw: WT 'bru < *ɴbru 'grain, seed'; WB myui[B] 'seed, seed grain' ⤲ ə-myui[B] 'race, lineage, kind, class, sort'

j 芴 a plant wù mjwət mut mət

芴 confused hū xwət huət hmə̂t

k 歾 mò mwət mət mə̂ = 30-18/492c

\- 昒 wú mjwət, xwət mut, hət mət, hmə̂t

\- [illegible] mèi mwât, mai[C] mɑt, mas mât, mrâts < môt

l 忽 careless hū xwət huət hmə̂t OCB *hmut

The Shijing rimes are ambiguous <> [T] Sin Sukchu SR xu (入); MGZY hu (入) [xu]

p 惚 hū xwət huət hmə̂t

m 笏 hù, hū xwət huət hmə̂t 'writing tablet'

no 吻刎 wěn mjwən[B] mun[B] mənʔ

qr 脗[illegible] wěn, mjwən[B], mun[B], mənʔ or munʔ,

mǐn mjien[B] 4 min[B] minʔ

30-21 = K. 531 Some or all OC finals could have been -ts.

Mand. **MC** **LHan** **OCM**

a 未 wèi mjwei[C] mus məs

[T] Sin Sukchu SR vi (去); MGZY wi (去) [vi]; ONW mui[C]

[D] Wu-Wēnzh, Guǎngzh mei[C], Fuzh mui[C], Xiam be[C]

g 味 wèi mjwei[C] mus məs

k 妹 mèi mwậi[C] məs mə̂s OCB *məts

[T] Sin Sukchu SR muj (去), PR, LR məj; MGZY mue (去) [muɛ]

[D] PMin *mhyai[C] (or *mhye[C])

n 昧 mèi mwậi[C] məs mə̂s

[T] ONW mɑi; BTD Skt. -mādhi

i 寐 mèi mi[C] 4 mis mis OCB *mjits

[T] MTang mɨ, ONW mii

[E] TB *r-mwiy > WT rmi-ba 'to dream', WB mwe[C] 'to sleep', Magar mis-ke

h	魅	mèi	mji^C 3	mɨs	mrəs or mris	= 30-22/522a
p	沬	mèi	mwậi^C	məs	mə̂s	
q	韎 leather	mèi	mwậi^C	məs	mə̂s	
	music	mài	mwăi^C	mɛs	mrə̂s	

30-22 = K. 522		**Mand.**	**MC**	**LHan**	**OCM**	
a	鬽	mèi	mji^C 3	mɨs	mrəs or mris	= 30-21/531h 魅

31 OCM rime *-ut, *uts, *-us Wù bù 物部 (2)

GSR 486 - 540

Baxter 1992: 437 ff. (§10.1.7)

See Table 28-1 for OCM rimes *-un / -wən, *-ut and *-ui / -wəi. See Intro. 5.2.3 about the removal of OCB medial *r in MC Div. 3/3 syllables.

Table 31-1: OCM rimes *-ut, *-wət, *-wit, *-ui, *-u(t)s, *-wəi, *-wə(t)s, *-wi(t)s

Div.	*-ut R.31	*-wət, *-wit R.31, 29	*-ui, *-u(t)s R.28, 31	*-wəi, *-wə(t)s, *-wi/(t)s R.28, 29
I	骨 kwət kuət *kût 突 tʰwət tʰuət *thût	汩 kwət kuət *kwə̂t	偎 ʔwậi ʔuəi *ʔûi 堆 twậi tuəi *tûi 對 twậiᶜ tuəs *tûts	塊 kʰwậiᶜ kʰuəiᶜ *khwə̂ih
III gr	屈 kʰjwət kʰut *khut			歸 kjwei kui *kwəi 貴 kjweiᶜ kus *kwəs 謂 jweiᶜ wus *wəs
3/3	—		夔 gjwi3 guɨ *gui 匱 gjwiᶜ3 guɨs *gus	
III ac	出 tśʰjwet tśʰuit *k-hlut		誰 źwi dźui *dui	
II	滑 ɣwǎt guɛt *grût	劀 kwǎt kuɛt *kwrît	褢 ɣwǎi guɛi *grûi 蒯 kʰwǎiᶜ kʰuɛs *khrû(t)s	
IV gr		穴 ɣiwet ɣuet *wît 血 xiwet huet *hwît		睽 kʰiwei kʰuei *khwî 惠 ɣiweiᶜ ɣues *wîs
3/4 w		橘 kjiwet4 kuit *kwit 矞 jiwet wit *wit 恤 sjwet suit *swit		癸 kwiᴮ4 kwiᴮ *kwiʔ 季 kwiᶜ4 kuis *kwis 維 jiwi4 wi *wi 穗 zwiᶜ zuis *s-wis

Shijing rimes *(-)wit and *-ut tended to mingle (Baxter 1992: 444ff); by LHan *-ut became > *-uit, it seems that this process had already started in Western Zhou times. This is parallel to *-in, *-un.

31-1	**= K. 486**	**Mand.**	**MC**	**LHan**	**OCM**
a	骨	gǔ	kwət	kuət	kût
	[T] Sin Sukchu SR ku (入); MGZY gu (入) [ku]; ONW kot <> [D] PMin *kot				
b	鶻	gǔ, hú, huá	kwət, ɣwət, ɣwǎt	kuət, guət, ɣuɛt	kût, gût grût
	MC kwət is probably just the reading of the phonetic gǔ.				
c	搰 dig	hú	ɣwət	ɣuət	gût
	搰 force	kù	kʰwət	kʰuət	khût

d	猾	huá	ɣwăt	ɣuɛt	grût	
e	滑 slipp.	huá	ɣwăt	ɣuɛt	grût	

[T] Sin Sukchu SR ɣwa (入); MGZY Xwa (入) [ɣwa]
[E] TB: JP gum^{31}-rut^{31} < gu-mrut 'slippery'

	滑 disturb	gǔ	kwət	kuət	kût	[T] BTD Skt. kūṭa

31-2	= K. 540	Mand.	MC	LHan	OCM	
ai	臾 > 蕢[1]	(guì >) kuì	gjwi^C 3	guɨs	gus	'basket'
j	簣 basket	kuì	gjwi^C 3, k^{h}wăi^C	guɨs, k^{h}uɛs	gus, khrûs	
g	匱	kuì	gjwi^C 3	guɨs	gus	OCB *grjuts R!

⋈ 4-7/986. [T] MHan 央匱 ʔɨɑŋ-guɨs Tocharian B ankwaṣ 'asafoetida'

hi	櫃蕢[2]	kuì	gjwi^C 3	guɨs	gus	
k	鞼	guì	gjwi^C 3	guɨs	gus	
l	饋	kuì	gjwi^C 3	guɨs	gus	~ 28-1/569r 餽
b	貴	guì	kjwei^C	kus	kwəs	OCB *kjuts

[T] Sin Sukchu SR kuj (去); MGZY gue (去) [kuɛ]; ONW kui. MHan 貴霜 Kuṣāṇa
[D] PMin *kyi^C <> [E] WT *gus-po 'costly, expensive' ⋈ gus-pa 'respect' ⋈ dkon 'valuable'

c	憒	kuì	kwậi^C	kuəs	kûs or kwə̂s	
d	潰	kuì	ɣwậi^C	ɣuəs	(g)wə̂s R!	OCB guts
e	繢	kuì	ɣwậi^C	ɣuəs	gûs or (g)wə̂s	
m	遺 reject	yí	jiwi 4	wi	wi	

[T] Sin Sukchu SR i (平); MGZY ywi (平) [yi]; BTD Skt. vi- (Coblin 1993: 907)

	遺 present	yì	jiwi^C 4	wi^C	wih	
q	壝	wéi, wěi	jiwi(^{B}) 4	wi(^{B})	wi, wiʔ	
f	頮	huì	hwậi^C	huəs	hwə̂s [Li]	= 4-9/988b 颒
o	僓	huài, tuí	xwăi^C	huɛs	hrûs	
p	聵	kuì !	ŋwăi^C	ŋuɛs	ŋrûs	
	隤穨頹	tuí				See 28-13/544.

31-3	= K. 510a	Mand.	MC	LHan	OCM	
a	凷	kuài	k^{h}wậi^C	k^{h}uəs	khwə̂s	~ 28-1/569g

This graph is said to be phonetic in 29-4/510b 屆. Possibly LH k^{h}uəi^C, *khûih

31-4	= K. 534	Mand.	MC	LHan	OCM
ab	蒯蔽	kuài	k^{h}wăi^C	k^{h}uɛs	khrû(t)s

31-5	= K. 523	Mand.	MC	LHan	OCM	
a	胃	wèi	jwei^C	wus	wəs	
d	謂	wèi	jwei^C	wus	wəs	OCB *wjəts

[T] ONW ui; BTD wuC: Skt. puṣa

c	媦	wèi	jwei^C	wus	wəs	
f	蝟 porcu.	wèi	jwei^C	wus	wəs 'porcupine' = 31-6/524	
g	喟	kuì, kuài	k^{h}jwi^C, k^{h}wăi^C	k^{h}uɨs, k^{h}uɛs	khus, khrûs	
-	渭	wèi	jwei^C	wus	wəs	OCB *wjəts

31-6	**= K. 524**	**Mand.**	**MC**	**LHan**	**OCM**	
a	彙	huì	jwei^{C}	wus	wəs	= 31-5/523f

31-7	**= K. 539**	**Mand.**	**MC**	**LHan**	**OCM**	
a	位	wèi	jwi^{C} 3	wɨs	wus or wrəts	OCB *(w)rjəps

[T] Sin Sukchu SR uj (去); MGZY xue (去) [ɦuɛ]; ONW ui; Han BTD wiC
See Intro. 9.2.4 and 5.2.3.

31-8	**= K. 495**	**Mand.**	**MC**	**LHan**	**OCM**
ab	鬱欝	yù	ʔjwət	ʔut	ʔut

= 25-17/260d 苑 <> [T] ONW ʔut

31-9	**= K. 525**	**Mand.**	**MC**	**LHan**	**OCM**
ab	a 尉	wèi	ʔjwei^{C}	ʔus	ʔuts
c	熨	wèi,	ʔjwei^{C}	ʔus,	ʔuts,
		yù	ʔjwət	ʔut	ʔut
de	慰罻	wèi	ʔjwei^{C}	ʔus	ʔuts

慰 [T] Sin Sukchu SR ʔuj (去); MGZY 'ue (去) [ʔuɛ]

f	蔚 artem.	wèi	ʔjwei^{C}, ʔjwet	ʔus, ʔut	ʔut, ʔuts
g	褽	wèi	ʔjwei^{C}	ʔus	ʔuts

31-10	**= K. 487**	**Mand.**	**MC**	**LHan**	**OCM**
ac	兀杌	wù	ŋwət	ŋuət	ŋût
bde	扤阢卼	wù	ŋwət	ŋuət	ŋût
f	軏	yuè, wù	ŋjwɐt, ŋwət	ŋyɑt, ŋuət	ŋot, ŋût

31-11	**= K. 488**	**Mand.**	**MC**	**LHan**	**OCM**
a	𠫓	tū	t^{h}wət	t^{h}uət	thût

31-12	**= K. 489**	**Mand.**	**MC**	**LHan**	**OCM**
a	突	tū	t^{h}wət, dwət	t^{h}uət, duət	thût, dût

[T] ONW dot <> [E] TB *tu, *du > PL *m-du^{2}, WB tu^{B} dig; Lushai t^{h}ut^{H} 'suddenly'

31-13 凸 tū, tú dwət, diet — 'protrude. convex', a later graph for 31-8/489a 突

31-14	**= K. 511**	**Mand.**	**MC**	**LHan**	**OCM**
a	對	duì	twậi^{C}	tuəs	tûts

⋇ 37-6/676a. <> [T] Sin Sukchu SR tuj (去); MGZY due (去) [tuɛ]; ONW tuɑi
[E] Tai: S. tɔp^{4} 'to reply, answer'

h	轛	duì, zhuì	twậi^{C}, ṭwi^{C}	tuəs, ṭuis	tûts, truts
i	懟	duì	ḍwi^{C}	ḍuis	druts

31-15	**= K. 512**	**Mand.**	**MC**	**LHan**	**OCM**	
a	退	tuì	t^{h}wậi^{C}	t^{h}uəs	thûs	OCB *hnuts < *hnups
-	腿	tuǐ	t^{h}wậi^{B}			

'Thigh', also 'lower leg' [Tang: Han Yu; GY]

31-16	**= K. 496**	**Mand.**	**MC**	**LHan**	**OCM**	
a	出 come	chū	tś^{h}jwet	tś^{h}uit	k-hlut	'come out'

[T] Sin Sukchu SR tʂ'y (入); MGZY chÿu (入) [tʂ'y]; MTang tśʰur < tśʰuir, ONW tśʰuit
[D] PMin *tšhuit > Xiam tsʰut^{D1} <> [E] TB: JP lot^{31}-lam^{33} 'outlet', Trung klɔ̆t 'come out'; KC-Chinbok hlɔt 'come out'

	出 bring	chuì	tśʰwi^C	tśʰuis	k-hluts	'bring out'	

'nephew' [E] TB *tu ~ *du 'nephew'

f	黜	chù	ṭʰjwet	ṭʰuit	thrut < k-hrut	

[D] M-Xiam lit. tut^{D1}, col. lut^{D1}

-	朏	kū	kʰwət	kʰuət	khût	

[E] ? WT rkub 'buttocks', WB lañ-kup. Cf. 30-17/530a

o	淈	gǔ	kwət, ɣwət	kuət, guət	kût, gût	
k	屈 bend	qū	kʰjwət	kʰut	khut	

[T] Sin Sukchu SR k'y (入); MGZY khÿu (入) [k'y]

	屈 Pl.N.	qū	kjwət	kut	kut	
	屈 short	jué	gjwət	gut	gut	
pq	堀窟	kū	kʰwət	kʰuət	khût	

[E] Tai: S. kʰut^{D1}S, Saek kʰut^6 < *kʰuut 'to dig'

r	倔	jué	gjwət	gut	gut	
-	崛	jué	gjwət	gut	—	[T] BTD Skt. kūṭa
sn	掘鈯	jué, jú	gjwət, gjwɐt	gut, guɑt	gut, got	

[D] PMin *guit

lm	詘誳	qū	kʰjwət	kʰut	khut	
g	絀	chù	tjwet	ṭuit	trut	
h	咄	duō	twət	tuət	tût	
i	拙	zhuō	tśjwät	tśuat	tot	
j	茁	zhuā, zhuó	tṣwăt, tṣjwät	tṣuɛt, tṣuat	tsrût, tsrot	

31-17 = K. 497		**Mand.**	**MC**	**LHan**	**OCM**
ac	朮秫	shú	dźjwet	źuit	m-lut

[T] ONW źuit. BTD 秫代 Skt. śuddha <> [D] PEMin *tsut^{D2}, PWMin tshut^{D2} (PMin *tʃhut?) 'glutinous (rice)' <> [E] MY *nblut 'glutinous, sticky', AN pulut 'sticky substance'

deg	術述鉥	shù	dźjwet	źuit	m-lut

術 [T] Sin Sukchu SR ʐy (入); MGZY cÿu (入) [dʐy]; ONW źuit. BTD 術闍 źuit-źa Skt. vidhya, Pali vijja; 那術 nɑ-źuit Skt. nayuta; 兜術陀 to-źuit-dɑ Skt. tuṣita

i	訹	xù	sjwet	suit	slut
h	怵	chù	ṭʰjwet	ṭʰuit	rhut or t-hlut ?

31-18 = K. 502 Acc. to SW 1271 yī 一 *ʔit is phonetic.

		Mand.	**MC**	**LHan**	**OCM**	
a	聿	yù	jiwet	juit	lut	
c	律	lǜ	ljwet	luit	rut	

[T] Sin Sukchu SR ly (入); MGZY lÿu (入) [ly]; ONW luit; BTD 拘律陀 kio-luit-dɑ Skt. kolita; 阿難律 ʔɑ-nɑn-luit Skt. aniruddha

d	筆	bǐ	pjet 3	pɨt	prut	OCB *prjut

[T] Sin Sukchu SR pi (入); MGZY bue (入) [puɛ]; ONW pit

31-19 = K. 529		**Mand.**	**MC**	**LHan**	**OCM**
a	類	lèi	ljwi^C	luis	rus

[T] ONW lui; BTD Skt. -rodh- (?). MHan 蒲類 bɑ-luis Bars (*barus) <> [E] TB: WT rus 'clan, lineage' (also 'bone'), Tamang ^{3}rui 'clan', WB rui^B 'lineage' (also 'bone')

b	纇	lèi	lwậi^C	luəs	rûs	
31-20 = K. 490		**Mand.**	**MC**	**LHan**	**OCM**	
a	卒 soldier	zú	tswət	tsuət	tsût	OCB *Stut
	[T] MTang tsur < tsuir, ONW tsuit					
	卒 finish	zú	tsjwet	tsuit	tsut	OCB *Stjut
	卒 brusq.	cù	tsʰwət	tsʰuət	tshût	
b	捽	zú	dzwət	dzuət	dzût	
c	崒	zú	dzjwet, tsjwet	dzuit, tsuit	dzut, tsut	
h	醉	zuì	tswi^C	tsuis	tsuts	[T] ONW tsui
def	倅啐淬	cuì	tsʰwậi^C	tsʰuəs	tshûts	
g	焠	cuì	tsʰwậi^C	tsʰuəs	tshûts	
i	翠	cuì	tsʰwi^C	tsʰuis	tshuts	
jkl	悴瘁顇	cuì !	dzwi^C	dzuis	dzuts	
m	萃	cuì	dzwi^C	dzuis	dzuts	OCB *dzjuts < *dzjups ?
o	晬	suì	swi^C	suis	suts	
p	粹	cuì !	swi^C	suis	suts	
n	碎	suì	swậi^C	suəs	sûts	
q	誶	suì	swi^C, suâi^C, dzjwet	suis, suəs, dzuit	suts, dzut	
31-21 = K. 528		**Mand.**	**MC**	**LHan**	**OCM**	
a-	祟㲚	suì	swi^C	suis	suts or sus	
31-22 = K. 1257hm			MC	LHan	OCM	
h[n]	戌鉞	xū	sjwet	suit	sut or swit	
m	怴	xù	xjwet 3	huɨt	hwit 'reckless'	
31-23 = K. 498		**Mand.**	**MC**	**LHan**	**OCM**	
a	率 follow	shuài	ṣjwet, ṣwi^C	ṣuit, ṣuis	srut(s)	
	= 31-19/499a 帥 <> [T] ONW ṣuit					
a-	率繂	lǜ	ljwet	luit	rut 'leather band'	
	[E] TB: WT rgyud < *r-jut 'string, cord'					
h	膟	lǜ	ljwet	luit	rut	[T] ONW luit-
e	逹	shuài	ṣjwet	ṣuit	srut	
g	蟋蟀	xī- shuài	-ṣjwət	ṣit-ṣuit	srit-srut	
31-24 = K.499		**Mand.**	**MC**	**LHan**	**OCM**	
a	帥 lead	shuài	ṣjwet, ṣwi^C	ṣuit, ṣuis	srut, sruts	= 31-18/498a 率
	[T] ONW ṣuit					
	帥 leader	shuài	ṣwi^C	ṣuis	sruts	
	[T] Sin Sukchu SR ṣuj (去), PR, LR ṣwaj?; MGZY (zhway >) shway (去) [ṣwaj]					

32 OCM rime *-in Zhēn bù 真部

GSR 361 - 392

Baxter 1992: 422 ff. (§10.1.4)

Table 32-1: OCM rimes *-in, *-it, *-(t)s, *-i in QYS categories

Div.	*-in R.32	*-it R.29	*-i(t)s R.29	*-i R.26
IV	賢 ɣien gen *gîn 天 tʰien tʰen *thîn	結 kiet ket *kît 跌 diet det *lît	淠 pʰiei^C pʰes *phîts	啟 kʰiei^B kʰei^B *khîʔ 米 miei^B mei^B *mîʔ 氐 tiei^B tei^B *tîʔ
IV w	犬 kʰiwen^B kʰuen^B *khwînʔ 泫 ɣiwen^B ɣuen^B *wînʔ	穴 ɣiwet ɣuet *wît 血 xiwet huet *hwît		睽 kʰiwei kʰuei *khwî
3/4	緊 kjien^B 4 kin^B *kinʔ 民 mjien 4 min *min	吉 kjiet 4 kit *kit 必 pjiet 4 pit *pit	棄 kʰi^C 4 kʰis *khis 畀 pi^C 4 pis *pis	伊 ʔi4 ʔi *ʔi 比 pi^{B}4 pi^B *piʔ
3/4 w	鈞 kjiwen4 kuin *kwin 勻 jiwen win *win 恂 sjwen suin *swin	橘 kjiwet4 kuit *kwit 矞 jiwet wit *wit 恤 sjwet suit *swit	季 kwi^C 4 kuis *kwis 檖 zwi^C zuis *s-wis	癸 kwi^{B}4 kwi^B *kwiʔ
III ac	真 tśjen tśin *tin 人 ńźjen nin *nin	室 śjet śit *lhit	至 tśi^C tśis *tits	死 si^B si^B *siʔ 維 jiwi4 wi *wi
3/3 gr	愍 mjen^B 3 mɨn^B *mrinʔ	密 mjet 3 mɨt *mrit		耆 gji3 gɨ *gri 戣 gjwi3 gwɨ *gwri
II	矜 kwăn kuɛn *kwrîn	秸 kăt kɛt *krît 劀 kwăt kuɛt *kwrît	屆 kăi^C kɛs *krîs	階 kăi kɛi *krî

Rimes in OCM *-in, *-ən, *-un are kept distinct in *Shijing*, but they interrime in *Chuci* where we find *xiān* 先 *sîn or *sən riming with *mén* 門 *mən and *yún* 雲 *wən, *tiān* 天 *tîn with *wén* 聞 *wən, *pī* 匹 *phit with *hū* 忽 *hmət.

See Table 33-1 for a comparison of OCM rimes *-in, *-ən, *-it, *-ət; Table 31-1 for OCM *-ut, *-wət, *-wit, *-ui, *-u(t)s, *-wəi, *-wə(t)s, *-wi(t)s; Table 34-1 for OCM rimes *-un, *-wən, *-win, *-ut, *-wət, *-wit.

32-1	**= K. 368, 377**		**MC**	**LHan**	**OCM**	
377a	臣	chén	źjen	dźin < gin	gin	OCB *gjin
	[T] Sin Sukchu SR dẓin (平); MGZY zhin (平) [ẓin]; ONW dźin					
g	挋	zhèn	tśjen^C	tśin^C < kin^C	kins	
368a	臤	qìn, qiān	kʰjien^{C}4, kʰăn	kʰin^C, kʰɛn	khins, khrîn	
h	腎	shèn	źjen^B	dźin^B < gin^B	ginʔ	
d	掔	qiān	kʰien, kʰăn	kʰen, kʰɛn	khîn, khrîn	

c 堅 jiān kien ken kîn

[T] Sin Sukchu SR kjen (平); MGZY gȳan (平) [kjɛn]; ONW kėn. LH 堅昆 jiān-kūn LH ken-kuən < kîn-kûn Qyrqyz < qyrqyŕ (Pulleyblank 1983: 455)

\- 掔 qǐn k^hien^B

e 賢 wise xián ɣien gen gîn

nave xiàn ɣien^C gen^C gîns

g 緊 jǐn kjien^B 4 kin^B kinʔ

[T] Sin Sukchu SR kin (上); MGZY gȳin (上) [kjin]; ONW kiin. MC unpalatalized initial k- is irregular <> [E] ? TB: Lushai k^hirʔ^L < *k^hirh 'to tie / bind', NNaga *C-k^hyin 'to tie'

1252a 鏗 kēng k^hɛŋ k^hɛŋ khrêŋ

32-2	**= K. 1250ab**		**MC**	**LHan**	**OCM**
ab	蕑蘭	jiǎn	kien^B	ken^B	kînʔ or kênʔ

32-3	**= K. 369**	**Mand.**	**MC**	**LHan**	**OCM**	
a	矜 shaft	qín	gjen 3	gɨn	grin	~ 33-5/480 穫 *grən
	矜 pity	jīn	kjəŋ	gɨn	grin R!	OCB *kjiŋ

⋇ 32-36/3871 憐 *rîn

	矜 widow.	guān	kwăn	kuɛn	kwrîn	OCB *k^wrin

~ 鰥 kwrə̂n 34-4/481a. This graph consistently rimes with *-in in Shījīng.

32-4 = K. 479 MC $k(^h)$iwen can only derive from *kwîn or *kwên; OC *kwən would result in MC kwən; OC *kwiən, *kiwən or *kiun do not exist.

		Mand.	**MC**	**LHan**	**OCM**	
a	犬	quǎn	k^hiwen^B	k^huen^B	khwînʔ	

[T] Sin Sukchu SR k'yen (上); MGZY khwȳan (上) [k'yEn] <> [E] ST *kwiʔ: TB *kwiʔ

e	畎	quǎn	kiwen^B	kuen^B	kwînʔ	= 34-6/422b 甽

32-5 = K. 366 Throughout this series, the OC forms could be either *gwîn or *wîn.

		Mand.	**MC**	**LHan**	**OCM**	
a	玄	xuán	ɣiwen	ɣuen	gwîn	
c	泫	xuàn	ɣiwen^B	ɣuen^B	gwînʔ	
e	鉉	xuàn	ɣiwen^B	ɣuen^B	gwînʔ	
d	眩	xuàn	ɣiwen(^{C})	ɣuen(^{C})	gwîn, gwîns	
hj	炫衒	xuàn	ɣien^C	gen^C	gîns	
fgm	弦絃誸	xián	ɣien	gen	gîn	[T] ONW ɣėn
i	蚿	xián	ɣien	gen	gîn	
k	牽	qiān	k^hien	k^hen	khîn	

[D] Xiang-Shuangfeng k^hĩ^{55}, Ke-Meix k^hian^{55}, Yue-Guangzh hin^{53}, Min-Xiamen k^han^{55}

l	鮌	gǔn	kwən^B	kuən^B	kwə̂nʔ	= 34-1/417i; 34-3/419a

32-6	**= K. 1250g**		**MC**	**LHan**	**OCM**
g	贙	xuàn	ɣiwen$^{B/C}$	ɣuen$^{B/C}$	(g)wînʔ/s or (g)wênʔ/s

32-7 = K. 391 OB distinguish between 391 and 392.

		Mand.	**MC**	**LHan**	**OCM**
391a	匀	yún	jiwen 4	win	win

392j	畇	yún,	jiwen 4,	win,	win,	
		xún	zjwen,	zuin,	s-win,	
			sjwen	suin	swin	
391fg	盷旬	xuán	ɣiwen	ɣuen	wîn	
1252b	訇	hōng	xweŋ	hueŋ	hwrêŋ	
		Acc. to SW 1047, 勻 is phonetic; it also has an alternate 'reading like' xuán 玄 *(g)wîn.				
-	惸	qióng	gjwäng	gyeŋ	gweŋ	
391e	鈞	jūn	kjiwen 4	kuin	kwin	
		[E] TB: WB kʰyin 'weigh, a balance'				
d	袀	jūn	kjiwen 4	kuin	kwin	
c	均	jūn	kjiwen 4	kuin	kwin	OCB *kʷjin
j	筠	yún	jwen 3	win	win	
h	h	—				

32-8 = K. 392 OB distinguish between 32-7/391 and 32-8/392.

		Mand.	**MC**	**LHan**	**OCM**	
392a	旬	xún	zjwen	zuin	s-win	
		[T] Sin Sukchu SR zyn (平); MGZY zȳun (平) [zyn]				
ef	徇狥 all	xùn	zjwen^{C}	zuin^{C}	s-wins	[E] ? ST *wir
	cause	xún	zjwen(^{C})	zuin(^{C})	s-win, s-wins	
gh	殉侚	xùn	zjwen^{C}	zuin^{C}	s-wins	
l	洵 far	xuán	xiwen	huen	hwîn	OCB *hwin
	洵 drip	xún	sjwen	suin	swin	
		[E] ST *(r)we: Mikir arwè ~ ruwè < r-we^{L} 'rain'				
k	恂 sincere	xún	sjwen	suin	swin	
	恂 fear	xún	sjwen^{C}	suin^{C}	swins	
		[N] Xùn may be partially phonetic / semantic in 830 qióng 惸 *gweŋ ('fear') below				
m	眴 scared	xuàn,	xiwen^{C},	huen^{C},	hwîns,	
		shùn	śjwen^{C}	śuin^{C}	hwins	
	眴 delud.	xún	sjwen	suin	swin	
nst	筍簨箰	sǔn	sjwen^{B}	suin^{B}	swinʔ	
830a	惸	qióng	gjwäŋ	gyeŋ	gweŋ	
		= 23-11/256b 嬛, 9-9/843g 煢 <> [N] xūn 恂 *swin may be partially phonetic / semantic ('fear'); *-win and *-weŋ do occasionally mix in phonetic series				
392u	栒	sǔn	sjwen	suin	swin	
		The reading chūn (ṭʰjwen), LH ṭʰuin, OCM thrun belongs to a synonym 34-17-l.				
o	荀	xún	sjwen	suin	swin	
p	詢	xún	sjwen	suin	swin	OCB swjin
q	迿	xùn,	sjwen^{C},	suin^{C},	swins,	
		xún	zjwen	zuin	s-win	
r	絢	xuàn,	xiwen^{C},	huen^{C},	hwîns,	
		xún	sjwen	suin	swin	

32-9	**= K. 370**	**Mand.**	**MC**	**LHan**	**OCM**	
ade	因茵絪	yīn	ʔjien 4	ʔin	ʔin	
		[T] Sin Sukchu SR ʔin (平); MGZY Yin (平) [ʔjin]; ONW ʔiin				
fg	姻駰	yīn	ʔjien 4	ʔin	ʔin	OCB *ʔjin

i	烟		yān	ʔien	ʔen	ʔîn	= 32-10/483h 煙
h	咽	gullet	yān	ʔien	ʔen	ʔîn	
		swallow	yàn	ʔien^{C}	ʔen^{C}	ʔîns	~ 23-15/243c 嚥
		drum	yīn, yuān	ʔjien, ʔiwen	ʔin, ʔwen	ʔin, ʔwîn	
j	恩		ēn	ʔən	ʔən	ʔôn	

32-10 = K. 483		Mand.	MC	LHan	OCM	
a	垔	yīn	ʔjien 4	ʔin	ʔin	
cde	陻堙湮	yīn	ʔjien 4	ʔin	ʔin	
fg	闉禋	yīn	ʔjien 4	ʔin	ʔin	
--	諲歅	yīn	ʔjien 4	ʔin	ʔin	
h	煙	yān	ʔien	ʔen	ʔîn	= 32-9/370i 烟

32-11 = K. 1251f			MC	LHan	OCM
f	印	yìn	ʔjien^{C} 4	ʔin^{C}	ʔins

32-12 = K. 367		Mand.	MC	LHan	OCM	
a	淵	yuān	ʔiwen	ʔuen	ʔwîn	
d	婣	yīn	ʔjien 4	ʔin	ʔin	= 32-9/370f 姻

32-13 = K. 1251a			MC	LHan	OCM
a	嚚	yín	ŋjen 3	ŋɨn	ŋrin or ŋrən

32-1/377a 臣 may be phonetic

32-14 = K. 1251b			MC	LHan	OCM
- b c	猌憖 c	yìn	ŋjen^{C} 3	ŋɨn^{C}	ŋrins or ŋrəns

32-15 = K. 361 The phonetic seems to be dīng 丁 *têŋ 9-11/833a.

		Mand.	MC	LHan	OCM
a	天	tiān	t^{h}ien	t^{h}en	thîn

[T] Sin Sukchu SR t'jen (平); MGZY then (平) [t'ɛn]; MTang t^{h}ian < t^{h}ɨan, ONW t^{h}ėn; BTD Old Iranian hin- (Coblin 1994: 156). <> [D] Yue-Guangzhou ^{53}t^{h}in^{A1} 'sky', Taishan ^{33}hen^{A1}. PMin *thien, Xiamen t^{h}ĩ^{A1}. Some Han period dialects have xiǎn 顯 xen^{B}, others tǎn 坦 t^{h}an^{B} for 'heaven' (Coblin *ibid.*). <> [E] TB: Kachin puŋdiŋ 'zenith, top'; Zemi (Naga) tiŋ 'sky'

d	吞	tūn	t^{h}ən, t^{h}ien	t^{h}ən	thôn or lhôn ?

[T] Sin Sukchu SR t'un (平), PR t'ən; MGZY th^{h}in (平) [t'ən]
[E] KT: PT *kl-: S. klɨɨn^{A1} 'to swallow'

32-16 = K. 375		Mand.	MC	LHan	OCM
a	真	zhēn	tśjen	tśin	tin

[T] Sin Sukchu SR tʂin (平); MGZY jin (平) [tʂin] <> [E] WT bden-pa 'true'

b	稹	zhēn, zhěn,	tśjen(^{B}),	tśin(^{B}),	tin, tinʔ,	(Lu Deming's reading)
		diàn	dien^{C}	den^{C}	dîns	(Zheng Zhong's reading)

[N] On the different readings, see Coblin 1983: 153

c	縝	zhēn, zhěn	tśjen(^{B})	tśin(^{B})	tin, tinʔ	
de	鬒黰	zhěn	tśjen^{B}	tśin^{B}	tinʔ	= 33-15/453a 㐱
g	瞋	chēn	tś^{h}jen	tś^{h}in	thin	
h	磌	zhēn, tián	tśjen, dien	tśin, den	tin, dîn	

i	慎	shèn	źjen^{C}	dźin^{C}	dins	= 32-17/376a 昚
f	鎮 precio.	zhēn, zhěn	tjen(^{B})	ṭin(^{B})	trin, trinʔ	
	鎮 press	zhèn	tjen^{C}	ṭin^{C}	trins	
jkl	傎蹎瘨	diān	tien	ten	tîn	
m	顛 full	tián	dien	den	dîn	
	顛 top	diān	tien	ten	tîn	⋇ 9-11/833e
	[N] MTang tian < tian, ONW tėn <> [E] Miao gliŋ 'to fall'					
n	巔 top	diān	tien	ten	tîn	
p	瑱 pend.	zhèn	tjen^{C}	ṭin^{C}	trins 'jade pendant'	
	瑱	tiàn	t^{h}ien^{C}	t^{h}en^{C}	thîns	
	瑱 jade	zhèn	tjen^{C}	ṭin^{C}	trins	
o	齻	diān	tien	ten	tîn	
uv	填嵮 bl.	tián	dien	den	dîn 'block, fill up'	
u	填 exhaust	diǎn	dien^{B}	den^{B}	dînʔ	
	填 old	chén	ḍjen	ḍin	drin	
	填 subdue	zhèn, tián	tjen^{C}, dien	ṭin^{C}, den	trins, dîn	
qrs	嗔闐搷	tián	dien	den	dîn	
	[T] MHan 于闐 wa-den Hvatäna (Khotan)					
t	窴	diàn	dien^{C}	den^{C}	dîns	
x	寘	zhì	tśje^{C}	tśes	tes	
	于寘	Yú-tián	-dien	wa-den	—	[T] Hwatäna (Khotan)

32-17 = K. 376		Mand.	MC	LHan	OCM	
a	昚	shèn	źjen^{C}	dźin^{C}	dins	= 32-16/375i 慎

32-18 = K. 373		Mand.	MC	LHan	OCM	
ad	陳 d arran.	chén	ḍjen	ḍin	drin R!	OCB *drjin [T] ONW din
	陳 array	zhèn	ḍjen^{C}	ḍin^{C}	drins	
f	陣 array	zhèn	ḍjen^{C}	ḍin^{C}	drins	
g	螴	chén	ḍjen	ḍin	drin	

32-19 = K. 362		Mand.	MC	LHan	OCM	
ade	田佃畋	tián	dien	den	lîn 'field, hunt'	
	[T] MTang dian < dian, ONW dėn <> [D] Y-Guangzh t^{h}in^{A2} 'wet field' [E] TB: Bumthang Zha ^{L}leŋ, Lep. lyaŋ 'field, land'; Cuona Monpa ^{13}leŋ; NNaga *lji:ŋ 'grow(th)', JP mǎ^{31}-liŋ^{33} 'forest'					
	cultivate	diàn	dien^{C}	den^{C}	lîns	
g	甸 domain	diàn	dien^{C}	den^{C}	lîns	
	甸 = 乘	shèng	(źjəŋ^{C}), dźjəŋ^{C}	źiŋ^{C}	m-ləŋh 'carriage'	

32-20 = K. 371		Mand.	MC	LHan	OCM	
a	引	yǐn	jien^{B}	jin^{B}	linʔ	
	[T] Sin Sukchu SR in (上); MGZY yin (上) [jin]; ONW in					
c	蚓	yǐn	jien^{B}	jin^{B}	linʔ	
	[D] Min *un^{B} = 螾 33-19/450j					
b	靷	yìn	jien^{C}	jin^{C}	lins	
d	紖	zhèn	ḍjen^{B}	ḍin^{B}	drinʔ < r-linʔ	= 32-21/372 紾

-	矧	shěn	śjen^B	śin^B	hinʔ < nhinʔ	= 26-19/560i

[N] The graph is late

32-21 = K. 372

		Mand.	MC	LHan	OCM
a	縥	zhèn	ḍjen^B	ḍin^B	drinʔ < r-linʔ

= 32-20/371d 紖 — 7-16/1238b 豸 *dreʔ is perhaps phonetic

32-22 = K. 385

		Mand.	MC	LHan	OCM
afg	申伸呻	shēn	śjen	śin	lhin
h	紳	shēn	śjen	śin	lhin
j	神	shén	dźjen	źin	m-lin

[T] Sin Sukchu SR ẓin (平); MGZY cin (平) [dẓin]

l	軙	yìn	jien^C	jin^C	lins
m	電	diàn	dien^C	den^C	lîns

[E] PYao *(?)liŋ 'lightning'; < TB-Chepang pliŋh-ʔo 'lightning'

32-23 = K. 386

		Mand.	MC	LHan	OCM
a	身	shēn	śjen	śin	lhin

[T] Sin Sukchu SR ṣin (平); MGZY shin (平) [ṣin]; ONW śin. MHan 身毒 śin-douk Hinduka

d	軥	tián	dien	den	lîn

32-24 = K. 469 The MC rime is ambiguous, it could derive from OCM *-win or *-un.

		Mand.	MC	LHan	OCM
ab	舜蕣	shùn	śjwen^C	śuin^C	hwins (or hjuns ?)

[T] Sin Sukchu SR ṣyn (去); MGZY shÿun (去) [ṣyn]

c	瞬	shùn	śjwen^C	śuin^C	hwins

= 33-19/450 瞚; 26-19/560k 眣

32-25 = K. 1251l The MC rime is ambiguous, it could derive from OCM *-win or *-un.

		Mand.	MC	LHan	OCM
l	尹	yǐn	jiwen^B	win^B or juin^B	winʔ or j/lunʔ

[T] MTang iun < iuin, ONW iuin

32-26 = K. 387

		Mand.	MC	LHan	OCM
ab	粦燐	lín	ljen(^C)	lin(^C)	rin, rins
cd	鄰獜	lín	ljen	lin	rin
gij	轔鄰麟	lín	ljen	lin	rin
k	鱗	lín	ljen	lin	rin

[E] Kam-Sui *krin⁵ 'scales'

efh	甐磷遴	lìn	ljen^C	lin^C	rins
l	憐	lián	lien	len	rîn

[T] ONW lėn <> [E] ST *rin: WT 'drin 'kindness, favor, grace'; WB rañ^B- 'love'

32-27 = K. 1251ij

			MC	LHan	OCM
ij	藺閵	lìn	ljen^C	lin^C	—

32-28 = K. 388, 364, 365

			MC	LHan	OCM
388a	人	rén	ńźjen	nin	nin

[T] Sin Sukchu SR rin (平); MGZY Zhin (平) [rin]; ONW ńin

f	仁	rén	ńźjen	ńin	nin	
364a	年	nián	nien	nen	nîn	

[T] Sin Sukchu SR njen (平); MGZY nen (平) [nɛn]; MTang nian < nɨan, ONW nėn
[E] TB *s-niŋ 'year'

365a	千	qiān	ts^{h}ien	ts^{h}en	tshîn < *s-nhin	OCB *snin

[T] Sin Sukchu SR ts'jen (平); MGZY tshy̅an (平) [ts'jɛn]

ef	阡芊	qiān	ts^{h}ien	ts^{h}en	tshîn	

32-29 = K. 378		Mand.	MC	LHan	OCM	
afg	晉搢縉	jìn	$tsjen^C$	$tsin^C$	tsins	
h	戩	jǐn, jiǎn	$tsjen^B$, $tsjän^B$	$tsin^B$	tsinʔ	= 32-32/381a 盡

32-30 = K. 379		Mand.	MC	LHan	OCM
a	進	jìn	$tsjen^C$	$tsin^C$	tsins

[T] Sin Sukchu SR tsin (去); MGZY dzin (去) [tsin]

32-31 = K. 380		Mand.	MC	LHan	OCM	
ae	秦螓	qín	dzjen	dzin	dzin	[T] ONW dzin
fg	榛溱	zhēn	tṣjɛn	tṣin	tsrin	OCB *tsrjin
hi	臻蓁	zhēn	tṣjɛn	tṣin	tsrin	

32-32 = K. 381		Mand.	MC	LHan	OCM
a	盡	jìn	$dzjen^B$, $tsjen^B$	$dzin^B$, $tsin^B$	dzinʔ, tsinʔ

[T] Sin Sukchu SR dzin (上去); MGZY tsin (上) [dzin]; ONW dzin

c	燼	jìn	$dzjen^C$	$dzin^C$	dzins

[T] Sin Sukchu SR zin (去); MGZY zin (平) [zin] <> [E] TB: WT zin-pa 'be finished, be at an end', Lushai $seeŋ^H$ / $seen^L$ 'use up, consume, completely'

def	藎贐 f	jìn	$dzjen^C$	$dzin^C$	dzins
g	津	jīn	tsjen	tsin	tsin

32-33 = K. 382		Mand.	MC	LHan	OCM	
a	辛	xīn	sjen	sin	sin	[E] TB *m-sin 'liver'
k	新	xīn	sjen	sin	sin	

[T] Sin Sukchu SR sin (平); MGZY sin (平) [sin]; ONW sin < *siŋ ?

n	薪	xīn	sjen	sin	sin

[T] 薪犁 xīn-lí LH sin-li Syr (Pulleyblank 1983: 455) <> [E] TB *siŋ > WT šiŋ 'tree, wood'

oq	親寴	qīn	ts^{h}jen	ts^{h}in	tshin

[T] Sin Sukchu SR ts'in (平); MGZY tshin (平) [ts'in]; ONW ts^{h}in

h	莘	shēn	ṣjɛn	ṣin	srin

~ 32-37/484 甡; 33-25/478n 詵

g	辛	shēn	ṣjen	ṣin	srin	
i	亲	zhēn	tṣjɛn	tṣin	tsrin	OCB *tsrjin

= 32-31/380f 榛

s	櫬	chèn	$tṣ^hjɛn^C$	$tṣ^hin^C$	tshrins

32-34 = K.1241l		**Mand.**	**MC**	**LHan**	**OCM**
--	囟顖	xìn	sjen^C	sin^C	sins or səns ? 'head'
1241l	細	xì	siei^C	sei^C	sîh ?

[N] 囟 was originally phonetic acc. to GY (GYSX: 664) <> [T] ONW sėi^C
[E] TB *ziy > West Tib. zi 'very small'; Limbu ci 'little, few'; WB se^B 'small, fine'

32-35 = K. 383		**Mand.**	**MC**	**LHan**	**OCM**
a	卂	xìn	sjen^C	sin^C	sins
b	迅	xùn	sjen^C, sjwen^C	sin^C, suin^C	swins
cd	訊䒖	xùn	sjen^C	sin^C	sins

32-36 = K. 384		**Mand.**	**MC**	**LHan**	**OCM**	
a	信 stay	xìn	sjen^C	sin^C	sins	
	信 true	xìn	sjen^C	sin^C	sins	OCB *snins 'sincere'

[T] Sin Sukchu SR sin (去); MGZY sin (去) [sin]; ONW sin

	信 extend	shēn	śjen	śin	lhin

= 32-32/385a 申伸呻

32-37 = K. 484		**Mand.**	**MC**	**LHan**	**OCM**
a	甡	shēn	ṣjɛn	ṣin	srin

~ 32-33/382h 莘; 33-25/478n 詵

32-38 = K. 389		**Mand.**	**MC**	**LHan**	**OCM**
a	賓	bīn	pjien 4	pin	pin

[T] MGZY bin (平) [pin]; Sin Sukchu SR pin (平); ONW *piin; BTD Skt. -bhijñ-; MHan 罽賓 kɨas-pin Kashmir <> [E] TB: WT sbyin-pa 'to give, bestow; gift', Lepcha byí, byí-n 'to give'

j	濱	bīn	pjien 4	pin	pin
ghi	儐擯殯	bìn	pjien^C 4	pin^C	pins
k	鬢	bìn	pjien^C 4	pin^C	pins
l	繽	bīn !	p^{h}jien 4	p^{h}in	phin
mo	嬪臏 !	pín	bjien 4	bin	bin
qr	髕臏	bìn	bjien^B 4	bin^B	binʔ

[E] TB: WT byin-pa 'calf of the leg', Lushai p^{h}ei^L 'foot, leg, lower leg'

p	蠙	pín, pián	bjien 4, bien	bin, ben	bin, bîn

32-39 = K. 390		**Mand.**	**MC**	**LHan**	**OCM**
a	頻	pín	bjien 4	bin	bin

[E] ? TB: Lepcha bí 'edge, border'; WT p^{h}yi 'outside, behind, after' ⋨ p^{h}yin 'outside, later' <> ? AN: PMal.-Pol. *te(m)biŋ 'bank, shore'

-cd	瀕嚬蘋	pín	bjien 4	bin	bin

32-40 = K. 457 According to Baxter, MC mjen 3 derives from an OC medial *r syllable. But a simpler explanation may be OCM *mun, see Intro. 5.2.3 and rime 28.

		Mand.	**MC**	**LHan**	**OCM**	GYSX: 524ff
a	民	mín	mjien 4	min	min	

[T] Sin Sukchu SR min (平); MGZY min (平) [min]; MTang min < min, ONW miin
[E] ST *mi : TB *r-mi(y) > WT mi 'man, human being', Rgyarung tərmi (i.e., tə-rmi)

c	泯	mín	mjien(^{B}) 4	min(^{B})	min, minʔ

e	眠 sleep	mián	mien	men	mîn	~ 9-30/841b 瞑
	[T] MTang mian < mɨan, ONW mėn <> [E] TB *myel > Chepang mel- 'close, shut eyes', Bahing mjel 'sleepy', WB myañ^B 'be sleepy, sleep'; JP mjen^{31}-mjen^{31} 'to sleep soundly'					
	眠 befool	miǎn	mien^B	men^B	mînʔ	
f	殀	miǎn,	mien^B,	men^B,	mînʔ,	
		mén,	mwən,	muən,	mə̂n,	
		hūn	xwən	huən	hmə̂n	
d	珉	mín	mjen 3	mɨn < muɨn	mun	
jk	昬昏	hūn	xwən	huən	hmə̂n	
	[T] ONW hon <> [E] TB: WT mun-pa 'dark' ⋇ dmun-pa 'darkened' ⋇ rmun-po 'dull, heavy, stupid'; WB hmun^A 'dim, dusky, blurred'					
mno	婚惛 o	hūn	xwən	huən	hmə̂n	
pq-	涽閽殙	hūn	xwən	huən	hmə̂n	
x	緡 cord	mín	mjen 3	mɨn	mun	OCB *mrjun
	緡 cumul.	mǐn	mjen^B 3	mɨn^B	munʔ	
rs	痻 s	mín,	mjen 3,	mɨn,	mun,	
		hūn	xwən	huən	hmə̂n = hmûn	
tuv	捪 uv	mín	mjen 3	mɨn	mun	⋇ 32-35/441e 捫
g	敃	mǐn	mjen^B 3	mɨn^B	munʔ	
	[N] Karlgren writes MC mjwen 3 because of the fǎnqiè speller 隕 (with *w*).					
y	暋 violent	mǐn	mjen^B 3	mɨn^B	munʔ	
	暋 sorry	mín,	mjen(^{B}) 3,	mɨn(^{B}),	mun, munʔ	
		hūn	xwən	huən	hmə̂n = hmûn	
z	愍	mǐn	mjen^B 3	mɨn^B	munʔ	OCB *mrjən (1992: 433)
	= 32-35/441 憫					

33 OCM rime *-ən Wén bù 文部 (1)

GSR 416 - 485

Baxter 1992: 425 ff. (§10.1.5)

Table 33-1: OCM rimes *-in, *-ən, *-it, *-ət

Div.	*-in R.32	*-ən R.33	*-it R.29	*-ət R.30
I gr		根 kən kən *kə̂n 本 puən^B pən^B *pə̂nʔ		勃 buət bət *bə̂t
IV gr	賢 ɣien gen *gîn		結 kiet ket *kît	
IV ac	天 tʰien tʰen *thîn	典 tien^B ten^B *tə̂nʔ	跌 diet det *lît	
III gr		近 gjən^B giən^B *gənʔ 分 pjuən pun *pən		乞 kʰjət kʰiət *khət 物 mjuət mut *mət
III ac	真 tśjen tśin *tin 人 ńźjen nin *nin	刃 ńźjen^C ńɨn^C *nəns	室 śjet śit *lhit	質 tśjet tśit *tət
3/4	緊 kjien^B 4 kin^B *kinʔ 民 mjien 4 min *min		吉 kjiet 4 kit *kit 必 pjiet 4 pit *pit	
3/3	愍 mjen^B 3 mɨn^B *mrinʔ	巾 kjen3 kɨn *krən 貧 bjen3 bɨn *brən	密 mjet 3 mɨt *mrit	乙 ʔjet3 ʔɨt *ʔrət ?

See Table 30-1 for OCM rimes *-ən, *-ət, *-ə(t)s, *-əi in QYS categories.

After labial initials ST / PCH -un and -ən had merged at the latest by Han times and sorted themselves out according to QYS divisions: Div. I > -ən (mén 門 LHan mən), Div. III > -un (wén 聞 LHan mun). Baxter (1992: 431) tried to identify the vowel of some words with the help of *Shijing* rimes. The OC rimes *-in and *-ən have merged in MC after acute initials and in Div. II. The OC rime is therefore often difficult or impossible to determine.

There is no distinction between QYS kjən and kjen 3 type syllables in dialects, not even in Min (both PMin *kyn or *kɯn); nor do Han and Wei-Jin rimes make a distinction. However, QYS syllables of the type kjen (LHan kɨn) are used in Han Buddhist transcriptions, while QYS type kjən syllables are completely absent. Therefore these two syllable types have also been distinct in LHan, and I suggest to write LH kɨn for QYS kjen 3, and LH kɨən for QYS kjən.

OC finals as in 人 ńźjen LHan ńin *nin and 刃 ńźjen^C LHan ńɨn^C *nəns have merged in MC after acute initials, but Min dialects keep the finals separate (-in vs. -ɨn) and confirm the OC categories.

After palatal and retroflex initials, one could write either LH -ɨn or -ən (MC ṣjen < LH ṣɨn or ṣən; MC ńźjen < LH ńɨn or ńən, etc.).

33-1	**= K. 416**	**Mand.**	**MC**	**LHan**	**OCM**
a	艮	gèn	kən^{C}	kən^{C}	kə̂ns
b	根	gēn	kən	kən	kə̂n

[T] Sin Sukchu SR kən (平); MGZY g^{h}in (平) [kən]; ONW kən

[E] AA: PVM *kəl 'tree (trunk)', PMon *t[l]gəl 'stump (of tree, etc.)', Khmer găl 'tree trunk'

-	齦	kěn	k^{h}ən^{B}	k^{h}ən^{B}	khə̂nʔ

[E] ? TB: Lushai k^{h}el^{F} 'eat the outside of a thing, gnaw off'

cm-	狠墾懇	kěn	k^{h}ən^{B}	k^{h}ən^{B}	khə̂nʔ
g	痕	hén	ɣən	gən	gə̂n
de	佷很	hěn	ɣən^{B}	gən^{B}	gə̂nʔ
i	限	xiàn	ɣăn^{B}	gɛn^{B}	grə̂nʔ
f	恨	hèn	ɣən^{C}	gən^{C}	gə̂ns
h	垠	yín	ŋjən	ŋiən	ŋən
k	銀	yín	ŋjen 3	ŋɨn	ŋrən

[T] Sin Sukchu SR ŋin (平), PR, LR in; MGZY ngin (平) [ŋin]; ONW ŋin

[E] WT dŋul 'silver', WB ŋwe, PL *C-ŋwe[1]

l	眼 eye	yǎn	ŋăn^{B}	ŋɛn^{B}	ŋrə̂nʔ

[T] Sin Sukchu SR ŋjan (上), PR jan, LR jen; MGZY yan (上) [jan]; ONW ŋän

	眼 knob	ěn	ŋən^{B}	ŋən^{B}	ŋə̂nʔ

33-2	**= K. 443**	**Mand.**	**MC**	**LHan**	**OCM**
ad	斤[1] > 釿 axe	jīn	kjən	kiən	kən

[T] ONW kin <> [E] ? TB: PLB *gyan[2] 'pick-axe'

a	斤[2] perspic.	jìn	kjən^{C}	kiən^{C}	kəns	
e	靳	jìn	kjən^{C}	kiən^{C}	kəns	
f	芹	qín	gjən	giən	gən	
g	近	jìn	gjən^{B}	giən^{B}	gənʔ	

[T] Sin Sukchu SR gin (上去); MGZY kin (上去) [gin]; ONW gin

	近	jìn	gjən^{C}	giən^{C}	gəns	[E] PVM *t-kiŋ 'near'
hjk	昕忻訢	xīn	xjən	hiən	hən	
i	欣	xīn	xjən	hiən	hən	
x	焮	xīn !	xjən^{C}	hiən^{C}	həns	
y	掀	xiān	xjɐn	xɨɑn	han	
m	頎 tall	qí	gjei	gɨi	gəi	
	extreme	kěn	k^{h}ən^{B}	k^{h}ən^{B}	khə̂nʔ	
l	圻 fief	qí	gjei	gɨi	gəi	
	border	yín	ŋjən	ŋiən	ŋən	
no	肵祈	qí	gjei	gɨi	gəi	[T] ONW gi
pt	旂蘄	qí	gjei	gɨi	gəi	OCB *gjəj
-	沂	yí	ŋjei	ŋiən !		

[N] Name of a river (Luò and Zhōu 1958: 199)

33-3	**= K. 445**	**Mand.**	**MC**	**LHan**	**OCM**
a	筋	jīn	kjən	kiən	kən

[T] ONW kin <> [E] PTai *ʔi̯en$^{A1 \sim A2}$ 'tendon, sinew'

33-4	**= K. 444**	**Mand.**	**MC**	**LHan**	**OCM**
a	巹	jǐn	kjən^{B}	kiən^{B}	kənʔ

33-5 = K. 480 The phonetic element was also used to write tàn 嘆 (24-35/152) and hàn 暵 (24-10/144) because of its meaning, not necessarily because of its sound.

		Mand.	MC	LHan	OCM	
aecj	a 堇[1]艱 j	jiān	kǎn	kɛn	krə̂n	OCB *krən
	'Distress' <> [T] ONW kän					
e	堇[2] clay	qín	gjen 3	gin	grən	
-	[illegible]	qín	gjen 3	gin	grən	= 32-3/369a 矜
mp	僅瑾	jǐn !	gjen^{C} 3	gin^{C}	grəns	
noqr	墐殣覲饉	jìn	gjen^{C} 3	gin^{C}	grəns	
--	廑瘽	jìn	gjen^{C} 3	gin^{C}	grəns	
vxyz	慬勤懃廑	qín	gjən	giən	gən	
t	堇 violet	jǐn	kjən^{B}	kiən^{B}	kən?	
	aconite	jìn	kjən^{C}	kiən^{C}	kəns	
u	謹	jǐn	kjən^{B}	kiən^{B}	kən?	
-	螼	qǐn	kʰjien^{C} 4 !	kʰin^{C}	khins	

33-6 = K. 482		**Mand.**	**MC**	**LHan**	**OCM**	
a	巾	jīn	kjen 3	kin	krən	OCB *krjən

33-7 = K. 446		**Mand.**	**MC**	**LHan**	**OCM**	
a	釁	xìn	xjən^{C}, xjen 3	hin^{C}	həns	= 33-8/447a 衅

33-8 = K. 447		**Mand.**	**MC**	**LHan**	**OCM**	
a	衅	xìn	xjən^{C}, xjen 3	hin^{C}	həns	= 33-7/446a 釁

33-9 = K. 448		**Mand.**	**MC**	**LHan**	**OCM**
a	殷 great	yīn	ʔjən	ʔiən	ʔən
	殷 thunder	yǐn	ʔjən^{B}	ʔiən^{B}	ʔən?
	殷 red	yān	ʔǎn	ʔɛn	ʔrə̂n
e	慇	yīn	ʔjən	ʔiən	ʔən

33-10 = K. 449		**Mand.**	**MC**	**LHan**	**OCM**
-	𤔔	yìn	ʔjən^{C}	ʔiən^{C}	ʔəns
-	㥯	yǐn	ʔjən^{B}	ʔiən^{B}	ʔən?
-	濦	yǐn			
a	隱 conceal	yǐn	ʔjən^{B}	ʔiən^{B}	ʔən?
	隱 lean on	yìn	ʔjən^{C} [GY]	ʔiən^{C}	ʔəns
b	檃	yǐn	ʔjən^{B}	ʔiən^{B}	ʔən?

33-11 = K. 476		**Mand.**	**MC**	**LHan**	**OCM**
a	典 norm	diǎn	tien^{B}	ten^{B}	tə̂n?
	[T] MTang tian < tian, ONW tėn				
	典 solid	tiǎn	tʰien^{B}	tʰen^{B}	thə̂n?
d	腆	tiǎn	tʰien^{B}	tʰen^{B}	thə̂n?

33-12 = K. 429		**Mand.**	**MC**	**LHan**	**OCM**	
abc	[illegible] b 臀	tún	dwən	duən	dûn	[E] TB *tun

		Mand.	MC	LHan	OCM	
d	殿 rear	diàn	tien^{C}	ten^{C}	təns	
	殿 palace	diàn	dien^{C}	den^{C}	—	

33-13 = K. 455		**Mand.**	**MC**	**LHan**	**OCM**	
a	辰	chén	źjen	dźɨn	dən ?	[T] ONW dźin
	[T] Sin Sukchu SR ẓin (平), LR dẓin; MGZY zhin (平) [ẓin]; ONW dźin					
k	宸	chén	źjen	dźɨn	dən	
hi	晨 i	chén	źjen, dźjen	(d)źɨn	(m-)dən	
lm	脤蜃	shèn	źjen^{B}	dźɨn^{B}	dənʔ	
nqrs	侲娠賑震	zhèn	tśjen^{C}	tśɨn^{C}	təns	
q	娠	zhèn	tśjen^{C}	tśɨn^{C}	təns	
	The reading MC śjen has been borrowed from shēn 身 32-23/386.					
p	振 shake	zhèn	tśjen^{C}	tśɨn^{C}	təns	
	[E] Perh. TB: Chepang dhər- 'to shake, vibrate...'					
	振 numer.	zhēn	tśjen	tśɨn	tən	OCB *tjən
	= 33-14/1251h 甄					
-	桭	zhēn	tśjen	tśɨn	tən	
t	辴	chěn, chī	ṭ^{h}jen^{B}, ṭ^{h}i	ṭ^{h}ɨn^{B}, ṭ^{h}ɨ	thrənʔ, thrəi	
uv	脣漘	chún	dźjwen	źuin	m-dun	
	[T] Sin Sukchu SR ẓyn (平), CPR dẓyn; MGZY cy̌un (平) [dẓyn]					

33-14 = K. 1251h		**Mand.**	**MC**	**LHan**	**OCM**	
h-	甄甀	zhēn	tśjen^{A} !	tśɨn	tən	= 33-13/455p 振

33-15 = K. 453		**Mand.**	**MC**	**LHan**	**OCM**	
a	㐱	zhěn	tśjen^{B}	tśɨn^{B}	tənʔ	
	= 32-16/375de 鬒黰 *tinʔ					
c	眕	zhěn	tśjen^{B}	tśɨn^{B}	tənʔ	
d	畛 path	zhěn	tśjen(^{B})	tśɨn^{B}	tənʔ	OCB *tjənʔ
	offer	zhèn	tśjen^{C}	tśɨn^{C}	təns	
e	紾 twist	zhěn,zhǎn	tśjen^{B}, tjän^{B}	tśɨn^{B}, ṭɑn^{B}	tənʔ, trenʔ or tranʔ	
	twisted	shàn,zhàn	źjän^{B}, ḍjän^{B}	dźan^{B}, ḍɑn^{B}	danʔ, dranʔ (or *-e-)	
fg	袗軫	zhěn	tśjen^{B}	tśɨn^{B}	tənʔ	
i	珍	zhēn	tjen	ṭɨn	trən	
l	診	zhèn, zhěn	ḍjen^{C}, tśjen^{B}	ḍɨn^{C}, tśin^{B}	drəns, tənʔ	
j	疹	chèn	ṭ^{h}jen^{C}	ṭ^{h}ɨn^{C}	thrəns	= 33-16/452a 疢
k	殄	tiǎn	dien^{B}	den^{B}	dənʔ	OCB *dənʔ
1241s	沴	lì	liei^{C}	lei^{C}	rə̂ts	
453m	饕餮	tāo-tiè	t^{h}âu-t^{h}iet	? t^{h}ɑ/ou-t^{h}et	?	
n	跈	diàn,	dien^{B},	den^{B},	də̂nʔ,	
		niǎn	nien^{B}, ṇjän^{B}	nen^{B}, ṇɑn^{B}	nə̂nʔ, nrenʔ or nranʔ ?	

33-16 = K. 452		**Mand.**	**MC**	**LHan**	**OCM**	
a	疢	chèn	ṭ^{h}jen^{C}	ṭ^{h}ɨn^{C}	thrəns	= 33-15/453j 疹

33-17 = K. 374		**Mand.**	**MC**	**LHan**	**OCM**	
a	塵	chén	ḍjen	ḍɨn	drən	OCB *drjən (1992: 433)
	[T] ONW din <> [E] TB: WT rdul 'dust'					

33-18 = K. 451		**Mand.**	**MC**	**LHan**	**OCM**	
ac	胤酳	yìn	jien^{C}	jɨn^{C}	ləns	

33-19 = K. 450		**Mand.**	**MC**	**LHan**	**OCM**	
a	寅	yín, yí	jien, ji	jɨn, ji	jən, jəi	
h	夤	yín	jien	jɨn	jən?	
j	螾	yǐn	jien^{B}	jɨn^{B}	jən?	
	[D] Min *un^{B} = 32-20/371c 蚓					
k	演	yǎn	jiän^{B}	jan^{B} ?	jan?	
	= 24-29/197a 衍 [T] ONW ian					
-	瞚	shùn	śjwen^{C}	śuin^{C}	—	= 32-24/469c 瞬

33-20 = K. 456		**Mand.**	**MC**	**LHan**	**OCM**	
ab	刃仞	rèn	ńźjen^{C}	ńɨn^{C}	nəns	
defg	牣肕訒軔	rèn	ńźjen^{C}	ńɨn^{C}	nəns	
h	紉	rèn, nín	ṇjen, ńźjen	ṇɨn, ńɨn	nrən, nən	
i	黏 glue	nì	ṇjet	ṇɨt	nrət	
	⤮ 29-26/404 昵, 暱 *nrit					
c	忍	rěn	ńźjen^{B}	ńɨn^{B}	nən?	
	[T] ONW ńin <> [D] PMin *niun^{B} ~ nin^{B} <> [E] TB: WT gñan-pa 'to be able, (not) be able'					
-	涊	niǎn, rěn	ńźjen^{B}	ńɨn^{B}	nən?	
j	認	rèn	ńźjen^{C}	ńɨn^{C}	nəns	
	[T] Sin Sukchu SR rin (去); MGZY Zhin (去) [rin] <> [D] PMin *nin^{C}					
	[E] TB: JP non^{55} 'to think, consider', WT gñan-pa 'to listen'					

33-21		**Mand.**	**MC**	**LHan**	**OCM**	
-	嫩	nèn, nùn	nwən^{C}			[T] ONW don (!)

33-22 = K. 432		**Mand.**	**MC**	**LHan**	**OCM**	
a	存	cún	dzwən	dzən !	dzôn	OCB *dzən
	[T] ONW dzon. Acc. to SW, cái 才 *dzə is phonetic.					
b	荐 grass	jiàn, zùn	dzien^{C}, dzwən^{C}	dzen^{C}	dzôns	~ 33-23/477a 薦
	荐 repeat	jiàn	dzien	dzen^{C}	dzôns	
cd	栫洊	jiàn	dzien^{C}	dzen^{C}	dzôns	

33-23 = K. 477		**Mand.**	**MC**	**LHan**	**OCM**	
a	薦 grass	jiàn	tsien^{C}	tsen^{C}	tsôns	~ 33-22/432b 洊荐
	[D] PMin *tsan^{C} 'straw mattress'					
	薦 repeat	jiàn	dzien^{C}	dzen^{C}	dzôns	

33-24 = K. 454		**Mand.**	**MC**	**LHan**	**OCM**	
a	齔	chèn	tṣʰjen$^{B/C}$	tṣʰɨn$^{B/C}$	tshrən?, tshrəns	
	GSR has the wrong MC initial category (Coblin 1983: 240).					

33-25 = K. 478		**Mand.**	**MC**	**LHan**	**OCM**	
a	先 before	xiān	sien	sen	sôn	

[T] Sin Sukchu SR sjen (平); MGZY syan (平) [sjɛn]; MTang sian < sian, ONW sėn

[E] TB: WT bsel(-ba) 'safeguard, guide' (as escorting a convoy); Chepang ⤮ syal?- 'to lead, go, do first, open way'

	先 lead	xiàn	sien^C	sen^C	sə̂ns	OCB *səns
f	毨	xiǎn	sien^B	sen^B	sə̂nʔ	

[E] TB: WT zil 'brightness, splendor'

gh	跣銑	xiǎn	sien^B	sen^B	sə̂nʔ
i	姺	xiǎn, xǐ	sien^B, siei^B	sen^B, sei^B	sə̂nʔ, sə̂iʔ
j	洗	xiǎn, xǐ	sien^B, siei^B	sen^B, sei^B	sə̂nʔ, sə̂iʔ

[E] WT bsil 'wash'; = 26-32/594g 洒

kl	侁佺	shēn	ʂjɛn	ṣin	srən
n	詵	shēn	ʂjɛn	ṣin	srən

~ 32-33/382 莘; 32-37/484 甡

o	駪	shěn !	ʂjɛn	ṣin	srən

33-26 = K. 439		Mand.	MC	LHan	OCM
a	畚	běn	pwən^B	pən^B	pə̂nʔ

33-27 = K. 440		Mand.	MC	LHan	OCM
a	本	běn	pwən^B	pən^B	pə̂nʔ

[T] Sin Sukchu SR pun (上); PR pən; LR pən; MGZY bun (上) [pun]; ONW pon, -> Tai-Wuming pløn^C1 'volume'

[E] TB *bul ~ *pul > Lushai bul^R < *buulʔ 'beginning, base, stump', NNaga pul 'tree', Garo bol 'root, stump'; JP pʰun^55 'tree, wood', ? WT sbun ~ spun 'stalk of a plant'

33-28 = K. 438		Mand.	MC	LHan	OCM	
ad	奔犇	bēn	pwən	pən	pə̂n	OCB pun

[T] BTD Skt. pal-. <> [E] TB *ploŋ: JP pʰroŋ^33 'flee, run away', Mikir arploŋ < *r-ploŋ 'run' ⋇ iŋploŋ < *m-ploŋ 'run, gallop', Lahu phɔ 'flee', ? WB hroŋ 'flee'

e	饙	fēn	pjwən	pun	pən
f	蕡	fén	bjwən	bun	bən

33-29 = K. 437		Mand.	MC	LHan	OCM
a	賁 brave	bēn	pwən	pən	pə̂n

[E] TB: Lushai pʰuur^R < pʰuurʔ 'eager'

	great	fén	bjwən	bun	bən
	ornate	bì	pje^C	piɑi^C	paih
ef	噴歕	pēn	pʰən(^C)	pʰən(^C)	phə̂n, phə̂ns

[E] TB-Lushai pʰuʔ^L 'to blow out of the mouth (water, smoke), squirt'; WT pʰu-ba, spun-pa 'puff of breath'

g	獖	bèn	bwən^B	bən^B	bə̂nʔ	
i	See 33-28/438e.					
j	饙	fēn	pjwən	pun	pən	
h	僨	fèn	pjwən^C	pun^C	pəns	
o	濆	fén	bjwən	bun	bən	

[E] TB: Lepcha bun-rí 'an edging, frame, border'

p	豶	fén	bjwən	bun	bən	= 33-30/471 豮
qr	蕡豶	fén	bjwən	bun	bən	
m	墳 tumulus	fén	bjwən	bun	bən	

[T] MTang bvun, ONW bun

	墳 swell up	fèn	bjwən^B	bun^B	bənʔ

n 憤 fèn bjwən^{B} bun^{B} bənʔ

[T] Sin Sukchu SR vun (上), PR vən; MGZY H(w)un (上) [vun]

s 轒 fén bjwən(^{B}) bun(^{B}) bən, bənʔ

t 幩 fén, fēn bjwən, p^{h}jwən bun, p^{h}un bən, phən

33-30 = K. 471 **Mand.** **MC** **LHan** **OCM**

a 分 fēn pjwən pun pən

[T] Sin S. SR fun (平), PR fən; MGZY H(w)un (平) [fun ?]; ONW pun, BTD Skt. piṇ[ḍa], puṇ[ḍa], pūrṇa

分 fèn bjwən^{C} bun^{C} bəns

[T] ONW bun <> [E] ST *pun: JP p^{h}un^{55} 'part' (unit of weight) ⋇ p^{h}un^{33} 'part' (monetary unit), Lushai buŋ^{H} / bun^{L} 'to cut, break or divide into two or more pieces for'; WB puiŋ^{B} 'divide' ⋇ ə-puiŋ^{B} 'division, part'

ef 翁翂 fēn pjwən pun pən

d 粉 fěn pjwən^{B} pun^{B} pənʔ

[E] ? ST *pul: TB-PKiranti p^{h}ùl 'flour', WB p^{h}un 'dust' <> PVM *bu:lʔ 'dust'

h 紛 fēn p^{h}jwən p^{h}un phən

jn 雰氛 fēn p^{h}jwən p^{h}un phən OCB *phjən 'mist, vapors'

i 芬 fēn p^{h}jwən p^{h}un phən OCB *phjən

g 忿 fèn p^{h}jwən$^{B/C}$ p^{h}un$^{B/C}$ phənʔ/s

[E] Area etymon: Lushai ti^{L}-puun^{H} 'to increase (as water, wound)' <> OKhmer vva(n)i, Khmer būna /puun/ 'to amass, accumulate, to heap, stack, pile'

m 枌 fén bjwən bun bən

n 氛 fén bjwən bun bən

r 棼 hemp fén bjwən bun bən

disorder fēn p^{h}jwən p^{h}un phən

k 弅 fèn bjwən^{B} bun^{B} bənʔ

l 扮 fèn bjwən(^{B}) bun(^{B}) bən, bənʔ

o 秎 fèn bjwən^{C} bun^{C} bəns

[E] ? TB: Lushai pɔɔl^{H} 'straw'

s 盆 pén bwən bən bə̂n

p 頒 fén bjwən bun bən

頒 bān pan pan prân

q 肦 bān pan pan prân = 33-34/474c

u 份 bīn pjen 3 pɨn prən

v 貧 pín bjen 3 bɨn brən OCB *brjən

[T] ONW bin <> [E] TB: WT dbul 'poor'

\- 邠 bīn pjen 3 pɨn prən = 33-31 豳 ?

x 盼 pàn p^{h}ăn^{C} p^{h}ɛn^{C} phrîns

OCB *phrins R! (Baxter 1992: 433) 'black and white in contrast'

33-31 **Mand.** **MC** **LHan** **OCM**

\- 豳 bīn pjen 3 pɨn prən = 33-30/471 邠

33-32 = K. 472 **Mand.** **MC** **LHan** **OCM**

a 糞 fèn pjwən^{C} pun^{C} pəns

[T] Sin Sukchu SR vun (去), PR, LR vən; MGZY H(w)un (去) [vun ?] <> [D] PMin *piun^{C}

[E] WT brun 'dung', Mru prün 'manure, filth'

33-33 = K. 473		**Mand.**	**MC**	**LHan**	**OCM**	
a	奮	fèn	pjwən^{C}	pun^{C}	pəns	

33-34 = K. 474		**Mand.**	**MC**	**LHan**	**OCM**	
a	焚	fén	bjwən	bun	bən	OCB bjun

[E] TB *ploŋ > Kachin proŋ^{33} 'to be burnt (as a house)', Mikir p^{h}loŋ 'burn the dead, cremation'; Lhota ^{1}ruŋ 'burn', Mishmi lâuŋ

c	彬	bīn	pjen 3	pɨn	prən	= 33-30/471u

33-35 = K. 441		**Mand.**	**MC**	**LHan**	**OCM**	GYSX: 420
a	門	mén	mwən	mən	mə̂n	OCB mən

[T] Sin Sukchu SR mun (平); PR, LR mən; MGZY mun (平) [mun]; ONW mon < mən; BTD Skt. maṇa, manā. MHan 桑門 saŋ-mən śramaṇa <> [E] TB *muːr > WT mur 'gills'; Limbu mura 'mouth, beak'

e	捫	mén	mwən	mən	mə̂n	⋇ 32-40/457t 揞
d	悶 unconsc.	mén	mwən	mən	mə̂n	
	悶 sad	mèn	mwən^{C}	mən^{C}	mə̂ns	
f	聞 hear	wén	mjwən	mun	mən	OCB mjun R!

[T] Sin S. SR vun (平), PR vən; MGZY wun (平) [vun]; MTang mvun < mun, ONW mun

	fame	wèn	mjwən^{C}	mun^{C}	məns	
g	問	wèn	mjwən^{C}	mun^{C}	məns	

[T] MHan 疏問 ṣa-mun^{C} (*sra-məns) Skt. śramaṇa

[E] TB *m-nəm: WT mnam-pa 'to smell of'; WB nam 'stink' ⋇ nam$^{B/C}$ 'smell', JP mă^{31}-nam^{55} 'to hear, smell' <> MY *nhoM^{B} 'to hear, smell'

i	閩	mǐn, mín	mjen 3! [GY]	mɨn	mrən	

33-36 = K. 475		**Mand.**	**MC**	**LHan**	**OCM**	GYSX: 525; 527
a	文	wén	mjwən	mun	mən	

[T] Sin Sukchu SR vun (平), PR, LR vən; MGZY wun (平) [vun]; MTang mvun, ONW mun; BTD 釋迦文 śak-k(j)a-mun Skt. śākyamuni; mañ[juśrī], man-

kl	蚊 1	wén	mjwən	mun	mən	

[D] PMin *mhun

h	抆	wèn	mjwən$^{B/C}$	mun$^{B/C}$	mənʔ, məns	
j	紊	wěn	mjwən^{C} !	mun^{C}	məns	
i	汶 a river	wèn	mjwən^{C}	mun^{C}	məns	
	dirty	mén	mwən [JY]	mən	mə̂n	
qs	閔憫	mǐn	mjen^{B} 3	mɨn^{B}	mrənʔ	OCB *mrjən(ʔ)

(p. 434, tone A!)

mno	忞旻玟	mín	mjen 3	mɨn	mrən (or mun?)	忞 = 6-24/1252d
t	吝	lìn	ljen^{C}	lin^{C}	rəns	

34 OCM rime *-un, *-wən Wén bù 文部 (2)

GSR 416 - 485

Baxter 1992: 425 ff. (§10.1.5)

See Table 28-1 for OCM rimes *-un / -wən, *-ut and *-ui / -wəi in QYS categories. See Intro. 5.2.3 about the removal of OCB medial *r in some MC Div. 3/3 syllables.

Table 34-1: OCM rimes *-un, *-wən, *-win, *-ut, *-wət, *-wit

Div.	*-un R.34	*-wən, *-win R.34, 32	*-ut R.31	*-wət, *-wit R.31, 29
I	困 k^{h}wən^{C} k^{h}uən^{C} *khûns 敦 twən tuən *tûn	壼 k^{h}wən^{B} k^{h}uən^{B} *khwə̂nʔ	骨 kwət kuət *kût 突 t^{h}wət t^{h}uət *thût	汩 kwət kuət *kwə̂t
III gr		君 kjwən kun *kwən 雲 jwən wun *wən	—	
III gr			屈 k^{h}jwət k^{h}ut *khut	
3/3	菌 gjwen^{B}3 guin^{B} *gunʔ	—	—	
III ac	春 tś^{h}jwen tś^{h}uin *thun 允 jiwen^{B} juin^{B} *junʔ		出 tś^{h}jwet tś^{h}uit *k-hlut	
II		鰥 kwăn kuɛn *kwrə̂n	滑 ɣwăt guɛt *grût	劀 kwăt kuɛt *kwrît
IV gr		犬 k^{h}iwen^{B} k^{h}uen^{B} *khwînʔ 泫 ɣiwen^{B} ɣuen^{B} *wînʔ		穴 ɣiwet ɣuet *wît 血 xiwet huet *hwît
3/4 w		鈞 kjiwen4 kuin *kwin 匀 jiwen win *win 恂 sjwen suin *swin		橘 kjiwet4 kuit *kwit 矞 jiwet wit *wit 恤 sjwet suit *swit

困 *khrun rimes with 輪 *run, 漘 *m-dun, 淪 *run, 鶉 *dun, 飧 *sûn (Shi 112,3)
麕 *kun rimes with 春 *thun (Shi 23.1)

34-1	= K. 417	Mand.	MC	LHan	OCM	
a	昆 elder bro	kūn !	kwən	kuən	kûn	OCB *kun

[T] ONW kon. MHan 鬲昆 gé-kūn LH kɛk-kuən < krêk-kûn, and 堅昆 jiān-kūn LH ken-kuən < kên-kûn Qyrqyz < qyrqyŕ (Pulleyblank 1983: 455)

c-d	崐崑琨	kūn !	kwən	kuən	kûn
hij	錕鯤鵾	gūn	kwən	kuən	kûn
efg	混緄輥	gǔn	kwən^{B}	kuən^{B}	kûnʔ

k	混 chaos	hùn	ɣwən^{B}	ɣuən^{B}	gûnʔ !	= 34-13/458b 渾
	a tribe	gūn	kwən	kuən	kûn	
l	焜	hùn, kūn	ɣwən^{B}, kwən	ɣuən^{B}, kuən	gûnʔ, kûn	

34-2	**= K. 418**	**Mand.**	**MC**	**LHan**	**OCM**	
abe	a 衮袞	gǔn	kwən^{B}	kuən^{B}	kûnʔ	

34-3	**= K. 419**	**Mand.**	**MC**	**LHan**	**OCM**	
a	鯀	gǔn	kwən^{B} !	kuən^{B}	kwənʔ	= 32-5/366l

34-4	**= K. 481**	**Mand.**	**MC**	**LHan**	**OCM**	
a	鰥	guān	kwǎn	kuɛn	kwrə̂n	OCB *k^{w}rən
					~ 矜 *kwrîn 32-3/369a	
c	瘝	guān	kwǎn	kuɛn	kwrə̂n	

34-5	**= K. 421**	**Mand.**	**MC**	**LHan**	**OCM**	
a	坤	kūn	k^{h}wən	k^{h}uən	khwə̂n	= 34-6/422a 巛

34-6 **= K. 422** OCM *-wən because it explains *kwîn better than *-un would.

		Mand.	**MC**	**LHan**	**OCM**	
a	巛	kūn	k^{h}wən	k^{h}uən	khwə̂n	= 34-5/421a 坤
bc	甽	quǎn	kiwen^{B}	kuen^{B}	kwînʔ	= 32-4/479e 畎
d	訓	xùn	xjwən^{C}	hun^{C}	hwəns	OCB *xjuns

34-7	**= K. 423**	**Mand.**	**MC**	**LHan**	**OCM**	
a	髡	kūn	k^{h}wən	k^{h}uən	khûn	

34-8	**= K. 424**	**Mand.**	**MC**	**LHan**	**OCM**	
a	壼	kǔn	k^{h}wən^{B}	k^{h}uən^{B}	khwə̂nʔ	OCB *k^{w}hənʔ

34-9	**= K. 420**	**Mand.**	**MC**	**LHan**	**OCM**	
a-	困睏	kùn	k^{h}wən^{C}	k^{h}uən^{C}	khûns	
	[T] Sin Sukchu SR k'un (去); MGZY khun (去) [k'un]; ONW k^{h}on					
cde	悃捆梱	kǔn	k^{h}wən^{B}	k^{h}uən^{B}	khûnʔ	
f	稇	kǔn	k^{h}wən^{B}	k^{h}uən^{B}	khûnʔ	= 34-11/485h 稛

34-10	**= K. 425**	**Mand.**	**MC**	**LHan**	**OCM**	
acd	圂慁溷	hùn	ɣwən^{C}	ɣuən^{C}	gûns	

34-11	**= K. 485**	**Mand.**	**MC**	**LHan**	**OCM**	
a	囷 granary	qūn	k^{h}jwen 3	k^{h}uɨn	khun	OCB *khrjun
d	麕 deer	jūn	kjwen 3	kuɨn	kun	OCB *krjun
	= 34-12/459i					
e	麇 deer	jūn	kjwen 3	kuɨn	kun	
	麇 bind	qǔn	k^{h}jwen^{B} 3	k^{h}uɨn^{B}	khunʔ	
b	箘 bamboo	jùn	gjwen^{B} 3	guɨn^{B}	gunʔ	
	Cassia	qūn	k^{h}jwen 3	k^{h}uɨn	khun	
c	菌	jūn !	gjwen^{B} 3	guɨn^{B}	gunʔ	

fg	攟	jùn	kjwən^{C}	kun^{C}	kwəns	
h	稛	kǔn	k^{h}wən^{B}	k^{h}uən^{B}	khûn?	= 34-9/420f 稇

[N] *GSR* writes this type syllable MC kjwĕn, but phonemically this final is the same as -juĕt after acute initials (see below); therefore I write kjwen.

34-12 = K. 459		**Mand.**	**MC**	**LHan**	**OCM**	
a	君	jūn	kjwən	kun	kwən	OCB kjun

[T] Sin Sukchu SR kyn (平); MGZY gyun (平) [kyn]; ONW kun

g	郡	jùn	gjwən^{C}	gun^{C}	gwəns	

[E] TB: WT k^{h}ul 'district, province'

-d	群羣	qún	gjwən	gun	gwən	OCB gjun

[T] Sin Sukchu 裙 SR gyn (平); MGZY 裙 kyun (平) [gyn]; 群 ONW gun, BTD guṇ
[E] ? TB *m-kul '20' ~ *kun 'all' > WT kun

f	裙	qún	gjwən	gun	gwən	
i	麕	jūn	kjwen 3	kuɨn	kun	= 34-11/485d
j	頵	qún,	k^{h}jwen 3,	k^{h}uɨn,	khun,	
		yūn	ʔjwen 3	ʔuɨn	ʔrun !	
l	窘	jiǒng	gjwen^{B} 3	guɨn^{B}	gun?	OCB *grjun?
h	焄	xūn	xjwən	hun	hwən	

= 461 熏燻纁薰 ONW hun

-	涒 vomit	tūn	t^{h}wən	t^{h}uən	—	SW

[N] The initial MC t^{h}- has perhaps resulted through paronomastic attraction from familiar words for 'spit' and the like, like tuò 唾 and tǔ 吐; a similar case is 4-61/999tu. Mundane possibilities must be ruled out before one assumes unusual initial clusters for late OC.

34-13 = K. 458		**Mand.**	**MC**	**LHan**	**OCM**	
a	軍	jūn	kjwən	kun	kwən	[T] ONW kun
cde	暈運餫	yùn	jwən^{C}	wun^{C}	wəns	

運 [T] Sin Sukchu SR yn (去); MGZY xwin (去) [ɦwin]; ONW un

fg	輝韗	yùn,	jwən^{C},	wun^{C},	wəns,	
		xuàn	xjwɐn^{C}	hyɑn^{C}	hwans	
-	緷	yùn	jwən^{C}	wun^{C}	wəns	OCB *wjən
b	渾 run. wat.	hún	ɣwən	ɣuən	gûn	
	渾 confused	hùn	ɣwən^{B}	ɣuən^{B}	gûn? !	= 混
h	葷	hūn !	xjwən	hun	hwən	
ij	揮暉	huī	xjwei	hui	hwəi	
lmn	輝楎翬	huī	xjwei	hui	hwəi	
k	煇 flame	huī	xjwei	hui	hwəi	OCB *hwjəj
	brightness	yùn	jwən^{C}	wun^{C}	wəns	

34-14 = K. 460		**Mand.**	**MC**	**LHan**	**OCM**	
a	云	yún	jwən	wun	wən	OCB *wjən
b	雲	yún	jwən	wun	wən	OCB *wjən

[T] Sin Sukchu SR yn (平); MGZY xwin (平) [ɦwin]; ONW un; BTD Skt. -hula
[D] PMin *hiun, W-Wenzh ɦyoŋ^{A2}, Guangzh wan^{A2}

c	妘	yún	jwən	wun	wən	= 23-10/277j
e	耘	yún	jwən	wun	wən	OCB *wjən

[E] TB: WT yur-ma 'the act of weeding'

d	抎	yǔn	jwən^B	wun^B	wən?	
f	芸 a plant	yún	jwən	wun	wən	[T] BTD Skt. -vajñ-
	芸 rich	yún	jwən(^{C})	wun(^{C})	wən, wəns	
g	䰟	hún	ɣwən	ɣuən	wən̂	

34-15 = K. 461		**Mand.**	**MC**	**LHan**	**OCM**	
ad	熏燻	xūn	xjwən	hun	hwən	OCB *xjun
	[T] ONW hun					
efg	薰勳獯	xūn	xjwən	hun	hwən	OCB *xjun
hi	纁臐	xūn	xjwən	hun	hwən	= 34-12/459h 焄
j	壎	xūn !	xjwɐn	hyɑn	hwan	

34-16 = K. 426		**Mand.**	**MC**	**LHan**	**OCM**	
acd	昷溫輼	wēn	ʔwən	ʔuən	ʔûn	
	溫 [T] Sin Sukchu SR ʔun (平); MGZY 'un (平) [ʔun]; ONW ʔon <> [E] ST *ur: TB-Lushai uur^H 'to smoke, to heat, distill; to warm'					
h	薀 a plant	wēn	ʔwən	ʔuən	ʔûn	
	accumul.	yùn	ʔjwən$^{B/C}$	ʔun$^{B/C}$	ʔun?, ʔuns	
i	蘊 accumul.	yùn	ʔjwən$^{B/C}$	ʔun$^{B/C}$	ʔun?, ʔuns	[T] ONW ʔun
f	縕 floss	yùn	ʔjwən$^{B/C}$	ʔun$^{B/C}$	ʔun?, ʔuns	
	influence	yūn	ʔjwən	ʔun	ʔun	
	brown	wēn	ʔwən	ʔuən	ʔûn	
e	慍	yùn	ʔjwən^C	ʔun^C	ʔuns	OCB ʔjuns
g	韞	yùn	ʔjwən^B	ʔun^B	ʔun?	
1244e	媼	ǎo	ʔâu^B	ʔôu^B ?	ʔû? ?	
	[N] The OC vowel *u, LH -ou, is suggested by the phonetic, but it could also be *âu					

34-17 = K. 427		**Mand.**	**MC**	**LHan**	**OCM**	
af	屯[1] > 芚	tún	dwən	duən	dûn	
	'To come out, emerge' (seedling) [SW, Fayan]					
	屯[2] hill	tún	dwən	duən	dûn	
	屯[3] difficult	zhūn	ṭjwen	ṭuin	trun	
deg	忳豘軘	tún	dwən	duən	dûn	
h	沌 chaos	dùn	dwən^B	duən^B	dûn?	
	confused	tún, dùn	dwən, dwən^B	duən(^{B})	dûn(?)	
i	鈍	dùn	dwən^C	duən^C	dûns	[T] ONW don
	WT rtul-po 'dull, blunt'					
j	頓	dùn	twən^C	tuən^C	tûns	
	[T] Sin Sukchu SR tun (去); MGZY dun (去) [tun]; ONW ton <> [E] PVM *dol^A 'hill'					
	頓	dú	twət	tuət		
	Alternate reading in the name Mào-dùn 冒頓, then read Mò-dú LH mək-tuət					
n	純 envelop	tún	dwən(^{B})	duən(^{B})	dûn, dûn?	
	[E] TB: WT t^{h}ul-pa 'to roll or wind up'; Nung rədul 'roll, wrap, enwrap'					
	純 silken	chún	źjwen	dźuin	dun	
	純 border	zhǔn	tśjwen$^{B/C}$	tśuin$^{B/C}$	tun?, tuns	
l	杶	chūn	ṭ^{h}jwen	ṭ^{h}uin	thrun	= 椿 ?

k	窀	zhūn, tún	tjwen, dwən	ṭuin, duən	trun, dûn

'Thick (as darkness in a grave)' [Zuo] (also zhūn / LHan ṭun or ṭuin)

m	肫 slice	zhūn	tśjwen, źjwen	tśuin, dźuin	tun, dun
	肫 sincere	zhūn	tśjwen	tśuin	tun

[E] TB: Chepang dunh- 'be dense, closely spaced'; TB *tow 'thick' (STC no. 319) > PL *tu^{l}, WB tu^{C} 'thickness' ⋈ thu 'thick, dense'

34-18 = K. 464		**Mand.**	**MC**	**LHan**	**OCM**	
af	𦎫醇	chún	źjwen	dźuin	dun	
e	淳 flow	chún	źjwen	dźuin	dun	
	moisten	zhūn	tśjwen	tśuin	tun	
	measure	zhǔn	tśjwen^{B}	tśuin^{B}	tunʔ	
gh	錞鐓 bell	chún	źjwen	dźuin	dun	
	cap	duì	dwậi$^{B/C}$	duəi$^{B/C}$	dûiʔ, dûih	OCB dujs, dun
j	鶉 quail	chún	źjwen	dźuin	dun	
	eagle	tuán	dwân	duɑn	dôn	
l	諄	zhūn	tśjwen	tśuin	tun	
r	焞 bright	tūn	tʰwən	tʰuən	thûn	
		tūn, tuī	tʰwən, tʰwậi	tʰuən, tʰuəi	thûn, thûi	
t	啍	tūn, tún	tʰwən, dwən	tʰuən, duən	thûn, dûn	
o	蜳	dūn	twən	tuən	tûn	
s	暾	tūn	tʰwən	tʰuən	thûn	

WT'tʰon-pa, tʰon 'to come out, go out', WB pə-tʰon^{B} 'come out (e.g., the sun)'

n	惇	dūn, zhūn	twən, tśjwen	tuən, tśuin	tûn, tun
p	敦 thick	dūn	twən	tuən	tûn

[T] ONW ton. MHan 安敦 ʔɑn- Antonius; 敦煌 -ɣuɑŋ Sogd. *ðruwan, Θρόανα (Dunhuang)

	chaos	dùn	dwən^{B}	duən^{B}	dûnʔ
	numer.	tuán	dwân	duɑn	dôn
	vessel	duì	twậi^{C}	tuəi^{C}	tûih
	carve	duī	twậi	tuəi	tûi
uv	憝譈	duì	dwậi^{C}	duəi^{C}	dûih
m	犉	rún	ńźjwen	ńuin	nun

34-19 = K. 463 Originally, the phonetic was 芚 34-17/427 (Qiu X. 2000: 20).

		Mand.	**MC**	**LHan**	**OCM**	
a	春萅	chūn	tśʰjwen	tśʰuin	thun	OCB thjun

[T] MTang tśʰun, ONW tśʰuin <> [D] PMin *tšhuin

cd	惷蠢	chǔn	tśʰjwen^{B}	tśʰuin^{B}	thunʔ

[T] Sin Sukchu SR tʂ'yn (上); MGZY (蠢) chÿun (上) [tʂ'yn]; ONW tśʰuin

e	椿	chūn	ṭʰjwen	ṭʰuin	thrun	=34-17/427e 杶 ?
f	鬊	shùn	śjwen^{C}	śuin^{C}	lhuns	

34-20 = K. 462		**Mand.**	**MC**	**LHan**	**OCM**	
a	川	chuān	tśʰjwän	tśʰuan	k-hlun !	OCB *KHju/on

(rime *-un) <> [E] Area word: TB *klu:ŋ > WT kluŋ 'river'; Kachin kruŋ 'valley, dale', OBurm. kʰloŋ, WB kʰyuiŋ^{B} 'stream'

		Mand.	MC	LHan	OCM	
c	順	shùn	dźjwen^C	źuin^C	m-luns	
	[T] Sin Sukchu SR zyn (去); MGZY cyun (去) [dzyn]; ONW źuin					
e	巡	xún	zjwen	zuin	s-lun	⋊ 34-21/465f 循
f	馴	xùn !	zjwen	zuin	s-lun	
	[E] TB: WT 'čhun-pa 'be tamed, subdued' ⋊ 'ǰun-pa, bčun, gžun 'subdue, punish, soften'					
d	紃	xún, chún	zjwen, dźjwen	zuin, źuin	s-lun, m-lun	
b	軕	chūn	ṭhjwen	ṭhuin	thrun	

34-21 = K. 465		**Mand.**	**MC**	**LHan**	**OCM**	
a	盾	dùn, shǔn	dwən^B,	duən^B,	lûnʔ,	
			dźjwen^B	źuin^B	m-lunʔ	
b	楯	shǔn	dźjwen^B	źuin^B	m-lunʔ	
e	遁	dùn	dwən$^{B/C}$	duən$^{B/C}$	lûnʔ, lûns	= 34-22/428d 遯
f	循	xún	zjwen	zuin	s-lun	⋊ 34-20/462e 巡
	[T] MHan 伊循 ʔi-zuin < -s-jun (< *s-lun) Ἰσσηδόνες (Issedones)					
c	揗	shǔn, shùn,	dźjwen$^{B/C}$,	źuin$^{B/C}$,	m-lunʔ, m-luns,	
		xún	zjwen	zuin	s-lun	
d	輴	chūn	ṭhjwen	ṭhuin	thrun	
g	腯 fat	dú	dwət	duət	lût	

34-22 = K. 428		**Mand.**	**MC**	**LHan**	**OCM**	
a	豚 pig	tún	dwən	duən	lûn	
	drag feet	dùn	dwən$^{B/C}$	duən$^{B/C}$	lûnʔ, lûns	
d	遯	dùn	dwən$^{B/C}$	duən$^{B/C}$	lûnʔ, lûns	= 34-21/465e 遁

34-23 = K. 468 MC initial ji- and ts- in a phonetic series indicate OC *j- rather than *l-.

		Mand.	**MC**	**LHan**	**OCM**
a	允	yǔn	jiwen^B	juin^B	junʔ
	[T] Sin Sukchu SR yn (上); MGZY yyun (上) [jyn]				
dgh	d 狁 h	yǔn	jiwen^B	juin^B	junʔ
jk	鈗 k	yǔn	jiwen^B	juin^B	junʔ
n	沇	yǎn	jiwän^B	jyan^B	jonʔ
m	吮	shǔn	dźjwen^B	źuin^B	m-ljunʔ
	[D] PMin *d̯zion^B <> [E] ST *mlyu-n: TB *m-lyun > Kanauri *myun 'to swallow'				
t	俊	jùn	tsjwen^C	tsuin^C	tsjuns
u	焌	jùn,	tsjwen^C,	tsuin^C,	tsuns,
		zùn	tswən^C	tsuən^C	tsûns
vxy	畯餕駿	jùn	tsjwen^C	tsuin^C	tsjuns
p	夋	qūn	tshjwen	tshuin	tshjun
q	竣	jùn !	tshjwen	tshuin	tshjun
s	鵕	qūn,	tshjwen,	tshuin,	tshjun,
		jùn	tsjwen^C	tsuin^C	tsjuns
	[E] TB *yu(w) ~ yun > Lushai sa^L-zu^F 'rat', sa^L-zu^L-pui^R 'hare' = 'big rat'; JP yu^{55} ~ yun^{33} 'rat, mouse', WB yun 'rabbit'. <> [N] The graphs in this series could be reconciled if we assume OCM *tshjun with 允 *jun as phonetic.				
r	逡 draw back	qūn	tshjwen	tshuin	tshjun
	逡 rapid	xùn	sjwen^C	suin^C	sjuns

za'	峻浚	jùn !	sjwen^{C}	suin^{C}	sjuns	浚 = 34-32/466a 濬
b'	b'	cún	dzwən	dzuən	dzûn	
d'	狻	suān	swân	suɑn	sôn	
e'	酸	suān	swân	suɑn	sôn, swân ?	
	[E] TB *suːr ~ *swaːr 'sour' > Kan. sur-k, Lushai tʰuur^{R} < tʰuurʔ, Mikir tʰor 'sour'					
c'	悛	quān	tsʰjwän	tsʰyan	tshon	
f'	捘	zuì, zùn	tswậi^{C}	tsuəi^{C}	tsûih	
g'h'	g' 朘	zuī	tswậi	tsuəi	tsûi	

34-24 = K. 470		**Mand.**	**MC**	**LHan**	**OCM**	
a	侖	lún	ljwen	luin	run	
cdf	倫淪輪	lún	ljwen	luin	run	OCB rjun
	倫 [T] Sin Sukchu SR lun (平去); MGZY lun (平去) [lun]; ONW lon					
e	綸 cord	lún	ljwen	luin	run	
	綸 cord	guān	kwan	kuan	krûn	OCB krun
b	論	lùn	ljwen, lwən(^{C})	luin, luən(^{C})	run, rûn, rûns	
	[E] TB: Lushai rɔɔn^{H} 'to ask advice, consult' ≈ rɔɔn^{L} < rɔɔnh (< rɔɔns) 'to suggest, advise'					
g	惀	lún, lǔn	ljwen, lwən^{B}	luin, luən^{B}	run, rûnʔ	
hij	崙 i 掄	lún	lwən	luən	rûn	

34-25 = K. 1251op 門 *mən 'door' is not necessarily phonetic, it simply may have been intended to suggest the notion 'in between something' (cf. jiàn 間).

		Mand.	**MC**	**LHan**	**OCM**
op	閏潤	rùn	ńźjwen^{C}	ńuin^{C}	nuns

34-26 = K. 430		**Mand.**	**MC**	**LHan**	**OCM**
aim	尊樽繜	zūn	tswən	tsuən	tsûn
	尊 [T] Sin Sukchu SR tsun (平); MGZY dzun (平) [tsun]; ONW tson				
	[E] TB: WT btsun-pa 'noble, honorable'				
jkl	僔噂撙	zǔn	tswən^{B}	tsuən^{B}	tsûnʔ
	撙 [E] TB: WT tsʰul 'way of acting, conduct, right way, orderly'				
n	蹲 squat	dūn //	dzwən	dzuən	dzûn
	蹲 posture	qūn	tsʰjwen	tsʰuin	tshun
o	鐏	zùn	dzwən^{C}	dzuən^{C}	dzûns
p	鱒	zūn	dzwən$^{B/C}$	dzuən$^{B/C}$	dzûnʔ, dzûns
q	遵	zūn	tsjwen	tsuin	tsun

34-27 = K. 431		**Mand.**	**MC**	**LHan**	**OCM**
a	寸	cùn	tsʰwən^{C}	tsʰuən^{C}	tshûns
	[T] Sin Sukchu SR ts'un (去); MGZY tshun (去) [ts'un]; ONW tsʰon				
cd	刌忖	cǔn	tsʰwən^{B}	tsʰuən^{B}	tshûnʔ

34-28 = K. 434		**Mand.**	**MC**	**LHan**	**OCM**	
ad	孫蓀	sūn	swən	suən	sûn	
	[T] ONW son <> [E] ? TB *śu(w)					
ef	遜愻	sùn, xùn	swən^{C}	suən^{C}	sûns	= 34-30/433a 巽

34-29 = K. 436		**Mand.**	**MC**	**LHan**	**OCM**	
a	飧	sūn	swən	suən	sûn	

34-30 = K. 433		**Mand.**	**MC**	**LHan**	**OCM**	
a	巽	sùn, xùn	swən^{C}	suən^{C}	sûns	= 34-28/434e 遜
b	簨	sŭn	sjwen^{B}	suin^{B}	sunʔ	
cd	c 僎	zūn	tsjwen	tsuin	tsun	
e	蹼	xuăn	sjwän^{C}	syan^{C}	sons	
f	選 select	xuăn	sjwän^{B}	syan^{B}	sonʔ	
	選 promote	xuàn	sjwän^{C}	syan^{C}	sons	
	選 count	suăn,	swân^{B},	suɑn^{B},	sônʔ,	
		xuăn	sjwän^{B}	syan^{B}	sonʔ	OCB sjonʔ
g	撰	zhuàn	dẓjwän^{B}	dẓuan^{B}	dzronʔ	
h	饌	zhuàn	dẓjwän^{C}	dẓuan^{C}	dzrons	
i	譔	zhuàn,	dẓjwän$^{B/C}$,	dẓuan$^{B/C}$,	dzronʔ(/s ?),	
		quān	tsʰjwän	tsʰyan	tshon	

34-31 = K. 467		**Mand.**	**MC**	**LHan**	**OCM**	
a	隼[1] falcon	sŭn	sjwen^{B}	suin^{B}	snunʔ ?	
c	毴	rŏng	ńźjwen^{B}	ńuin^{B}	nunʔ	
a	隼[2] quail	chún	źjwen	dźuin	dun	
		Loan for 34-18/464j 鶉 'quail'; a graph may write similar sounding items with similar meaning, thus 鶉 also writes tuán 'eagle'				
d	準	zhŭn	tśjwen^{B}	tśuin^{B}	tunʔ	

34-32 = K. 466		**Mand.**	**MC**	**LHan**	**OCM**	
ab	a 濬	xùn	sjwen^{C}	suin^{C}	sjuns	= 34-23/468a' 浚
c	璿	xún, xuán	zjwen	zuin	s-jun ?	

35 OCM rime *-ap, *-ep Hé bù 盍部

GSR 628 - 642

Baxter 1992: 543 ff. (§10.3.2)

Table 35-1: OCM rimes *-am, *-ap, *-em, *-ep in QYS categories

Div.	*-am	*-ap	*-em	*-ep
I	甘 kâm kɑm *kâm 藍 lâm lɑm *râm	盍 ɣâp gɑp *gâp		
IV			兼 kiem kem kêm 溓 liem lem *rêm 拈 niem nem *nêm	頰 kiep kep *kêp 牒 diep dep *lêp
III gr	嚴 ŋjɐm ŋɨɑm *ŋam 凡 bjwɐm buɑm *bam	胠 kʰjɐp kʰɨɑp *khap 法 pjwɐp puɑp *pap		
III ac		涉 źjäp dźɑp *dap 枼 jiäp jap *lap	佔 ṭʰjäm ṭʰam *threm	
3/3	窆 pjäm^C 3 pɨam^C *prams 柑 gjäm 3 gɨam *gam !			
II	監 kam kam *krâm	甲 kap kap *krâp		
II			歉 kʰăm^B kʰɛm^B *khrêm?	狹 ɣăp gɛp *grêp 臿 tṣʰăp tṣʰɛp *tshrêp

The relationship between MC and OC finals in *-p is parallel to finals in -m, see the table. After acute initials MC -jäp can derive from OCM *-ap and *-ep; MC -iep can reflect OCM *-îp and *-êp. OCM *-âp can reflect PCH, ST and foreign *-ap or *-op; OCM *-ap (MC -jäp) can reflect PCH, ST and foreign *-ap, *-ep, and *-op.

35-1 = K. 642 For qù 去 *khah and the graphs GSR 642a-g, see 1-8; for fǎ 法, see 35-21.

		Mand.	MC	LHan	OCM	
g	胠	qū, qiè	kʰjɐp	kʰɨɑp	khap	
	The reading MC kʰjwo has been borrowed from the meaning 'enclose'					
hi	劫刧	jié	kjɐp	kɨɑp	kap	
	[T] BTD Skt. kalpa. MHan 劫貝(娑) kɨɑp-pas(-sɑ) kārpāsa					
j	怯	qiè	kʰjɐp	kʰɨɑp	khap	
no	盍盇	hé	ɣâp	gɑp	gâp	
p	嗑 shut	hé	ɣâp	gɑp	gâp	
	laugh	xiā	xap	hap	hâp	(probably not *hrâp)

qr	蓋葢 thatch	hé	ɣâp	gɑp	gâp	
	conceal	gài	kâi^C	kɑs	kâts < kâps	OCB *kats < **kaps

[T] Sin Sukchu SR kai (去); MGZY gay (去) [kaj]
[E] WT 'gebs-pa, bkab... 'to cover', JP mă³¹-kap³¹ 'lid'

s	闔 shut	hé	ɣâp	gɑp	gâp	OCB *ɦkap
t	榼	gē	kʰâp	kʰɑp	khâp	
u	溘	kè, kē	kʰâp, kʰəp	kʰɑp, kʰəp	khâp, khə̂p	
v	磕	kē,	kʰâp,	kʰɑp,	khâp,	
		kài	kʰâi^C, kʰât	kʰɑs, kʰɑt	khâts, khât	
x	饁	yè	jäp 3	wɑp	wap	

[D] PMin *jiap (or *jiat ?) 'to eat'

35-2	**= K. 629**	**Mand.**	**MC**	**LHan**	**OCM**	
a	甲	jiǎ	kap	kap	krâp	

[T] Sin Sukchu SR kja (入); MGZY gya (入) [kja]; ONW käp <> [D] PMin *kɑp ~ kap
[E] WT kʰrab 'shield, fish scales'

efg	匣柙狎	xiá	ɣap	gap	grâp	
-	呷	xiá	xap	hap	hrâp (or hâp ?)	

[E] WT hab 'mouthful', WB hap 'bite at', Lushai hap^H 'bite, snap'

h	押	yā	ʔap	ʔap	ʔrâp	

35-3	**= K. 630**	**Mand.**	**MC**	**LHan**	**OCM**	
a	夾 sides	jiā	kăp	kɛp	krêp	OCB *krep; ONW käp
	夾 handle	jié	kiep	kep	kêp	'sword handle'
d	郟	jiá	kăp	kɛp	krêp	
e	狹	xiá	ɣăp	gɛp	grêp	OCB *ɦkrep

[T] ONW ɣäp <> [D] PMin *ḫap <> [E] MY *nGep, PTai *g-: S. kʰɛɛp^D2 <> TB-JP lă⁵⁵-kap⁵⁵ 'tweezers'

f	梜	jié, jiā	kiep, kap	kep, kap	kêp, krêp	
ghi	莢頰鋏	jiá	kiep	kep	kêp	
jno	匧愜篋	qiè	kʰiep	kʰep	khêp	= 36-7/627d 慊
k	俠	xiá	ɣiep	gep	gêp	
l	挾 hold	xié	ɣiep	gep	gêp	= 35-4/639b 協
	挾 hold	jiē	tsiep	tsep	tsêp	'hold, all around'

MC tsiep may belong to a synonym 'hold'

m	浹 all around	jiá	tsiep	tsep	tsêp	
-	痰	qiè	kʰiep	kʰep	khêp	
-	瘞	yì	ʔiep	ʔep	ʔêp	

35-4	**= K. 639**	**Mand.**	**MC**	**LHan**	**OCM**	
a	劦	xié	ɣiep	gep	gêp	
bc	協叶	xié	ɣiep	gep	gêp	= 35-3/630l 挾

For 叶, see also 37-3/686.

d	拹 break	xié	xjɐp	hɨɑp	hap	
1254a	擸 break	lā	lập	ləp	rə̂p	

The reading lā MC lập has been transferred from a syn. lā 拉 'break' (GSR 1254a).

639e	脅	xié	xjɐp	hɨɑp	hap (from hrap ?)	

[T] ONW hap <> [E] JP gă³¹-rep³¹ 'rib', Kanauri *hrip, Chepang rip, WT rtsib < rhjip

f	嗋	xié	xjɐp	hɨɑp	hap

35-5	**= K. 640**	**Mand.**	**MC**	**LHan**	**OCM**
a	業	yè	ŋjɐp	ŋɨɑp	ŋap

[T] Sin Sukchu SR ŋje (入); ONW ŋap

35-6	**= K. 634**	**Mand.**	**MC**	**LHan**	**OCM**	
a	涉	shè	źjäp	dźap	dap	[T] ONW dźap

35-7	**= K. 628**	**Mand.**	**MC**	**LHan**	**OCM**
a-	𦐇榻	tà	t^hâp	t^hɑp	thâp
-	搨	tà	tâp	tɑp	—
b	蹋	tà	dâp	dɑp	dâp

35-8		**Mand.**	**MC**	**LHan**	**OCM**
-	耷	dā	tâp	tɑp	—

[E] Tai *tu:p 'hanging ears (of dog)'

35-9	**= K. 632**	**Mand.**	**MC**	**LHan**	**OCM**	
a	耴	zhé	tjäp	ṭɑp	trep	
b	輒 side	zhé	tjäp	ṭɑp	trep	'side of carriage box'
	paralysed	dié	tiep	tep	têp	
c	踂	niè	ṇjäp	ṇap	nrep	

35-10 = K. 633 The phonetic is actually 21-23/339 世 *lhats < lhaps.

		Mand.	**MC**	**LHan**	**OCM**
ade	枼葉鍱	yè	jiäp	jap	lap or lep

[T] ONW iap <> [E] TB *lap 'leaf'

h	蝶 in 胡蝶	hú-dié	ɣuo-diep	gɑ-dep	gâ-lêp

[E] TB:Lepcha ha-kljóp, WT p^hje-ma-leb < *pem-a-lep

g	牒	dié	diep	dep	lêp

= 35-11/1255a 疊; ~ 37-12/690g 褶 <> [T] ONW dẹp

[E] TB *lyap > WT ldeb 'leaf, sheet', JP gă^{31}-lep^{31} 'flat', Lushai dep^F 'flat'

fijk	堞褋諜蹀	dié	diep	dep	lêp
-	喋血	dié (xuè)	diep	dep	— (blood) flowing [Shiji]
l	擛	yè	jiäp, siep	jap, sep	lep, slêp
mn	偞 n	yè, xiè	jiäp, xjäp 3	jap, hɨap	lap, hap
o	韘	shè	śjäp	śap	lhep
p	屟	xiè	siep	sep	slêp

35-11	**= K. 1255a**	**Mand.**	**MC**	**LHan**	**OCM**
ab	疊 b	dié	diep	dep	lêp

= 35-10/633g 牒; ~ 37-12/690g 褶 <> [T] ONW dẹp

35-12	**= K. 637**	**Mand.**	**MC**	**LHan**	**OCM**
ai	巤鬣	liè	ljäp	liap	rap
cdg	儠擸邋	liè	ljäp	liap	rap

f	躐	liè	ljäp	liap	rap

[E] TB *rap > KN-Lushai rap^L / raʔ^L 'to tread (upon), trample upon'

e	獵	liè	ljäp	liap	rap

[E] TB *lip / *lep 'turtle'

j	臘	là	lâp	lɑp	râp

[T] Sin Sukchu SR la (入); ONW lɑp

-	蠟	là	lâp		—

[E] TB: Maru rap 'lac insect', Nung k'ə-rap 'wax' <> Viet. sáp 'wax'

35-13 = K. 638 The OCM vowel in some or all of these words could also be *e.

		Mand.	MC	LHan	OCM	
a	聶[1]	niè	ṇjäp	ṇɑp	nrap	
-	鑷	niè	ṇjäp	ṇɑp	nrap	[T] ONW nap

[E] ST *s-njap ~ *r-njap: WT rñab-rñab-pa 'to seize or snatch together'

b	躡	niè	ṇjäp	ṇɑp	nrap
c	讘	rè	ńźjäp	ńap	nap
d	懾[1]	shè	śjäp	śap	nhap

[E] MK: Khmer sɲap

e	攝	shè	śjäp	śap	nhep	OCB *hnjep

[T] ONW śap

a	聶[2]	zhé	tśjäp	tśap	tap
d	懾[2]	shè	tśjäp	tśap	tap

⋈ 37-12/690h 慴; 37-8/685h 慹. <> The words MC tśjäp are first attested in the Liji; they are therefore late applications of this phonetic

35-14 = K. 1255e		**Mand.**	**MC**	**LHan**	**OCM**	
e	苶	niè	niep	nep	nêp or nîp	'exhausted'

35-15 = K. 635		**Mand.**	**MC**	**LHan**	**OCM**	
ad	妾踥	qiè	ts^{h}jäp	ts^{h}iap	tshap	
ef	接椄	jiē	tsjäp	tsiap	tsap	[T] ONW tsiap
g	翣	shà	ṣap	ṣap	srâp	

35-16 = K. 636		**Mand.**	**MC**	**LHan**	**OCM**
ab	a捷	jié	dzjäp	dziap	dzap

[E] MK: Khmer, OKhmer cā'pa /cap/ 'to grasp..., seize, catch'

c	疌	jié, zǎn	dzjäp, tsậm^B	dziap	dzap
d	睫	jié	tsjäp	tsiap	tsap

35-17 = K. 631		**Mand.**	**MC**	**LHan**	**OCM**	
ab	臿插	chā	tṣ^{h}ăp	tṣ^{h}ɛp	tshrêp	OCB *tshrjop

= 扱 1254b

c	歃	shà	ṣăp, ṣjäp	ṣɛp, ṣap	srêp, srep

[E] Tai: S. čap^4 'to smear over, paint'

35-18 = K. 1254b		**Mand.**	**MC**	**LHan**	**OCM**	
b	扱	chā	tṣ^{h}ăp	tṣ^{h}ɛp	tshrêp	= 35-17/631a 臿

The element 及 'reach' is perh. partially semantic. See also 37-2/681.

35-19 = K. 1255c		**Mand.**	**MC**	**LHan**	**OCM**	
c	燮	xiè	siep	sep	sêp or sîp	'harmonious; march'

35-20 = K. 641		**Mand.**	**MC**	**LHan**	**OCM**
a	乏	fá	bjwɐp	buɑp	bap

[T] MTang bvuap, ONW buap < bap <> [E] WT 'bab-pa (< *ɴbab), babs 'fall down' ⋇ 'bebs-pa (< *ɴbebs), p^{h}ab 'to throw down' = 氾

b	泛	fàn	p^{h}jwɐm^{C}	p^{h}uɑm^{C}	phams

=36-27/626c 氾; 36-26/625f 汎 <> [E] WT 'byam-pa < *ɴbjam 'to flow over, be diffused'

d	貶	biǎn	pjäm^{B} 3, pjɐm^{B}	pɨam^{B}	pramʔ

[E] TB: OTib. 'p^{h}am-ba, p^{h}am 'to be diminished'

c	窆	biǎn,	pjäm^{C} 3,	pɨam^{C},	prams
		bèng	pəŋ^{C}	pəŋ^{C}	pə̂ms

35-21 = K. 642		**Mand.**	**MC**	**LHan**	**OCM**
lk	灋法	fǎ	pjwɐp	puɑp	pap

[T] Sin Sukchu SR fa (入); ONW pap > puap. 法 is a later simplification, hence qù 去 *khah is not phonetic.

36 OCM rime *-am, *-em Tán bù 談部

GSR 606 - 627

Baxter 1992: 537 ff. (§10.3.1)

See Table 35-1 for OCM rimes *-am, *-ap, *-em, *-ep in QYS categories.
Words in MC -jäm after acute initials (sjäm, tśjäm, etc.) can derive from OCM *-am and *-em; MC -iem can reflect OCM *-îm and *-êm.

OCM *-âm can correspond to PCH, ST and foreign *-am or *-om; OCM *-am (MC -jäm) can reflect PCH, ST and foreign *-am, *-em, and *-om.

36-1	**= K. 606**	**Mand.**	**MC**	**LHan**	**OCM**	
acd	甘泔d	gān	kâm	kɑm	kâm	
	[T] Sin Sukchu SR kam (平), PR kan; MGZY gam (平) [kam]; ONW kɑm					
	[E] TB *klum 'sweet', OCM *kâm < *klam (prob. < **kluam < **klom)					
g	酣	hān	ɣâm	gɑm	gâm	
hi	拑鉗	qián	gjäm 3	gɨam	gam	[D] PMin *ghiam 'pincers'
jl	柑箝	qián	gjäm 3	gɨam	gam	
k	紺	gàn	kậm^C	kəm^C	kə̂ms < kləms	
	[E] PTai *kləm^{B1} 'dark red, purple, dark, black' <> AN *kelam 'dark'					

36-2	**= K. 607**	36-1 was originally not part of the graph and therefore not phonetic.				
		Mand.	**MC**	**LHan**	**OCM**	
a	敢	gǎn	kâm^B	kɑm^B	kâmʔ	
	[T] Sin Sukchu SR kam (上), PR kan; MGZY gam (上) [kam]; ONW kɑm					
	[E] ST *k-wam: TB *hwam 'dare'					
d	闞 Pl.N.	kàn	kʰâm^C	kʰɑm^C	khâms	
	闞 roar	xiǎn, hǎn	xăm^B, xam^B, xâm^B	ham^B	hâmʔ, hrâmʔ or hrəmʔ	
	[E] Area word: MK-PMonic *grəəm > Nyah Kur 'to growl (of tiger or dog)' <> TB-Lai hraam 'to growl, groan'					
e	矙	kàn	kʰâm^C	kʰɑm^C	khâms	
f	厰	kǎn, tǎn, yín	kʰâm^B, tʰâm^B, ŋjəm	kʰɑm^B, tʰɑm^B, ŋɨm	khâmʔ, thâmʔ ? (or rhâmʔ ?), ŋəm	
h	嚴	yán	ŋjɐm	ŋɨɑm	ŋam	OCB *ng(r)jam
	[T] Sin Sukchu SR jem (平), PR, LR jen; MGZY ngem (平) [ŋɛm]; ONW ŋam					
l	巖	yán	ŋam	ŋam	ŋrâm	~ 36-6/613fg 險嶮
	[T] ONW ŋäm <> [E] TB: WT rŋams-pa 'height'					
k	儼	yǎn	ŋjɐm^B	ŋɨɑm^B	ŋamʔ	OCB *ng(r)jomʔ (?)
m	玁	xiǎn	xjäm^B	hɨam^B	hamʔ (or hŋamʔ)	

36-3	= K. 608	Mand.	MC	LHan	OCM	
a	銜	xián	ɣam	gam	grâm	

38-3/652a 金 is probably partially phonetic

36-4	= K. 624	Mand.	MC	LHan	OCM	
a	欠	qiàn	k^{h}jɐm^C	k^{h}ɨɑm^C	khams	

[T] Sin S. SR k'jem (去), PR, LR k'jen; MGZY khem (去) [k'ɛm] <> [E] TB *kam 'to yawn'

c	芡	jiàn,	gjäm^B 3 !,	gɨam^C	gams	
		qiàn	gjɐm^C			
d	坎	kǎn	k^{h}ậm^B	k^{h}əm^B	khə̂mʔ	= 38-5/672e 埳
-	砍	kǎn	k^{h}ậm^B	'to chop' (wood, a tree)'		

[D] PMin *kham^B 砍 'chop' <> [E] ST *kəm: TB-Chepang k^{h}amh- 'fell tree'

36-5	= K. 609	Mand.	MC	LHan	OCM	
a	監^1 see	jiān	kam(^{C})	kam	krâm	
ac	監^{2}鑑 m.	jiàn	kam^C	kam^C	krâms	'mirror'

[T] Sin Sukchu SR kjam (去), PR (kjan), LR kjen; MGZY (gȳam >) gyam (去) [kjam]

	鑑 basin	hàn	ɣam^C	gam^C	grâms	
d	礛	jiān	kam	kam	krâm	
e-f	嚂壏檻	hǎn !	ɣam^B	gam^B	grâmʔ	
g	檻	jiàn, hàn	ɣam^B, ɣâm^B	gam^B, gɑm^B	grâmʔ, gâmʔ	

[E] TB: WB k^{h}ram 'fence, enclosure' ⋈ ə-ram 'fence forming an enclosure'

k	藍	lán	lâm	lɑm	râm	OCB *g-ram

[T] ONW lɑm <> [D] PMin *lam <> [E] Area word: AN *taɣum 'indigo'; PTai *gram^{A2} 'indigo' <> WT rams 'indigo', WT ram(-pa) 'quick grass', Mru charam 'indigo'

- -	籃襤	lán	lâm	lɑm	râm	籃 OCB *g-ram

籃 [D] Min *l̥am: Jiànōu saŋ^{C1} 'basket'

l	覽	lǎn	lâm^B	lɑm^B	râmʔ	

[T] TB: JP mă^{31}-ram^{55} 'to observe, view'

oi	攬擥	lǎn	lâm^B	lɑm^B	râmʔ	

[D] Gan-Nanchang lɔn^{213}, Ke-Meix nam^{31} 揇 (tone B), Yue-Guangzh lam^{23} (tone B), Min-Xiamen lam^{51} (B) <> [E] Area: TB-Lushai hrɔɔm^R < hrɔɔmʔ 'grip, grasp' <> Tai: S. rɔɔm^{A2} < *rɔm^A 'to collect, gather together' <> AA: OKhmer rāma /ríiəm/ 'to gather'

h	爁	làn	lâm^C	lɑm^C	râms	
j	濫 overflow	làn	lâm^C	lɑm^C	râms	
	join	lǎn	lâm^B	lɑm^B	râmʔ	
	tub	hàn	ɣâm^C	gɑm^C	gâms	
m	嚂	hǎn	xâm^B	hɑm^B	hâmʔ	
n	鹽 salt	yán	jiäm	jam	jam < r-jam	

[T] Sin Sukchu SR jem (平), PR, LR jen; MGZY yem (平) [jɛm]; ONW iam. BTD Skt. yama, -śām[-bi] <> [D] PMin *ziem 'a white encrustation formed from saltwater or brine'
[E] TB: WT rgyam-ts^{h}wa < *r-jam 'a kind of salt', WB yam^B 'saltpeter'

	鹽 to salt	(yàn	jiäm^C)	jam^C	jams	[D] PMin *ziem^{C2}

36-6	= K. 613	Mand.	MC	LHan	OCM	
a	僉	qiān	ts^{h}jäm	ts^{h}iam	tsham < k-sam	

[N] Three XS point to a very early cluster *k-s... > *tsh... and *s-k... > *kh...: 36-6/613; 20-1/279; 20-11/309; see EDOC §5.9.1; see §5.8.1 for *s-k... > *kh...

bc	憸譣	qiān,	tsʰjäm(^{B}),	tsʰiam(^{B}),	tsham(ʔ) < k-sam(ʔ),	
		xiān	sjäm	siam	sam	
i	劍	jiàn	kjɐm^{C}	kɨɑm^{C}	kams	[T] ONW kam
d	檢	jiǎn	kjäm^{B}, kjɐm^{B}	kɨam^{B}	kamʔ	
e	儉	jiǎn	gjäm^{B}	gɨam^{B}	gamʔ	
	[E] TB: Lushai kaam^{H} 'to decrease (as water, wages, etc.)' ⋈ kiam^{R} 'to lessen, to reduce'					
-	臉	liǎn	lǎm^{B} [GY],			
			kjäm^{B}	kɨam^{B}	kramʔ	
	[E] Tai: S. kɛɛm^{C1} 'cheek'. TB: WT 'gram-pa 'cheek', 'gram-rus 'cheekbone, jawbone'					
fg	險嶮	xiǎn	xjäm^{B} 3,	hɨam^{B},	hŋramʔ	~ 36-2/607l 巖
			xjɐm^{B}	hɨɑm^{B}		
h	驗	yàn	ŋjäm^{C}	ŋɨam^{C}	ŋrams	
k	獫	lián	ljäm($^{B/C}$)	liam($^{B/C}$)	ram, ramʔ, rams	
l	斂 accumul.	liǎn	ljäm$^{B/C}$	liam$^{B/C}$	ramʔ, rams	
	斂 enshroud	liàn	ljäm^{C}	liam^{C}	rams	
	[E] AA: OKhmer rum [rum] 'to wind, roll, coil, surround, encircle, wrap (a corpse)'					
m	蘞	liǎn	ljäm(^{B})	liam(^{B})	ram, ramʔ	

36-7	**= K. 627**	**Mand.**	**MC**	**LHan**	**OCM**	
a	兼	jiān	kiem(^{C})	kem(^{C})	kêm, kêms	
	[T] ONW kėm <> [E] MK: PMonic *ckiəm, OMon ckem 'to grasp, pick up'					
b	蒹	jiān	kiem	kem	kêm	
d	慊 dissatisf.	qiǎn	kʰiem^{B}	kʰem^{B}	khêmʔ	
	慊 satisfied	qiè	kʰiep	kʰep	khêp	= 35-3/630n 愜
c	嗛	qiǎn	kʰiem^{B},	kʰem^{B},	khêmʔ,	
			ɣiem^{B}	gem^{B}	gêmʔ	
e	歉	qiàn	kʰiem^{B},	kʰem^{B},	khêmʔ,	
	歉		kʰăm$^{B/C}$	kʰɛm$^{B/C}$	khrêmʔ, khrêms	
f	謙	qiān	kʰiem	kʰem	khêm	
j	嫌	xián	ɣiem	gem	gêm	
k	鼸	xiàn	ɣiem^{B}	gem^{B}	gêmʔ	
g	溓	lián	liem	lem	rêm	
	[N] GSR nián is a ghost reading (Coblin 1983: 151).					
i	熑	lián	liem, ljäm	lem, liam	rêm, rem	
l	廉	lián	ljäm	liam	rem	
	[T] ONW liam <> [E] Tai: S. liam^{B1} (WSiam hli:am]					
mn	磏鐮	lián	ljäm	liam	rem	

36-8	**= K. 614**	**Mand.**	**MC**	**LHan**	**OCM**	
a	奄	yǎn	ʔjäm^{B} 3	ʔɨam^{B}	ʔamʔ	
	= 36-9/615ab 弇揜 [T] ONW ʔam. MHan 奄蔡 ʔɨam^{B}-sɑ^{C} Abzoae, Ἀόρσιοι					
-	唵	ǎn	ʔậm^{B}	ʔəm^{B}	ʔə̂mʔ	[T] ONW ʔɑm
-	庵	ān	ʔậm, ʔập	ʔəm, ʔəp	ʔə̂m, ʔə̂p	
b	掩	yǎn	ʔjäm^{B} 3, ʔjɐm^{B}	ʔɨam^{B}	ʔamʔ	
c	淹	yān	ʔjäm 3	ʔɨam	ʔam	
e	晻	yǎn,	ʔjäm^{B} 3,	ʔɨam^{B},	ʔamʔ,	
		ǎn	ʔậm^{B}	ʔəm^{B}	ʔə̂mʔ	

d	閹	yān, yǎn	ʔjäm(^{B}) 3, ʔjɐm^B	ʔɨam(^{B})	ʔamʔ	
-	晻	yè	ʔjɐp	ʔiɑp	ʔap	

[E] TB: WT yab-pa ~ g-yab-pa (< *g-ʔjap) 'to lock, cover over', yab-yab-pa 'hide, conceal'

-	黤	yǎn	ʔăm^B	ʔɛm^B	ʔrə̂mʔ	= 38-4/671k

36-9	**= K. 615**	**Mand.**	**MC**	**LHan**	**OCM**	
a	弇	yǎn	ʔjäm^B 3, kəm^B	ʔɨam^B	ʔamʔ	= 揜; 36-8 奄
b	揜	yǎn	ʔjäm^B 3	ʔɨam^B	ʔamʔ	

= 弇; 36-8 奄 [T] ONW ʔam

c	渰	yǎn	ʔjäm^B, ʔjɐm^B	ʔɨam^B	ʔamʔ	
d	黭	yǎn	ʔậm^B	ʔəm^B	ʔə̂mʔ	

36-10	**= K. 616**	**Mand.**	**MC**	**LHan**	**OCM**
ad	猒饜	yàn	ʔjiäm(^{C}) 4	ʔiam(^{C})	ʔem, ʔems

[T] ONW ʔiam <> [E] PTai *ʔim^{B1} 'full, satiated'

c	厭 satiate	yàn	ʔjiäm^C 4	ʔiam^C	ʔems
	content	yān	ʔjiäm 4	ʔiam	ʔem
	cover	yǎn	ʔăm^B	ʔɛm^B	ʔrêmʔ
	press	yè	ʔjäp 4	ʔiap	ʔep
e	懕	yān	ʔjiäm 4	ʔiam	ʔem
g	擪	yǎn, yè	ʔjiäm^B 4, ʔjäp 4	ʔiam^B, ʔiap	ʔemʔ, ʔep
-f	黶檿	yǎn	ʔjiäm^B 4	ʔiam^B	ʔemʔ
h	壓	yā	ʔap	ʔap	ʔrâp

[T] Sin Sukchu SR ʔja (入) <> [D] M-Xiam col. ɑʔ^{D1}, ɑʔ^{D2}, lit. ɑp^{D1}

36-11	**= K. 619**	**Mand.**	**MC**	**LHan**	**OCM**	
ab	詹噡	zhān	tśjäm	tśam	tam	[E] TB *C-lam
c	瞻	zhān	tśjäm	tśam	tam	OCB *tjam

~ 占 36-12/618a

d	幨 cut out	chān	tś^{h}jäm	tś^{h}am	tham
	coat	chàn	tś^{h}jäm^C	tś^{h}am^C	thams
e	襜	chān	tś^{h}jäm	tś^{h}am	tham
f	贍	shàn	źjäm^C	dźam^C	dams
mn	憺澹	dàn	dâm$^{B/C}$	dɑm$^{B/C}$	dâmʔ, dâms (or dlâmʔ/s ?)
l	膽	dǎn	tâm^B	tɑm^B	tâmʔ < tlamʔ

[T] ONW tśam <> [E] AA: PNBahn. *klàm 'liver', PVM *lɔːm, Katuic *luɑm; on the other hand, there is the form PPal. *kəntɔːm 'liver'

hi	儋甔	dān	tâm	tɑm	tâm < tlam
k	擔 carry	dān	tâm	tɑm	tâm < tlam

[T] ONW tɑm <> [D] PMin *tɑm 'to carry'

	擔 burden	dàn	tâm^C	tɑm^C	tâms

[D] PMin tɑm^C 'a load' <> [E] Area word: Khmuʔ klam 'carry on the shoulder', PWa *klɐm <> Kam-Tai: PT *t^{h}r-: S. haam^{A1} 'two or more people carry' <> WB t^{h}am^B 'to carry on the shoulder', JP t^{h}am^{55} 'carry'

	擔 function	shàn	źjäm	dźam	dam
g	檐	yán	jiäm	jam	lam

36-12 = K. 618		**Mand.**	**MC**	**LHan**	**OCM**	
a	占	zhān	tśjäm	tśam	tem	OCB *tjem
	[T] ONW tśam. BTD Skt. cam- ~ 瞻 36-11/619c					
cd	沾霑	zhān	ṭjäm	ṭam	trem	
	[T] MTang ṭam, ONW tam <> [E] AA: Khmer /tram/ 'to soak, steep'					
f	佔	chān	ṭ^{h}jäm	ṭ^{h}am	threm	
g	覘	chān	ṭ^{h}jäm(^{C})	ṭ^{h}am(^{C})	threm, threms	
h	怗 discord.	zhān !	tś^{h}jäm	tś^{h}am	them	
	submit	tiē	t^{h}iep	t^{h}ep	thêp	
j	痁	diàn,	tiem^{C},	tem^{C},	têms,	
		shān	śjäm(^{C})	śam(^{C})	lhem, lhems	
k	坫	diàn	tiem^{C}	tem^{C}	têms	
lm	玷刮	diàn	tiem$^{B/C}$	tem$^{B/C}$	têmʔ, têms	
n	點	diǎn	tiem^{B}	tem^{B}	têmʔ	
e	阽	yán	jiäm	jam	lem	
-	煔	shǎn	śjäm^{B}	śam^{B}	lhemʔ	= 36-14/617i 覢
i	苫	zhān !	śjäm(^{C})	śam(^{C})	lhem, thems	
pq	呫帖	tiē	t^{h}iep	t^{h}ep	— (*nhêp)	'to taste'
	呫 [Yupian: Guliang] <> [E] WT sñab-pa 'to taste, savor'					
-	貼	tiē	t^{h}iep	—	'To stick to, glue to' [GY]	
o	拈	niān !	niem	nem	nêm	
-	黏	nián	ṇjäm	ṇem ?	—	

36-13 = K. 1247a		**Mand.**	**MC**	**LHan**	**OCM**
ab	a 豔	yàn	jiäm^{C}	jam^{C}	jams < r-jams
	[E] Tai: S. riam^{B2} 'beautiful'				

36-14 = K. 617		**Mand.**	**MC**	**LHan**	**OCM**
a	炎[1] blaze	yán	jiäm 4 [JY]	jam	lam
	[T] ONW iam <> [E] ST and area word: TB *(s-)lyam > Tamang me-lahm 'flame' (me 'fire'), Lepcha lim 'to flame up' ⋟ ă-lim 'flame'; JP lam^{31} 'to flash'				
	炎[2] brilliant	tán	dâm	dɑm	lâm
	炎[3] blaze	yán	jäm 3 [GY]	wam	wam
	[N] Early MC wiam (Pulleyblank) <> [E] TB: Lushai vaam^{L} / vam^{F} 'red-hot glowing' <> Tai: S. wɛɛm^{A2} in wɔɔm^{A2}-wɛɛm^{A2} 'brilliant, glowing (of fire)' <> Sino-Vietn. viêm				
c	錟	yàn	jiäm^{B}, jiäm^{C}	jam^{B}	lamʔ or jamʔ ? = 剡
def	剡掞琰	yǎn	jiäm^{B}	jam^{B}	lamʔ or jamʔ ? = 錟
	[E] ST *r-jam 'sharp' = 38-16/646a 覃				
k	惔	tán	dâm	dɑm	lâm
l	談	tán	dâm	dɑm	lâm
	[T] Sin Sukchu SR dam (平), PR dan; MGZY tam (平) [dam]				
o	淡	dàn	dâm$^{B/C}$	dɑm$^{B/C}$	lâmʔ, lâms
	[D] Yue-Guǎngzh t^{h}a:m^{B} 'insipid'				
p	餤	tán, yán	dâm, jiäm	dɑm, jam	lâm, lam
m	倓	tán, dàn	dâm(^{C})	dɑm(^{C})	lâm, lâms
n	啖	dàn	dâm^{B}	dɑm^{B}	lâmʔ
	~ 38-5/672k 啗; 38-16/646f 嘾				
j	菼	tǎn	t^{h}âm^{B}	t^{h}ɑm^{B}	lhâmʔ

i-	覢䀈	shǎn	śjäm^B	śam^B	lham?	=36-15 閃

[T] Sin Sukchu SR ʂjem (上); MGZY shem (上去) [ʂɛm]; ONW śam

g	裧	chān	tś^{h}jäm	tś^{h}am	k-hlam
h	燅	xián	zjäm	ziam	s-lam

= 36-16/646d 燂; 38-5/672o 爓 <> [E] TB: WT slam-pa 'to parch'

--	䀈烒	tiǎn	t^{h}iem$^{B/C}$	t^{h}em$^{B/C}$	lhêm?, lhêms

36-15		Mand.	MC	LHan	OCM	
-	閃	shǎn	śjäm^B	śam^B	lham?	= 36-14/617i 覢

[T] Sin Sukchu SR ʂjem (上); MGZY shem (上去) [ʂɛm]; ONW śam

36-16 = K. 621 'Tongue' 舌 in this group is more semantic ('pointed, lick, sweet') than phonetic.

		Mand.	MC	LHan	OCM	
a	銛	xiān	sjäm	siam	sem	

[E] TB *syam > WB saṁ, Rgyarung śom 'iron', Nung śam 'iron, sword'

-	甜	tián	diem	dem	lêm	OCB *līm sweet

[E] TB *lim 'sweet'

b	恬	tián	diem	dem	lêm

[E] TB: Lepcha glyám 'be calm, to calm', Lushai thleem^R 'to comfort, pacify'

36-17 = K. 1247c		Mand.	MC	LHan	OCM	
c	忝	tiǎn	t^{h}iem$^{B/C}$	t^{h}em$^{B/C}$	lhêm?, lhêms	
-	舔	tiǎn	t^{h}iem^B	t^{h}em^B	lhêm?	OCB *hlīm? lick

[D] Yue: Guǎngzh li:m^{B1} (< *lim?) 'lick'

[E] TB *(s-)lyam 'tongue', Kanauri lem 'lick'. <> KS: Mulam *lja:m^5 'lick'

-	添	tiān	t^{h}iem	t^{h}em	—

[D] PMin *diem^B 'full' <> PTai *tl- > S. tem^{A1} 'full'

36-18 = K. 622		Mand.	MC	LHan	OCM
ab	a 冉	rǎn	ńźjäm^B	ńam^B	nam?
e	呥 to chew	rán	ńźjäm	ńam	nam
f	姌	rǎn,	ńźjäm^B,	ńam^B,	nem?,
		niǎn	niem^B	nem^B	nêm?
h	袡	rán	ńźjäm	ńam	nam
jk	顃髯	rán	ńźjäm(^{C})	ńam(^{C})	nam, nams
l	枏	nán	nậm	nəm	nəm
mn	聃	dān!, nán	t^{h}âm, nâm	t^{h}ɑm, nɑm	nhâm, nâm

36-19 = K. 623		Mand.	MC	LHan	OCM
a	染	rǎn	ńźjäm$^{B/C}$	ńam$^{B/C}$	nam?, nams

[T] Sin Sukchu SR rjem (上去); MGZY 'em [> rem] (上去) [rɛm]; ONW ńam

[E] Tai: PTai *ńuɔm^{C2} 'to dye'; Old Sino-Viet. nhuom

36-20		Mand.	MC	LHan	OCM
-	尖	jiān	tsjäm	tsiam	tsam or tsem= 36-21/620 鐵

36-21 = K. 620 The OC rime could be either *-am or *-em.

		Mand.	MC	LHan	OCM	
af-	𢦏殲鑯	jiān	tsjäm	tsiam	tsam	鑯 = 36-20 尖
g	瀸	jiān	tsjäm	tsiam	tsam	
	= 36-22/611f 漸; 38-11/658l 湛					
e	纖[1] prick	jiān	tsjäm	tsiam	tsam	
	纖[2] fine	xiān	sjäm	siam	sam	
cd	韱孅	xiān	sjäm	siam	sam	
h	攕	xiān, shān	ṣăm	ṣɛm	srêm	

36-22 = K. 611

		Mand.	MC	LHan	OCM	
a	斬	zhǎn	tṣăm^{B}	tṣɛm^{B}	tsrâmʔ	OCB *tsrjamʔ
c	慙	cán	dzâm	dzɑm	dzâm	
de	暫蹔	zhàn !	dzâm^{C}	dzɑm^{C}	dzâms	
g	塹	qiàn	ts^{h}jäm^{C}	ts^{h}iam^{C}	tshams	
f	漸 moisten	jiān	tsjäm	tsiam	tsam	
	= 36-21/620g 瀸; 38-11/658l 湛					
	漸 gradual	jiàn	dzjäm^{B}	dziam^{B}	dzamʔ	
	[E] AA: Khmer jāṃ /coəm/ 'wet, soaked, permeated, steeped'					
	漸 craggy	chán	dẓam	dẓam	dzrâm	
h	蔪	jiàn	dzjäm^{B}	dziam^{B}	dzamʔ	
	[E] TB: WT sdom-pa, bsdams 'to bind, tie up'					
b	摲	shān, shàn	ṣam	ṣam	srâm	= 36-25/610a 芟
	[E] TB: Kuki-N. *(s-)rjam 'sharp'					

36-23 = K. 612 Almost all graphs have MC double readings with /a/ and /ă/, the OC vowel could therefore have been *a or *e, possibly also *ə. We write *a by default, supported by one *Shijing* rime. It is not clear if 4-46 belongs to this series.

		Mand.	MC	LHan	OCM	
a	毚	chán	dẓăm, dẓam	dẓɛm, dẓam	dzrâm	
b	欃	chán	dẓăm	dẓɛm	dzrâm	
e	鑱	chán, zhàn	dẓam(^{C})	dẓam(^{C})	dzrâm, dzrâms	
d	讒	chán	dẓăm, dẓam(^{C})	dẓɛm, dẓam(^{C})	dzrâm, dzrâms	OCB *dzjom
c	儳 uneven	chán, zhàn	dẓam, dẓăm^{B}	dẓam, dẓɛm^{B}	dzrâm	
	儳 mixed	chàn, zhàn	tṣ^{h}am^{C}, dẓăm^{C}	tṣ^{h}am^{C}, dẓɛm^{C}	tshrâms	

36-24 = K. 1154

		Mand.	MC	LHan	OCM
-a--	彡髟 衫杉	shān	ṣam	ṣam	srâm

[T] Sin Sukchu 衫 SR ṣam (平), PR ṣan; MGZY 衫 sham (平) [ṣam]
[E] TB *(C-)sam 'beard' <> [N] The graph 髟 also writes a synonym biāo 13-71/1154

36-25 = K. 610

		Mand.	MC	LHan	OCM	
a	芟	shān	ṣam	ṣam	srâm	= 36-22/611b 摲

36-26 = K. 625 風 and 楓 rime in *-əm and *-im in Han poetry (Luo and Zhou p. 215).

		Mand.	MC	LHan	OCM	
a	凡	fán	bjwɐm	buɑm	bam	

[T] Sin Sukchu SR vam (平) PR van; MGZY Hwam (平) [vam]; MTang bvuam < buam, ONW bam. <> [E] TB: Lushai pum^H 'whole, all, everywhere'; WB pum 'form, model, pattern'

		Mand.	MC	LHan	OCM	
d	帆	fān	bjwɐm	buɑm	bam	
e	軓	fàn	bjwɐm^B	buɑm^B	bamʔ	= 36-27/626b
-	梵	fàn	bjwɐm^C	buɑm	—	[T] BTD Skt. brahmā
f	汎	fàn	p^{h}jwɐm^C, bjuŋ	p^{h}uɑm^C, buəm	phams, bəm	

= 35-20/641b 泛; 36-27/626c 氾

		Mand.	MC	LHan	OCM	
g	芃	péng, féng	buŋ, bjuŋ	buəm	bə̂m, bəm	[E] ST *pum
j	鳳	fèng	bjuŋ^C	buəm^C	bəms	OCB *p(r)jə/um

[D] Min: Xiam (lit.) hoŋ^{C2}

		Mand.	MC	LHan	OCM	
hi	風[1] 飌 wind	fēng	pjuŋ	puəm	pəm	OCB *p(r)jə/um

風 [T] Sin Sukchu SR fuŋ (平); MGZY hwung (平) [fuŋ]; MTang pfuŋ, ONW puŋ
楓 [T] BTD Skt. brahm(ā)

		Mand.	MC	LHan	OCM	
	風[2] criticize	fèng	pjuŋ^C	puəm^C	pəms	
n	楓	fēng	pjuŋ	puəm	pəm	

[T] BTD 楓摩 puəm-mɑ Skt. brahma

		Mand.	MC	LHan	OCM	
o	諷	fěng !	pjuŋ^C	puəm^C	pəms	OCB *p(r)jə/um
p	渢	féng, fēng	bjuŋ	buəm	bəm	OCB *b(r)jə/um
-	葻	lán	lậm	ləm	—	SW 388
-	嵐	lán	lậm			ONW lɑm

<- Indic *vairambha, veramba*. The element 風 has been chosen for its meaning; it does not prove a medial liquid in this phonetic series.

36-27 = K. 626		Mand.	MC	LHan	OCM	
a	犯	fàn	bjwɐm^B	buɑm^B	bamʔ	
b	軓	fàn	bjwɐm^B	buɑm^B	bamʔ	= 36-26/625e
d	範	fàn	bjwɐm^B	buɑm^B	bamʔ	
e	范	fàn	bjwɐm^B	buɑm^B	bamʔ	
c	氾 overflow	fàn	p^{h}jwɐm^C	p^{h}uɑm^C	phams or phjams ?	

= 35-20/641b 泛

		Mand.	MC	LHan	OCM	
	氾 disperse	fàn	bjwɐm^C	buɑm^C	bams	

36-28		Mand.	MC	LHan	OCM
-	奣	mǎn, miǎn	mjwɐm^B, miem^B	muɑm^B	—

37 OCM rime *-əp, *-ip Qī bù 緝部

GSR 675 - 696

Baxter 1992: 555 ff. (§10.3.4)

See Table 38-1 for OCM rimes *-əp and *-əm, *-im, etc. in QYS categories.

MC -jəp after guttural initials (kjəp type syllables) are here transcribed with the LHan vowel ɨ (kɨp), this syllable type has probably developed from OCM kəp to kɨəp > kɨp > later kip.

MC -jəp can derive from OCM *-əp or *-ip; when a preceding velar consonant is palatalized to MC tśj- etc., the rime was *-ip, when not, the rime was *-əp. After acute initials, MC -jəp can go back to either OCM *-əp (when in contact with MC -ập), or to *-ip (when in contact with MC -iep). When there is no revealing xiesheng or rime association, the final remains ambiguous. MC -iep IV can derive from OCM *-îp or *-êp (rime 35), depending on the phonetic series. MC -ập /jəp can correspond to foreign *-əp, *-ip, and *-up. This final is parallel to no. 38 *-əm, see the table there.

37-1 = K. 675, 687

		Mand.	**MC**	**LHan**	**OCM**	
a-e	合盒迨	hé	ɣập	gəp	gə̂p	OCB *gop

[T] Sin Sukchu SR ɣa (入); PR, LR ɣɔʔ; MGZY Xo (入) [ɣɔ]; ONW ɣɑp

[E] MK *kup: Khmer gwpa /kúuəp/ 'to join, bring together, unite', ga'pa /kup/ 'to join, unite, meet with, visit often', Mon inscr. sakuip /səkøp/ 'lid'

hi	蛤閤	gé	kập	kəp	kə̂p	
j	韐	jiá, gé	kập, kăp	kəp, kɛp	kə̂p, krə̂p	
mn	洽祫	qià	ɣăp	gɛp	grə̂p	
p	給	jǐ, gěi	kjəp	kɨp	kəp	
l	鞈	jiá	kăp	kɛp	krə̂p	
k	跲	jiá, jiē, jié	kăp, kjɐp, gjɐp	kɛp, kɨɑp, gɨɑp	krə̂p, kap, gap	
o	袷	jié	kjɐp	kɨɑp,	kap	
687a	拾 pick	shí	źjəp	gip	gip	

= 37-3/686a 十 [E] PTai *kjəp

	alternate	jié	gjɐp	gɨɑp	gap	
675qrs	翕噏歙	xī	xjəp	hɨp	həp	
tu	潝闟	xī	xjəp	hɨp	həp	
-	欱	hē	xập	həp	hə̂p	= 21-1/313k 喝

37-2 = K. 681

		Mand.	**MC**	**LHan**	**OCM**
a	及	jí	gjəp	gɨp	gəp

[T] Sin Sukchu SR gi (入); MGZY ki (入) [gi]; ONW gip

[E] WB kʰap 'arrive at', JP kʰap[51] 'to carry, reach'

di	彶級	jí	kjəp	kɨp	kəp

h 汲 jī kjəp kɨp kəp

[E] TB *ka:p: LB *C-kap, WB k^{h}ap 'dig up, draw water'

g 急 jí kjəp kɨp kəp

[T] Sin Sukchu SR ki (入); MGZY gi (入) [ki]; ONW kip

mo 极笈 jí gjäp 3 gɨap gap or grap

kl 圾岌 jí ŋjəp ŋɨp ŋəp

j 吸 xī xjəp hɨp həp or hŋəp [D] Min: Xiam khip^{D1}

1254b 扱 (xī) xjəp 'to collect', see also 35-18/1254b.

37-3 = K. 686 Mand. MC LHan OCM

ae 十什 shí źjəp dźip < gip gip =37-1/687a 拾

[T] Sin Sukchu SR ʐi (入); MGZY zhi (入) [ʐi]; ONW dźip <> [D] PMin *džep

[E] TB *gip > WB kyip, Mikir kep < kip <> PMiao *ge̱u^D

f 汁 zhī tśjəp tśip < kip kip

[T] ONW tśip <> [D] PMin *tšep

\- 叶 xié ɣiep gep gîp

Old graph for xié 35-4/639c

37-4 = K. 682 Mand. MC LHan OCM

a 爗 yè jäp 3, jiəp wap, jəp wap, ləp

[E] WT lhab-lhab-pa 'to flutter to and fro, to glimmer, glisten' <> KT: Siam. lɛɛp^{D2L} ~ ma-lɛɛp 'to flash (as lightning)'; PHlai ɬjip^7 'lightning' <> Tai: S. wɛɛp^{D2}-wap^{D2} 'glittering, flashing'

37-5 = K. 683 Mand. MC LHan OCM

a 邑 yì ʔjəp ʔɨp ʔəp OCB *ʔ(r)jup

gfh 挹悒浥 yì ʔjəp ʔɨp ʔəp

i 唈 yì ʔjəp, ʔập ʔɨp, ʔəp ʔəp, ʔə̂p

37-6 = K. 676 The element 37-1 合 is probably semantic ('fit, agree').

Mand. MC LHan OCM

a 答 dá tập təp tə̂p < tûp ⋇ 31-9/511a 對

\- 搭 dā tập təp tə̂p

[T] 答 Sin Sukchu SR ta (入); ONW tɑp

[E] 搭 WB tap 'put in, fix' // WT t^{h}ab-pa 'to fight, quarrel'

b 荅 bean dá tập təp tə̂p OCB *k-lup

[E] MY *dəp 'bean'

c 嗒 tà t^{h}ập, t^{h}âp t^{h}əp, t^{h}ɑp thə̂p, thâp

\-- 塔墖 tă t^{h}âp t^{h}ɑp — 'pagoda'

37-7 = K. 684 Mand. MC LHan OCM

a 㚔 zhí tjəp ṭip trəp =37-8/685f 縶

37-8 = K. 685 The OC vowel could be *i or *ə.

Mand. MC LHan OCM

a 執 zhí tśjəp tśip təp [T] ONW tśip

kmn 摯贄鷙 zhì tśi^C tśih təts < təps

[E] ? TB: WT č^{h}ab 'power, authority'

f	縶	zhí	tjəp	ṭip	trəp	

= 37-7/684a 㚔 [T] ONW tip

g	蟄	zhé !	ḍjəp	ḍip	drəp	
h	慹	zhí, zhé	tśjəp, tśjäp, niep	tśip, tśap, nep	tip, tep, nîp	
j	鷙	zhì	ṭi^{C}	ṭɨs	trəts < trəps	
o	墊	diàn	tiem^{C}	tem^{C}	tîms	
i	執	jí	tsjəp	tsɨp	tsəp	

37-9	**= K. 677**	**Mand.**	**MC**	**LHan**	**OCM**	
ab	沓誻	dá	dâp	dəp	lôp	

= 37-10/678e 遝 [T] ONW dɑp

37-10	**= K. 678**	**Mand.**	**MC**	**LHan**	**OCM**	
ae	眔遝	dá	dâp	dəp	lôp	= 37-9/677a 沓
f	嚃	tà	t^{h}âp	t^{h}əp	lhôp	

37-11	**= K. 689**	**Mand.**	**MC**	**LHan**	**OCM**	
a	襲	xí	zjəp	zip	s-ləp	= 37-12/690a 習

37-12	**= K. 690**	**Mand.**	**MC**	**LHan**	**OCM**	
abcd	習謵槢騽	xí	zjəp	zip	s-ləp	= 37-11/689a 襲

[T] Sin Sukchu SR zi (入); MGZY zi (入) [zi]; ONW zip

[E] WT slob-pa, slabs 'to learn, teach' ⋈ slobs 'exercise, practice'

g	褶	dié	diep	dep	lêp (or lîp ?)	

= 35-10/633g 牒; 35-11/1255a 疊 <> [E] WT ldab-pa < *ɴlap 'to do again, repeat', ldeb-pa 'to bend round, double down' ⋈ ltab-pa, bltabs < *ɴlap 'to fold'

-	摺	zhé	tśjäp	tśap	tep	[T] ONW tśap
h	慴 to fear	zhé	tśjäp	tśap	tep	
f	熠	yì	jiəp, jəp	jəp, wəp	wəp	= 37-4/682a

37-13 = K. 692 Aspiration and *l in the initial are the common denominators.

		Mand.	**MC**	**LHan**	**OCM**
a	濕 to flap	shī, chī	śjəp, tṣ^{h}jəp	śip, tṣ^{h}ip	lhəp, tshrəp < k-srəp
	濕 dry	qì	k^{h}jəp	k^{h}ɨp	khəp
b	隰 wet	xí	zjəp	zip	s-ləp

37-14	**= K. 693**	**Mand.**	**MC**	**LHan**	**OCM**	
a	溼 wet	shī	śjəp	śip	lhəp	[T] ONW śip

37-15	**= K. 694, 520**		**MC**	**LHan**	**OCM**	
aef	立笠粒	lì	ljəp	lip	rəp	OCB *g-rjəp

[T] 立 Sin Sukchu SR li (入); MGZY li (入) [li]; ONW lip <> [E] TB *g-ryap 'to stand' <>

[D] 笠 Min: Jiànyōu sɛ^{C2}<> Tai: Wuming klop^{D1S} < *kl- 'bamboo hat'

g	苙	lì, jí	ljəp, gjəp	lip, gɨp	rəp, grəp	
hi	泣湆	qì	k^{h}jəp	k^{h}ɨp	khrəp	

[T] 泣 ONW k^{h}ip <> [E] TB *krap 'to weep'

j	⿸厂立	là	lâp	ləp	rôp	
l	拉 break	lā	lâp	ləp	rôp	cf. 35-4/639d 協

520						
abc	泣莅蒞	lì	lji^{C}	lis	rəts < rəps ?	

37-16 = K. 695		**Mand.**	**MC**	**LHan**	**OCM**	
a	入	rù	ńźjəp	ńip	nəp < nup	OCB njup
	[T] Sin Sukchu SR ri (入), PR, LR ryʔ; MGZY Zhi (入) [ri]; ONW ńip					
	[E] TB *nup > WT nub-pa 'to fall, sink, set'					
e	內 inside	nèi	nwậi^{C}	nuəs	nûts < nûps	
	[T] Sin Sukchu SR nuj (去), LR nuj; MGZY nue (去) [nuɛ]; ONW nuɑi					
	This graph already had a final dental in OC, hence it could be used for items with OC *-t.					
	內 bring in	nà	nập	nəp	nə̂p < nûp	
hi	納軜	nà	nập	nəp	nə̂p < nûp	
	[T] Sin Sukchu SR na (入); ONW nɑp					
j	訥	nè	nwət	nuət	nût	
kl	吶㕯	nè	nwət, ńźjwät, ṇjwät, ṇwat	nuət, ńuat, ṇuɑt, ṇuat	nût, not, nrot	
n	枘	ruì	ńźjwäi^{C}	ńuas	nots	
	[E] AA: Khmer tnota /tnaaot/ 'impaling pole, skewer, spit' < ṭota /daaot/ 'to impale, run into...'					
op	汭蜹	ruì	ńźjwäi^{C}	ńuas	nots	
q	芮	ruì	ńźjwäi^{C}	ńuas	nots	
rs	焫蜹	ruì	ńźjwäi^{C}, ńźjwät	ńuas, ńuat	not, nots	

37-17 = K. 696		**Mand.**	**MC**	**LHan**	**OCM**
a	㚔	niè	ṇjäp	ṇɑp ?	nrep
	[E] MK: OKhmer ñyāp /ɲap/ 'to tremble, fear'				

37-18 = K. 679		**Mand.**	**MC**	**LHan**	**OCM**
ab	帀匝	zā	tsập	tsəp	tsə̂p

37-19 = K. 688 The vowel could also be *i.

		Mand.	**MC**	**LHan**	**OCM**	
a	咠	qī, jī	ts(^{h})jəp	ts(^{h})ip	tsəp, tshəp	
b	緝 hem	qī	ts^{h}jəp	ts^{h}ip	tshəp	
	babble	qī, jī	ts(^{h})jəp	ts(^{h})ip	tsəp, tshəp	
c	葺	qì	ts^{h}jəp	ts^{h}ip	tshəp (< s-ʔip ?)	
	[E] WT skyibs (< *s-ʔips ?) 'a shelter from above (from rain, etc.)'					
d	輯 collect	jí	dzjəp	dzip	dzəp	OCB *dzjup [T] ONW dzip
	gather up	zhí	tṣjəp	tṣip	tsrəp	
ef	戢濈	jí	tṣjəp	tṣip	tsrəp	
	[E] ? AA: PMonic *cap, Nyah Kur '(bird) to settle on, perch', Mon *cɔp 'to adhere to, cleave to'; OKhmer /ɟap/ 'touch, join, meet, cling, adhere'					
g	揖 cluster	jí, zhí	tsjəp, tṣjəp	tsip, tṣip	tsəp, tsrəp	
	salute	yī	ʔjəp	ʔɨp	ʔəp	
hi	楫檝	jí	tsjäp	tsiap	tsap	[E] JP šap < tšap 'oar'

37-20 = K. 691		**Mand.**	**MC**	**LHan**	**OCM**	
a	集	jí	dzjəp	dzip	dzəp	OCB *dzjup
	[T] ONW dzip <> [E] AA: Khmer cwpa /cùuəp/ ~ jwpa /cúuəp/ 'to join', intr. 'to meet, come together'					
d-	雜襍 mixed	zá	dzəp	dzəp	dzə̂p	[T] ONW dzɑp

37-21 = K. 680		**Mand.**	**MC**	**LHan**	**OCM**
a	颯	sà	sập	səp	sə̂p

37-22		**Mand.**	**MC**	**LHan**	**OCM**	
-	澀	sè	ṣjəp	ṣip	srəp	[T] ONW ṣip

38 OCM rime *-əm , *-im Qīn bù 侵部

GSR 643 - 674

Baxter 1992: 548 ff. (§10.3.3)

MC -jəm after guttural initials (kjəm type syllables) is here transcribed with the LHan vowel ɨ (kɨm); this syllable type has probably developed from OCM kəm to kɨəm > kɨm > later kim.

MC -iem can derive from OCM *-îm (when associated with MC -jəm), or from *-êm (when associated with MC -jäm), but MC -ậm can only derive from OCM *-ə̂m.

After acute initials, MC -jəm can go back to either OCM *-əm (when in contact with MC -ậm), or to *-im (when in contact with MC -iem). When there is no revealing *xiesheng* or rime contact, the final remains ambiguous.

Table 38-1: OCM rimes *-əm, *-əp, *-im, *-ip in QYS finals

Div.	*-əm	*-əp	*-im	*-ip
I	含 ɣậm gəm *gə̂m 南 nậm nəm *nə̂m 菡 dậm^B dəm^B *lə̂mʔ	合 ɣập gəp *gə̂p 答 tập təp *tə̂p		
IV			念 niem^C nem^C *nîms	叶 ɣiep gep *gîp 褶 diep dep *lîp
III lab	風 pjuŋ puəm *pəm 熊 juŋ wəm *wəm			
3/3	稟 pjəm^B pim^B *prəmʔ			
III	今 kjəm kɨm *kəm 禁 kjəm^C kɨm^C *krəms	及 gjəp gɨp *gəp	箴 tśjəm tśim < kim *kim	十 źjəp dźip < gip *gip
III ac	心 sjəm sim *səm 林 ljəm lim *rəm 任 ńźjəm ńim *nəm	執 tśjəp tśip *təp 立 ljəp lip *rəp 入 ńźjəp ńip *nəp	merged with *-əm	merged with *-əp
II	咸 ɣăm gɛm *grə̂m	洽 ɣăp gɛp *grə̂p		

38-1		**Mand.**	**MC**	**LHan**	**OCM**	
-	柬	hàn	ɣậm^{B}	gəm^{B}	gə̂mʔ	
	'God of the West' [OB: Sōrui 481; SW 3037], in Shūjīng (Yáo diǎn) erroneously written 夷					

38-2	**= K. 643**	**Mand.**	**MC**	**LHan**	**OCM**	
ab	a 函 cont.	hán	ɣậm	gəm	gə̂m	'contain'
	= 38-3/651l' 含 [T] ONW ɣɑm					
	函 Pl.N.	xián	ɣăm	gɛm	grə̂m	
g	涵	hán	ɣậm	gəm	gə̂m	
h	菡	hàn	ɣậm^{B}	gəm^{B}	gə̂mʔ	

38-3 = K. 651, 652 I suspect that the graph 今 was originally invented for *hàn* 頷[1] *gə̂mʔ 'jaw', see Indro. 9.2.7.

		Mand.	**MC**	**LHan**	**OCM**	
651an'	今[1] > 頷[1]	hàn	ɣậm^{B}	gəm^{B}	gə̂mʔ	'jaw'
	See Intro. 9.2.7. <> [E] TB *gam: Lepcha kam 'jaw' <> PMK *tga(a)m 'jaw'					
n'	頷[2]	ǎn	ŋậm^{B}	ŋəm^{B}	ŋə̂mʔ	'nod the head'
	= 38-3/652j 顉					
l'	含	hán	ɣậm	gəm	gə̂m	'hold in mouth'
	= 38-2/643a 函. BTD Skt. -gama, -gāmin					
	含	hàn	ɣậm^{C}	gəm^{C}	gə̂ms	'put in mouth'
	= 38-4/671p 憾 <> [T] ONW ɣɑm <> [E] TB *gam > WT 'gam 'put into the mouth'					
m'	唅	hán	ɣậm	gəm	gə̂m	
a	今[2] now	jīn	kjəm	kɨm	kəm	OCB *k(r)jəm
	[T] Sin Sukchu SR kim (平), PR, LR kin; MGZY gim (平) [kim]; ONW kim. BTD 基耶今波羅 kiə-ja-kɨm-pɑ-lɑ Skt. keśakambala <> [E] PTai *ɣəm^{A2} 'gold' ⋇ S. ka:m^{B1} 'bright, striking'					
i	坅	qǐn, yǐn	k^{h}jəm^{B}, ŋjəm^{B}	k^{h}ɨm^{B}, ŋɨm^{B}	khəmʔ, ŋəmʔ	
	[T] ? NTai dial. *k^{h}- or *k-: Po-ai kam^{C1} < *k- 'cave', KS *ka:m^{1} 'cave'					
t	岑 bank	qīn, qín, yǐn	ts^{h}jəm, ŋjəm^{B}	ts^{h}ɨm, ŋɨm^{B}	tshəm, ŋəmʔ	⋇ 38-3/652f 嶔 [E] TB *r-ka[:]m 'bank of river'
	岑 hill	cén !	dẓjəm	dẓim	dzrəm	
	Jīn is only partially phonetic [rime] <> [T] BTD Skt. sum					
f	紟	jìn	gjəm^{C}	gɨm^{C}	gəms	
g	衿 lapel	jīn	kjəm	kɨm	kəm	= 38-18/655l
	string	jìn	gjəm^{C}	gɨm^{C}	gəms	
h	衾	qīn	k^{h}jəm	k^{h}ɨm	khəm	
v	戡	kān	k^{h}ậm	k^{h}əm	khə̂m	= 38-11/658q 戡
r	黔	qín, qián	gjəm, gjäm 3	gɨm, gɨam	gəm, gram ?	
jn	禽擒	qín	gjəm	gɨm	gəm	[T] ONW gim
opq	芩靲琴	qín	gjəm	gɨm	gəm	
s	吟	yín	ŋjəm	ŋɨm	ŋəm	
u	趻	chěn	ṭ^{h}jəm^{B}	ṭ^{h}ɨm^{B}	thrəm	= 38-11/658g 踸
	OC is uncertain; it could also be OCM rhəm or k-hrəm.					
652	(GSR 651 continues below)					
ad	金淦	jīn	kjəm	kɨm	kəm	
	According to SW, 今 *kəm is phonetic <> [T] Sin Sukchu SR kim (平), PR, LR kin; MGZY gim (平) [kim]; ONW kim					
e	錦	jǐn	kjəm^{B}	kɨm^{B}	kəmʔ	

fk	欽嶔	qīn	kʰjəm	kʰɨm	khəm	= 38-3/651t 芩
l	廞	xīn	xjəm	hɨm	həm	
g	唫 shut	jìn	gjəm^B	gɨm^B	gəm?	
	precipit.	yín, qīn	ŋjəm, kʰjəm	ŋɨm, kʰɨm	ŋəm, khəm	
j	顉	ǎn, hàn	ŋậm^B	ŋəm^B	ŋə̂m?	= 38-3/651n' 頷
h	趛	yǐn	ŋjəm^B	ŋɨm^B	ŋəm?	
651						
xa'	侌黔	yīn	ʔjəm	ʔɨm	ʔəm	
y	陰[1]	yīn	ʔjəm	ʔɨm	ʔəm	OCB *ʔ(r)jum
	[T] ONW ʔim					
yb'c'	陰[2]蔭廕	yìn	ʔjəm^C	ʔɨm^C	ʔəms	
d'	酓	yǎn	ʔjiäm^B 4	ʔiam^B	ʔem?	[E] MY *ʔiːm^A 'bitter'
h'	黯	ān	ʔậm	ʔəm	ʔə̂m	
i'	歓	yǐn	ʔjəm^B	ʔɨm^B	ʔəm?	= 38-8/654a 飲
k'	嬸	ǎn	ŋậm^B	ŋəm^B	ŋə̂m?	

38-4	**= K. 671**	**Mand.**	**MC**	**LHan**	**OCM**	
ae	咸諴	xián	ɣǎm	gɛm	grə̂m	[T] ONW käm
f	鹹	xián	ɣǎm	gɛm	grə̂m	
	[D] Min: Xiam kiam^{A2} / ham^{A2} 'salted, salty' <> [E] TB *r-gyum > Kiranti *rum 'salt'; Kachin dʒum^{31} 'salt' ⋈ ʃum^{33} 'be salted'					
g	減	jiǎn,xiàn	kǎm^B, ɣǎm^B	kɛm^B	krə̂m?	[T] ONW käm
i	緘	jiān	kǎm	kɛm	krə̂m	
k	黬	jiān,	kǎm	kɛm	krə̂m	
		yǎn	ʔǎm^B	ʔɛm^B	ʔrə̂m?	
l	感	gǎn	kậm^B	kəm^B	kə̂m?	
	[T] Sin Sukchu SR kam (上), PR kan; MGZY gam (上) [kam]; ONW kɑm					
p	憾	hàn	ɣậm^C	gəm^C	gə̂ms	
	= 38-3/651l' 含 <> [T] ONW ɣɑm					
m	顑	kǎn	kʰậm^B,	kʰəm^B,	khə̂m?,	
			xậm^C	həm^C	hə̂ms	
no	箴鍼	zhēn	tśjəm	tśim < kim	kim	
	[T] ONW tśim <> [D] PMin *tšim ~ *tšem					
	[E] OC -> Viet. kim 'needle', -> Tai: Saek kim^A					

38-5	**= K. 672**	**Mand.**	**MC**	**LHan**	**OCM**	
acd	臽陷錎	xiàn	ɣǎm^C	gɛm^C	grə̂ms	
	[T] Sin Sukchu SR ɣjam (平), PR ɣjan, LR ɣjen; MGZY Hyam (平) [ɣjam]; ONW ɣäm					
	[E] ST *grəm: WB gyam^B < gram^B 'a trap'					
g	淊	hàn	ɣậm^B	gəm^B	gə̂m?	
ef	埳欿	kǎn	kʰậm^B	kʰəm^B	khə̂m?	= 36-4/624d 坎
i	窞	tàn (!)	dậm^B	dəm^B	lə̂m?	
j	萏	dàn	dậm^B	dəm^B	lə̂m?	
k	啗	dàn	dậm$^{B/C}$	dəm$^{B/C}$	lə̂m?, lə̂ms	
mn	閻壛	yán	jiäm	jam, wam ?	lam	
	[T] MHan Vim(a)					
o	爓 bright	yàn	jiäm^C	jam^C	—	(a late word)

		Mand.	MC	LHan	OCM	
	爓 boil	xián	zjäm	ziam	s-lam	
	= see 36-14/617 燅燂					
	爓 sacr.	xín	zjəm	zim	s-ləm	
	= 38-17/662a 尋; 38-28/660k 鬵 <> [T] ONW zim					
lp	諂讇	chǎn	ṭʰjäm^{B}	ṭʰɑm^{B}	rhamʔ or k-hramʔ ?	

38-6	**= K. 674**	**Mand.**	**MC**	**LHan**	**OCM**	
a	熊	xióng	juŋ	wɨm < wəm	wəm	
	[T] Sin Sukchu SR ɣjuŋ (平); MGZY Hȳung (平) [ɣjuŋ]; ONW ɣuəm?? > ɣuŋ (?) > huŋ, BTD Skt. -hm- <> [D] Min: Amoy him^{A2}, Fú'ān hem^{A2}, Yǒng'ān ham^{A2} 'bear' <> [E] TB *d-wam					

38-7	**= K. 653**	**Mand.**	**MC**	**LHan**	**OCM**	
ac	音愔	yīn	ʔjəm	ʔɨm	ʔəm	
	音 OCB *ʔ(r)jəm; 愔 OCB *ʔjim					
d	喑 dumb	yīn, ān	ʔjəm, ʔậm	ʔɨm, ʔəm	ʔəm, ʔə̂m	
	喑 pent up	yìn	ʔjəm^{C}	ʔɨm^{C}	ʔəms	
	[E] ST *ʔum: TB *um 'hold in the mouth'					
ef	瘖 (厂+音)	yīn	ʔjəm	ʔɨm	ʔəm	
h	暗	àn	ʔậm^{C}	ʔəm^{C}	ʔə̂ms	
	[T] Sin Sukchu SR ʔam (去); PR ʔan; MGZY 'am (去) [ʔam], ONW ʔɑm^{C}					
i	闇	àn	ʔậm$^{B/C}$	ʔəm$^{B/C}$	ʔə̂mʔ, ʔəms	
-	黯	àn	ʔậm^{B}	ʔəm^{B}	ʔə̂mʔ	[T] ONW ʔɑm
j	歆	xīn	xjəm	hɨm	həm	

38-8	**= K. 654**	**Mand.**	**MC**	**LHan**	**OCM**	
a	飲 drink	yǐn	ʔjəm^{B}	ʔɨm^{B}	ʔəmʔ	= 38-3/651i' 歙
	[D] PMin *əm^{B1} 'rice water'					
	飲 give dr.	yìn	ʔjəm^{C}	ʔɨm^{C}	ʔəms	OCB *ʔ(r)jum(ʔ)s

38-9	**= K. 644**	**Mand.**	**MC**	**LHan**	**OCM**
a	儑	àn	ŋậm^{C} !	ŋəm^{C}	ŋə̂ms

38-10	**= K. 673**	**Mand.**	**MC**	**LHan**	**OCM**
a	嵒	yán	ŋăm, ŋjəm	ŋɛm, ŋɨm	ŋrə̂m, ŋəm
-	喦	yán	ŋăm	ŋɛm	ŋrə̂m

38-10A	㐺	yín	ŋjəm	ŋɨm	— SW 3659

38-11	**= K. 658**	**Mand.**	**MC**	**LHan**	**OCM**	
a	甚	shèn	źjəm$^{B/C}$	dźim$^{B/C}$	dəmʔ, dəms	OCB *Gjumʔ
	[T] Sin Sukchu SR ʐim (上去), LR ʐim (上); MGZY zhim (上) [ʐim]; ONW dźim					
	[E] ? ST: TB *tyam ~ *dyam 'full', KN-Tiddim dim 'be full'					
bc	煁諶	chén	źjəm	dźim	dəm	
e	揕	zhèn	ṭjəm^{C}	ṭim^{C}	trəms	
i	葚	shèn	dźjəm^{B}, źjem^{B}	(d)źim^{B}	dəmʔ	
h	斟	zhēn	tśjəm	tśim	təm	[T] ONW tśim
f	椹	zhēn	ṭjəm	ṭim	trəm	

l 湛 deep zhàn ḍăm^{B} ḍɛm^{B} drə̂mʔ 'deep, soak'
[E] PYao *rjɛm 'to water, soak'
sunk in dān tə̣̂m təm tə̂m
soak jiān tsjäm tsiam tsem or tsam

n 黮 tăn t^{h}ə̣̂m^{B}, də̣̂m^{B} t^{h}əm^{B}, dəm^{B} thə̂mʔ, də̂mʔ
[E] MK-Khmer ṭaṃ /-dɑm/ 'be dark', daṃ /-tum/ 'be ripe, dark'

g 踸 chěn ṭ^{h}jəm^{B} ṭhim^{B} thrəm = 38-3/651u 趻
OC is uncertain; it could also be OCM rhəm or k-hrəm.

o 糂 săn sə̣̂m^{B} səm^{B} sə̂mʔ
= 38-29/647f 糝 [T] ONW sɑm

j 媅 dān tə̣̂m təm —

p 堪 kān k^{h}ə̣̂m k^{h}əm khə̂m OCB *khum
[T] Sin Sukchu SR k'am (平), PR k'an; MGZY kham (平) [k'am] <> [D] Xiam k^{h}am^{A1}
[E] ST *kəm: WB k^{h}aṁ^{A} 'receive, endure' ⋈ ə-k^{h}am^{B} 'suitable appendage', JP k^{h}am^{31} 'endure'

r 嵁 kān, k^{h}ə̣̂m, k^{h}əm, khə̂m,
qiān, k^{h}ăm, k^{h}ɛm, krə̂m,
án ŋə̣̂m ŋəm ŋə̂m

q 戡 kān k^{h}ə̣̂m k^{h}əm khə̂m
[D] Xiam k^{h}am^{A1} 'to suppress (a rebellion)' <> [E] ST *kum: Lushai k^{h}um^{F} 'upon, on top of, inside, against, over...', vb. 'to put on, wear' ⋈ k^{h}uum^{F} vb. 'to surpass, excel, beat, over, beyond'; WT'gum-pa, bkum 'to kill' ⋈ 'gum-pa, gum, *ɴgums 'to die'

\- 勘 kān, kàn k^{h}ə̣̂m^{C} k^{h}əm^{C} khə̂ms [D] Amoy k^{h}am^{C}

\- 磡 kàn k^{h}ə̣̂m^{C} k^{h}əm^{C} khə̂ms [D] Amoy k^{h}ĩ^{A1}-k^{h}am^{C1}

\- 歁 kăn k^{h}ə̣̂m^{B} k^{h}əm^{B} khə̂mʔ
[E] WT skom 'thirst', skom-pa 'to thirst', skam-po 'dry', skem-pa, bskams... 'to make dry'

\- 歁 kăn xə̣̂m^{B} həm^{B} hə̂mʔ
[E] TB: WT ham-pa 'avarice, covetousness, greed'

38-12 = K. 659 **Mand.** **MC** **LHan** **OCM**

a 闖 chèn ṭ^{h}jəm^{C} ṭ^{h}im^{C} thrəms or rhəms
The OC rime could be *-əm or *-im.

38-13 = K. 665 **Mand.** **MC** **LHan** **OCM**

a 審 shěn śjəm^{B} śim^{B} lhəmʔ

b 瀋 chěn tś^{h}jəm^{B} tś^{h}im^{B} k-hləmʔ = 38-14/656b 沈

38-14 = K. 656 **Mand.** **MC** **LHan** **OCM**

a 冘 yín jiəm jim ləm

b 沈 sink chén ḍjəm ḍim drəm < r-ləm
[T] Sin Sukchu SR dẓim (平), PR, LR dẓin; MGZY chim (平) [dẓim]; ONW dim
sacrif. chén, zhèn ḍjəm(^{C}) ḍim(^{C}) drəm, drəms < r-ləm, r-ləms
juice chěn tś^{h}jəm^{B} tś^{h}im^{B} k-hləmʔ = 38-13/665b 瀋
a state shěn śjəm^{B} śim^{B} lhəmʔ

ef 酖鴆 zhèn ḍjəm^{C} ḍim^{C} drəms < r-ləms
[E] AA-Khmer ralāṃ /rloəm/ 'be soaked, drenched, drowned'

h 忱 chén, shén źjəm dźim dəm

g 枕 zhěn tśjəm$^{B/C}$ tśim^{B} < kim^{B} kimʔ OCB *Kjumʔ
[T] ONW tśim <> [E] ST *kum ~ *kim: TB *Nkum > JP k^{h}um^{55} 'headrest, pillow'

l	耽	dān	tâm	təm	tâm < tləm	
	= 38-11/658l 湛 [T] ONW tam					
i	抌	dǎn	tâm^{B}	təm^{B}	tâmʔ	
	[E] Tai: PTai *t-: S. tam^{A1} 'to pound', esp. in a mortar					
j	眈	dān	tâm(^{B})	təm(^{B})	tâm, tâmʔ	
k	紞	dǎn	tâm^{B}	təm^{B}	tâmʔ	
n	黕	dǎn	tâm^{B}	təm^{B}	tâmʔ	
o	醓	tǎn	tʰâm^{B}	tʰəm^{B}	thâmʔ	
m	髧	dàn	dâm^{B}	dəm^{B}	dâmʔ	

38-15 = K. 657 The OC rime in this series could be *-əm and / or *-im.

		Mand.	MC	LHan	OCM
ab-	㸒淫霪	yín	jiəm	jim	ləm
	淫 [T] Sin Sukchu SR im (平), PR, LR in; MGZY yim (平) [jim]				

38-16 = K. 646		Mand.	MC	LHan	OCM	
a	覃 spread	tán	dâm	dəm	lâm	
	覃 sharp	yǎn	jiäm^{B}	jam^{B}	lemʔ	= see 36-14 剡琰
j	簟	diàn	diem^{B}	dem^{B}	lêmʔ or lîmʔ	OCB *limʔ
l	驔	diàn	diem^{B}	dem^{B}	lêmʔ	
b	潭	tán	dâm	dəm	lâm	
	[E] KS *tʰlam[1] (but many KS lgs. have initial d) < AN, cf. Malay kolam 'pond, well, pool'					
c	譚	tán	dâm	dəm	lâm	
	[E] TB: WT gtam < *g-lham 'talk, discourse', Mikir -lám 'word, speech, language', Lushai lam^{R} < lamʔ 'say, pronounce, ask for'					
d	燂	xián, qián, tán	zjäm, dzjäm, dâm	ziam	s-lem ?	= see 36-14 爓 燅
e	鐔	tán, yín, xín	dâm, jiəm, zjəm	dəm, jim, zim	lâm, ləm, s-ləm	
fg	嘾禫	dàn	dâm^{B}	dəm^{B}	lâmʔ	
h	撢	tān	tʰâm	tʰəm	lhâm	
i	鱏	yín, xún !	jiəm, zjəm	jim, zim	ləm, s-ləm	

38-17 = K. 662		Mand.	MC	LHan	OCM	
a	尋 warm	xín	zjəm	zim	s-ləm	
	= 38-5/672o 燖; 38-28/660k 鬵. [T] ONW zim <> [E] TB *lum^{A} 'warm'					
	尋 meas.	xún	zjəm	zim	s-ləm	'a measure'
	[T] Sin Sukchu SR zim (平), PR, LR zin; MGZY zim (平) [zim]; ONW zim					
	[E] TB: Lush hlam^{H} < hlam 'measure with arms extended', WT 'dom 'fathom'					

38-18 = K. 655		Mand.	MC	LHan	OCM	
a	林	lín	ljəm	lim	rəm	OCB *C-rjəm
	[T] Sin Sukchu SR lim (平), PR, LR lin; MGZY lim (平) [lim]; ONW lim <> [D] PMin *lam					
	[E] TB-NNaga *C-ram 'forest, jungle', Lushai ram^{H} 'forest, jungle, country, land'					
efh	淋霖琳	lín	ljəm	lim	rəm	
	淋 [T] Sin Sukchu SR lim (平), PR, LR lin; MGZY lim (平) [lim]					
	[D] Min: Amoy lam^{A2} 'long rain'					
-	啉	lán	lâm			[D] Min: Amoy lit. lam^{A2} 'to drink'

ij	婪惏	lán	lậm	ləm	rə̂m	
--	郴綝	chēn	ṭʰjəm	ṭʰim	rhəm	SW 5823
k	禁	jìn	kjəm^{C}	kɨm^{C}	krəms	[T] ONW kim

[E] TB *krim > WT kʰrims 'rule, right, law' ⋈ 'kʰrims 'fear, terror, awe'. MC kjəm^{C} can also derive from OCM *kəms or *krims (not *kims).

l	襟	jīn	kjəm	kɨm	krəm	
m	噤	jìn	gjəm$^{B/C}$	gɨm$^{B/C}$	gəmʔ, gəms	⋈ 38-3/651l'

38-19 = K. 668 The OC rime in this series could be *-əm and / or *-im.

		Mand.	MC	LHan	OCM	
ab	稟 b rat.	lǐn	ljəm^{B}	lim^{B}	rəmʔ	'rations'
	稟 receive	bǐng	pjəm^{B}	pim^{B}	prəmʔ	

[T] Sin Sukchu SR pin (上); MGZY bim (上) [pim]
[E] WT 'brim-pa 'to distribute, hand out, deal out'

c	廩	lǐn	ljəm^{B}	lim^{B}	rəmʔ
d	懍	lǐn	ljəm^{B}	lim^{B}	rəmʔ

38-20 = K. 669 The OC rime in this series could be *-əm and / or *-im.

		Mand.	MC	LHan	OCM	
a	品	pǐn	pʰjəm^{B}	pʰim^{B}	phrəmʔ	

[T] Sin Sukchu SR p'in (上); MGZY phim (上) [p'im]. MHan 臨兒 lim-ńe Skt. Lumbini
[E] ? TB: WT rim-pa 'series, succession, order, method'

e	臨 oversee	lín	ljəm	lim	rəm	OCB *b-rjum
	臨 wail	lìn	ljəm^{C}	lim^{C}	rəms	

[E] TB: Lushai rim^{R} < rimʔ 'to court, inspect / make enquiries about (a girl)', WT rim-(')gro 'honor, homage, offerings'

38-21 = K. 645 Contra SW, 今 *kəm is not a phonetic, see Introd.

		Mand.	MC	LHan	OCM	
a	貪	tān	tʰậm	tʰəm	rhə̂m	⋈ 38-18/655j 惏

See Intro. 9.2.7. [T] Sin Sukchu SR t'am (平), PR t'an; MGZY tham (平) [t'am]; ONW tʰɑm

b	嗿	tǎn	tʰậm^{B}	tʰəm^{B}	rhə̂mʔ

38-22 = K. 649		**Mand.**	**MC**	**LHan**	**OCM**
a	男	nán	nậm	nəm	nə̂m

[E] Area word: TB-PKiranti *nam 'man'; PTai *hn-: S. num^{B1} 'young man, young'; etc.

38-23 = K. 650		**Mand.**	**MC**	**LHan**	**OCM**	
-	羊	rěn	ńźjəm^{B}	ńim^{B}	nəmʔ	SW (931)
a	南	nán	nậm	nəm	nə̂m	

[T] Sin Sukchu SR nam (平); PR, LR nan; MGZY nam (平) [nam]; ONW nɑm. The graph, a drawing of some kind of building (?), was perhaps intended for an obsolete AA-OC word for 'house': cf. Laven ʰnɔːm 'house'.

-	揇	nǎn	nậm^{B}	nəm^{B}	nə̂mʔ

38-24 = K. 670 Contra SW 4661, 今 *kəm is not a phonetic, see Introd. 9.2.7.

		Mand.	MC	LHan	OCM	
a	念	niàn	niem^{C}	nem^{C}	nîms	OCB *nims

See Intro. 9.2.7. [T] Sin Sukchu SR njem (去); MGZY nem (去) [nɛm]; ONW nėm

[E] WT ñam(s) 'soul, mind, thought' ⋈ sñam-pa 'to think, mind'

de	稔腍	rěn	ńźjəm^B	ńim^B	nimʔ	

[E] AA: PMonic *cnaam 'year', Mon hnam, Khmer cnam, PVM *c-n-əm 'year'

fg	淰諗	shěn	śjəm^B	śim^B	nhimʔ	諗 OCB *hnjimʔ
-	捻	niē	niep	nep	nîp	

[E] LB: *nip ~ ʔnip ~ ʔnjit 'to squeeze, press'

h	敜	niè	niep	nep	nîp

[E] TB: WT sñobs = sñoms-pa, bsñoms 'make equal with ground, destroy'

38-25 = K. 667 The OC rime in this series could be *-əm and/or *-im.

		Mand.	MC	LHan	OCM	
a	壬	rén	ńźjəm	ńim	nəm	
f	任 carry	rén	ńźjəm	ńim	nəm	
	burden	rèn	ńźjəm^C	ńim^C	nəms	
ik	妊姙	rèn	ńźjəm^C	ńim^C	nəms	

[T] Sin Sukchu SR rim (去), PR, LR rin; MGZY Zhim (去) [rim]

[E] WT snom-pa, bsnams 'to take, seize, hold, put on'

l	紝	rèn !, nín	ńźjəm, ṇjəm	ńim, ṇim	nəm, nrəm	

[E] AN anem, IN ańam 'plait'

m	絍	rèn	ńźjəm^C	ńim^C	nəms	
no	衽袵	rèn	ńźjəm$^{B/C}$	ńim$^{B/C}$	nəmʔ, nəms	
p	飪	rèn	ńźjəm^B	ńim^B	nəmʔ	= 38-24/670e 腍
q	恁	rèn	ńźjəm^B	ńim^B	nəmʔ	
r	荏	rèn, rěn	ńźjəm^B	ńim^B	nəmʔ	

[E] WB ñam 'leguminous plant'

t	賃	lìn !	ńźjəm^C	ńim^C	nəms

38-26 = K. 666 The initial consonant in this series is very uncertain; it could be n or l or something more complex.

		Mand.	MC	LHan	OCM	
ab	罙突	shēn	śjəm^A	śim, tś^{h}im	nhəm	'deep'
c	深 deep	shēn	śjəm^A	śim, tś^{h}im	nhəm	OCB *hljəm

[T] ONW śim; BTD śim Skt. sīma <> [D] PMin *tšhim, CYue *sim

	depth	shèn	śjəm^C	śim^C	nhəms	
e	琛	chēn	ṭ^{h}jəm	ṭ^{h}im	nhrəm	

[T] Sin Sukchu SR tʂ'im (平), PR, LR tʂ'in; MGZY chim (平) [tʂ'im]

[E] Tai: S. ta-nim 'jewel'

f	探	tān	t^{h}âm	t^{h}əm	nhâm

38-27 = K. 661 The OC rime in this series could be *-əm and/or *-im.

		Mand.	MC	LHan	OCM	
ac	㑴侵	qīn	ts^{h}jəm	ts^{h}im	tshəm < k-səm	

[T] Sin Sukchu SR ts'im (平), PR, LR ts'in; MGZY tshim (平) [ts'im]; ONW ts^{h}im

e	綅	qīn	ts^{h}jəm	ts^{h}im	tshəm	OCB *tshjəm

[E] ? TB: JP ă^{31}-tsam^{31} 'string', WT 'ts^{h}em-pa 'to sew'

also	jīn,	tsjəm,	tsim,	tsəm,
	xiān	sjäm	siam	sem or sam

f 寑 qǐn ts^{h}jəm^B ts^{h}im^B tshəmʔ < k-səmʔ / k-simʔ
OCB *tshjim <> [E] TB: WT gzim-pa 'fall asleep, sleep'
k 鋟 qǐn, ts^{h}jəm^B, ts^{h}im^B, tshəmʔ,
qiān ts(^{h})jäm ts(^{h})iam ts(h)em or ts(h)am
l 駸 qīn, chēn ts^{h}jəm, ts^{h}im, tshəm,
tṣ^{h}jəm tṣ^{h}im tshrəm OCB *tsrjim
n 祲 jīn tsjəm(^{C}) tsim(^{C}) tsəm, tsəms
mo 浸濅 jìn tsjəm^C tsim^C tsəms OCB *tsjims
[E] TB: WB cim 'steep, soak' <> Tai: čim^3 'to dip into, immerse'

38-28 = K. 660 Mand. MC LHan OCM
a 兓 jīn tsjəm tsim tsəm
ce 朁憯 cǎn ts^{h}ậm^B ts^{h}əm^B tshə̂mʔ
f 噆 in mou. cǎn ts^{h}ậm^B ts^{h}əm^B tshə̂mʔ < sʔə̂mʔ ? ONW ts^{h}ɑm
o 噆 suck zá tsập tsəp tsə̂p
[E] TB *dzo:p 'suck, milk'
g 簪 pin zān, zhēn tsậm, tsjəm tsəm, tṣim tsrəm
[E] Area word: AN-PCham *jurŭm, IN daɣum 'needle'; AA-PNBahn. jarŭm, PSBahn. ɟərum, Sre jurum
簪 quick zhēn tṣjəm tṣim tsrəm
h 鐕 pin zān tsậm tsəm tsə̂m =g 簪
j 譖 zèn tṣjəm^C tṣim^C tsrəms
i 蠶 cán dzậm dzəm dzə̂m
[T] Sin Sukchu SR dzam (平), PR dzan; MGZY tsam (平) [dzam]
l 僭 jiàn tsiem^C tsem^C tsêms
m 熸 jiān tsjäm tsiam tsem
n 潛 wade qián dzjäm dziam dzem
潛 to hide jiàn dzjäm(^{C}) dziam(^{C}) dzem, dzems
k 鬵 xín zjəm, dzjäm zim, dziam s-ləm, dzem
= see 38-5/672o 尋燖 [T] ONW zim

38-29 = K. 647 Mand. MC LHan OCM
a 參 three cān ts^{h}ậm ts^{h}əm tshə̂m < *k-sə̂m
[T] Sin Sukchu SR ts'am (平), PR ts'an; MGZY tsham (平) [ts'am]
[E] TB *g-sum > WT gsum 'three', PL *C-sum^2, WB sum^B; Garo git^{h}am, Digaro kəsaŋ
參 stars shēn ṣjəm ṣim srəm OCB *srjum
參 uneven cēn tṣ^{h}jəm tṣ^{h}im ts^{h}rəm
c 驂 cān ts^{h}ậm ts^{h}əm tshə̂m < *k-sə̂m OCB *srum
e 慘 cǎn ts^{h}ậm^B ts^{h}əm^B tshə̂mʔ
loan for 16-30/1134l 懆 cǎo
f 糝 sǎn sậm^B səm^B sə̂mʔ =38-11/658o 糂
[T] ONW sɑm <> [E] ? TB: WT rtsam-pa < *r-tsam or *r-sam ? 'roast flour'
g 槮 shēn, ṣjəm, ṣim, srəm,
chēn tṣ^{h}jəm tṣ^{h}im tshrəm < k-srəm
h 摻 grasp shǎn ṣăm^B ṣɛm^B srə̂mʔ
tender shān ṣăm ṣɛm srə̂m

38-30 = K. 648	**Mand.**	**MC**	**LHan**	**OCM**	
a 三 three	sān	sâm	sɑm, səm	sə̂m	OCB *sum

[T] Sin Sukchu SR sam (平), PR san; MGZY sam (平) [sam]; ONW sɑm; BTD Skt sam[ādhi]
[E] TB *sum

三 thrice	sàn	sâm^C	sɑm^C, səm^C	sə̂ms	

38-31 = K. 663	**Mand.**	**MC**	**LHan**	**OCM**	
a 心	xīn	sjəm	sim	səm R!	OCB *sjəm

[T] Sin Sukchu SR sim (平), PR, LR sin; MGZY sim (平) [sim]; ONW sim
[E] TB *sam: Bahing sam 'breath, life'; Limbu sam 'soul', WT sem(s) 'soul, spirit, mind'

- 沁	qìn	$\text{ts}^\text{h}\text{jəm}^C$	$\text{ts}^\text{h}\text{im}^C$	tshəms < k-səms	

38-32 = K. 664	**Mand.**	**MC**	**LHan**	**OCM**
a 森	sēn	ṣjəm	ṣim	srəm

[T] Sin Sukchu SR ṣəm (平); MGZY $\text{sh}^\text{h}\text{im}$ (平) [ṣəm]; ONW ṣim, BTS ṣim
[N] 38-18/655a 林 lín may be partially phonetic

GSR NUMBER = *GSC* NUMBER

GSR=	GSC
1	18-1
2	18-5
3	18-8
4	18-9
5	18-13
6	18-10
7	19-1
8	19-7
9	19-11
10	19-14
11a	19-16
11b	19-9
12	19-21
13	19-22
14	19-18
15	18-4
16	18-15
17	18-18
18	19-4
19	19-8
20	19-13
21	18-6
22	18-7
23	18-11
24	18-14
25	18-16
26	18-17
27	19-6
28	19-5
29	19-12
30	19-15
31	19-17
32	1-11
33	1-12
34	1-13
35	1-14
36	1-15
37	1-34
38	1-16
39	1-68
40	1-73
41	1-21
42	1-22
43	1-23
44	1-27
45	1-38
46	1-57
47	1-47
48	1-48
49	1-1
50	1-2
51	1-3
52	1-4
53	1-6
54	1-7
55	1-17
56	1-5
57	1-18
58	1-29
59	1-35
60	1-30
61	1-28
62	1-36
63	1-46
64	1-37
65	1-58
66	1-59
67	1-31
68	1-61
69	1-51
70	1-52
71	1-53
72	1-64
73	1-65
74	1-10
75	1-45
76	1-54
77	1-55
78	1-18
79	1-31
80	1-33
81	1-32
82	1-42
83	1-43
83n	1-44
84	1-39
85	1-18
86	1-41
87	1-60
88	1-62
89	1-45
90	1-62
91	1-63
	1-6
92	1-49
93	1-50
94	1-56
95	1-19
96	2-7
97	1-23
98	1-24
99	1-25
100	1-26
101	1-66
102	1-67
103	1-69
104	1-71
105	1-72
106	1-70
107	4-64
108	10-1
109	10-2
110	10-3
111	10-4
112	10-5
113	10-6
114	10-7
115	10-8
116	10-13
117	10-12
118	10-16
119	10-33
120	10-27
121	10-9
122	10-10
123	10-29
124	10-11
125	10-23
126	10-24
127	10-22
128	10-18
129	10-19
130	10-21
131	10-35
132	10-36
133	10-30
134	10-31
135	10-32
136	10-39
137	10-40
138	4-64
139	24-1
140	24-2
141	24-3
142	24-4
143	24-5
144	24-10
145	24-15
146	24-11
147	24-21
148	24-23
149	24-22
150	24-20
151	24-24
152	24-35
153	24-39
154	24-40
155	24-41
156	24-44
157	25-1
158	25-2
159	25-3
160	25-4
161	25-5
162	25-6
163	25-16
164	25-12
165	25-7
166	25-8
167	23-12
	25-13
168	25-24
169	10-16
170	25-22
171	25-28
172	25-23
173	25-42
174	25-43
175	25-44
176	25-36
177	25-37
178	25-31
179	25-32
180	25-33
181	24-47
182	24-48
183	24-57
184	24-9
185	23-7
186	24-15
187	25-9
188	25-10
189	25-34
190	24-53
191	23-5
192	23-6
193	24-45
194	24-46
195	24-54
196	23-4
197	24-29
198	24-7
199	24-19
200	24-14
201	24-26
202	24-27
203	24-30
204	24-28
205	24-25
206	24-42
207	24-31
208	24-43
209	23-21
210	23-23
211	23-22
212	24-38
213	24-32
214	24-33
215	24-34
216	24-37
217	24-36
218	23-24
219	23-28
220	24-55
221	23-25

GSR	GSC
222	24-58
223	23-31
224	23-26
225	23-29
226	25-11
227	23-10
228	23-17
229	25-29
230	25-30
231	25-25
232	25-26
233	25-27
234	25-38
235	25-39
236	23-14
237	25-40
238	25-35
239	23-3
240	23-1
241	23-2
242	23-16
243	23-15
244	23-18
245	23-20
246	23-27
247	23-32
248	23-9
249	24-8
250	24-18
251	24-16
252	24-17
253	24-12
254	24-13
255	25-14
256a	25-15
256h	23-11
257	25-19
258	25-20
259	25-21
260	25-17
261	25-18
262	24-49
263	24-50
264	24-51
265	24-52
266	24-56
267	21-26
268	21-8
269	21-9
270	1-28
271	21-14
272	21-24
273	22-7
274	22-9
275	21-30
276	21-31
277	21-37
278	29-2
279	20-1
280	20-4
281	20-14
282	21-3
283	21-4
284	21-5
285	20-7
286	21-20
287	21-19
288	20-10
289	21-11
290	20-8
291	21-25
292	20-15
293	21-38
294	20-19
295	22-10
296	22-16
297	22-18
298	22-19
299	22-14
300	24-1
301	22-2
302	22-1
303	22-5
304	22-4
305	22-6
306	22-8
307	21-33
308	21-34
309	20-11
310	20-12
311	20-18
312	20-3
313	21-1
314	21-2
315	21-15
316	21-13
317	21-12
318	21-27
319	21-29
320	21-35
321	22-3
322	22-8
323	10-21
324	22-13
325	10-35
326	21-26
327	20-2
328	20-17
329	21-6
330	20-13
331	20-6
332	21-7
333	21-22
334	21-18
335	21-17
336	21-16
337	21-28
338	21-21
339	21-23
340	21-26
341	20-16
342	28-5
343	22-11
344	22-12
345	22-17
346	22-5
347	21-10
348	21-36
349	18-2
350	18-12
351	19-2
352	19-3
353	27-12
354	19-19
355	19-23
356	18-19
357	19-10
358	7-25
359	7-20
360	7-31
361	32-15
362	32-19
363	9-13
364	32-28
365	32-28
366	32-5
367	32-12
368	32-1
369	32-3
370	32-9
371	32-20
372	32-21
373	32-18
374	33-17
375	32-16
376	32-17
377	32-1
378	32-29
379	32-30
380	32-31
381	32-32
382	32-33
383	32-35
384	32-36
385	32-22
386	32-23
387	32-26
388	32-28
389	32-38
390	32-39
391	32-7
392	32-8
393	29-1
394	29-12
395	29-13
396	29-19
397	29-21
398	29-18
399	29-30
400	29-31
401	29-32
402	29-17
403	29-23
404	29-26
405	29-41
406	29-44
407	29-42
408	29-38
409	29-6
410	29-7
411	29-36
412	29-37
413	29-15
414	29-27
415	29-16
416	33-1
417	34-1
418	34-2
419	34-3
420	34-9
421	34-5
422	34-6
423	34-7
424	34-8
425	34-10
426	34-16
427	34-17
428	34-22
429	33-12
430	34-26
431	34-27
432	33-22
433	34-30
434	34-28
435	23-9
436	34-29
437	33-29
438	33-28
439	33-26
440	33-27
441	33-35
442	18-18
443	33-2
444	33-4
445	33-3
446	33-7
447	33-8
448	33-9
449	33-10
450	33-19
451	33-18
452	33-16
453	33-15
454	33-24
455	33-13
456	33-20
457	32-40
458	34-13
459	34-12
460	34-14
461	34-15
462	34-20
463	34-19
464	34-18
465	34-21

GSR	GSC
466	34-32
467	34-31
468	34-23
469	32-24
470	34-24
471	33-30
472	33-32
473	33-33
474	33-34
475	33-36
476	33-11
477	33-23
478	33-25
479	32-4
480	33-5
481	34-4
482	33-6
483	32-10
484	32-37
485	34-11
486	31-1
487	31-10
488	31-11
489	31-12
490	31-20
491	30-13
492	30-18
493	30-10
494	29-29
495	31-8
496	31-16
497	31-17
498	31-23
499	31-24
500	30-14
501	30-16
502	31-18
503	30-19
	30-20
504	30-5
505	30-7
506	29-35
507	29-11
508	30-6
509	30-11
510a	31-3
510b	29-4
511	31-14
512	31-15
513	28-20
514	30-12
515	30-2
516	30-9
517	30-1
518	29-34
519	26-24
520	37-15
521	29-39
522	30-22
523	31-5
524	31-6
525	31-9
526	29-9
527	29-10
528	31-21
529	31-19
530	30-17
531	30-21
532	29-25
533	29-8
534	31-4
535	29-3
536	30-3
537	30-8
538	29-5
539	31-7
540	31-2
541	27-1
542	28-4
543	28-12
544	28-13
545	28-16
546	27-13
547	27-4
548	27-2
549	27-6
550	27-5
551	26-17
552	26-6
553	26-7
554	26-28
555	26-29
556	26-21
557	26-34
558	26-35
559	26-36
560	26-19
561	26-20
562	26-22
563	26-25
564	29-28
565	26-37
566	26-38
567	27-14
568	27-16
569	28-1
570	28-2
571	28-5
572	29-19
573	28-9
574	28-10
575	28-11
576	28-14
577	28-15
578	28-17
579	27-8
580	27-9
581	27-10
582	27-11
583	27-17
584	27-18
585	27-15
586	26-1
587	26-2
588	26-4
589	26-12
590	26-14
591	26-15
592	26-26
593	26-27
594	26-31
595	26-16
	26-32
596	26-16
	26-33
597	26-23
598	26-39
599	26-9
600	28-6
601	28-11
602	26-8
603	27-3
604	26-13
605	26-10
606	36-1
607	36-2
608	36-3
609	36-5
610	36-25
611	36-22
612	36-23
613	36-6
614	36-8
615	36-9
616	36-10
617	36-14
618	36-12
619	36-11
620	36-21
621	36-16
622	36-18
623	36-19
624	36-4
625	36-26
626	36-27
627	36-7
628	35-7
629	35-2
630	35-3
631	35-17
632	35-9
633	35-10
634	35-6
635	35-15
636	35-16
637	35-12
638	35-13
639	35-4
640	35-5
641	35-20
642	35-1
642a-g	1-8
642kl	35-21
643	38-2
644	38-9
645	38-21
646	38-16
647	38-29
	13-63
648	38-30
649	38-22
650	38-23
651	38-3
652	38-3
653	38-7
654	38-8
655	38-18
656	38-14
657	38-15
658	38-11
659	38-12
660	38-28
661	38-27
662	38-17
663	38-31
664	38-32
665	38-13
666	38-26
667	38-25
668	38-19
669	38-20
670	38-24
671	38-4
672	38-5
673	38-10
674	38-6
675	37-1
676	37-6
677	37-9
678	37-10
679	37-18
680	37-21
681	37-2
682	37-4
683	37-5
684	37-7
685	37-8
686	37-3
687	37-1
688	37-19
689	37-11
690	37-12
691	37-20
692	37-13
693	37-14
694	37-15
695	37-16
696	37-17
697	3-2
698	3-1
699	3-29
700	3-12
701	3-30
702	3-47
703	3-48

GSR	GSC
704	3-53
705	3-54
706	3-22
707	3-23
708	3-24
709	3-64
710	3-3
711	3-5
712	3-6
713	3-4
714	3-16
715	3-18
716	3-17
717	3-19
718	3-20
719	3-37
720	3-38
721	3-35
722	3-36
723	3-31
724	3-34
725	3-32
726	3-33
727	3-49
727m	3-50
727r	3-51
728	3-41
729	3-52
730	3-42
731	3-55
732	3-39
733	3-56
734	3-40
735	3-43
736	3-44
737	3-45
738	3-46
739	3-26
740	3-57
741	3-58
742	3-65
743	3-66
744	3-67
745	3-11
746	3-12
747	3-13
748	3-14
749	3-15
750	3-59
751	3-60
752	3-7
753	3-8
754	3-9
755	3-10
756	3-21
757	3-61
758	3-62
759	3-63
760	3-68
761	3-69
762	9-32
763	3-25
764	3-27
765	3-28
766	2-1
767	2-9
768	2-15
769	2-34
770	2-33
771	1-67
772	2-39
773	2-36
774	2-6
775	2-12
776	2-2
777	2-30
778	2-7
779	2-10
780	2-22
781	2-37
782	2-38
783	2-7A
784	2-8
785	2-3
786	2-4
787	2-5
788	2-14
789	2-11
790	2-25
791	2-19
792	2-23
793	2-24
794	2-20
795	2-17
796	2-28
797	2-29
798	2-32
799	2-35
800	2-27
801	2-16
802	2-40
803	1-9
804	2-18
805	2-13
806	2-31
807	2-26
808	9-4
809	9-6
810	9-5
811	9-23
812	9-25
813	9-3
814	9-10
815	9-15
816	9-16
817	9-27
818	9-14
819	9-22
820	9-21
821	9-24
822	9-2
823	9-19
824	9-29
825	9-26
826	9-31
827	9-33
828	9-7
829	23-11
830	32-8
831	9-1
832	9-2
833	9-11
834	9-12
835	9-17
836	9-18
837	9-20
838	26-26
839	9-27
840	9-28
841	9-30
842	9-8
843	9-9
844	8-4
845	8-15
846	8-16
847	8-9
848	8-24
849	8-5
850	8-12
851	8-8
852	8-17
853	8-19
854	8-1
855	8-2
856	8-10
857	8-18
858	8-13
859	8-21
860	8-6
861	7-7
862	7-4
863	7-13
864	7-3
865	7-5
866	7-14
867	7-6
868	8-14
869	7-26
870	7-27
871	7-28
872	7-24
873	7-11
874	7-29
875	7-10
876	7-1
877	7-12
878	7-21
879	7-8
880	7-9
881	6-1
882	6-2
883	6-9
884	6-19
885	6-18
886	6-20
887	6-5
888	6-3
889	6-6
890	6-8
891	6-11
892	6-24
893	6-13
894	6-12
895	6-15
896	6-10
897	6-16
898	6-17
899	6-21
900	6-22
901	6-4
902	6-23
903	5-1
904	5-38
905	5-11
906	5-24
907	5-23
908	5-28
909	5-32
910	5-4
911	5-5
912	5-18
913	5-20
914	5-8
915	5-9
916	5-14
917	5-15
918	5-16
919	5-12
920	5-13
921	5-19
922	5-25
923	5-26, 29-30
924	5-27
925	5-29
926	5-30
927	5-31
928	5-21
929	5-6
930	5-7
931	5-2
932	5-22
933	5-33
934	5-35
935	5-36
936	4-1
937	4-2
938	4-30
939	4-25
940	4-42
941	4-43
942	4-44
943	4-45
944	5-22
945	4-38

GSR	*GSC*
945j	6-14
946	4-39
947	4-64
948	4-65
949	4-66
950	4-20
951	4-56
952	4-4
953	4-5
954	5-17
955	4-21
956	4-23
957	5-10
958	4-22
959	4-40
960	4-34
961	4-26
961l	4-29
962	4-27
963	4-28
964	4-47
965	4-48
966	4-49
967	4-32
968	4-33
969	4-50
970	4-51
971	4-52
972	4-53
973	4-54
974	4-55
975	4-52
976	4-30
977	4-31
978	4-35
979	4-36
980	4-37
981	4-40
982	4-41
983	4-57
984	5-34
985	4-6
986	4-7
987	4-8
988	4-9
989	4-10
990	4-3
991	4-11
992	4-12
993	4-13
994	4-14
995	4-17
996	4-18
997	4-19
998	4-24
999	4-61
1000	4-62
1001	4-63
1002	15-3
1003	15-13
1004	15-12
1005	15-9
1006	15-1
1007	15-6
1008	15-8
1009	15-7
	27-20
1010	15-4
1011	15-5
1012	15-11
1013	15-10
1014	15-14
1015	15-2
1016	14-5
1017	14-2
1018	14-15
1019	14-8
1020	14-11
1021	14-12
1022	14-13
1023	14-14
1024	14-10
1025	14-6
1026	14-7
1027	14-19
1028	14-22
1029	14-20
1030	14-21
1031	14-18
1032	14-16
1033	14-17
1034	14-23
1035	14-25
1036	14-24
1037	5-39
1038	14-3
1039	14-1
1040	13-1
1041	13-3
1041p	16-8
1042	13-4
1043	13-5
1044	13-9
1045	14-4
1046	13-28
1047	13-29
1048	13-38
1049	13-51
1050	13-53
1051	13-54
1052	13-52
1053	13-55
1054	13-56
1055	13-43
1056	13-44
1057	13-64
1058	13-65
1059	13-66
1060	13-67
1061	13-68
1062	13-74
1062a	5-37
1063	13-75
1064	13-8
1065	13-6
1066	4-15
1067	4-16
1068	13-7
1069	13-45
1070	13-11
1070m	13-7A
1071	13-14
1072	13-15
1073	13-23
1074	13-24
1075	14-9
1076	13-50
1077	13-32
1078	13-27
1079	13-30
1080	13-33
1081	13-34
1082	13-31
1083	13-26
1084	13-19
1085	13-19
1086	13-20
1087	13-61
	13-20A
1088	13-12
1089	13-13
1090	13-22
1091	13-21
1092	13-57
1093	13-58
1094	13-35
1095	13-39
1096	13-36
1097	10-37
1098	13-62
1099	13-40
1100	13-41
1101	13-42
1102	13-38
1103	13-8
1104	13-46
1105	13-48
1106	13-71
1107	13-69
1108	13-70
1109	13-76
1110	13-77
1111	13-59
1112	13-60
1113	13-72
1114	13-47
1115	13-16
1116	13-25
1117	17-1
1118	17-2
1119	17-6
1120	17-5
1121	17-12
1122	17-13
1123	17-9
1124	17-7
1125	17-8
1126	17-4
1127	17-15
1128	17-11
1129	16-1
1130	16-13
1131	16-15
1132	16-15
1133	16-16
1134	16-30
1135	16-23
1136	17-14
1137	16-41
1138	16-3
1139	13-8
1140	16-12
1141	16-10
1142	16-11
1143	16-17
1144	16-21
1145	16-20
1146	16-18
1147	16-19
1148	16-31
1149a	16-33
1149e	16-22
1150	16-34
1151	16-24
1152	16-27
1153	16-35
1154	13-71
1154a	36-24
1155	16-37
1156	16-38
1157	16-39
1158	16-44
1159	16-43
1160	16-17
1161	16-45
1162	16-4
1163	16-5
1164	16-14
1165	17-3
1166	16-6
1167	16-7
1168	16-9
1169	16-32
1170	16-40
1171	16-42
1172	12-1
1173	12-13
1174	12-2
1175	12-6
1176	12-9
1177	12-20
1178	12-21
1179	12-23
1180	12-14
1181	12-27

GSR	GSC
1182	12-3
1183	12-5
1184	12-4
1185	12-10
1186	12-10A
1187	12-11
1188	12-8
1189	12-7
1190	12-13
1191	12-22
1192	12-12
1193	12-15
1194	12-16
1195	12-17
1196	12-18
1197	12-25
1198	10-2
1199	12-19
1200	12-24
1201	12-26
1202	11-14
1203	11-1
1204	11-6
1205	11-11
1206	11-18
1207	10-29
1208	11-15
1209	11-16
1210	11-22
1211	11-23
1212	11-24
1213	11-4
1214	11-5
1215	11-10
1216	11-9
1217	11-7
1218	11-13
1219	11-19
1220	11-14
1221	11-20
1222	11-21
1223	11-17
1224	11-12
1225	11-2
1226	11-3
1227	11-8
1228	11-15
1229	10-34
1230	10-38
1231	13-78
1232	10-20
1233	13-73
1234	10-17
1235	10-15
1236a	7-25
1236b	19-18A
1236c	1-15
1237a	30-4
1237c	26-18
1237i	27-7
1237k	27-6
1237l	26-5
1237m	26-30
	29-40
1237q	4-36
1237r	4-59
1237s	28-3
1237u	28-11
1237v	28-18
1237x	28-19
1237y	4-60
1237a'	4-58
1238a	18-3
1238b	7-16
1238d	7-15
1238e	7-18
1238f	7-19
1238jk	19-20
1239a	28-8
1240a	4-30
1240b	4-45A
1240ce	7-33
1240fg	7-7A
1240h	28-7
1241a	26-3
1241b	7-2
1241dh	26-5
1241i	26-11
1241j	29-14
1241l	32-34
1241m	30-14
1241n	29-24
1241oq	7-22
1241r	7-23
1241s	33-15
1242a	16-10
1242b	1-40
1243a	12-5
1243b	10-25
1243c	10-26
1244ab	16-2
1244c	13-2
1244d	13-10
1244e	34-16
1244f	16-28
1244g	16-28A
1244h	13-18
1244ij	16-29
1244k	17-16
1245ab	13-17
1245cd	16-26
1246a	10-14
1246b	10-28
1246c	13-37
1247a	36-13
1247c	36-17
1248a	12-8
1248b	9-11
1248c	23-13
1249a	25-41
1250ab	32-2
1250cd	9-25
1250e	23-19
1250f	23-8
1250g	32-6
1251a	32-13
1251b	32-14
1251f	32-11
1251h	33-14
1251ij	32-27
1251l	32-25
1251op	34-25
1251q	4-64
1252a	32-1
1252b	32-7
1252d	6-24
1253	15-15
1254a	35-4
1254b	35-18
	37-2
1255a	35-11
1255c	35-19
1255e	35-14
1256a	20-5
1256bc	20-9
1256de	29-21
1256f	23-11
1257ab	29-20
1257c	29-22
1257d	5-14
1257ef	29-33
1257g	29-43
1257h	31-22
1257m	31-22
1258a	1-1
1258b	2-21
1258e	16-4
1259a	2-10A
1259b	7-3
1260a	5-3
1260b	5-20A
1260c	8-11
1260d	8-3
1260e	8-22
1260f	8-7

PINYIN INDEX

子 *GSC* number / *GSR* number

ā
阿 18-1 / 1

āi
唉 4-30 / 938
埃 4-30 / 976
毐 4-22A
欸 4-30 / 976
哀 27-5 / 550

ǎi
挨 4-30 / 976
藹 21-1 / 313

ài
艾 21-10 / 347
侅 4-2 / 937
硋 4-2 / 937
礙 4-23 / 956
醷 5-10 / 957
噫 5-10 / 957
阨 8-4 / 844
隘 8-5 / 849
愛 30-6 / 508
曖 30-6 / 508
薆 30-6 / 508
僾 30-6 / 508

ān
安 24-11 / 146
鞍 24-11 / 146
喑 38-7 / 653
諳 38-3 / 652

ǎn
唵 36-8 / 614
晻 36-8 / 614
閹 36-8 / 614
顉 38-3 / 652
⿰女酓 38-3 / 652

àn
按 24-11 / 146
暗 38-7 / 653
闇 38-7 / 653
黯 38-7 / 653
儑 38-9 / 644
犴 24-1 / 139
豻 24-1 / 139
岸 24-1 / 139
24-15 / 139

āng
佒 3-20 / 718
鴦 3-20 / 718

áng
卬 3-29 / 699
昂 3-29 / 699

àng
盎 3-20 / 718

āo
坳 13-16 / 1115
凹 13-16A

áo
翱 13-1 / 1040
囂 16-12 / 1140
敖 16-13 / 1130
遨 16-13 / 1130
嗷 16-13 / 1130
嗸 16-13 / 1130
摮 16-13 / 1130
螯 16-13 / 1130
熬 16-13 / 1130
獒 16-13 / 1130
鷔 16-13 / 1130
鼇 16-13 / 1130
謷 16-13 / 1130

ǎo
夭 16-10 / 1141
⿸鹿夭 16-10 / 1141
媼 34-16 / 1244

ào
奧 14-4 / 1045
澳 14-4 / 1045
隩 14-4 / 1045
傲 16-13 / 1130

bā
八 20-14 / 281
巴 1-68 / 39
笆 1-68 / 39
疤 1-68 / 39
芭 1-68 / 39
豝 1-68 / 39

bá
犮 21-31 / 276
拔 21-31 / 276
茇 21-31 / 276
胈 21-31 / 276
跋 21-31 / 276
魃 21-31 / 276
坺 21-31 / 276
軷 21-31 / 276

bǎ
把 1-68 / 39

bà
杷 1-68 / 39
耙 1-68 / 39
垻 21-35 / 320
霸 2-39 / 772
罷 18-17 / 26

bái
白 2-38 / 782

bǎi
百 2-37 / 781
柏 2-38 / 782
捭 7-29 / 874

bài
拜 20-17 / 328
稗 7-29 / 874
粺 7-29 / 874
敗 21-35 / 320

bān
班 24-53 / 190
斑 24-53 / 190
般 24-48 / 182
搬 24-48 / 182
頒 33-30 / 471
肦 33-30 / 471

bǎn
阪 24-49 / 262
板 24-49 / 262
版 24-49 / 262
眅 24-49 / 262
鈑 24-49 / 262

bàn
半 24-47 / 181
靽 24-47 / 181
絆 24-47 / 181
姅 24-47 / 181
釆 24-54 / 195
辨 23-28 / 219
辦 23-28 / 219
瓣 23-28 / 219

bāng
邦 12-25 / 1197

bàng
傍 3-57 / 740
膀 3-57 / 740
謗 3-57 / 740
榜 3-57 / 740
蚌 12-25 / 1197
棒 12-25 / 1197

bāo
胞 13-72 / 1113
包 13-72 / 1113
苞 13-72 / 1113
褒 13-64 / 1057

báo
雹 13-72 / 1113

bǎo
飽 13-72 / 1113
寶 13-66 / 1059
鴇 13-67 / 1060
保 13-64 / 1057
葆 13-64 / 1057
褓 13-64 / 1057

bào
豹 17-16 / 1244
袍 13-72 / 1113
抱 13-72 / 1113
鮑 13-72 / 1113
鞄 13-72 / 1113
虣 13-68 / 1061
報 13-65 / 1058
瀑 17-14 / 1136

bēi
桮 4-61 / 999
杯 4-61 / 999
卑 7-29 / 874
碑 7-29 / 874
裨 7-29 / 874
陂 18-16 / 25
悲 27-8 / 579

běi
北 5-32 / 909
俾 7-29 / 874
髀 7-29 / 874

bèi
倍 4-61 / 999
背 5-32 / 933
偝 5-32 / 933
葡 5-34 / 984
備 5-34 / 984
糒 5-34 / 984
犕 5-34 / 984
僃 5-34 / 984
被 18-16 / 25
貝 21-35 / 320

bēn
奔 33-28 / 438
犇 33-28 / 438
賁 33-29 / 437

běn
本 33-27 / 440
畚 33-26 / 439

bèn
獖 33-29 / 437

bēng
伻 9-26 / 825
祊 3-57 / 740
蒡 3-57 / 740
鬃 3-59 / 750
崩 6-20 / 886
繃 6-20 / 886
絣 9-29 / 824

běng
鞛 4-61 / 999
紺 12-25 / 1197
唪 12-25 / 1197
琫 12-25 / 1197
菶 12-25 / 1197

bèng
塴 6-20 / 886
迸 9-29 / 824
廲 7-29 / 874

bī
屄 7-30
逼 5-33 / 933
偪 5-33 / 933

bí
鼻 29-39 / 521

bǐ
匕 26-38 / 565
匕 26-38 / 566
朼 26-37 / 565
妣 26-38 / 566
疕 26-38 / 566
比 26-38 / 566
秕 26-38 / 566
粃 26-38 / 566
枇 26-38 / 566
彼 18-16 / 25
鄙 4-57 / 983
俾 7-29 / 874
鞞 7-29 / 874
筆 31-18 / 502

bì
碧 2-38 / 782
畀 4-59 / 1237r
紱 5-36 / 935
韍 5-36 / 935
湢 5-33 / 933
婢 7-29 / 874
庳 7-29 / 874
髀 7-29 / 874
裨 7-29 / 874
辟 8-19 / 853
擗 8-19 / 853
壁 8-19 / 853
躃 8-19 / 853
甓 8-19 / 853
避 8-19 / 853
璧 8-19 / 853
嬖 8-19 / 853
薜 8-19 / 853
臂 8-19 / 853
愎 14-23 / 1034
鞁 18-16 / 25
跛 18-16 / 25
詖 18-16 / 25
敝 20-16 / 341
幣 20-16 / 341
弊 20-16 / 341
斃 20-16 / 341
獘 20-16 / 341
蔽 20-16 / 341
鷩 20-16 / 341
牝 26-38 / 566
秕 26-38 / 566
庇 26-38 / 566
坒 26-38 / 566
陛 26-38 / 566
梐 26-38 / 566
畢 29-42 / 407
罼 29-42 / 407
斁 29-42 / 407
彈 29-42 / 407
篳 29-42 / 407
縪 29-42 / 407
蹕 29-42 / 407
韠 29-42 / 407
鷩 29-43 / 1257
弼 29-44 / 406
弼 29-44 / 406
畀 29-39 / 521
頙 29-40
必 29-41 / 405
珌 29-41 / 405
怭 29-41 / 405
抋 29-41 / 405
駜 29-41 / 405
苾 29-41 / 405
飶 29-41 / 405
柲 29-41 / 405
毖 29-41 / 405
泌 29-41 / 405
祕 29-41 / 405
閟 29-41 / 405
閉 29-37 / 412
覕 29-41 / 405

biān
鞭 23-25 / 221
邊 23-26 / 224
籩 23-26 / 224
蝙 23-27 / 246
編 23-27 / 246
猵 23-27 / 246

biǎn
貶 35-20 / 641
窆 35-20 / 641
扁 23-27 / 246
惼 23-27 / 246
褊 23-27 / 246
辡 23-28 / 219

biàn
卞 24-55 / 220
弁 24-55 / 220
抃 24-55 / 220
拚 24-55 / 220
便 23-25 / 221
徧 23-27 / 246
遍 23-27 / 246
辨 23-28 / 219
辯 23-28 / 219
辮 23-28 / 219
變 25-31 / 178

biāo
髟 13-71 / 1154
彪 13-71 / 1106
滮 13-71 / 1106
猋 16-37 / 1155
飍 16-38 / 1156
儦 16-40 / 1170
瀌 16-40 / 1170
穮 16-40 / 1170
鑣 16-40 / 1170
熛 16-39 / 1157
標 16-39 / 1157

biǎo
表 16-35 / 1153
苞 13-72 / 1113

biào
摽 16-39 / 1157

biē
鼈 20-16 / 341
鱉 20-16 / 341
憋 20-16 / 341

bié
別 20-15 / 292
蹩 20-16 / 341

bīn
賓 32-38 / 389
濱 32-38 / 389
繽 32-38 / 389
彬 33-34 / 474
豳 33-31
邠 33-30 / 471
份 33-30 / 471

bìn
儐 32-38 / 389
擯 32-38 / 389
殯 32-38 / 389
鬢 32-38 / 389
髕 32-38 / 389
臏 32-38 / 389

bīng
冫 6-21 / 899
冰 6-21 / 899
兵 3-63 / 759
掤 6-20 / 886
屏 9-29 / 824

bǐng
丙 3-61 / 757
怲 3-61 / 757
炳 3-61 / 757
昺 3-61 / 757
邴 3-61 / 757
秉 3-62 / 758
綆 23-25 / 745
鞞 7-29 / 874
稟 38-19 / 668

bìng
柄 3-61 / 757
病 3-61 / 757
棅 3-62 / 758
並 9-28 / 840
并 9-29 / 824
併 9-29 / 824
屏 9-29 / 824
偋 9-29 / 824
枋 3-57 / 740

薵 14-5 / 1016
腯 34-21 / 465

dǔ
竺 14-8 / 1019
篤 14-8 / 1019
堵 1-38 / 45
帾 1-38 / 45
睹 1-38 / 45
覩 1-38 / 45
賭 1-38 / 45

dù
杜 1-36 / 62
肚 1-36 / 62
度 2-16 / 801
渡 2-16 / 801
妬 2-17 / 795
妒 2-17 / 795
蠹 2-17 / 795
託 2-22 / 780
斁 2-25 / 790
殬 2-25 / 790
稌 1-42 / 82

duān
耑 25-24 / 168
剬 25-24 / 168
端 25-24 / 168
竱 25-25 / 231
褍 25-24 / 168
鍴 25-24 / 168

duǎn
短 10-16 / 169

duàn
段 25-23 / 172
鍛 25-23 / 172
腶 25-23 / 172
斷 25-22 / 170

duī
堆 28-11 / 575
𠂤 28-12 / 543
追 28-12 / 543
敦 34-18 / 464

duì
奪 22-9 / 274
兑 22-13 / 324
鋭 22-13 / 324
駾 22-13 / 324
祋 10-21 / 323
碓 28-11 / 575
陮 28-11 / 575
對 31-14 / 511
轛 31-14 / 511
懟 31-14 / 511
隊 29-9 / 526
憝 34-18 / 464
譈 34-18 / 464

dūn
蜳 34-18 / 464
惇 34-18 / 464
敦 34-18 / 464
蹲 34-26 / 430

dùn
沌 34-17 / 427
鈍 34-17 / 427
頓 34-17 / 427
盾 34-21 / 465
遁 34-21 / 465
豚 34-22 / 428
遯 34-22 / 428
敦 34-18 / 464

duō
多 18-8 / 3
剟 22-10 / 295
掇 22-10 / 295
咄 31-16 / 496

duó
度 2-16 / 801
剫 2-16 / 801
鐸 2-25 / 790
澤 2-25 / 790
敓 22-13 / 324
挩 22-13 / 324
脱 22-13 / 324
剟 22-10 / 295
奪 22-9 / 274

duǒ
朵 19-14 / 10
埵 19-17 / 31
鬌 19-16 / 11

duò
剁 19-14 / 10
惰 19-16 / 11
隓 19-16 / 11
隓 19-16 / 11
墮 19-16 / 11
鬌 19-16 / 11
舵 18-9 / 4
柁 18-9 / 4
痑 18-8 / 3
憚 24-21 / 147
癉 24-21 / 147

é
額 2-1 / 766
詻 2-1 / 766
俄 18-5 / 2
娥 18-5 / 2
鵝 18-5 / 2
峨 18-5 / 2
睋 18-5 / 2
莪 18-5 / 2
誐 18-5 / 2
蛾 18-5 / 2
譌 19-6 / 27
訛 19-8 / 19
吪 19-8 / 19

ě
旑 18-1 / 1
猗 18-1 / 1

è
啞 2-13 / 805
堊 2-13 / 805
惡 2-13 / 805
咢 2-14 / 788
顎 2-14 / 788
愕 2-14 / 788
鄂 2-14 / 788
遻 2-14 / 788
諤 2-14 / 788
鍔 2-14 / 788
鶚 2-14 / 788
噩 2-15 / 768
鱷 2-15 / 768
閼 1-28 / 270
戹 8-4 / 844
厄 8-4 / 844
軛 8-4 / 844
軶 8-4 / 844
扼 8-4 / 844
阸 8-4 / 844
阨 8-4 / 844
搤 8-5 / 849
隘 8-5 / 849
餓 18-5 / 2
櫱 21-11 / 289
枿 21-8 / 268
歹 21-9 / 269
遏 21-1 / 313
頞 24-11 / 146
櫱 24-17 / 252
額 2-1 / 766
詻 2-1 / 766

ēn
恩 32-9 / 370

ěn
眼 33-1 / 416

ér
而 4-41 / 982
栭 4-41 / 982
聏 4-41 / 982
胹 4-41 / 982
鴯 4-41 / 982
鮞 4-41 / 982
兒 7-11 / 873
唲 7-11 / 873

ěr
尒 7-20A
耳 4-40 / 981
珥 4-40 / 981
衈 4-40 / 981
餌 4-40 / 981
爾 7-20 / 359
邇 7-20 / 359

èr
二 29-28 / 564
貳 29-28 / 564
樲 29-28 / 564
刵 4-40 / 981
佴 4-40 / 981
咡 4-40 / 981
眲 4-40 / 981

fā
發 21-30 / 275

fá
乏 35-20 / 641
伐 21-33 / 307
茷 21-33 / 307
筏 21-33 / 307
罰 21-34 / 308

fǎ
法 35-21 / 642
髮 21-31 / 276

fān
帆 36-26 / 625
拚 24-55 / 220
犿 24-55 / 220
番 24-54 / 195
蕃 24-54 / 195
翻 24-54 / 195
藩 24-54 / 195
幡 24-54 / 195
旛 24-54 / 195
轓 24-54 / 195

fán
凡 36-26 / 625
棥 24-50 / 263
樊 24-50 / 263
煩 24-51 / 264
蹞 24-51 / 264
繁 24-52 / 265
蘩 24-52 / 265
笲 24-55 / 220
燔 24-54 / 195
璠 24-54 / 195
膰 24-54 / 195
蹯 24-54 / 195

迈 4-4A
紀 4-5 / 953
記 4-5 / 953
忌 4-5 / 953
認 4-5 / 953
跽 4-5 / 953
嬰 5-25 / 922
稷 5-25 / 922
繼 7-2 / 1241
繫 8-1 / 854
罊 8-1 / 854
蹟 8-14 / 868
迹 8-14 / 868
寂 14-18 / 1031
家 14-18 / 1031
輯 37-19 / 688
戢 37-19 / 688
濈 37-19 / 688
揖 37-19 / 688
徛 18-1 / 1
寄 18-1 / 1
錡 18-1 / 1
瘈 20-1 / 279
紒 20-2 / 327
祭 21-28 / 337
穄 21-28 / 337
際 21-28 / 337
計 26-3 / 1241
訐 24-1 / 300
劑 26-27 / 593
嚌 26-27 / 593
薺 26-27 / 593
癠 26-27 / 593
懠 26-27 / 593
穧 26-27 / 593
霽 26-27 / 593
濟 26-27 / 593
覬 27-2 / 548
冀 27-3 / 603
驥 27-3 / 603
髻 29-1 / 393
季 29-5 / 538
悸 29-5 / 538
嫉 29-29 / 494
瘈 20-1 / 279
洎 30-4 / 1237
垍 30-4
塈 30-2 / 515
髻 29-1 / 393
罽 21-5B

jiā

介 20-2 / 327
加 18-4 / 15
枷 18-4 / 15
珈 18-4 / 15
迦 18-4 / 15
嘉 18-4 / 15
夾 35-3 / 630
梜 35-3 / 630
家 1-11 / 32
葭 1-12 / 33
豭 1-12 / 33
佳 7-8 / 879
揩 26-9 / 599

jiá

莢 35-3 / 630
頰 35-3 / 630
鋏 35-3 / 630
郟 35-3 / 630
浹 35-3 / 630
韐 37-1 / 675
鞈 37-1 / 675
跲 37-1 / 675
戛 30-5 / 504

jiǎ

甲 35-2 / 629
叚 1-12 / 33
假 1-12 / 33
椵 1-12 / 33
斝 1-13 / 34
檟 1-16 / 38

jià

嫁 1-11 / 32
稼 1-11 / 32
賈 1-16 / 38
價 1-16 / 38
駕 18-4 / 15

jiān

幵 23-3 / 239
枅 23-3 / 239
豜 23-3 / 239
尖 36-20
奸 24-1 / 139
豻 24-1 / 139
飦 24-1 / 139
𢦏 36-21 / 620
殲 36-21 / 620
鑯 36-21 / 620
瀸 36-21 / 620
纖 36-21 / 620
漸 36-22 / 611
兼 36-7 / 627
監 36-5 / 609
礛 36-5 / 609
緘 38-4 / 671
黬 38-4 / 671
熸 38-28 / 660
肩 23-1 / 240
猏 23-1 / 240
閒 23-5 / 191
間 23-5 / 191
蕑 23-5 / 191
淺 24-41 / 155
湔 23-20 / 245
煎 23-20 / 245
鬋 23-20 / 245
腱 24-8 / 249
鞬 24-8 / 249
犍 24-8 / 249
姦 24-9 / 184
菅 25-1 / 157
堅 32-1 / 368
堇 33-5 / 480
艱 33-5 / 480
湛 38-11 / 658

jiǎn

儉 36-6 / 613
檢 36-6 / 613
減 38-4 / 671
趼 23-3 / 239
簡 23-5 / 191
柬 23-7 / 185
揀 23-7 / 185
揃 23-20 / 245
翦 23-20 / 245
剪 23-20 / 245
鬋 23-20 / 245
蹇 24-5 / 143
攓 24-5 / 143
謇 24-5 / 143
囝 24-6
揵 24-8 / 249
楗 24-8 / 249
帴 24-41 / 155
諓 24-41 / 155
錢 24-41 / 155
戩 32-29 / 378
繭 32-2 / 1250
襺 32-2 / 1250

jiàn

見 23-2 / 241
漸 36-22 / 611
蔪 36-22 / 611
劍 36-6 / 613
儉 36-6 / 613
監 36-5 / 609
鑑 36-5 / 609
檻 36-5 / 609
僭 38-28 / 660
潛 38-28 / 660
澗 23-5 / 191
諫 23-7 / 185
箭 23-20 / 245
建 24-8 / 249
腱 24-8 / 249
健 24-8 / 249
揵 24-8 / 249
楗 24-8 / 249
鍵 24-8 / 249
俴 24-41 / 155
踐 24-41 / 155
餞 24-41 / 155
賤 24-41 / 155
諓 24-41 / 155
濺 24-41 / 155
荐 33-22 / 432
栫 33-22 / 432
洊 33-22 / 432
薦 33-23 / 477
芡 36-4 / 624

jiāng

江 12-1 / 1172
姜 3-5 / 711
羌 3-6 / 712
將 3-49 / 727
蔣 3-49 / 727
漿 3-49 / 727
畺 3-3 / 710
僵 3-3 / 710
壃 3-3 / 710
彊 3-3 / 710
疆 3-3 / 710
薑 3-3 / 710

jiǎng

蔣 3-49 / 727
獎 3-49 / 727
滰 3-7 / 752
講 10-2 / 1198

jiàng

匠 3-52 / 729
醬 3-49 / 727
虹 12-1 / 1172
降 15-2 / 1015

jiāo

交 16-6 / 1166
茭 16-6 / 1166
蛟 16-6 / 1166
鮫 16-6 / 1166
郊 16-6 / 1166
咬 16-6 / 1166
姣 16-6 / 1166
釗 16-5 / 1163
椒 14-18 / 1031
膠 13-45 / 1069
澆 16-14 / 1164
徼 16-4 / 1162
喬 16-3 / 1138
憍 16-3 / 1138
鷮 16-3 / 1138
驕 16-3 / 1138
焦 16-31 / 1148

jūn
鈞 32-7 / 391
袀 32-7 / 391
均 32-7 / 391
君 34-12 / 459
麏 34-12 / 459
麕 34-11 / 485
麇 34-11 / 485
菌 34-11 / 485
軍 34-13 / 458

jùn
儁 25-39 / 235
箘 34-11 / 485
攟 34-11 / 485
郡 34-12 / 459
俊 34-23 / 468
焌 34-23 / 468
竣 34-23 / 468
晙 34-23 / 468
鵔 34-23 / 468
餕 34-23 / 468
駿 34-23 / 468
峻 34-23 / 468
浚 34-23 / 468
濬 34-32 / 466

kǎ
咯 2-1 / 766

kāi
開 27-1 / 541

kǎi
豈 27-2 / 548
凱 27-2 / 548
愷 27-2 / 548
塏 27-2 / 548
闓 27-2 / 548
鎧 27-2 / 548
楷 26-9 / 599

kài
磕 35-1 / 642
愾 30-1 / 517
嘅 30-2 / 515
慨 30-2 / 515
愒 21-1 / 313

kān
刊 24-1 / 139
栞 24-1 / 139
𢦔 38-3 / 651
堪 38-11 / 658
嵁 38-11 / 658
戡 38-11 / 658
勘 38-11 / 658

kǎn
坎 36-4 / 624
砍 36-4 / 624
厳 36-2 / 607
顑 38-4 / 671
欿 38-5 / 672
埳 38-5 / 672
歁 38-11 / 658
侃 24-3 / 141

kàn
看 24-4 / 142
磡 38-11 / 658
矙 36-2 / 607
衎 24-1 / 139
虷 24-1 / 139

kāng
康 3-12 / 746
㝩 3-12 / 746
穅 3-12 / 746
糠 3-12 / 746
忼 3-1 / 698
慷 3-12 / 746

kàng
亢 3-1 / 698
抗 3-1 / 698
伉 3-1 / 698
囥 3-1 / 698

kāo
尻 4-12 / 992

kǎo
丂 13-3 / 1041
攷 13-3 / 1041
考 13-3 / 1041
栲 13-3 / 1041
槁 16-1 / 1129
藁 16-1 / 1129

kào
犒 16-1 / 1129

kē
柯 18-1 / 1
軻 18-1 / 1
苛 18-1 / 1
溘 35-1 / 642
磕 35-1 / 642
薖 19-4 / 18
科 19-7 / 8

ké
欬 4-2 / 937
咳 4-2 / 937
殼 11-3 / 1226

kě
可 18-1 / 1
渴 21-1 / 313
鶡 21-1 / 313
㵣 21-1 / 313

kè
克 5-1 / 903
尅 5-1 / 903
剋 5-1 / 903
客 2-1 / 766
喀 2-1 / 766
恪 2-1 / 766
貉 2-1 / 766
溘 35-1 / 642
刻 4-2 / 937
堁 19-2 / 351
課 19-2 / 351

kěn
肯 6-2 / 882
肎 6-2 / 882
齦 33-1 / 416
狠 33-1 / 416
墾 33-1 / 416
懇 33-1 / 416
頎 33-2 / 443

kēng
坑 3-1 / 698
阬 3-1 / 698
硜 9-1 / 831
誙 9-1 / 831
牼 9-1 / 831
鏗 32-1 / 1252

kōng
空 12-1 / 1172
悾 12-1 / 1172
鞃 6-5 / 887

kǒng
孔 12-2 / 1174
空 12-1 / 1172
恐 12-1 / 1172

kòng
空 12-1 / 1172
控 12-1 / 1172
矼 12-1 / 1172

kōu
摳 10-10 / 122
袧 10-1 / 108
竘 10-1 / 108

kǒu
口 10-3 / 110

kòu
叩 10-3 / 110
扣 10-3 / 110
釦 10-3 / 110
寇 10-4 / 111
敂 10-1 / 108
怐 10-1 / 108
詬 10-5 / 112
彀 11-3 / 1226

kū
枯 1-1 / 49
楛 1-1 / 49
刳 1-23 / 43
挎 1-23 / 43
哭 11-1 / 1203
堀 31-16 / 496
窟 31-16 / 496
朏 31-16 / 496

kǔ
苦 1-1 / 49

kù
庫 1-10 / 74
褲 1-10 / 74
袴 1-23 / 43
絝 1-23 / 43
酷 14-1 / 1039
嚳 14-3 / 1038
搰 31-1 / 486

kuā
夸 1-23 / 43
誇 1-23 / 43
姱 1-23 / 43
荂 1-23 / 43
挎 1-23 / 43
咼 19-4 / 18

kuà
跨 1-23 / 43
髁 19-2 / 351

kuāi
咼 19-4 / 18
喎 19-4 / 18

kuài
快 20-3 / 312
廥 22-3 / 321
旝 22-3 / 321
澮 22-3 / 321
膾 22-3 / 321
禬 22-3 / 321
噲 22-3 / 321
塊 28-1 / 569
剻 31-4 / 534
蒯 31-4 / 534
凷 31-3 / 510
喟 31-5 / 523

kuān
寬 25-7 / 165

kuǎn
梡 25-19 / 257
款 25-6 / 162
窾 25-6 / 162

wán
丸 25-16 / 163
芄 25-16 / 163
紈 25-16 / 163
樠 24-57 / 183
刓 25-19 / 257
頑 25-19 / 257
玩 25-19 / 257
园 25-19 / 257
翫 25-19 / 257
完 25-19 / 257

wǎn
晚 24-58 / 222
脕 24-58 / 222
輓 24-58 / 222
晩 25-17 / 260
宛 25-17 / 260
婉 25-17 / 260
畹 25-17 / 260
椀 25-17 / 260
碗 25-17 / 260

wàn
曼 24-56 / 266
蔓 24-56 / 266
萬 21-26 / 267
掔 22-7 / 273
捥 25-17 / 260
腕 25-17 / 260
忨 25-19 / 257

wāng
汪 3-26 / 739
尪 3-26 / 739

wáng
王 3-26 / 739
亡 3-65 / 742

wǎng
往 3-26 / 739
枉 3-26 / 739
迋 3-26 / 739
罔 3-65 / 742
網 3-65 / 742
惘 3-65 / 742
网 3-67 / 744
蛧 3-67 / 744
魍 3-67 / 744

wàng
迋 3-26 / 739
妄 3-65 / 742
望 3-65 / 742
忘 3-65 / 742
朢 3-66 / 743
朢 3-66 / 743
譼 3-66 / 743

wēi
危 19-12 / 29
委 19-10 / 357
倭 19-10 / 357
痿 19-10 / 357
萎 19-10 / 357
逶 19-10 / 357
偎 28-9 / 573
煨 28-9 / 573
隈 28-9 / 573
威 28-10 / 574
葳 28-10 / 574
敚 27-18 / 584
微 27-18 / 584
薇 27-18 / 584
嵬 28-1 / 569
巍 28-1 / 569

wéi
為 19-6 / 27
危 19-12 / 29
巍 28-1 / 569
犩 28-1 / 569
韋 28-5 / 571
違 28-5 / 571
幃 28-5 / 571
闈 28-5 / 571
圍 28-5 / 571
惟 28-11 / 575
唯 28-11 / 575
維 28-11 / 575
帷 28-11 / 575
壝 31-2 / 540

wěi
痏 4-17 / 995
鮪 4-17 / 995
偽 19-6 / 27
闖 19-6 / 27
委 19-10 / 357
骩 25-16 / 163
尾 27-17 / 583
娓 27-17 / 583
浘 27-17 / 583
嵬 28-1 / 569
偉 28-5 / 571
煒 28-5 / 571
瑋 28-5 / 571
韙 28-5 / 571
韡 28-5 / 571
葦 28-5 / 571
緯 28-5 / 571
薇 27-18 / 584
喂 28-9 / 573
餵 28-9 / 573
崣 28-9 / 573
猥 28-9 / 573
鷕 28-11 / 575
蜼 28-11 / 575
亹 27-15 / 585

wèi
未 30-21 / 531
味 30-21 / 531
偽 19-6 / 27
餧 19-10 / 357
諉 19-19 / 354
蜼 28-11 / 575
䲁 28-11 / 575
胃 31-5 / 523
謂 31-5 / 523
媦 31-5 / 523
蝟 31-5 / 523
位 31-7 / 539
畏 28-9 / 573
魏 28-1 / 569
衛 28-5 / 342
䡺 28-5 / 342
躗 28-5 / 342
尉 31-9 / 525
熨 31-9 / 525
蔚 31-9 / 525
慰 31-9 / 525
罻 31-9 / 525
褽 31-9 / 525

wēn
昷 34-16 / 426
溫 34-16 / 426
緼 34-16 / 426
薀 34-16 / 426
轀 34-16 / 426

wén
文 33-36 / 475
蚊 33-36 / 475
聞 33-35 / 441

wěn
紊 33-36 / 475
抆 33-36 / 475
脗 30-20 / 503
吻 30-20 / 503
刎 30-20 / 503

wèn
絻 24-58 / 222
問 33-35 / 441
聞 33-35 / 441
抆 33-36 / 475
汶 33-36 / 475
紊 33-36 / 475

wēng
翁 12-13 / 1173

wèng
瓮 12-13 / 1173
罋 12-4 / 1184
甕 12-4 / 1184

wō
蝸 19-4 / 18
踒 19-10 / 357

wǒ
我 18-5 / 2
婐 19-2 / 351

wò
腛 11-6 / 1204
偓 11-6 / 1204
喔 11-6 / 1204
幄 11-6 / 1204
握 11-6 / 1204
渥 11-6 / 1204
矱 2-8 / 784
臒 2-8 / 784
沃 16-10 / 1141
臥 19-11 / 9
臤 22-7 / 273

wū
於 1-28 / 61
烏 1-28 / 61
鳴 1-28 / 61
汙 1-23 / 43
污 1-23 / 43
洿 1-23 / 43
圬 1-23 / 97
杇 1-23 / 97
巫 1-72 / 105
誣 1-72 / 105
屋 11-6 / 1204
剭 11-6 / 1204

wú
吾 1-29 / 58
梧 1-29 / 58
吳 1-35 / 59
毋 4-64 / 947
无 1-70 / 106
無 1-69 / 103
蕪 1-69 / 103
膴 1-69 / 103
譕 1-69 / 103
昒 30-20 / 503

wǔ
午 1-30 / 60
仵 1-30 / 60
忤 1-30 / 60
迕 1-30 / 60
五 1-29 / 58
伍 1-29 / 58
舞 1-69 / 103
廡 1-69 / 103
甒 1-69 / 103
憮 1-69 / 103

ABOUT THE AUTHOR

Axel Schuessler studied classical Chinese, Tibetan, and other Asian languages, as well as Indo-European languages and linguistics, at the Universität München, where he received his doctorate in 1966, He is now professor emeritus at Wartburg College in Iowa, where he taught until 1996. He has written articles and papers on Old Chinese phonology and has compiled an inventory of the Early Zhou Chinese lexicon *(Dictionary of Early Zhou Chinese)* and an *Etymological Dictionary of Old Chinese,* both published by the University of Hawai'i Press.